Don't Be a Norwegian All Your Life

Earl Ronneberg

D1307922

Table of Contents

Memory

Blessed reader, whoever you are, how can you believe what I am about to tell you? You may ask of me, pseudo-Christian that I am, 'will I follow Luther?' expecting that my reply to your question will be that 'the just shall live by faith!' But perhaps you or I or all of us are not just; we live by intuitions that have nothing to do with faith. Either way, then, to an outside observer, we must seem to live by deeds, by actions for which we take personal responsibility.

But what do deeds have to do with memory? I will tell you of my deeds from times seemingly immemorial to the present; but to me they are not beyond the pale of memory; that mine still contains riches. Now, whether there be good or bad ore, or even fool's gold, if I give you tales from that cerebral repository, per se, do you think that will bridge the gap? Will it cause you to prospect further within this underground mine of endless words, to stake a claim for authenticity? For veracity? For some gleam of transcendent truth?

I must warn you that the land of that region, my memory, has a checkered history. You will ask how can such variety be thought to convey reality. I will answer that it is only from your perspective, my reader, that you can assemble the judge and the jury that will announce the verdict. I am reminded of words that were recorded within my eighty-five billion brain cells, each with up to ten thousand connections, close to eighteen years after that repository came into existence, to wit: 'Aided by Him to whom your most inner thought, worthy or unworthy, is an open page, you, yourself, must measure the sincerity of your purpose.'

But before we turn back the leaves of the forest floor to seek the dark soil lying below such an old growth of timber, I take pains that you know that memory recordings such as those which occurred eighteen years after this timber was planted, originated from adjacent trees. We have already spoken of the difference between motives and deeds, intuitions and faith. May I suggest an example?

As a child, I often wondered what motivated my father's actions. There were numerous arenas of activities within which this child was captivated. When father was left on his own devices in the early mornings of his free time he sat at a desk in his remodeled back porch and played with his stamp collection, endlessly recataloguing the tiny pieces of paper with their perforated edges, tallying up their total value, page by page, year after year.

Each new stamp was christened with a baptism that began by pouring tiny drops of benzene in a covered glass font which, when opened and possessing that highly volatile hydrocarbon, would cause, by some magical process, the appearance of a mysterious design, which he called a watermark, to appear when the stamp was submerged. This mark, together with other philatelic tokens such as color, design, denomination, and further signs of identity, were then used to enter the pages of a volume much larger than a family Bible, yet possessing pages every bit as thin as that holy book.

From that catalogue, assuming the preliminary efforts were all correct in every way, a unique identity could be found much the same as a fingerprint except that multiple, identical stamps, unlike a human fingerprint, were possible. The catalogue thus fixed the identity of the tiny initiate within the bounds of skill of my father. The final step in this process, for it did involve multiple steps, was to use the catalogue information to locate a home for the stamp within one of many albums that were bound with blank pages each possessing squares for the inevitable attachment of the correct stamp by use of a tiny piece of folded paper, or hinge, which, when appropriately licked by the collector's tongue, could then be pressed into its correct location.

The title of each album consisted of the country of origin and after the newborn entry was properly pressed into its place, father then, using a pencil with a sharp point, wrote the value of the stamp and the necessary catalogue number below the stamp. This writing added a personal touch to the process; it seemed to be an artistic stroke that crowned all of the other efforts of identification.

While there were new, unused members of father's collection that were submitted to this numismatic ritual, with certain steps added or deleted, by far and away, most of those joining his albums were taken from letters written decades and even centuries long since passed and even from countries that no longer existed, thereby marking the stamp catalogue as being an old testament text.

But we must speak of one other arena of activity. For this we shall use those occasions when, as a child navigator, I sat alongside father as he piloted his single-engine Fairchild across the country from one origin to a specific destination. For this orientation, other kinds of markings were needed as a reference. I was engaged in a search that involved identification using another type of coordination with a single pane of paper information that pointed upward from my lap where, below the pane, one could see all of the other folded portions of the map that were not below us at the time.

With this appropriate portion of a larger map resting on my seat belt I was engaged in a search that scanned the land passing beneath our flight for the evidence of an object that had once existed in the past but was now abandoned much like a used postage stamp that performed its original function of facilitating transportation from one location to another. While the postage stamp operated during all hours of the day and night, my efforts were limited to the daytime, and even to periods when the ground could be observed. Father referred to this as flying by VFR or Visual Flight Rules as distinct from a flight involving electronic instrument rules.

This new search was akin to looking for an envelope where the stamp had been removed; in this instance, the sighting on my part of a marking that revealed the present lack of the object for which it had once been used, made that loss efficacious for my efforts. I was searching, of course, for the lines on the earth marking the location of an abandoned railroad.

Unlike a watermark pattern, the evidence was a straight line clearly apparent to the eye of a searcher from above; it required no petrochemicals except the aviation gas and engine oil that powered and lubricated the Fairchild's

Ranger engine. Because the cartographers who drew and maintained the Sectional Aeronautical Charts were wise enough to mark those charts so that even a child could confirm this man-made line, an orientation between the ground and the chart could occur. The magic words "we are here" could be pronounced and reinforced with a pointed finger thereby causing a quick glance from father followed by a nod before he returned to his piloting.

But these two searches for patterns arising from early childhood snippets of history, are but two stones skipped upon calm waters; so many scenes of action occurred during my childhood that, like the seemingly endless progression of peturbances of smaller and smaller skip waves, there existed hundreds of environments, as endless and as fascinating as an entire bag of excellent and perfect skippers, each of which made permanent pathways and connections in my brain.

But while actions carry the hallmark of our perception, there are also words, thoughts, concepts, metaphors, and all the other like-minded categories such as beliefs or life strategies – things that were articulated but required other mental pathways beyond mere perception occurring within an activity. And in these genres there were fewer sources that found a permanent place in my memory. Their paucity was enhanced by the increased frequency with which they were pronounced by both parents. They were spoken, too, at unexpected times; they needed no particular arena of action.

They were cautionary pronouncements and my mother claimed, by how often she spoke them, to have as many in her repertoire as father. It was clear from what my mother said that she not only had beliefs but, ultimately, I was shown what, explicitly, those beliefs were. From my father's admonitions, I could never completely unlock his deepest beliefs. This requires an example. I shall begin with one of the most enigmatic statements that I heard as a child. It was pronounced when I was in the company of a loyal employee of my father. I should announce that father owned a small architectural engineering firm of ten employees; this particular employee often performed supervisory functions. Whenever we met during the period of my boyhood from age eight through ten, he would address me with the warning "Don't be a Norwegian all your life!"

I never could formulate a reply to this seemingly important piece of advice; in retrospect so akin to some kind of practical wisdom; yet how could I act upon it? In my mind I questioned the idea that I could be classified as a Norwegian. I supposed that through some kind of osmosis I was a Norwegian of sorts since my grandfather came over from Norway as early as 1893 and, ultimately, started the architectural engineering firm that father took over at the end of the great Depression. I knew that during World War II my mother and father sent food packages to Norway when it was occupied by the Germans. My father's stamp collection was especially strong in Norwegian stamps; father traded with his Norwegian cousin, Sigurd.

At Christmas time I learned to make Fattigmann and two other kinds of Norwegian cookies; Fattigmann translates to 'poor man's pastry'. The process of making these cookies appealed to my imagination, my sense that I was participating in a Norwegian ritual. After mixing the Fattigmann dough, one ingredient of which was eighteen egg yolks, the dough was refrigerated until it became stiff, so stiff that portions had to be cut out with a knife; it required effort; but that was just the beginning. The ritual of making Fattigmann went on for several additional hours; it required that the dough be rolled out in the freezing cold, outside. Instead of an apron I wore my warmest winter garments; gloves were not used.

After a card table was set in the snow outside the kitchen together with all the paraphernalia, with my bare hands I began by carving out a portion of the dough, flowered it on both sides, and then began rolling it on a large bread board, making sure that it did not stick by using flour. The dough was rolled into a very large and very thin sheet. Then, using a Fattigmann roller which had a crimped edge all around the one and a half inch circumference, I made elongated diamonds varying from eight inches from tip to tip to four inches; tip to tip here refers to the longest dimension of the diamond; the shortest dimension of the diamond was usually two inches; the result reminded me of the perforations on the edges of my father's stamps; but I was still not done with the small quantity of dough.

This was because the recipe made more than six hundred cookies; any given carved-out portion of dough might, with luck, make only twenty five diamonds. Before the diamonds could be removed from the bread board, using the Fattigmann roller a second time, a two inch slit was made in the middle of each cookie, aligned along the tip to tip axis; once this was done I could proceed to the next step. Carefully putting a spatula under each diamond so as not to destroy the shape by tearing it, I lifted it up and now that it was free in my freezing fingers, I pushed one of the tips down into the slit and then further so that there was a twist in the middle of the cookie; the twist gave each Fattigmann cookie its very characteristic shape. Naturally, one had to be very careful not to rip the dough as the tip was pulled through the slit; the dough was thin and had to be handled with kid gloves; except there were no gloves allowed!

After the first two portions of dough were rolled out into twenty five cookies, given their distinctive shape, and placed on multiple cookie sheets supplemented by anything else that was flat and would hold the cookies, my hands were freezing and I had to try and warm them up. This form of semi-frozen hand torture went on and on and the cookie sheets were kept outdoors as well. After all that work, a huge pot of corn or Mazola oil was heated on the inside stove. Tiny scraps from my rolling were used to test the ability of the near boiling oil to brown the cookies. The now frozen cookie sheets were then introduced into the kitchen, one by one, where, each cookie was gently dropped into the top surface of the oil where they briefly sank but then floated. After a short interval they were flipped; that caused the other side to get slightly brown; once this was done and all of the cookies were both floating and browned on both sides, they were all quickly moved to huge sheets of brown paper where they cooled; the brown paper absorbed any excess oil.

From freezing cold, then, I took my turn at the hot stove! After the cookies were at room temperature they were then put in tins of varying sizes, all lined with waxed paper. I thought this ritual made me a Norwegian, but there were three rituals that had to be endured each Christmas and I had only performed the first, the Fattigmann rite; a few days later I would face the Krum kaka process. Like Fattigmann, the dough contained cardamom, but unlike Fattigmann, it was like a cake dough before the cake is made. The actual making of a Krum kaga involved hours at a hot stove. On a burner of that stove rested a two-sided iron griddle, similar to a waffle iron but with a very delicate pattern carved into each inner side. Using the precise temperature for the griddle, one then placed a teaspoon of dough into the center of the bottom side and closed down the top. After an interval which I knew and which made me a Norwegian, I turned the grill at the precise moment, and then, a short time later, I opened it.

Surprise! I now had a very delicate piece of lace which had been browned on both sides and was extremely thin and hot. I carefully transferred it to brown paper – a delicate operation – and quickly, so as not to let it harden by losing its heat, I rolled it up using a tapered wooden roller. This produced a rolled up cookie, an eight inch long cylinder-like cookie that had a circular opening at one end about three-quarters of an inch in diameter, and, at the other end, about an inch and a quarter in diameter. I gently removed the tapered cylinder from the wooden roller and let the Krum kaka cylinder get to room temperature; at that temperature it was extremely delicate. Storing a Krum kaga was an art in itself; the tins were handled with great care. For some reason, the name Krum kaka stood for 'bent or curved cake.'

Finally the third rite of cookie-making time arrived and we were enlisted to make Sandbakkels. The name Sandbakkels stood for 'sand tarts.' The agony of the ritual began the day before and consisted of cracking enormous amounts of almonds in the shell. Step number two was blanching the almonds in boiling water so as to be able to remove the brown coverings. Step numbers three and four were removing the skins and then grinding the almonds into an almond meal.

There are those non-Norwegians that use flour and almond extract; for a true Norwegian that would be sacrilege. It would be like using skies to go down and then up ski slopes; true Norwegians knew that skis were used for getting from one location to another. The use of hand-shelled almonds were a must! But back to the Sandbakkels. A dough was made using the ground almonds and then the dough was pressed into fluted tins of various shapes and sizes. The tins were baked in the oven, cooled, and then, very carefully, they were removed so as not to break the shapes. The final step was a another gentle packing in a tin.

I never thought that the consumption of these three Christmas cookies made me any more of a Norwegian – everyone who tasted them couldn't stop – but the Norwegians also ate fish. After the Second World War my family received two items from the Ronneberg canning factory, the second such factory in Norway. You see, my great-grandfather was very proud of the career change that took him away from the Ronneberg farm outside Stavanger and into his canning factory; he also had the first automobile in that area and we always thought that father having his own plane was an attempt to follow in his footsteps.

In any event, we received sardines – the number on the bottom of the tin, 246, meant it came from the Ronneberg canning factory – and fiskeboller. Acquiring a taste for fiskeboller and the brown cheese Gjetost, goat cheese, was a distinct effort for me as a child. I say this because those two stood in contrast to Lutefisk, an aged fish. I was excused from having to be at a table where Lutefisk was being served. This was because many native-born Norwegians felt exactly the same way as I did.

It was perplexing; how could I follow Erling, my father's respected employee, and implement his advice not to be a Norwegian all my life? Returning then, to my mother and father, and to those statements that came out over and over again during times when I could be engaged in any number of heterogeneous activities and unrelated activities, it was also perplexing that while I could take action on many of my father's pronouncements, I still could not fathom his beliefs.

Since we have used the term beliefs to characterize my dilemma it is well to go one step further on that score. Whenever it became necessary to identify (within the context of one of the numerous stories that father told while in the company of anyone who would listen – his friends, and business clients, for example) the church to which he sent his children, father would pronounce that the institution so chosen was "The one nearest our house." Presumably, then, it made little difference which denomination's sanctuary was to receive the family offspring; the choice was made when the purchase of the brick bungalow was finalized in the realtor's office.

This arbitrary choice was pronounced in the presence of friends, business clients, and even the owners of general contracting organizations, plumbing and electrical supply outfits, and other established owners within the building trades. It cast a spell over what I was learning in Sunday School. Further complicating my analysis, was the realization that my father's upbringing in Oak Park, Illinois, was in a house on Cuyler Avenue in that city, and his Bible, dated 1914, was from the Cuyler Avenue Methodist Episcopal Sunday School. This Bible was located on the bookshelves above the cabinets that housed his stamp collection. So there was a double instance of serendipity with respect to the juxtaposition of home and church. The germ of what I would later come to know as the notion of duplicity entered my mind at an early age and darkened my conjectures concerning my father's true beliefs.

But before we proceed to more direct and unambiguous epithets that were directed toward my actions by my father, we should pause a minute to relate a further example of ambiguity that came about through pure curiosity. There were, of course, other books than a Bible and Scott's Stamp Catalogues in those bookshelves. The very secretive obscurity of one of the smallest denizens of those shelves, tucked away on the highest shelf, caught my attention when I was very young. It was a thin, black, poetry book and it had an intriguing title: *King of the Black* Isles. It was published in Chicago in 1926, a year in which my father's brother and sister, as well as my mother, were all enrolled in the University of Illinois in Champaign Urbana, Illinois.

Sometime, at a very early age, I managed to reach for this book by standing upon a chair in my father's study. This 'study' was formerly a porch area that was remodeled to house a desk, cabinets, book shelves and other amenities. I saw from the Table of Contents in the front of the book that each poem might serve as a kind of fairy tale text for older children but I wondered if their content was as scary to an eight year old as were those of Hans Christian Andersen?

Intrigued by a poem entitled *In Babylon, in Babylon* I instantly read it and found that it added to the mysteries of father's belief system.

In Babylon, in Babylon

In Babylon, in Babylon
    They made a harlot queen,
And all the gold of all the world
    Was gathered there, I ween,
And love was always young, there
    And beauty always gay
Upon the streets of Babylon,
    Before they passed away.

In Babylon, in Babylon
    It was a queen's delight
To seek along the dark ways
    For lovers in the night;
And men they came in armor
    And men they came in skins
To eat the meats of Babylon
    And sip the wine of sins.

In Babylon, in Babylon
    The walls are fallen down
And gone are all the princes
    And merchants of the town,

The little laughing ladies
      And lords of bitter wars
In all the halls of Babylon
      Are quiet as the stars.

Even at such an early age I sensed that I needed to examine another book; they couldn't all be the same and I shouldn't judge my father's tastes from just one book chosen at random; but what else was there? *The Norwegian Migration to America*, a very thick volume, seemed too dull, and *The Illustrated Tales of Edgar Allen Poe*, too scary. Then I spied a better candidate, *Poems in Praise of Practically Nothing*, published in 1928. I sought a second poem that I could average in with *In Babylon, in Babylon*, after all, the book, *Poems in Praise of Practically Nothing*, must be innocent. There was a section entitled "Love-Songs, At Once Tender and Informative" it sounded just like what I needed; I picked poem XIII at random, ignoring in my haste the choice of number thirteen:

XIII

Your little hands,
Your little feet,
Your little mouth –
Oh, God, how sweet!

Your little nose,
Your little ears,
Your eyes, that shed
Such little tears!

Your little voice,
So soft and kind;
Your little soul,
Your little mind!

The first thing that occurred to me was that these two volumes were gifts from my father's friends and I began a process of determining who the gift givers were. It was hopeless; all my father's friends were the most upright individuals I knew, happily married, distinguished in their careers, many were brilliantly successful; there were honest, hardworking owners of companies in the building trades who, when I was introduced to them for the first time, never failed to tell me how grateful they were to employ father as their architect; they never hesitated a second, their comments were unrehearsed, spontaneous, heartfelt, and genuine!

I recalled a close friend who was self-educated, and possessed expertise in cardboard; he had wit. We were sitting at a Park Dairy luncheonette in Pentwater, Michigan, and the waitress asked Mr. Zimmerman what he would like on his hamburger. There was a pause, followed by a slowly spoken reply "I think . . . I'd like a little more hamburger." As a child, I thought it was brilliant.

Needless to say, I returned the volume with no further enlightenment as to my father's beliefs, but I had an intuition that whispered to me that these books came to father during the 1920s when father was vice president of his college fraternity. One of father's stories focused on that vice presidency; he always remarked that the president of the fraternity was either a scholar – who had academic honors – or an athletic hero; this was a student that could be put on display for prospective new members. What did this leave for the vice-president? The vice president *ran* the fraternity; I concluded that the vice president's position was much more important and from that notion I just knew that these books were gifts from his fraternity brothers; retaining them was a gesture of proper protocol! But what about those pieces of advice which seemed straight forward maxims on how to live one's life?

Surely these pronouncements were as simple to understand as a nursery rhyme line like 'I do not like thee, Doctor Fell, The reason why I cannot tell;' or the moral of Goldilocks and the Three Bears, involving a warning not to stray away from home. My father's comments were spoken within the context of a prior situation that called forth for the umpteenth time an object lesson to be learned from the conjunction of the situation and the implicit applicability of recalling the warning or admonishment. One of these notions was pronounced ubiquitously across many, seemingly unconnected consequences of my actions, except for the fact that something had gone amiss due to my being lazy; the observation by father was "You are only happy when you work!"

We shall soon see that my mother used a much more subtle version of this idea, a version that called for the doing of specific works, as well as a more appealing reward than just being happy. In any event, the idea of my father's seemed to imply that both work and happiness belong to a cause and effect pair where any kind of work leads to the same result. The words were ambiguous to me; why was this so?

It was clear to me that father loved playing; he played poker with the young scout leaders on weekend camping excursions; he possessed a passion for cribbage; he often played Mahjong with other couples of relatives and close friends. His extensive community involvement was a form of play; the stories he told of his clients, and of the times before taking over the architectural engineering firm of his father, the stories he told about those experiences as a government agent during the Depression, as G-man, were all humorous; he formed good friends in every working situation. It could be said that where there were people, there he found enjoyment. His work at his office was fun; I listened to him tell the same tales, over and over again, and they were always funny. My reciprocal reply to his 'you are only happy when you work' could easily have been "Life is play!" but these are not the thoughts of a child.

But other references to life's dilemmas were more direct: "You always put off doing something until the last minute of the last hour of the last day in which you can act." This for when I failed to accomplish something on time; a crisis involving a deadline had arisen unexpectedly and caused a 'flail,' a term where people were 'flailing around' trying to overcome the lack of time.

But whether it was putting things off to the last minute or any other action, I was reminded that "For the rest of your life you will be ranked by others." This, of course was true, there were grades for every class I was to attend, there were military fitness reports, and yearly evaluations by future employers. A corollary of the ranking admonition was always to have a career goal in mind for your education and, if that was not enough, I was to avoid 'idle driving,' another metaphor for purposeless activity.

The mystery of father's beliefs remained obscure simply because the tenet of how to live a practical life jumped over the idea of an underlying belief system, thereby expressing nothing more than a truth pronounced by an older and wiser person; there was no mystery revealed, the reality of the inner motivation underlying the reproof remained unknown.

Quite a different situation arose with respect to my mother's words of wisdom; in her words I could detect moral notions that formed the foundation of her beliefs; her practical wisdom was rooted within deeper levels of meaning, levels which Abraham Lincoln's observation "All that I am, or hope to be, I owe to my angel mother." expressed. Lincoln's words assume that both the practical wisdom he exhibited as an adult as well as the moral underpinnings which drove his actions were both attributed to his mother. His prowess as a log splitter, store clerk, father, political figure, and all his other roles, could only have come from his mother. The implication is that the very core of his belief system, his foundational moral upbringing, responsible for the buds that were to become the blossoms of his future deeds – all that I am, or hope to be – he owed to his mother.

These were strong words. The use of his term 'angel mother' implies a spiritual component. Let me defend this claim. It could be said, by those who use a modern dictionary, that angel in Lincoln's words merely pointed out a person regarded as beautiful, good, innocent, etc. But I would point out that when the 1889 copy of Webster's Dictionary is consulted, that usage – beautiful, good, innocent, etc. – does not appear in the 1889 tome I have before me. The only applicable definition from that enormous volume is: a messenger of God, a spirit or spiritual being employed by God to communicate his will to man; a ministering spirit.

I take pains to point this out because my own mother's words spoken by way of providing me with practical wisdom were closer to Lincoln's mother; through my mother's words I received a ministering spirit. Let me give you an example.

What could be more necessary to a young man than his preparation for an institution that he will most certainly face in his adulthood? Recall that my father's efforts were reminders about working, timeliness, being ranked by others, and having a job in mind when pursuing education, as well as avoiding idle pursuits. I am suggesting that in just three of my mother's off quoted observations, as regarding the institution of marriage, there were the hallmarks of more explicit means of how exactly to achieve happiness within the married state; the single term of my father's – work – as a way to happiness, was now, in the case of my mother's notions, richer. Her observations were "No woman will marry a man who does not know how to wash floors," "You should go camping with a future spouse before you marry her," and "When you marry a woman you marry her family."

Now, it could be argued that the result of her first observation – the one about the washing of floors – kept me constantly washing the kitchen and bathroom floors of our home. But I sensed there was more going on; my mother wanted to protect me from the designs of potential mates. Rudyard Kipling's *Just So Stories*, especially 'The Elephant Child' was one of my favorites but I had never read his poem *The Ladies*. My mother spoke, on certain occasions, the last two lines of that poem:

> *For the Colonel's Lady an' Judy O'Grady*
> *Are sisters under their skins !*

Mother kept no slim volume of Kipling's poems stashed away that I could surreptitiously find and discover how racy the rest of *The Ladies* poem was.

While father never spoke openly to me about his beliefs, he did discuss business ethics and even a practice that he observed with respect to individuals, sharpers, who may have tried to 'pull a fast one.' I heard him explain to interested parties one ethical practice that N. Ronneberg & Co. performed for their clients. This was a service that involved taking bids from the various trades – general contractors, heating and air conditioning outfits, electrical and plumbing contractors, and so on. This process began by choosing those companies that were to participate in each of the necessary areas. These firms received copies of both the plans and written specifications from which their estimators would determine the cost of services that they were to provide. Father related the way in which an unscrupulous architect might operate.

The unscrupulous architect would solicit bids form many general contractors and subcontractors. By having a large number – way beyond what was necessary – there was bound to be a mistake by some poor soul; some estimator had taken off the wrong values from the plans or specifications and his total costs were way out of line with all the others which were clustered within reasonable high and low limits. The cause could have been a simple misunderstanding, lack of time for a thorough job, a simple blunder in reading a value, or just inexperience. The unethical act was that of actually *using* these bids to perform the work.

By recommending to his client the use of all these way-out-of-line low bids, father felt that the unethical architect wanted to look good to his client by causing his building not to cost him as much as he thought. For my father's clients, he never asked for more than three bids for a given building trade. If one of the bid values was way out of line with respect to the other two, i.e., too low, he sent it back to be checked. This saved the client the agony of thinking he had the right price for his building when overruns occurred; he saved the contractor from a blunder, and he saved himself from a lot of headaches. This latter point was true because N. Ronneberg & Co, also allocated payments to contractors as the work progressed – 25%, 50%, 75%, and so on – from monies set aside by the bank, i.e., in escrow. Only reputable contractors were chosen to begin with – firms that had been in business and had demonstrated competency in all aspects of the work including the ability to accurately estimate the cost of the work.

But there were one or two occasions where father did discuss with me how *he* handled a sharp operator. I might mention that in addition to his architectural/engineering degree from the University of Illinois – a five year program – he also finished a law degree during the 1930s which he would often mention was just as valuable as the achitectural/engineering degree. After I understood what happened with the sharp operator, I thought the situation would end up in court but father finished his tale with the comment "and I forgave him."

When I recall how my mother revealed her beliefs I find that she was much more explicit. Ultimately she shared with me the source of what I took to be those beliefs; it came from a book entitled *101 Famous Poems*; it was first printed in 1916. My mother's copy was covered with brown paper; it showed that she may have used it a great deal since that year; it was a very worn volume. In it I could easily find lines that found their way into her spoken words; the examples were easy to locate. I was constantly reminded, especially in Michigan at our summer home, to reflect upon the world of nature vis a via the world of 'getting and spending,' for this, she quoted the first lines from William Wordsworth's sonnet "The World Is Too Much With Us"

> The World is too much with us; late and soon,
> Getting and spending, we lay waste our powers;
> Little we see in Nature that is ours;
> We have given our hearts away, a sordid boon!

To emphasize the active vis a via the passive life, she quoted the first stanza from Alice Cary's poem "Nobility"

> True worth is in *being*, not *seeming* –
>   In doing, each day that goes by,
> Some little good – not in dreaming
>   Of great things to do by and by.

Instead of listening to any form of discouragement that could be tackled with more effort and a broader view of life as a whole, she quoted the first lines and last lines of Longfellow's poem "A Psalm of Life"

Tell me not, in mournful numbers,
    Life is but an empty dream! –
For the soul is dead that slumbers,
    And things are not what they seem.

. . .

Let us then be up and doing,
    With a heart for any fate:
Still achieving, still pursuing,
    Learn to labor and to wait.

To counter the effects of a whole range of societal evils and emphasize one's work in the world, one's usefulness, she quoted the first two stanzas of Longfellow's poem "The Builder

All are architects of Fate,
    Working in these walls of Time:
Some with massive deeds and great,
    Some with ornaments of rhyme.

Nothing useless is, or low:
    Each thing in its place is best;
And what seems but idle show
    Strengthens and supports the rest.

But she was not oblivious to the problems that confront the individual when facing the harsher side of society and for this, she quoted lines from Ella Wheeler Wilcox's poem "Solitude."

Laugh, and the world laughs with you;
    Weep, and you weep alone.
For the sad old earth must borrow its mirth,
    But has trouble enough of its own.

. . .

Rejoice, and men will seek you;
    Grieve, and they turn and go.
They want full measure of all your pleasure,
    But they do not need your woe.

. . .

Feast, and your halls are crowded;
    Fast, and the world goes by.
Succeed and give, and it helps you live,
    But no man can help you die.

There were many more poetic examples from *101 Famous Poems* by Roy J. Cook; I never forgot them. Which brings us, my readers, back to the subject of memory, or, the question of what does it mean to 'not forget?' Given the emphasis on action, not dreaming – True worth is in *being*, not *seeming* – it seems natural that when it comes to memory, I would have an 'action plan' as it might be called in modern parlance, a 'to-do list,' the kind of list that results from a weekly material inspection by the Captain of a U.S. Naval combatant ship like a Destroyer.

As the years progressed an action plan for memory was put in place and there were other factors that reinforced my action plan; factors that strengthened my resolve to enhance my memory. However, during my first eight years I had no name for the sequence of memory enhancing acts I performed, nor was I consciously aware of what was going on, nonetheless, with respect to my memory, and from a retrospective viewpoint, the collective actions exhibit a pattern, a strategy to fight the 'battle of memory!'

It all began as a result of the same factor that drove me to search for books on the top shelf of the library in my father's study: curiosity. I distinctly remember sitting alone in one of the very comfortable stuffed living room chairs; it was winter and I was pondering a question. Blessed reader, whoever you are, let me assure that this story will not be a recasting of Descartes' famous lines of skepticism in his first of six *Meditations* where he says:

"But it is possible that, even though the senses occasionally deceive us about things which are barely perceptible and very far away, there are many other things which we cannot reasonably doubt, even though we know them through the senses – as for example, that I am here, seated by the fire, wearing a 'winter' dressing gown, holding this paper in my hands, and other things of this nature. And how could I deny that these hands and this body are mine, unless I am to compare myself with certain lunatics whose brain is so troubled and befogged by the black vapors of the bile that they continually affirm that they are kings while they are paupers . . . such men are fools."

Descartes, however, does go on to doubt, beginning with the doubt that he is not sure that he is dreaming. I am not going to tell you, blessed reader, that as a young child of six, I was concerned with the issue of whether I was dreaming. My meditation was much more childish and was never written down so as to become a reference point in the history of Analytic Philosophy; a definite point for explicating Cartesian skepticism. All I asked myself was whether, if I willed it to happen, I could force myself to remember this room, this chair, this vow to remember this particular moment the rest of my life. And it so happens that the answer was yes, I could.

It is interesting to note that when I was sixteen years old, I again experienced similar words being pronounced to me and others who were participating, as initiates, in a ceremony where the individual conducting the ritual remarked at the outset "The next twelve hours will bring to you a memory which shall abide with you for life." The amazing thing was that I had begun the experiment, on my own, a full ten years before the profound words of the ceremony were heard! How marvelous, then, the thoughts of a child.

But even with the best of intentions towards the execution of a memory-plan program, the next step of my plan was initiated by a source none other than the Methodist church Sunday School; let me illustrate for you, my reader, how things can go amiss. I am referring to the next piece of memory work that comes to mind during this early period of my development: Psalm 23. This feat of memorization was not, in itself, a difficult task. You will recall the first line "The LORD is my shepherd; I shall not want." My excerpt is taken from the Cuyler Avenue Methodist Episcopal Sunday School Bible of 1914.

Nor is it worthy of note to even mention the fact that I retained the line these many years. What *is* of note, however, is how I interpreted the first line. This admittance on my part will stretch my claim on your belief system, blessed reader, but I will have you know that for most of my life, until just a few years ago, my interpretation was: "I shall not want the LORD!" To me the words were explicit – I didn't need a shepherd!

It is well that we proceed to the next scene of my memory-play, however unknown as a drama it was at the time of which I speak; this scene was another externally initiated one only this time the trigger for the effort came from being chosen as the Interlocutor in the yearly Cub Scout Minstrel Show. In my role as Interlocutor I wore a tuxedo and a black top hat, much like Abraham Lincoln wore; I was the voice that took the audience through both acts, always announcing solo numbers, the three quartets, the ensemble numbers, and participating in the back-and-forth dialogue that formed the repertoire of many jokes; these jokes were always between myself and six 'end-men' who sat at the ends of the semi-circle and were in black-face.

One of my mother's best friends not only rehearsed all of the music with the various groups – from a single number through the quartets to the ensemble pieces – but also played the piano backstage throughout the two acts of the Minstrel show, as well as during the intermission when a style show of young cubs, dressed as women, kept the audience laughing. During the style show cubs walked onto the stage, turned, and then came down a runway into the audience. Music accompanied each cub and an original piece of introductory poetry was read; every year those poetic pieces were completely rewritten by another friend of my mother's, and, in fact my own den mother; she was a brilliant and creative woman.

The speaking parts for the Minstrel Show were rehearsed on Sunday afternoons in the basement of my father's friend, Peter Orlebeck; father was Cub Master for seventeen years, and Peter was Chairman of the Cub Pack Committee for seventeen years. Peter Orlebeck wrote the shows and used three, rotating scripts, that formed a round-robin during a three year cycle of shows. Since many Interlocutors had difficulty memorizing all the lines, the entire script was put on cards that fit, one after the other, in the Interlocutor's top hat.

The strategy was to look down at the cards – when the top hat was taken off and in the Interlocutor's lap – only if necessary; to keep current, however, it was necessary to remove the cards, one by one, and surreptitiously drop them behind the Interlocutor's chair in the center of the semi-circular ring of performers; this, of course, was necessary whether or not they were used as memory aids. I can remember the jokes; one began when the end man, Tambone, started weeping:

Interlocutor: Tambone, why are you weeping?
Tambone: Oh, it was awful Mr. Interlocutor, it was awful!
Interlocutor: What was awful?
Tambone: Oh, it was terrible!
Interlocutor: What was terrible, Tambone?
Tambone: It happened last Sunday.
Interlocutor: What happened last Sunday, Tambone?
Tambone: It was a steamboat, it left New Orleans last Sunday.
Interlocutor: But why was that awful?
Tambone: It went upstream.

Interlocutor: Well, then what happened?

Tambone: It went upstream and struck an obstacle and all the passengers drowned!

Interlocutor: Did you have friends aboard, Tambone?

Tambone: No, but it was awful.

Interlocutor: Was a member of your family aboard?

Tambone: No, but it was awful, Mr. Interlocutor.

Interlocutor: Were any of your relatives aboard?

Tambone: No, but it was awful.

Interlocutor: Well, if you had no friends, family, or relatives aboard, why are you so upset?

Tambone: I'm upset because my mother-in-law *missed* the boat!

When I first read my script for that joke, I remember recalling my mother's saying "when you marry a woman you marry her family." But there was another pronouncement of my mother's which I haven't shared with you, my blessed reader. Tambone's repetition of 'it was awful' recalls my mother's words; my mother repeated these words ever so many times; and 'words' they were as we shall see. My mother's words in this particular pronouncement of hers all came about because I was obliged to memorize twelve distinct definitions in order to advance myself, in order to obtain a favorable 'ranking' as father would have it; and it did involve, rather explicitly, a rank. So now I have raised the question "what kind of a story involved the repetition of words in conjunction with the memorization of twelve definitions, pursuant to the achievement of a rank and a ranking?"

The story begins with my graduation to the Boy Scout troop belonging to the Methodist Church, the same church that was closest to home, and where Peter Orlebeck was the leader for the Sunday School for the girls and boys in the sixth through eighth grades. My Scoutmaster, George Simmons, Jr., insisted that when learning the Scout Law, "A Scout is Trustworthy, Loyal, Helpful, and so on," it was necessary to learn it the way he learned it years ago; this meant that he insisted that we recite the Scout Law in what he called the 'Long Form,' more particularly, the words that explained what these twelve individual words meant.

The Long Form that was currently in effect dated from 1911, and Mr. George Simmons, Jr. learned it that way. George's father, George Simmons, Sr., a prior Scoutmaster, insisted that his son and everyone else joining the troop and achieving the Tenderfoot rank needed to memorize those twelve definitions; you might call it a family requirement. Now, let me make it perfectly clear that when I joined the Boy Scouts there was no official requirement for memorization of the Long Form! The requirement came about due to the Simmons family tradition; as a result I began memorizing the Long Form, beginning with A Scout is Trustworthy: 'A Scout's honor is to be trusted. If he were to violate his honor by telling a lie or by cheating or by not doing exactly a given task, when trusted on his honor, he may be directed to hand over his Scout Badge.' and ending with A Scout is Reverent: 'He is reverent toward God. He is faithful in his religious duties, and respects the convictions of others in matters of custom and religion.'

So how did all this become beneficial for my mother? The answer was both simple and obvious; once having heard the long form of the Scout Law, she immediately incorporated all of those definitions into her belief system: Now she had a more extensive repertoire; it didn't require reference to a nineteenth century poem, albeit that the poem might well be relevant; more importantly, it didn't require recalling something that might be temporarily forgotten! Quite the contrary, her son had *memorized* these twelve definitions; he wore the tenderfoot scout badge!

Imagine the power and simplicity of a new admonition that mother now had at her command! Suppose I had not been as helping in washing or drying dishes, or even washing a bathroom floor. She knew that I had memorized A Scout is Helpful "He must be prepared at any time to save life, help injured persons, and share the home duties. He must do at least one good turn to somebody every day." Suppose I woke up a bit grumpy; she knew that I had memorized A Scout is Cheerful "He smiles whenever he can. His obedience to orders is prompt and cheery. He never shirks nor grumbles at hardships." And the beauty of the whole plan was that the reminder she used applied to all twelve points of the Scout Law! All she had to say was "Words, words, words!"

But enough of these parental pronouncements; we must return to what could be called my 'motives for memory.' You might, dear reader, expect a completely new motive to arise within this history; and you would be quite correct in your guess. For example, if you were a teenager during the times of this memory saga, you might wonder if my parents were concerned with my becoming a 'type' that William H. White identified in his book, *The Organization Man*. Father was a small business owner; he took over his father's business after a lapse of time toward the end of the Depression, during which period he held a number of jobs. One of the major jobs he held during this period was a Justice Department G-man. N. Ronneberg & Co., founded by my Norwegian grandfather was a very successful business. Natal Ronneberg first came to Chicago in 1893. Because of this, you would certainly be correct in identifying my mother's worry of my becoming an Organization Man as defined in White's book.

I sensed this from the way the book was read and discussed in the family; it seemed to me that the type was so fearful to mother that she needed to make certain that the necessary sharp contrasts between father and grandfather were publically compared with White's Organization Man. Closely associated with White's work at this time was David Riesman's (and other co-authors) concept of an inner-directed versus an other-directed individual. God forbid that my parents should raise an other-directed child!

But returning to the motive that sparked my next span of self-imposed memorization, the source was, geographically speaking, even closer than the Methodist church. This was because a mere half block away from our home — within the entire adjacent city block area to the west — was the furthest northwest elementary school in the City of Chicago, Ebinger School. And it was by virtue of a complete misunderstanding of what went on one day while I was in sixth grade that the genes of my inner-connectedness took charge of the direction of my memory odyssey. Or, maybe my tale will show that it was a combination of genes and environment; I'll let you decide.

To be sure, there had been ripples, undetected gravity waves, present in earlier classrooms as regards my memory. In the fifth grade I became aware of the importance of spelling. I fall to remember the teacher's name but that is of no matter as I distinctly remember her teaching strategy. Each week, an extensive spelling list was assigned with a date and time specified for a test involving the entire classroom; all the words in the list were assigned. That, of itself, was nothing to write home about.

What was new was her use of those weekly spelling tests to seat the entire class on the strength of those spelling test scores, thereby introducing a very obvious spatial dimension of understanding into her stress on the subject, and, in my own case, causing that famous commentary of father to be reawakened "For the rest of your life you will be ranked by others." But it was, perhaps, neither my fifth grade teacher, nor even my father, who had the last word. I rather think it was my mother. How could that be?

First we must point out that I came to the conclusion that there was a contrasting degree of arbitrariness – vis a via ranked seating assignments – when it came to spelling words from the English language. The upshot of that analysis was a further vote of confidence for using memorization skills, such as they were. Thus it was that my reasoning was joined with my inner-directedness in such a complimentary way that I began to receive grades of one-hundred percent on the weekly trials of my memory. But that did not solve the problem. What *was* the problem?

The problem was that a young woman, Paulette by name, who wore two braids of hair that hung down in back of her head, also received one-hundred percent scores every week. For some strange reason that I never completely understood, Paulette began her sequence of one-hundred percent correct grades at a point in time before my streak. This, of course, was not Chicago Cubs baseball, nor even Chicago White Sox baseball.

What we are focusing on was the privilege of sitting in the front seat of row number one. I, of course, was unable to move forward to that seat and was forced to have those braids facing me week after week! In one sense, though, it was like baseball: I was number two in the line-up behind the lead-off hitter and, because of our batting averages, the manager had no reason to change things.

My home-room teacher during that period, Miss Anderson, played another game that involved memory; this game did not involve competition with respect to the position you played from – to use the baseball analogy – but it was more akin to your success as a fielder, and, in one sense, I had the impression that sitting in the back of the rows of seats – the outfield – allowed me to field more balls.

All this makes no sense without the rules of engagement. The game was a reading game and a weekly student newspaper from some educational publishing house was the vehicle that made the game work. Each student simultaneously read the same assigned article during a fixed period of time. The publishing house furnished Miss Anderson with a list of questions pertinent to each article. When the reading time was up, everyone covered their newsprint and Miss Anderson read the first question. If you thought you knew the answer, you quickly raised your hand.

If you were fast enough, Miss Anderson identified you as the first to raise your hand and she called on you to give your answer. If your answer was correct you were given one additional vertical mark on a wall chart which was also a seating chart because it was filled with squares and each square had a student's name and a tally of that student's marks. As the weeks progressed these four-vertical-marks-with-a-horizontal-line groups grew in number if you were both fast and a reader who understood what you were reading.

Obviously, there was no misunderstanding how the game worked; it forced a person to quickly memorize what was read; it seemed more competitive to me because the marking groups were public and so were the answers. If, for example, Paulette and I had the same tally, there was the chance that both our tallies represented a point on a normal curve that included the entire class; that seemed a better public representation than a seating chart. But I would add, parenthetically, that the public display of all grades of all students, a system in effect at Princeton University during my freshman year, has changed my view and I now strongly feel that all grades should be kept secret.

Be that as it may, in Miss Anderson's reading class, I sensed that I discovered a strategy to win more points in this game. First, I felt that in a tie where two students raised their hands simultaneously, for some reason or another, pupils like myself sitting in the back of the classroom were more likely to win the tie; this might have been because Miss Anderson wore her reading glasses. My second strategy applied only to me; what I decided to do was risk my reputation by raising my hand while Miss Anderson was still reading the question! After all, I was inner-directed! That meant that I felt so confident from just hearing how the first two-thirds of the question was put, that I just *knew* that I had the answer!

Before we proceed to see how this early raising of the hand occurred in the Navy many years later, we must remark on what can only be described as my 'ultimate audacity' with respect to an exam in Mrs. Perry's geometry class in High School. In one instance, I felt that this test was so easy, and so trivial, that I put nothing on the answer sheet, marked the sheet with a grade of one-hundred percent, and passed it forward with a written remark to the effect that the test questions were so easy that I had done all of them in my head and I had all of them correct!

One piece of audacity deserves another only this time things backfired for the teacher. I was encouraged to take five and six major subjects in High School by my father; we even visited the High School Principal, Mr. Hoefer, to get his permission; I can remember the visit – on his desk was a sign 'Luck is when preparedness meets opportunity.' My father's encouragement and the Principal's permission led me to take typing as a minor and then go on and take typing as a major subject. At that time in the history of feminism, I was the only male in the class. The teacher was a very sarcastic, elderly woman, who spoke to the class as though she didn't expect anyone in the class to achieve sixty words per minute; that meant absolutely no mistakes! I, of course, being the only male she might have seen in the past decade or two, immediately began a program to put her sarcasm to use.

The tests were all precisely timed and everyone took the test on a Friday. The teacher checked any claims for sixty words per minute herself; she was particularly concerned that someone would claim a score and the test would have an overstrike. As the weeks rolled on she would address the class with a statement like, "I don't suppose anyone has yet arrived at sixty words per minute? . . . Well, there's always next week." It seemed so matter of fact, so sarcastic, that I couldn't wait to raise my hand. Then it came; according to the typing test book, I was over sixty words a minute.

I waited for the usual statement and then, from the back row, raised my hand. Her original look of disdain quickly turned to disbelief followed by confidence in her ability to put down, of all things, a male. "Bring your paper up to me, Mr. Ronneberg," she pronounced, again with the look that the whole thing was a waste of time. She took out the magnifying glass to check for overstrikes. She scanned the test a second time, paused, as though looking for the possibility of some kind of sabotage; perhaps that kind of thing would have been reported by the students sitting to my left and right. She didn't want to admit that a miracle had occurred in her class, but everyone was looking at her; finally she had to give in and make some kind of brief acknowledgement.

But returning now to Miss Anderson's room and my strategy to answer up before she finished the question; the same kind of ploy took place while I was in the U. S. Navy on active duty on the Destroyer, USS *Hank* (DD-702), crossing the Atlantic ocean to join up with the Sixth Fleet in the Mediterranean. The Commodore of our Destroyer Squadron recognized a problem that was inherent in joining the Sixth Fleet: how could he get all of his junior officers to read the voluminous binders of information, the hundreds of memos and other documents that were necessary to running that Fleet. The Commodore decided to use a game to sharpen our skills and call attention to the need to read this rather dull material.

The game was played like this; at a designated time, all those junior officers not on watch were required to report to the Combat Information Center where a complete set of the volumes was made available to the group of players. Each ship competed against all the other ships in the squadron and they did this by earning points for correctly answering questions that were sent by a staff officer who worked directly for the Commodore; the staff officer, a Lieutenant, used the common radio telephone circuit for the Squadron; he began by restating the rules and then began asking explicit questions.

If *Hank* was the first to reply, the Commodore's lieutenant gave Auditorium, the *Hank's* code name, permission to answer, whereupon *Hank's* operations officer, Mark Godfred, used the radiotelephone in his hand and replied with an answer 'Sixth-fleet Daily Operational Dress Requirements for Eastern Mediterranean Deployments, Section 3.1.4 – Uniform of the Day, normal working hours, enlisted ranks, March through October – Undress Whites.'

The contest ran for fifteen minutes and *Hank* was winning; Mark was exhibiting an uncanny ability to know exactly where to find the answer, rarely needing the other officers to supply information, but suddenly, the USS *English*, a Destroyer in Destroyer Division twenty-two, our division, became both fast and accurate – they had scored two hits – this was not live ammunition – in a row. This caused Mark to be concerned; he wanted the *Hank* to win and, like my raising my hand before Miss Anderson finished reading the question at Ebinger School, Mark spoke out 'Auditorium Ready,' before his fingers had thumbed through the correct volume and found the answer!

The Commodore's Lieutenant, always suspecting tricks, spoke out immediately "Your answer Auditorium?" on the radio telephone just as quickly as Mark announced we were ready. There was a pause as Mark held the radio telephone handset in one hand and frantically flipped through volumes of directives in the other. But no delays were allowed and the Lieutenant quickly spoke again "Your answer, please, Auditorium?"

At this point everyone on the *Hank* could feel the laughing and remarks that were going on in the Combat Information Centers in the rest of the squadron; people were commenting to each other that the *Hank* was now caught! Most likely, they had all found the right pages and were just itching to get permission to speak. Then, just at the very last minute, before the Lieutenant could disqualify *Hank*, Mark pressed the talk button and began "This is Auditorium, my answer, Sixth-fleet Standing Engineering Orders for Blowing tubes while in Company with Task-force Commanders . . ." We all breathed a sigh of relief.

Before we return to Ebinger School from our detour to the Combat Information Center on the USS *Hank* (DD-702) as it steamed the North Atlantic to rejoin the Sixth-fleet, it is fitting that we comment on the quality of Ebinger school in relation to other elementary schools then operational in the Chicago area. This further digression is necessary for those readers who may have heard of the pejorative reputation of the entire population of Chicago Public Schools. For those readers inclined to think that I am picking on my elementary school – perhaps because of what I have alluded to in the fifth and sixth grade class rooms – I plead innocent; my remarks are chosen in the purely rational cause of analyzing memory.

In defense of this argument I will merely point out that the USS *Hank* (DD-702) was commissioned in 1948 and saw service in the Pacific during World War II. (Parenthetically, I will be speaking of a teacher who also saw service in the Pacific during World War II.) The battle stripes on the *Hank*, some dating from a Kamikaze attack at the entrance to Tokyo Bay, are witness enough to that ship; I shall not proceed further at this time to answer the question of how a World War II Destroyer could be considered battle-ready eighteen years later when it took part in the Cuban Crisis of 1962, a crisis that this writer enjoyed for several reasons while on active duty on the *Hank*.

No, it is only the accepted reputation of Chicago Public Schools that prompts my commentary. On the whole, I would give a grade of 'Good,' 'G,' on Ebinger's Report Card. I support my ranking in the spirit of my father's "The rest of your life you will be ranked" as applying to institutions. Toward that end I present an examination of two teachers at Ebinger who occupied opposite ends of a spectrum. My focus will be on that important criteria that many parents use to evaluate what goes on in a classroom: discipline!

I begin my analysis by pointing out that I find it extremely unusual for a sixth through eighth grader to have as a science and reading teacher – during the three years of departmental methodology – who was one of the most outstanding former Boy Scouts of my own troop, a troop that was led at that time by the father of my own scoutmaster, Mr. George Simmons, Sr. The teacher, Robert Nelson, was not only an Eagle Scout and Vigil Honor member of the Order of the Arrow, but he was also trained as a weatherman at the University of Chicago during World War II and, as previously pointed out, saw service in the Pacific. While teaching science and reading at Ebinger, he attended the University of Chicago Law School during his evenings, and, yes, he was married and raising a young family.

He held the position of Assistant Scoutmaster of my troop, was the head of the High School Sunday School at the Methodist Church, and also participated at the District level of the Boy Scouts; one summer while I was serving on the Camp Wilderness staff at Owasippie Scout Camps in Michigan, he took the troop to Scout Camp for two weeks. Robert Nelson was a role model, clean cut, good looking, and an athlete; when challenged by an Ebinger School student to run a one-hundred yard race with her, he complied, and ran as fast as if it was only the day before that he had earned Athletics Merit Badge; much of the school comprised the audience for the race. He was an accomplished naturalist and, as a former weather expert, spearheaded a great science class. I can still remember how he told us about how raindrops begin to form around what he called 'condensation nuclei.'

But why would I choose a role model who led an outstanding Sunday School class I attended, mentored the Scout Patrol Leaders in my troop and, as well as mine own activities as a Junior Assistant Scoutmaster? Why a person who organized troop competitions for the entire Boy Scout district, competitions that were held during Camporees and in which I excelled? The reason, to my own dismay, was that he could not successfully discipline his Ebinger school classroom!

There was a group of troublemakers in the three departmental grades and the members of this group knew Mr. Nelson from his Scout Troop activities; he was such a good scout in so many ways that when told to stop talking, the troublemakers ignored their teacher and began talking again. This caused Mr. Nelson to go to the blackboard and give the offender still another 'conduct check.' This went on and on until much of the teaching time of the class had been taken up with the sequence of: talking, interruption, another conduct check, and resumption of the business at hand.

After one or more of the troublemakers achieved twenty-five conduct checks the class sensed that the situation was absurd; the offenders kept on talking with complete impunity! As far as I was concerned I felt only sympathy for a person who was giving so much time to my own outside activities while pursuing a law degree and raising a family. To an astute reader the question may arise as to why these individuals, who knew Mr. Nelson as an Assistant Scoutmaster, did not observe the discipline that was present at troop meetings? This question deserves an answer as it forms the basis of one of the many things I liked about the scout troop.

We have already remarked about the need to learn the Scout Law in the long form; it was a holdover going back to Mr. George Simmons, Sr., the earlier Scoutmaster. I cannot say, one way or another, if the Scout Troop discipline used by George Simmons, Jr. was inherited from his father. All I *can* say was that it was extremely effective and, if I may be so bold to emphasize, was loved, even revered, by the scouts. The importance of Scouting to veterans that served in World War II cannot be overestimated. George Simmons, Jr. often related how his scouting experiences helped him survive in the forests of Germany.

As soon as George Simmons Jr. took over the Scout Troop, he explained his disciplinary methods. For this explanation he introduced a long 'paddle' which he made in his shop. It was about three feet long and eight inches wide; it had a grip at one end so it could be grabbed like a baseball bat; it was beautifully varnished; he called the paddle "Allah." Whenever someone violated 'rules' George assigned the miscreant an 'Allah.' What that meant was that, at a later time in the meeting, the miscreant was called forward, told to make a bow to the Allah and then bend over. George gave the miscreant's fanny an Allah. Unlike twenty-five conduct checks, this solved the problem. But, of course, Mr. Nelson couldn't use this approach in a Chicago Public School.

There are, for sure, children who are never exposed to this kind of physical discipline at home; most of these children, I would argue, just don't get out of hand. On the opposite side of that coin, there are spoiled children, bullies, and a whole host of young individuals who think they can get away with anything! Now I was raised in the first group of children but I was given one Allah; George made no exceptions. Let me describe the circumstances.

We were attending a District Camporee at White Pines State Park. The troop was camped on a lovely site and my tent mate, Raymond Schifelbein, and I had retired. We were told that it was 'lights out,' it was tattoo, and if it were the U. S. Navy, the quartermaster of the watch would already have piped 'Keep Silent About the Decks!' Unfortunately, Raymond and I were good friends and, from the seclusion of my Arctic tent, we felt we could continue our earlier conversation. What we didn't know was that like any good Scoutmaster, George Simmons, Jr. made the rounds of the site to see that all was well. He listened outside all of the troop's tents and our tent might have been the only one where talking, albeit subdued, was going on!

The first thing I heard was "All right Schifelbein, that will be one Allah." Raymond and I didn't need to be told why. Raymond crawled out the circular opening in the Arctic tent and I heard a sound of the Allah against Raymond's fanny. The next thing I heard was "All right Ronneberg, you're next." Needless to say, a warm fanny does help one get to sleep.

What ever happened to Mr. Nelson? It was unfortunate that, although he executed a live audition over the course of a week for the position of a television weatherman, he came in second place. Instead of going into television, he acquired the skills of a patent lawyer and then accepted a position at Standard Oil of California in their legal department in California. (For more information on Mr. Nelson and George Simmons, Jr., see Appendix A.) But, my blessed readers, I promised you that I would discuss a dichotomy, the flip side of the discipline coin I began looking at when I spoke about Mr. Nelson, and therefore I must segue to Mrs. Hoff!

Mrs. Hoff taught mathematics. She was not young, she had a piercing stare and her words were brief and cutting! The departmental system required that one class, the current sitting class in Mrs. Hoff's room, be changed with students from another, incoming class. For this swap, the incoming class came through the door between the two classrooms and stood along the side and back-of-the-room aisles of the classroom – where there was standing room – while the sitting class, once the incoming class had their aisle positions, exited, row by row, through the common doorway.

It was always interesting to watch a new class make their first encounter into Mrs. Hoff's class. The exchange was a perfect time for loud whispers and even talking, but as soon as a single word was audible, Mrs. Hoff cut the offenders down with a sharp rebuke as though they had committed a misdemeanor of extraordinary proportions. Naturally, the new arrivals were informed by their friends what to expect; Mrs. Hoff's words were beyond their worst imaginings. But there was an explicit, follow-on punishment that was very real – and, in its way, painful – for offenders who dared to open their mouth a second time, and it was not conduct checks ad nauseam! No, the offender was sentenced to one hour of after-school punishment, the famous long division and multiplication papers of Mrs. Hoff!

During that hour after school you were assigned a number of these papers on which were written long division problems like: 798,643 divided into 1,682,498,301 and multiplication problems like 987,682 times 348,496. Not only was it necessary to get the results exactly correct – including the remainder, if any, to the division problems – but if, in the not rare circumstance you did not complete your quota of papers, you were obliged to appear the next day, and the next, ad infinitum! Certain offenders achieved a bit of peer notoriety by announcing to their friends that they had just completed their second month of after-school hours in Mrs. Hoff's classroom doing papers. One such student, the eldest son of my Cub Pack den parents, spent an entire year in after-school mathematics in Mrs. Hoff's room; after High School he went to the University of Chicago.

When Mrs. Hoff stared her iron-mask stare at you, her words, the tone of her voice, and the knowledge that you had pleasant things to do after school which were much more fun than doing 'papers,' caused even the most intransigent talker to pause for, in most cases, the talker knew several individuals who were still doing papers with no end in sight. The upshot of being in Mrs. Hoff's classroom for learning mathematics was that for a full one-hundred percent of the class time you were learning, and it was quality learning. I can still recall that wonderful lead-in to Algebra that she put on the board "Coat, hat, and gloves all cost \$4.83; the coat cost twice the cost of the hat, the hat cost twice the price of the gloves; how much did each cost?"

So, I imagine, there were extremes in all schools. I, too, had a saying with respect to the quality of my education; it worked like this. As we drove past a good looking school – it could be new construction, site, or just the architecture – I commented to my parents "Boy, could I get good grades in *that* school!" There were certainly extremes in my Chicago Public High School; there were two teachers who had PhD's, and then there was an English teacher who merely read short stories to the class, and a young, good looking, unmarried history teacher who could not control the ducktail hoods in the back rows making personal comments. At least, in High School, the disciplinary officer held a weekend job as a bouncer at a night club and he was feared, but all that is another story. Our task is to return to the misunderstanding concerning memory that occurred during my sixth-grade time at Ebinger Elementary School. To do that we must first examine another teacher, Miss Day.

As they say in the U. S. Navy, Miss Day wore several hats; she was the eight-grade home-room teacher, the assistant principal, and the disciplinarian teacher, all at the same time; she did not moonlight during weekends as a bouncer at a nightclub! I can honestly say that I never learned anything from Miss Day; in the sixth-grade we sat in her room for music. When I remark that I learned nothing whatsoever, that vacuum refers to any pieces of music that we sang. The criteria I use in this judgment involves a comparison with the large number of ensemble pieces that I retain to this day from the two Minstrel Shows I participated in, and these were worth knowing for the rest of one's life; they would include

Grand Old Flag

You're a grand old flag
You're a high-flying flag,
And forever in peace may you wave.
You're the emblem of the land I love,
The home of the free and the brave.

Hot Time In the Old Town

When you hear those bells go ding-a-ling
All join 'round and sweetly you must sing
And when the verse is through, and the chorus all joins in:
"There'll be a hot time in the old town tonight!"

Ida

Ida sweet as apple cider
Sweeter than all I know

Down at the Old Picnic Grounds

The ants held their convention the day that we held ours,
Down at the old picnic grounds.

The chiggers and mosquitos were hiding in the flowers,
Down at the old picnic grounds.
Beside a babbling brook my girl and I thought we would take a rest.
She said "Here is the place to tell me who you love the best."
Then I sat on a fishhook, she sat on a hornets nest,
Down at the old picnic grounds.

Bill Bailey

Won't you come home Bill Bailey,
Won't you come home?

Strawberry Blond

Casey would waltz with the strawberry blond
And the band played on.

If I contrast these songs with the Ebinger School Song that I learned in Miss Day's music class, all I have to show for my total time at Ebinger is "Ebinger, Ebinger, our school, where we work and play," followed by a repeat of the same words. There might have been another line to the effect of "guide us on our way" but I did not care to retain them.

The misunderstanding concerning memory, per se, in the sixth-grade, occurred during a 'special session' which, for all I knew, involved our class visiting Miss Day's classroom to perform a task dictated by her being the assistant principal. But either way, whether it was a special class or a music class, I can truly say that I learned nothing in that classroom; what that special session did for me was strictly a matter of motivation.

After taking our seats Miss Day announced that we were called to her room for a memory test. She explained that she was going to show us cards upon which were printed numbers – some were a single digit, some two digits; each card would be displayed for about ten seconds then another would be displayed; an example would be: 7 19 86 3 55 17 43 26 97 11 2 74 56 93 12 84 33 1 19 52. After all the numbers were displayed, Miss Day asked questions and we were asked to write down the answers on a form with numbers. The questions were similar to the following:

> What was the fifth number?
> What number was after 11?
> What numbers had the digit 3?

The second part of the test did the same type of thing using single letters of the alphabet: an example would be: P L F T U B W M X Z Q K O S R C N B. The questions were similar: What was the letter after X? What was the 9th letter? And so on. The papers were then graded; there was no attempt to explain the test beyond what I have related. I, of course, felt that I had failed, and since there was no explanation of the test, nor any help given with respect to why everyone had failed, I, as well as everyone else, I am sure, came away with the opinion that they had a bad memory. Nothing was mentioned about the test being a test of short term memory! Nothing was said about the difference between short term memory and long term memory. I was convinced that I had a bad memory, period!

Once again my inner-direction came to the fore, my propensity to act – True worth is in *being*, not *seeming* – caused me to begin memorizing long poems that I enjoyed reading; I began with *Paul Revere's Ride* by Henry Wadsworth Longfellow; it was in my mother's book of *101 Famous Poems*:

Paul Revere's Ride

> Listen, my children, and you shall hear
> Of the midnight ride of Paul Revere,
> On the eighteenth of April, in Seventy-five;
> Hardly a man is now alive
> Who remembers that famous day and year.

I would love to have listened to Miss Day explain what the test was all about, but it was too late! A process began that incorporated future memorization tasks arising from many different promptings. At the time I began *Paul Revere's Ride*, I had no idea about where this process would take me, no inkling as to what kind of future encounters with life would rekindle the flame. It was as though a single gleam of light had been lit in the belfry's height – my brain cells – and then, as I lingered and gazed on the world, a second lamp in my belfry was lit, not from a spark arising from the pebbles of Paul Revere's horse, but a kind of internal spark that flew every bit as fearless and fleet as it kindled my motive for memorization into a flame with its heat.

The next encounter at age eleven came, literally out of the flames of a burning campfire; from that initial campfire there arose a whole sequence of major memory efforts, more than I could imagine at the time when only the very first piece of memorization was completed. I have already alluded to the seriousness of my Scoutmaster, George Simmons, Jr., when it came to how his scouting experiences helped him survive in the forests of Germany; some of these so called survival skills were camping tricks that made life in the outdoors more bearable. In this category were things like how to make a night's sleep more restful on the forest floor.

I took an interest in this kind of information because I was subjected to the inconveniences of outdoor living throughout my scouting career. One of the first instances of those trials came when I was only eleven years old; it occurred in conjunction with attending my first National Jamboree in 1950 held at Valley Forge, Pennsylvania. There were reasons why adults and even the U. S. Government were interested in these types of massive camping experiences where contingents of troops – composed of individuals from many source-troops – came together for a week from every state in the union.

A Boy Scout National Jamboree had not been held in the United States since 1937 – this was, of course, due to World War II – but the feat of bringing together tens of thousands of scouts formed into troops – implying they did not know each other – and patrols within those troops, who were to live together for a week, was an undertaking not to be taken lightly. With merely a weekend to prepare for the event, eight person patrols would have to learn to work together in order to cook all their meals, keep their food fresh without any on-site refrigeration, take care of laundry, fresh drinking water, the washing of dishes using very hot water, cooking with charcoal briquettes, the issues of supply, communication, entertainment, fellowship, and so on; it was no mean trick.

It was an open fact that such an accomplishment could no longer be carried out by the U. S. Army; by 1953, the next Scout Jamboree, after 1950, the attendance rose to fifty-thousand! And this next Jamboree was held on a very parched piece of California, the Irving Ranch; after one week of camping, small, circular grass shoots began to appear below the huge canvas lister bags – much like a monk's tonsure – where the fresh drinking water had dropped during the week. At Valley Forge, Pennsylvania, in 1950, the weather was not as bad as the year General George Washington encamped with his troops during the winter; nor was there the lack of foliage in Pennsylvania as there was in California in 1953; both Jamborees took place in the summer. Each troop – typically put together from a large city – was allotted a square of ground that was eighty feet in both directions.

Nor did Valley Forge have any of the problems that George Simmons, Jr. encountered in the forests of Germany during World War II; we camped out in the open. What, then, could it have been that sorely taxed the Chicago troop and many others? We attended a pre-jamboree camping experience at Camp Kiwanis south of Chicago where we built our picnic table from raw lumber and a set of instructions, started our charcoal briquette fires with homemade wax and particle board starters, and cooked our meals precisely as outlined in the detailed instructions for each and every meal. We rotated the positions of cook, assistant cook, dishwasher, assistant dishwasher, and fire starters. We learned to make frying fires and boiling fires; we could set up our dining fly with the picnic table below it in a wind storm if necessary, and we knew how to store our cooking equipment in the large, wooden, kitchen trunk as it stood on its four legs while one side, the hinged side, was open so as to provide a horizontal working table.

No, it was something that no one ever could have dreamed of! When each patrol was shown its two pieces of ground – within the eighty by eighty foot troop area – where the dinning fly, and the patrol's two-person tents were to be pitched, the first thing we saw was that the entire troop square was covered with poison ivy plants! Needless to say, George Washington had winter weather but we had poison ivy; we became obsessed not with how we were to cross the Delaware river, but with how to avoid poison ivy for seven consecutive days!

For several reasons, dear reader, it is necessary to supply a footnote to this experience of surviving poison ivy at Valley Forge, Pennsylvania. One reason is that my return from Pennsylvania involves a lapse of memory which remains unaccountable to me; another reason is that what followed after Valley Forge is an excellent segue to the next major source of my memorization of large amounts of material. Perhaps I was too tired from thinking about poison ivy or too familiar with flying with father long distances. The memory lapse came about because the 1950s Jamboree was held the first week of a two-week camping period for my Chicago troop at camp Dan Beard in Michigan. George Simmons, Jr. took the troop that year and if I took the train back from Pennsylvania to Chicago, I would arrive too late to spend the second week with my Chicago troop at Dan Beard; the Dan Beard camp was to be my first opportunity to attend an Owasippie Scout camp. Father reasoned that the only way out of this dilemma was for him to fly his single-engine aircraft to Valley Forge, pick me up, and fly me directly to Michigan.

Of course, the whole idea, in retrospect, seems quite bizarre! But looking at it from my father's standpoint, it seems reasonable for several reasons: Point one – I would be able to attend the second week at the Michigan camp with my own troop and could relate my experiences at the first Scout Jamboree held since 1937. Point two – I would have George

Simmons, Jr. as my Scoutmaster in camp, and Point three – my father's friend, Peter Orlebeck, was Camp Director at Camp Beard all summer long, a job he held for many years.

By virtue of Peter being a friend, my swap from one camp to another would be a simple task; why was this? Every Friday afternoon – during the summer vacation months – father flew from Elmhurst airport west of Chicago, around the bottom of Lake Michigan, and then north to Bass Lake, north of Pentwater, Michigan, where his family was in residence at the family summer home. His children would listen for the sound of his plane circling the lake all Friday afternoon and when identified, run out to the end of the pier, wave beach towels at the plane whereupon he would level off and land nine miles to the north at Ludington, Michigan, airport. My mother would then pick him up for residency at our summer home on Bass Lake for the weekend.

All that was necessary to perform the swap was to alert Peter Orlebeck of the day on which he would circle Owasippe Lake and the location of the tiny airstrip near Rothbury, Michigan. Peter would turn over the camp to his assistant director, drive to the Rothbury site, pick me up together with my duffel bag and take me to rejoin my own troop at their campsite. Father would take off and within twenty minutes would circle Bass Lake to the north, and would soon be back with the rest of the family. So what was the lapse in this odyssey?

The lapse was that I have no memory whatsoever of the flight except the final pickup and delivery to my new troop site! Once there, I remember the hike to Ergang's Lake and Headwater Hill, and I can also remember taking classes in First Aid Merit Badge from Harold Donovan, a scoutmaster of many, many years at St. Juliana School; the two troops always booked a Beard campsite together; it was a tradition; the churches were close to each other. The two camping locations, Ergang's Lake and Headwater Hill, were popular camping locations in the Owasippe system which comprised thousands of acres. George Simmons, Jr. had another tradition that he enforced – the insistence that a troop leave a campsite cleaner than how they found it.

What this meant was that before the troop left the site everyone was assigned an area and given the task of going over the ground 'as with a fine tooth comb.' Any piece of paper, however tiny, needed to be picked up, in fact, it was more than just paper; any man-made item, i.e., any item that was not placed at the campsite by mother nature was to be picked up and carried away. There was an inspection carried out by George before the troop moved out; it took only one inspection for everyone to know just how miniscule a bit of plastic needed to be before it should be picked up. It was a collective task that every scout related to; somehow it was translated into a procedure that marked the entire troop as possessing an outdoor culture that we were proud of; I can't think of anyone who resisted the effort.

At the same time, even as an eleven year old, I was proud of the things I was learning during those two weeks, one in Pennsylvania, the other in Michigan. Obviously I was proud of learning how to cope with poison ivy. Another item might seem obvious but with respect to comfort I felt it was very important; it had to do with my sleeping bag. Father purchased two arctic sleeping bags from World War II surplus. These were down bags that had an inner bag, much like a mummy bag, and an outer bag; everyone also used a ground cloth to put under the sleeping bag. It was clear that I did not need the outer bag for summer camping but the inner bag was extremely warm; the alternative was another army surplus item, a wool bag that itched! The poison ivy experience and the hot weather at Headwater Hill forced me to seek relief; the answer was simple. The outer bag had a thin covering; by merely using the very fluffy and comfortable arctic inner bag as a mattress and the thin covering as a sheet – that adequately kept mosquitoes away – I ended up with a good solution. In the event of a cold spell in the evening, I could easily slip into the inner, mummy bag.

But there was one other event that stood out; I ask you, astute reader that you are, what could that be? Can you guess? For me it was being a witness to a famous Allah delivered to a bully and a spoiled brat, a fellow who was big enough to push anyone around just for fun. What made the Allah special beyond the mere fact that he broke a rule, and his mean personality, was that the Allah was delivered after swimming period in Owasippie Lake; it was 'the smack heard around the campsite and a bit beyond!' But poison ivy, dear reader, as you might have already surmised, has nothing to do with my motivation for more memory effort; for that, we must return to that pre-jamboree camping experience at camp Kiwanis.

I was to be expected that, like any Scout camping experience, there would be a campfire with songs and entertainment in the evening. It was at the entertainment in the evening of this pre-jamboree camping weekend that the spark that began another burst of effort was experienced. The boys and leaders who would take the train to Valley Forge had enough on their hands during the weekend at camp Kiwanis just to get familiarized with how to build a picnic table from scratch, how to set up new types of sleeping tents, the dining fly, starting charcoal fires – including actual practice with how to make a 'frying' fire and a 'boiling water' fire used to heat the water for washing dishes; and let's not forget the important culinary art of making Jamboree Stew.

The upshot of all this learning was that the entertainment part of the program was assigned to one of the professional Scout Executives who were appointed by their boss, the Chief Scout Executive of Chicago, to look after this. To make a long story short, one of these Scout Executives recited *The Cremation of Sam McGee* by Robert Service and, after the campfire, handed me a small pamphlet with about ten of Service's most popular poems. You, my reader, must have heard it recited; it was the one that began with eight lines at the beginning which were repeated at the end:

> *There are strange things done in the midnight sun*
> *By the men who moil for gold;*
> *The Arctic trails have their secret tales*
> *That would make your blood run cold;*
> *The Northern Lights have seen queer sights,*
> *But the queerest they ever did see*
> *Was that night on the marge of Lake Lebarge*
> *I cremated Sam McGee.*

The Scout Executive who recited the poem was both humorous and an entertainer. I was impressed with the recitation, couldn't understand why I was given the pamphlet, and I ended up memorizing the entire poem.

But I didn't stop there; I kept on going. It took time but I soon memorized *The Shooting of Dan McGrew*:

A BUNCH of the boys were whooping it up in the Malamute saloon;
The kid that handles the music-box was hitting a jag-time tune;
Back of the bar, in a solo game, sat Dangerous Dan McGrew,
And watching his luck was his light-o'-love, the lady that's known as Lou.

The Ballad if Hard-Luck Henry

Now wouldn't you expect to find a man an awful crank
That's staked out nigh three hundred claims, and every one a blank;
That's followed every fool stampede, and see the rise and fall
Of camps where men got gold in chunks and he got none at all;
That's prospected a bit of ground and sold it for a song
To see it yield a fortune to some fool that came along;
That's sunk a dozen bed-rock holes, and not a speck in sight,
Yet sees them take a million from the claims to left and right?
Now aren't things like that enough to drive a man to booze?
But Hard-Luck Smith was hoodoo-proof – he knew the way to lose.

and *The Men That Don't Fit In*

There's a race of men that don't fit in,
        A race that can't stay still;
So they break the hearts of kith and kin,
        And they roam the world at will.
They range the field and they rove the flood,
        And they climb the mountain's crest;

Theirs is the curse of the gypsy blood,
    And they don't know how to rest.

I put these poems under my belt or, put another way, captured within those eighty-five billion brain cells, each with their ten-thousand connections, the words of these poems so that I, too, could recite them at campfires. In fact, I can distinctly remember when the Sam McGee poem came in very handy; you might say it was an instance of that little saying that stood on the desk of my High School Principal, Mr. Hoefer, 'Luck is when preparedness and opportunity meet.'

After graduation from High School I took a nine week job as Head Ranger at the Chicago Council's Owasippie Scout Camp, Camp Stuart. Every two weeks a group of two hundred and fifty new scouts and their leaders arrived by train from Chicago. At the opening campfire each department head was responsible for a skit; I used the Sam McGee poem for the Ranger Department; I gave it four times that summer. First, I picked a ranger on my staff to act out the part of Sam. I used a very lean, gaunt looking ranger to take that part, the epitome of the words:

Now Sam McGee was from Tennessee, where the cotton blooms and blows,
Why he left his home in the south to roam 'round the Pole, God only knows,
He was always cold, but the land of gold seemed to hold him like a spell;
Though he'd often say in his homely way that "he'd sooner live in hell."

I used other ranger staff members as well to take roles like the narrator of the poem and to act out the team of huskies.

By the time of the Ranger Department skit at Camp Stuart, the big campfire was burned down to coals. The Stuart campfire rink was set in the woods on a beautiful promontory; just beyond the trees that formed a wonderful, circular sweep, was a natural prairie with a tiny woodland lake. The audience could easily imagine seeing Lake Lebarge ahead, through the woods. Lake Lebarge is the destination of the poem, where the cremation takes place. It was the campfire, however, that suggested the site even more forcefully than the lake in the woods; the marge of Lake Lebarge has a derelict cabin with a boiler inside:

> Some planks I tore from the cabin floor, and I lit the boiler fire;
> Some coal I found that was lying around, and I heaped the fuel higher;
> The flames just soared, and the furnace roared – such a blaze you seldom see;
> And I burrowed a hole in the glowing coal, and I stuffed in Sam McGee.
> Then I made a hike, for I didn't like to hear him sizzle so;

But while we are on the subject of this group of Robert Service poems, I should mention that it didn't take a campfire with an audience of two hundred and fifty scouts, all looking down from their seats on logs arranged in semi-circular rows, to provide me with an opportunity to recite one of these poems. No, there was a one-on-one recital with one of my wife's aunts; the recital occurred many years later and we were discussing one of my wife's cousins. I asked my wife's aunt if she ever heard *The Men That Don't Fit In?* She replied "no" and I recited it for her. Readers, let me assure you that there is nothing so powerful as a source, no matter what it is, that explains to a parent the actions of her child; and I should add that if you, my reader, are that child, I can only say that I made your mother very, very happy that day; she affirmed my recitation line by line, as though it was a piece of prophecy!

But we must return to that path that leads forward; it was a mere two years later, again, at a scout camp in the summer time, that another spark was ignited which would cause memorization all through High School and even beyond. That event was my initiation into the Order of the Arrow, a society of scout campers who perpetuate the founding myth of Chingachgook, the aged chieftain of the Lenni Lenape tribe of Delaware Indians, and his noble son Uncas. Rallying the Delawares, viewed as their brothers, they went on a journey to recruit those who were willing to spend themselves in other's service.

It is not my intention, blessed reader, to compromise the secrets of the Order of the Arrow but to examine the nature of the sparks that lit such a long-lasting flame. And for this we must focus on another dimension of our memory which, as human beings, plays as active a role as those poems that were cached in my long term memory. I refer to *visual memory*, a memory of vivid impressions, set pieces that speak to us like great art, and individuals whose presence means something to us; such memories can be seen through a telescope or even a high powered magnifying glass. There are, then, as many visual images vying for permanent membership alongside the uncounted thousands that have already won their place by virtue of an attraction that was so penetrating to our consciousness that we willed that it never leave our memory; in that sense they are like that first willing that I made as a child.

Who can forget the maternity ward nurse when she held up the first infant born to a family? Who can willingly disremember the first time she opened her eyes underwater? Who can forget the exquisite stem of tiny Helleborine Orchids when first seen through a magnifying glass? Because of these kinds of images and their effect upon us, I have chosen to speak of this population of visual impressions that made their way into my permanent memory as if they had found a long lost home. When combined with the words that were uttered in the context of the life experiences I am about to describe, I find there is no other way to describe the totality of the effect except as a *romance*! My topic, then, is simply 'The Romance of the Order of the Arrow.' And I will go so far as to say that though love between a man and a woman, a love affair, might possibly occur 'across a crowded room' and be driven by a perception that encapsulates love at first sight, the Romance of the Order of the Arrow seems to involve a more complex conjunction of parts, parts that strongly appeal to values that we have already internalized.

And now I must make an apology to you, my reader, for, in the examination of the romance of the Order of the Arrow, I must needs begin with a mystery; I cannot omit the mystery that forms the prologue to everything that followed; it is intended that it be that way – "In its (The Order of the Arrow's) ceremonies it employs the element of mystery, for the sake of its effect on the Scouts who enter. Its Ceremonies are NOT put on in public at a camp because of the knowledge that this would decrease their appeal to the boy as he first participates in them." My apology is to the readers who have already been exposed to the following short exposition, *The Coming of the Chief.* Coming as it does following my first exposure as an eleven year old with my troop at Camp Beard in 1950, it sets up the first scene of the romance. Readers already familiar with that scene may scan or skip it as you will, the essential building blocks of the Romance follow the prologue:

* * *

The Coming of the Chief

There was only one point in time toward which all thoughts converged during the first week of that particular year at summer camp. At dusk on the second Sunday, the entire camp would silently wend their way down to the beach, like monks attending vespers, and arrange themselves into the form of a huge triangle. At each corner was placed a tinder-dry pine fire ready to burst instantly into crackling flames at the touch of a torch. Each leg of the triangle was actually a double row of boys separated by perhaps fifteen feet so that each person could look into the faces opposite him, but, even more importantly, could see what would transpire behind those who would become the chosen few.

The enforced silence itself was unusual, and campers who had never paused for reflection in the afterglow of a summer sunset were prompted to do so now by the beauty of the scene. Those who had witnessed the ceremony before knew where to look for the tiny point of light across the lake that would grow in intensity as the canoe came across the mirror-like surface with a masculine Indian standing in the center holding a flaming torch.

The paddlers were more primitively dressed and stripped to the waist; they impressed with their muscles, the accuracy of their stroke, and the sweat that stood out amongst the war paint, all illumined by the torch and its reflection on the glassy surface. The standing figure however, was no mere brave, for his headdress, double trailer, and stature bespoke the quiet dignity of a Chief.

As if the glow of the sunset itself were returning in the red, yellow, and orange of the flames, thousands of eyes refocused until the canoe gently nudged the sandy shore. No one was prepared, however, for the sudden alteration in mood that now occurred, for no sooner had the party embarked than one of the braves took up the torch, leaving the Chief standing with folded arms across his chest. In a burst of raw energy he ran the triangle at a speed that seemed impossible given the sand. "Could he extinguish the flame with such speed?" was the question on all minds as he raced between the rows and the flame noisily brightened in the breeze of his effort.

As if by magic, the three corner fires had been lit, and the darkness of summer night was now illumined by the four fires with the first magnitude stars Vega and Deneb all but obscured. When the brave returned to his starting point, a procession of three now began a slower walk through the assembled rows, a torch bearer in the lead, followed by the magnificent Chief, again with his arms folded, and finally the second brave with a bow and quiver.

At this time the uninitiated could observe small branches of white pine boughs being held over the heads of a certain few individuals in the opposite row by assistants who wore white sashes with red arrows across their chests. The lead torch-bearer would stop so that the Chief, by turning ninety degrees, could face the individual so chosen. Maintaining an unflinching gaze and raising a bronzed and muscular arm fitted with a pad of leather over the palm, the Chief raised his arm and came down hard upon the shoulder of the chosen one with a resounding sound of leather upon flesh. This was repeated twice more, whereupon the Chief turned and moved one pace further with the torch-bearer.

Now the third Indian drawing an arrow from his quiver turned toward the tapped candidate and, pulling the bow to its full extent, pointed the arrow directly at the forehead, slowly lowered it on a line dissecting the body, and discharged the shaft into the sand between the feet of the person he faced. As the three-person ceremonial team moved forward to locate the next of the chosen few, a quiet assistant was seen to attach a small live white pine bough to the person who had been tapped.

The process continued until all so designated had been tapped and marked. The three Indians then returned to their canoe and, in the same manner as their arrival, disappeared into the dark recesses of the lake until the torch, now only a small point of light, extinguished itself in an instant like the last ray of the sunset itself at a far horizon disappears leaving only a memory of its intensity.

Without the need of spoken words the camp disappeared from the beach, leaving only the group that stood with arrows between their legs and pine branches fastened to their persons. For those who walked silently to their tents, the answer to the question of what it all meant would now be deferred until another summer.

* * *

Have you, my reader, ever been kept past your usual bedtime and told to remain completely silent while returning to your tent with the mission of gathering up your sleeping bag in preparation for a night alone at a place unknown? When you returned to the beach of the above related ceremony you were told to follow two Indian guides – both carrying blazing torches, one in front and the other in back of a long line of candidates like yourself – deep into a portion of the forest where you never travelled before, nor even knew of the path. If so, can you recall that line of tired scouts weaving along a narrow track with only a full moon to supplement the light and eerie blazing of the torches held high by the two braves, their muscles gleaming bronze in the torchlight?

And then, my reader, can you recall that first time you glanced forward – after what seemed a long journey – and saw the glow of a blazing fire within a hidden rink? As you approached you saw that the rink was formed with posts around its circumference and atop each post other pots of flame were mounted. As you entered through a gateway you saw a mighty chief in full dress together with his guard and guide; the chief had returned to the secret rink from far across the lake where you last saw the light of his torch and his canoe disappear into the darkness. The chief tells you what you already knew: that it was your fellow troop members who elected you; he outlines the solemn and serious steps you will need to take in the next twenty-four hours; he calls the experience an ordeal; he gives every candidate an opportunity to go no further on the journey without a shadow of discredit to one so inclined.

From the romantic setting of the calling out ceremony – as per *The Coming of the Chief* – to the intensity of the campfires, the torches, the silence, the winding path, the hidden rink, the night alone that still lies ahead, and the words of what have been said, a multitude of impressions have entered your consciousness, but that is only the second scene of the first act; an even deeper and more romantic scene, tinged with the sense of the unbelievable, awaits. You hear the guide admonish you to, in strictest silence, and with courage, take up your blanket; you begin a second journey.

The new path takes you from the rink in the dark forest out into a sandy area on the edge of the forest where you perceive a medicine man fully dressed. From the distance as you leave the tree line, the medicine man stands up from the edge of a small lake surrounded by reeds and sedges; there is a full moon over the medicine man and he stands tall like a set piece, immobile in the strength and power of his statuesque pose; his arms are crossed; he is painted so that the left side of his face is white and the right side black; the borderline splits his eyes, nose, lips, and continues further down and under his chin; the closer you come, the more you feel his dramatic presence.

The two Indians, the guard Indian and the guide Indian, have joined the medicine man. The torch-bearing guides arrange themselves so that the light of their torches falls on the faces of the three Indians. You are arranged in a semicircle; words are spoken. Unless you are a completely insensitive person, most of those words pierce your heart, mind, and spirit; you cannot but want to memorize them, to burn them into your memory as soon as the opportunity arrives; you sense they are words that will guide you through life.

After the initial lines are spoken – lines which refer, in part, to the Scout Oath and the pledges made therein – the medicine man gives advice in the form of admonitions to listen to for guidance on your journey. These words crystalize prior feelings towards the out-of-doors and nature, in such a way that you find them relevant every time you recall them:

> Long ago, when bear and bison
> Swarmed the forest and the prairie,
> Then the great and mighty chieftain,
> Looked with love upon his children;
> Saw them striving, fighting, battling
> With the evil that abounded;
> And he spoke and said in this wise:
> You who love the haunts of nature,
> Love the moonlight on the water,
> Love the sunshine on the meadow,
> Love the shadow of the forest,
> Love the wind among the branches,
> Ever murmuring, ever sighing,
> Love the rushing of great rivers
> Through their palisades of pine trees,
> Love the thunder in the mountains,
> Whose innumerable echoes
> Leap and bound from crag to cliffsides;

Listen to these admonitions
For your guidance in your journey!

Scene three ends with a prayer given by the medicine man; it encapsulates notions that resonate with Biblical passages. But the scene ends with the last two lines of the prayer, lines that must be the hope of every person who lives in the world today for they scream out two words so sorely needed; two simple lines that, hopefully, might allow Sunni and Shiite, Muslim and Hindu, Catholic and Protestant, and so many other combinations all across history to be reconciled. The words are so simple: *"Pray you now in reverent silence, Each of you in your own fashion."*

Call you now upon your Father,
Great Creator of all nations.
To grant blessings on His children,
From His high and holy station
Guiding you upon your journey.
That His hand be stretched out to you,
As you ever help His people;
That His light may ever lead you;
As you lead the wayward to Him;
That His love be ever with you,
As you love your fellow mortals.
That His Spirit rest upon you
Till at last He calls you Home.
Pray you now in reverent silence,
Each of you in your own fashion.

(Pause for at least one minute, for silent prayer.)

And what are the two words that need to be screamed out? Pluralism! Tolerance! And how propitious, then, the last line of the last tenet of the Scout Law "A Scout is Reverent. A scout is reverent toward God. He is faithful in his religious duties. *He respects the convictions of others in matters of custom and religion."* We must return to the Romance of the Order of the Arrow.

There are overtones of Longfellow's *Hiawatha* throughout the ceremonies of the Order; this, too, affected anyone who had memorized *Paul Revere's Ride* and knew of *Hiawatha*:

* * *

At the door on summer evenings,
Sat the little Hiawatha;
Heard the whispering of the pine-trees,
Heard the lapping of the waters,
Sounds of music, words of wonder;

. . .

Saw the moon rise from the water,
Rippling, rounding from the water,
Saw the flecks and shadows on it,

* * *

The meter of the poetry and the images of Hiawatha were awakened once again in the audience that stood in the moonlight and heard the lines that began "You who love the haunts of nature," but there was more for the Legend of the Order also reflected the calm and peace of *Hiawatha's Childhood*:

Years ago, in the dim ages
In the valley of the Delaware,
Lived a peaceful tribe of Indians –
Lenni Lenape their name was.
Deer and bear, wildcat and panther
Through the forest oft they hunted.
On the bosom of the river
Peacefully they fished and paddled.

Round their busy village wigwams
Still the chase they nimbly followed.
In this state of bliss so happy
Many moons they lived contented,
Springtime blossomed into summer,
Summer into autumn ripened,
Autumn died on winter's bosom;
Thus the seasons in succession
Never ending seemed to pass on.

* * *

By the shores of Gitche Gumee,
By the shining Big-Sea-Water,
Stood the wigwam of Nokomis,
Daughter of the Moon, Nokomis.
Dark behind it rose the forest,
Rose the black and gloomy pine-trees
Rose the firs with cones upon them;
Bright before it beat the water,
Beat the clear and sunny water,
Beat the shining Big-Sea-Water.

* * *

But another factor in the Romance of the Order deals with the way the Scout Oath and Law are central, not only to many lines in the ritual, but are particularly emphasized in the closing ceremony of the Lodge where candles are extinguished; a typical passage is the first of three given by the Guard of the Lodge:

"As guard of this Lodge, I would be ever mindful of my duty faithfully to exemplify the points of the Scout Law represented by these candles which I now extinguish as we close our Lodge: A scout is Cheerful; A

Scout is thrifty; A Scout is Brave; A Scout is Clean; and always to live that part of our Scout Promise which describes our duty to ourselves: To keep ourselves physically strong, mentally awake and morally straight. May it be our steadfast purpose that, although we snuff these candles as we leave this circle, the virtues which they represent may glow the brighter in our hearts and consciences."

Another, more elaborate rink, again, deep in the forest, was used for the closing ceremony and for explaining the Ordeal or first level of the Order. Twelve candles represented the Scout Law and three candles the Scout Promise. The closing lines, delivered as they were after the formal ceremony, seemed an appropriate capstone to the entire suite of romantic elements. But what effect did these ceremonies, these words, these images, even the true identity of the Indians who spoke the lines, have upon me. First, I wanted to learn them simply because of their beauty and wisdom; they sealed my experience. Secondly, I wanted to partake in the activities of the Order and speak the lines during the ceremonies.

I speak of ceremonies because I took the second degree, the so-called Brotherhood level of membership; and, after that ceremony, I began memorizing the lines appropriate to it. Finally, I was nominated for the Vigil Honor. This caused me to make an elaborate Indian costume appropriate to the Vigil Honor member, and to memorize the lines of that ceremony. Altogether, then, *The Coming of the Chief* caused a new way of life to emerge within my High School years and beyond and a major, life-long component of that particular activity was the memorization of the lines of those three rituals.

Just as the final spark of my memory journey occurred between High School and College – the summer of my induction into the Vigil Honor – so too, the sporadic aftershocks came to an end after college. There seemed to be no further motives for long-term memory projects, in fact, the short-term memory demands were ubiquitous, even daily. One could make the claim that I became addicted to learning something every day! The Navy, correspondence courses, IBM, masters degrees, and auditing classes were the drivers of this passion which still remains. But there were pin pricks of light that we should examine before we close this recital of memory sparks. The first of these came while still in High School, one at home, the other in school.

For some reason or other I was watching a television show; I hasten to remark that I never owned a television once I left my family for the married state. It was a show hosted by Dave Garroway; in the context of that show he presented a poem, *Etiquette*, written by William Schwenk Gilbert of Gilbert and Sullivan fame; I knew immediately that it deserved a place in my long-term memory – and so it remains.

* * *

The Ballyshannon floundered off the coast of Cariboo;
And down in fathoms many went the captain and the crew;

. . .

* * *

The second point of light came in my High school chemistry class.

In that chemistry class I realized that if I outlined each chapter of our Chemistry Book, *Modern Chemistry*, written by Charles E. Dull, H. Clark Metcalfe, and William O. Brooks, I could achieve a high grade on every test. I can remember Mr. McCalmont, our High School teacher speaking to the chemistry class before he handed back each test; he spoke slowly with a pronounced and profound emphasis: "Some of you have clearly indicated that you have never opened (he held up a copy of *Modern Chemistry*), let alone read, any words by Messer's Dull, . . . Metcalfe, . . . and Brooks!"

The other two demands that exercised my need for short-term memory proficiency were inorganic chemistry taught by Professor John Turkevich at Princeton University and my Architectural history classes at that same institution. Professor Turkevich was a performer; he was named one of the most popular lecturers, was fluent in Russian, a pioneer in catalytic research, and worked on the Manhattan Project. He possessed a broad smile, was ambidextrous, and switched the chalk stick from left to right as he wrote out the important points of his lecture. He often threw out experiences of what went on at Oak Ridge, Tennessee, and the chemical methodologies for the isolation of Uranium. His favorite classroom experiment – taken from a huge repertoire of 'show piece' digressions – was an explosion!

This experiment began by pointing out a glass tube about fourteen inches high, two inches in diameter, and filled with oxygen and hydrogen gasses. The tube was surrounded by hardware cloth with one-quarter inch square holes. With the smile and gestures of a mad scientist he explained for the nth time "A mixture of oxygen and hydrogen, we need a catalyst!" He then cut a strip of magnesium about two feet long, and lit the strip with a match; it burned like a welder's rod; the class was tempted to look away. "The Catalyst! – Light!" he shouted as he moved the burning strip to a point just outside the hardware cloth.

There was a huge explosion, and an enormous smile that was like a child's who has caused a shock to those that are looking on; Professor Turkevich turned quickly to the blackboard and with both hands working, from left to right, one after the other, wrote the following on the blackboard:

$$2H_2 + O_2 = 2H_2O$$

while exclaiming "Hydrogen plus Oxygen . . . equals Water!" as though a new and exciting chemical discovery had just been made.

There was no textbook in the Inorganic Chemistry class at Princeton. I likened Professor Turkevich's creating water and other stunts to Mr. McCalmont's: "Some of you have clearly indicated that you have never opened (he held up a copy of *Modern Chemistry*), let alone read, any words by Messer's Dull, . . . Metcalfe, . . . and Brooks!" More importantly, I quickly realized that I needed to take detailed notes of every word spoken in the lecture and then, in order to get ready for a written test, outline all the lectures before that test! It worked again, I did quite well in Inorganic Chemistry.

For my final scene, I see myself sitting in the dimly lit lower level of the Princeton University hall that housed Architectural studies; I am the only student that seeks this basement-like area. In my hands are hundreds of small slips of paper on which I have written words and dates that must be exactly memorized so that if used in a future essay exam – an exam that uses 'unknown' photographic images projected at the front of the exam room – there will be no spelling errors nor any incorrect dates in those essays. The words are the names of architects, buildings, and locations of buildings, loggias, gateways, and in fact, anything that an architect from the past may have designed, built, or even just put in a volume he wrote on the subject; the slips are spellings in various languages. We shall look at two of such slips:

* * *

German Rococo
Balthasar Neumann
Vierzehnheiligen
Franconia
1743 to 1772

* * *

16th Century Italian
Renaissance
Andrea Palladio
Villa Rotunda
Vicenza
1567

* * *

And so it went, hour after hour. Only after such periods of preparation could I respond with the precise analysis, the thought process that sifted known buildings and architectural motifs toward the solution of the 'unknown,' so unlike the 'unknown' inorganic substances we identified in Chemistry lab which all appeared as white powers! In the Architectural History class I could support my identification of a façade as being so very much like Filippo Brunelleschi's Foundling Hospital in Florence, begun in 1419. With such precise points of memory supporting my essay, I could, ultimately, spring to my verdict as to exactly where, when, and by whom did the responsibility belong for the image on the screen of an unknown; and I would not lose points for misspelling, no matter what it took to arrive at my conclusion; it would help my class rank.

Home

If you have come this far, blessed reader, without turning back, then I congratulate you! You have been submitted to environments as diverse as Valley Forge, Pennsylvania, the forests of Michigan, and the bookshelves of my father. Now we seek a new dimension: the concept of home, the place where one lives, the place where one was born or raised, a place thought of as home, and a household and its affairs.

Again I must pose the warning that gets issued from the forests of Michigan "Let any of you who, facing this Ordeal, if, for reasons that need be known only to yourself, you desire to go no further on this journey, you may now retire in silence to your quarters without shadow of discredit to yourself." I have, of course, not explained the nature of any Ordeal you may encounter in the next twenty-four hours. But these words *do* remind one of the difference between home and quarters; quarters are mere lodgings. But what, then, characterizes a home? It is well that we ask this kind of question before the scope of 'home' extends from the cities of Illinois, New Jersey, and California, and from the forests of Michigan, and Illinois, to the high seas.

That question occupies our attention in the same way as I once struggled to discover and then articulate the belief systems of my mother and father. Across the spectrum of 'a place one lives,' a 'place where born or raised,' 'a place *thought* of as a home,' 'and a household and its affairs,' there must exist, somewhere, an even longer and more diverse list of criteria that injects some kind of rational analysis, some kind of unifying structure for this important concept. Further, the choice of the five homes that father owned might yield some insights into his belief system. But there are three times that number of homes that will come within the rubric of this concept.

"Home is where the heart is," is too simple an answer. "There are more things in heaven and earth, Horatio, than are dreamt of in your philosophy." was meant to refer to belief systems, but there are, too, more things within those eighty-five billion brain cells, each with ten-thousand connections, that allow us to pronounce the high honor extended to homes. These are the environments, the incidents, the surroundings, the people, and many other kinds of associated values, good or bad, that merit the ultimate knighting of a mere lodging, or even a cave, to the high honors of a home.

And these knighted homes, arising as they do from within a lifetime, present to the committee recommending knighthood, differing reasons that are offered as a function of the committee member's age. One might allow for the fact that from the child's perspective the environment defining the home – as with a place of birth – differs from the parental environment of 'a household and its affairs.' The focus, the criteria, and the analysis of the mature adult are a mélange of all the homes experienced, from the latter back to the former.

The task, then, is to articulate across time how this growing sequence of checkered residences comprise a story that exhibits some kind of consistency and maybe even a perspective on the human condition; but we must begin! Not only shall we begin from a child's perspective but we shall borrow from that visual image of an Architectural History student memorizing words written on small slips of paper in preparation for identifying 'unknowns' in the context of an examination; let us choose a paper slip; ah, here it is:

Chicago Depression Era
Architecture
Red Brick Bungalow
7240 West Pratt Avenue
Edison Park
Chicago
1930s

As one drives up and down the residential streets of Chicago it becomes apparent that for a certain, extended period in Chicago's architectural history, the so called 'brick bungalow' was built by the tens of thousands. Whether it be the far Northwest side or the West side, the traveler who pays attention to these things cannot but be amazed at the sheer numbers – block after block – of this genre of dwelling. The Art Institute of Chicago searches for original blueprints or ink-on-linen plans; we sense the story of the disappearance of the Passenger Pigeon being played out in the form an original copy of the designs for these tiny residences.

Now 'tiny' is a pejorative term but if the Depression didn't influence the affordability of residential tastes for the middle class, certainly the quantity of alterations and additions that the bungalow needed was dictated by the shortages of resources for that kind of construction during World War II. The home buyer of the late 1930s was limited to what was already built; what was already built was very spare and economical by comparison with post World War II luxury.

The result of these historical eras was that a young child, born into one of these Depression-built structures might, in retrospect, marvel at their primitive nature and at the lack of amenities that his parents were obliged to accept and make do with during the war years. And, like the built-up forces of inflation that were released after the war, that child, still young, would recall the large number of home alterations that came in one continuous sequence of major 'home remodelings' during the child's postwar years of residence.

So, despite the fact that the predecessor to N. Ronneberg & Company, N. Ronneberg, Inc., designed Chicago bungalows – principally in the period from 1915 through the early 1920s – these bungalows were by no means a major source of commissions as compared to many other types or kinds of structures including apartment houses, laundries, and other buildings; certain it is that the bungalow at 7240 West Pratt Avenue was not designed by that firm. Probably the most important proof of that was the total lack of commentary toward that end made by the adult occupants, both of whom knew well the professional activities of Natal Ronneberg. For the curious reader who desires proof of what grandfather *was* involved during the period of 1915 through the early 1920s, I have excerpted printed material from family archives and placed the information in Appendix B.

Returning to the bungalow on Pratt Avenue, we can affirm that with two children, the first born in 1935, and the second born in 1938, the physical space of that particular home – and those homes occupying the entire block to the east and to the west – was identical to that of its neighbors, and all their living spaces were tiny. Returning to Appendix B and the plan referenced on page 46, a plan of a five-room bungalow pictured in the Marketing Material for Ronneberg, Pierce & Hauber, Architects and Engineers, the first floor plan in many ways looks identical: two bedrooms 11'- 6" x 11'- 0", a kitchen 10' x 11', a dining room 14'- 0" x 13'- 8", and a living room 11'- 6" x 17'- 6".

All of the homes on the Pratt Avenue block had slightly different facades but were, inside, essentially similar. Imagine then, if you can, such a home: the basement is unfinished with open 2 inch by 10 inch beams supporting the first floor. A large enclosed coal bin occupies one corner of the basement since gas heating does not arrive until after World War II; at that time the waiting period for conversion of coal powered furnaces explodes to a length of twelve months and more.

How are clothes washed in such close proximity to coal dust? The answer: not so far away from the coal bin are two, adjoining wash tubs and an old-fashioned clothes washer amounting to a large, circular barrel with a wringer mounted on the side of the wash barrel. By manually forcing wet clothes through the two rubber-coated cylinders of the wringer, rinse water was expelled preparatory to hanging the clothes outside – or inside in the basement – in order to dry.

There was no clothes washer or dryer, and, for the time being, this was a blessing in disguise. That blessing deserves a brief digression. As late as 1953, the time of the Second National Jamboree, father took a staff job at that Jamboree in Irving, California. Although the job was a cooking advisor, actually a type of inspector, he did have telephone duties at the regional headquarters tent during the evening hours for the benefit of the adult leaders.

It so happened that a large rainstorm hit Chicago during Jamboree week in 1953. The storm sewer system in large sections of residential Chicago was as ubiquitously inadequate as the space in many bungalows. The water had nowhere to go but up and this led to rain water coming up through the multiple basement floor drains in the basements of thousands of homes. On the night of the 1953 storm Mr. Ronneberg, Sr. had 'phone duty.' There was also a scout messenger to take the transcribed phone message to the correct leader, asleep in his tent.

The phone began to ring; the first message went something like: "There is two feet of water in the basement and it is rising; I'm afraid of getting an electric shock. Come home immediately! Your wife, Elaine." The second was from a braver woman: "I have lassoed the freezer which was floating and tied it to the steel post that holds the flooring; what should I do next? Shelia."

And so the messages came in all night and the messenger became exhausted! All this by way of pointing out that once purchased after World War II, the washer, dryer, and freezer at 7240 West Pratt Avenue were given concrete platforms well above the basement floor. As the owner of an architectural/engineering firm, father had no difficulty in obtaining the services of employees from Enger Brothers Construction Company, a general contractor that was jointly run by the four Enger brothers and had access to individual laborers who were expert in just about every field. When concrete work – like the platforms – was called for, the people who came were workers who had good rapport with a child onlooker. I can remember the carpenter who did all the work in my father's study and made use of ash planks that were very carefully examined for cracks in the boards. Both of these events remind me to return to the first floor, the only floor that could be lived in at 7240 West Pratt Avenue. It remains a complete mystery how so many people could have lived in that first floor space; the occupants were: two children, two parents, one grandmother, and one dog. There *were* two small bedrooms with two tiny closets; there is that word 'tiny' again! I cannot claim to call a four foot by five foot closet space as any size other than tiny.

A single, tiny, bathroom served all five human beings; the dog, a wire-haired fox terrier, was obliged to use one of the basement tubs for his bath. I hasten to add that mother continually referred to her retirement wish by including dogs; after raising children, her wish was to live where it was very hot – preferably near the Rio Grande river in Texas – and raise dogs. There is a famous baby picture that was taken when I was still in a high-chair; there were, at that time, two wire-haired fox terriers in the family, both of who were in the picture; I was in tears! Mother could have been trying to say that raising four children – the ultimate limit for the family – was, perhaps, equivalent to dogs? Or, maybe, it was just a ploy to get me to wash the single dog in one of those basement tubs, or even both ideas; after all, if dogs are equivalent to children, then, presumably, if you marry a woman similar to your mother – I want a girl, just like the girl, that married dear old dad – then, by analogy, you, too, would have a dog, and, also, by analogy, 'No woman will ever marry a man who cannot wash dogs!'

In actual fact, the bathroom was not too time consuming for me to wash; it was getting behind the radiator and the water closet that presented the challenge, especially when the criteria of washing a floor was making certain that it dried quickly. The kitchen took longer, even though, for a kitchen, it, too, was very small; it had a radiator, and behind-the-refrigerator-and-stove areas, as well as a tiny closet – three feet by three feet – which, as you may accurately surmise, was filled with mops, brooms, and such-like, all of which had to be removed before washing the floor. But the kitchen was small because of a large pantry that adjoined it. The pantry had a trapdoor that opened out to the back porch and allowed a milkman, or any type of delivery person, like a driver delivering cloth baby diapers, to drop off his delivery. The refrigerator had one of those coiled condensers on top of it, the kind you see in movies of the 1920s; there was no dishwasher, and the stove was gas.

But a memory, you could call it a recollection from the remotest past of my brain cells, of my paternal grandmother sitting in an easy chair in one of the downstairs bedrooms and doing beadwork, might probably be the earliest memory I can claim; I certainly don't remember sitting in a baby chair with two wire-haired fox terriers nearby – I was crying at the time! When I visited my grandmother I was probably only three or four years old; she was at work with a form of Norwegian beading where each seed bead is sewed to the fabric one-bead-at-a-time; I was fascinated with the colors of the seed beads – they were all mixed together in a jar which seemed, upon later reflection, to impose the most tedious requirements on the worker; first, there was the lack of a loom – each bead had to be picked up individually – second, there was the fact that all the colors were jumbled in the jar – which taxed the eyesight of the worker – and third, there was the problem of making a mistake, a wrong color or a lapse in memory, as there was no paper pattern in use; any one of these problems precipitated the terrible consequence of removing the bead from the cloth, rethreading the needle, and starting over!

All these several complications occur to me now, having spent many weeks and months of loom-based beading while constructing my Indian costume. But equally perplexing was the fact that my grandmother must have had a room of her own. Just where everyone else in the family slept – two adults and two children at the time – remains a mystery. When it came to the outdoor areas of 7240 West Pratt Avenue, the situation was reversed.

When taken outside to play in the large backyard, I remember that there were no houses on the south side of Farwell Avenue, the east-west street to the north; it was prairie! The prairie was even more extensive a block south of Touhy Avenue, 7200 North – Pratt was 6800 North. This area became the site for numerous 'victory gardens' where vegetables were grown by families who came to their 'plots' after dinner time and tended their gardens; it became a site of social interaction; children helped pull weeds and pick ripe vegetables; neighbors spoke to neighbors across the plots.

North of Touhy avenue there was a wilderness of high grass prairie, extending further north as far as the eye could see – Oakton Avenue and beyond. Narrow paths *were* present amongst the grass and these were, for me and my friends like Raymond Schifelbein, a call to adventure beyond vegetable farming. I wondered how I would be found if I lost my way or sprained an ankle; what would happen if I was bitten by a garden snake? The reality of these fears came one day when Raymond and I braved the prairie paths to see how far we could get. We encountered some older boys who made a fortress within a pile of logs; they were armed with BB guns! How very much like the real, wild west, where pioneers braved the tall grass in covered wagons, it was just that we had no wagons to arrange in a circle so we had to suffer the sound of BB balls at long range while fleeing back to the safe territory below Touhy Avenue.

But as a young child, I was not aware of any constraints upon my activities within the home; this might have been due to the spacious backyard. It seemed natural that the narrow, bricked-in space in the front of the basement should be used to store the cans of vegetables from the victory garden. Father purchased a canning machine from the Sears Roebuck catalogue; the machine sealed the cans with covers so they could be boiled in a large pot. This must have been another Ronneberg goal that arose from Norway where father's grandfather, Terres, owned the second canning factory built in Norway.

Unfortunately, the result of the Chicago canning operation was not as successful as the Norwegian Canning company; I enjoyed the sardines and even the fiskeboller. What spoiled the canned vegetables was their taste! For example, the carrots absorbed the metallic flavor of the cans! That seemed natural even to a child; after all, they had been boiled for an hour after being sealed inside the can using the canning machine. Their taste was enough to make 'spam' a delicacy. My sense of depravation during the war years was limited to the dinner table and did not include the space that I occupied. No sooner than VE day was celebrated however, my sense of living in a tiny space – basement, backyard, first floor, and attic – began to change with a vengeance! One of those changes was responsible for providing me adventures akin to my sojourn north of Touhy Avenue with Raymond; but first, we must examine some of the earliest changes.

The kitchen was remodeled in a flash! In a very short time the pantry was gone, replaced by a large, L-shaped row of cabinets – above and below – together with lots of counter space; now I could stretch and breathe. More importantly, we had space for the Fattigmann, Krum kaga, and Sandbakkels rituals. The refrigerator – the kind you see in museums exhibiting the prior ways of life in Chicago – was replaced, a dishwasher added, a gorgeous electric stove – with back-lit, colored buttons – replaced the gas stove that was put in the basement to facilitate making grape jelly. Ultimately, even a garbage grinder was installed below the kitchen sink.

You might think, blessed readers, that the grape jelly goes to make up for the carrots and other canned food, and I would not fault you for that conclusion. Like so many things in life however, reality took over there as well. While father, most likely, had a good upbringing with respect to 'things of the kitchen' I feel certain that his family, the Cuyler Avenue, Oak Park family, never grew grapes, nor had father ever made good things to eat other than Fattigmann, Krum kaga, and Sandbakkels. I say this because the grapes for our jelly came from a grocery store; but that was not the cause of the problem. After a lengthy process of squeezing the grapes in a cloth bag so as to extract the juice – which left one's hands purple for many days – the next step was to mix the juice with Certo, a product that facilitated turning the sugar-sweetened liquid into the consistency of a jelly; mixing was followed by boiling the mixture for a certain time. Nor was it the leaving out of the Certo that caused the problem with the grape jelly, in fact, it was just the opposite.

A large number of jars of grape jelly were made. The process ended with the liquid jelly being poured into the jars which were first boiled in water; once the jars were filled with jelly and cooled, a layer of wax was placed over the surface of the jelly and was followed by a metal cap that protected the wax – there was no way that the metal could get at the jelly. No, the problem was with the Certo; the instructions were, perhaps, ambiguous – that is a generous interpretation on my part. When the first jar was opened, the jelly had the consistency of 'artificial rubber!' It had to be sliced with a sharp knife! I knew about the need for rubber during World War II and reasoned that the grape jelly should be sent to the War Department to help that effort; after all, that's why we brought cans of grease to the butcher.

Aside from these 'victory garden' and 'grape jelly' activities, one of the most onerous wartime tasks for father was an effort that kept him very busy in the basement, especially during the winter months. The task was building up a coal fire in the coal furnace from paper and wood kindling. Once started, the nascent blaze was supplemented with coal from the coal bin so that it did not go out. The process was, thankfully, replaced with a gas furnace which consisted of a refitting of the coal furnace to use gas instead of coal. The repercussions were huge and, fortunately, it came soon after VE day. This was because Paul Langren, a fraternity brother and employee of Peoples Gas Company, managed to get our house to the top of the conversion list; his efforts were pure wizardry and their consequences profound.

Overnight, the space occupied by the huge coal bin disappeared; the coal dust was no more and the coal bin walls were torn down and thrown away. That entire space of the basement was converted into a large workshop that provided many hours of enjoyment. The workshop had two large work benches, a drill press, band saw, jig saw, wood lathe, planer, grinding wheel and a table bench saw. Tools were put in their proper place with peg boards, cabinets, and drawers; wood was kept in under-table storage areas. My older sister soon had a beautiful hand-made, multi-story dollhouse with glass windows, curtains, and other amenities that were all exquisitely cut and pieced together from paper plans. I was to undertake many projects and became adept at using the wood lathe. Father kept a nice piece of black walnut wood and I used a great deal of that wood making small bowls – face plate work – with covers; wood turning merit badge was one of the thirty-nine merit badges that I earned.

As previously mentioned, not far away from the workshop were a clothes washer, clothes dryer, and a large freezer box – all were raised up on concrete structures – and a pool table. Father took over the task of doing all of the laundry; everyone threw their clothes down the basement stairs and when father returned from work, he swept all the clothes down to the bottom of the stairs with his feet and began the laundry work. When my friends came over and played pool, I served bottled water with crystal-clear ice cubes from Jefferson Ice Company; it was a new center of socialization where children could join in with adults.

One of the favorite pool games involved the use of marble-like spheres that were kept in a leather bottle. Each player took a sphere before a regular game of rotation pool was played, noted the number, and pocketed the ball. On the sphere was a number corresponding to one of the pool balls. If you sunk a pool ball and another player held the sphere with that number, the other player gave you a dime; if you sunk your own ball, every player gave you a dime. It was very exciting when the game reached the point where, by the process of elimination, all players knew that the lone, remaining pool ball, corresponded to a specific player's sphere.

"Now just wait a second," said one blessed reader, "what could a leather bottle used in a game of pool have anything to do with anything?"

"OK, good question," replies the writer; a conversation ensues.

"Don't you remember the story about the Norway Spruce?" asks the writer.

"You're not going to tell me that in Norway they use Norway Spruce for pool ques?" asks the reader.

"You missed my point."

"All right, tell me about that."

"Let's suppose you are a writer."

"God forbid!" replies the reader, "but, OK, I'm a writer now."

"And let's further suppose you are writing a story, a mystery story that involves the discovery of millions of dollars of gold. The story begins when you discover that an old friend – a fellow officer on the USS *Crichton*, a Destroyer – lives nearby and you go with your wife to his mansion for a dinner party."

"I can imagine what's coming next: you and your Navy colleague reminisce about an island you explored together while on liberty and you decide to go back and investigate?" said the reader, "since I already know you were in the Navy I can see how that kind of tale grows out of your military experience. But what I don't see is how that story of finding gold grows out of your playing pool in the basement of your Chicago home; how it causes a new growth – al la the layering propagation of the Norway Spruce – that is, how exactly the 'parental nutrient' arises out of a game of rotation pool."

"Excellently put! And let me add that Robert Louis Stevenson's *Treasure Island* doesn't need any modern improvements. So let's see if I can show how the layering metaphor or leitmotif gives us a grip on what you are looking for."

"Exactly!" replies the reader.

"For that we need an excerpt. Our excerpt is from the first chapter of the first story in the book *Old Friends and Other Stories*. From the first story, 'Old Friends,' and the first chapter, '*An Unexpected Party Favor*,' we will excerpt the last two pages of that story:

* * *

After dinner Skip asked the men, who wanted to play pool, to follow him to the first floor poolroom while Phyllis took all of the women guests and a few of their spouses on a house tour. After the first game of rotation pool was played on a table that Skip thought was built in 1850 – when it had been overhauled a bit of a newspaper clipping had been found with that date – Skip pulled out a little leather bottle, wide at the bottom and then tapered to a narrow circular opening at the top, altogether about seven inches tall. "I've always wondered what this was for," Skip asked me.

"You're in luck," I replied, "I just happen to know because we grew up with a pool table in our basement. I used to serve my friends store-bought crystal clear ice cubes and bottled water, but that's beside the point. There are fifteen ivory balls inside and each one has a portion cut back so as to make a flat edge large enough to engrave a number from one to fifteen.

"At the start of each game, the bottle is shook up, each person gets a ball with his or her own number, makes a mental note of it, and places it in their pocket. So, for example, if I got the ivory ball with the number seven engraved on it, my number would be seven, which correlates with the number seven-ball on the table."

"I see," said Skip.

"Now," I continued, "we all play a game of rotation pool, just as before. If you or anyone else sinks the seven-ball, I pay that person a dime and return the ball to the tapered leather container."

"Okay, what happens if you sink the seven-ball yourself?" he asked.

"Very astute question," I said, "if I sink my own ball everyone pays me a dime! Sometimes, if you are on the fifteen-ball, and there is only one person left who hasn't returned his ball, everyone else is cheered on so as to prevent lots of dimes from flowing into one pocket – pants pocket, that is."

"Sounds fun, let's try it," said Skip. We all put our own ball in our pocket, racked the balls, and Skip used the cue ball to break them up and start the game. Halfway through the game one of Skip's guests pointed to an oil painting near the pool cue rack. "I never noticed this before," he said to Skip.

"What's that?" he replied.

"This picture, it's an oil painting of Angel Island in San Francisco Bay. I was there last week on a deal and, if I'm not mistaken, it was painted from Alcatraz."

"That's interesting," said Skip, "it came with the house like everything else. I have no idea who painted it."

The women had just come through the pool room and felt we could have one more game before it was time to end the party. Skip's guest, the one who liked the painting, did the honors with the leather bottle and starting with me, tilted the bottle to pour me out my ivory ball and new number, only this time two balls dropped into my hand; one was ivory and one was metal. I turned away from the other players' eyes to examine them and then pocket my number, but I also pocketed a 24-carat gold marble just under three quarters of an inch in diameter. I made the decision then and there to discuss the extra spherical object in private with Skip rather than announce it, disrupt the game, bring the ladies back, and cause a lot of future phone calls from Skip's friends.

* * *

Having finished discussing the basement alterations, we again move upstairs. Once the kitchen expansion was done, two follow-on projects came in the wake of that effort. The first, an enclosed back porch just beyond the kitchen door, provided a protected space from Chicago's winters and a storage/staging area for many items. The second project was much more extensive and was facilitated by the way in which the pantry disappeared and by the enclosed back porch. In effect the stage was set to transform the unheated back porch that remained into father's study.

The back porch space was insulated and then paneled with ash boards. The stamp album cabinets and the library shelves above the stamp collection were built along one wall; a hide-a-bed sofa, steel sash windows – one a large picture window – and a gas wall heater completed the effort. The carpenter was one of those highly skilled, old-world, carpenters employed by Enger Brothers. I developed a good rapport with the carpenter. I am certain that part of the reason was my tagging along with father when he visited the 'headquarters' of Enger Brothers General Contractors. Each morning there would be one or two of the brothers in the basement of the family home, their headquarters. Their mother lived above and father would drop in for coffee-and. Rudy was a gentleman and always showed me such deference; I felt special, and there was always some comment about my going into the construction business, or, if not that, continuing in father's footsteps.

I, of course, always thought they were talking about becoming an architect/engineer and following in my father's footsteps even when they forgot to bring the subject up, and I did follow those footsteps until other attractions caused me to change course; there was, then, some kind of hidden agenda in these visits – the notion of becoming a third-generation architect/engineer. But some of my father's friends were more literal; these were any number of acquaintances who knew of my father's close relationship with general contractors – like Enger Brothers – and made a request to have their sons placed in these organizations for summer work. What most parents did not know, however, was the enormous strength and the daily, ongoing, physical effort required. So, for several years, father *did* manage to obtain a summer job for those sons; the acquaintances sensed that a general contractor could not exactly say no to an architect that caused a lot of business to come their way.

What invariably happened, however, was that after several days of very rigorous work – lifting bricks, using a wheelbarrow, working in the hot sun, and other tasks – the young person took sick and then missed a week of work. This happened so often that father finally explained to the parent who asked for a favor, exactly what was involved and the results. After the continuing sequence of the same results, he stopped accommodating parental requests for summer construction work.

But there was one other type of request that father received from friends and it was very much akin to those parental requests for summer construction jobs for their sons. It came about in a very natural and logical fashion. Invariably, someone who was associated with the building trades, would come to serve on the 'building committee' of a church; there would be a need for an addition/alteration or anything that required the services of an architect from start to finish – plans, specifications, bidding, recommendations, getting the project through the City of Chicago's Building Department for a permit – the list was quite long. Naturally, the building committee met during the evening and always interviewed several architects – many of whose names were proposed by committee members.

It was as difficult a task for father to decline being interviewed as it was for the owner of a general construction company not to accept the son of a friend of my father's for summer work. Nine times out of ten there was always some business tie to the building committee member – for example, a plumber who worked for Sievert & Company – and father didn't want to embarrass that individual. The problem was that all of father's after dinner free time was already tied up with volunteer work which was very extensive; I should say that was the first problem. The second problem was that he never won a church contract. And often, he would have to attend more than one meeting.

His volunteer work trumped this extra effort; he was especially put out by having to come back more than once and then, not obtaining the business. He decided to do something about the problem. The next time he was invited to bid on a church building job, he handled things differently. It so happened that while waiting for the committee to call him in, he recognized a very prominent Chicago architect sitting in the waiting room; that acquaintance, for they knew each other, prompted him to act. When it was his turn and he had marketed his firm, the committee came to their final question which was always the percentage he charged for his fee. There was only one way to get out of the situation, especially in view of his thinking he could not compete with his acquaintance, the other architect; he announced that his fee was twelve percent! He left very proud of himself that he figured out a way to stop the need for additional after-dinner meetings.

Very soon after, he received a call at work from the prominent Chicago architect. "Earl, I heard you landed that church job where we last met. What fee did you ask for? I quoted them three percent! Are you giving your work away for nothing?" The caller explained that he was just curious; he had made a low bid for several reasons. Father replied that he bid twelve percent! The story, then, was that when dealing with committees with only one member associated with the building trades, the majority of the other members always felt that the highest fee was the best. After that experience he continued along the same path and landed many church jobs.

But I must apologize, dear reader, for that digression; we are focusing on the subject of a home. My only excuse goes back to father who, among his other sayings, always insisted that a church "should be a second home." Returning to 7240 West Pratt Avenue, there is no doubt in my mind that the entire upstairs, the attic, was the area that received a complete face lifting and created places where, as a child, I could have adventures! I have no idea where my sister and I slept prior to the end of World War II, but after the attic remodeling, she enjoyed a back-bedroom in the attic with knotty-pine walls, oak flooring, and a nearby closet that was quite large.

I moved into an even larger space in the form of a front-bedroom; again, my walls were four feet high on the sides, made of knotty-pine, and I had the same oak flooring; I, too, had a huge walk-in closet with lots of shelves – even a shelves for shoes! Between the two bedrooms was a hallway of oak flooring, but the largest item in between the two rooms was a second bathroom! It had a shower, window, sink, water-closet, and a linen closet. It was enclosed in a dormer that rose from the slanting east-side roof. Each of the two bedrooms had a pair of small windows facing to the north and south, respectively, but the bathroom window was large; it let you see much more of the sky, and the roof of the next-door neighbor.

I remember father working on weekends up in the attic; it seems impossible that he did all the work himself. Two incidents stood out that showed an attachment to the remodeling effort of the attic. The ceiling that began at the top of the four foot tall knotty-pine walls, slanted its way to the center of the room – right below the peak of the roof. My sister's and my own bedroom thus had a tent-like ceiling; it was white fiberboard and no doubt insulation was installed between it and the roof. In any event, one event marks just how young I was when the room was finished.

This idea for this event occurred when I looked up from my bed and saw above me what seemed a perfect surface to draw upon. You know, those childish drawings that parents often claim are the work of an artist-to-be. I had a set of water paints, the kind that have multiple, colored circles of hard paint; you take a wet brush and work at the surface and soon your brush has paint on it. I began my masterpiece on the slanted fiberboard; it looked like it was installed for that purpose. Of course, painting on a slanting surface reduced my genius but, nonetheless, I continued. Facing upward, much like Michelangelo painting the Sistine Chapel, I began my own four year painting. After a minute or so, I left the bed, stood up and examined my work; I had painted – using one color, pink – what might easily be taken as a couple of primitive stick figures! They were so unappealing that I stopped my work and thought I should erase what I had done and start over again. Alas! That was not a valid option.

There was, of course, a reaction, first from my mother – which was not exactly filled with praise – and then from father when he returned from work – which was much more pejorative. But years later, after a trip to Texas – the one where I remember looking for all those abandoned railroad tracks – the sloping fiberboard roof was used for another type of aesthetic purpose, and not just to cover up the vague remains of my pink stick figures which, like a shadow, never completely disappeared.

It came about by way of the planning that occurred prior to that multi-day sojourn to the south. Father brought home the huge Sectional

Aeronautical Charts that we needed to get from Illinois to Texas and back; using an architect's mechanical pencil – the kind with a very thick, orange lead, used for marking up blueprints – he traced out and across all the Charts, the path that he intended to fly to Corpus Christi where he was visiting another architect on a job; the trip was a business trip. It was that thick, orange line that I used to follow along the world below us as we progressed south.

After we returned from that trip I had the idea that if we merely cut out those charts – they wouldn't be used again – so that there was a band about three feet wide with the orange line in the middle – then we could attach – with thumbtacks – that long, green set of Charts beginning at the top of the knotty-pine wall above my bed and proceeding – zigzag fashion – up to the top of the bedroom ceiling, and then down to the top of the knotty-pine wall across and over a bit from the bed area.

This made a beautiful mosaic of the entire trip! Some might go so far as to call it a collage! I could point out to any interested party where Tyler, Texas, was – we stayed there one night. I could point out the destination Corpus Christi, Texas, where, for all I knew, my mother might retire and start raising dogs, even though it was not exactly on the Rio Grande River. The most exciting experience on the trip, however, occurred at Little Rock, Arkansas, where we made a landing to refuel on the flight down. There was a terrific wind and father made a power-on landing. Just at the end of that landing, a gust of wind caught the Fairchild and began tipping the left wing down toward the grass! Whatever it was that father did to correct the tip, it worked. All I knew was that we seemed to do a fast U-turn, the result of which was that we were facing the opposite way, and were no longer tipping either the left or the right wing. We taxied up to the building where we could refuel and several employees, whose eyes were glued on the Fairchild as it landed, ran out and began commenting on the landing; it was then I realized that the landing required real skill.

But there was nothing adventurous about what I have described so far as part of the attic renovation; for that, we must explore further into the depths of the attic – the deep, dark, depths – where one enters – like the airport at Little Rock, Arkansas – at one's own peril! The cause of these adventures was, in fact, are you ready for this, reader? A tunnel! I'll go one step further. A tunnel implies an engineered enclosure – dark, straight, and without obstructions. There were cave-like aspects to my attic tunnel which gave it a hybrid nature. For example, it was not altogether dark, there were some forty watt bulbs here and there but there *were* sections where the light from those bulbs did not completely find its way.

While the terms 'straight' and 'without obstructions' conjure up a uniform structure, my tunnel, I should say tunnels because there were three of them, had the heterogeneity of a cave – it varied in width from open, tall spaces, to narrow, confined spaces where a child could not stand up but was obliged to crawl. Finally, there were obstructions planted along the route which constrained the crawler with a varying array of objects; these – the objects, that is – of course heightened the urge to investigate them for they appealed to my curiosity as much as the journey from one end of the tunnel to another.

One needed to be cautious with respect to the length of the journey, especially those which might be prolonged by the examination of several of the obstructions in the dim light – by use of a flashlight – while traversing the tunnel. This caution was enhanced by the entrance doorways to the several tunnels. The four principal entranceways – there were others which, in their way, were different – all had a metal latch that could easily be slipped, either inadvertently when the entranceway was closed or, by another member of the household; either way caused the exit from the tunnel to be blocked!

This latter fear might seem misguided but it was not. Most of the time when exploring a tunnel, the explorer did not want anyone outside to know that he or she was engaged in that exploration; the tunnel was not completely clean and might call for a change of clothing upon exit and, perhaps, more importantly, the exploration of an item in the tunnel might expose the explorer to discoveries that were not intended for the eyes of a child. Obviously father was not concerned about my discovering the *King of the Black Isles* but was that also true about the objects that I came across in the tunnels?

The upshot of these young ruminations was that a young person whether entering alone or with a companion, always pushed the entranceway door closed but left it unlocked. This would hide any light from appearing around the edges of the door. Despite this extra effort there was always a fear that an unknown person would throw the metal latch to the closed position – it was so easy! The tunnel would then become a trap and the entranceway a trapdoor!

There is, obviously, at this point, a need to explain all of this mystery and what better way than by taking you, my reader, on that first trip of discovery? We will take our cue, then, from those lines of Joaquin Miller the poet who, in 1908, wrote:

> Behind him lay the *gray* Azores,
>   Behind the *Gates* of Hercules;

We will see that once through the *Gates* of Hercules – the entranceway – the portion of the tunnel already traversed was quite *gray*. But we must begin with a different geometry. If you have a four foot high bedroom wall of knotty-pine, then behind that wall or, more accurately, working one's way outward toward the gutters of the roof of the Chicago bungalow, you have a triangular space. As already mentioned, the *gray*, dusty floor of the unfinished attic forms the bottom side of this right triangle, and the roof with its exposed beams, forms the hypotenuse.

One is quite correct in pointing out that this triangular space extends from the front of a Chicago bungalow to the rear in a uniform fashion, but for several reasons, that was not the case. In the first instance, consider the corners of a bungalow attic: the geometry changes to a larger space. It was at these four corners where the four entranceway doors were positioned. Between those corners and running back along the long dimension of the bungalow, that is, between my bedroom and my sister's, one might surmise that the four foot high knotty-pine wall was uniformly present. That, however, was not the case; the two large closets intervened and they narrowed the right triangle so that all three sides were shortened; one was constrained, as with a cave, to a more restricted passageway.

Upon entering the tunnel at those four corners – there were three, additional entranceways – the explorer found herself in a larger tent-like space, a space that sloped in two directions; one direction was immediately perceived to be a much taller wall that sloped toward the window area of the bedroom; the other slope was of the size of the unconstrained triangle which ran back in the other direction, i.e., the tunnel direction.

The east side tunnel was not continuous; two obstructions occurred that divided the east side tunnel into two sections of tunnel. The first obstruction was the new bathroom and the second obstruction were three, large drawers, the fronts of which were also knotty-pine. The drawer pulls of these three monstrous drawers were in my bedroom; one side of the drawer space – which extended toward the bungalow gutter – was the bathroom wall, the other faced into the short, stubby tunnel that remained.

Once having entered, then, the new explorer closed the entranceway door – the *Gates* of Hercules – behind him, and stood, for a moment in the larger, corner space. Courage was needed on that first investigation: what lay ahead in the darkness of the tunnel for it was all unknown? Even the new explorer knew of the possibility of the latch being thrown into the lock position. What actually lay ahead of the crawler – for that was the chief method of making forward progress – were not shoreless seas, quite the contrary. Instead the ghosts of shores consisted of boxes, items of furniture, and other bric-a-brac that couldn't fit anywhere else in the bungalow.

In this latter category were precious items that were saved during the Depression – and even before that period – that would, hopefully, find their way into a future summer home after the war, a home that was known in Norway as a seter – a simple wooden cottage in the mountains with a barn for cattle, goats, and sheep, now, more commonly, a summer home in the mountains that removes the occupants from the heat and humidity of a larger city in the valley below. These miscellaneous objects became the unexpected, cave-like obstructions that, with a dim light, could only vaguely be seen ahead while crawling but were, intrinsically, objects that heightened the traveler's curiosity.

I have alluded to the fact that the corner spaces that one encountered immediately beyond the entranceway doors, were spacious. My evidence in support of this claim is that my sister and several of her friends used this space for a special purpose; it had, of course, two slopes where the roofs joined, the north-south roof and the east-west roof. That area was large enough to accommodate the secret society meetings of the BVD Club!

While such a meeting was being held – the members having entered through the entranceway door in my sister's bedroom – I could enter at the opposite end of this short tunnel using another door; this was a large door in the hallway between the two bedrooms; the purpose of the large door was to facilitate storing larger pieces of furniture for the seter. While my sister and her friends held the meeting of the BVD Club and read by the forty watt bulb just above their heads, I used the light to find my way through the furniture to a point where I could listen in without being seen.

Although they never revealed the meaning of the club's name, it is a measure of my sister's loyalty to her brother that she told me the meaning of BVD – there were no evidences of that meaning when I secretly examined the contents of their lair! It meant "But Very Determined" and it had to do with obtaining a husband!

Christopherson Cottage
Bass Lake, Pentwater, Michigan
Unknown Architect
Unknown Date
Estimated Date of Construction: 1920

While the attic tunnels of 7240 West Pratt Avenue held the objects that could be used to furnish a Norwegian-like seter, the problem of locating the seter was more difficult than how it would be furnished. Illinois and much of the rest of the Midwest are flat; there are no mountains! Especially a range of mountains that would offer respite from the high temperatures and humidity that, during the summer months, predominated in that city. Fortunately for Earl Ronneberg, Sr. the solution was suggested by his secretary, Marie Christopherson, who spent her summers as a child at Bass Lake, Pentwater, Michigan.

While Marie identified the location there were still other problems that to be solved. Marie's estimate of the driving time to travel to that location from Pratt Avenue was eight hours, one way. During the war years this long drive presented problems: automobiles were not air conditioned, there were no Interstate Highways, the route consisted of two-lane highways that went through many fairly large cities; these cities had stop signs, and stoplights; and, last but not least, automobile gas was rationed!

In the Norwegian seter converted to a summer home from its earlier existence as a high altitude farm, presumably, the male parent of a family spending their summer months at a seter, could climb or ride up the mountain – from his place of employment far below in a city – to join his family in less than eight hours. Perhaps the generous vacations offered by many Scandinavian countries limited these up and down weekend trips to only one or two during the time the seter was occupied, after all, the key decision nowadays in some of these countries is whether to work or not, the latter option being a valid one due to the generous welfare benefits arising from North Sea oil revenue.

Today's social welfare benefits in Norway belie the lifelong efforts and accomplishments of Natal Ronneberg; even as he pursued his impressive engineering career – see Appendix B – his list of books read during that time, the purpose of which was acclimating his mind and values to his adopted country, was impressive; he kept a list, in the form of a 'books read diary,' that is a testament to his intellectual energy.

The lack of extensive vacation time provided by generous country-wide social welfare policies was a problem for a small business owner like Natal's son, Earl Ronneberg, Sr., who needed to be on hand to manage his company throughout the year; his principal job was bringing in the business and he was the only one who dealt directly with the client decision makers. The problem of transportation, then, to such a far flung seter, had to be solved; eight hours of driving, i.e., twice driven for a weekend visit in an un-air-conditioned car, was unacceptable, even if gasoline was not rationed.

My father's strategy became obvious when several factors presented themselves. The first factor was a suggestion by Marie Christopherson that her family's summer cottage, now occupied by her brother, Sydney, could well be rented for the season; all that would be necessary would be to visit Sydney and ask him if this was so. The cottage was referred to as Christopherson Cottage but would later be called Chris Cot. The visit would also allow Marie's employer to inspect the cottage and the environment.

The second factor was the realization that aviation gasoline was not rationed during the war years; the upshot of this was that an aircraft would have to be purchased but Mr. Ronneberg, Sr. was conscious that he could use a plane in his business. By having a plane that could be used for both business and pleasure, he could commute on weekends in two hours – or one and three quarter hours with a tail wind – rather than eight. Owning a plane carried with it another prerequisite: a pilot's license.

Fortunately, Palwaukee Airport was not far from 7240 West Pratt Avenue and, anticipating a need for a home for a future airplane, Elmhurst Airport, west of Chicago was not far from father's office at 3906 North Harlem Avenue; Harlem Avenue was 7200 West, hence it was already eight miles west of Chicago's Loop. From these several factors an action plan was laid out. Weekend flying lessons at Palwaukee Airport were kept secret; only my sister accompanied her father. Then, one day, he returned home with a cartoon certification showing a young bird being kicked out of a nest, a celebration of his solo flight. Our focus, however, is on the notion of a home and we shall soon examine that summer home, Chris Cot, in more detail. Before that examination, we must remark that people – neighbors to the north and the south, the iceman, the garbage man, and the milkman – made strong impressions on me, a six-year old, and some of these early Chris Cot impressions can be read about in Appendix C.

It would be incongruous to imagine that the amenities of Chris Cot were an improvement over 7240 W. Pratt Avenue. Chris Cot possessed a huge iron wood-stove, reminding us of the old basement clothes washing machine with its ringer but the Chris Cot wood stove was the only source of heat in a completely uninsulated cottage. In the summer it was used for burning papers. The icebox and the delivery of blocks of ice by an iceman was even more primitive than the first refrigerator in Chicago with its compressor coils on top; it was a relic from the days before electricity, the days when kerosene lamps were the source of light, a time before rural electrification. Even so, the word 'icebox' was carried forward: I can never quite forget using the word; to this day, from deep within those brain cells, ostensibly filled while at Chris Cot, comes forth the word 'icebox' in place of refrigerator!

The kerosene stove had a distinct smell – it smoked – and it was not easy to deal with. My mother needed to learn its idiosyncrasies; the task was way beyond just turning up the original gas stove in Chicago. And, yes, the hot water tank was also heated by kerosene; a large tank with metal struts stood outside; when it was sounded with a stick and discovered to be in need of replenishment, a service person needed to be informed in person because there was no telephone at Chris Cot. While father experienced cooler temperatures and much less humidity in Michigan than in Chicago, that was not entirely the case with his two children who both slept in the upstairs bedroom of Chris Cot.

I might be imagined that the two, new attic bedrooms, one in back for my sister, and one in front for my usage, afforded some kind of relief from the oppressive summer heat of Chicago when we were in residence; I can assure you that such was not the case! They were hot, no air passed through the windows, and the heat extended to the tunnels which, if one had to travel them during the summer season, were very close to an un-ventilated coal mine far below the earth's surface. Fetching something in a tunnel that legitimately needed to be used was not a pleasant experience for the scorching sun beat down on the asphalt roof all day long. At Chris Cot, it was only when we were outside of that bedroom, in the cool of the forest, with the prevailing west wind coming from Lake Michigan a half mile away, or on the pier experiencing the breeze from across Bass Lake that we had any inkling of 'air conditioning.' At those times the temperature and humidity differences between Chicago and Bass Lake were pronounced.

The cooler environment of a Norwegian seter was very apparent, however, to father during his weekend sojourns to Bass Lake from Friday afternoon to Monday morning when he returned to Chicago. Of course he always hoped for rain Monday morning but it never, ever, came. As soon as he achieved his flying altitude – a mere 3,000 feet – after he took off from Elmhurst Airport, the air and the cockpit was cooler. I can't count the number of times he told a story to his friends that emphasized this environmental change. He related his Friday afternoon conversational exchange when he flew over Muskegon, Michigan, a mere forty miles south of Bass Lake. The control tower at Muskegon airport had little business from private planes, and, even today, seems little used, so there was no reason to be worried about using the airways:

Father: Muskegon Tower, this is NC77657, radio check, over.

Muskegon Tower: How the H . . . are you, Earl? I bet you'll be glad to get to Bass Lake. I hear the temperature *and* the humidity were both above ninety last week, all week long! Have a good weekend!

Father: Roger!

My sister and I had an inkling of how hot it was – and would be when we returned – because of the upstairs bedroom at Chris Cot. The bedroom had a single window facing east toward Bass Lake, but by virtue of the fact that the stairwell downstairs cut off any air from the west, the direction from which a cool breeze from Lake Michigan would arrive, if it could, through the sky and the half mile of cool forest that lay between Chris Cot and the big lake, we never felt *any* breeze. It was doubly frustrating because in the stairwell, the builder placed a large window to the west! Fortunately the bathroom at Chris Cot had a west window above the Victorian tub.

Father always claimed that it took him three years, 1944-46, to search out land where he could build his own summer home, his own seter. These were the years when he rented Chris Cot. During those three years I was left on my own devices but I spent a great deal of time with the neighbors to the immediate north (Proctors were to the south.) and that summer cottage became my home away from home as related in Appendix D.

I think that it is fair to say that a new awareness came to me during my experience of a summer home: the adults who surrounded me – who varied from the anonymous group of garbage man, ice delivery man, and milkman, on to the southern neighbors, the Proctors with whom we had a speaking relationship, and then on to the best relationship of all, the relationship that influenced me the most, the one with Scottie and even Lady. With the start of construction of Jerp House in 1946, the last year of renting, the presence of people involved in the context of 'home' would greatly increase; it would grow beyond my limited friendships in Chicago – Raymond Schifelbein, for example – yet it also included Raymond. Jerp House was also the only home where I would witness the construction of its prefabricated parts as delivered to the forest site from New Jersey; once all the parts were on the brown leaves of the forest floor, it would be assembled from a thick book of instructions very much in the fashion of the wooden model airplanes of this period.

Jerp House
Bass Lake, Pentwater, Michigan
Prefabricated Summer Home
Designed By
The Home Ola Corporation of New Jersey
Delivered by truck from New Jersey to site
And constructed by three workers
In three weeks
July-August 1946

I have no idea what father paid for his first plane, a Piper Cub Super Cruiser, a three-seater – two back seats – before he traded it in for the four-seater Fairchild, the plane we used to fly to Texas. What I do know was the price he paid for Jerp House – delivered to the site by the truck from New Jersey – and the cost of the Fairchild; they were both the same: $3,000. Ironically, Home Ola, the New Jersey maker of prefabricated homes, was going out of business and Jerp House was bought during the 'fire sale' of that decision.

The Fairchild aircraft, too, was offered at a reduced price – its manufacture was being discontinued; there were only three left. Father closed the deal, flew the Piper Cub Super Cruiser down to Wichita, Kansas, traded in the Super Cruiser, took some lessons on how to fly the Fairchild, and then flew back to Chicago. The Fairchild purchase was seamless; there was no further work that needed to be performed after the sale; in fact, by law, only a licensed mechanic was allowed to open up the cowling that covered the engine and reduced drag.

With JERP House the transaction was completed when the truck delivered its load about twenty-five feet from the shoreline of Bass Lake, but the house remained to be put together! JERP stood for Jenny, Earl, Ronnie, and Peter, the family children. The thick set of instructions came in a book and was much more than just plans; it had sequenced, step by step tasks, completely written out on how to put the pieces together; things like where to begin, what had to be painted or otherwise made ready before any given step, how to mix the paints, caulk the bathtub, etc., etc., etc.

I, of course, was driven by pure curiosity to abandon part of my morning or afternoon with Scottie so as to be able to observe the goings on at the construction site, a mere hundred yards to the north. Only three existing homes lay between Chris Cot and the JERP house site. The first to the north was where Scottie and Lady lived during the summer, the second was owned by the Astors, and at the third site – the neighbor next-door to the south of JERP house – the home, in one sense, was the most interesting. Back in the 1930s it was a hotel but the hotel burned down and from those vacationing at the time, I learned that it remained in that state for a few years. It was purchased by a retired carpenter, Mr. Linneman, and his wife. Mr. Linneman built the new house. Out in back, the only thing Mr. Linneman kept from the hotel were a set of concrete stairs and a sidewalk.

I mention this at this time because of an interesting aspect that could be found in the history of the property – the property abstract – that accompanied the deed. The hotel acquired the JERP house property by 'squatter's rights.' It seems that the hotel threw some of their garbage on the property and that was enough to acquire the land by squatter's rights – they had squatted on the land. A few years after Jerp House was built, the family was raking the leaves in the back in preparation for setting up things like swings and hammocks for J, E, R, and P. Lo and behold, a glass bottle was discovered that had an address – in the glass itself – from Chicago using the street system then in effect; my mother grew up near the address, recognized it, and recalled the street numbering system then in vogue! But back to my curiosity and the construction of Jerp House.

The man in charge of the three-week construction project was none other than Erling Berg, my father's employee, the man who befriended me earlier and pronounced that admonition of "Don't be a Norwegian all your life!" Erling had lost the use of his left hand but you wouldn't know it as you watched him perform any manual task. He could make architectural drawings, swim in Bass Lake, and handle pieces of Jerp House as well as his two assistants. One of these assistants was 'Ole' who was older than Erling; he, too, could do anything when it came to the building trades. A third, younger man, whose name I can't recall, completed the trio, a team that worked together like clockwork. Erling's two assistants worked for Enger Brothers General Contractors in Chicago.

It was very fascinating for me, an eight-year old, to watch these three at work; here was a two-story, insulated home, arising from the forest floor. It used steel beams for floor supports, screens and storm windows, and the shipment included all that the men needed: all the plumbing, bathroom and kitchen fixtures, an oil furnace, a fuel oil hot water heater, everything came on that truck! Of course, a septic tank was dug, a well driven – hand driven thirty feet down to tap the pure, cold, sand filtered Lake Michigan water below the 'hard-pan' – an underground fuel oil tank was buried, and an electric oil pump purchased, and attached to the kitchen wall to bring up the fuel oil.

But I must, dear reader, skip to the time one year later, 1947, when the family spent its first summer in residence. I was instantly surprised by the fact that it was furnished! All the furniture, rugs, bric-a-brac, and the other amenities from the dark tunnel-storerooms of 7240 West Pratt Avenue were magically transported and, just as magically, properly placed in Jerp House. I could recognize some pieces from earlier years; for example, a dark green leather couch that came from father's office.

There were, of course, new purchases. In one of the two upstairs bedrooms, there was a double decker bed; I climbed the ladder each night to sleep in the upper bed while, ultimately, both Ronnie and Peter, shared the lower bed with pillows at each end – half a bed/child. My sister had her own bed across from her three brothers. To relieve the summer heat that we suffered in Chris Cot, the children's bedroom sported a window that caught the breeze from Bass Lake; I enjoyed my own tiny electric fan attached to the railing of the upper bunk. Our parents slept in the other upstairs bedroom; there were six huge closet/storage spaces in both bedrooms.

As if taking a cue from the post-World War II additions to 7240 Pratt Avenue, the additions to Jerp House came fast and furious. The first of these arrived as a result of taking advantage of another Home Ola fire sale; it was an enclosed front porch with a flat roof that spanned the entire front of Jerp House. A concrete flat slab was poured in front of the porch for outdoor chairs.

The front porch was followed by a small, open, back porch but that was quickly replaced by a larger, roofed, screened-in porch which housed a park-like, rustic dinner table; father and I added all the screens to the framework; now the kitchen opened to a long dining table that used seat pads snapped to the bench seats; the pads came from army surplus parachute packs. It took many months of searching through hardware stores to find the screws which had a snap-head that could be screwed into the bottom of the bench and would accept the female portion of the snap that was attached to straps from the parachute pack seat pads.

I must remark, in passing, that bath towels, washcloths and even comforters, also came from army surplus. Those bathroom items were a drab, military grey. To brighten these items mother crocheted their edges with colored edgings; they became iconic. Many decades later I felt the urge to obtain some of these army surplus towels; I felt a longing to hold the un-crocheted towel once more, just to get the feel of it. I saw an advertisement for army surplus towels and ordered two. They came but they were very thin, the wrong color – brown – and the wrong army: they came from the surplus supplies of the Pakistani Army! They are now used for miscellaneous laundry activities like drying sweaters.

The next addition, a tent house, was built according to the plan of an Owasippie Scout Camp staff tent minus the front porch. A description of the tent house follows from the third chapter 'A Word From the Past' found in a story called 'Double Eagles,' the first story in the book *Western Michigan Tales of Mystery and Adventure*. As before, I refer to myself as John Sherman.

* * *

Mr. Sherman constructed the tent house on a design he had seen at the Owasippe Scout camps near Whitehall, Michigan. Mr. Sherman's best friend, Peter Orlebeck, served as camp director at one of the camps there. Mr. Sherman's design was a smaller, less luxurious version of Peter's tent-house. In the woods, seventy-five feet behind his summer house, Mr. Sherman planted a set of concrete blocks on the ground, their long sides vertical. On these he placed two-by-six-inch joists, and on those joists he constructed a wooden floor, six by eight feet.

A wooden baseboard about two-and-a-half feet high rose from the floor on three sides. Screening rose another three feet above that. The wooden baseboard and screening flanked both sides of the screen door in the front of the tent house. A heavy, canvas, army-surplus tent fitted over a simple ridgepole frame above the sides so that when first installed the four sides of the tent came down over all four screens about four inches below the edges of the screening.

A set of looped cords on all four sides allowed one to pull up the canvas sides into a bunch at the top, exposing the screening throughout and allowing a breeze to enter from any direction. When the canvas was pulled up, the cords were wrapped around cleats attached to the wooden sides.

When a guest from Chicago or Lansing slept in the tent house, Sherman took the single cot on one side and the guest took the bottom cot of a double-decker on the other side. Occupants always rolled up the tent flaps as the night began. If it started to rain or if lightning woke up the sleepers, someone had to exit in their pajamas to roll down the flaps, hopefully before drops started to be blown through the screening.

Two small dressers, a rug, and a table between the two cots, constituted the rest of the furniture. For light, they either hand-pumped a Coleman lantern that burned white gas or used flashlights.

There were many advantages to sleeping in the tent house with a friend. First, there was the independence: Sherman and his friends could come and go at will without anyone knowing of their existence or whereabouts. During the day, the tent house became a private retreat that Sherman visited even without a friend near at hand.

There were, to be sure, many other aspects of the tent house experience that appealed to the sensibilities of Sherman and his guests. They could hear whip-poor-wills at dusk. A breeze blew on many nights and they could see fireflies whenever atmospheric conditions were propitious. When the wind came through the nearby white pine trees, its sounds soothed Sherman as he fell asleep. Even after he returned from lowering the tent flaps – catching the early drops on his face while he tied them down – and before he turned in once again, there was always the sound of rain on the canvas to listen to as he tried to regain his slumber.

* * *

The tent house was a great place to sleep with friends who flew up to Bass Lake on a Friday afternoon, stayed nine days, and then returned to Chicago on the Monday of the following weekend. In one instance, there occurred a very hot summer when both my sister and I had friends for this extended week. For some reason or other everyone drank lots of milk. Father, on the Sunday before he departed with our two visitors, picked up the milk bill for the week and, during lunch, examined it: "Ninety-four Quarts!" he exclaimed; he couldn't understand the size of that bill.

But long before our Chicago friends started coming up, my responsibilities extended to the boat house – a structure that was built with ordinary, lumber yard lumber, by the crew of three that built Jerp House – our boat, and the wooden pier that extended twenty feet out – through lily pads – from the shoreline. From the end of the pier I could cast a fish line another ten feet to the drop off – a place where the water became much deeper. Using a bobber to indicate a bite and to position the hook with a worm at the correct depth, I could catch a stringer of pan fish – bluegills, sunfish, and occasional dwarf perch and regular size crappies. The boat house became the site for cleaning these fish.

The boat house was built at the water's edge by the same trio that constructed Jerp House; it was set on concrete blocks. Two large doors that swung out to the left and right gave access through a padlock made by the Chicago Lock Company, a client of my father's. Father wanted about twenty five locks that all used the same key and he asked one of the executives at Chicago Lock for a batch of those locks; it could only have been the President of the company who would grant such a favor. "I'm going to give you twenty-five Chicago Lock Company locks; they are all marked with number 1012, which is only used by one other organization," the President announced. "And who may that be?" father asked. "The Chicago Board of Education!" We referred to these locks as "ten twelves" and they were used ubiquitously across all of my father's real estate; there was something special about having a key that opened all of those schools; especially for children that were hundreds of miles away from Chicago schools all summer long. The key seemed to give me power over that huge administrative system that engaged my attentions for twelve years. But back to the boat house.

Once through the two large doors, and assuming there was nothing in the way, you could walk to the far end where there was a screened window that caught the Bass Lake breeze and below that window was a sink, a pedestal sink – it had four legs – that my parents saved from the 1920s; it, too, must have been deep within the tunnel for I never set eyes on it before opening the boat house doors for the first time. A hand pump with the well point sunk ten feet into the sand below the boat house allowed Bass Lake water to be pumped into the sink. Once filled, the fish – from a pail, stringer, or net – could be dumped into the sink water where they splashed around. I always feared they would jump out or move the flat rubber piece we placed over the drain hole. To the left of the sink basin was a flat surface where we cleaned the fish on newspaper, salted them down and then put them in a clean container for the Jerp House refrigerator.

The rule was: every fish that was caught was cleaned and eaten; this extended to the seven to eight inch long perch which were fried along with the other species; they were delicious! Bass Lake offered the excitement of catching bullheads and cleaning them. By lowering a hook with a worm to the bottom of the lake, the probability of landing a bullhead was increased; once caught, they put up a fight, and had to be handled carefully – they possessed sharp spines on the front of their fins. A needle nose pliers was used to extract the hook while holding the bullhead so as to avoid the spines. Since they had no scales, they were nailed to a tree where they were skinned. This was, invariably, a bloody operation that attracted mosquitoes but it was worth it; when cooked they were a delicacy; they tasted like chicken and there were large fillets without any tiny bones.

In the early days Jerp House had just one watercraft, a fishing boat made of plywood; it was completely safe for children because it was so wide that a child could lean over the gunnel and not tip the boat over. In addition to keeping the boat house neat – a place for everything and everything in its place – I also swept and washed the floor. This cleaning extended to the pier and the inside of the boat. After any rain, I bailed the boat and even dried it out; it was always as ready as a Coast Guard lifeboat except the mission was fishing!

A single pair of oars were the preferred method of locomotion but in order to travel to the beach through the channel – a natural, winding, and beautiful stream that led to the Lake Michigan beach – father ordered a five horsepower outboard motor from the Sears Roebuck catalog. Being a person who read and followed the instructions included with his purchases, he learned that it was recommended that only 'white gas' – appropriately mixed with oil – be used. This warning caused him to purchase a fifty-five gallon drum for storing white gas. It occupied a space near the two swinging doors. When filled it took great strength to turn it from its upright position to a horizontal posture and then roll it so that the spout projected over the edge of the front of the boat house.

Once in place, the white gas could be put into the smaller, two gallon tank that was carried in the boat. When the fifty-five gallon drum was half empty I could wrestle it down and fill the two gallon tank with white gas and a small, measured amount of oil. Numerous experiences occurred while on the pier either fishing or observing others. There was an incident that happened when Raymond Schifelbein was visiting from Chicago. We noticed the huge quantities of frogs and decided to cook frog legs – all we needed were two frogs. Huge lily pads grew right up to the north side of the pier and the boat house contained a multi-pronged ice fishing spear. All of a sudden we spied a frog sticking its neck above a lily pad. Raymond went back for the spear and we speared it. As we lifted the spear up, we realized that this was no frog! We had speared a snapping turtle that was about a foot across.

Before Raymond flew up with father I visited the Morphy cottage located in back of Jerp House and beyond the tent house. Mr. Morphy said he was having a friend up for the weekend from Lansing, Michigan, who was a chef. I immediately informed Raymond that if we could lift the turtle Mr. Morphy's friend would cook it for us and we could have some turtle meat for dinner. We carried the heavy turtle back to the Morphy cottage and Mr. Morphy's friend was delighted; the next day we were given turtle meat. But another experience – I was to give an adult something and expect something back – on the pier turned out differently.

Very early in my career as caretaker of these several pieces of the waterfront – boat house, pier, and boat – I was taking a break from my labors and fishing off the end of the pier when I became aware of an inboard boat – the only inboard on the lake – approaching the pier. It was Mr. Wallace, the so called Carrot King, who hailed from Texas and who owned a lovely house with lots of adjacent property at the north end of the lake. The house had an artesian well that fed a stream from the source of the well and that flowed down one edge of the grass lawn; the house was built with a long row of floor to ceiling windows across the front; it looked southern.

As the craft approached me I could see the shine of the varnish applied over the mahogany wood. "I'm, out of gas," Mr. Wallace declared, "do you have any gas?" Of course we had gas, we had a fifty-five gallon drum! "Yes," I replied, and hurried back to the boat house for the two gallon tank. I felt there was something tragic about that beautiful motorboat not being able to cut through the lake at high speed. Mr. Wallace took the tank, unscrewed a cap, began pouring, and the entire two gallon tank disappeared in a flash. He handed me back the tank, said "Thank you," and in an even more dramatic flash, started the engine, turned the steering wheel toward the north, and gunned his sleek possession in a burst of speed; he was never seen again!

There were two incidents that I witnessed from the end of the pier that stood out as being tragic/comic; they both involved the second Jerp

House watercraft: an aluminum canoe. In the beginning, there was a canoe! Or rather, there was the arrival of a canoe that was not a matter of either creationism or evolution; it was much simpler in its way, although it did have a complication. You will recall, blessed reader, that father was active at the District level in the Boy Scout hierarchy of Chicago. That involvement brought him in contact with the highest level of Scout Executives, a group just below the Chief Scout Executive of Chicago and above the twenty-six District executives. For many years, father was a District Chairman for a northwest side district.

Father befriended a member of that illustrious intermediate level of Scout Executives – I was given that Robert Service pamphlet of ballads by another member of the group. That gift occurred earlier and we already examined its consequences. One day I found myself following father around the City of Chicago Department of Buildings while he was shepherding a set of plans through the various departments so as to obtain the necessary signatures for a building permit. You may ask what I was doing at so young an age. I found out when father replied to another architect's question.

There were two lines in the room where you paid your fee and received the final permit. One line was the true, final, line and the other was a line for obtaining a signature from one of the departments; it could have been heating and air-conditioning, plumbing, or electrical, but it made no difference. He directed me to get in line at the queue that was lined up at the last, final, window. A mere ten feet away, he entered the line for the last signature from the department window – maybe it was the structural department and he knew all was well. In any event, he quickly arrived at the head of his line and everything was stamped and signed; then he crossed the ten foot interval between us and took a place in line ahead of me. Someone behind me commented, "hey, what's going on here?" obviously thinking he was butting in line ahead of him. Father's reply was, "I'm paying that assistant good money, $7.00 an hour!" Everyone laughed. But there is need at this point for a digression; after that, we'll get back to the Scout Executive friend.

'Why do we need an interruption from your standing in line at the Department of Buildings in City Hall?' you ask. The answer is that there was a Norwegian connection at the City of Chicago's Department of Buildings and it was more than just having your child standing in line at the rate of $7.00/hour. 'What do you mean by a connection?' I'll go you one step further: it was a high-level connection on both sides for the Ronneberg family. 'All right, I suppose some well-known Norwegian meets another,' you reply.

No, I'm not talking about the most famous Norwegian hero in World War II, Joachim Rønneberg, connecting up with an American Ronneberg. Joachim has enough notoriety for several lifetimes after leading a daring raid on the Nazi heavy water plant in Norway and blowing it up; there are books, and movies enough about that feat. Ah, so you thought Joachim Rønneberg and I were are related? We are! The Ronneberg family genealogy Data Base indicates that Joachim is my 9th cousin once removed.

But let's not get carried away by Ronneberg family genealogy! When the trio that maintains the Web Site and Data Base give a presentation, they remind the audience that in Norway, the first generation, from which all Norwegians are descended, is made up of the Gods of Norway. They are followed by the Kings of Norway. The Kings of Norway are the progenitors of everyone who came after them; they were quite prolific!

Instead of relating a story of genealogy, let me tell you a World War II Norwegian story that involves father. OK, it begins when I was eleven or twelve years old. There was a political rite-of-passage event that was held on a yearly basis for certain youngsters in Chicago that allowed children of that age to become, for one day, the Department Head of a City Government Office. I don't know how it happened that I was chosen, it might have been the Boy Scouts again, but I was named Building Commissioner for a Day. There was a luncheon and other events, but the only thing I remember was the story that the Building Commissioner, Roy T. Christiansen, told me when father and I came into his office at City Hall.

Commissioner Christiansen knew father, they were both architects and, of course, father spent a lot of time waiting in line to see the employees that worked for Commissioner Christiansen in the various sub-departments like plumbing, electrical, and so on; the guys who checked and approved the plans so that a Building Permit could be issued. But that's not what Mr. Christiansen talked about. In World War II he was a Colonel in the Paratroop Division of the Army Air Corps. When the time came to liberate Norway from the Germans, Colonel Christiansen parachuted into Norway with his regiment.

He told me how he landed in a field, gathered up his parachute, pulled his things together, and then looked around for a member of the Norwegian Underground, his contact person. All of a sudden a man sprinted out from a nearby hiding place and ran across the field towards him; he spoke English. The first question the Norwegian asked was, "Where are you from?" Christiansen replied, "Chicago." The Norwegian smiled, "do you know a Ronneberg in Chicago? I am related to him." The answer was, "yes," for the man was father's cousin! and, instantly, one more bond was added to all the others! Now we can return to father's Scout Executive friend.

After writing a check and folding up the plans with the building permit, father announced that we were going to have lunch with Manny Goldberg, his friend. I became aware earlier that Manny was independently wealthy; we might say he was a dollar-a-day Scout Executive. What I remember from the lunch, however, was that he was also a gourmet. The old Scout Office was not too far from City Hall and we met at a very fine Greek restaurant in the Loop that was halfway between these two empires. Naturally, we ordered a lamb dish. Manny encouraged me to pick an item from the menu and that's where I began a lifelong taste for lamb. Manny talked about the Greeks and their history with respect to lamb; I was impressed and father may even have picked up the tab. But what does all this have to do with a canoe at Jerp House, a summer home away from home, that we are investigating? I'm getting to that, hang in there!

Manny, of course, knew how to pull strings at scout headquarters downtown in the Loop as well as at the Owasippie Scout Camp system outside Whitehall, Michigan. If one of my father's best friends, Peter Orlebeck, Camp Director at Owasippie Scout Camp Dan Beard for the entire summer for many years, could leave his job to pick me up on my return from Valley Forge, Pennsylvania, then why couldn't Manny arrange for the private purchase of a new Grumman aluminum canoe? Since the Owasippie system bought a quantity of new Grummans every Spring, it would be so easy for father to pay the Scout Office price for a new one and then make the short drive down to Whitehall from Bass Lake to pick it up and carry it atop the family car to Bass Lake. All it would take was asking a favor from Manny.

Everything seemed to be going according to plan and father departed Jerp House to pick up the new Grumman canoe. As already mentioned, his children never had any experience in a watercraft that was as tippy as a canoe. The family canoe arrived from Owasippie; there was only one thing wrong: it didn't look very new! There was a minor snafu and the canoe was sent to the put-in site on the White River which is a river used by many scout troops on their first canoeing excursion. As luck would have it, the canoe was already familiar with the White River; you could say that it had its maiden voyage because no one set it aside for a private pick up; in fact we could see that because the number 96 was painted on the air pocket in the bow of the canoe; there were also a few bottom dents, but who cared? We now possessed a canoe with a history.

None of these alterations made any difference. None whatsoever! We had our own family canoe courtesy of the Scout Office, but no one knew how to canoe! Father was a Boy Scout in Oak Park, Illinois; he saved his various cards and records of merit badges and advancements; I perused them when I started in the movement. Although never discussed, it was highly likely that he knew the skill from his past. He even told a story about a so-called 'junket' he took earlier on the White River. It was a picnic kind of a canoe trip for District Chairmen and a few of those high-level Scout Executives like Manny Goldberg. Peter Orlebeck, by virtue of his being a long time Camp Director, was also invited however, quite a few of the attendees had never been in in a canoe.

When the canoeing portion of the junket began a group of non-canoeists scrambled to find a partner who could paddle in the stern seat. As you might imagine, the few Scout Executives were quickly grabbed as partners, the assumption being that they were, most likely, Eagle Scouts with Canoeing Merit Badge as well, but there were not enough of these individuals who knew the J stroke to go around. Then one District Chairman who was still looking for a stern paddler spied Peter Orlebeck and knew him to be a long time Camp Director; he reasoned that the next best thing to a Scout Executive would be a Camp Director from way back.

As might be expected there *were* a number of tip-overs. But a Scout is cheerful – he smiles whenever he can . . . He never shirks or grumbles at hardships. And for this august company of District Chairmen, there was an award for those who had tipped; it was called 'initiation into the Wet Fanny Club.' The membership ceremony consisted of receiving a necklace of sorts, a circle of grocery store string on which was attached a white Life Saver candy!

The canoes of the junket arrived at the put-out point on the White River and preparations for lunch began. Then someone remarked "where is the Orlebeck canoe?" No sooner than the words were spoken, the Orlebeck canoe appeared from around the last bend with two additional candidates for initiation into the Wet Fanny Club. The moral: there is no safety in a reputation that does not match your true skills!

Returning to Bass Lake and the arrival of canoe number 96, we children reasoned that father, either because he had canoeing experience as a scout or because he was not initiated into the Wet Fanny Club the way his friend, Peter Orlebeck, was, possessed the necessary skill to demonstrate to his children how to canoe. Once the new canoe was alongside the pier he took the back seat – which kept the Grumman front air tank (the one with the 96 on it) out of the water. After pushing off from the pier he paddled south toward the channel and then made a left turn which took him over the drop-off. But either he should have kneeled in the center of the canoe – rather than sitting in the stern seat – or he should have had more experience. Just as he attempted his one hundred and eighty degree turn, the canoe tipped over!

We remarked that we would hold our own ceremony to award him membership in the Wet Fanny Club; all we needed was a package of Life Savers. But recall, reader, that when father made that landing at Little Rock, Arkansas, to refuel the Fairchild, his skills *were* up to recovering from that one hundred and eighty degree turn; through training and keeping calm he was able to recover; he exhibited prescience.

As a footnote to this first incident observed from the end of the pier, it is well to note that the Grumman canoe was fitted at a later time with an aluminum bracket that was clamped behind the stern seat to the gunnels of the canoe; it held a slanted piece of wood about two inches thick; that piece of wood was used to fasten a one and a quarter horsepower Sears Roebuck outboard motor. This was an excellent addition for expediting a canoe trip that might otherwise have included a night of camping: for example a day trip from Scottville, Michigan, down to the bridge on U. S. 31 that crossed over the south branch of the Pere Marquette River. The only downside was that the motor disturbed the quiet of the river.

In sharp contrast to a quiet paddling of a Michigan river and the observation of birdlife like a Rose-Breasted Grosbeak, the second incident observed from the end of the pier involved not only the canoe but also a large audience, lots of noise from a much more powerful outboard motor than a one and a quarter horsepower outboard, as well as an exciting rescue. My brother Ronnie was allowed to operate a speedboat that was loaned to him for a brief spin. We watched him speed around on Bass Lake without making any attempts to extend his journey across the lake – the journey was, essentially, back and forth along the shoreline about fifty yards into Bass Lake. In this sojourn he was making quick turns at the end of each run. One of those turns was clearly much too sharp and the speedboat tipped and threw him into the water. Ronnie was wearing a life preserver and the speedboat continued speeding without its driver at the wheel! There was a fortunate and an unfortunate aspect to what happened next.

Ronnie was about seventy-five yards from shore when he was thrown into the lake; he began swimming toward the shore. The speedboat, however, with the motor running at full speed ahead, had a different notion of where it wanted to go; it began circling around him because the motor was stuck at an angle – most likely the same angle that was used to turn the craft back for its next run down the lakeshore. What made matters even worse was that we soon noticed that the circling was not a circle! It was going around and around in what, at a distance, started to look like a circle of the same diameter but, in actual fact, upon closer examination, the circle was a spiral that was growing smaller and smaller with each trip around Ronnie for he always remained at the center, no matter how much he tried to gain the safety of the shallow water.

Everyone began wondering how Ronnie could survive this speeding threat; it posed the problem of how to contend with the rotating propeller of the outboard. My brother-in-law, standing next to me on the pier, was quick to the rescue; he jumped into the Grumman – he was an expert canoeist – and J stroked with very powerful strokes into the heart of the spiraling disaster. He was able to get the speedboat under control by throwing a rope that entangled the propeller and caused it to slow down and, ultimately, stop. Needless to say, this scene was watched with much more anxiety than father's tip over.

So much, then, for the Boat House. We must return to Jerp House itself and the next 'big addition', but that will require some background. The carpenter for that addition, a bedroom, was Mr. Graham of Pentwater. Like the Enger Brothers General Contractor carpenter who paneled the back porch in Chicago with ash, Mr. Graham was very skilled and would, later on, be asked by father to build a modern house in Pentwater. The question that needs to be asked now is why would father be building another home?

The answer is very simple: when Social Security was created there was no provision for architects; father felt that by building homes in Chicago and Michigan, homes that could be rented or sold on contract, i.e., one month at a time through long-term rentals, he could develop a source of retirement income. There were periods when his office experienced a lessening of engagements and he could use an architect in his own office, an employee, to produce the plans. These motives caused him to build at least two homes in Chicago.

I did not get to know Mr. Graham well because the Jerp House addition was not done during the summer months; like the magic appearance of the furnishings for Jerp House when I first stepped inside, the bedroom addition just happened. It used the side doorway to the south – toward the Linneman's – for the door to the bedroom. Mr. Graham constructed a large, flat roofed bedroom with a big steel framed picture window facing Bass Lake – towards the east – and smaller windows to the west. It sported two, tiny closets, lots of room for a dresser and a table below the picture window made from half an oak table that was saved during the Depression; my parents immediately moved in and the upstairs bedroom became free.

While I visited the two Chicago homes once or twice while they were being rented, I had a much greater involvement with the Pentwater home that Mr. Graham built from plans made in the Ronneberg firm. It was a one story, very modern home, with varnished tongue and groove vertical boards applied vertically. The windows were large floor-to-ceiling thermopane and the views outside were magnificent. The story of how the property was acquired fascinated me as a child; it was just as interesting as the tale of where the lumber came from and the cost of the construction materials.

The property story began with Mr. Shaw, a Pentwater realtor. Mr. Shaw was a Methodist, a distinguished-looking fellow, who was active in civic affairs and could have befriended father when he found the property for Jerp House. He also assisted father after the summer of 1957 in a very interesting real estate transaction; he facilitated a property situation at that time, but that is not our current focus; we'll look at that later.

Mr. Shaw approached father one day and announced that he wanted father to purchase a piece of property in the Village of Pentwater; the initiation of the transaction was strictly due to Mr. Shaw; father had never seen the parcel. The realtor's reasons were that the property contained the oldest white pine trees in Pentwater, virgin white pine, trees that had not been cut in the 19ᵗʰ century when the lumber barons went through the State of Michigan and cut everything. The trees on the property were easily four feet in diameter or more; Mr. Shaw made it clear to father that he knew father would never cut them down! The property included a stream that ran across a corner of the piece.

Upon further examination, the property was pronounced absolutely gorgeous: it was dark, possessed enormous hardwood trees, which were all as straight as an arrow, and a large spread of Trout Lilies that bloomed every spring. The purchase price was $800. Mr. Shaw knew his man and the deal was closed. Very soon after purchasing the property father began to imagine carving out a trout pond within this primeval paradise; the stream, a beautiful waterway already, would provide the cold water for the pond.

Father was curious as to what the actual value of all the timber over eight inches in diameter was; he hired a forester to make an estimate; the estimated value of the trees was more than twice the purchase price. In any event, no trout pond was constructed and no trees were touched except by me. Noticing that the thickness of the branches going up to the top of one of the largest white pines I ever saw, were very large, I resolved to climb the tree and see what I could see. The tree I climbed extended well above its deciduous neighbors and I soon had a three hundred and sixty degree view of Pentwater and vicinity. I can still see that view; it, too, was magnificent.

What did come to pass was the construction of the modern house on an open piece of land at the edge of the property, a house that would support father's retirement. Mr. Graham agreed to build it and all that was needed to begin were the materials. Father dropped off a set of plans and specifications at the Pentwater Lumber Company and asked them for an estimate. A week later he picked up their estimate for the lumber for the entire dwelling. He thanked the Pentwater company, returned to Chicago, and gave a set of plans to a Chicago lumber company; he specified that he wanted a price that included "delivery to the site from Chicago."

The following week he returned to the Pentwater Lumber Company and began a conversation with the owner to the effect that it was always his desire to engage the local tradesmen of Pentwater: he mentioned 'Shorty,' the plumber, Harold Shaw, the Realtor, and Mr. Graham, the carpenter. Then he presented the two price estimates from Pentwater and Chicago – there was a huge difference! The owner of the Pentwater Lumber Company looked at the two documents; it took but a brief moment, so the story goes, for the owner to announce very forcefully, "Mr. Ronneberg, we will *meet* all Chicago prices!"

Aside from dreaming about a future trout pound, and often walking through the property just to experience the almost hallowed nature of the property, I had only one 'working' experience that engaged me for a couple of days: one summer, I was asked between rentals, to varnish the exterior.

But again, dear reader, we must return to our theme of home and the current domicile that we are examining, Jerp House. You must recall that socialization was included in the rubric of that topic. Jerp House expanded my social contacts; to be sure, Raymond Schifelbein came up for nine day visits during the summer but I also made friends with four more individuals who lived the rest of the year in Lansing, Michigan, and who summered at Bass Lake for the entire season. But, by far and away, the high point of Bass Lake socialization that occurred during all of the years of summer residence at Jerp House, were the Tuesday and Thursday evening square dances at Camp Morrison.

The square dances were an ideal venue for the age groups that gathered on those two evenings. If we were to examine each grade from the 7th grade through the end of High School we would see that there was something for every one of those groups; at times the eight people in a square dance or the twelve or more in a Virginia Reel, would overlap by one or at most, two years, in terms of their ages, but there was something else that kept each square appropriate for all eight dancers – a sense of solidarity that we will examine. Parents sat on the sidelines and I suspect most of the parents were more interested in the younger dancers of their families; they never danced.

I can speak for every one of my friends when I say that the square dances extended acquaintances to many young women whom they never would have approached on the beach nor even been introduced to by virtue of the location of their summer home on the lake; for myself, some of these acquaintances were permanent summer residents, some were the daughters of adults known to my parents or, in one case, the daughter of the owner of Camp Morrison, and some were visiting at summer homes around the lake owned by my friends from Lansing, Michigan, or had no connection to anyone known to my friends. As previously pointed out, for every child, ages eight through eighteen, the dances were the quintessential high points of the social season. The reasons for this needs to be examined as those causes were very particularly linked to the essential nature of the activity; it was as though someone figured out exactly how something so simple as a square dance could make Bass Lake – the entire expanse – a home in a very special way.

First, I think it fair to say that the square dance was another link in the bonds that made every child, no matter where they came from, and no matter whether they stayed all summer long or not, feel that they shared an additional, common piece of culture, a multi-faceted heritage everyone understood and enjoyed; what were these components? At the top of that unique set of features we must place the physical beauties of the collective surroundings and their effect on anyone who experienced them. We begin with the lake itself.

Every child rowed, sailed, canoed, or even swam in the lake. Many, from early childhood onward, enjoyed the warm, shallow waters; they were fascinated with the clams and tiny shell creatures that crawled along the sand and left interesting trails behind them; they saw the small depressions where the sunfish and bluegills came to lay their eggs and, later, observed the minnows acting like a coordinated group as they swam in the waters at the end of the family pier; they knew about the drop-off for they were warned not to swim or splash around that far out or, they had already set their hook – below their bobber – to the greater depth needed when throwing the line so as to fish beyond the drop-off.

The older children rowed out to the Bass Lake Property Owner's Association raft anchored in the middle of the lake, tied up their boat and then dove off the raft; in this they enjoyed greater *freedom* than at a camp they might have attended where life guards were always watching. Many observed the Bass Lake Property Owner's Association weed cutter as it slowly ploughed the lake – back and forth, back and forth – cutting the weeds down to where there was now three feet of pure water instead of the tops of the weeds almost breaking the surface or, starting to interfere with the propeller of their outboard motor. They knew that the next morning after weed cutting there would be clumps of floating weeds at their pier and at the shoreline nearby. Those that maintained the waterfront, like myself, would then bring the rake from the Boat House and rake them up so as not to cause motors to be lifted up and unburdened of the weeds that were entwined to such a degree that their boat was slowed to a standstill.

But in the simple act of merely going to the Lake Michigan beach, they encountered an enchanted waterway that began as they approached the corner of Bass Lake at the start of their journey. Here began the 'channel' and, after a mere hundred yards, one motored, rowed, or canoed under the bridge that marked the entrance to the winding, very slow moving stream that, ultimately, ended at the dam where the warm, yellow tinted waters of the lake fell over the boards of the dam, entered a pond below the dam, and then became a meandering channel through the Lake Michigan sand eventually joining the crystal clear and much colder waters of Lake Michigan.

But returning back to that entrance way, before the bridge, no child could ever forget what they saw to either side as they approached the narrowing of Bass Lake for the first time; year after year they would recall that first experience and no matter how many times the Lake Michigan beach was visited in a summer, there was not a soul who didn't anxiously await the entire experience from beginning to end and back again; it was very special. To each side of the open water channel were what seemed like acres of white, fragrant, water lilies with their flowers and leaves floating on the water. You could lean over the gunnel to smell the fragrance for you must never pick one! Even to a six-year old child that would have been a sacrilege.

But what is it that I hear and see, flying and then alighting atop a cattail? A redwing blackbird; look! Another and then another, a call that once heard is never forgotten, the very harbinger of Spring. And then, below, where the driftwood is caught between the Virginia Rose blooms of the marsh beyond and the lily pads and their flowers, one spies the painted turtles sunning themselves, never in a hurry.

And do you want a pet turtle for a day? For you must never keep a turtle longer than that. Go to where there is a thick, green cotton that appears nearby in the undisturbed, sunny water near a turtle log. You will soon see a tiny turtle head poke above the green, floating, transparent-up-to-a-point, cotton candy. Quickly grab a clump of this soft green. Inside your hand you will find a turtle, perhaps as large as a fifty cent piece. Free it from the gauze and let it crawl in your hand or, for a moment, in the bottom of your craft. Better yet, you don't need a pet; let it go; your memory is just as precious.

Paddle further, almost to the bridge; now you see some Yellow Water Lilies; nice in their way. The bridge marks the entry point for the channel, an enchanted, twisting path. On one bank rise the moss-covered slopes with hemlocks and wintergreen growing below with the ghost-like Indian Pipes scattered in between the wintergreen and moss after the rain. On the other side rises a proliferation of bushes; again the Virginia Rose and Jewelweed; here, at the turn, the slope is all Sassafras trees from top to bottom – a very shady slope – and opposite? The glorious Swamp Mallow Roses rising above everything else aesthetically and physically! And now, a small side channel filled with wild plants rising from the water and shore, a place where no one ever paddles.

But everywhere to the south, and just beyond the untouched banks of green, we feel the presence of the wooded slopes of Eagle Top. Finally we have turned the last bend and we feel the sound, and the breeze of Lake Michigan; there are the spikes of Cardinal Flowers on the left bank where they always are; here is the dam ahead where the warm, yellow-tinted waters of Bass Lake fall to join the final channel carved into the sand of the beach. For the adventurous, the journey continues over the dam and beyond through the warm channel waters where young children are at play building sand castles along the shoreline or herding tiny minnows into their hand-made pools in the sand. We are more adventurous and we continue out into the cold waters of Lake Michigan in our canoe.

We shall use a fictional narrative of what happens next where the adventure of canoeing the breakers is related. It is taken from *Western Michigan Tales of Mystery and Adventure* from the story 'What's Past is Prologue' Pages 513-14:

* * *

"I'm pleased to meet all of you," said Raoul, "your uncle spoke very highly of you and I now can see why. I suspect you have known uncle Alex since as far back as you can remember and, I am certain, that would include many Bass Lake experiences?"

"Uncle Alex was keen on taking all three of us out into Lake Michigan in an aluminum canoe," spoke up Jennifer, the youngest sibling.

"You mean to paddle to Pentwater, or to go north to swim where the beach was less crowded?" asked Raoul.

"Oh no," said Alexandra, "uncle wanted to surf the big rollers that came in toward the end of August; at that time you can't even *think* of swimming. With four paddlers the object was to keep the canoe at the top of a wave crest and ride it in like they do in Hawaii!"

"That sounds like fun," said Raoul, "but what do you do when you slam into the beach?"

"That's just it," answered Alexandra, "with four people, two sitting on the seats and two on the thwarts, it's quite top-heavy, quite! top-heavy, and so you never make it that far. You paddle out beyond where the rollers are breaking, quickly do a one-hundred and eighty degree turn, and then paddle like mad to catch the top of a big wave just before it starts to curl."

"OK," remarked Raoul.

"That's the easy part, and you *do* stay poised, let me say balanced, at the top, and you *do* get propelled forward at the speed of the breaker. But you quickly begin to swerve to the side; one or two paddlers attempt to keep the bow straight ahead, but it becomes impossible to ride in all the way – except on extremely rare occasions."

"Alexandra, tell José what usually happens," said Alice.

"Well, first of all, with four of us, any slight tip at the top of the crest causes some water to come in over the gunnel. That, of course, increases the weight and makes the canoe even tippier because the water is sloshing from side to side. From then on, any attempts to keep the canoe on course *and* not tipping, become more and more frantic. At the same time there is another motion going on; the wave crest is inherently unstable because rotation can't be prevented. By rotation I mean the tendency to twist from the center of the canoe so that the bow is now going clockwise or counter-clockwise like the seconds hand on a wrist watch.

"The more a front paddler tries to help uncle Alex in the stern, the more the canoe veers the bow towards either Pentwater or Ludington, as the case may be, and that augments the tip, and with a bit more water over the gunnel, whoosh! Over we go right into the wave as it is curling! This, of course, ends up in a mess: water with a lot of crash and foam, four paddles and a canoe adrift, all caught up in the crash of the wave not to mention four canoeists, coming up for breath before the next roller crashes down! Sometimes there is even fear as we come up for breath, because we are not certain whether we are going to be touched by a waterlogged canoe that is now a moving, mostly underwater, hazard."

"So you've probably been doing this kind of thing since you were able to swim," offered Raoul.

"Alexandra and I learned to swim before our parents would let us go out," said Deborah, "but Jennifer could swim when she was three years younger than when we learned, and she felt cheated when she was still too young and wasn't allowed to go out and get capsized."

"*That* I *can* understand," remarked Raoul.

* * *

So these and many other adventures link the square dancers before the dancing begins; experiences like the climbing of Eagle Top, the exploration of Devil's Pond, the night spent sleeping on the beach – the bonfire of driftwood, the hard sand for a pillow, the shooting stars, and the sunset – the full moon rising over Bass Lake, the Milky Way, and shooting stars seen from a Bass Lake pier long after the sun has set.

Another aspect of the square dance that enhanced the confidence of all of the dancers with respect to their social skills and the ease of talking to partners from an early age, was the fact that everyone memorized the calls to all the dances! That implied knowing all of the movements that were announced by the caller: first couple, out to the right, swing as you meet, circle four in the middle of the floor, allemande left with your left hand then meet your partner with a right and left grand, ladies all lead to the left of the ring,

salute your partners all, do-se-do your partner, swing your corner lady, grab
that lady by the wrist and around that lady with the grape vine twist, back
to the center, cut a figure eight, circle to the left and to the right, promenade.

From what other source could that confidence come from, a confidence that allowed you to walk up to a girl whom you knew or never
saw before, and ask her to dance with you as the first couple? The process
seemed so natural so enjoyable. Here, taken from a John Sherman story
called 'New Friends' from the book *Western Michigan Tales of Mystery and
Adventure*, is more about the Camp Morrison square dance:

* * *

"So you square dance on Tuesday and Thursday nights, every week, all
summer long at Camp Morrison?" asked Winston.

"Yes," said Sherman, "we all know the calls, and not a child from
eight years old through the end of high school would miss it."

"Tomorrow is Thursday," said Winston, "and we want you to have a
good time."

Camp Morrison was an institution on the lake long before Sherman's
family began renting from Sherman's father's secretary's brother. It consisted
of a large screened-in, wooden-floored dining hall situated on the top of a
small wooded hill and was surrounded by forty or so sleeping cottages with
washroom facilities. All these small cottages were spread throughout the
remaining property of several acres. A bell was rung fifteen minutes before
the first dining room sitting and families could hear the gong at the beach
and hike the trail around the base of Eagle Top, a large wooded dune, so as to
arrive for lunch or dinner. There were also activities back behind the dining
hall for children like storytelling and campfires. On Tuesday and Thursday
evenings there were square dances for any child from eight to eighteen and
even for adults, but adult squares were rare.

To prepare for the dance, the dining tables and chairs were pushed to the edges of three sides of the dining hall, and rows of chairs were set up for parents and children of all ages along the edge. By the time Sherman started to attend, phonograph records and a seventeen-year-old caller were responsible for the music and calling the dances. Before that time, an elderly fiddle player together with Mr. Morrison, who called the dances, provided joint entertainment for the evenings. During the years Sherman attended, the new procedure was always the same. Bob, the caller, would pick up a microphone and announce, "fill up the floor for an old-fashioned square dance!"

Every male who wanted to dance would then pick out a partner and join a square until the entire floor was filled. There were usually one or two squares of eight-to-ten-year-olds, then some for the next two years, and so on. Even before joining a square, an eight-to-ten-year-old dancer would know the calls by heart. Once the squares were formed, Bob would put on the appropriate record and start the call, which invariably began with an "Allemande left with your left hand then meet your partner with a right and left grand." Three dances would be called before an intermission, then three more, another intermission, and then the final three before everyone went home.

When he was twelve years old, Sherman was always being encouraged to ask partners to dance who were chosen by his friends and who were a year or two older than he was. Sherman's friends wanted him to bring a new girl, their age, into their square. As a result, Sherman often found himself dancing one of the three sets with an older girl and usually the second set with a girl his age, and the last set with a girl one or two years younger. After years of dancing it was easy to bring a new boy or girl into a square; often they were the only one in the square who had not memorized the call and done the dance many times.

There were dances that were danced to the music of the Arkansas Traveler and were variations on a simple idea which became more complex. For example, the simplest and least tiring was a call that went like:

First couple out to the right,
Behind that couple take a little peek,
Back to the center and swing your feet.
Behind that couple, peek once more,
Then back to the center and swing all four.
Lead right on to the next.

It took a little more energy to dance the next variation:

First couple out to the right,
Behind that couple swing as you meet,
Back to the center and swing your feet.
Behind that couple swing once more,
Then back to the center and swing all four.
Lead right on to the next.

By far the most energetic call was a crack-the-whip call known as the grape vine twist called to a tune called Possum in a 'Simmon' Tree. 'Simmon stood for persimmon and Sherman wondered if the Algonquian origin of the word was responsible for the intensity of the dance:

First couple out to the right,
Grab that lady by the wrist
And around that lady with the grape vine twist,
Back to the center, cut a figure eight,
And around that gent with the same old gait.
Circle four in the middle of the floor,
And lead right on to the next.

By the time the last couple was reached, the girl at the end of the six-person chain was hanging on with both hands as the figure eight was cut for a second time. She was literally being whipped at the end of a crack-the-whip chain. Invariably, Bob would call the grape vine twist at the end of a set of three dances and everyone would pour outside into the back porch open veranda with a soda or just to cool off.

Sherman and his partner finished the grape vine twist and he left to go outside while his partner exited to the washroom to freshen up. He pushed the screen door to move into the night air and the lake breeze. He could see the moon and stars except for some intervening trees. He decided to walk down the few steps where he could see better from the campfire circle where young children were told stories around a blazing fire.

* * *

The environment at Bass Lake could even lead to romance. Here is another John Sherman extract from the book *Stories of Groups* taken from the story 'Archers':

* * *

Years passed. Sherman's family now lived in Jerp House all summer long. Sherman's sister Julia constantly played her forty-five rpm records every day. Songs like Frankie Laine's "Mule Train" and "(Ghost) Riders in the Sky" vied with more romantic tunes like "Harbor Lights" and "Once I Had a Secret Love." Sherman's father flew Julia's and Sherman's friends from Chicago to Bass Lake and back for ten-day visits. These guests stayed in the Tent House. Sleeping in a separate structure was part of the experience.

Sherman was alive to the attractions around him. The lyrics of his sister's records began stirring his heart beyond its faint awareness of the girls he asked to dance with him during the Tuesday and Thursday evening square dances. Often the moon rose across the lake as the square dancing began. It would be overhead when the last dance finished; the mottled light filtered down through the trees enchanting the forest.

Sherman remembered the time when his mother first spotted the moon and its long golden path on the lake. Even through the dining room windows at Chris Cot, the image permanently impressed him.

These were very happy times for Sherman. He sang a song into the air as he performed his chores for the day. The song he sang the morning after a square dance could easily be the music and call of a dance. "Ladies all lead to the left of the ring / When they get there, you give them a swing / When you do that, remember the call / It's allemande left and promenade all." Then one day his sister put on another record. The magic of its tune and the suggestions of its lyrics clarified feelings he had felt for some time.

There was something attractive and fun about square dancing. The music was part of it, along with the fact that Sherman knew all the calls and dances by heart. Some of the friends Sherman palled around with were a bit girl-crazy. His friend Bob H's parents invited Bob's cousin's family to stay at Bob's cottage for a week. Bob's cousin was eleven, Sherman's age. Bob often asked Sherman to invite older girls to join Bob's square and now it was Bob's turn to reciprocate.

"I want you to dance a lot with my cousin," said Bob before the first set of three dances.

"OK," replied Sherman. He liked Bob's cousin Linda as soon as he saw her. Things didn't change during the evening. Linda not only was good-looking, but also seemed to be a good friend – easy to talk to, gracious, and something else he couldn't put his finger on. It was just the feeling that he wanted to be with her, near her.

At Bob's urging after the dance, Sherman walked Linda home, three-and-a-half city blocks away. There was no moon out that evening, but Sherman knew the way by heart. He had held Linda's hand for six of the nine dances and it seemed natural to hold it again as they walked together in the dark with only the starlight to make out the road. Sherman felt sorry that she was staying for so short a time.

It was this experience that caused Sherman to remember the tune and lyrics of Julia's new record. It clarified his thinking. Like the moon coming up over the lake that first time at Chris Cot, that tune and its words permanently imprinted themselves on him. Sherman often found himself returning to it as time passed. The record caught the imaginations of millions of others, too. The first stanza ran:

> Somewhere there's music
> How faint the tune
> Somewhere there's heaven
> How high the moon
> There is no moon above
> When love is far away too
> Till it comes true
> That you love me as I love you
> How high the moon

Sherman doubted that he was now oblivious to the return of the moon; the language left room for interpretation. He felt the line "How high the moon" was a reflection of his new consciousness. The notion of heaven changed and the height of the moon was merely a figurative reminder of the depth of a new emotion. The second stanza was no less haunting.

> Somewhere there's music
> How near, how far
> Somewhere there's heaven
> It's where you are
> The darkest night would shine
> If you would come to me soon
> Until you will, how still my heart
> How high the moon

Music seemed important to Sherman. It reminded him of the square dance. There was a suggestion in the lyric "How near, how far" that the distance of the tune from Sherman's hearing now reflected his distance from another square dance exactly like the one where he had danced with Linda.

"How near, how far" suggested the stars in a constellation. So long as the constellation formed an object, it was of no importance how separated the stars were from one another. The important things were a recognizable image and a new definition of heaven. More particularly, a dark night, like this one as he walked Linda back home, would shine with the return of someone. Without that someone, the singer's heart would remain still and as faint as the tune he is searching for.

What crept into Sherman's consciousness was an element of the bittersweet, the idea that bright things can pass away; that there are often two sides to the splendors of the objects that reside in the heavens. The cosmos and heavenly things are as ephemeral as a campfire on the beach and will soon cease to be, passing with time into oblivion.

Campfire

You always have an inner heart of coals
Despite your goal of self-destruction bright.
Your flames warned Clytemnestra's evil soul,
But most you warm and cheer good hearts the night.

Your yellow flame invokes our ancient past,
A catalyst we can't resist to know
For from the camps and caves 'cross centuries vast
The brain we now retain began to grow.

The trees you seize no longer feel the breeze
Your flames unique, an endless dancing treat.
Pure dazzling feat of heat, consume with ease.
Whate'er we please to sacrifice, you eat.

You warm without regard to friend or foe
Yet warn the beast how far to go, secure
When near we lose our fear, you melt the snow,
Ward off the winter's cough, sure mental cure.

And when you're down to ash and sparks at night,
You link with heaven's burning points of light
And rival all the shooting stars their flight
But then with final flame, give up the fight.

* * *

Our examination of the Jerp House home requires that we speak of Devil's Pond. We will do this through a fictional chase by John Sherman into Devil's Pond. The story begins from a home that is yet to be discussed; it is included here because it introduces Devil's Pond. An unknown gunman has, with a single, lucky, shot, broken the plastic cord that holds one of his most beloved hummingbird feeders – one that cannot be replaced. The excerpt describing the chase is taken from *Western Michigan Tales of Mystery and Adventure* in a story called 'Red and Green.'

* * *

John Sherman looked out through the window above the kitchen sink in his summer home, Idlewild, to watch a ruby-throated humming bird drink sugar water from a small feeder attached to a low branch of a white oak tree that grew but four feet from the wall of his home. The feeder was one of his favorites and was now unobtainable from commercial sources. This was particularly disturbing to Sherman. Every time he picked up a copy of *Enjoying Hummingbirds* by Nancy Newfield, published in 2001, he would turn to page nine and there, in a picture attributed to Charles W. Melton, was a young woman holding the feeder!

The result of this inability to purchase an exact replacement of the same style of feeder, not to mention additional ones, led Sherman, over the years, to repair his only representative of the product. The red plastic top had long since broken open, but electrical friction tape was adequate to fix that problem. The bent piece of glass tubing that conveyed the sugar water from the reservoir to the end, where the hummer poked its long bill, was broken at one end but was still serviceable if Sherman put the jagged end into the reservoir through the plastic cork, always being careful not to cut himself when cleaning the feeder.

John used four active feeders in the summer months, and he always hung them with old shower curtain hooks. A branch of small diameter, growing low on the white oak tree, supported the kitchen-window feeder's shower curtain hook (from the end that would have rolled along a shower curtain rod, were it still hanging in a bathroom). With the hook thus attached to the branch and its narrow portion pointing toward the earth, it could easily be opened and closed to allow removal, cleaning, and refilling of the feeder.

Sherman's other feeders also hung from tree branches using shower curtain hooks, but he hung these hangers at the end of a long loop of ten-pound fishing line. To attach the line to a tree limb, he first attached a metal weight to the line and then threw the weight up and across the limb. This resulted in a feeder that seemed to float in the air as the fish line was transparent. It was important to keep the feeder well away from the trunk of the tree so that squirrels would not be tempted to jump from the trunk to the feeder.

After pointing its bill into the end of the glass tube outside the kitchen window, a ruby throat began to drink. Within a second or two, a small air bubble made its way up the tube and slowly rose; the sugar water was like syrup because it was made with one cup of sugar added to one quart of boiling water. The air bubble arrived at the glass reservoir where it rose further and ultimately joined the ever-increasing body of air at the top of the feeder.

John liked to watch these tiny air bubbles rise and merge. He was glad to be free of the constraints of a chemistry lab where clear glass containers and tubes were also connected. He remembered the frenzy to finish experiments in his chemistry labs, the rush to determine the unknown chemical compound he had been working on and to fill out the laboratory worksheet before the next class came in to use the university chemistry lab. Now, the slow motion of the air bubble as it rose through the liquid was more to his liking.

The hummer was beating its wings at an enormous number of beats per second, but it was the slow ascent of the tiny bubble that always fascinated Sherman in these encounters. At summer's end he could never imagine how many times he had blended quarts of boiling water with a cup of sugar to make the liquid for all his feeders.

There must be something very satisfying and relaxing in all this, thought Sherman as another small bubble rose up the glass tube. The chemistry of flying all the way to southern Mexico and beyond, as far south as Costa Rica, to winter, all while competing with other birds for nectar, could only be matched with the nonstop, eighteen-hour return trip across the Gulf of Mexico, and all these feats began in a nest the size of a walnut!

But suddenly, as if the peace of his thoughts were too calm for the human race, John heard the unnatural sound of a gunshot fired at close range. He saw the ruby throat withdraw its long beak and the feeder, as if responding to the shot, detach itself from the shower curtain hook falling to the oak leaves below. Some lucky shot, or unlucky one, Sherman could not tell, broke the remaining fragment of plastic at the top of the feeder releasing it to the effects of gravity. It could not be otherwise, for there, hanging from the shower curtain hook itself, was the red-wire cord and, at its end, a small piece of plastic.

For a moment, Sherman was happy to realize that friction tape would repair the irreplaceable feeder; the other feeders hanging from fish line would meet the demands of the hungry birds, which defended their food sources with a vengeance. The same vengeance that caused the hummingbirds to dive-bomb each other with a loud, raspy squeal, now took hold of John, for he, too, could defend his territory. He threw open the kitchen screen door and saw a young man standing in the woods about thirty yards away, and holding a single-shot target pistol with a long barrel. . . .

After the hummingbird feeder dropped into the leaves, John, with vengeance in his heart, yelled at the young man to stop, for he could see that the man turned and was running toward the lake. As long as the young man kept moving and did not reload his weapon, pursuing him would just be a matter of strength and will. In a moment, the gunman jumped into a neighbor's canoe, grabbed a paddle from the pier, and pushed off for the north end of the lake, paddling furiously. John ran for his own aluminum canoe, grabbed the longest stern paddle, and was soon in hot pursuit, using the J stroke from the midsection, and feathering his paddle blade on the return to gain any small advantage.

The north end of the lake was a largely desolate and swampy area of brush with enormous clumps of cattails growing at the shoreline, with adder bushes, wild rose bushes, elderberry, and other species growing behind the cattails. The only way into this maze of vegetation was to paddle upstream the very narrow, sluggish, and torturous waterway that twisted between Devil's Pond and the lake. For decades, young adventurers pushed through the cobwebs and spiders, the brush and muddy bottom, of the almost stagnant channel into the tranquil and quiet open space of shallow water known as Devil's Pond, principally because of the treacherous bog that surrounded it, a sphagnum-covered and dense bushy area that quickly absorbed one's first step into it, often up to the knees.

After the young man negotiated his way into the pond, he could only escape by paddling directly toward a point on the shore, where he would encounter a dense wall of brush and moss. Once there, he'd have to attempt to support himself by stepping on bent-over live branches or scrambling along on his stomach and crawling across whatever dead or live material he encountered. Live material might include any native species of snakes he might find along his path. The only benign creatures were the dwarf perch that seemed unwilling to leave the pond.

John soon felt that fate was on his side, for as he struggled to reduce the distance between the two canoes, he noticed a pair of flippers left in the bow of his canoe from an earlier diving expedition. In the excitement of finding a waterlogged dagger board, lost from a sailboat a year ago, the last user had forgotten to return the flippers to the boathouse after diving the prior day. By putting on the flippers while he was still crossing from the shoreline of Devil's Pond to the bog surrounding it, John knew he would have an advantage chasing his human prey across the moss and underbrush.

Sherman could still hear the efforts of the man he pursued. Branches were breaking and the sides of the canoe were scraping those and other branches; in effect the gunman was both blazing the trail and clearing the path for John in his own canoe. Then he heard the canoe being dragged across Lattin Road, the entrance road to Bass Lake. The young man had reached the culvert that ran under Lattin road and was pushing his craft up, across, and then down, back into the channel. It seemed only a minute before John duplicated that effort and only a few more before he emerged into the quiet solitude of Devil's Pond.

John's path of further pursuit was now obvious; the gunman paddled the stolen canoe into brush along the pond's shore, and was immediately rebuffed by the bushes. The unknown man with the pistol must have then jumped out and started negotiating the almost impenetrable obstacle course that lay between him and solid ground. Probably, in response to the gunman's jump ashore, the canoe had floated back from the shore, almost in the middle of the pond; only the disturbed Virginia Rose bushes marked where the gunman entered the ring of bog land.

Sherman strapped on the flippers, tied his canoe to the nearest rose bush, and began his own attempt at traversing the terrain. The new path was blazed with markers, broken branches, and huge depressions in the sphagnum, as well as crushed plants. Pools shaped like a footprint and outlined by green sphagnum moss immediately filled with muddy water up to a depth of about half a foot.

Sherman remembered the feeling from when he was younger – the first time he was caught in the moss – and he heard once again the squish that came from stepping into the moss as it sank below his flipper and ankle. Long ago, he felt the water rise up higher and higher as he grabbed for anything he could use to check the downward motion of his shoe before both shoes were equally drawn into the morass. But now the flippers were helping; the sinking was not as fast or as deep. Forward progress was still a struggle but extracting each foot was easier. He knew he must be going faster than the man ahead of him; it was only a matter of time before he would catch up with him.

And then, as he labored with the dead logs and branches immediately before him, Sherman saw the object of his pursuit suffering an even worse struggle with the underbrush. In such a situation, there was no time even to think of loading a cartridge, turning, and firing a shot at one's pursuer. The gunman clearly had to focus all his mental concentration on planning and negotiating his next step, looking out for handholds in the small pines that managed to grow in the environment, and somehow mustering the energy for the next step; each movement was an effort, and exhaustion beckoned him at every moment.

Sherman started to yell at the young man but his voice was soon cut off by a noise he heard many times before but which was now completely unexpected. For the past dozen years, a full-time resident on Lattin Road, who lived but a quarter of a mile away, had been in the business of offering rides on a motorized aircraft, a powered paraglider, as it was known in the trade.

A huge, brightly colored plastic airfoil, called a paraglider, or wing, that bowed up in the middle, was attached by strong lines at both ends to a platform on which was mounted a paramotor situated behind two platform seats. The paramotor was actually attached to a propeller in a wire cage, and provided thrust going backward so as to propel the craft forward.

The upper portion, or paraglider, looked exactly the same as non-powered paragliders used by individuals who jump out of aircraft and then manipulate themselves to land in front of a reviewing stand, or at the front end of a Fourth of July parade about to start.

The Lattin Road entrepreneur purchased a two-seater powered paraglider. The Lattin Road entrepreneur offered this form of flight for a fee, and carried his customer over the trees, above the lake, across the forest and wooded hills along Lake Michigan, and even over the farmlands and orchards of Mason and Oceana Counties.

Before Sherman could call out at the gunman, this familiar aircraft swooped down above the treetops and over the lake beyond, making its usual loud roar. Flying at slow speed, the paraglider's operator swung a harness hanging below the platform into the waiting arms of the destroyer of Sherman's peace of mind, the gunman, thereby causing that destroyer to be plucked from the clutches of sphagnum moss, or whatever else he was currently caught up with, and lifted into the freedom of the sky.

* * *

Before we leave Bass Lake and the chase to Devil's Pond, there is another kind of chase that occurred many times both in Chicago and at Bass Lake; this family of chases were not fictional by any means! They interrupted everything that the family was doing for they demanded immediate attention. The chase was a multi-vehicle affair that involved four drivers and, of course, four cars. We're going to use an excerpt from a diary that John Sherman kept. In the excerpt we'll see just what those chasses were all about and learn another one of mother's reminders. The excerpt comes from *Stories of Groups* in a piece called 'Sherman's Diary.'

* * *

If you have been keeping track, diary, you know that there were four cars in use during the years when both my sister Julia and I lived at home. But, once again, it seemed that having lots of cars hearkened back to my grandfather who was a very successful architect and engineer. He lived in Oak Park, an upscale suburb of Chicago – my father could remember conversations with Frank Lloyd Wright on the front porch of their Cuyler Avenue home. My grandfather sent three children through the University of Illinois, all at the same time!

Father made it known that, as a child, he had a car that he used to take a trip out west, just to see the landscape. For some reason he drove through Cape Girardeau Missouri on the way. I hesitate, diary, to call his trip idle driving because there must have been some additional purpose. Maybe it was the equivalent of that world tour that upper class children took in Europe during the nineteenth century and that we read about in novels and social commentary of that period.

I felt that having a fleet of cars was the result of my father's desire to compete with his own father. My sister and I could take the bus to High School but I couldn't imagine my father and his siblings not having cars at the University of Illinois and I wouldn't be surprised if they all didn't have cars to attend the equivalent of a University, Oak Park High School.

In any event, having cars to drive per se would not have caused an "embarrassment of riches;" it was out of character for the neighborhood but not beyond the pale of imagination. No, it was the interjection of a wire-haired fox terrier that caused the embarrassment. Here, diary, I must confess that I do not know for sure that I am on firm ground for I am not certain that our wired-haired fox-terriers – we went through ownership in a serial fashion – acquired their most prominent characteristic by virtue of genes passed through their parents. That characteristic was, of course, to bolt through any open door or gate and run away at great speed to remote locations that were miles away from home.

This was a very frequent family occurrence and the first family member to notice the situation would shout out, "The dog is out!" Nothing else was required, all other activity ceased and everyone dropped what they were doing. Quadrants of the surrounding neighborhood were imprinted – like on a duck gosling – on our minds from prior canvassing of the streets and alleys surrounding our home. It was like the beginning of an auto race where the official voice is heard to say, "Drivers start your engines!" and all the drivers – all four of us in Fords – dashed to our vehicles.

Once started, windows were rolled down – in any weather – and the search began. Alleys, with their smells and backyard access to other canine species, seemed to be preferred by wire-haired terriers. Up and down, up and down, north to south and east to west, four open-windowed cars searched the neighborhood byways and from each vehicle could be heard a voice getting more and more hoarse as it yelled, "Here Sugar, here Sugar!" hour after hour.

There seemed to be no better way. Sometimes Sugar or Butzie – Sugar's successor – was found two miles away! Imagine, diary, a circular area of 12.56 square miles. In Michigan, the dog often ended up across the lake where roads were difficult to negotiate. Each vehicle needed to use the single lane, mossy road that led up to a summer cottage; it was necessary to get to the lake, call out for the dog, and then negotiate turning back and locating the next road in.

It became so bad that one year Mother – who wanted to raise dogs after four children – read somewhere that chasing cars – I should mention, diary, that this trait was also inherited and tended to optimize the travelled distance at the start of or during an organized search – could be curtailed by firing a squirt gun filled with lemon juice into the eyes of a barking dog that ran alongside a car. I might add that when we watched our wired-haired fox-terrier chase a car we were preoccupied with only one thing – it always looked like the dog was about to be run over by the front wheels – and the fearful proximity to that event recurred over and over again as the chase continued.

But back to the squirt gun filled with lemon juice. Sugar was re-leased and I, in the passenger seat, was given the task of firing the gun. It didn't work! A long search around the perimeter of Bass Lake was our reward for the failure.

Dear Diary,

I'm trying to explain why my upbringing was so confusing and I see that I've just scratched the surface. I've already told you about the "royalty" aspect. This was reinforced by mother when she wanted to get me to do something I might rebel against. She would remind me that "Nobility had its obligations." Elsewhere, I've talked about her warning me that boys must learn to wash bathroom floors and kitchen floors because "no woman would marry a man if he could not wash floors." It seemed to me as a child then that even a crown prince like myself had to wash floors and drive up and down alleys yelling, "Here Butzie, here Butzie!" and make a fool of himself because "Nobility had its obligations!"

* * *

There are many more characteristics that made Bass Lake, Pentwater, Michigan, a home away from home for those young denizens who were fortunate enough to spend their entire summers exploring the hills, lakes, beach, shorelines, channel, and Devil's Pond while also enjoying the social amenities of their friends and square dance partners at Camp Morrison. Our intent is not to exhaust this list but to continue the variety of this progressive diversity in its historical sequence. To continue that trajectory it is necessary to return to Illinois:

Customize-Your-Own
Insulated Log Cabin
With
Vertical Log Panels
Buyer Designed
Woodland Acreage
Adjacent to
Silver Lake
North of Cary, Illinois
Early 1950s

I suspect there were several reasons why father decided to incorporate a third family home into the existing routines of his family. Like the two year search for a piece of lakefront property on Bass Lake, a search which ended the three years of renting Chris Cot, an inadvertent discovery led to locating the property on which he would construct what many would describe as a

Fall/Winter/Spring weekend seter, a seter that was about an hour and a half trip by automobile from 7240 West Pratt Avenue.

The story of the discovery of that property begins with a flight path that the Fairchild took that brought its pilot over a wooded and hilly area northwest of Fox River Grove, Illinois. This flight path was repeated many times most likely because of its relationship to Elmhurst Airport as well as a succession of business trips in either Illinois or Wisconsin. However that may be, as father looked below him just before crossing the Fox River north of Fox River Grove, he spied a large tract of uninhabited wooded property; in the middle of the property was a man-made lake surrounded by wooded slopes – a small dam was used to create the lake – and there was a second lake nearby with a more open shoreline, i.e., fewer trees.

There were no homes on any of this property. Another point of interest that he could see from the air was an expansive prairie adjacent to one corner of the entire tract of woodland and the two lakes. Such a prairie at this late hour in Illinois' history could only imply some kind of game preserve – most likely for pheasants.

The next clue, or motive – whichever you prefer – was a large advertisement in the Sunday Chicago Tribune; it advertised lots for sale on and around Silver Lake, north of Cary, Illinois, and intimated that a very large estate was being subdivided for the benefit of Chicago and northern Illinois buyers. The ad triggered a trip by car on the following Sunday and the discovery of a sales office together with a crew of salesmen ready to guide interested parties around the entire estate.

On this tour the potential buyer could see that roads were built, lots were staked out, and there were lakefront lots as well as wooded lots away from the lake; there were out-in-the-open prairie lots. A sandy beach existed with facilities for swimming, a pier, and even some play equipment for small children. The lake was reputed to be an excellent fishing spot as it was stocked by the former owner with bass and bluegills; at a later time this claim was verified. In no time at all, father purchased a couple of wooded lots at the far edge of the forested expanse of land. The site was a wooded hillside; by building a home just below the top of the hill, the occupants would have a view into the trees below. My father's secretary, Marie Christopherson, soon decided to purchase lots across the road with a view to building her own, small, getaway home.

As the design of the Silver Lake home took shape on the drawing boards, Mr. Ronneberg, Sr., felt that if he purchased the entire block of wooded property to the north, which consisted of five or six acres, then he would achieve a degree of isolation. No road would have to be put through since no one else would be building on the entire parcel. Beyond the block that father purchased was the extensive game preserve which he saw from the air; it stretched north another half mile and then east for more than a mile before it turned and went further. The block was, on the east and north sides, in the corner of the entire estate; this was because further up the hill from the site, and running all along the eastern edge of the block, was undeveloped, private, and open prairie.

To facilitate purchase of the entire block to the north, the sales office offered father a discount on every lot when bought in a group; they did not have to put in a road stretching all along the east side of the block, nor did they have to survey any lots in the block and stake out those parcels. The rest of the block was purchased and the family now owned a huge forest; even the road at the bottom of the hill was not built beyond the Silver Lake home; that extended the owned property by virtue of the large expanse of un-owned, adjacent property, accessible only by foot. I quickly saw that I could walk through an enormous expanse of uninhabited Illinois forest with small, rolling hills, and the biodiversity of an adjacent prairie – some of which was swamp-like. This was a new environment from Michigan with Shagbark Hickory and Burr Oak trees. There was the potential for discovering natural elements that I was never exposed to.

One could, I imagine, say that one motive of purchasing Silver Lake was to extend the property that was owned and adjacent to the Silver Lake home vis a via the property in Michigan. The problem with that analysis was that already, at that point in time, Chris Cot had been purchased from Marie Christopherson who inherited it from her brother, and, an additional twenty acres of Michigan woodland had been purchased two miles south of the Bass Lake outlet in a plat known as Pentwater Beach Addition No. 1, about a mile north of the village of Pentwater; some of that property was Lake Michigan lakefront property.

I truly believe that a major need for father was isolation; the Silver Lake land was, for many years, a private nature preserve. The second goal was to extend the idea of a weekend Norwegian seter to an accessible location relative to an eight hour drive to Bass Lake by car or a two hour flight by private plane. Implicit in this goal was the idea of extending the Bass Lake experience to his family *all year long*, and this especially emphasized being exposed to nature. Finally, there was the very real desire to ski in during the winter. From the main country road at the point where we turned to follow the subdivision road for two blocks to get to the Silver Lake home, we could see the ski lift and downhill slopes owned by the town of Fox River Grove. When we commented on the activity that we saw across a half mile of prairie, I can distinctly remember father commenting that in Norway the purpose of skiing was to get from one place to another. This was perplexing simply because I knew that the only trip to Norway to visit grandparents from the Oak Park home was made when father was in the first grade.

That Norwegian trip was a long one; the family stayed a year! Of course the trip had its share of family legends but they were limited to immediate family members. More particularly, there was the story of Gordon, my father's brother, attempting to slice a banana by submitting the peeled banana to the blades of an electric fan! During the voyage to Norway Gordon also became enamored with the desserts that were served. During some rough weather Gordon recognized that individuals were staying in their cabins and avoiding the desserts. Wanting to take advantage of the extra quantities of desserts, so the story goes, he publically put his finger in his mouth and then stuck his finger in many of the desserts.

The most oft repeated story of that trip was the one involving my father's losing his ability to speak the English language. Upon return to Oak Park he was demoted back to kindergarten! Natal Ronneberg was so upset that he put his foot down: no more Norwegian would be spoken in the Ronneberg household! The maid would immediately start night school! Thus it was that I came to have an actual family resolution, instituted by no less a person than my grandfather, Natal Ronneberg, not to be a Norwegian all your life, assuming, of course, that speaking the Norwegian language constituted a huge percentage of what being a Norwegian amounted to. I never doubted these stories even though uncle Gordon was too kind an uncle to have been so mischievous. What I doubted was that at the age of kindergarten/first grade father could have developed such an allegiance to the real purpose of skiing. With the acquisition of Silver Lake, this could be tested.

In proof of this last idea we can footnote the fact that skies *were* purchased from the Sears catalog, and on *one* occasion, the family car was left parked on the main country road – right at the point where we had observed the Fox River Grove ski lift in the distance. The family *did* ski in the two blocks to get to our Silver Lake home; we carried backpacks with the groceries that we purchased at the Cary, Illinois, grocery store a few miles away. After that one-time ski trip the skis were retired to the rafters where they remained forever after.

I suspect that another motive was to make up for all those summer weeks when he was working in Chicago while the family was in Michigan. With a fall/winter/spring home, a compensating strategy could be put into play: he would have, close at hand, his entire family every weekend. But however true the principal was, the elements that made Silver Lake a home were different; they complimented the Bass Lake summers and while never as extensive as the glorious aspects of Michigan, the delights of the Silver Lake home were the frosting on the cake, and were complimentary, and synergistic with respect to Michigan.

What we experienced in Illinois opened up new vistas for me; the spirit of what father achieved for his family in Michigan was in effect even though the visits were limited to weekends; I experienced new dimensions with respect to the out of doors and these would come to cross pollinate my Michigan summers. It is necessary, then, that we examine this new environment not only as a home, but also as a place to know more intimately the other three seasons of the year.

The buyer of a home like Silver Lake – a log home with logs put together vertically rather than horizontally – picked a standard design to begin with and then altered it in such a way so as to accommodate variations he felt were necessary. The basic plan was a large L-shaped room; a small bathroom with a shower and a tiny kitchen were back-to-back in one corner of the large room. Two big picture windows faced the downhill side, but there were many windows on all the walls.

One adjustment to the standard design was leaving an opening for a large stone – crab orchard stone – fireplace. Half of the fireplace faced inward and operated with a heatilator which was an iron three sided wall set into the fireplace. The walls were hollow; two fans picked up cold air from two, grated, input vents at the bottom of the stone work on either side and those fans blew the air through the heatilator and out through two exit grates above the input grates and about a foot below a huge slab of stone that was the mantle.

I point out that this was half a fireplace because outside, on a screened in porch, and behind the inside fireplace, was another, outside fireplace that opened out to the porch that ran all along the north side of the house that faced all of the additional property; it had no heatilator. It took an experienced mason to cut and lay the crab orchard stone – two huge fireplaces and then a double chimney running up to the peak of the roof and beyond; it was a work of art! It also took a long time and, during construction, the Silver Lake home was exposed by virtue of the opening.

But the time and cost was well worth the effort. Having an oak log fire was a highlight that was new to the family; it became central to our enjoyment of the home. Splitting oak logs with axe, wedges, and sledge hammer became a new weekend task that linked my exertions with past generations; I felt closer to Abraham Lincoln, the log splitter; the effort was associated with a fundamental human need – heat; it served a higher purpose than the recreational collection of driftwood for use in fires that I built with friends when spending a night on the Lake Michigan beach; splitting wood brought me closer to adulthood.

A trapdoor in the kitchen floor led to a concrete enclosed pump pit, big enough to stand in. The design allowed the entire house to be winterized in minutes. The well went down two hundred feet to Lake Superior limestone; much deeper than the well points we drove by hand in Michigan to a depth of thirty feet, enough to pierce the hard-pan and tap the pure, sand filtered waters from Lake Michigan a mere half mile away. Of course the water was hard but we put up with it.

The pump pit and well also served Marie Christopherson's home across the road that ran up the hill between the two log cabin homes; a pipe was laid under the roadway. The upshot was that coming and going in the winter was much easier than it was on the few occasions when the family went to Jerp House in December – driving to Milwaukee, Wisconsin, boarding the Chesapeake and Ohio Railroad car ferry to Ludington – where opening and closing the water was much more cumbersome as it involved winterizing the plumbing system when leaving.

Although a hide-a-bed sofa faced the fireplace, the entire family slept in a large bedroom. This was a room that ran along the entire uphill side of the main room. It had two bunk beds on opposite walls and a double bed between them. An oil stove in the main room gave thermostat controlled heat and was supplemented by the warm air of the heatilator.

The house was cozy. We occasionally swam in Silver Lake and fished; we kept a small, wooden rowboat at the lakeshore but the experiences I treasure most were, aside from the warm winter fires, all outside. As already mentioned, they were encounters with nature and with the fall, winter, and spring seasons; there was a seasonal magic in those weekends that I could never know in the summers in Michigan – which were by no means devoid of their own magical charm – nor in the city. This, more than anything, heightened my appreciation of Silver Lake.

From a very early age I had hiked and explored the wooded and uninhabited hills that rise up along the Lake Michigan lakefront. Even in the winter on those rare occasions that we opened Jerp House in all the glory of the snow and the foot thick ice on Bass Lake, there were memories of things that were impossible in the summer: ice skating on the mirror-like clear ice where the wind seemed to polish the frozen water into transparent glass; walking and skating across the lake just to add it to the list of ways Bass Lake had been crossed.

There were the times when we cut a hole in the ice and fished. Father built an ice hut using aluminum corrugated siding. He placed the hut on two two-by-eight boards used as runners so that it could be pushed beyond the drop-off. Once in place over a hole we could see the light coming up into the darkness of the hut; we lowered a wooden lure without hooks and sat looking down at the lure, an ice-fishing spear close at hand with a line attached to the top end. But it was cold inside and we envisioned hours of waiting. Like the skies at Silver Lake that were used only once, the ice hut followed the same trajectory. The only difference was that we could tolerate the skies in the open rafters of the main room at Silver Lake; the ice hut was an eyesore and we eventually tore it down and used the aluminum pieces to cover some firewood for a tiny fireplace that was added to one corner of the bedroom addition.

How different, then, were those fall and spring walks that I took at Silver Lake! It was as though I had my own private forest that I could explore without seeing or hearing civilization in any of its forms. The early leaves of the Shagbark Hickories and Burr Oak trees gave a whole new aspect to the forest. In one area, the path rose slightly above the swamp-like, lower land and I could see the Skunk Cabbage and Marsh Marigolds that were already pushing up through the snow. Instead of the miles of placid Lake Michigan waters on the horizon, viewed as I walked the Lake Michigan beaches to the north and south from the outlet, or viewed from atop the hills I climbed to pick blueberries in the summer, I had a prairie that stretched as far as the eye could see in one direction, and in another, about half a mile distant, were more woods, just like those to my left.

The density of the forest was not the same; I could see *into* the slope to my left, and up as high as the ridge line, a mere ten feet higher. This rise seemed more interesting than the forests of Michigan; the light penetrated down to the ground; there was more green. There were wildflowers everywhere and they caught my attention and left me looking for their return year after year.

My eyes were opened wider at Silver Lake; there were new wildflowers that I had never seen and wherever I walked they were present. The exposure to those new species led to a lifelong interest; they were a catalyst for further examination of Michigan's species which were always present but I needed the additional spark of beauty that I saw in the Spring. What, then, were these flowers that began this journey? Coming up through the snow of winter I saw Skunk Cabbage; it is easy to see how this led to a reverence for Jack-in-the-Pulpit flowers in Michigan. For the first time I saw May Apples. Sure, there were bracken ferns in Michigan but no May Apples.

Was it the white flower of the May Apple that led me to never again ignore the fragrance of the hundreds and hundreds of Lily-of-the-Valley plants that grew near Jerp House and elsewhere? But in the natural forest floor at Silver Lake below where we parked at the top of the hill I first glimpsed the glories of Bird-foot Violets! A mere twenty feet into the woods beyond the Silver Lake screened in porch I couldn't believe what I found: Shooting Stars. What can compare with locating your first clump of these beauties? They were everywhere in the forest at Silver Lake.

The Marsh Marigolds came close upon the heels of Skunk Cabbage. Did that yellow of the Marsh Marigolds cause me to worship so many yellow blooms in Michigan: Evening Primrose, Blue-Stemmed Goldenrod, Butter-and-Eggs, and Jewelweed? As a seven-year old my mother asked me to identify Orange Hawkweed; she also loved Butterfly Weed and Cardinal flowers. The Silver Lake flowers prompted me to find a Purple Fringed Orchid, hundreds of Cardinal flowers, the pink, orchid-like, Fringed Polygala, and Starflowers in the spring.

The combination of these two environments, Illinois and Michigan, intensified my searches for every species in Michigan, and that, in turn, would dominate my poetry; for when I chose the 365 poems – one for each day of the year – for *A Love Affair With Flowers Fair* – the choice of the title reflected this inner passion that would never leave me. We see this in the sonnet Bird-foot Violet:

Bird-foot Violet

There was a place where you did hold the pace
Near shaggy caps of burr oak on the ground.
The fragile beauty of your grace erased
All thought within till just your face was found.

Marsh marigold did lead the way but soon
Was just another boon. Mayapple shy
Once found brought no complexity for eye
Like your bouquet, the sunset in your bloom.

And when the bark of burr so rough and dark
Did hark how tough the world, your fairy ark
Did lift the heart from woodland stark to fly
Like frilly butterfly to God on high.

And there you keep through winters deep and cold
To bloom and rise again as sight grows old.

It can be paired with Purple Fringed Orchid, a sonnet from my Michigan discovery:

Purple Fringed Orchid

A beauty on the border of the swamp,
An exclamation point of frilly grace,
Fair creature from the past, supply our want
There's nothing in the world can take your place.

Transcendent through the centuries you came
To stand in isolation all your own.
Did local natives worship you by name,
Was it only through the spirit you were known?

Through consecrated alter of your hue,
In you the clustered galaxies unfold.
We humbled worshippers would pay our due.
Eternity will ne'er release your hold.

And so you stand beyond the bounds of time,
Beyond the comprehension of a rhyme.

Here was a wildflower that was placed under the date of August 28th, my wedding anniversary! But you, my blessed reader, may ask if there were any untoward experiences at Silver Lake? Was there an embarrassing weekend moment like a canoe tipping or, even, a threatening and scary experience? Was everything completely idyllic? A fair question to ask; let us begin. You recall my love affair with splitting wood? Down at the bottom of the hill in a very lovely area within the clumps of green bushes, there was a pile of oak logs, just the kind that are ready to split and give the splitter that solid satisfaction of making firewood that would burn with glowing colors!

I recall the day I approached this kind of mini-glen with extra alertness for I had heard the distinctive call of a Chinese Ring-necked Pheasant in the woods. The call was common from the game preserve but were they moving into the forest? The call disappeared as I approached my splitting area, and I began the effort. There is, of course, some randomness in the splitting of wood – a miss that frustrates by slicing off a mere sliver of oak, or a solid hit that embeds the axe head! This later event requires great effort to remove the axe head and then, after the steel wedge is inserted, it seems impossible to drive the wedge in no matter how hard your blow with the mallet.

Was that the untoward experience? You ask. Of course not, hang in there. In fact, one of the well-aimed swings of the axe caused a beautiful cleanly-split piece of oak to fly off into the bush. I immediately retrieved it so as to be able to enjoy the aesthetic beauty of a piece so accurately cleaved. It was then that I spied the destination of the Ring-Necked Pheasant making that *kork-kok* noise. She must have seen me coming for as I picked up my splitting masterpiece I saw the nest: sixteen brown eggs! Quite a brood! I backed out, nor was that the tragedy; hopefully she returned to the nest. The tragedy happened to the piece of split wood!

Fires in the crab orchard stone fireplace, as already mentioned, were a highlight – no pun intended – of Silver Lake weekends. Glowing coals of oak were not only beautiful to look upon and meditate as to their meaning, but the warmth coming out of the heatilator grew hotter and hotter. It was only human nature, then, that caused me to make a wood pile just outside the screened in porch door and up against the house. As soon as a few more pieces were needed I could step out – even in the snow – and quickly retrieve more pieces of firewood whose final destiny was to bring us warmth.

But there came a Fall day when my sister and her friend decided to sleep on the hide-a-bed in front of the fire; in Michigan this would have been the equivalent of hiking down the mostly uninhabited beaches to the north and south of the channel, building a driftwood fire and then, with the background lapping of waves – the heatilator in Illinois – trying to fall asleep before the fire was out, waking up and finding that the sand had somehow crept into your wooly – itchy – army surplus sleeping bag, and that the fire was merely a pile of ashes.

Imagine how different it was to fall asleep at Silver Lake; there was the warmth of an oak fire, and the ease of replenishing the fire with just two more pieces if that was even necessary. Picture the soft sofa with sheets, and blankets with *pillows*! Why, that must be like coffee mit schlag. What could be more idyllic? What could possibly disturb such a slumber?

Slowly but inexorably the coming disturbance grew to epidemic proportions within the heart of that woodpile outside the screened-in-porch door. Then, at the precise time that my sister and her friend fell asleep, the growing menace made itself known! An insect of some type dropped from the ceiling. It did not drop upon the wheel or spokes of the wagon-wheel chandelier that I made for the Silver Lake living room; I put a great deal of energy into sanding those weathered spokes so that they could be varnished to reveal their original state.

There was a loud scream and the lights in all eight globes of the wagon-wheel chandelier came on – I wired it so that the wires were hidden on the upper side of the wheel. What were they? I use the plural because more of the insects soon followed the first; they had feelers – long whiskers – they looked menacing; the problem was that there were a lot of them; it was an unanticipated attack prompted, perhaps, by the heat way up there at the peak of the roof. The family jumped into action.

I grabbed the step-ladder, put the long extension on the end of the Electrolux vacuum cleaner tube so I could reach the peak of the roof and began vacuuming without the need for an attachment. Another family member reasoned that they came from the woodpile with its neat stacks built against the side of the house, and began moving the pile away to a new location.

Father had the foresight to bottle up a couple of the insects; he knew it would be good to spray or dust the woodpile and that he needed the services of an expert to diagnose the species and prescribe an antidote. My sister, her friend, and the family survived; the Electrolux had bottled up – beaten off – the invaders; it had been a skirmish.

Within a week father announced who the invaders were: Pennsylvania Wood Roaches! Shortly thereafter a canister of powder arrived for the woodpile; a teaspoon of the powder in the Electrolux bag would do the trick in the mopping up operations that followed. But was there a Silver Lake experience like the tip-over of the canoe from Owasippie? you ask. If so, how could that be? We were half a mile from Silver Lake, had a small fishing boat and rarely went fishing.

In fact, truth be known, father gave a ten-twelve key to Art Fritsche, a friend *and* a fisherman, and he used the boat more than the family. Despite the low usage by the family, accidents have a way of happening. Thankfully I wasn't there; it was relayed to me by mail but I was very familiar with the circumstances. You will recall that a corner of the Silver Lake main room was devoted to the small bathroom and kitchen? Good. Well, above those two spaces was a flat, wood floor; it was open like a loft and used for storage. I can remember climbing up there and looking around; it was like what I expected to find in a real log cabin from the past similar to the ones in New Salem State Park. I could see through the picture windows, inspect the top of the old fashioned oil lamp – converted to use an electric bulb – that hung over the dinner table; it was warm up there.

There was, however, a single, permanent item in that space that existed among the transient items: an electric hot water heater. There was a fuel oil hot water heater in Chris Cot and a fuel oil hot water heater and furnace at Jerp House. Since there was an electric heater with a thermostat at the bottom of the pump pit below the kitchen trap door at Silver Lake, all that was necessary to winterize the house was to drain the kitchen, bathroom, and hot water heater pipes. It was fast work compared to Michigan. If Marie Christopherson visited her house across the road – she was unmarried – the pipe below the road was still usable for fresh water; Marie's access was independent from our house.

There is one important difference in the steps for winterization of an electric hot water heater as compared with a fuel oil hot water heater: the person performing the work must always turn off the electricity to the hot water heater before it is drained – usually by throwing the circuit breaker. If you don't take this precaution the heating element is exposed to the air in the tank which ruins it and you must buy a replacement. To recover from a ruined element you take the following steps: with the replacement in hand you open the side panel, move aside the insulation covering the electrical connections to the element, detach the wires to the element, unfasten the bolts holding the element, take the element and its gasket out, insert the new element, and then do all the steps in reverse. The electricity must be off before you begin the replacement.

I received news of the incident by mail for I was occupying one of those several homes that became my places of residence after High School. Father had forgotten to turn off the hot water heater electricity before winterization! He obtained a replacement element and set about to rectify his procedural blunder the following week. Are you ready for this, reader? No, he remembered to turn the electricity off before he climbed the ladder to the loft with the element, a screw driver, and a wrench. I ask you, what else could have happened?

That's right! I had a hard time picturing it from my home away from home. He would be sitting with his legs crossed in front of the outside panel and using the screwdriver to remove the outside plate that allowed access to the element; I pictured him pushing aside the insulation and removing the electrical wires. So far, so good. But then, how could he have started to remove the element and the gasket between it and the tank while the tank was still full? No, I can't imagine it either!

The only excuse/sequence I have ever been able to come up with was that: 1. He inadvertently kept the water heater on during winterization, the electricity was on and the water tank was drained to prevent the water freezing, 2. He came prepared to fix the element at a later time, and 3. He routinely turned on the water *throughout* the house but inadvertently didn't think about draining the tank! I, too, have a hard time with this, but you asked for a tip-over moment and there it is.

There were other events that brought High School groups to Silver Lake for a day; typical of these would be the Methodist Youth Fellowship where the house was used for a retreat, and an Explorer Scout group that earned money going door-to-door selling hard candy, life savers actually, but not the 'wet fanny club' type but the ones in packages containing six rolls of fruit flavored life savers, for the price of a quarter. The Explorer group didn't know what to do with their earnings except to finance an outing that involved swimming and a great meal.

We, however, must not dwell any longer on the Silver Lake experiences if only because a new sequence of homes began to appear in 1956 and these residences were truly not at all like the homes we have already discussed. Before we begin to look at that very heterogeneous group of residences, we will add a footnote relative to the three homes – 7240 W. Pratt Avenue, Jerp House, and Silver Lake – that we have already examined.

Once Silver Lake was fully operational you can imagine the successive segues that were then imposed upon mother. All summer long she managed four children at Jerp House, but that was just the tip of the iceberg. There were also those children from Chicago and from Bass Lake itself – for example young men who were interested in knowing my sister and listening to her records. Besides my own and my sisters friends from Chicago, there were week-long visits – perhaps I should say visitations – of my two female cousins from Itasca, Illinois.

Shortly after my two Itasca cousins appeared on the scene a greater quantity of young males dropped by at Jerp House. Their intentions exceed a simple courtesy call for my cousins caused their admirers to occupy adjacent beach towels when at the Lake Michigan beach and their presence (the admirers) extended further into the evening hours so as to include, in the summer time, hours of total darkness; Jerp House became a place to hang out.

Mother was also secretary of the Bass Lake Property Owners Association at a time when, strange as it seems, she made house calls to collect dues for the association. Then there were Association family picnics at the beach which she coordinated as well as the usual household tasks: cooking, cleaning, shopping, laundry, washing dishes, and so on and so forth.

At the end of the summer there occurred the eight hour drive from Jerp House to 7240 W. Pratt Avenue; she arrived to find a home that was occupied all summer long by a bachelor: dirty dishes in the sink, not much in the refrigerator, and stacks of unopened junk mail piled in the living room chairs: newspapers in one chair, mail-order catalogs in another, miscellaneous mail in a third, and important letters in a forth; elsewhere there was unsorted laundry.

Despite the herculean efforts that were immediately needed to put a dinner on the table, she knew that on the very next weekend, after the first week of school, there would be the need to pack up what was necessary to start the Silver Lake fall/winter/spring season. The phrase my mother often used with her friends to articulate her situation was that her life involved going from: "Sink, to sink, to sink!"

So now we must leave the sink to sink environment for new horizons and there is no better time to begin than with the summer of 1956 and with the first home away from home of that summer:

Owasippe Scout Camp Reservation
Camp Director's Tent
Owasippie Lake
Near
Whitehall, Michigan
Camp Robert E. Stuart
Erected 1956

The best description of this home away from home comes from *Western Michigan Tales of Mystery and Adventure* in a story called 'Across the Lake.' Although the description from the story implies that all camp staff members occupied a staff tent as described – a staff tent with a porch – that was not the case. The description applies only to the quarters of the Camp Director; such were the lodgings of Peter Orlebeck at Camp Dan Beard – directly across Owasippie Lake from Camp Stuart – during those many summers he served as Camp Beard's director:

* * *

About a third of the way down those log stairs, an opening in one of the railings allowed a walker to exit to an ordered row of large and spacious staff tents. These tents, so unlike the more simple ones elsewhere, possessed wooden plank floors and wooden walls that rose three feet above the floor; there were screens above those wall planks that circled around all sides of the tented space, except for the front where, in the middle, there was an opening out to a porch by way of a screen door that gave entrance to the inside. In effect, it was a tent house, because a tent was placed over the upper wooden and screened structure, and, during most days, the canvas sides of the tent were rolled up exposing the screens.

The porch itself was also a luxury. It was covered above with a separate piece of canvas, falling away on either side from a common ridge member at the top, but the sides were open as no canvas existed that could be rolled down to prevent rain from being blown into the porch. The roll-down canvas on the sides of the tent house were always kept up, thereby allowing a three hundred and sixty degree access to any breezes from any direction to pass through the screens and cool the sleeper on his cot. The porch had furniture, typically a rustic table and chairs, where, from on high, a staff person could sit outside with a colleague and discuss the events of the day, observe through the trees the waterfront activities at the beach far below, or just pass any free time he had by reading or enjoying the bird life.

There was very little of written history to assist a thoughtful child with the answers to his questions, only conjectures of his own making. It would be nice to rise in the world and occupy a staff tent; the amenities of such a tent were obvious when compared to an unscreened and wooden-floored tent with two iron double-decker bunk beds.

* * *

It is necessary to back track a bit to understand why a recent graduate of a Chicago Public School would, within a mere week or so after graduation, come to occupy the Camp Director's lodgings at one of the three large scout camps on Owasippie Lake. The Director's tent was located in the premier position at the end of a row of staff tents at Camp Stuart. From the front porch the occupant, from a lovely, wooded hill above the shoreline, viewed the waterfront with its sandy beach, piers, diving board, raft, floating lines of brightly colored buoys, canoes, and rowboats, as well as a beach staff tent for the Aquatic Director and his assistant. One could also see the entire expanse of the lake; across the lake were camps Beard and West, and a very short distance to the right, just after the Camp Stuart Church seats – logs in the side of the hill – were several private cottages.

But one shoreline element was left out in this view from the Director's tent and it was that missing element that allowed the Head Ranger, myself, and my senior assistant, Bob Nakamura, to occupy this prestigious piece of real estate. That element was the fourth camp, the Owasippie Lake Family camp, adjacent to Camp Stuart but serving the families of married camp staff and scout leader's families with the full set of family oriented facilities: meals, singing, campfires, story-telling, waterfront instructors for children, crafts, and all the other programmatic amenities of a family camp.

Conveniently located down a wooded path from Camp Stuart, the Owasippe Lake Family camp required but a few minutes of walking for the Camp Stuart Director and his assistant to join their families after dinner. We have already observed the opening campfire and the presentation of *The Cremation of Sam McGee* by the ranger staff. The campfire location therein described was no less attractive than the entire camp. The ranger staff worked out of two buildings; the first was a log version of a fort – two stories with the square, larger story, set upon a smaller square, ground story. Nearby was a crafts lodge and a nature pond which was also the responsibility of the ranger staff.

It is time to examine the contents of the Directors tent with its porch; if we do, we may come to understand some of the duties of a Head Ranger. There were two hats that I wore that summer – the Head Ranger's hat – as Navy jargon would have it – and a volunteer hat that I wore by virtue of being appointed the Summer Chief of the Owasippie Lodge of the Order of the Arrow. I served as the Vice Chief of the Lodge during the prior ten months and the Chief of the Lodge was not a staff member at the Owasippie camp system so he appointed me to the position.

There were two bunk beds as well as a desk and chair inside the tent proper; I appropriated them for my use. Below my bunk and located in an oblong, locked, wooden box were rifles that were used during very specific hours at a skeet shooting site. This activity was entirely under my control even though it was a new activity introduced that year into the Owasippie system. Troops would sign up for a skeet shooting session and, using a mechanical skeet launcher, a skeet would be shot into the air. The rifle, loaded with a 22 caliber shell which contained tiny balls – al la a shotgun – was fired in such a way that the balls intercepted a fragile, ceramic skeet, and disintegrated it in a puff. The sessions were scheduled in the daylight hours.

My desk drawer contained the notes I developed for the second activity that I appropriated for myself. This activity was conducted when it was pitch dark and required a small hike to a special location; a moonless night was preferred although some troops had to put up with a moon or a portion of the moon. The activity was called a Star Hike which amounted to a hike to an open space where the entire panoply of the heavens could be observed. My notes were organized by constellations and specific stars within them and I spoke about the legends of various cultures with respect to the constellations and stars.

There was one other object that appeared to be very much out of place beneath my cot where it lay near the skeet shooting box. It looked like a record keeping book with pages of handwritten names and dates on each page going back many years. It was heavy and the back and front covers were substantial with shiny metal borders running around the edges. This object was normally kept under lock and key at Scout Headquarters in the Chicago Loop but years of following written procedures caused it to be in possession of the Owasippie Scout Camp Summer Chief of the Owasippie Lodge Order of the Arrow. It contained the names and dates of initiations into the Order of the Arrow arranged by the three honors, Ordeal, Brotherhood, and Vigil.

It is well to ask if there were *any* duties that I performed in my capacity as Summer Chief. A case could be made that, at this particular time in Owasippie Order of the Arrow history, the position was a sinecure with neither income nor work. This was because with the arrival of twenty-six district chapters of the Chicago lodge, the Owasippie ceremonies as previously outlined in *The Coming of The Chief* were no longer being performed in Michigan. Instead, each chapter had their own, chapter ritual team and those teams performed induction ceremonies at their Fall and Spring fellowships near Chicago. What, then, were the duties, if any, left for the Summer Chief? I never wrote entries into the ledger book below my cot because that clerical effort was performed downtown; this included entries for the third honor, the Vigil honor, simply because those nominations were approved at the national level.

The answer to the question, though, from the standpoint of the work I actually *did* perform, was my work taking a major role in the ceremony for the second degree of the order, the Brotherhood level, and which I had memorized earlier. A group of us performed the Brotherhood induction ceremony for Ordeal members from all the camps who, after eighteen months of membership, nominated themselves for initiation into that level.

What went on during that ceremony – acts that quite exceeded what was in the official ceremony – is captured in the book *Black Friends* where I relate my experience of performing the Brotherhood ceremony with my friend, Norville Carter:

* * *

As mentioned, starting with my lodge meetings as a junior in high school, I developed a friendship with another member of the executive committee, Norville Carter. Norville had a sense of humor – and a smile to go with it – that were the epitome of what it meant to be a member of a 'brotherhood of cheerful service.' This went beyond the scout law of being cheerful: a scout smiles whenever he can, his obedience to orders is prompt and cheery. We hit it off; he probably served on my lodge banquet committee but the funniest time we had together occurred the next summer.

I was appointed summer chief for the Owasippe scout camps in Michigan and I was employed the entire summer as head ranger at camp Stuart on Owasippe Lake. Norville was working at camp Blackhawk – miles away on Big Blue Lake – and we didn't see too much of each other until we decided to put on a brotherhood ceremony. There was a group of first level members of the order who had been members for eighteen months after their initial ceremony. They felt they deserved the second level of membership; the decision was made in the depths of their own conscience and there were no others who could veto their decision. This was unlike the first level of membership and the third level where the individual member had no control over his becoming a member to begin with and other members were completely in charge of nominating second level members the third level of membership.

During the third two-week period in the summer there were enough brotherhood candidates to hold a ceremony. My chapter provided the costumes and we decided to hold the ceremony indoors in the huge dining hall of camp Beard on Owasippe Lake. Norville came down from camp Blackhawk and we rehearsed with the other members of the ritual team. Norville took the part of Allowat Sakima, Mighty Chief (pronounced Al'-lo-wot Sa-kee'-ma.) I spoke the role of Meteu, the Medicine Man. Together, we had the two leading roles.

While rehearsing, Norville explained that there was one member who would be receiving the brotherhood degree from his chapter and who Norville felt had not done enough during his first eighteen months. Norville intended to add some additional features to the ceremony – for this fellow only – that were not in the officially certified ceremony; he had prepared some surprises. I had no idea what he was up to.

One of the several acts I carried out with Norville's help during the ritual was the mingling of blood. The instructions for this were: Meteu with a sterile needle makes a prick in the thumb of Allowat Sakima and then of the first candidate in the line. They allow the blood to flow together and then the first candidate mixes his with that of the second candidate, and with the third, and so on 'til all have had their thumbs pricked.

I carved a small wooden arrow, painted it red, and put a tiny needle at its point; I used a pad soaked with an antiseptic to clean the tiny point – probably only 1/32nd of an inch long. As Norville and I made our way down the line and as I pricked thumbs, we came nearer and nearer to Norville's 'unworthy' candidate. There was, already, some anxiety about having your thumb pricked with a needle. Because it was indoors – there might have been rain in the forecast – we used candles in the Beard dining hall for light. As we approached the candidate with Norville ahead of me, I sensed that the candidate recognized that Norville was up to something. As we came up to the unworthy scout, Norville withdrew a sheath knife that caught the candlelight. Norville stopped so that I could not proceed, faced the member and stared at him with a stare that could only be interpreted that he was going to bypass the thumb prick.

I was astonished! If I had let myself go, it would have been like laughing in church – this *was* a solemn ceremony. Finally, Norville relented but others had observed his ploy.

Another part of the ceremony was passing your hand through the fire of cheerfulness. Because we were indoors, we lit a group of three candles and put them on a mess stool bench to the left of the main table for the ceremony which had candles representing the three main points of the scout oath and twelve points of the scout law. To begin the sequence, I spoke lines of what was to be done and Norville stood behind the mess stool and demonstrated by passing his hand through the flames, palm side down.

Again, each candidate followed suit. This time, when Norville's unqualified candidate passed his hand through the candle flames, he looked up at Norville with a kind of meek, anticipatory look. And for good reason! Norville, again, acting beyond the written instructions, grabbed the member's wrist, and slowly moved his hand through the flames once again only this time, the duration was much longer than before, in fact it was much longer than any of the prior members and, I felt, it was too long, but I was again prevented from distracting the ceremony.

The final act involved taking a heavy weight or burden from the shoulder of one brother and, walking a short distance, moving it to the shoulder of another. This continued until all new candidates had shouldered the burden. The task, as I explained later in my memorized lines was to be a metaphor for the candidate's resolve to 'willingly and cheerfully bear the loads of their brothers all through their life.' True to form, when it came to the unqualified candidate, Norville caused this particular member to perform the bearing of the burden an additional time as if he didn't get the point the first time!

I never lost the memory of how Norville laughed after the ceremony was finished but it also became a good story to tell to other members about Norville and what he did to correct things. Those that knew him recognized his character but for myself, it was an adventure with a friend, an adventure in the spirit of brotherhood.

* * *

We have already resorted to the use of a fictional narrative to explicate the real life experiences that describe the environment of a home.

Before we leave the1956 summer home of the Camp Director's tent at Camp Stuart, we shall excerpt two fictional passages from *Western Michigan Tales of Mystery and Adventure* taken from a story called 'Across The Lake.' These two excerpts involve a fictional character other than John Sherman; his name is Scott Spenser and he is an Aquatic Director not a Head Ranger; his assistant is Bob and the story is a love story.

Regardless of those aspects of the plot, the excerpted sections illustrate several activities that I experienced at Camp Stuart during the nine weeks of my employment; these include: coaching the war canoe team, leading songs after dinner, a description of the waterfront, teaching a pioneering merit badge class involving lashings, knots, and the building of a tower, as well as a brief description of a star hike:

* * *

The Invitation

The first period campers arrived and Scott and Bob were busy setting up buddy tags for every person in camp. Each new arrival was, in the absence of written documentation, given a swim test whereby they demonstrated their level of proficiency in the water. On the strength of the swim test or written evidence, each person was given a circular buddy tag which had his name printed on it and a number from one to eight. The criteria for the numbers were based on skills in the water according to the following scheme:

1 – Beginner, Non-swimmer
2 – 50-Yard Swimmer
3 – 100-Yard Swimmer, 50 yards on back
4 – Swimming Merit Badge
5 – Scout Life-Guard/Life-Saving Merit Badge
6 – Junior Red Cross Life-Saver
7 – Senior Red Cross Life-Saver
8 – Red Cross Water Safety Instructor

After dinner every evening there was a period of rowing and canoeing on the lake according to a set of rules: To take out a rowboat, two people totaling at least four points were needed so that a beginner, for example, could go out with a person who could swim 100 yards. A canoe required eight points – two paddlers who both had swimming merit badges or any other combinations such as 1 + 7, 2 + 6, or 3 + 5.

In two days, it was Scott's turn to lead the mess hall in singing after dinner. He chose for one of his songs a game song called *John Jacob Jingleheimer Schmidt*. It, too, had rules. A person was chosen and sent out of the mess hall while everyone decided on a strategy. While gone, an object was chosen like a particular item hanging on the wall, a cabinet, or even a person sitting at a mess hall table.

The person sent out was then asked back in and the singing was begun. To succeed in the game, the person sent out was now required to guess the object. When he walked closer to the chosen object, the song became louder and louder and, as he walked farther and farther away, softer and softer, until the intensity was that of a whisper.

John Jacob Jingleheimer Schmidt,
That's my name too,
Whenever I go out, the people always shout:
JOHN JACOB JINGLEHEIMER SCHMIDT!
TRA–LA–LA–LA–LA–LA–LA.…..(REPEAT)

On the second time around, with a new person sent out, Scott chose Bob as the object to be discovered. Initially, Bob was casually standing and leaning against a wall. The song began and the intensity grew as the new person walked toward Bob, but then the person turned away from Bob and Bob quickly shifted to the other side of the mess hall. The person sent out didn't see Bob move but everyone was singing in a whisper now, so he turned back toward where the singing had been louder – to where Bob used to be standing – but to no avail! Finally he caught on to what was happening.

After this they were ready for a new song, *Down by the Old Mill Stream*. It required learning words and gestures.

Down by the Old Mill Stream

(Sign Language to music using hands to make motions while singing.)

Down (point downward) by (motion good-bye)
The old (as though stroking beard) mill
Stream (a zigzag motion).
Where I (point to eye) first (finger raised)
Met (handclasp) you (point),
With your (point) eyes (point to eyes) of
Blue (point to sky) dressed (touch clothing)
In gingham (point) too (two fingers);
It was there (point) I (point to eye) knew
(point to head) that you (point) loved
(hand to heart) me (point to yourself) true;
You were sixteen (on hands), my (point) village
Queen (make crown movement overhead);
Down by the old mill stream (same as first line).

For his dismissal song, Scott chose the *Tramping* song. Each table with ten persons seated, sit at attention with arms crossed on their chests. As they sing, Scott and Bob give the nod to a table that is singing well and they are dismissed with that nod.

Tramping

Tramping over the mountains,
On hard tack and pork and beans,
While the plutocrats in their Cadillacs
Proceed on gasoline,
Tramp, tramp, tramp, tramp,
Tramp, tramp, tramp, tramp. (return to first line)

There was an advantage in being dismissed early; the waiters and dishwashers could get a jump start on clean-up, inspection of washed and dried dishes, and sweeping up around the tables. The last few table teams had to stay late and sweep the mess hall floors not immediately around the ten-person mess hall tables.

Scott and Bob now made their way to the waterfront. Bob began processing the line that formed for rowboats and canoes and Scott mustered the war canoe team.

"We'll be going around the lake this time out. I'll be varying the stroke count and all we want to do is build up those paddling muscles."

The team members nodded. Then Scott explained once more how to feather the paddle when bringing it forward, against the wind, so as to cut down on wind resistance before dipping it into the water for the next stroke.

The team members took their places by kneeling on the bottom of the canoe, alternately from front to back, and Scott took his place in back sitting on the wooden tail piece with a very long steering paddle. He began by calling a slow stroke and gradually turned the canoe in a wide arc so as to get it parallel with the shore and about two hundred feet out from the land.

Slowly, he began increasing the stroke, and he could feel the breeze of the forward motion get stronger and stronger in his face. The crew was enjoying its efforts and Scott was calling time with the words: *stroh...oh, stroh...oh, stroh...oh.* On and on they went, and as Scott wanted a stronger breeze, he increased the pace – it was like turning up an electric fan with a variable speed control knob.

They crossed over to the other side of Big Blue and ahead lay Camp Emory. They, too, were putting out rowboats and canoes. Scott wanted to pass by at a slower speed so he reduced his pace. By now the *stroh...oh* calls were second nature and Scott began thinking again of the lines in the song: "With your eyes of blue," "It was there I knew that you loved me true," "You were sixteen, my village queen."

Then, all of a sudden, he saw her. He reduced the pace to an even slower count and edged the canoe closer inshore. The team was all concentrating on feathering the paddles and staying in sync with the count.

"I'm going to let you paddle together without my counting, so just hold this rhythm and concentrate on keeping together." To give his commands Scott used a small, tapered megaphone.

He reasoned that she must be a young staff member from Camp Emory because she was sitting on the raft by herself watching the canoes and rowboats, her own canoe having been tied by a painter to the raft itself.

"Hello there," yelled Scott.

"Now that's the way to travel," she replied. Her voice was soft and feminine, and she wore a fantastic smile that made him want to spend more time with her on that raft, or better yet, in a canoe. "I bet she is sixteen," thought Scott.

There wasn't much time to think, the war canoe would soon be past the raft. "I'm from Camp Seaton, across the lake. We have our free weekend on Saturday the fifteenth. My name's Scott, I'm the aquatic director."

"Glad to meet you, Scott. I'm Alice and I'm the assistant waterfront director. We're having a party that night; I'll have the director invite you and your staff; you can canoe across."

"Thanks Alice, there's just Bob and myself. Thank you again, goodbye."

Scott caught her smile again as he turned back and then took up the *stroh...oh, stroh...oh,* rhythm once more. Bob would be delighted, he thought to himself as he increased the speed once more and began the wide arc that would head them back to Camp Seaton.

* * *

The campers for the second period arrived Sunday and John, Seaton's camp director, decided to start implementing his new job rotation plan for the staff during the second period. After the new campers were all classified with the buddy tag system and given their tags, the rotation plan called for changes to be made on Tuesday. Bob was to take Scott's position as aquatic director, Scott was to move to the head ranger's job, and the head ranger was to take Bob's position on the waterfront.

For Scott, this would only involve Tuesday and Wednesday, and he was going to be performing activities that he enjoyed; on both days he would start teaching lashings and splicing to the pioneering class, and on Tuesday night he would take out one campsite on a star hike before the full moon came up on Wednesday.

During the first Tuesday of the first period, a headquarters truck took the pioneering class on a trip to visit a huge growth of aspen trees to obtain logs for the pioneering project that would be used four times during the summer – a four pole watchtower constructed with rope lashings and built on an open hill behind the camp. After the bark was peeled, the tower was built, photographed, and taken down before that period's campers returned to Chicago. All of the ropes for the lashings were kept and the logs piled together at the top of the hill.

Scott planned to teach splicing on Tuesday and then move the class to the hill for practice in various lashings before the actual tower and its platform on top were reconstructed. It was also a good time to ask if everyone remembered how to tie timber hitches and clove hitches from earlier instruction as these would be used for the lashings. He also pointed out that a project of this size, or any pioneering project, for that matter, required teamwork, and that should always be kept in mind.

The splicing class quickly made it clear to Scott that this was a sharp group that caught on immediately; it was obvious they had already read about splicing. They were quickly able to make the required splices and their work, now as souvenirs, were ready to take back to Chicago. As a reward, Scott taught them all how to tie a Turk's head, a trick that once learned was never forgotten; it was also an impressive knot to tie for younger children and to give away as a gift.

For the lashing class on Wednesday, he decided to lash together the tower platform frame on the ground, stabilize it with some logs that would involve diagonal lashings, and finish the top using square lashings. This would give everyone lots of practice and a great deal would have to be repeated after the structure of the tower below the platform was raised later in the week.

Scott was also glad to have the opportunity to review his notes for leading a star hike. Much of this amounted to a review of the northern constellations with tips on how to jump from one to another and brief stories about each. Just as important were all the other points he wanted to cover: Sagittarius – the teapot – the teaspoon, the four major star cloud groups in the Milky Way, the summer triangle and its constellations, Scorpius, Albireo, the famous Blue-Orange double star, where to look for the M31 Andromeda galaxy, and a few other things.

* * *

As with any of the homes we are looking at, it becomes necessary to make a segue to the next residence. Certain of these home to home transitions provide contrasts that are abrupt; such a one occurred during the summer of 1956. Within a very short space of time I experienced a sequence of location movements that involved such disparate locations as: Camp Stuart Head Ranger, an all-night vigil spent alone in a forest in Michigan, the acquisition of fatigue, termination of my Head Ranger job, return to Jerp House for a brief convalescence, a flight in my father's Fairchild from Ludington, Michigan, to Chicago, some few days at 7240 W. Pratt Avenue, an overnight train trip – with a single-bed Roomette – to Princeton, New Jersey, and an introduction to my next home – for two years – which involved purchasing furniture, discovering how to obtain food, hauling stuff up three flights of stairs, and a whole lot more.

I had never visited Princeton University, let alone New Jersey, nor had I applied to, let alone visited, any other institution of higher learning. By virtue of my father's Boy Scout activities – and extensive Cub Scout activities across seventeen years – he became aware of a Robert D. Stuart, Jr. Eagle Scout scholarship to Princeton in the amount of $250 per year for those Eagle Scouts who lived in the City of Chicago. Camp Stuart on Owasippie lake was named after this gentleman who graduated from Princeton in 1937. I suspect that father was more interested in that part of his resume for the years 1984 through 1989 when he was Ambassador to Norway; what other role model could be more vivid than Robert Stuart's presumed desire to 'be a Norwegian all his life'?, surely it was the next best thing to having been born there.

In the course of researching that scholarship – which was never awarded to a Chicago Eagle Scout (It was always given to a New Trier High School eagle or an Evanston High School eagle – or suchlike suburban eagle.) – he became aware of a Regular NROTC Scholarship awarded by the U. S. Navy. This was a much more lucrative scholarship offering full tuition, uniforms, books, $50/month, summer cruises for three years, and a commission as an Ensign, USN, second lieutenant in Army terms. The USN designation was not USNR, instead USN was the same designation received by Naval Academy graduates, hence the use of the term Regular. In return, the Navy asked for three years of service; I received a letter in April of 1956 from the Chairman of the Princeton Club of Chicago's Schools Committee announcing that I was accepted under the Navy ROTC program and was one of a group of thirty-nine Regular NROTC students in the incoming freshman class.

We have already alluded to the many contractors – such as Enger Brothers – and clients – (for example Leon Sausage not previously alluded to) – where I was invariably asked the question if I was going to be a third-generation Ronneberg engineer. Of course, I had no answer; my only thoughts were Erling Berg's admonition: "Don't be a Norwegian all your life!" Despite what Erling said I followed my father's suggestion that I matriculate in the Civil Engineering Department.

We referred to my Norwegian Grandfather's education in Appendix B which included studies in England, Norway, and Germany. Left unsaid was my father's graduation from the University of Illinois in 1929 with a five-year degree in Architectural/Engineering. Parenthetically, we should point out that my mother graduated from the University of Illinois in the same year, 1929, with a degree in Law. These ancestral educative digressions are merely to point out that in order to follow my father's educational curricula, I would have needed to obtain a three-year Master's Degree in Architecture.

Faced with the careers of these illustrious ancestors, it was no wonder, then, that I embarked on the Civil Engineering curriculum – leading to a BSE, Bachelor of Science in Engineering – and I coupled that with eight NROTC classes – leading to my commission as an Ensign, USN. The seriousness with which I pursued my father's joint Architectural/engineering path can only be seen when one examines a transcript for those four years and discovers that I received grades in four Architectural courses: Architectural Drawing, Architectural History – Mediaeval Architecture, Architectural History – Renaissance Architecture, Architectural History – Modern Architecture. The latter three have already been alluded to when discussing memorization that went on in the lower level of Princeton's McCormick Hall in preparation for midterm and final exams; the building was shared by the Departments of Art and Archeology.

The decision to attempt to follow in the footsteps of father and grandfather without having the slightest idea of what my likes and dislikes were or, put another way, what would interest me, given my personality and who I actually was, I say this unpreparedness was to plague me for the next nine years – it was as though I was pointed in a direction – call it my personal momentum – by a directive force that, when articulated, ran: "Go there, young man!" and I never altered course until many years later. I mention this because we are now able to discern the approach of my next home:

High Victorian Gothic
William A. Potter and Robert H. Robertson
441 Witherspoon Hall
Princeton University
Princeton, New Jersey
Commissioned 1875
Occupied 1877

And it is quite possible that, since my upbringing was sympathetic to late 19th century values, from the standpoint of the physical characteristics of Witherspoon Hall, I had, by some unknown set of circumstances, been vectored into a dwelling that resonated with my upbringing. We shall have more to say on that subject.

For now, let us merely remark that with respect to the personalities of my Grandfather and Father, there are some clues that would suggest that I was a completely different person. Setting aside the fact that I graduated from a Chicago Public High School with high grades after taking five, six, and even seven major subjects at the same time, there were only two classes where – without citing any excuses – I did not achieve a superior grade. The first class was an English class taught by a brilliant teacher, and the second, a series of Latin classes taught by a teacher with a PhD from Yale. The Latin teacher was an excellent shot when it came to throwing erasers at students but for two years I did not achieve an S, superior, grade but languished with E grades, excellent.

From these classes we can surmise that I did not have the knack for languages that Natal Ronneberg had – Norwegian, English, German, and French. We should add, parenthetically, that my maternal grandfather was fluent in English, German, French, Italian, and Spanish. By fluent I mean that he could speak in the dialects of different regions in those countries as well as write poetry in many tongues and, in 1938, submit a French thesis to the University of Chicago.

Father was much more of a social animal than I; everyone enjoyed his company; they sought him out, publically praised his personality, and spoke highly of his professional abilities. My mother was much more responsible for encouraging my interests in intellectual pursuits – rather than earning merit badges, my father's forte – and in establishing values to live by. In summary, then, I think it safe to point out that my total unpreparedness for my home in Witherspoon Hall mirrored, was a metaphor for the entire four-year Princeton experience; we shall examine a detailed critique of that assertion at a later time. For now, we need to back-track to the last week of August 1956 before we return to New Jersey and the first week of September 1956.

There is no denying that the all-night Vigil ceremony and the loss of sleep caused me to struggle during my last two weeks of employment as Head Ranger at Camp Stuart; I felt worn out and tired but plodded on trying to service the excellent scout leaders of the troops who showed up for the final, two-week, fourth period of the summer season. My sponsor during the period of those ceremonies was my father's friend, Peter Orlebeck, who was a Vigil member. I can remember one instance where, due to demands on my staff, I was obliged to take on some strenuous work immediately after my return from the night in the forest and the start of the fourth period.

After weathering that period I drove north to Bass Lake and quickly took to an upstairs bed for recuperation. There was a Princeton imposed early deadline that drove my parent's attempts to bring back my health as quickly as possible. Unlike the Liberal Arts students in the Freshman Class of 1960, the Engineering students – from all the Engineering disciplines – were required to report three weeks earlier than their Liberal Arts classmates – essentially, the first week of September – for a three-week period of classes that were, collectively, a period of intellectual intensity.

Three classes were crammed into that six-day-a-week, three-week period along with a series of lectures that were, for the most part, delivered by the Department Heads of the Engineering disciplines – Civil, Mechanical, Aeronautical, Electrical, Chemical, and Basic. That made six additional lectures. The first graded course was *Elementary Surveying*; there were lectures every morning, homework problems every evening based on the lectures and reading assignments in the Elementary Surveying textbook, a three hour graded field lab exercise every afternoon – which called for dexterity with a surveyor's transit and other equipment – a mid-term exam, and a final exam.

The second class was entitled *The History of American Technology*. It was introduced by the head of the Mechanical Engineering Department. He began by outlining several books that he read on the subject, held them up to show the class, and mentioned their strong and weak points; there were no questions from the class. He then held up the text he chose for the class: it was seven hundred and fifty pages long! I don't recall any pictures or diagrams. The chosen text wasn't perfect but it came out on top; the bookstore had an adequate number of copies for the entire class; there were no questions from the class.

He finished his remarks by announcing that if there were no further questions as far as the History of Technology class was concerned, he had only two additional points. First, there would be no lectures; more than two hundred students breathed a collective sigh of relief. He went on to remark that the next time the class would meet – when he would see us again – would be in this classroom – a Physics classroom with seats rising up like a football stadium – for the final exam. The exam would be a series of essays that we would write in response to the test questions. He assured us that if we read the entire text we would have no problems. He asked for questions; there were no questions from the class. What he didn't mention was the appeal of the topic; after all of the work we had to do after dinner for the other two classes, we picked up the tome and became enthralled with topics such as how Cyrus McCormick came to invent a mechanical reaper that revolutionized farming!

The final, third class, was how to use the Keuffel & Esser Log Log Duplex Decitrig slide rule that every student purchased, as per earlier, mailed instructions. This class *did* have lectures and in-class exercises every day and was taught, in sections, by a jovial Civil Engineering professor, Professor Bigelow, who was also a Carillion expert – he knew a great deal about bells and could, no doubt, play the instrument as well. There were also in-class exams principally oriented on how to solve problems with the Keuffel & Esser Log Log Duplex Decitrig slide rule in the most efficient fashion.

One day during the three-week slide rule class professor Bigelow related his involvement with the new, Franklin fifty cent piece; you will remember that it had a Liberty Bell on the obverse side of the coin. Early in 1948 there was an inauguration ceremony sponsored by the U. S. Mint and professor Bigelow was invited to speak; he was a consultant for the coin. The Vice President of the United States, Harry S. Truman, was also a speaker. Professor Bigelow announced that he received more applause than the Vice President!

Although not intimately familiar with the rigor of this set of three-week classes, taught during a very hot September of 1956, my parents expended every effort to nurse me back from what seemed like a malaise. I was flown back to Chicago rather than driven; I was given a one-way ticket to Trenton, New Jersey, that included a single-person roomette as my parents wanted me to try and sleep reasoning that it was the all-night Vigil that had precipitated my lethargy.

I have never been able to sleep on trains; the trip from Chicago to Trenton was no exception despite the roomette. I must have made some kind of recovery – perhaps it was the pills – for I was able to catch a local train from Trenton to Princeton Junction as well as transfer to the PJAB – Princeton Junction And Back – trolley, more commonly referred to as the 'dinky.' The station was a quarter of a mile from Witherspoon Hall and I remember asking for directions.

Fortunately, in anticipation of over two-hundred Freshmen Engineers, a member of the Orange Key Society – a group that, among other activities, gave campus tours – was available to answer questions; they were kind to strangers. I can't say exactly whether or not the Orange Key Society helper commented that when Witherspoon was first occupied in 1877 it was the most expensive and sought-after dormitory on campus. If he did, I am certain that he did not go on to mention that it quickly became one of the least desirable places to room.

In any event, he didn't need to add any further remarks; as soon as I began climbing up the three flights of wooden stairs – they were, I am sure, the original, well-worn stairs – I became aware of Witherspoon's age. I have no idea how I obtained a key to the room; my roommate, a Liberal Arts student from New York City, would arrive three weeks later. Fortunately I became aware that there would be no furniture whatsoever, nor any curtains for the windows. Upon entry I saw that the room was, truly barren.

But the Orange Key member at the 'Dinky' station took mercy on me – it was a very hot day – and offered the suggestion that I visit the large tent erected by the Student Furniture Exchange student organization; they were known to stay open past dinner time. Under the 'big top' I would find objects to purchase like a bed! Unless I preferred the floor?

With a little further effort I might encounter a member of the Student Linen Exchange and have something to place on the mattress the very same evening that the Student Furniture Exchange delivered. Oh, yes, the Student Linen Exchange would also deliver towels. Returning to the outside of Witherspoon Hall, I asked a student that was relaxing for directions to the furniture tent and once inside the tent quickly purchased a desk, chair, dresser, and a bed making a mental note to send my mother the window dimensions so that she could sew a set of curtains.

It should be obvious by now that there were no such things as 'dorm parents,' 'resident assistants,' or any other kind of on-site help. Such things did not exist, they were unheard of, nor, it seemed did anyone ever imagine the need since times immemorial. My communications back home would through use of a Webster Electric tape recorder; I never became aware of a telephone being available anywhere for the next four years. It is important to explain why such a modern instrument as a tape recorder – it weighed fifteen pounds – should be brought to a dorm room first occupied in 1877; it had to do with my father's popularity with his clients.

N. Ronneberg & Company designed a factory for Webster Electric and on many occasions father was called back to the President's office for additions, alterations, and such like requests; for our explanation, it makes no difference. After each of those calls the President encouraged father to go to the end of the production line and take home a tape recorder, courtesy of Webster Electric. Accordingly, by the time I departed for New Jersey, he had accumulated five!

I'll return to Webster Electric in a moment; I think it important to mention that this kind of thing happened elsewhere. The most famous incident occurred with Schwinn Bicycle Company where N. Ronneberg & Company also built a factory; this led to numerous conversations with, as father called him, 'Old Man Schwinn.' I suspected that they formed a two-person mutual admiration society. Anyhow, one day Old Man Schwinn became aware of the birth of father's first grandson, my sister's first child. The discussion of this wonderful event was delayed until my nephew was old enough to require a two-wheeler bicycle.

Old Man Schwinn insisted that father go to the end of the production line and take the right size bike for his grandson, courtesy of the Schwinn Bicycle Company. There was one caveat however; a bike from the end of the production line would not have an official serial number applied to the bike on a metal band. Old Man Schwinn promised all his dealers that he would never let such a bike out of his factory. Father had to promise that he would never bring the bike into a dealer's shop. The bike survived without any dealer help for many years for the rule was that it was to be passed on from one grandchild to the next and so on. With that digression behind us, we now return to the Webster Electric tape recorder.

My parents wanted to keep track of their eldest son who was destined for seven years of absence, the final three on the high seas. Also, I must ask, who needs five fifteen pound tape recorders? It was decided that one of these behemoths would be a time saver for a child so occupied. In addition to using the large eight inch diameter reels of tape, the recorders could also handle the small, four inch diameter size, a size that was just perfect for a busy student or Naval Officer, assuming he could find the time to dictate his letter and put it in a small manila envelope, apply an address, and mail it.

Because father was a G-man, an investigator for the Justice Department, during the Depression, he was an expert with train schedules and the facility to ship parcels ahead of time 'on a ticket' as the saying goes. He shipped the tape recorder on my ticket in a wooden box along with a trunk of necessary items like clothing; the trunk was used many times by my sister and I should say trunks because there were several of them; I do believe that these trunks were saved from his own university days and were hidden in the attic tunnels. Did I have to haul the tape recorder and the trunk a quarter of a mile to Witherspoon Hall? The answer is no; I hired a taxi to transport these objects from the 'Dinky' station freight room – there was no Student Package Transportation Agency. Despite that oversight, I did have to lug these objects up three flights of wooden stairs.

After the furniture arrived and I possessed sheets, towels, and a pillow case, I could take time to look out the windows and take in the adjacent views of Blair Hall and Richardson Auditorium as well as the Elm trees. Later in the year I would learn how to get to the open tower area of Witherspoon through a trap door in the ceiling at the end of the 5th floor corridor. The view was spectacular especially the sunsets to the west.

There *were* shared washroom facilities on the fourth floor; many other would-be engineering students had arrived. Several of these fellow fourth-floor engineering students who used what, in Princeton terminology, was called an entry – a shared entrance to a group of dorm rooms – knew how to find the dining hall area for freshmen and sophomores and also at what time dinner would be served.

For two years undergraduates take their meals in several common dining halls which are opened in a sequential fashion; long lines are formed outside the doors and each hall is filled with row upon row of ten-person tables; when one hall fills the next is opened. In one sense such halls become part of a home away from home and should be mentioned in more detail. I shall not discuss that aspect of my home away from home except to share with you, my reader, the names of certain dishes that were repeatedly served during those first two years. Freshmen and sophomore students added the following menu entrées to their vocabulary: Mystery Meat, The Green Death, The Yellow Death, and Elephant Balls!

After returning from my first experience of the dining halls I did get some sleep after what seemed like a long day that included the train trip from Chicago and my first half-day at Princeton; I didn't give a thought about when, or how, I would be awakened; I had no alarm clock. But even if I had given such a trivial detail as when to wake up in time for breakfast any thought, I awoke and realized that I would never need to worry about reveille.

I was assigned a corner room with windows facing the north (Richardson Auditorium) and the west (Blair Hall), that is to say that my mother would have more curtains to make than the rest of the freshmen who lived down the hall, albeit they had fewer steps to walk to the washrooms. My next-door neighbors were also early arrivals as they, too, were thinking about pursuing an engineering course of study. One of the two engineers next-door wanted to exhibit the prowess he already acquired; I suspect he was an electrical or mechanical engineering student. In any event, he knew how to attach his alarm clock to his LP record player in such a way that the reveille notes from a bugle at Camp Stuart were altered to the words and music of a Frank Sinatra song currently in vogue:

You make me feel so young
You make me feel like spring has sprung
Every time I see you grin
I'm such a happy individual

The moment that you speak
I want to run and play hide-and-seek
I want to go and bounce the moon
Just like a big toy balloon

Messrs. Potter and Robertson did not believe in sound-proofing walls between one Witherspoon room and another. The words and music came through loud and clear; my bedroom wall separated my bed from the adjacent living room of my neighbors where the stereo set was set to alert the denizens of that room that another day was beginning; I sprung out of my bed as though every day was a spring day; I never did purchase an alarm clock.

Returning to the total lack of House Parents, Resident Assistants, and such like, there was one contact I made at this early date with the University. The incident, I am sure, is the kind that every Freshman student recalls. It would seem that the Admissions Office, that secretive department responsible for looking at examinations, personal interviews, forms, essays and other accomplishments, was not completely satisfied with the predictive value of their efforts; they wanted to have some further guarantee that each freshman would graduate in four years.

Now there were non-academic circumstances which caused a student to be politely asked to leave his studies; every incoming freshman was told of these rules. There was the rule that you could go to any, for example, clothing store on Nassau Street and buy something on credit. The proprietor knew that if there was any balance due before graduation, he could merely walk across the street and report the situation to an office in Nassau Hall; if not paid, the student would not receive his degree.

Another non-academic reason which caused a student to be politely asked to leave his studies was the discovery that he was the owner of a nearby automobile. Then there was the rule of not having a wife – either nearby or elsewhere. I say elsewhere because after the NROTC cruise through the Panama Canal to Valparaiso, Chile, in 1957, one of my NROTC freshman colleagues was observed being greeted back home by a young woman on the pier in Norfolk, Virginia, with a very enthusiastic embrace that was observed by the officer who accompanied the midshipmen, the Midshipman Liaison Officer. The Liaison Officer felt that the young woman so embraced was the midshipman's wife and reported his hunch to Princeton. He was correct and the gentleman was asked to leave the university; I'm certain that a validation occurred; the midshipman was from Little Rock, Arkansas.

Still another reason for expulsion was any violation of the Honor Code; all incoming students signed a statement that they understood the code and agreed to follow it. The signing indicated that the student pledged to never falsely sign the statement at the end of every exam which began: "I pledge my honor as a gentleman . . ." The code also required that every student report any observed infractions. A final reason for dismissal was the 'required chapel' rule: every Freshman was obliged to attend religious services at least 50% of the time while he was a student. In every place of worship in the town of Princeton each member of the class, who was in attendance for the entire service, was given a white card as evidence of attending that service. On vacation cards were available for use in institutions outside the Princeton community. The cards were turned in to an office in Nassau Hall.

I found myself attending several different denominations during the Freshman year and one was the First Presbyterian Church, a mere stone's throw from Witherspoon Hall. On one occasion I attended the entire service but for some reason or other one of the Ushers didn't observe my attendance and I picked up an attendance card. This was a very zealous Presbyterian and he singled me out as having bypassed the service and then surreptitiously creeping back in to steal a card! I protested; people were starting to leave in large numbers; they were looking at us; I offered to outline, from memory, the key points of the sermon. Only then did he stop his protestations. The so-called required attendance rule was abandoned, after two-hundred years, my sophomore year.

Having finished this digression we return to the strategy that the Admissions Office implemented to give new students a better, 'warm fuzzy' feel about the Freshman class actually graduating: it was a test. The test came at a later time when the entire class was on campus and on a day I was very tired; I struggled with the questions but, in reality, I couldn't care less about my score. I received a notice a few days later that encouraged me to seek counseling which notice I ignored. I am happy to report that I did graduate with honors, period, end of report.

But while the Admissions Office wanted to give freshmen a 'warm fuzzy,' that motive was not completely true of the faculty, especially those who taught freshmen. Since I attended a Chicago Public High School, there were no honors classes and, although I took four years of math, I never heard the word 'calculus.' I believe it was a young PhD student that was assigned by the Math Department in Fine Hall to tackle the task of teaching integral and differential calculus to these underprivileged freshmen like myself. In the first part of the class, the differential calculus portion, everything went smoothly without any problems but people began having trouble with integral calculus.

Finally, one day, in a fit of obvious frustration, the PhD student declared to the class of about eighteen students the following words. They were delivered in crisp, short sentences, just as though he was enduring some kind of torture. "Well, many say that integral calculus is an art; if you're an artist that can grasp it, fine, if not, there are other things to do in life! So, what I am going to do is put up an integral calculus problem on the board and I'll let you know if you have acquired the art. Any questions? . . . Good; here is the problem." Whereupon he wrote the problem on the blackboard.

"I'll give you five minutes and then I will come around and see how each of you are doing." He sat down, set his watch, and looked at some papers. After five minutes, he stood up, and began looking at each of the papers for the first nine students in the front row and made comments out loud so the rest of the class could benefit. At the first student he quickly remarked, "You haven't understood a word I have said since the beginning of the class." He moved on to the next front-row student and remarked, "Brilliant! You are well on your way to becoming an artist."

I was sitting in the back row and the PhD student could walk behind us. The commentary given to the front row was not helpful for concentration; nor was it very uplifting; most of his analysis was cutting, and quite pejorative. It reminded me of Mrs. Hoff at Ebinger even though it was only a single problem. I had no idea what he would say about my work; I was sitting in the middle of the back row and as he approached me, the back row was not doing any better than the front row. He paused as he looked over my shoulder and then remarked in kind of a clipped voice, "Well, there's hope!" It is now time to return to the surveying class in early September as my new home, 441 Witherspoon Hall, was the site of those reading assignments, homework problems, and slide rule exercises along with preparation for exams.

It became clear to me that one of the purposes of the three weeks of three classes and supplemental information talks about each engineering field was to cause a large percentage of the class to decide they didn't want anything to do with engineering of any kind! These were classmates who, unlike myself, would take seriously an earlier warning like "Don't be a Norwegian all your life!" by simply switching to liberal arts; after all, Princeton was known for its liberal arts but as one individual said to me years later "Whoever heard of a Princeton engineer?" When another person was informed of my current profession, he kindly remarked "I've always wondered where those Princeton engineers go after graduation."

One of the stories about a student that did not pursue engineering, arose from his daily three-hour surveying lab on the hot, grassy fields not so far from the football stadium. It was a long hike and carrying the surveying transit with its tripod took energy; before the transit could be used it had to be calibrated as per the textbook which called for any number of calibration procedures to make it *accurate*! Even measuring a distance between two points – two stakes in the ground set there for the lab – involved a correction formula that included the temperature of the tape – taken from a thermometer attached to the tape so the bulb touched the metal – the tension of the tape – a spring scale at one end was used to remove a portion of the 'sag' – but it was the force of the spring, the actual, precise tension on the tape, that was absolutely necessary for precision and for the correction formula; holding that scale steady in the hot sun was easier said than done because there were two fellows involved; it was a tug-of-war with a spring, of all things, on one end!

Reference points, like property stakes, survey markers, boundary lines and many other kinds of in-ground points of steel, are the stock and trade of surveying. Some get imbedded in five inch concrete circular monuments, and others become nails hammered into concrete sidewalks. So, too, are the notes taken down and recorded in a strict, documented, fashion; only in this way can they be understood by individuals who use those notes later. After each lab the graduate Civil Engineering student, who was in charge of the lab, graded the quality of the notebooks with the field notes. Legibility was one thing, an obvious given, but following the precise way in which things were to be set down was infinitely more important.

The story about one of the students who decided not to continue with any further engineering studies involved the use of a reference point that he used in his field notes. In the notes, he was asked to identify a remote marker that was used to establish a critical line of sight that was needed in the next lab for reorientation purposes. When the student asked the Graduate Civil Engineering student in charge of the lab for assistance, the graduate student asked him what he used for a reference marker and was told that he had used the "antenna of a blue Ford parked near the stadium!"

A frustration with acquiring the art of surveying came one day during the lecture. Professor Kissam not only wrote both the Elementary and Advanced Surveying texts but he also stared in all the photographs! He was always dressed in very plain clothes. When Professor Kissam lectured he would turn the bowl of his pipe to the side in order to re-lite the pipe. He spoke quickly if only because he knew everything that was in the book by heart. When demonstrating a long sequence of complex adjustments made by twisting knobs a half turn clockwise, followed by looking through the telescope at the crosshairs, and then six more steps, they were not time-consuming sequences. Professor Kissam went through them with the rapidity of having done them several thousand times. If anyone was taking notes and asked him to slow down his reply was that "It's all in the book!"

The lectures were now at a point about halfway through the three weeks, the mid-term was behind everyone, and Professor Kissam was speaking to the class about what an outside observer might call a trench, when a student raised his hand with a question and was given the nod by Professor Kissam; "Professor Kissam," he asked, "are you surveying a new sewer, or are you surveying a sewer that is already there?" A terrible look came upon Professor Kissam's face, a look that no one had ever seen in all of his pictures in the Elementary Surveying Text. What made matters worse for Professor Kissam was that when he looked up at the rest of the class he realized that a huge majority of the class thought it was a very good question!

My New York roommate arrived after the three week period. It was immediately clear that his main interest in High School was being knighted by the New York Fire Department as a 'Fire Photographer!' He quickly showed me his high quality camera and, perhaps an even more precious possession, a card in his wallet that designated him by name as an Official New York Fire Department Photographer. With this card he was allowed to cross lines where others could not go! How did this affect our home, 441 Witherspoon Hall?

Ed immediately looked at the two bare walls in the main room and announced that came with objects that would remove the boredom of those walls whereupon he put up huge black and white photos – two feet wide by three feet tall – of smoke pouring out of different kinds of buildings! A regular gallery of smoking buildings! But he also was convinced that the pictures would attract an audience. To prove his point he held a party every weekend and invited anyone he saw. He had no qualms about adding some alcohol from a flask to his punch bowl. Supposedly the proctors – plain-clothes policemen employed by the university to look for infringements of the rules – would not be able to discern any extra ingredients in the punch.

At the start of his parties Ed put on a record of what seemed to be his only musical interest: Kurt Weill's *The Threepenny Opera* with lyrics by Bertolt Brecht. Then he sat back and waited for his friends to arrive, sipped his punch and listened to the same record over and over again. It was like listening to Frank Sinatra singing "You make me feel so young, You make me feel like spring has sprung" every morning, except it was 'The Ballad of Mack The Knife' played over and over again "Oh the shark has pretty teeth dear, And he shows them pearly white, Just a jack-knife has Macheath dear, And he keeps it out of sight"

I, of course, could not study and went to the library but my friends reported that I was not alone; they looked in and reported that, invari-ably, no one showed up to enjoy the 'Smoke' Gallery or to taste the punch. I eventually spoke with the administration in Nassau Hall, reported my woes – which went beyond those outlined here – and was told that I could retain the room as a single for my Sophomore year.

My mother's curtains arrived; they looked great; she used the same material as my typewriter cover and they would be used for another year. Somehow, I now had my High School typewriter and a stand and I was us-ing it to earn $1 per page for papers and thesis work for liberal arts students in the dorm. Once more I shall resort to the use of an excerpt from *Stories of Identity* wherein there is a fictional conversation of John Sherman with Michel de Montaigne, the French essayist born in 1533. The beginning portion – prior to the conversation – and the conversation itself summarizes the social aspect of the Freshman year which was present, to a large degree, during the entire four years:

* * *

The final ceremony was held at dawn, and Sherman was given his Indian name, "Be known, my brother, as Petachdonamen Weuchsowagan, which, being interpreted, means He Who Seeks Knowledge."

With the lines of the vigil ceremonies still ringing in his ears, Sherman walked down the platform to catch the train that would carry him to a campus he had never seen to live among people he had never known. How appropriate was the name Petachdonamen Weuchsowagan he thought. If anything was certain, it would be that he was going east to seek knowledge. He of course hoped that the next four years would bring him something beyond mere knowledge of engineering and naval science subjects.

He realized that he would have to make new friends and acquire social skills that he sensed were already present in the large groups from the suburban communities, outside the City of Chicago that sent big delegations to Princeton for decades. He doubted his own high school education. He always received top grades but had the suspicion that his high school was not a top school. He never spent time studying; perhaps he was considered a minority student.

He questioned how he could contribute to the university as an undergraduate in view of his never having practiced a sport. He doubted his expertise with the clarinet was adequate for the Princeton Marching Band. He wondered whether his church experiences would provide him with the fortitude to succeed. Another unanswered question was how he would transition, after he graduated, so as to achieve honor under the rubric of "Princeton in the Nation's Service." Military service of three years following a full NROTC scholarship was not what the Princeton motto was supposed to be about.

The story of Sherman's first year at Princeton is facilitated by the transcription of a lengthy dream that Sherman had, after it was all over. The vividness and extent of the dream caused him to write down its details. It reminded him of Scrooge and the Ghost of Christmas Past except that Sherman sensed that he had done nothing wrong. The ghost that accompanied him was identifiable as one Michel de Montaigne, the French essayist born in 1533.

During the course of the dream journey they took together, it became clear that in many respects they were soul mates. Prior to the dream, he was reading Montaigne's essay, *On presumption,* and Montaigne quoted those lines to him during their sojourn together. Sherman realized that they resonated thoroughly with his own thoughts, despite the fact that the Frenchman's history was so completely different from his own. In his written transcription of the dream, Sherman decided to put in *italics* the lines Montaigne spoke from his essay, *On presumption.*

The Dream Transcription

I awoke from my slumbers to find a short and what some might call an unhandsome gentleman standing at the foot of the bed. "Who are you and why have you come?" I asked him.

"I am Michel de Montaigne and I have come to help you understand your freshman year. *Now, I am a little below middle stature, and this defect is not only ugly, but a disadvantage in those who hold commands and offices. For the authority conferred by a fine presence and dignity of body is lacking.*"

"But I am afraid I have a bad memory," said Sherman, "as a child I memorized lines and lines of rhymed stories to tell around campfires by way of self-improvement, and these I remember, but I've devoted little time in my past studies to further this ability."

"You will find," spoke Montaigne, "that we are soul mates and as for memory, *the memory is an instrument of wonderful utility, and without it the judgment can hardly perform its duties; I am almost completely without it. Anything that is put before me must be presented piecemeal. I am obliged to call the men who serve me by the names of their offices or their provinces, for I find it very hard to remember a name. And, if I live long enough, I am not sure that I shall not forget my own name, as others have done.*"

I decided to put my soul mate to a further test. I then told Montaigne, "I also know little about the world and have kept track of major gaps in my knowledge where everyone around me seems to know these gaps as common knowledge." Following this I reiterated a list of memorized embarrassments that I knew and that included items similar to some recent additions like:

+ I never knew the meaning of the word circumcision when my son was born, and falsely communicated with the doctor.
+ Even after serving three years in the Navy, I never assumed that I was a veteran. A veteran was, to me, one who fought in World War II. I lost thousands of tax-free education benefits, even on appeal, because ignorance of the law is no excuse.
+ I never knew where Ireland was in relation to England.
+ I failed to know, after I retired, that my pension was fully deductible on my state income tax form.
+ I never understood the meaning of the first line of the Twenty-third Psalm, "The Lord is my shepherd, I shall not want." For years I thought the writer was rejecting the shepherd.

Montaigne replied to this test by recounting, *"There is no mind so inept as mine, or so ignorant of many common things of which a man cannot be ignorant without shame. . . . I do not even know the names of the commonest farm implements, or the plainest principles of agriculture which are familiar to boys; and I know even less of the mechanical arts, of trade and merchandise, of the nature and variety of fruit, wines, and food, of training a hawk, or physicking a horse or a dog."* He went on to add that just recently, he *"was caught in ignorance of the fact that leaven is used in bread-making and of the purpose of putting wine into vats."*

Sherman remembered the Indian drum in the darkness of the night, the words that were spoken, the ending, and the feeling of solidarity he felt with vigil members of the lodge for he now was feeling a strong solidarity with Montaigne. It was though he were saying, "My brother, I too have kept the vigil."

Before a moment passed however, Montaigne took me to a vantage point from which we could see a Princeton party in progress. Well-dressed young men in tweed coats, college ties and loafers were dancing with young women, with what appeared to Sherman to be professional competence. Others were drinking beer from kegs at a bar nearby. There was a certain kind of haircut then in vogue causing many Princeton students to wear their hair swept to one side. The young women all wore camel hair coats and Princeton scarves, making it difficult, Sherman thought, to find one's own coat on the rack in the hallway.

Sherman mentioned to Michel that he had never tasted beer, and recalled for him his feelings about his classmates. Huge percentages of the freshman class had graduated at the top of their high school class and had served as class president or equivalent. Huge numbers were proficient at one or more sports, and huge numbers had gone to preparatory schools where social skills were honed to at least an eastern seaboard standard.

Large numbers of students already knew friends from their prep schools and suburban high schools–they socialized with them and they could actually dance with their sisters, who were often in attendance at nearby eastern girls' schools. Dress was the most obvious mark of these polished freshmen. They wore tweed jackets, loafers, crew-neck sweaters, club-like ties from Langrocks on Nassau Street, or from Brooks Brothers, spoke of other Princeton graduates in the family, and they were good at sports which Sherman had to look up in the dictionary: lacrosse, rugby, crew, and soccer. They acted in plays, sang in operas, and were members of a-cappella groups. They could play tennis, swim, play golf, shoot baskets, or were already specializing in fencing and squash.

Montaigne replied to these remarks, "*I do not know how to please or to delight, or to amuse; the best story in the world becomes dry and withers in my hands. I can only speak seriously and am altogether without that easy knack, which I see in many of my friends, of entertaining chance comers and keeping a whole company amused, or of holding the attention of a prince with all kinds of small talk, and never boring him. Such men never lack a subject, thanks to their gift of knowing how to use the first that comes, and to adapt it to the humour and understanding of anyone they may have to do with.*

"I admire the assurance and confidence that everyone has in himself, while there is hardly anything that I am sure of knowing, or that I dare answer to myself that I can do. I never have my means marshaled and at my service, and am only aware of them after the event. I am as doubtful of myself as of anything else."

I told Michel that I made efforts to overcome these deficiencies and mentioned that I never went to my high school senior prom. "I bought a tuxedo at the student tailor shop but not the top hat that I wore as interlocutor in the minstrel show. I asked a town girl, a senior from Princeton High School, to the freshman prom at Dillon Gym," I explained to Montaigne.

He replied, "Let's take a look at that," and before I knew it we were watching my freshman classmates dancing in Dillon gym.

"There, there I am," I said excitedly to Michel, "but I'm hardly moving; the best you can say is that I'm not stepping on my partner's toes. But look around. Everyone seems to be having a great time because they know how to dance. I spent my time with church and scouting activities and carried this incompetence to Princeton. My competency on the dance floor made it an experiment in futility and there were no ballroom dancing classes in the curriculum."

Michael replied, *"My works are so far from pleasing me, that every time I look at them they annoy me."*

"Skill and agility were never mine."

"In dancing, tennis, or wrestling, I was never able to acquire more than a very slight and ordinary competence; in swimming, fencing, vaulting, and leaping, none at all."

"But let me tell you about the clarinet," I said to Michel, "that was a different variation."

"By all means," he replied, "go right ahead."

"Clarinet playing was one activity I considered an extraordinary failure. No well-rounded individual can exist without playing a musical instrument. My sister took piano lessons at home, and I, too, had a year or so of piano lessons.

"The high school band director was famous, a very involved person. He entered the band and orchestra in competitions, and they did quite well, but, alas, this was during the time my sister played viola. The students loved him. He taught a group class at a local field house near the high school for younger musicians. Ten different types of instruments were thrown together, and there was little time for any private attention. Just when I started with the clarinet, the famous high school teacher died, and I had no private lessons. A person who was non-descript took over at the field house and I received very bad lessons from the outset.

"Thus, when arriving at high school, I was barely able to make a noise on the instrument, and was relegated to playing fourth clarinet in the ROTC marching band, which was a group of rag-taggle guys, who wanted to get out of both ROTC and gym by goofing off for one hour, without any supervision from the new High School music teacher, who, in turn, was only interested in getting people to take private lessons from him! Squeaking away as a fourth clarinet for four years and marching once a year in the City of Chicago's Cadet Day Parade was an agonizing failure.

"But things became worse. During the summers, my mother reacted to this by driving me to the nearest town in Michigan where our summer home was. She signed me up for private lessons from the local High School teacher in Ludington. This was even worse, for I can still remember mother paying this man with real money to listen to me squeak, as I had not even picked up the instrument from one week to the next. Thus the clarinet was a worrisome token with respect to the true measure of my competence since I saw others who could actually play the overture to Mozart's Impresario and I would have given my eye teeth to have any ability, but it seemed beyond my reach."

Michel nodded and said, "I suppose this carried over into Princeton?"

"Right on," I replied, "I put down on the application that I could make some contribution to the school, and of course the clarinet seemed to be the only skill I brought. If you can imagine a fourth clarinet from a City of Chicago High School ROTC band, dominated by what we then called 'hoods,' a person with no private lessons, who could barely read notes, you would understand the absurdity of such a one trying out for a marching band."

"We don't have to imagine," said Montaigne, and to my amazement we were on the balcony in Alexander Hall, watching the Princeton marching band rehearse. There I was, squeaking away and looking at unfamiliar notes in strange songs, played in a fast tempo and all printed on extremely small pieces of paper, about four and a half by seven inches in size.

"Why a person can be so totally ignorant of where he stands remains a question," I said to Michel.

Michel replied to this last comment by speaking of his own case, "*I think it would be difficult for any man to have a poorer opinion of himself, or indeed to have a poorer opinion of me, than I have of myself. I regard myself as one of the common sort in all save this, that I do so regard myself. I plead guilty to the meanest and most ordinary failings; I neither disown nor excuse them; and I value myself for nothing except that I know my own value.*"

"Should we go on in this way?" I asked Michel, "you see how all these things end up, and we haven't even started looking at failures where my miscalculations involved things I knew nothing about."

"Yes, go on," he said and then gave his reasons for continuing. *"From these articles of my confession you can imagine others to my discredit. But whatever I make myself out to be, provided that I show myself as I am, I am fulfilling my purpose. So I will not apologize for daring to put in writing such mean and frivolous things as these. The meanness of my subject compels me to do so. You may condemn my project if you will, but not my way of carrying it out. However that may be, I see well enough, without anyone pointing it out, how little weight and value all this has, and how foolish my plan is. It is sufficient if my judgment, of which these essays are the proof, has not gone lame."* I took heart and continued, for some power had sent me a soul mate.

"I decided to develop a sport, Michel. I thought that anyone could run, and reasoned that, of course, freshman cross-country would be a matter of pure will. In Cub Scout softball father once remarked on how fast I ran to first base. My high school lacked a track team so I reasoned that I came from a disadvantaged environment."

Michel interrupted, "as I have said *skill and agility were never mine . . . while I have seldom met anyone who did not excel me in any (physical exercise) but running, at which I was moderately good."*

"The freshman track coach would accept anyone, and I began the painful effort of running as far and as fast as I could through the woods around Lake Carnegie in the late afternoon." Now we found ourselves high above the trees looking down at a stretched out group of freshmen runners coming up along the side of Washington Road as they ascended from the bridge at the lake. Way at the end Sherman spotted himself; he was being encouraged to run faster by another boy coming up fast behind him.

"Yes," he said to Michel, "I can remember that day. I liked him for trying to keep my spirits up. What happened on that very day as I began to put out more effort was that my feet went flat. Another coach I spoke with in the large gym said it was a bad sign, and that very few cross country runners with flat feet ever won a race. I transferred into a gym class.

"But the absurdity of it all! There were freshmen who ran all four years in prep school, whose muscles were developed in hundreds of hours of practice, and the winning of many races. Perhaps after four years of effort and losing constantly, and still trying, something could have been achieved; these were my thoughts."

Michel replied, "*The uncertainty of my judgment is so evenly balanced in most cases that I would willingly refer the decision to a throw of the dice.*"

"The upshot of these failures," I told Michel, "at the time, when I could not take more definitive action due to the demands of my studies, was to take solace in the mean."

"Yes," said Michel, "*we may thus conclude that virtue or excellence is a characteristic involving a choice, and that it consists in observing the mean relative to us, a mean which is defined by a rational principle, such as a man of practical wisdom would use to determine it. It is the mean by reference to two vices: the one of excess and the other of deficiency.*"

"My flat feet made me fear that I would lose my NROTC scholarship because I heard that during the Depression, people were not allowed to join the Navy because of flat feet. At the next annual NROTC physical that was done on campus, I asked a machinist mate who was performing some of the work about this, and he replied not to worry, there were a lot of flat footed sailors in the Navy.

"Even gym was an awakening as I had taken no gym classes in high school, having opted to take high school ROTC instead. Having failed with a sport and then cycled through various sports in gym, about which I knew nothing, such as tennis, fencing, and squash, perhaps it was a touch of ambition that prompted my next move. I went to try out for a part in Thornton Wilder's play, *The Skin of Our Teeth,* which was being put on at Miss Fine's School for Girls, a private High School nearby. This, too, was a terrible underestimate of what it took to act. I witnessed accomplished high school students get all the speaking parts, and ended up getting a walk-on role in the crowd scenes."

This time Michel replied with sentiments that I realized were closer to my true feelings. By going to Miss Fine's school I ignored those inner promptings and was carried away. Michel replied, *"As for ambition, which is a neighbor*t *or rather a daughter— of presumption, if fortune had wished to advance me, she would have had to come and lead me by the hand. For to give myself trouble for an uncertain hope, and to submit myself to all the difficulties that attend men endeavoring to force themselves into favor at the beginning of their career, that I could never have done.*

"For the strongest and most general ideas that I possess are those which, in a manner of speaking, were born with me; they are natural and wholly my own. I brought them forth crude and simple; at their birth they were bold and vigorous, though a little confused and imperfect."

"But after my experience at Miss Fine's I did carry away something from being a walk-on."

"What was that?" asked Michel.

"It was those lines from Act Two of the play, where Mr. Antrobus tells his wife of five thousand years that he is going to leave her, and she replies back to him. I've never forgotten them."

ANTROBUS: Maggie, I'm moving out of the hotel. In fact, I'm moving out of everything. For good. I'm going to marry Miss Fairweather. I shall provide generously for you and the children. In a few years you'll be able to see that it's all for the best. That's all I have to say.

MRS. ANTROBUS: *Composedly with lowered eyes.* George, I can't talk to you until you wipe those silly red marks off your face.

ANTROBUS: I think there's nothing to talk about. I've said what I have to say.

SABINA: Splendid!

ANTROBUS: You're a fine woman, Maggie, but . . . but a man has his own life to lead in the world.

MRS. ANTROBUS: Well, after living with you for five thousand years I guess I have a right to a word or two, haven't I?

ANTROBUS: *To* SABINA. What can I answer to that?

SABINA: Tell her that conversation would only hurt her feelings. It's-kinder-in-the-long-run-to-do-it-short-and-quick.

ANTROBUS: I want to spare your feelings in every way I can, Maggie.

BROADCAST OFFICIAL: Mr. Antrobus, the hurricane signal's gone up. We could begin right now.

MRS. ANTROBUS: *Calmly, almost dreamily.* I didn't marry you because were perfect. I didn't even marry you because I loved you. I married you because you gave me a promise.

She takes off her ring and looks at it.

That promise made up for your faults. And the promise I gave you made up for mine. Two imperfect people got married and it was the promise that made the marriage.

ANTROBUS: Maggie, . . . I was only nineteen.

MRS. ANTROBUS: *She puts her ring back on her finger.*

And when our children were growing up, it wasn't a house that protected them; and it wasn't our love, that protected them – it was that promise. And when that promise is broken – this can happen!

MRS. ANTROBUS: *Claps her hands peremptorily.*

Stop your noise. – I'm taking her back to the hotel, George. Before I go I have a letter . . . I have a message to throw into the ocean.

Fumbling in her handbag.

Where is the plagued thing? Here it is.

She flings something – invisible to us – far over the heads of the audience to the back of the auditorium.

It's a bottle. And in the bottle's a letter. And in the letter is written all the things that a woman knows.

It's never been told to any man and it's never been told to any woman, and if it finds its destination, a new time will come. We're not what books and plays say we are. We're not what advertisements say we are. We're not in the movies and we're not on the radio.

We're not what you're all told and what you think we are: We're ourselves. And if any man can find one of us he'll learn why the whole universe was set in motion. And if any man harm any one of us, his soul – the only soul he's got – had better be at the bottom of that ocean, - and that's the only way to put it. Gladys, come here. We're going back to the hotel.

"But the words did something else Michel. They made me realize that I must be missing something. There are things you hear or read that stay with you for a lifetime, and others that disappear from memory. Even during freshman year, having taken only a single English course, I had the premonition that I would not be remembering physics, chemistry, calculus, elementary strength of materials, or naval science 101. No, it was always the material from the one or two English classes, or a course in mediaeval

Christian thought that I audited, and was able to squeeze in, that stayed
with me; and it's been that way ever since.

"This occurred with a play, a poem, a short story, or even a random passage that was discovered as a result of picking up a random book in the stacks
at Firestone Library. All these things were like Kierkegaard's *Purity of Heart
is to Will One Thing,* or like the lines of the rituals I had memorized, lines like,

> Call you now upon your Father,
> Great Creator of all nations,
> To grant blessings on His children
> From His high and holy station
> Guiding you upon your journey.
> That His Hand be stretched out to you,
> As you ever help His people;
> That His light may ever lead you
> As you lead the wayward to Him;
> That his love be ever with you
> As you love your fellow mortals.
> That His Spirit rest upon you
> To direct and rule and guide you
> Till at last He calls you Home.
> Pray you now in reverent silence,
> Each of your in your own fashion.

"There was engendered, in those few exposures during four years, a hunger
for something beyond pure knowledge. And I began to question why I stayed
with my plan of studies when I felt that empty void that was not being filled."

Michel replied, "*I readily relapse into my reflections on the uselessness of our
education. Its aim has been to make us not good and wise, but learned; and in this
it has succeeded. It has not taught us to follow and embrace virtue and wisdom, but
has imprinted their derivations and etymologies on our minds. We are able to decline
virtue, even if we are unable to love it; if we do not know what wisdom is in fact and
by experience, we are familiar with it as a jargon learned by heart.*"

"All around me were classmates who were taking philosophy and others who could read Shelley's poetry so that I can still remember the sound of the words."

The Cloud

I bring fresh showers for the thirsting flowers,
From the seas and the streams;
I bear light shade for the leaves when laid
In their noonday dreams.
From my wings are shaken the dews that waken
The sweet buds every one,
When rocked to rest on their mother's breast,
As she dances about the sun.
I wield the flail of the lashing hail,
And whiten the green plains under,
And then again I dissolve it in rain,
And laugh as I pass in thunder.

"I was as much in need of this side of my personal development as ballroom dancing, clarinet lessons, proficiency in a lifelong sport, and social skills."

"Enough," said Michel, "my time is getting short. What did you resolve to do?"

I answered Montaigne as quickly as I could "I would start an elaborate beaded Indian costume in the Navy to fulfill my obligations to the Order of the Arrow, so as to further the effort that I promised to follow in the vigil ceremony. I would build my own single scull wherry from a mahogany kit, and be a one-person crew. I would learn to dance at Stanford. I would make many beautiful things with my own hands, and assimilate a creative, aesthetic component into my existence. I would formally acquire a philosophy of life that would be a working philosophy and have significance for my everyday activities. I would spend the rest of my life studying the liberal arts. I would write hundreds of sonnets, a dozen short plays, many other essays, and books.

"I would find a wife and raise a family. I would seek a job where nothing depended on any Princeton person or thought, and where everything depended on new knowledge and one's ability to work and acquire that knowledge. I would take clarinet lessons and play in an orchestra, and band, and would enjoy the instrument. I would give service back to my community. I would keep physical fitness at the top of my list. I would never own a television."

"Good," said Michel, "my service is over."

I awoke from my dream feeling refreshed.

End of Dream

* * *

The dream, being fictional, takes the liberty of looking into the future at its end; but having, as it does, a conversation with a Philosopher from the past, we apologize for the oversight. In any event, our story will not jump into the future but merely continue into the summer of 1957 and the first NROTC cruise. My new home?

Iowa-class Battleship
Philadelphia Naval Shipyard
USS *Wisconsin* (BB-64)
Launched December 7, 1943
Commissioned April 16, 1944

I feel certain that parenthood begins at birth and only ends after the demise of both parents. One might imagine that having a son finish his Freshman year at Princeton and possessing orders to report to Norfolk, Virginia, for an eight-week cruise, would provide some relief for parents with two more sons in the pipeline, so to speak. Upon my return to Chicago from New Jersey and before the NROTC cruise this was certainly not the case.

We have already commented upon father's expertise with respect to obtaining railroad tickets; a skill perfected during the Depression. My railroad return, then, from Princeton to Chicago was a reversal of my arrival with one exception. By reversal I mean a short trip on the 'Dinky' from Princeton to Princeton Junction, a local train trip from Princeton Junction to Trenton, New Jersey, followed by a coach seat trip to Chicago.

Father became aware that if I traveled in my NROTC uniform I could obtain a round trip ticket for $50. There would, of course, be no roomette which necessitated losing a night's sleep. As far as I can recall, however, I was never sick nor exhausted when I began this journey and there was an interval of a week before I was due at Norfolk, Virginia.

I arrived in Chicago with a duffel bag full of uniforms: this was a US Navy Sea bag that was made of white canvas and stood forty or so inches tall; it was close to twenty inches in diameter. The uniforms looked just like the typical summer uniforms worn by enlisted men except that the white cap sported a black, one inch wide band of cloth all around its upper edge thereby announcing that the wearer held the rank of a Midshipman (4th class).

Mother immediately set to work as all of the uniforms needed to be washed and starched, followed by ironing, and then carefully packed in the duffel bag. Father's work was with the transportation aspects of the forthcoming cruise – Norfolk, Virginia, to and through the Panama Canal, south to Valpariso, Chile, returning by the same path in reverse except for a brief stop at Guantanamo Bay, Cuba, some gunnery exercises at Culebra Island, Puerto Rico, followed by the final leg to Norfolk. In short, father's challenge was how to parlay a return ticket from Chicago to Trenton, New

Jersey, into a ticket that went from Chicago to Washington, D. C., and then continued further south via the Richmond, Fredericksburg and Potomac Railroad and the Atlantic Coast Line Railroad to Norfolk, Virginia.

Father *did* accomplish this task; I received a tremendously long ticket; it was as long as those modern drug store free offerings that stretch out two feet. The problem with the drug store special deals is that you don't want or need most of the stuff. The problem with my return ticket that now went to Norfolk – via three railroads – was that I left Chicago at 11:45 P. M. in a coach seat.

Arriving at Washington, D. C., in the midst of the usual summer weather – intense heat and humidity – I was exhausted from lack of sleep. Oddly enough, it seemed that the only comfortable place to rest was in a telephone booth! I dragged the heavy sea bag to the booth, closed the doors and attempted to sleep. The phone both provided an upright side to lean against and a relief from the noise of announcements; I imagined that it was cooler in there as well. The effort was only partly successful. By the time I boarded the Richmond, Fredericksburg, and Potomac Railroad passenger train I was so tired that I fell asleep sitting upright hoping that my being a military passenger would protect me from burglars dispossessing me of items at the top of my sea bag.

I can't remember changing trains to the Atlantic Coast Line but I did make it to Norfolk and found bus transportation to the USS *Wisconsin* (BB-64). I arrived, like many other Midshipmen, a day early, but what a fortuitous thing to do! It so happened that the sleeping quarters were being filled on a top-down basis. That meant that I was assigned a main-deck living compartment near a door that opened to fresh air, albeit it was hot fresh air in Norfolk before the *Wisconsin* was underway.

As the other eight hundred 4th and 1st class midshipmen arrived, they were escorted 'below decks' where it was hot 24/7, all the way to Valpariso, Chile, and back. The one night in the phone booth paid off in weeks of comfort. The early arrivals were the envy of everyone who came on time the next day. I became aware of the plight of the on-time arrivals in a rather awkward fashion.

Never having set foot in, let alone lived in, any type of U. S. Naval warship, I had little idea of the rules and regulations that facilitated living in such crowded quarters. There were regulations that mandated using the 'customary terminology' of the Navy. Some of these were in the Freshman NROTC curriculum, others were not. Examples covered a range of words and commands: floors were decks, ceilings were overheads, walls were bulkheads, ropes were lines, bits were where mooring lines were fastened to the ship, and bollards were where mooring lines were fastened on the pier. Living on a ship also required knowing the commands that were announced in customary phraseology over the *Wisconsin's* public address speakers, a system called the '1 MC' things like: 'Now knock off ship's work,' 'Commence Holiday Routine,' 'Go to your stations all the Special Sea and Anchor Detail,' General quarters, general quarters, all hands man your battle stations,' ' The Smoking Lamp is out in all Authorized Spaces,' 'The Officer of the Deck is switching his watch to the bridge,' and 'Up all Idlers.'

There were also rules of conduct that were not announced, for instance it was not a good idea to 'Skylark,' i. e., fooling around, nor was it correct to be seen in the wrong uniform during certain times of the day; at those times one must be in the 'uniform of the day.' Some classifications seemed ridiculous like the difference between 'Dress Whites,' and 'Undress Whites.' One of the rules involved the term 'Gear Adrift.' No, this was not equipment that was thrown overboard and spotted by a sailor looking over the 'Fantail,' the stern of the ship. Gear Adrift applied to the misdemeanor of leaving personal items out of your locker. I was not a person who, by nature, Skylarked. But I did have a problem with storage; something as simple as a washcloth presented problems: how was such an item to dry?

In the list of items to put in my sea bag there were more objects than starched and ironed uniforms. Mother decided to have me pack her colorfully embroidered Jerp House WW II Army Surplus washcloths; this was highly appropriate as the *Wisconsin* served in the Pacific with Admiral Halsey's 3rd Fleet. It seemed the natural thing to do with a washcloth – leave it out to dry – but dry or not dry, it was Gear Adrift! As such it was an infraction of the customary rules. To emphasize this, a court was held that followed the trappings of 'Captain's Mast' – the non-judicial punishment that was granted Naval Ship Captains by the UCMJ, the Uniform Code of Military Justice. Of course, for Midshipmen, the officer handing out punishment was not the Captain of the *Wisconsin* but the NROTC Liaison Officer.

After several sea bags of 'gear' that was drifting about was confiscated by a few 1st class Midshipmen and then stowed in a locked compartment, most 4th class Midshipmen resolved to part with whatever object(s) that were missing; after all, many 4th class Midshipmen had, most likely, brought more than one paperback novel on the cruise and they were still locked up in the single locker that everyone was given.

I, however, did not want to lose even as much as a single possession, especially a washcloth that was embroidered by my mother! Accordingly, I went to the locked compartment at the time posted as to when it would be open, and I sorted through the confiscated objects and located my washcloth. For identifying myself as the culprit I was told to report at a later time to undergo 'Captain's Mast' as previously discussed, in order to fix my punishment.

My punishment was to stand 'guard duty' in one of those 'lower deck' compartments where the 'on-time' arrivals were billeted. This guard duty was quite revealing. In the main deck compartment where I slept, the racks – sleeping frames with a stretched piece of canvas on which was placed a mattress – were built in tiers where there were only two racks to a tier, one rack above the other. Below decks where I worked off my guard duty, there were six racks in tier after tier; everyone slept in their 'skivvies'

I stood my watch near the 'scuttlebutt' the refrigerated drinking water fountain; there was a lot of traffic all during my watch which was during a night watch. Unlike my own compartment where I rarely felt thirsty, there was a continuous stream of sleepers who climbed down the tiers, arrived at the deck, and walked to the scuttlebutt; many popped a salt tablet with their liquid refreshment.

The cruise soon settled into days of routine activities. There were classes every day with workbooks to fill out. There were watches to stand in various spaces – engineering, combat information center, main deck lookout stations, and the bridge. Meals were delicious and we all saw the shipboard Marines who operated the Wisconsin's Brig bring their charges through the mess spaces to the mess tables designated for miscreants; the crew members of the *Wisconsin* who were given Brig time were under the discipline of Marine Corps supervisors; we were, collectively, impressed; I was thankful that my extra duty didn't involve a brig. While we were eating our meals on the mess decks, we could always tell when the Brig contingent was about to arrive; they, too, used the customary phraseology of the service to alert everyone: "Make a hole! Prisoners! Make a hole! Prisoners!"

After transiting the Panama Canal we steamed south and crossed the equator and were all initiated through the rituals of the 'Ancient Order of The Deep,' the realm of Davy Jones. The Midshipmen were baptized in a very large group on the fantail that was set up for the ceremonies. The baptizers employed garbage, fire hoses, and other ritual items. From our lowly status of being 'pollywogs' we emerged as members of a much higher class of creatures: 'Shellbacks!'

For many days before crossing the equator we were alerted to the idea that some ceremony was about to occur. Certain of the ship's crew, dressed as pirates, were accompanied by leading and trailing crew members – dressed as usual – who paraded back and forth while the lead sailor shouted out: 'Make a hole! Shellback!' These were the assistants of the legendary Davy Jones. After the ceremonies many midshipmen felt that their fraternity initiation was mild by comparison.

In my own case, I experienced what I felt many other pollywogs might also have endured. At one point we were crawling along for a long distance on the wooden decks of the fantail of the *Wisconsin* while being sprayed with salt water fire hoses. Those decks were polished every day with holystones by crews of polishers who sang a catchy song as they moved from one board to the next; it went something like "A one, and a two, and a three and four . . . thirteen, fourteen, fifteen, sixteen, seventeen, eighteen, nineteen SHIFT!" When 'shift' was pronounced they all moved to the next board and began polishing it and repeating the song. A lot of the midshipmen learned the song and joined in the work – it was like a conga-line.

Despite the daily polishing with holystones, the boards, which were white and very clean, were still rough; a holystoning did not make them smooth by any means. The upshot was that the trousers that I and everyone else were wearing soon were torn at the knees and the knees were soon scratched by the boards and the salt water entered those scratches.

But now, dear readers, we shall refer you to a short play, *The Midshipman Cruise*, which will relate more of this cruise in a fashion that mixes much fact with the fiction of the principal characters: two female midshipmen! Take your seats!

* * *

The Midshipman Cruise

Characters:

Deborah Stevens, *Midshipman 4th Class*
Sheila, *Midshipman 4th Class*
Commander Higgins, *Midshipman Cruise Liaison Officer*
Captain John Hornsby, *Commanding Officer, USS Wisconsin, BB-64*
DelMundo, *Filipino Steward*
A Marine Sentry

Setting:

The action takes place aboard the USS Wisconsin, BB-64, during a routine Midshipman Summer cruise through the Panama Canal to South America and back. At various times the background lights dim and the focus is on Deborah or Shelia who reread lines from letters they have written to friends at home.

Scene One:

A topside living compartment for 4th class Midshipmen aboard the USS Wisconsin. Deborah and Sheila are seen unpacking their duffel bags and stuffing small canvas bags into lockers below standard horizontal Navy "racks," or canvas frames with mattresses.

Focus on Deborah who rereads her letter for the first time.

DEBORAH *(reading)*: So, for once I was glad my father insisted on getting here early as Sheila and I have been given a living compartment on the main deck where we have a breeze!

Lights come up, both women unpacking.

DEBORAH: Sheila, have you been able to find a place for all of your things?

SHEILA: No, these lockers were made for seamen, not women who have to keep a lot more uniforms, and, as you might imagine, when they were building battleships, they had no idea that that kind of midshipmen would ever occupy these spaces.

DEBORAH: And have you noticed that even though we have a topside compartment everyone keeps walking through it? I thought we could put curtains on the portholes, but I just don't know what we will do tonight. I want to leave that door open and I can't imagine wanting to sleep with anything on in this heat. We were lucky to have come early for assignments. Have you seen some of those spaces down below? It must be over a hundred down there!

SHEILA: Well, I suppose we'll have to post watches at all the doors, ladders, and other points. By the way I just threw some stuff under my mattress pad.

DEBORAH *(coming up to Sheila and whispering.)*: I was just talking with Carol, that first class midshipman from school, and she said they eventually go after that kind of stuff. It's all in the locker or not at all! They call it gear adrift and you go to captain's mast and get demerits and extra duty, and all that kind of stuff. Besides, you might not be able to get it back at all if you can't find it again.

SHEILA: Well I'm going to complain to the Secretary of the Navy. She has no idea what she says when she talks about the transparent integration of women in the Navy as a fait accompli. I'd like to see her get some of her outfits in this locker.

DEBORAH: Sheila, did you see that marine on the quarter-deck when we came aboard?

SHEILA: Deborah, if you are going to start that type of thing you might as well put on your bathing suit and go out there on that wooden paradise of a fantail and get some sun.

DEBORAH: What I meant was that he was as neat as a pin, his trousers were pressed, and there wasn't a crease anywhere, shirt, trousers, or hat. Those marines must have a way of keeping this stuff without having to put it triple folded in a small locker.

A LOUD VOICE NEARBY: Attention on deck!

Sheila and Deborah snap to attention. Commander Higgins enters the compartment.

HIGGINS: At your ease. I just wanted to stop by and see how things are coming. You girls topside should consider yourself lucky. I was just down three levels and those compartments are rapidly filling up as the buses arrive. There will be inspections by first class you know, and it goes without saying that everything will have to be put away. I see towels, cosmetics, what's this? Undies! Well! I'm glad I came by. Women! There will be men coming through this compartment! We haven't arranged all the details yet. As you know the heads on the port side have been marked for women but we may still get absentminded crew who don't know or care to read signs.

SHEILA: Commander Higgins, what do you suggest we sleep in?

HIGGINS: Well, they do have regular issue pajamas at the ship's store, and if used with a sheet, I think that may be adequate. You should all have robes issued already?

ANOTHER MIDSHIPMAN: Commander, we have all been reading a lot in the papers these days about sexual harassment. Could you give us the procedures that will be in effect for this cruise?

HIGGINS: All cases should be discussed with me immediately. I will post instructions as to my hours and a general outline of what constitutes something worthy of discussion. I don't expect any problems. Well, I see you all have more unpacking to do, so I will see you later. I hope you get a lot out of this cruise. Remember, anything a man can do on this ship you can do also. That should be your motto for the next eight weeks. Thank you.

A LOUD VOICE NEARBY: Attention on deck!

Sheila and Deborah snap to attention as the Commander leaves and the lights fade.

Scene Two:

The Wisconsin *is passing through the Panama Canal and is rising in a lock. Sheila and Deborah are standing amidships watching the concrete side of the lock slowly rise some few inches distant from the outer surface of the ship. Across the way in an adjacent lock, the cruiser, USS* Albany, *is rising along with the* Wisconsin.

Focus on Deborah, who reads her letter again.

DEBORAH (*reading*): The jungles of Panama, bird life, and close proximity to the shore have really been fascinating, and during the passage, the voice on the ship's speaker, like a luxury liner announcer, pointed out items of interest, like the huge mountain that was cut out for the canal, all done at a time when there was no cure for malaria.

Lights come up. Both women on deck.

DEBORAH (*pointing to the concrete wall of the lock itself*): Look, Sheila, where this stone in the concrete has been scraped out – some sailor has stuffed in a penny! I think it says 1923.

SHEILA: You know that these locks were designed so that a battleship could just fit?

DEBORAH: Wasn't it the other way around? I think these locks were built much before this ship.

SHEILA: Deborah, I still don't know why you think attending a medical lecture on venereal disease is inapplicable to woman midshipmen, embarrassing, degrading, and sexually harassing? After all, you will be leading men who will have liberty opportunities, men who will know that condoms and penicillin can be had for the asking, and your duties as a future officer require you to be familiar with what can go on.

DEBORAH: I know; that's the Navy's argument.

SHEILA: Panama is notorious for these things, and you may want to purchase straw hats on the beach, but it's just conceivable that others will do a different type of shopping.

DEBORAH: Well, I guess you're right. Sheila, just look at those men on the bridge of the *Albany*; they're focusing every binocular on us! You'd think the Officer of the Deck would stop those guys from staring at our group.

SHEILA: I don't know what you expect from them. After all, they have been at sea for three weeks, and I don't think any of us were assigned to cruisers, as they just weren't big enough to divide up the way we have things arranged here.

DEBORAH: Sheila, I think you and I have different opinions on men. You seem to always be making excuses for them, and I think they need to shape up or ship out. Just because women are in the military now doesn't mean we can be ignored.

SHEILA: I don't think those deck officers are ignoring you, Deborah.

DEBORAH: That, of course, is not what I mean. We can bring to these ships a level-headed, competent, and intelligent force for getting the job done, and that needs to be recognized by people who understand that the world has changed. Corporate boardrooms know this, and there exists a no-nonsense respect and deference there that the Navy needs to emulate.

SHEILA: So, I guess you would never think of marrying a shipmate?

DEBORAH: That depends.

SHEILA: Depends on what?

DEBORAH: Well, I think you have to realize that with the responsibilities one has, there just won't be a lot of time for that sort of thing.

Besides, an officer needs to watch herself because actions speak louder than words.

SHEILA: That's what I am trying to point out to you. Those deck officers there are carrying out their responsibilities of seeing to it that all is well during this canal transit, keeping track of the mules, maintaining radio contact and so on, even though the ship is restricted. Those actions with the binoculars speak much louder than the ship's announcing system, and you are saying that there won't be any time for that sort of thing. Just exactly how would you handle these situations?

DEBORAH: Sheila, you and I both know that women, even in non-military situations, can easily control these attentions, or whatever you want to call them. Given the extra emphasis of a rank thrown in, I don't see a problem.

SHEILA: But what about attentions coming from an equally ranked person? Or suppose the captain invites you for a private dinner in his quarters? You don't think any Filipino steward is going to intervene with what goes on?

DEBORAH: Sheila, you do have a vivid imagination! Most captains of major combatants have been married for years with scores of children. If they didn't think a Filipino steward would keep track of what was going on, they would fear other officers close to them in the chain of command who could sense what was happening.

SHEILA: But that's just what doesn't seem to be happening. Time and again, people are looking the other way, giving the wink to these kinds of things. Only after some congressional committee or hotline is set up and a woman realizes that that very captain is on the board of inquiry to eliminate these improprieties, do we come forth and use some of that no-nonsense, level-headed competence to set the world straight. But by then, it is too late.

DEBORAH: Well, I don't think I would have any problem with the captain of this or any other ship, for that matter. And I don't think it is an issue because I don't think there is any reason that a captain would be interested. So I think, Sheila, we should drop the subject.

Scene Three:

The Engineering spaces of the Wisconsin. *On one side of a bulkhead Deborah is on watch, taking temperature and pressure readings; on the other side, on Broadway, a long polished passageway, Sheila stands and rereads a letter she has written.*

SHEILA *(reading):* I just don't think Deborah knows how attractive she really is. I think she has more experience with boys than with men. The other midshipmen try to get near her using almost any ploy, like standing next to her in a chow line, or sitting at the same mess table, all trying to have a conversation with her and receiving her gorgeous smile.

I know you've never met her, but she is like one of those fashion models in J. Crew: dimples, enthusiasm, and a pleasing personality. When she's on watch in an engine room she is even more attractive, as the vents blow-dry her hair and tiny droplets of sweat add extra luster to her complexion.

Light fades on Sheila and focuses on Deborah, who reads her letter in the engine room.

DEBORAH *(reading):* Broadway is this wonderful polished deck that runs the length of the engineering spaces. It has been polished to a beautiful burnished steel mirror using an electric polisher with small wire elements that bring out an old-world patina that reminds one of the aura of an oil painting. Inside an engine room one can wear whites instead of dungarees, things are so polished. It looks like everything was just built in the shipyard. Well, I've turned some valves, climbed some ladders, and had my exercise in a sauna! Time to finish this watch and find the cool air of the sea once again.

Deborah puts the letter away and passes through the bulkhead to Broadway to stand where Sheila read her letter. She pauses. A Filipino steward approaches.

DELMUNDO: Ms. Stevens?

DEBORAH: Yes.

DELMUNDO: Letter for you, from captain.

The Filipino boy smiles and then is off down Broadway. Deborah is curious and decides to read by the light of Broadway before she goes topside.

DEBORAH *(reading)*:

On board USS *Wisconsin* (BB-64)
July 15, 19__

My Dear Ms. Stevens:

Permit me to introduce myself as Captain Hornsby, your captain for this midshipman cruise. I am certain you are surprised at receiving this letter through my steward, but I have chosen not to use the chain of command for this communication. I will be attending the Naval War College after this cruise, and as my request involves matters academic, I have chosen to follow the ways of the less formal college campus.

More to the point, I will be required to submit a paper (actually one of many) on the subject of "Women in the Service" and am using this cruise and the close proximity of so many midshipmen to do some interviewing toward that end. Although there are a number of other women officers available to assist me in this, such as Commander Higgins, I am focusing on the attitudes and opinions of the woman who will best reflect the current views of our society, unbiased by naval career experience.

If you should care to assist me in this endeavor, I would be glad to perform that effort with you over dinner in my sea cabin at 1930 hours on Tuesday next. You may find this space on the port side just aft of the bridge area. Please show the marine posted there the ID enclosed for entry.

Signed,

John Hornsby
Commanding
USS *Wisconsin* (BB-64)

P.S. I would rather you not discuss this with other midshipmen, as my duties allow me to interview only a tiny fraction of the first-class and fourth-class midshipmen aboard. I look forward to our talk.

Deborah tucks the letter into her dungaree pocket as the lights fade.

Scene Four:

Underway at sea in the Pacific Ocean, amidships, topside, on deck in the same location as in Scene Two.

Focus on Sheila as she reads a letter.

SHEILA *(reading):* At last, we are at sea again in the beautiful, blue, romantic Pacific! Huge swells have greeted us as we make our way down the west coast of South America. Rolling in from far across the Pacific, they seem to make life more interesting, and we can see the tiny destroyers in our group climbing up the swells and then moving down the other side like toys, or even "tin cans," as the Navy calls them, as they are caught in the immense power of the ocean.

Even the *Wisconsin*, which was as stable as a gyroscope, is now tilting in a rhythmic fashion as tiny amounts of foam come up and wash the white boards of the fantail. We have to keep track of our metal trays when we eat.

The effect is delightful, but Deborah and I can only wonder at what must be going on in those destroyers during mealtime. Tonight, we will watch another breathtaking sunset. Deborah seems to be quieter than usual.

Lights come up. Both women on deck in the glow of a sunset.

SHEILA: Something is on your mind; you just haven't been as talkative as usual.

DEBORAH: All right, you are my best friend and I know you can keep a secret, so I'll tell you but you are not going to believe this, and you will see he has asked me to keep this a secret, so I trust you will not let this get beyond the two of us?

SHEILA: Of course—so there is a "he"? Who can this person be?

DEBORAH: I was coming out of one of the forward engine rooms the other night and a Filipino handed me this.

Deborah takes a crumpled letter from her pocket and hands it over to Sheila who reads it in the remaining daylight.

SHEILA: Well, I knew there were pranks played on midshipmen, but I didn't think you would be a victim. It even looks realistic.

DEBORAH: Sheila, this letter was delivered to me by a Filipino steward, one of the crew who serves the wardroom.

SHEILA: Anyone can pass a few dollars to a steward, find some of the captain's stationery in the ship's office while doing some routine paperwork there and get the prank going.

DEBORAH: But what about this ID?

Sheila takes the ID card and examines it in the fading daylight.

SHEILA: Kind of like a driver's license sealed in plastic; looks like an official ship's seal and the words "Captain's Guest, USS *Wisconsin*, BB-64"

DEBORAH: No, Sheila, I think you are wrong this time. It's quite conceivable that the War College does require more senior officers to get in touch with what is going on, and an officer who makes good use of his time would use this cruise to get his prerequisite material in order.

SHEILA: And how do you explain that it requires the presence of one of the best looking midshipmen on this ship to "get in touch with what is going on?"

DEBORAH: Sheila, I thought you had more sense. It's clear to me that I was chosen at random!

SHEILA: And I suppose people were looking at you randomly back there in the canal? Deborah, there's no question in my mind that he's after you. Have you ever read such an excuse? No officer ever uses his first name, no officer tries to conceal what he is doing, and no officer makes such private appointments. Under the circumstances, he protects himself by at least having his chief of staff or executive officer around. How can you stand there and tell me that this is innocent? And think of the topic and what it could lead to! I can see now what that paper is going to say: "Upon closer questioning, a full sixty-five percent of the younger women of the Navy admitted to wanting to know their commanding officer on a more intimate basis, whereas many of the older women, eighty-three percent to be exact, said that intrinsic job satisfaction was more important." And all of this collected under the guise of a college campus! (*pause*) What are you going to wear?

Focus on Deborah, who reads her letter.

DEBORAH (*reading*): So, I have been thinking about this ever since Sheila and I talked. Sheila didn't ask me how the captain had found me out, or how he knew when I was standing an engine room watch. Either this whole thing is as innocent as cherry cobbler, or there must be several individuals helping the captain choose his interviewees and that group of people must be sworn to secrecy. I could talk to Commander Higgins, but that would ruin the whole thing.

First, it would ruin things if she were over suspicious of what was a very polite and valid request for information and Commander Higgins would not like having to see her name in the note. It would also ruin the romance of the thing, if there were any to be had. Not every young woman who has just completed her freshman year could say that during the summer, in the southern tropics, on an ocean voyage in the South Pacific, she had been invited to a private and discreet dinner party in the captain's sea cabin, admittance through a Marine Corps bouncer by prearranged guess pass!

Besides, the captain might just be unmarried, a lonely man in command of a World War II battleship on a mission of training midshipmen in waters where perhaps only research vessels working on El Niño sail. Is there anything wrong in answering a few questions on "women in the Navy" for such a one as he? It is obvious that this is not to be a captain-to-subordinate situation and that I am being treated like a fellow student at the War College who does not have the same rank.

I can't wear my blue dress folded up in the bottom of my locker, so I guess I will just have to try some jewelry and wash my hair. I have the next watch so I will have to sign off for now.

Scene Four:

The Captain's sea cabin on the after bridge of the USS Wisconsin. *On one side of the bulkhead, stands a marine sentry. Deborah Stevens is seen quickly touching her hair and attaching a pair of earrings as she approaches the marine. She is wearing a bracelet. She flashes an ID card and the Marine Corporal snaps to attention and then opens the door for her. She passes through the bulkhead and*

*enters the sea cabin. The door closes behind her. A male voice speaks from behind
a curtained-off space.*

HORNSBY: Is that you, Ms. Stevens?

DEBORAH: Yes, Captain.

HORNSBY: I will be with you in a minute. Make yourself
comfortable.

*Deborah sits down on a comfortable couch, takes in the surroundings and then
reads again from a letter. Lights focus on her alone.*

DEBORAH *(reading):* The first thing I noticed was the sheer intimacy and extraordinary taste in the décor. I had always known that uniforms
were of impeccable taste in almost every arena but I had never imagined
how the same could be said for the functional integration and design of a
sea cabin on a battleship.

First, it was comfortably air conditioned; the lighting was subdued
and the greens of the décor were coordinated from the paintwork to the
fabrics. It was as though some naval architect working away during World
War II had taken some special pains, but yet had not strayed from the
expected patterns and functional needs of his country. Toward the center of the space was a table set for two using the traditional cutlery and
service of the wardroom: white napkins with pewter holders, heavy silver
utensils, and sturdy goblets that were wet with condensation from the ice
and water inside, vessels that would not tip in the swells the ship was still
experiencing.

An uncluttered desk with comfortable leather-upholstered chairs
gave one area the atmosphere of an office. Radiotelephones and internal
communication equipment were within easy reach. Still another area or
space was that associated with a bed. It was more like a Pullman car
space in that it was recessed, had its own lighting, fan, and communication

equipment, as well as a speaking tube to the bridge in the event of a power failure. Here too, curtains were used and they were open and I could see a small reading light had been left on over an impeccably made-up pillow and spread. It was the kind of space where one would want to escape and curl up inside with a good novel before turning off the light and giving oneself over to the wonderful rolling swell of the waves.

There were also a library area, and a private wash area. Several other functions were beautifully woven into the elements that flowed unobtrusively from one to the next. One of these was a small private galley from which meals could be served and it was from this area that the voice had come and from which emerged an enormously handsome young man who seemed too young to be captain of a battleship, for he was certainly in his thirties. He offered me his hand.

Lights come up and Hornsby makes his appearance.

HORNSBY: Ms. Stevens? John Hornsby. I am sorry to have kept you waiting, but I let DelMundo have the night off and I needed to look after a few things. Have a seat. How are you enjoying the cruise?

DEBORAH: Well, I can see why everyone wants to go through the canal. There is such a wonderful transition between the open ocean and the green of the jungle. I imagine there is no other place in the world where that occurs. And, of course, I loved the shopping. *She adjusts her bracelet and glances at it for just a moment.*

HORNSBY: You're right; it never ceases to fascinate me. It's almost like coming into this cabin. From the open space of a huge ship to the quiet, cool, green center where one's mind can refocus. Why don't we have something to eat? DelMundo left things in pretty good shape. I, too, bought some things in Panama but I can't show them quite as publicly as that bracelet. If you can keep a secret we can try some of this cabernet I picked up in one of the Panamanian wine shops.

You know, years ago, our predecessors in the British service drank wine with every meal.

Hornsby helps Deborah with her chair and removes the warming covers exposing a delicious meal with several choices. He pours the wine.

DEBORAH: You know, I have wanted to ask you, Captain, how can such a young man be in command of a ship like this?

HORNSBY: Well, it's called accelerated promotion. If you keep doing the right things, concentrate on your work, and have luck, the Navy rewards all that with early promotion and the hope is that you will reward the Navy by staying here for several more years than usual. My War College tour coming up is another example of this thinking; I hadn't thought I would get there this soon.

Focus on Deborah, again reading.

DEBORAH *(reading):* He was extremely personable. He had that ability to put people at ease, to find common topics of conversation, and to intrinsically play down the fact that he was extremely handsome, as well. His uniform set off his sharp features, and the insignia of his rank only added to the synergism of all these visual impressions acting on me at the same time.

His life was the Navy, yet he was able to converse on just about any topic I could bring to bear from my freshman studies and talk about them intelligently.

Lights come back up.

HORNSBY: You know, some men join the Navy to escape women. They see life aboard ship as an exclusive male club with all the amenities. Others, I am certain, have the view of women that those lectures on venereal disease make so important, and if you were watching when we crossed the equator, you saw some rather ferocious passions come to the surface.

DEBORAH: Yes, Captain, there are a number of facets to the issue. But do you really think that I can add anything original concerning these things? This is my first cruise; I am just a midshipman, fourth class. I know that I can't turn those engine room valves as fast as the crew or even male midshipman. I am the one that should be asking you questions.

HORNSBY: Let me put it another way. Suppose you were on a ship, a ship like this one, and you started falling in love with another person. How would you handle that? You could ask for a transfer but that wouldn't solve the problem. You could resign and then find yourself married to a spouse who went on six-month cruises. Suppose this person was a superior or inferior in rank. I imagine the person could be from the enlisted ranks. How would you act, how should the Navy set policy based on its mission, and do you want to place yourself in a situation where these kinds of things are potential mines that can be run into?

Focus on Deborah, again reading.

DEBORAH *(reading):* When he started asking me these types of questions, I knew that I wanted to fall in love with him and, in fact, in the subdued light of that cabin, I wasn't certain that I hadn't already. There was no way I could answer such questions by myself. Two people needed to examine the consequences together and come up with whatever could be said on the subject and that analysis might be different depending on who these two were. At the same time, I had had several glasses of that glorious wine and the red of that liquid seemed to reflect my emotions.

Lights come back up.

Deborah holds the glass between her thumb and her forefinger and, twisting the glass, looks up at Hornsby.

DEBORAH: Captain, would you like to kiss me? If you would, the feeling is mutual.

Scene Five:

Inside the USS Wisconsin. *A loudspeaker is blaring "General Quarters, General Quarters, All Hands Man Your Battle Stations, General Quarters, General Quarters." Deborah and Sheila are striving to get to their battle stations, a gunnery control space containing the mechanical computer used to aim the big sixteen-inch guns.*

They both try to go through a door, but the crew has set Condition Zebra and they must find another route. Finally, they arrive inside their assigned space.

Focus on Sheila, reading her letter.

SHEILA: Deborah and I have our battle stations way down in the space where the computer controls the firing of the big sixteen-inch guns. We were going to fire them off the island of Culebra, near Puerto Rico, and I was worried about the goats that wander around the island. We barely made it to our battle stations during gunnery practice and I heard the bearings and ranges being fed into the computer. Finally, I heard the observing officer say, "check sight clear," which was the check to see that no goats had been sighted around the target. Shortly thereafter the entire ship shook.

Particles of dust came down from the cable tiers above. I looked across at Deborah and we both knew we would have to wash our hair that evening. Then the spotter's voice came over the sound-powered phones, "two thousand yards short." Now I began to be worried about some of the fish offshore. Either the final liberty in Panama was too much for the crew or there had not been enough practice. In any event, I still don't know what happened with Deborah and the captain, but maybe some frozen daiquiris will get her talking again.

Scene Six:

Guantanamo Bay Naval Base at the southern tip of Cuba. Deborah and Sheila are drinking frozen daiquiris at the bar.

SHEILA: So you still love him?

DEBORAH: Sheila, I don't know what happened, but if it could happen again, I would welcome the experience.

SHEILA: What kind of answer is that? You have dinner with John – I imagine he would have lit candles if he could have – and you are going back to school with what? A memory? Has he invited you to the War College for house parties?

DEBORAH: Well, let's suppose I had spent these eight weeks in Brooklyn or even San Francisco. Could I have met anyone like him?

SHEILA: I don't know, perhaps yes, perhaps no. You haven't even told me if he was married. You liked the wine and the atmosphere, and I don't think those cities have anything to compare. Was the same marine still on duty when you left?

DEBORAH: I don't remember and I didn't have those kinds of questions on my mind at the time.

SHEILA: What kind did you have?

DEBORAH: Oh, I guess just the loneliness of the sea, of command, of that inner longing for someone with whom to share a secret.

Curtain.

* * *

There is an old saying that 'Truth is stranger than fiction.' If I were asked if my return from the Midshipman Cruise of 1957 to Valpariso, Chile, would present me with a tale that involved so many aspects of what we have already discussed – all woven into a new pattern – I should have believed that feat impossible. I remember father picking me up at the old Illinois Central Railroad Station on Michigan Avenue in Chicago; my ultimate destination was Michigan – Jerp House – and the tale was a Michigan tale; perhaps, that all ties together like the tale itself? In any case, the Sophomore year at Princeton did not begin with a three-week class for engineers, consequently, that allowed me time in Michigan to unwind from the USS *Wisconsin* and points further south. After briefly discussing the cruise with father, the conversation quickly turned to the story he had to tell.

Father began by informing me that the day after I was to arrive at Bass Lake, at about 10 AM, I could expect a visitor to drive up to Jerp House in a white Cadillac to have a word with me. Father suggested I should be sitting in a lounge chair on the concrete platform in front of the Jerp House front porch. The story as to who the visitor was and why he wanted to speak with me involved a plethora of diverse elements: my father's career mindset (architect), my earlier September 1956 class (Elementary Surveying), a common interest I shared with father (scouting), my mother's mindset as to how to relieve the anxiety of untoward situations (mother's action plan), a Pentwater realtor (Harold Shaw), and father's purchase of additional property (the purchase of land *sight unseen.*)

Father purchased additional forested land from the State of Michigan in the amount of twenty acres; it was located in a plot of land laid out in 1903 called Pentwater Beach Addition No. 1 and was halfway between Pentwater and Jerp House. The story included one more factor, an $80,000 get-away summer home on the Lake Michigan waterfront; in the 1956-57 timeframe, that price tag was only for the wealthy. I shall refer to the visitor as Mr. T, and shall relate the situation as it was told to me soon after returning from my cruise.

"As soon as we return to Bass Lake, you will encounter Mr. T," began father, "he wants to talk to you and you will know him by the white Cadillac he drives."

"I see."

"He is an industrialist from Grand Rapids,"

"O. K."

"Mr. T was very anxious to build a lavish summer home on the Lake Michigan shore on lots adjacent to that fifty foot wide lot I own."

"There are two lots," I remarked, "because you own four-hundred feet back, and that takes two."

"That's right," agreed father, "the key thing though, is that those two lots form a land corridor for anyone having a residency, or even using some of the 'back twenty acres' to get to the Lake Michigan beach."

"Yes, they do."

"All right," continued father, "Mr. T was very anxious to build his $80,000 summer place; in fact, he was so anxious that he told the contractor to build a road across the land leading up to his dream home without a survey!"

"That can lead to problems," I remarked.

"There was another factor in the construction of his retreat: Mr. T told the contractor that the eve line – the south edge of his peaked roof – should be built so that it was right up to the edge of what he thought was the boundary line between our two lots and his property."

"That's not the usual practice," I said, "there should be *some* space left on his side; this is not the city."

"Well, after everything was built, someone, perhaps a friend or visitor, suggested he survey his land. Mr. T protested by saying that there was only one place to build his access road: on the flat ground where he built the road; the other back-portion of his land contained a small, wooded hill, and for this reason he put through the access road on the low ground."

"I think I sense what is coming," I said.

"Yes, you remember that those lot lines slant a bit; Mr. T's access road cuts across our property; he built the road without a survey and, most likely, thinks that money talks and that he can easily buy out the adjacent owner."

"But why does he want to talk to me?" I asked.

"When Mr. T drove up to talk to me while you were on your cruise, I told him that I gave over the future *use* of that land to my son who is currently on a cruise with the U. S. Navy to South America."

"O. K.," I replied.

"'Have you any idea what your son's intentions are?' asked Mr. T. "Yes, I have, was my reply. Then I went on to describe the back twenty acres of land that we owned. I explained that my son was very active in scouting, and that he intended to build a small Scout Camp for inner-city scouts on the back property. Because swimming is part of the scouting program, that land (implying the lots where Mr. T built his access road) is the only way that those boys will have access to Lake Michigan and the beach."

"I suspect that he didn't smile."

"I think it took only a moment for Mr. T to imagine groups of inner-city scouts running – and shouting – as they charged to their swimming period instruction. Here was a situation developing where an $80,000 rather secluded and private residence offered the view of noisy swimmers during the cocktail hour!"

"Precisely!"

"So now, Mr. T will be driving up at 10 AM on Saturday and asking you to confirm or deny these intentions."

To assuage their anxiety while I was on the *Wisconsin*, my mother insisted that her husband design a 'spite house.' It would be built next to Mr. T's house, eve-to-eve! Presumably, with a north window in the spite house facing the south windows in Mr. T's house, the neighbors would be able to both hear and see each other. Very cozy! But that was not necessary; Mr. T and father agreed to a *swap* of land. Mr. T would buy *four* lots to the south – one-hundred feet of Lake Michigan waterfront – from whoever owned them, and trade those four for the two lots over which he built his access road. He also agreed to put a road in on the back of the four lots for owner access.

But where did Mr. Shaw, the Pentwater realtor, come in? Mr. T hired Mr. Shaw to purchase the four lots for the swap. Later, after the swap deal was completed, Mr. Shaw told father that two of the lots were owned by a California woman who sensed that something was up and held out for what was then, a large sum $7,500. Father obtained his two lots for $200.

Here ends, then, a busy year. As far as Jerp House was concerned the 1957 Midshipman Cruise left two small evidences within that house. On a window pane between the main house and the front porch I pasted a colorful eight-inch square sticker commemorating the cruise. Less obvious was the Llama wool blank I purchased on a one-night side trip to Santiago, Chile; mother put it on a couch on the front porch of Jerp House.

Returning to Chicago and then, ultimately, to Princeton, New Jersey, I enjoyed 441 Witherspoon Hall for a second year as a single room! The Nassau Hall group that administers rooms kept their word after listening to my tale of woe with respect to my New York roommate. Regarding my room during the Sophomore year, my home away from home experienced no further changes; the furniture, curtains, tape recorder, cover for the typewriter, and the view to the west and north were all the same; the three flights of stairs were a bit more worn down but that couldn't be noticed.

The food at the dining halls was the same; when a freshman or sophomore brought a date into one of the dining halls, she received the same reception that other women received from time immemorial: all the male diners picked up their spoons and hit the tables with them; there was a cacophony of sounds until the date was seated; every single spoon in all the halls was pounded so that the normally curved portion of the spoon was now flat. This group action was a way to relieve the anxiety that awaited the sophomores in the spring; they were all anticipating their matriculation into the eighteen upper class eating clubs on Prospect Street. The process was called 'bicker.'

I shall not review the more-than-infamous Bicker of 1958. Suffice it to say that it made the front page of the New York Times! We are concerned with the topic of homes and, at the start of the junior year, both my physical residence – where I slept – and my eating location – eating club – changed as well as the number and nature of my roommates.

Collegiate Tutor Gothic
Cope and Stewardson
Blair Hall (First Floor Room – Junior Year)
6 Blair Tower (Tower Room – Senior Year)
Princeton University
Princeton, New Jersey
1897

I was asked by two classmates to join them in forming a 'triple' during the week-long bicker process. This simply meant that the three of us would be in a dormitory room together during the designated bicker hours. The eating clubs would send their representatives to conduct simultaneous interviews during those hours. We also joined together to enter the junior year room draw which meant that we would need a room accommodating three individuals.

The room we drew was on the ground floor of Blair Hall in a single-story wing that was separated by a sidewalk from Witherspoon Hall. The room was at the end of that wing and had a spacious living room with two large windows with good views. Below those windows were long built-in seats with cushions, a very typical architectural touch for the 1880's. Another touch was the fireplace. There were two bedrooms. One of my roommates, John, was a Philosophy major and a serious student. He went on to Harvard Law School and was soon a renowned Constitutional Law Professor and Dean of Stanford Law School.

We were right in giving John the larger bedroom; he had a desk, bed, a dresser, and a single window that was high up so he would not be distracted by people walking on the sidewalk between 'Spoon' and Blair. The room was quiet and John could study in his room and write his Junior Thesis on David Hume. Karl and I occupied the other room and used a double-decker bed.

We needed one addition to the living room: a mounted White-Tail Deer head trophy. Because I had a summer home in Michigan, I accepted the assignment of obtaining the deer trophy before the junior year began. My brother-in-law located an appropriate, used, trophy and I dutifully carried it on the train back to New Jersey, this, despite my attracting comments from youngsters on the train to their parents like "Mother, there's a Navy guy sitting up ahead and he has a deer head! I didn't think the Navy allowed those things." We felt it was unsafe to ship a mounted deer head on my ticket, no matter how many times we did that with trunks and no matter my having a father that could arrange it.

While John joined one eating club during bicker, Karl and I both joined another; it was well that John could be independent. The eating clubs were many blocks toward the east and one had to be on time for dinner, dressed in coat and tie. Elm Club possessed a lovely dining room with tables that were not long benches, neither were the spoons all flat on their bottoms. There were pleasant views through the windows unlike the Lower Eagle dining hall which had no windows and the other dining halls where the windows were so high up you couldn't see anything.

A trained staff served meals at Elm Club unlike the students at the dining halls; Elm, like all the clubs, had its own kitchen, the menu items varied – there was, for example, no Mystery Meat – and conversations were quiet. After dinner demitasse coffee was self-served in the Red Room, a tastefully-appointed, sunken room; this served to prolong the dinner hour – the living was genteel! You could, if so motivated, wear the Elm Club tie; since it was a silk, red and green tie, it seemed doubly appropriate before Christmas break.

The junior year, then, took on a different tone. In the first year there were the antics of my freshman roommate from New York; I can recall only one tale that involved playing a trick on a number of students, myself included, I'll talk about that in a moment. Karl, my roommate, was a math and economics major and he brought back many stories about the math and physics department professors. Karl always attended the afternoon teas in Fine Hall, a math department building, where both departments gathered – the two buildings, physics and math, were connected with a hallway. There were enough foibles going on with the math and physics departments to make for interesting conversations. I had no equivalent stories to tell about my department's foibles; it was quite deadpan, by comparison. I was, however, admonished by one professor, Professor Irish, more of that later as well.

Having grown up with a father who told stories endlessly – with many repeats of the same story – I felt that stories were very much part of home life and so it seems fitting that they should be resurrected for they are part of the fabric that was woven while occupying this New Jersey home, so different in their nature from the stories that occurred while occupying my next residence; a few from Princeton will suffice.

We begin with the trick played on a number of students who, like myself, were taking Physics 103 during the freshman year. It is important understand, my reader, that there were three freshman physics classes offered to each class; these were not sequential, i.e., you didn't go from Physics 101 to Physics 103 to Physics 105. Instead, you took, or were placed in, one of the three. Physics 101 was for Liberal Arts students, those fellows who couldn't stand the first three weeks of engineering, or died-in-the-woods Liberal Arts students from the get-go, like most of the student body and who, for some reason, took Physics 101 just because they wanted to know something about physics.

The Physics 103 class was for all the engineers; it used calculus – you were expected to pick up calculus while taking Physics 103 if you were, like myself, a student from a High School where it was never taught, albeit that I had four years of math at High School. Physics 105 was a honors physics class for those, probably private school students or elite public High School graduates, who had both calculus *and* an honors physics class 'under their belt' upon entry to Princeton.

The Professors who taught Physics 103 and Physics 105 were, by no means, unknown! They were brilliant physicists with worldwide reputations. John A. Wheeler who taught my Physics 103 class was a theoretical physicist renowned for his work in general relativity. Robert Dicke who taught Physics 105 was known for contributions to astrophysics, atomic physics, cosmology, and gravity.

John Wheeler's personality was the kind that brightens your day; he had a warm and caring smile; he looked distinguished, but he was kind, soft spoken, and unassuming; he was a fantastic teacher; he prefaced what he was about to teach with the truly confused nature of past thinkers who did something about their lack of understanding. Professor Wheeler never used notes and made great use of a huge, roll-up blackboard to great advantage. He had a full-time staff person who set up all his in-class experiments; before class we could watch this person making final adjustments to the equipment for those experiments.

Every experiment was ingenious; they reinforced his board work, there was a magical quality about them that fascinated everyone, and both before and after he performed the experiments he explained the principals and equations that articulated the laws of physics under discussion; historical perspectives were integrated seamlessly into his lecture, wherever necessary, to reinforce the learning process.

Graduate PhD students led the 'sections' where homework was discussed along with other topics. The PhD students competed with one another to write the midterm and final exam problems which were also, extraordinarily ingenious. I can still remember one of those exam questions; it involved a vertical thin-wire ring, a circle that was eight inches in diameter. At the top was a bead which went down one side of the ring to the bottom; the bead experienced no friction as it traversed the half circle – that was given as an assumption – nor were there any other effects like air resistance or the altitude of the ring, that were relevant. The bead did, however, have a mass. The exam question asked the student to develop the equations of motion so that you could find its velocity and acceleration at any given point from the top of the ring to the bottom. But I digress.

For some strange reason, I received a good grade on the Physics 103 midterm; I suspect it was due to pure fear! In any event, all the grades were public – like the final course grades that were posted in Richardson Hall after all classes. After the midterm, someone told me that my name was on a letter that was posted on the Physics Department bulletin Board. I actually took the time to walk down to the Physics building to look because I couldn't imagine what it could be about.

Sure enough, there was the letter written on the Physics Department's stationary; the letter stated that the following list of Physics 103 students are being promoted, transferred, to Physics 105! They should talk to So and So in the Physics Department. This was a blatant joke but because I hadn't failed the midterm – because I came from an underprivileged High School, you could say I was Mr. Gullible. I walked into the Physics Department office and asked for Mr. So and So; a PhD student was kind enough to say that someone was playing tricks.

My roommate, Karl, told stories about the Math and Physics Department faculty and two of his tales were about Professor Bargman, a Mathematics Professor. Professor Bargman had the nasty habit of checking out *all* the single copies that the Fine Hall library received for every new math book that arrived; he didn't want anyone else to read them before he had a chance to peruse them. The librarians were unable to say no to his insatiable curiosity; Professor Bargman knew when they were delivered and were available; he knew there were no limits on the quantity he could check out; no one could stand up to Professor Bargman and it appeared that he *did* read them; more about that in a moment.

But what happened when a student or, better yet, a Physics or Mathematics Professor wanted a volume that was due in on a specific date? Perhaps a friend failed to give him a complimentary copy but wanted to discuss something. It made no difference what the reason was, the book was never available, it had been checked out!

"By whom?" asked the upset Professor.

"Professor Bargman," answered the Librarian.

"Bargman again! This is the fifth time! Where *does* he keep all of those books?" asked the Professor.

"I suggest you look in the trunk of his car!" answered the Librarian.

Karl overhead that conversation and the tale was told at the Fine Hall teas but it was just a prelude to a Bargman-Wheeler encounter that my roommate told many times; in that sense, Karl was like my father. The story began with an announcement of an important lecture to be given by John Wheeler; being a theoretical physicist, the lecture promised to involve mathematics. The lecture was held in the large Physics classroom where the Introductory Surveying class was held by Professor Kissam and where John Wheeler taught my Physics 103 class.

You will recall the steep tiers of seats, rising up for a distance that accommodated large audiences. Professor Wheeler used the same roll-up blackboard; it resembled a twelve-foot roller board that Professor Wheeler could crank around – forward or back – thereby giving him twenty-four feet of clear space to write out equations, diagrams, etc.

The house was packed; the entire Math and Physics Department faculties were in the audience as well as all the PhD students from both those departments and all of the lesser students in those disciplines as well. Karl, my roommate, was there because he majored in Math and Economics; Professor Bargman took a front row seat on the right-hand side of the center aisle that ran upward. As per his usual delivery, Professor Wheeler used no notes.

The lecture – seminar – began and went along quite peacefully for some time; the early equations and diagrams had already begun to disappear at the top of and behind the roll-up blackboard and were being rolled downward when Professor Wheeler made a brief pause before proceeding with his math; John Wheeler was facing the roll-up blackboard and Karl said he sensed some slight hesitation but then Professor Wheeler continued in his usual fashion and rolled up the board about a foot.

All of a sudden from the front row there came a loud "NO!" Professor Wheeler turned around and saw that it came from Professor Bargman! Here was a distinguished, kind, and soft-spoken individual being abruptly interrupted by another person at the opposite end of a spectrum of personality types. You sensed that every Physics and Math Professor in the audience was hoping against hope that Bargman would be put down; after all, how many times had they wanted a new book but were afraid to pick the lock on Bargman's trunk!

But a put down was not John Wheeler's way. Professor Wheeler acknowledged his interruption with a quiet reply of "Yes, Professor Bargman," rolled back his most recent equations and began again. But Professor Bargman was still not satisfied, he let out another "NO!"

The process was repeated and began with Professor Wheeler's reply "Yes, yes, quite right, Professor Bargman." Professor Wheeler again rolled down what he had just written and revised his equation for a second time. The audience held their breath. The blackboard was rolled up and Professor Wheeler continued without interruption until the end of his lecture and asked for questions.

There was a third incident that Karl related that centered around a midterm exam that Karl took in a math class taught by Professor Spenser. It was a take-home exam and Professor Spenser graded the papers and passed them back. Professor Spenser returned the exams at the end of the class but one student was able to ask "Professor Spenser, are you going to review the answers to the midterm?" Everyone in the class wanted to ask the same question. "Oh, yes, bring that up at the start of our next meeting," was the reply.

At the next class meeting Professor Spenser did review the midterm; every problem except the last. At the next class the same spokesperson-student for the class asked "Professor Spenser, you didn't go over the last question. Are you going to review it?" Professor Spenser replied in the affirmative and gave a review of how to go about solving the problem of the last exam question; it was a procedural outline.

The next class arrived and Professor Spenser was again interrupted "Professor Spenser, several of us tried to follow your instructions but were unable to arrive at a solution. Could you please show us how your methodology works?" Professor Spenser realized that he had to put aside his prepared material for that class and revisit the last question on the midterm. He spent the entire class time on the problem but he couldn't find a way to make things come out correctly. He apologized and remarked "I think I have a solution at home; I'll bring it next class."

"At the next class Professor Spenser handed out copies of a thirty-three page paper that he published when he was ten years younger. "There, I knew I had a copy somewhere," he remarked as he handed the stack to the front row to pass back, but that was still not enough! At the next class a student began with a question about an equation on page 24; he didn't see how the transition between earlier equations and the particular one on page 24 could be made; how does it work? He asked. Again Professor Spenser focused his attention on the midterm exam question but he couldn't find his way and ne needed to teach the material he promised in the syllabus; how could he stop this hemorrhaging of his time?

Before the class ended he said that first: the paper received extensive peer review and second: it would not have been published without there being no problems throughout the entire text, but he had lost the thread, the link that now remained hidden after ten years passage of time! He needed to get on with the rest of the class material. It being common knowledge that professional mathematicians strive to perform the most complex aspects of their work before they arrive at the ripe old age of 36, the class acquiesced with Professor Spenser's wishes.

Having enough time brings us to my own experience when I was taken aside and strongly admonished by a Civil Engineering professor, Professor Irish. This advice was given to me in my Junior year, the year that all the Civil Engineering students took Advanced Surveying. It, too, used a book by Professor Kissam, Advanced Surveying. And, yes, it had many more photos of Professor Kissam. The class, as would be expected, had many hours of field labs where each team submitted solutions to surveying problems. One of the labs involved a survey that tied together existing monuments on either side of Lake Carnegie, a body of water where the Princeton Crews practiced rowing. The lab exercise involved lots of triangulation and the determination of distances between markers in the ground on either side of Lake Carnegie, distances that could not be measured with a steel surveyor's tape.

Because there were no digital computers that could be used for performing a large number of calculations in the Fall of 1958, the standard document, Peters Tables, put together in Germany between 1919-1922, was used. The tables consisted of ten place logarithms for all the numbers from 1 to 100,000 as well as logarithms for the trigonometric functions – sine, tangent, etc. – between 0 and 90 degrees for every thousandth of a degree. Using a Slide Rule for multiplication was reduced to adding two logarithms for the two numbers you wanted to multiply; the distance on a slide rule between one number and the next was equivalent to the logarithm so to multiply two numbers, you simply placed the vertical cross-hair on one of the numbers and then, using the sliding portion of the rule, added the second number – distance – to the first; adding was merely getting the two distances alongside each other; at the end of the distance, you glanced down and read off the result. By using logarithms multiplication became addition.

Peters Tables were enormous volumes; they took three years to create. By knowing the slide rule and the tiny distances between the numbers, you could imagine how much more accurate were the use of Peters Tables; between one number, say 34, and 35, you would have to have an infinitude of intermediate positions between 34 and 35 to get the cross-hair exactly on top of 34.463; with Peters Tables you would merely find the logarithm for 34,436, say 4.4589720861, adjust it to $4.4589720861 \times 10^{-3} = 1.4589720861$ and then add it to the other number's logarithm. This turned all of the otherwise enormous multiplications into a problem of looking up the logarithms, adding the numbers and then converting the resulting logarithm back to the final answer by using Peters Tables.

Despite the use of Peters Tables to simplify the work, the lab exercise was extensive and there were lots of calculations and re-calculations to adjust the field work according to standard surveying practices. At a certain point in time I sensed that we – our team of four – were not organized; at the rate we were going many hours would be added to the effort. The process was iterative and used electric calculators, and steps that included handling errors that couldn't be ignored.

I decided to take charge; I began organizing the work and developed a flow from one person to another; the result was a faster process where everyone understood which portion was being done by whom and what needed doing first. Two years later, as an Ensign in the U. S. Navy, I came to understand what I had implicitly done to complete the survey across Lake Carnegie. At that time, two years later, Chief Petty Officer Cox was the senior petty officer in my Division, R Division; he was an electrician by rate. When he organized a working group on the *Hank* (DD-702), the Destroyer I served on for three years, he used an expression to explain to me his rule: "Organize, Deputize, Supervise!"

I liked Chief Cox and whether it was the right or wrong thing to do, I made a batch of fudge and sent it down to the Chief Petty Officer's Quarters with my compliments to Chief Cox; the gesture was talked about but since many observers believe that it is the Chief Petty Officers that actually run the Navy, there was absolutely no way anyone would dare to question the gesture. A few months later, the Wardroom received a batch of fudge courtesy of Chief Cox. This digression is getting ahead of ourselves but with a close reading of what follows you will discover more about my fudge making as compared to Chief Cox's.

Professor Irish looked in on the collective effort to do all the analysis, adjustments, and final steps to complete the cross-lake survey. He observed my steps to organize, deputize, and supervise my peers. Before we finished the work he took me aside and said he was upset with the way I took charge; it was not the way to handle a group in the real world; he added that it would be a lesson for me on how not to lead a group with a common goal! I can't remember receiving any other pejorative comments during my four year stay in New Jersey.

As for Senior year at Princeton, Karl and I took a Blair Tower room, 6 Blair Tower; our bedroom was now octagonal! We put the double decker in the room but it always looked awkward; instead of a round peg in a square hole it was a rectangular bed in an octagonal tower room. Karl liked one feature of the room, a secret that he learned from the former occupant before he graduated. In the top of a big closet there was a trap door! We opened it and saw a huge, empty space; with a light bulb, or even with a candle, we saw that it was a hideout, and the prior occupant used it for just that. He often moved his date for the weekend into the space when there was a threat of the Proctors inspecting his room – the fateful knock on the door when there is a woman in the room after hours!

But like so many things during that four year stay in New Jersey, what I remember from that Senior year was a poem by Wallace Stevens; it seems that every time I took an English class – there were two of them – or an Architectural History class – there were three of them – or audited a Theology class – I kept, remembered, what I learned. It was as though the information, itself, was intrinsically, so fascinating that I retained it. This certainly was true of the poem I memorized from Carlos Baker's class, *The Emperor Of Ice-Cream* by Wallace Stevens:

The Emperor Of Ice-Cream

Call the roller of big cigars,
The muscular one, and bid him whip
In kitchen cups concupiscent curds.
Let the wenches dawdle in such dress
As they are used to wear, and let the boys
Bring flowers in last month's newspapers.
Let be be finale of seem,
The only emperor is the emperor of ice-cream.

Take from the dresser of deal.
Lacking the three glass knobs, that sheet
On which she embroidered fantails once
And spread it so as to cover her face.
If her horny feet protrude, they come
To show how cold she is, and dumb.
Let the lamp affix its beam.
The only emperor is the emperor of ice-cream.

It now becomes necessary to orient you, my reader, to the strategy we are about to pursue. I use the term strategy because we are talking about switching from a four-year home, Princeton University, more specifically Witherspoon Hall and Blair Hall, to a three-year home, USS *Hank* (DD-702), a General Purpose Destroyer:

Allen M. Sumner-Class Destroyer
Federal Shipbuilding and Drydock Company
Kearny, New Jersey
USS *Hank* (DD-702)
Launched May 21, 1944
Commissioned August 28, 1944

For those readers who are fascinated by numbers I should point out that another major event was to occur on August 28, 1965: my marriage to Christiane Wills in Youngstown, Ohio; in one sense, then, the *Hank* and I were 'commissioned' on the same day. Also note that while the *Hank* was launched on the 21st of the month, my own launching, as it were, occurred exactly 21 years later. But our interests lie with the notion of a home; for those pursuits it is important to note that the *Hank*, like Princeton before it and the Midwest – Illinois and Michigan – before that, will have more than one location as regards the act of sleeping – Forward Officer's Country and After Officer's Country – but the entire ship, like the entire campus of Princeton and Prospect Street, will be the scene of action.

I use these military terms because I have chosen to use a series of discrete tactical incidents to link these broader environments: a University and a Destroyer. The incidents are organized around a subtext which progressively links the two locations: Naval Air. However inexplicable this subtext appears at this point in our story, its employment will become clearer. We start this 'journey of transition' from late January 1957; the First Princeton Semester is finished and a brief rest period is offered before the second Semester starts.

In the John Sherman excerpt that follows we see the first of the Navy's attempts to interest a group of future officers – Princeton NROTC Freshman – in making a career as a Navy pilot at a point in time that was more than three years in the future. The trip is true in every detail, only John Sherman, my fictional name, is just that, fictional. The excerpt is taken from *Stories of Identity*:

* * *

Sherman had his own experience with naval aviation. Between semesters, during his freshman year at Princeton, in late January, the NROTC program offered a trip to Pensacola, Florida, to become more familiar with the Naval aviation program. Many signed up. When everyone arrived in Florida, it appeared that they would have opportunities to fly with an instructor in a high-powered, single-engine prop plane, and to go out on a carrier to watch pilots qualify for their final test, landing on a carrier.

When they were in the clouds over Pensacola, Sherman told the instructor in the two-seater aircraft, that his father owned a single engine aircraft since 1944, and had used it on business, and to fly to Michigan every weekend in the summer. He never did any acrobatics, but was very conservative and followed the shoreline of Lake Michigan using visual flight rules. On one occasion, one of his father's instructors conned him in to flying across Green Bay in Wisconsin, and then, in the middle of the bay, had turned off the engine, forcing Mr. Sherman to try to glide to the beach using the glide ratio of thirteen to one.

That glide ratio was not enough, and the aircraft was getting very close to the surface of Green Bay, before the instructor switched on the engine. "Don't ever do that again!" he told Mr. Sherman.

Now Sherman realized he could ask his pilot for "the works," the kinds of things you see in air shows, wing-overs, loops, dives, twists; he did not know the names exactly. He told the instructor that his father had never done any of those things but they were what he wanted. The instructor did as Sherman asked; perhaps he felt Sherman would be a very good prospect for the Naval Air program after he was commissioned, or maybe he just didn't get enough opportunity for that kind of thing in training new pilots. Sherman would never forget performing acrobatics among the cumulus clouds.

The next day, they went out on an aircraft carrier in the Gulf of Mexico. They were on an outside deck on the superstructure with a speaker turned on, so they could hear the pilot and a coaching instructor talk to each other as the pilots came in for their first aircraft landings. They practiced on land using a strip marked out the size of the carrier. Now the prospective carrier pilots had to catch the hook on the deck, and perform five out of seven landing attempts without getting a wave-off from the landing signal officer. If they failed, they would get switched into a land-based flight program.

Sherman and the other NROTC students could hear the coach as each aircraft approached, "You're looking good, pull her up a little, that's good, OK." Some of the group took a pencil and pad and kept track of the score. Wave-offs occurred at the last minute, requiring the student pilot to gun the aircraft, and get back up into the air for another precious try. There were failures and successes, and the coach knew when a pilot was on his last try and needed a final landing to continue this kind of training. It was every bit as hair-raising as the acrobatics.

* * *

One aspect of the Pensacola trip that was not related in the excerpt was the flight through a thunderstorm on the way to Florida. Flying through a thunderstorm was to be repeated on the second NROTC Midshipman 'Cruise' between the Sophomore and Junior years. On that cruise the time was not spent on a Navy ship nor did the Princeton NROTC students leave the United States. The first weeks were spent at Little Creek, Virginia, a Naval base, where we lived in Quonset huts, marched as a platoon to the mess hall, and participated in an amphibious landing al la the Pacific landings in WW II.

Our amphibious landing craft carried only personnel but the front dropped down and we climbed out through the shallow water and charged the enemy with our unloaded rifles and canteens of water; it was very hot! Ahead of us were instructors who fired blank shells and always retreated while firing so as to indicate where we were to pursue them. The idea behind these first weeks at Little Creek was to convince some of the NROTC students to sign up for the Marine Corps option, an option which redirected a NROTC student to Marine Corps studies and a different summer curriculum. The Marine officer who taught the program at Princeton was Major Minor!

Halfway through the summer cruise that wasn't a cruise, we again boarded a Navy piloted transport plane to fly us – through another thunderstorm – to Corpus Christi, Texas, on the Gulf of Mexico, for the second half of our summer training, a half devoted to Naval Air. But let me just interject the comment that flying through a thunderstorm is not just a hair-raising experience. There is a very special aesthetic dimension to viewing the flashes of lightning as they illuminate the huge cumulus clouds that you are flying through and around; the colors are spectacular, the clouds light up and are set pieces seen in all their glory; the effects are very special and are never forgotten; they really do take your mind off the idea that lightning might strike the plane.

After our arrival at Corpus Christi we assembled in a small auditorium for our introduction. A Naval officer came out for the first presentation, a preview of coming attractions. I remember two things that brought the house down. He began by asking his audience, "And where are you guys from?" and was appropriately answered "Princeton." He paused and then replied, "Oh, I remember now, that's where they give you an attitude instead of an education!" The second item I remember involved a story he told about training World War II pilots, an Instructor/Student story. Here it is as an excerpt from *Stories of Identity*:

* * *

Sherman remembered another story that was told about naval air training. One of the key goals of an instructor was to get the student to land the plane, completely on his own, as soon as possible. Sherman could remember the day his father soloed, they gave him a certificate. There was a cartoon on it that showed a small baby bird being more or less kicked out of a nest by its parent.

The Naval air story involved an instructor who used two ways to get a student to land the plane when the student was ready but just wouldn't do it. Using the first method, the instructor would call the student's attention to himself, and then bend over, and remove the bolt that held the "stick" in place; this was the stick that controlled the aircraft. He would raise the stick above his head to the student, and then, forcefully, throw it out of the aircraft. This forced the student to use his own stick to land the plane.

The second method was merely to bail out of the plane. One student, so the story went, knew that he was going to be tested and sensed to the day when the instructor might pull something to get him to land the training aircraft. On that day, he managed to locate an extra stick and place it under his seat. Sure enough, after being in the air for an hour, the instructor in the front seat called the student's attention to himself, bent over, and after detaching his stick, held it up, and threw it out of the aircraft. The student then reached for the stick under his seat and tapped the instructor on the shoulder. The instructor turned around in time to see the student hold the stick above his own head and throw it out of the aircraft.

This time the student *did* have to land the plane on his own; the instructor bailed out! Sherman decided not to sign up for the naval air program at graduation.

* * *

Corpus Christi is base for Navy Seaplanes and one of the coming attractions was a takeoff, flight, and landing in a seaplane; I recall a lot of vibration. But the real highlight was a trip in a Navy jet. The flight did not begin from the deck of an aircraft carrier but it was a two-seater, just like the prop trainer was at Pensacola during freshman year and it flew a lot faster. I gave the instructor who took me up the same story I gave at Pensacola: father never did acrobatics, flew visual flight rules, etc., ending in my plea for 'the works.'

The instructor started doing tricks but suddenly noticed that someone didn't refueled the aircraft and he had to go back; he was sincerely sorry that he couldn't put the plane through all that it was capable of. To keep the kettle boiling, with respect to a career in Naval flying, in the minds of NROTC students, especially those on a summer cruise between the Junior and Senior year, the Navy used the aircraft carrier USS *Valley Forge* (CV-45) for that eight week cruise.

Essex-class Aircraft Carrier
Philadelphia Naval Shipyard
USS *Valley Forge* (CV-45)
Launched July 8, 1945
Commissioned November 3, 1946

In the mere space of nine years – 1950 to 1958 – I had progressed from Valley Forge, Pennsylvania, to the USS *Valley Forge* (CV-45), with ever so many intermediate stopping points. It is instructive to compare these two homes, one a brief week, lived under a canvas tent on land, the other, an eight-week cruise in the Atlantic ocean, lived, as we shall see, under the busy flight deck of an aircraft carrier. You guessed correctly: keeping awake in one environment would center around poison-ivy anxiety, and in the other, keeping awake was no worry at all, the nightly take-offs and landings would do the trick.

On the *Valley Forge* cruise I was a First Class Midshipman and there was an expectation that, collectively, the First Class Midshipmen would be assisting the 4th class Midshipmen on their first cruise. On the USS *Wisconsin*, as far as I can recall, the First Class Midshipmen had their own quarters; on the USS *Valley Forge* 4th and 1st class Midshipmen shared the same living compartment. This consisted of tiers of racks – six racks to a tier – that rose, one above the other like a huge ladder of racks, in a large compartment under the flight deck. Sleepers on the top racks became adept at climbing up the lower racks to arrive at their place of repose. This was similar, rack-wise, to those lower deck compartments on the USS *Wisconsin* where I stood watches as a penalty for gear adrift; the difference was that on the USS *Valley Forge* there was plenty of fresh air for all residents of the compartment. As already alluded to, there was another factor to disturb everyone's slumbers: the nightly flight operations. All the Midshipmen became aware that the USS *Valley Forge* pilots were on a training cruise as much as we were.

It made no difference as regards noise whether you were a third-tier sleeper – like I was – or directly under the flight deck at the top of the tier. There was some respite from these seagoing interruptions because the *Valley Forge* visited Bermuda and Halifax, Nova Scotia; in Halifax a social event was scheduled that included a mixer and, for this Midshipman, a subsequent trip to a summer home outside Halifax. But the idea that the 1st class Midshipmen should be teaching something to the 4th class Midshipmen didn't seem to have any purchase on the cruise.

That lack of educational influence on the 4th class Midshipmen held sway until this seeming idleness began to occupy my thoughts. Thinking back to what the First Class Midshipman did on the USS *Wisconsin*, I recalled that they did very little. Then one day the conjunction of two ideas crystalized in my mind what it was that we should do. I leave it to the psychologists to explain how these bright ideas are hatched. For now, I can only explain what they were.

The first idea arose from the admonition I received from Professor Irish during the early part of my Junior year; you know, the one that I was taken to task for 'organizing, deputizing, and supervising' my colleagues in our surveying team. In order to implement my plan on the *Valley Forge* I had to do just that; I had to explain to my fellow Princeton NROTC 1st class Midshipmen exactly what it was that I felt we should be doing and then suggest the organization plan which involved enlisting volunteers to execute the plan, not to mention, bringing the plot to the attention of the Midshipman Liaison Officer. In all this I assumed the supervisory role.

The germ of the second idea was staring me in the face ever since the first day of the cruise. Whenever I climbed up to my third-tier rack I glanced upward to those racks belonging to those racks and mattresses occupied by, hopefully, more athletic Midshipman, and I spied a flagrant breach of Naval Discipline: Gear Adrift! Here was a cherished rule of the Navy being flouted by all kinds of clothing and other 'stuff' that was peeking out from under mattresses throughout the compartment; we First Class Midshipmen needed to bring this to the attention of the Midshipman Liaison Officer and offer our services to collect all those items into several sea bags, lock up the bag in a space, and facilitate their return so that a 'Captain's Mast' could be convened to award extra duty hours to the miscreants.

My plan was welcomed by all involved including the Midshipman Liaison Officer who, as is usual on such cruises, is looking for things to do. In no time at all, five or six First Class Midshipman filled several sea bags of drifting gear and locked the bags in a space assigned to us by higher authority. To demonstrate my own leadership amongst my peer group, I personally assisted in the collection effort. With one blow I had assuaged my own extra duty hours awarded to me for my miscreant washcloth on the *Wisconsin*, and proven to myself that, in some social environments, the organize/deputize/supervise ethic *is* an applicable, if not welcome tactic!

As you must recall, blessed reader, we are following a strategy oriented around the theme of Naval Air which will facilitate the transition from Princeton University to the USS *Hank* (DD-702). There are three experiences that prompted me to check the option 'Small Combatant' on the standard form that all Seniors filled out and that was used by the Navy's Personnel Department to assign ships to newly commissioned officers, i.e., Ensigns.

My first experience was a conversation I had with a Chief Petty Officer while on the flight deck of the USS *Valley Forge*. We were both watching a destroyer that was refueling from the *Valley Forge* about fifty yards away on the starboard side of the carrier. Midshipmen, like so many others who understand the Navy, recognize the wisdom and intelligence of Chief Petty

Officers when it comes to all matters Naval; we, too, agree that they ran the Navy and so it is no wonder that I posed a question to the Chief standing near me. I asked about what type of request, i.e., what type of ship should I put down at the end of the academic year. The excerpt that describes this conversation is taken from *Stories of Identity*, p. 89, and begins with a paragraph on the discernment of character:

* * *

For Sherman, the Navy seemed to be a laboratory for the exact discernment of character, from the Captains of the *Hank,* Captains O, D and M, to each and every person aboard. A smaller ship felt a greater demand for highly visible competence and expertise. Everyone's effort was subject to close scrutiny and there was an implicit demand that every individual be skilled and reliable. Often multiple skills were present in a single individual who must be relied on.

This attitude was reinforced when Sherman was on his final midshipman cruise on the aircraft carrier *Valley Forge.* He had never set foot on a destroyer, and was standing on the hangar deck, watching the destroyers come alongside, one by one, to be refueled. He was chatting with a Chief Petty Officer, and felt he needed to know the answer to a question. "In a short time, I'm going to have to fill out a form that asks for the kind of ship I want to serve in during active duty. What type should I put in for?"

The chief pointed to the destroyer currently alongside. "On a destroyer, you eat every meal with the Captain in the wardroom, sitting at the end of the table. A Chief Engineer, head of the Engineering Department, is a Lieutenant Junior Grade on a destroyer, and stands watches on the bridge and qualifies as an Officer of the Deck Underway. On this ship, the Chief Engineer is a full Commander, the same rank as a Captain of a destroyer but he's only a department head. You have full responsibility for everything when you are Officer of the Deck. Usually on a ship this size, as you've seen on the bridge, you are never given full command at so young an age.

"Mind you, third class petty officers on a destroyer, if they have the smarts, are given full control of an engine room or boiler room watch."

"I see," said Sherman.

The chief continued, "Everyone has to pull his weight. Merit is immediately obvious. Jobs performed by Chief Petty Officers, and a few subordinates on an aircraft carrier, are done by third and second class petty officers over there," and he again pointed to the destroyer that was starting to pull away from the *Valley Forge.* "Skills are seen and recognized by everyone; even during peacetime, destroyers make heroes. There's no comparison; put in for a destroyer."

Sherman was convinced and took the Chief's advice. During his junior year, he was able to read Joseph Conrad and he realized, like Marlow in *Youth,* that this might be his only opportunity to internalize those last lines that ended with words that would never leave him:

* * *

Ah! The good old time – the good old time. Youth and the sea. Glamour and the sea! The good, strong sea, the salt, bitter sea, that could whisper to you and roar at you and knock your breath out of you.

He drank again.

By all that's wonderful it is the sea, I believe the sea itself – or is it youth alone? Who can tell? But you here – you all had something out of life: money, love – whatever one gets on shore – and, tell me, wasn't that the best time, that time when we were young at sea; young and had nothing, on the sea that gives nothing, except hard knocks – and sometimes a chance to feel your strength – that only – what you all regret?

And we all nodded at him; the man of finance, the man of accounts, the man of law, we all nodded at him over the polished table that like a sheet of brown water reflected our faces, lined, wrinkled; our faces marked by toil, by deceptions, by success, by love; our weary eyes looking still, looking always, looking anxiously for something out of life, that while it is expected is already gone – has passed unseen, in a sigh, in a flash – together with the youth, with the strength, with the romance of illusions.

* * *

As Sherman saw the destroyer pull away from its refueling position, he knew that he, too, was a victim of the romance of illusions; what the chief said and more, came true. The second experience, as quoted in the last excerpt, was my reading of Joseph Conrad's stories at Princeton when I was able to take one of those rare classes that were not engineering, architectural, or NROTC pursuits. The story was called *Youth* and it has been read many, many times; we will soon excerpt from another story that was read in that class, *The Shadow Line*, and in many respects, the *Hank* experience *was* a shadow line experience. But we are interested in what it was that cemented my choice and it was a romance with the reality of a destroyer that did the trick even though, as remarked in the excerpt, I had never set foot on a destroyer, nonetheless I knew that type of ship was what I wanted; it happened this way.

After the cruise on the USS *Valley Forge* was finished, I found myself about a hundred yards away from a pier of tied up, nested, destroyers; there was a grassy field between where I stood and the group of destroyers side-by-side. I am moved to paraphrase those words from the musical *South Pacific* that suggest that "Some enchanted evening, You may see a stranger, You may see a stranger, Across a crowded room, And somehow you know, You know even then, That somewhere you'll see her, Again and again."

In the excerpt that follows I speak about how I felt when I spotted that group of destroyers in the nest; the excerpt is taken from *Dawn* and I refer to myself as 'child:'

* * *

The child recalled the first time he *really* observed a destroyer at the Norfolk, Virginia, Naval base. His summer cruises in the NROTC program were never aboard a small combatant; they were, instead, on the battleship U. S. S. *Wisconsin* (BB-64) and the U. S. S. *Valley Forge*, an aircraft carrier. At that particular, almost cathartic moment – in the sense of relieving the child's emotions – he focused intensely, almost frozen in his gaze, for an extended period, on a particular destroyer; it was the first time that he actually *saw* a destroyer; the other times he had merely glanced at that type of ship. The time was approaching when he would have to decide on what category of ship he would request for his three years of active duty. For some reason, the *presence* of a destroyer as a generic symbol had not as yet transfixed his focus; now the time had come and, like a feminine face seen at a distance, the unknown ship left a life-long impression.

Across a quarter of a mile of open space the child looked up and saw for the first time a creation that was both beautiful and unique. She had everything that a large combatant – like a cruiser or a battleship – but it was more, for it was all compressed into a tightly mixed complexity of distinctly functional elements. In one sense it possessed the attraction of a model ship where every mast, radar, antenna – in short, every detail – was present but the architecture – miniature as it was, yet unified in its own special way – held him in a state of suspension and wonder. What would it be like to live on so small yet so beautifully designed piece of naval architecture? The fascination of the miniature captured his imagination; he fell in love at first sight! The child as a NROTC midshipman knew in an instant that if he were to go to sea for an extended period of time he would need that intimate feeling of *romance* to sustain and reinforce the time spent, a period that, perhaps, would even redefine him. The ship worked its magic upon him; it possessed that quintessential sense of loyalty, excitement, and touch of feminine personality that only a long and perfect marriage could supply.

* * *

As we approach the *Hank* I suspect there are misconceptions that need to be addressed before we 'request permission to come aboard' to the Officer of the Deck. There was a time when I was wary of spending three years away from my alleged – imagined – profession – pursuing Civil Engineering through one of the numerous branches of that discipline. If I were asked what type that would be I would have answered a Structural Civil Engineer, even though there are more Civil Engineers of that particular stripe employed in the manufacture of aircraft. I certainly did not envision becoming involved in: water supply and sanitation, highways, dams and other large construction projects like bridges, tunnels, waterways, soil mechanics, and traffic and transportation studies although the foundations for many of those disciplines were set in place at Princeton. At a later time in this saga we shall examine a letter, *My Purpose and General Plan for Graduate Work*, and will be able to see if any alterations occurred during my time on the *Hank*.

Returning to our examination of misconceptions, it is certainly true that an even greater fear of total concentration on things naval was the loss of expertise through time and focus on matters that had nothing to do with an engineering career. This fear was one aspect of a larger question: What would be the effect on my entire life? How would these three years look to me from a perspective of ten, twenty, or even more years in the future? Would those years stand up against so many other future endeavors? Wouldn't they be some kind of, to use Professor Wheeler's terminology, a Black Hole, where the event horizon sucked me in never to be seen again due to the unknown bourn into which I was entering and would have difficulty returning from?

Heaven help the person who fears a future that turns out to be a joyful, and nourishing experience! My verdict that those days aboard the *Hank* were the birthplace of values and future pursuits to the extent that those three years not only have a lifelong effect that I am particularly grateful for, but that the only metaphor appropriate to that period, is the birth of stars and the explosion of supernova wherein we discern the origin of many elements that help one fashion the stuff of the rest of one's life.

Unlike the Princeton experience then, which focused on the acquisition of knowledge and would be overlaid, again and again, by more knowledge, the effects of the Naval experience would never be overlaid, never lost, never forgotten, and could never be overlaid; it possessed a cornucopia of unending fascinations that poured forth in a constant stream; it became part of my personhood to a degree that I could never have predicted. And so the *home* that is responsible for this phenomenon must be examined very carefully. It was no idle show for it strengthened and supported not only the military objectives of the *Hank* but was the perfect antidote to the sequestered life of a New Jersey student who needed to act, act in the living present, as per Longfellow's *A Psalm of Life*:

> Trust no Future, howe'er pleasant!
>> Let the dead Past bury its dead!
> Act, – act in the living Present!
>> Heart within, and God o'erhead!

But we must return to that claim of a supernova-like experience to see the sparks before we look closer into several of those antidotes to four years of Princeton and how they cast their spell, and achieved such lasting effects. We spoke earlier of the external attraction of a nest of Destroyers seen from across a crowded field, but what does that stranger bring you after three years? For "somehow you know, you know even then that somewhere you'll see her again and again."

There is something that is intrinsically comforting in life aboard a Destroyer, in experiencing all the three-hundred and seventy-six feet of a home. Part of this has to do with the peace, the regularity, the orderliness, the predictability of a military life. Tolstoy begins to explain this feeling in Book five of Chapter 13 of *War and Peace* when Nicholas Rostóv returns to his regiment. I have placed that excerpt and another from Joseph Conrad's story, *The Shadow-Line*, in Appendix F.

But these two excerpts speak of a *return* – to a regiment – and an arrival to a sailing ship; but there is something else, something that, over time, becomes an ever present memory of a home that you can never leave, a concentrated presence within your permanent memory; this presence includes the affinities of a home because of the intimate familiarity with the physical details of every space; it includes the smell of freshly baked bread wafting up to the bridge on the midwatch; it includes the joy, the sheer excitement, of conning your ship to a new station at high speed or exactly following in the colorful wake of an aircraft carrier as it makes its wide turn to a new course; it includes the wonder of seeing for the first time the sights that surround you as you enter harbors throughout the world and are too numerous to list; it includes all the stories that recount the personal interactions involving the conjunction of events and individuals; it includes the aesthetics of sunrise and sunset, the crystal waters of the ocean with flying fish and dolphins puncturing the sunlit surface; it includes the heat at the bottom of the Red Sea and the bitter cold in Genoa, Italy, in the depths of winter; it includes the blessing of having work to do while cruising the world, the ability to return home from a trip ashore to your own, familiar, private space where you can grab a peanut butter sandwich before retiring into the security of your surroundings.

None of these things are truly understood at the outset; they have to be lived! Literature can only give us a hint but if we are sensitive to the transformation that is going on we can see our own, individual, Shadow-Line being crossed and leaving us changed in whatever mysterious ways the exigencies of fate have brought all these treasures to our attention. Let us, then, look at the beginning, not from the standpoint of a Nicholas Rostóv or a newly appointed Captain, but from the standpoint of a child as per this excerpt from *Dawn*:

* * *

But the child as an Ensign, USN, still had never set foot on a destroyer, let alone the U. S. S. *Hank*, the ship destined to be his chosen companion for three years. He longed to get on board, to begin the life that he had envisioned but a delay of two weeks was caused by the *Hank* being at sea; his Captain-to-be enrolled him in two one-week classes. Sherman received the following letter while still at Princeton:

* * *

Ensign John Sherman, USN
6 Blair Tower
Princeton, New Jersey

Dear Mr. Sherman:

Thank you for your letter in which you indicate your reporting date of 19 June. I take this opportunity to welcome you. *Hank* is a 2200-ton short hull, Sumner class general purpose destroyer that can do any job she is called upon to do, and we pride ourselves in doing every job well.

Perhaps your immediate concern is our operating schedule. At this time our schedule is not firm but I will give my best predictions:

6 June – 3 July   Escort Newport – Bermuda Yacht Race
3 July – 10 July   Upkeep, Des-Sub Piers, NorVa
11 July – 11 Aug   To be assigned
12 Aug – thru end of year   ASW ready groups *
11 Jan – 15 April   Shipyard overhaul, NorVa

*The "ASW ready groups" is part of the Hunter-Killer Force which spends alternately 2 weeks at sea and 2 weeks in port.

So you see from the above we will probably be enroute to Bermuda on 19 June so I have arranged for you to attend Courses 401 and 402A (Basic and Advanced Damage Control), at the Fleet Training Center, Norfolk. These are one week courses held at the Main Naval Base in Norfolk. As you will be reporting while *Hank* is at sea, I have modified your orders and you will report to ComDesFlot 4 aboard the U.S.S. *Sierra* (AD-18). Have your orders endorsed and then report to BOQ at NOB (Main Naval Base) to get a room for two weeks. The BOQ will provide you with a room at no cost and you will be able to get meals there at a reasonable price.

We expect to return to Norfolk the first week in July and will be looking forward to seeing you.

Sincerely,
M. H. O.
Commander, U.S.N.
Commanding

* * *

The child as Ensign finished the two classes and transferred his belongings to U. S. S. *Sierra* (AD-18) a destroyer-submarine tender – the kind of ship that stays alongside a pier for months on end.

He slept well during that single night that he stayed on the *Sierra*, woke up, took an inner passageway to the wardroom, and ordered a good breakfast. The child knew that a 'nest' of destroyers had come alongside during the night and were now aligned in a row of ships outboard from the *Sierra* like cordwood; it required walking across the amidships passageways of every intervening ship for any individual to reach the far edge of the nest if the outer ship were his destination. The new reporting Ensign was not certain he could identify *his* ship amongst the nestlings but he savored the attempt all during breakfast and resolved, once his cloth napkin had been returned to the green tablecloth, to exit by the starboard side door to the main deck of the tender and peek from above, as it were, down into the nest where one of the ships *must* be the destination wherein he would find the fulfillment of all his expectations. His perusal of the *Hank* from above, without using the practiced eyesight of a destroyer man, had both differences *and* similarities with respect to the new captain in Conrad's story, *The Shadow-Line*:

* * *

"My rapid glance ran over her, enveloped, appropriated the form concreting the abstract sentiment of my command. A lot of details perceptible to a seaman struck my eye, vividly in that instant. For the rest, I saw her disengaged from the material conditions of her being. The shore to which she was moored was as if it did not exist. What were to me all the countries of the globe? In all the parts of the world washed by navigable waters our relation to each other would be the same – and more intimate than there are words to express in the language. Apart from that, every scene and episode would be a mere passing show. The very gang of yellow coolies busy about the main hatch was less substantial than the stuff dreams are made of. For who on earth would dream of Chinamen? . . .

"I went aft, ascended the poop, where, under the awning, gleamed the brasses of the yacht-like fittings, the polished surfaces of the rails, the glass of the skylights. Right aft two seamen, busy cleaning the steering gear, with the reflected ripples of light running playfully up their bent backs, went on with their work, unaware of me and of the almost affectionate glance I threw at them in passing toward the companion-way of the cabin."

* * *

The child as naval officer needed no assistance to find the *Hank* – she was the first ship in the nest – and he could slowly walk the deck of the *Sierra* from the *Hank's* fo'c'sle to her stern and stare down directly into all the elements that naval architects designed into her physiognomy. This encompassed a distance of 376 feet every detail of which, both above and below, would be indelibly imprinted on the child's memory during the next three years; even the underwater profile would be known from the two periods in dry dock during her routine overhaul every eighteen months. His survey was one of continuous fascination! It all beckoned to him and it seemed as though every object had a tinge of romance as though their functionality was christened with that quality at birth.

The men and officers of the *Hank* seemed all asleep – tired, perhaps, from their exertions in connection with the Bermuda Yacht Race – except for one seaman below him on the forward part of the ship. Again, his emotions seemed to take hold of him for the child as naval officer could remember forcing an intense stare downward to the solitary individual who was oblivious not only to the stare but also to its intent. And, if the truth be told, the child could not have articulated his own purpose as well. He remembered the single seaman at work just the same. He worked in the 'deck force' and would have no contact with an officer in the engineering department – the child's ultimate destination.

But well over a year later Drost, for that was his name, achieved a small bit of notoriety. The *Hank* was entering the port of Piraeus, Greece, while assigned to the Sixth Fleet in the Mediterranean for six months. All the ships of the squadron were in column formation, one behind the other at the prescribed distance. The child was dressing before going up to the wardroom for a bite to eat and was alerted by the 'One MC' – the general ship-wide announcing system – with the boatswain's call "Man overboard, man overboard, all hands muster on station!" He assembled on the fantail with 'R' division; the child was the division officer for R division and re-ported to the bridge that all men were present and accounted for. Others knew that it was Drost who fell overboard – they threw him a life preserv-er. He was putting up the awnings in preparation for Piraeus and liberty in Athens, when he overreached and fell into the channel – the only *actual* man overboard in the child's three years of active duty.

Like the hummingbirds that flew long distances from their far-flung places of origin to the feeders hung from the branches of many trees sur-rounding his summer home in Michigan, the child unconsciously thought that this, as yet unseen assemblage of souls, now asleep, were resting in their tiny nests of warmth, companionship, challenge, esprit de corps, soli-darity, adventure, and, yes, even romance. It was as though the nest of the squadron's destroyers was merely a metaphor for their unseen and tiny rest-ing place, a collection of unique personalities that, at the same time, was the living, breathing, human legacy, handed down from crew to crew, and officer to officer, across sixteen years.

The child as Ensign saluted the Officer Of The Deck and requested permission to come aboard. Now he would be walking the deck toward forward officer's country where he would be bunked in the most forward living space in this starboard-side suite of three sections. It was awkward to descend the narrow ladder that led down from the forward main deck house to the forward most cramped environment of his new quarters. The child was assigned the uppermost bunk in the space; his roommate was a year ahead of him and also a Princeton graduate assigned to the operations department. Many years later the child researched the *Hank's* history and learned how *Hank* had earned the WW II battle decorations he had spotted from the *Sierra*; they were due, in part, to an attack of five kamikaze planes while she and the destroyer *Borie* patrolled the entrance to Tokyo Bay on August 9, 1944.

The child's living space in forward officer's country was hot – his bunk was only three feet below the main deck which was warmed by the sun – but there was a fan for circulation and, like every compartment on the *Hank*, the muffled roar of supply and exhaust fans within the ventilation system could be heard. As his three years progressed, the child was to migrate from forward officer's country to, ultimately, the Chief Engineer's quarters in after officer's country, but that would occur almost two years after he had stepped aboard for the first time. In the meantime every ladder, passageway, compartment, engine room, boiler room, and engineering space, storeroom, living compartment, in short almost every compartment that was, in one way or another his responsibility by virtue of ubiquitous responsibilities that extended to the engineering department, were being imprinted on the child's permanent, long-term memory. He knew this to be true for, the child as an adult, had lived for all his married life – forty-six years as of the year 2011 – but a mere three-quarters of a mile from Chicago's Museum of Science and Industry where, he could, in a basement exhibit, peek inside the large eight foot long cutaway models of WW II destroyers and recall that everything was modeled as it should be; he was prompted, now as a museum spectator, to remember his experiences in specific spaces during those three brief years.

The Chief Engineer, his department head and another Princeton Engineering graduate, assigned him as the R division officer; the personnel responsibilities of that position included a miscellaneous group of ratings from electricians and interior communications specialists to damage control, ship fitters, and auxiliary equipment specialists. Every piece of morale-building equipment was R division's responsibility from the laundry to the air conditioners and scuttlebutts (drinking fountains); from the care of the single motor whaleboat (used for ferrying liberty parties back and forth to the liberty ports in the Mediterranean and elsewhere, and to pick up downed pilots and astronauts) to the high and low pressure air compressors (that powered the numerous air-driven tools used to remove paint and perform other tasks), refer compressors (cold storage for food), movie projectors, emergency fire pumps, the gyroscope, everything electrical in the entire ship (like fans, every motor in the entire ventilation system, ovens, and stoves in the galley), and emergency diesels.

The child as R division officer stood behind the Captain as he made his weekly material inspections; as R division officer – which also made him *Hank's* Damage Control Officer – he became an expert on the signage of every detail that needed to be stenciled in color coded information – in every compartment – in the event of an emergency. Sailors had a habit of forgetting to repaint, using a stencil, over the prior information, information which was legion; it required the use of many kinds of stencils. R division personnel took the lead in Damage Control and formed the core of organized Damage Control Parties who inventoried and accessed Damage Control Lockers and were the first individuals to the scene of a fire or an actual area of enemy damage like a hole in the hull of the *Hank*. R division maintained the portable pumps that were used in emergencies to, for example, pump out flooded compartments, as well as the *atomic attack water wash-down system* which, in the event of an atomic attack, was like a car wash for, when activated, and in working condition, it was capable of enveloping the *Hank* with spray.

* * *

The child as adult reflected years later and came to the conclusion that his first job aboard the *Hank* and his Princeton career were similar.

The similarity between the two environments came about because the child's superior for his first year on the *Hank* was a brilliant Princeton graduate – there were three Princeton officers on board the *Hank* for that first year – in aeronautical engineering. This Princeton graduate, the Chief Engineer, was very personable, popular, an extremely competent naval officer and, as affected the new R division officer, made clear that one of his *major* objectives was to have every single piece of equipment on the *Hank repaired and working at all times!* This strategy took up the entire efforts of the new R division officer and his men. Every leaking valve in the engineering spaces was pursued with a vengeance so that a 'tight plant' would have a surplus of fresh water for the crew and officers, laundry, and galleys where meals were prepared.

But the flip side was that damage control drills – the kinds of training that prepared you for a real war *or for getting a satisfactory grade at GTIMO where the Hank would be put through simulated exercises in the hot sun south of the island of Cuba* – suffered; it was one or the other, there was just not time enough in a day for both. The child accepted this but feared the unknown; the child's boss, the Chief Engineer, had been through GITMO once before and the child had no recourse but to follow orders. The child attended basic and advanced damage control classes while awaiting the *Hank*; his first orientation, then, were classes that emphasized preparedness. Whenever any small piece of time became available he did things like have an R division damage control specialist inventory the damage control repair lockers; he found them incomplete and reasoned that without funds being spent on the required inventory, any repair party crew, even if they did have the time to train, could not possibly have a valid training session. He wrote up directives which outlined these purely inventory requirements but, alas, funds in peacetime also had to have goals relative to departmental objectives. He realized that his men *did* know of these lacks but he knew that they had probably submitted requisitions before and were told that other supplies were more important.

In one sense, however, it *was* like Princeton: you had to keep after studies day after day, night after night, in order to get a degree in engineering and a commission as a Naval Officer, all in four years and that meant sacrificing one thing for another. Although his situation could be viewed in simple terms the child as Naval Officer viewed the situation as a potential embarrassment; he finally was able to get parts for the *Hank's* water wash-down system – the one that was turned on during a real or simulated atomic attack – but the parts came late. The system also needed constant attention simply because it was constructed of plastic or PVC pipe and the crew of the *Hank* when making a false step during a routine operation could step on or otherwise put weight on an element of the system and break it.

* * *

Returning to the period of destroyer exercises, Sherman felt that training at Guantanamo Bay at the southeast tip of Cuba provided him with some of his most vivid memories. The weeks at Guantanamo were part of an eighteen-month cycle. That also included a six month tour of duty with the Sixth fleet in the Mediterranean. The cycle included a major shipyard overhaul in dry dock, followed by training at Guantanamo Bay, Cuba, and then the Mediterranean period. So, for example, during his first shipyard period, the motor whale boat davits were reinforced to pick up a Project Mercury capsule in the Arabian Sea.

During a stay at Guantanamo, (GITMO) Sherman's first GITMO training experience, in the year 1961, he was very wary of earning a satisfactory grade in Damage Control. He was the ship's Damage Control Officer, a position that reports to the Chief Engineer; he was also Division Officer for men in the auxiliary, electrical, and repair sub-divisions of R Division. The men in these three sub-divisions, called the A, E, and R divisions, held major responsibilities in the area of Damage Control, but, as previously mentioned, Sherman was unable to carry out drills that would have sharpened their skills.

In the two engine rooms and two boiler rooms, steam leaks were pursued with the intensity of the Spanish Inquisition. A tight engineering plant, with not a single drop of wasted feed water or steam was the goal. The evaporators, which made both fresh water and feed water, were to be in such shape that they could make seven hundred gallons per hour. The less used by the engineering plant, the more for the crew. Daily Navy showers (turn water on to wet the body, turn water off, soap down, turn water on to quickly rinse, turn water off) were absolutely mandatory for everyone.; the laundry must never be down; every air conditioner must work, period! Under the tutelage of the Chief Engineer, Sherman became an expert on getting repairs done, both on the ship – his men ran the machine shop – and through tenders and shipyards. The *Hank*, in one sense, was like a cruise ship. Nothing broke down, or if it did, it was fixed instantly; it was hard to believe that it was built in 1944.

According to the legend of the Order of the Arrow, volunteers join with the Chief of the Delawares in the journey to warn their entire nation of the enemy. After the enemy is driven back, the chief promotes those who have served their brethren. After this, he makes known his reason, "For," said he, "he who serves his fellows is, of all his fellows, greatest!" The rest was history, for the order was founded upon the wish to make that principle permanent in the memory of all future generations.

Sherman felt that conspicuous crew members enjoyed such notoriety from their fellows. Among these were the evaporator men, and a first class Petty officer who repaired and looked after air conditioners, water coolers, and the reefers. Other conspicuous crew members that enjoyed praise from the crew and that worked for Sherman were men who could repair laundry equipment including the equipment that pressed uniforms, and even the group that kept all the movie projectors running and properly serviced.

While the engineering department was always in the limelight, by virtue of being called upon to come up to cruise ship standards, the gunnery department faced the implicit problem that they could only gain expertise with the ship's guns once every eighteen months while at Guantanamo Bay

(GITMO). For short periods of time, they fired at targets on the island of Culebra. Having infrequent time to practice skills was also the case with respect to anti-submarine warfare personnel; only at GITMO were there actually subs that tried to attack and launch hollow torpedoes. These torpedoes would bounce off the hull of the *Hank* if evasive action was ineffective, and come to the surface for recovery. One other instance was with the Sixth fleet during Mediterranean cruises where war games were played that involved real subs from different countries.

Submarines trained their crews as well during these games. Sherman remembered one incident when he was standing a bridge watch, during "holiday routine" in the Caribbean. The anti-submarine warfare officer, an ensign named Jack B who had joined the Hank at the same time as Sherman, walked up to the very tip of the fo'c'sle in his bathing suit, probably to watch dolphins and flying fish. He looked down in the water and saw the loom of a sub making practice runs on the *Hank*. This was a problem as the sub was only a few yards away. Jack pointed down into the water and then looked up at the bridge and waved his arms with a big smile on his face. "All back full," was the next order to the lee helmsman. "Main control answers all back full, sir," came back from the lee helmsman. The next voice was from Combat, "*Angle Fish* apologizes; they weren't watching their range rate."

Despite these limitations on training, Captain D still hoped the *Hank* would pass enough exercises to earn an overall satisfactory grade. He wasn't worried about engineering drills, but rather about damage control, gunnery, anti-submarine warfare and an atomic attack, as the plastic wash-down system was always breaking when people inadvertently stepped on it, and parts were hard to come by. This was the system that was turned on to completely wash down the entire ship after an atomic attack and reminded one of a car wash.

Every morning, a dozen lean observers would come aboard dressed in short khaki pants and holding clip boards and grading forms. They needed no signs of their rank and merely wore short pants and white T-shirts, but their authority was a given; they could do anything they wanted and cause any and all kinds of havoc. They knew what should be done, what the physical preparation of the ship should be for any emergency or drill, what training was exhibited, and what grade to assign the effort.

This crew that tested the ship in all aspects of its preparedness could lock up the Captain in his cabin and then tell the executive officer or any other officer, for that matter, to get the ship underway. While leaving Guantanamo Bay, they could schedule a man-overboard drill, and while everyone was mustering on the main deck to find out who had fallen overboard and report the missing person to the bridge, they often used the Captain, and the officer of the deck, after no one was missing, thought the *Hank* had failed to identify who fell into the sea. Then, when the officer of the deck turned around to report to the Captain that the identity of the man overboard could not be ascertained, fearing his wrath, the Captain wouldn't be there! While this was going on, the observers would cause a real submarine attack.

While the damage-control crews were rigging emergency power to the after-steering engines that controlled the rudders, and working out on the main deck, the observers would cause an atomic attack and inform the ship that an atomic device had just gone off four miles away. The GITMO observers liked surprises, and they checked for discrepancies before, during, and after their exercises, wrote everything down, and assigned grades of "sat" or "unsat."

Hank was getting its comeuppance. The wash-down system did not completely spray the entire ship like the inside of a car wash. Captain D was hoping that the anti-submarine warfare exercise would earn a "sat" but either a sonar contact was missed or the correct evasive action for a torpedo was not taken–the torpedo hit and bounced off the hull of the *Hank*–and *Hank* earned an "unsat" there, too. Captain D was dejected; damage control failed as well. The *Hank* returned to Norfolk with an "unsat" for the entire ship and everyone wondered whether the *Hank* would be allowed to go to the Mediterranean and join the sixth fleet.

Sherman remembered the show that was put on to keep morale up as the *Hank* steamed home. He was standing the bridge watch but could hear the words from some of the song sheets that were printed. One of the songs was "Bye, Bye GITMO" sung to the tune of "Bye, Bye Blackbird:"

> Gunnery practice gone astray, lunch is cold
> another day, Bye, Bye GITMO.
> Sonar contact can't decide, torpedoes bouncing
> off the side, Bye, Bye GITMO.

Chorus

> No one seems to know or understand us,
> Look at the "unsats" they all hand us.
> We're so glad we're sailing away,
> 'Cause at last we can say, GITMO Bye, Bye!

Upon return to home port, Norfolk, Virginia, the crew of the *Hank* soon became aware that they would have to continue damage-control exercises in port after normal working hours, in order to raise their grade to a "sat." The effort would become very embarrassing.

Sherman had never been to the Mediterranean. The trip would involve many of the usual ports, such as Marseille, Genoa, Naples, Athens, Crete, and Malta, to name a few. *Hank* was also to be dispatched to steam, by herself, through the Suez Canal, and then make stops at Assab, Ethiopia, Jeddah, Saudi Arabia, Djibouti, French Somalia, Britain's Aden Protectorate, and then up into the Persian Gulf with stops at Bahrain Island, and further north. The romance of illusions again captured Sherman. The *Hank* would rendezvous in the Arabian Sea with the destroyer coming back from the Persian Gulf, exchange ninety movies with its crew and even go fishing at the bottom of the Red Sea with spectacular results. Sherman was worried about missing the cruise; he was still unmarried.

The *Hank* crew's embarrassment came from the remedial damage-control drills they performed in the hot sun while the off-duty crews of neighboring destroyers watched them put out simulated fires by lowering the motor whaleboat with a portable pump-and-fire-hose attachment in the bow, and then motoring around to put out an imaginary fire on another ship. For the off-duty men on the other destroyers, it was a form of entertainment. Finally the *Hank* raised itself to a "sat," and sailed with its squadron to the Med.

* * *

There were certain qualifications that required a long period of hands-on experience before one became officially qualified. One of these was being certified as an Officer of The Deck Underway. Training in one of the eight Princeton NROTC classes only began the process of qualification by, for example, teaching students how to solve 'Maneuvering Board Problems.' The rest of the training required that the officer stand watches as a Junior Officer of the Deck under the tutelage of a qualified colleague, and that, in turn, depended on the time actually spent 'underway' as opposed to being in port, in a shipyard for a three month overhaul or alongside a tender for lesser repairs.

The common time to achieve this Officer of The Deck Underway qualification was eighteen months. When on the Bridge underway, the actions one took, the commands one gave, the use of the Radio Telephones for communication, the recognition from memory of the Task Force Commander's encoded commands, and the proper answering protocol, the implementation of the Captain's Standing Night Orders, all these and many more arenas of action, had to become second nature, established habits, where one could switch from one task to another seamlessly. It is appropriate then, that after examining my arrival on the *Hank*, that we look at this activity, this 'acquired skill.' The fictional excerpt involving John Sherman is taken from *Stories of Identity* in the first story of that book, 'A Biography of the Spirit Part One The Early Years.' This excerpt captures the essence of the Officer of The Deck's job when underway with a screen of Destroyers that are protecting an aircraft carrier:

* * *

It usually took eighteen months on a destroyer to qualify as an Officer of the Deck Underway. This was partly due to the time spent in port, shipyard and tender overhaul periods, as well as time at sea when not steaming with an aircraft carrier. When with a carrier, destroyers were deployed in a semicircular screen spread out in front of the carrier or, as a single destroyer, following in the stern of the carrier on what was known as a plane guarding station.

Sherman tried to capture what a watch at night was like by telling a story about a very ambitious young Naval Academy Ensign who had come aboard and given everyone the impression that he knew everything and could do everything–this fictional person was certainly not a humble person. Perhaps his schoolwork was the best it could possibly be.

In any event, the story began with Sherman standing the midwatch, 0000–0400, as Officer of the Deck and with the young ensign, Mr. Jones, in the capacity of Junior Officer of the Deck. Sherman had given Mr. Jones the "conn" meaning that he had the job of giving orders to the helmsman, the sailor steering the ship, and to the lee helmsman, the sailor controlling the engine order telegraph, the device that sends speed instructions to the engine rooms and which must be answered by those engine rooms.

All was peaceful. The *Hank* is at station 5 in an eight-ship destroyer screen forming a semicircle of ships, spread out in front of an aircraft carrier at the center of the circle. Station-keeping responsibilities had also been given to Mr. Jones. These consisted of staying at the same distance from and bearing–angular degrees from the course of all ships in the task force– from the carrier until instructions to the contrary were received–it involved very slight adjustments in the course and revolutions of the propellers, one way or another. It also involved checking the adjustments by use of the radar screen on the bridge.

All of a sudden, a small loudspeaker on the bridge was heard as it came to life with a human voice.

In the following exchanges, commands that are given using radiotelephone protocol—required by all users—are capitalized. In addition, commands from outside the Hank *appear in quotation marks.*

"Test Run Papa, this is Razor Blade, Immediate Execute, Corpen 270, I Say Again Immediate Execute, Corpen 270, Over."

Sherman: Are you going to answer the Task Force Commander Mr. Jones? I thought you were covering Pri Tac. (Pri Tac is short for Primary Tactical Circuit, the voice circuit through which commands are sent to ships and acknowledged.) We're alphabetically the first to answer.

Jones is not certain where the handset is for the Pri Tac Radiotelephone as there are three handsets, one for Pri Tac, one for Sec Tac (the Secondary Tactical Circuit), and one for the captain's cabin.

Sherman *Picking up the Pri Tac radiotelephone:* This is *Auditorium*, Roger out. – Auditorium *is the code name for the* Hank.

In rapid fashion Sherman asks Jones some questions.

Sherman: Do you have a course and speed to our new station Mr. Jones? Are we reorienting the screen by method rum or method coke?

Jones cannot answer either of the questions and Sherman must do the work.

Sherman: This is Mr. Sherman, I have the conn.

Two" Aye, aye, sirs" *are heard in reply.*

Sherman: Left standard rudder, all ahead full to twenty knots, come to course 290.

Two replies come back from inside the pilot house: "Left standard rudder course 290 sir." "All ahead full to twenty knots sir." "Main control answers all ahead full to twenty knots sir."

Sherman *Answering the pilot house replies:* Very well. *He then addresses Mr. Jones.* Did you read the night orders?

Jones *Giving a halfhearted reply:* Yes.

Sherman: I knew the carrier would start launching aircraft into the wind at 0130, and knew he would be turning to course 270, as the wind is still coming from that direction. So I had worked out the maneuvering board problem ahead of time.

Jones: Yes.

Sherman: We are reorienting the screen by method coke. Why don't you do the maneuvering board problem to our new station? It probably needs an adjustment.

It is clear that Jones is not certain where to look for the maneuvering board, paper, parallel rulers, and pencil so that he can carry out the suggestion.

Helmsman: Steady on 290 sir.

Sherman: Very Well. *Sherman picks up the telephone handset to the captain's cabin and buzzes the Captain. He hears the Captain reply "captain."* Captain we've come to 290 at twenty knots and are proceeding to our new station.

The Captain replies: Give me a call when we're on station. *Sherman replies:* "Very well sir, *and hangs up the phone.*

Sherman takes out the maneuvering board, plotting paper, and parallel rulers from the cabinet below the bridge plotting table, and turns on the red light just above the table. Jones begins constructing the speed and direction vectors using the parallel ruler. Jones, responding to the suggestion of a needed course correction, walks over to the radar screen and gets a new distance and bearing from the carrier. After checking what the neighboring destroyers are doing, he turns to Sherman.

Jones: Yes, that carrier turns in a wide arc. I recommend 295 at this speed.

Sherman: Have you checked that with Combat. *(Combat Information Center is a group of operations personnel inside the ship that support the bridge in everything it does. The Allen M. Sumner class destroyers were the first class to have a special space designated as such.)*

Jones *To the Starboard Lookout:* Ask combat how 295 looks at this speed.

Starboard Lookout: *The Starboard lookout speaks words into his sound powered phone and then quickly replies* Combat concurs with 295 at this speed, sir.

Sherman *Without hesitation:* Come right to 295.

Helmsman: Right to 295, Sir. *Within a moment he speaks up again* Steady on two nine five, sir.

No sooner than Sherman replied, "Very well," to this last information from the Helmsman, a voice is again heard over the Pri Tac loudspeaker:

"Test Run Papa, this is Razor Blade, Immediate Execute, Charlie Bravo Three, I say again, Immediate Execute, Charlie Bravo Three, Out."

Sherman asks Jones if he understood the signal and he answers No. He recommends that until such time as he has memorized them, it's a good idea to write them down, especially those that don't require any answer. Often while you go through the pages looking for the meaning you can forget the signal.

Sherman then asks Jones, "Will you use the salmon-colored NATO pages in the signal book, or the white ones?"

Jones replies, "White."

"Right," said Sherman, "when we get to the Med (Mediterranean, sixth fleet) we'll switch to the pink ones."

Sherman knew that this particular signal, Charlie Bravo Three, "I intend to launch aircraft in five minutes," was the same for both the white and salmon colored pages.

The *Hank* arrived on-station at the new distance and bearing from the carrier, Sherman set the course to 270 and then gave back the conn to Jones so as to give him more practice at station-keeping, while Sherman observed the launching of planes. He called the Captain, "We're on station, course 270, Sir, *Atlas* will be launching aircraft any minute now." The Captain replied, "very well," and went back to sleep. Sherman was accustomed to calling the carrier by its code name, *Atlas*.

Jones was busy station-keeping with minor additions to the turns of the propellers and one-degree course changes, but Sherman wanted him to know that for everyone on the bridge, multitasking, the doing of many things at once, some automatic and some less so, was the essence of the job. To make his point, after the launch he asked Jones, "Did you check that the bridge lookouts counted the number of aircraft launched?" He knew the answer would be no.

* * *

There were other operations that were, shall we say, more dynamic, and potentially more open to embarrassment; these required several officers on the bridge to keep track of things, not to mention the entire crew. One of these operations occurred while in the Mediterranean and it was called

'High Speed Replenishment.' The *Hank* was informed that it was a new kind of operation for the Sixth Fleet and that made us all the more fascinated. Here is how that operation was described in the book *Stories of Identity*:

* * *

Another day went by and, with the exception of his tasks, the day was uneventful. The ruby-throated hummingbirds visited the feeders all day long, the goldfinches took advantage of the thistle tubes that hung but ten feet from the table where meals were served on the screened front porch, and the young mallard ducks, all seven of them, were now almost indistinguishable in size from their two parents. They came en masse to the pier in search of food underneath it. They reminded Sherman of the high-speed replenishment operations carried out in the Mediterranean while Sherman's destroyer squadron was deployed with the Sixth Fleet.

In that replenishment operation, several columns of supply ships (oilers, reefers, ammunition and supply ships), were steaming in formation at a slow speed – twelve knots, for example. The combatant group, made up of an aircraft carrier and its surrounding squadron of destroyers, was steaming at twenty knots on an angular course to intercept the supply ship formation. This combatant group maintained its high-speed approach until it was given orders to break formation and proceed alongside the first supply ship designated for each combatant in the replenishment plan. The signal produced a melee, as each ship took a direct course to get alongside its first supply ship. The excitement consisted of several factors.

First, each destroyer took its own path; that could mean crossing between one or two columns of supply ships while steaming at high speed, all while watching out to avoid a collision with any supply ship, or another ship of the squadron that was also proceeding to its first station alongside a supply ship. Second, the bridge had to know the whereabouts of every single ship. If your own ship quickly finished refueling from the port side of an oiler and was to proceed to the starboard side of a reefer for her supplies by prearranged plan, it was important to know which reefer, where it was, what other ships were in queue on either side of that reefer, how far back in the correct queue your ship's place in line was, and how best to weave your way quickly back through the columns of supply ships with their queues of perhaps one or two other ships waiting in line.

In the meantime, the crew had to strike down refueling apparatus and stations and ready themselves to come alongside the reefer. This involved setting up high-lines, lines stretched between the two ships and across which crew members manually hauled all supplies. Once on deck, the large pallets of edible supplies had to be quickly stored below, either in the reefers, refrigerated storage compartments, or the appropriate storerooms. No matter the weather or sea conditions, this had to be done quickly simply because within a minute or so, another pallet was on its way and deck space was not typically available for multiple pallets on a destroyer.

With the exception of those on watch, the entire crew was fully employed either on deck or below deck at one or more levels, and each working party had to be told exactly where to store every edible commodity they received. This kept the supply department hopping, ensuring not only they sent the correct goods across, but also that they put them in the proper place and secured them properly, ready for subsequent inventory control.

If this was not enough, there were movies to be exchanged and repair parts to be high-lined across. Usually these came from the carrier that had just received important parts not stored on board any ship, along with mail by courier aircraft. In all this, someone on the bridge had to be able to answer such questions from the Captain as, "We refuel following the *English*; – the destroyer division flagship – after we finish getting our mail and movies from the carrier, where will the *English* be?"

A quick reply like, "*English* is first in line on the port side of the *Mississiniwa*, and the *Borie* has just finished refueling ahead of her; refueling lines are just being taken in by the oiler, sir," was required.

Sherman realized that more maneuvering took place in that one day than during three weeks of routine plane guarding exercises. A sense of relief permeated the ship after everything was stowed below, the dinner meal served on time, and the squadron arranged itself once again in normal screen formation.

* * *

But while these two prior excerpts focus on what I was doing on the bridge after qualifying as an Officer of The Deck Underway, there are several other documents from *Glimpses of My First Two Years of Naval Service* that date from my being a Division Officer for R Division. The first of these, ' My Policy and Ship's Policy Concerning Duties and Liberty in the Mediterranean,' is prefaced with the following: "On the 26th of September 1961 we found ourselves in an operating fleet. Standards of smartness and adherence to regulations were considerably upgraded. I found it necessary to write this instruction to my Division in order to clarify what would be required of them. I think I achieved a large amount of my objectives as can be seen in the last letter in this booklet." I have placed the Policy Letter in Appendix G.

There are two letters in *Glimpses of My First Two Years of Naval Service* that suggest that the personnel in R Division were taking me seriously. The first letter is to the entire Division and the second is a Letter of Commendation for a Third Class Engineman Petty Officer. I have placed these in Appendix H.

But what about the humorous incidents on the *Hank*, you ask? By the time March 1962 rolled around I was a Lieutenant Junior Grade; that meant that I acquired a perspective on what were the sources of humor on the *Hank*. I thought it could be summarized with the words: A Good Navy Flail. But what is a flail? Towards the end of the Mediterranean six month trip I put together *The Elements of a Good Navy Flail* as an attempt to define the idea:

* * *

The Elements of a Good Navy Flail

First and foremost, I would say that a good flail must involve a misunderstanding, a partial truth or a supposed injustice frankly stated and in agreement with the facts. Next, it requires a personal expression of this misunderstanding in terms of harsh language, sarcasm, a heated argument or the rousing of one person's temper and the subsequent influence he has on someone else below him in the Chain of Command. The more suspecting one person is of the other, the more strained the relationship, the better the flail. The more unsuspecting the victim of a superior's temper is in response to a 'discovery,' the better the flail.

On the other hand, if one person gives in, the flail is quickly killed. Fortunately however, a new flail can easily arise from the ashes of an old one. By suggesting the obvious bias or prejudices of one party to the flail – as brought out in the argument – a new flail is easily born, the basis of which lies in everyone's inability to see himself as others see him.

The secret of a good flail, then, involves selecting the victim and gaining his confidence. Next, relay the truth to him in as abrupt and surprising a way as possible. The success of your flail will rest on the sincerity of your story because a good flail always rests on a solid misunderstanding. The weakest form of flail is started by an allegation to hearsay. An example or two would be "So and said that – you are being given the extra watch – liberty has been canceled – you cannot take leave." Only the most unsuspecting person will be puzzled by such statements without further confirmation.

A much stronger start involves the use of 'inside dope' simply stated. Examples of these would be: "Captain, the motor whaleboat is adrift," "You have been extended indefinitely," "Captain, we are dragging anchor," "The insurance policy doesn't cover this situation," "Captain, the message you did not want the Commodore to see was sent to his Flagship by mistake." This type of flail has broader consequences, a greater capacity to spread and break out into smaller flails. It can unlock smoldering discontents, unfounded references to previous flails, accusations, and breaches of respect.

Ultimately, however, the Master Flail involves all this and more. It throws everything into a turmoil which continues to rumble down the days and weeks that follow. Such a flail is beyond the genius of any individual to recognize and start. Like a latent avalanche in the mountains which starts of its own accord or by a chance pistol shot, the Master Flail always begins by a chance discovery, usually by the Captain, and this discovery leads to more and more rumbles as it builds and finally ends in the abyss of discontent, fallen pride, the schism of purge, and incompetence. Examples of several small Master Flails follow.

One day, the sonar men on watch went to the head on their own accord and because of this they missed a sonar contact. This caused rumbles down the Gunnery Department Chain of Command and the 'decision for remedy' was to have each and every sonar man from then on, ask for permission 'to go to the head' from the Officer of The Deck via the intercommunication system. The speaker for this system is immediately in front of the Captain's chair on the bridge.

One morning – it was either the previous evening's meal or a particular characteristic of sonar men that caused it – this "request permission for so and so to go to the head," "permission granted" sequence became particularly obnoxious. The Captain, who has respect for Petty Officers assuming responsibility, especially sonar watch supervisor type Petty Officers – and for smooth, uninterrupted bridge watches, sat quietly in his chair until this diatribe of second and third requests for certain people became too much for him.

He jumped out of his chair, called for the Gunnery Officer, and shaking his fist demanded an explanation of why his policies had been violated. He pointed out how absurd the whole thing was. The Gunnery Officer insisted that he would not tell the sonar men to stop since his policy was to let his Anti-Submarine Warfare officer handle things as he wished and that he was going to back up his Anti-Submarine Warfare officer. The Captain continued insisting on the absurdity of the whole thing, the ridiculousness of it, and on his ship, at that! The Gunnery Officer said it was a matter of backing up his junior officers, supporting the Chain of Command, a show of confidence for the Anti-Submarine Warfare officer, instead of the enlisted sonar watch officer as the Captain insisted upon.

It then became clear that the Gunnery Officer was fed up with the Captain for his lack of support, change in policy, and for his disappointment with the Gunnery Officer. The Captain began to realize the pig-headedness of the Gunnery Officer and his lack of practicality in remembering that "every wish of the Captain should be considered as a command." In the next scene, the Anti-Submarine Warfare officer made his appearance and by this time, the Gunnery Officer was finally convinced, and so the flail rumbled down into the sonar room where it ultimately came to a halt.

The Gunnery Department has multiple Divisions. In addition to Fox Division (which contains the sonar men) there is the 1st Division, and the 2nd Division. These last two Divisions, according to standard Destroyer organization, contain about ½ Gunnersmates and ½ Boatswainsmates. On the *Hank*, however, the Gunnery Officer decided, administratively, to put all the Boatswainsmates in 1st Division and all the Gunnersmates in the 2nd Division. There was still a division of Boatswainsmates into two groups however, which was 'understood' throughout the ship – 1st Division, which took care of the forward part of the ship, and 2nd Division which took care of the after half of the ship. Also, for battle purposes, there were, administratively, 1st Division Boatswainsmates sleeping in the 2nd Division compartment aft with Gunnersmates, and this compartment was considered a 'deck force' compartment. Likewise, in 1st Division's compartment forward, there were 2nd Division Gunnersmates.

It was during Commander Destroyer Division Twenty-Two's Inspection when the Division Commander began to inspect 2nd Division aft on the fantail when this flail was born. Unfortunately, the Commodore asked one seaman what Division he was in and this brought out confusion both in the seaman's mind and in the Commodore's. Later, in the Wardroom, the Commodore, an old Destroyer man himself, wanted the Captain to explain how the man could be confused, i.e., how could he be in both 1st and 2nd Divisions. The Gunnery Officer insisted that the 'administrative/divisional' arrangement was similar to a 'book entry' and shouldn't confuse the Commodore, let alone a seaman. The answer was unacceptable to the Captain and the Commodore who both wanted a more specific explanation. After they received this they were even more confused. Finally, the Commodore left the matter with the Captain to decide.

This next flail might be entitled "a weekend with the Squadron Commander." The Squadron Commander, a very serious, dedicated, principled man, much respected, and well-liked, had a way of causing flails unlike any other man in the Squadron. Walking up to the Bridge one day, he observed from his Flagship several signalmen sacked out in the canvas covers of the flag bags of the USS *English,* the Flagship of the Commodore for Destroyer Division Twenty-Two. He called the *English* on the Primary Voice Radio net and said (We will use the Code Name *Razor-Blade* for the Squadron Commander and *Goldfinch* for the *English.*) "*Goldfish* this is *Razor-Blade*, reveille in the flag bags, out." The word 'out' at the end of his message means that an acknowledgement to his voice message is not required. This first message had no effect because several minutes later he called up the *English* again and said "*Goldfish* this is *Razor-Blade*, reveille in the flag bags, over." The word 'over' demanded an acknowledgement from the *English.*

One weekend in Naples, Italy, the *Hank* was with berthed with the Squadron Commander during a tender period. The Squadron Commander had a particular desire that Destroyers in the nest have an officer back on the fantail each morning and evening to observe colors. On Sunday morning, just prior to colors, he looked across the nest of ships and saw no officer on *Hank's* Fantail. Instead, he observed a fist fight between two men. Informing the Division Commodore of this on the USS *English*, he later traveled over to the *Hank* for a personal call.

There he was greeted by the Messenger of the Watch, no officer again, and he asked where the Officer of the Deck was. He told the Messenger that he had better get the Officer of the Deck, wherever he was – there was a sentry on the fo'c'sle who was writing a letter while on watch. Finally, the Squadron Commodore found the Officer of the Deck, the Captain, and the Executive Officer, and explained the reason behind his Sunday morning visit. The blame for this was shifted to the Command Duty Officer who had the mid-watch and was up until 0600. At the time he was trying to catch up on his sleep.

Following this, the Division Commodore came over for a visit. This was the same man who would steal the Officer of the Deck's long glass when he wasn't habitually carrying it and bring it to the Captain. Despite the previous incident with the sentry on the fo'c'sle, his being put on report and his chewing-out by the Captain, Executive Officer, and the Officer of the Deck, the Division Commodore had just noticed the same man sitting down on his watch and talking to a buddy. The Division Commodore wanted a new man on this watch, this morning, not just disciplinary action. It is of interest to note that this man was transferred to the deck force of the Division Flagship a few weeks later.

* * *

But you, blessed reader, are quite correct in wondering if these *Glimpses of My First Two Years of Naval Service* tell you what I was *really* thinking? That must be an important question if only because there just have to be many Norwegians that make a career of the Norwegian Navy. It may be that you, blessed reader, see no reason why I did not continue this exciting pursuit. What you need is some kind of personal journal, a diary, if even for a short period, especially a stressful period like the time on the *Hank* from the 5th of June, 1961 to the 28th of June, 1961.

This was a period when Destroyer training at Guantanamo Bay, Cuba, was interrupted to take care of a threatening situation in the Dominican Republic! If that wasn't enough, there was the terrible question on everyone's mind that if the Dominican Republic situation was taken care of, would the *Hank* be required to return to Guantanamo Bay to complete that interrupted training? We feared those instructors that came aboard every morning and put the *Hank* through all kinds of *graded* drills that were either satisfactory or unsatisfactory. And, heaven forbid, what would happen if the entire ship was unsatisfactory? Would they let us sail with the Squadron to the Mediterranean or would we have to languish in Norfolk, Virginia, the laughing stock of the Destroyer Submarine piers? We have already discussed the results of that return.

Fortunately a chance event, the discovery of an old journal, suggested that I keep a journal during that period; you'll find it in Appendix E. . . . Eleven months after the last Journal entry, 28 June 1961, on May 28, 1962, Captain Dinwiddie appointed me to the position of Engineering Officer. As of that day the Wardroom Stewards began putting my napkin in the Napkin Ring that was engraved with the words 'Chief Engineer.' I moved into the Chief Engineer's Quarters in After Officer's Country; those quarters were quite spacious as compared to my first bunk, an upper bunk, in Forward Officer's Country. I had my own telephone; on the outboard bulkhead, there was a slot where I could pass papers to the Engineering Department Office; when underway, I began writing the Engineering Department Night Orders – more of that in a moment.

What seemed the most luxurious touch were the green wall curtains that hung on two bulkheads of my bunk area; this was extravagance with a capital E. For ports like Genoa, Italy, where the bitter cold air came out of the mountains to the North, I enjoyed the fact that the deck in my Quarters was the overhead for the After Engine Room. I could hear certain operations that called for more steam during the times at sea; thus it was that I was never far from what the M and B Divisions (Machinist Mates and Boilermen) were doing. I hesitate to copy in the words in that letter from the Captain, J. M. Dinwiddie, but as they were brief, I shall:

* * *

From: Commanding Officer, USS *Hank* (DD-702)

To: LTJG EARL F. RONNEBERG

Subj: Relieving as Engineering Officer, USS *Hank* (DD-702)

Ref: (a) U. S Navy Regulations 1948, Chapter 9 (section 1 and 5) and Chapter 10 (section 3 and 4)

1.   You are hereby directed to relieve LTJG ROBERT H. DIEFENBACH-ER 593261/1105 as Engineering Officer of U. S. S. *Hank* (DD-702), by reason of the impending detachment of LTJG DIEFENBACHER.

Relief of LTJG DIEFENBACHER is to be effected on or about 29 May 1962.

2.   You are to familiarize yourself with the provisions of reference (a) (particularly article 0908) and (b) and appropriate OPNAV, Fleet and Type Commander directives associated with the duties of Engineering Officer.

3.   Submit a joint report to the Commanding Officer, in accordance with article 0908 of reference (a).

J. M. DINWIDDIE

Copy to:
LTJG DIEFENBACHER
Ships Secretary

* * *

The Night Orders for the Engineering Department were instructions issued to all of the Petty Officers in charge of the Forward Engine Room, After Engine Room, Forward Fire Room, and After Fire Room, for the 2000-2400, 0000-0400, and 0400-0800 watches. I often added the Evaporator Watch in the Forward Engine Room and the Oil King who managed the fuel tanks. Each person in charge was required to initial the orders every night while the *Hank* was underway.

A standard Navy Department form was used which included: Ship Name, Date, Enroute (From/To) or At, Standard Speed, Anticipated Speed Changes, Boilers in Use, Stand-by Boilers, Plant Operation (Split or Cross-connected), How Boiler Super Heaters were to be used (Lighted-off or Secured), Superheat Temperature Instructions, Electrical Generators in Use, Stand-By Generators, Evaporators in Use, and Instructions for Distilling to Potable Water Tanks and to Reserve Feed Water Tanks. In addition, there was a place for my remarks. I began by printing those remarks out since my handwriting was never legible despite the efforts of teachers at Ebinger Elementary School. I also emulated my Scout Leader, Robert Nelson, in this, as his handwriting was never in use when he posted the names of obstreperous individuals, the ones he gave all the conduct checks to. In my own case, however, my printing was soon remarked upon by some brave soul, who remained anonymous, to the effect that he could not read what I printed. After that, I typed my remarks which often overflowed onto the back side of the single page of the Night Order.

The copies of the Night Orders that I retained and, ultimately, bound together, were called, collectively, *Glimpses of My Third Year of Naval Service*, and spanned dates from 4 June 1962 to 23 November 1962; that period, seven months, I suspect, qualified the effort as being one which involved *Glimpses.* I found the remarks section to be a very important way of communicating with the entire Engineering Department, albeit that only sixteen key Petty Officers were required to initial that they read them. This confirms an old Navy axiom that "Word gets around!" I used the non-technical remarks for any number of purposes: transmitting what was actually going on (this would prevent false scuttlebutt from spreading), disseminating my philosophy for running the Engineering Department, praising individuals and groups that deserved public praise, providing information that would allow Petty Officers to anticipate what was coming up by way of tender and overhaul periods, ordering supplies, and procedures.

There were a lot of other things that I put into the Night Orders. I will go so far as to remark, that I probably abused them to a very tiny degree. For example, upon review, I see that I quoted from Macbeth – Tomorrow and tomorrow . . . – but I cannot precisely find the exact reason except that I was taking a Shakespeare Correspondence course while on the *Hank* and something came up which prompted the entire quote. On the other hand, I used my very first Night Order, 4 June 1962, to remark, on what I felt Captain Dinwiddie did when he appointed me: "3. As you know, the Captain has demonstrated a great trust and confidence in every member of this department by making me Chief Engineer. I am studying every day to learn this job. Without the experience of Chiefs, First Class, and even Second Class and Third Class Petty Officers, I am sure that he would have insisted on another man. I know that you will live up to every one of his expectations."

Examining the booklet, *Glimpses of My Third Year of Naval Service*, I happened upon the period of 14 October 1962 to 28 October 1962, the days of the Cuban Missile Crisis. Much later, after leaving the Navy, I came to understand my parent's views of the Crisis, and even, briefly, read some academic analysis. What, then, was the perspective that I had at the time? And what were the remarks that I put into the *Hank's* Engineering Night Orders? This would be an ex post facto review and I had no idea of what I would find. The only information, excerpted below, pertains to Night Order remarks relative to the Crisis:

* * *

On the night of 15 October 1962 *Hank* was steaming in the Mayport, Florida, Operations Area with the Aircraft Carrier *Independence* and the Destroyer *English*. I gave orders to be prepared for 27 Knots on 2 Boilers at Any time, and for 31 Knots on 4 Boilers at 30 a minute notice. There was, as yet, no direct mention of what we were actually doing; I wrote "The way things look now, we will be detached at 1200 Wednesday, and will refuel either Tuesday or Wednesday prior to our leaving to participate in another exercise to the South. We will try to re-fuel with the oilers in this other exercise. Friday afternoon prior to dark, we will try to transfer Mr. Seely from the *English* who will observe a 25 Knot economy run. We will probably be in Sunday night. We then commence a week of upkeep."

On the night of 16 October 1962 *Hank* was steaming in the Jacksonville, Florida, Operations Area with the Aircraft Carrier *Independence* and the Destroyer *English*. My concern in the Night Order book was merely that we had a large leak in the Forward Engine room; on both these nights all the men on the Evaporator watch and all the officers in the Department were required to initial the Night Orders.

On the night of 17 October 1962 *Hank* was at the Jacksonville, Florida, Operations area, heading North to avoid Hurricane Ella, in company with *Independence* and *English*. I alert the signers of the Engineering Night Orders to "Watch all missiles closely and tie down everything. There is still a possibility that we will get more of Hurricane Ella. Watch all H. T. AL. paint! (High Temperature Aluminum Paint). Division Officers and Leading Petty Officers make Certain that head-to-toe sleeping is being observed."

On the night of 18 October 1962 *Hank* was enroute to ? with *Independence, English*, and (others?). I write: "For electricians. Mr. Brockman desires continuous power to Mounts 33 and 34 after General Quarters."

On the night of 19 October 1962 *Hank* was at the East Atlantic Coast, South of Hatteras (500 miles) with *Independence*, and *English*. I write: "The Commodore has requested that we stay with the carrier until *Hank* refuels. This will occur when the weather picks up. Right now, the hurricane is between this formation and Norfolk. In order to get back now, it would be necessary to head in toward the coast and then move up the coast to Norfolk."

On the night of 20 October 1962 *Hank* is enroute to ? with *English* twelve miles astern and *Independence* 3-4 miles ahead. I write: "Be prepared to refuel at any time tonight or tomorrow morning. It is still unknown why we have been ordered south. As soon as information is received as to where and why we are going south, the word will be passed."

On the night of 21 October 1962 I write: "Everyone take plenty of salt tablets and avoid heat exhaustion. We still don't know what we are doing here. We have been told to halt and to go no further south unless otherwise ordered. We will steam back and forth on a north south course most of tonight at 12 knots. There might be occasional bursts to 20+ knots for station keeping purposes or for carrier launchings."

On the night of 22 October 1962 *Hank* was north of Cuba with *Independence*, and *English*. I write: "Yesterday the Commodore sent a message to the *Hank* which stated that because of the situation we are in, as much casualty control training should be conducted during regular steaming hours. I feel that this is especially important in view of the fact that we have many new men. Despite the heat, this training MUST be conducted. Following the Night Orders are changes to the casualty control manual. Each Chief in Charge must personally make changes and initial the back of the sheet. Report to me if you can't find your Casualty Control Manual."

On the night of 23 October 1962 *Hank* is in company with *English* and *Independence* enroute to ?. I write: ". . . continue casualty control training with Firemen Apprentices learning the basic steam cycle. Peebles will be boat engineer during General Quarters for Boarding and Search Details. Other Petty Officers names have been submitted to the Executive Officer for this type of duty. They are Bowers, Parker, Paulsen, and Cowart. Engineering Condition III: Propulsion machinery manned and ready for operational speed, full power available on two hour notice. Internal

Communication systems shall be sufficiently manned to enable the immediate control of all batteries that are manned and to provide for necessary ship control. Condition III watch is the normal watch under wartime conditions when surprise attack is possible. A part of the armament is ready for immediate action and the remainder at short notice. Chiefs continue making changes to Casualty Control Manual."

Night of 24 October 1962 *Hank* enroute to join up with Amphibious Forces. I write: "OIL KING, CONTINUE MAKING THIEF SAMPLES OF ALL TANKS ON A 6 HOUR BASIS. Wake Mr. Hulme and Myself at 0330 Sharp."

Night of 25 October 1962 At a point near Jamaica, Haiti, and Cuba 17° 45' N Equator. I write: "Keep after evaporators on 8-12, secure fresh water showers at 2200. Take saltwater showers rigged on fantail. Everyone is to voluntarily censor his own mail. DO NOT include *Hank's* present position or what we are doing. Right now we are destined to stay with the carrier and our reliefs (*Barton* and *Haynsworth*) have been ordered to the Amphibious Group. The *John R. Pierce* boarded and searched a Lebanese Merchantman today. This is the first incident of the blockade."

Night of 26 October 1962 *Hank* off *Haiti* with *English* and *Independence, Corry* and *O'Hare* on picket duty.

Night of 27 October 1962 *Hank* in Operations Area off Haiti, Jamaica, and Cuba with *English* and *Independence*. I write: "From now on, the Officer of the Decks are going to be concerned about any black smoke out of the stacks. Black smoke or blowing tubes during daytime will give our presence away. The following policies will hold for blowing tubes. Blow tubes once just after sunset, again at 0100, and a third time just prior to sunrise. Do not blow tubes during daylight hours. Watch smoke very carefully. Do not dump trash during the day. Dump all trash after dark and be certain to puncture all tin cans so they will sink. Standby to fuel tomorrow at any time. Continue submitting chits for supplies and tender jobs. This is very important. They will probably send out chits by mail for delivery by AKS and if we don't get our necessary orders in, we will be out of luck. Try to anticipate what materials we need if we were to stay in this area for another month with a tender period in San Juan the first of December and about a week in Norfolk for Christmas. With this in mind, order supplies up to 1 January 1963."

Night of 28 October 1962 *Hank* steaming in Operations Area, eventual destination Norfolk, Virginia. I write: "There is still no further word as far as I know on mail or what we will be doing this next week. I imagine that the following events will occur. 1. We will refuel twice, 2. We will replenish, 3. We will receive 14 personnel. The importance of the United States success in backing a strong foreign policy in Cuba in so far as we are concerned is twofold. First, this represents the first in what I expect will be a series of more and more powerful moves by this country to achieve its aims in as direct a manner as possible. The Navy's role in the future will be greatly enhanced and more funds and importance will be attached to our branch of the service than in the past. This is good, for the public needs to be aroused and impressed with our versatility. Secondly, more at home, the current operations stress how very much subject to change, the present situation is in the world. This means that each and every job that we do alongside a tender or in an upkeep status, takes on larger and larger proportions when the chips are down. In case you haven't noticed it is not just by coincidence that we are without problems such as #1 generator overheating, refer machinery out of commission, evaporators with low output, boilers with excessive leaks, entire plant with excessive leaks, 150 pound steam system completely shot, and many other items. No, the object lesson so apparent now is that everything we do all of the time is extremely important and one small thorn in our side can hurt us. I expect that this lesson and its spirit will be carried forward into the future. We owe this to the hundreds of conscientious personnel, Machinist Mates and Boiler Technicians, who have taken care of *Hank* before us with the hope in mind that someday she would again preserve the peace."

* * *

After the last word, peace, for the Night Orders for the 28th of October 1962, some anonymous individual penciled in the following: "AMEN" A long time after the brief period of the Cuban Missile Crisis I realized how little I knew of the goings-on; my parents, for example, were very fearful as compared with the relative ease with which the *Hank* carried out her duties of, for the most part, plane guarding for the Aircraft Carrier *Independence*, a task we performed millions of times. One incident, however, stood out above all others. What could that possibly be? It isn't even mentioned in the Night Orders, nor, I am sure, anywhere else in the Navy's record keeping.

The incident involved another aspect of the Navy joined with, are you ready for this my reader? the personality of the Vice President of the United States! Not since we examined father's flight to Corpus Christi, Texas, have we spoken of the Lone Star State. That was a business flight; our new focus will be a flight of fancy that involves a Destroyer, the USS *Wren*. A ship that appeared out of nowhere to join our squadron and became an heroic ship at a time when heroics didn't seem to be at play.

The USS *Wren* (DD-568) was part of the Naval Reserve Force and was used by a Naval Reserve unit in Houston, Texas, and was based in Galveston, Texas, in the early 1960's after a distinguished career ever since her commissioning the 20th of May, 1944. A Naval Reserve Force is a ship manned on weekends by Navy Reservists. I was the only person on the *Hank* that actually set foot on the *Wren* simply because I was highlined between the two ships, and back, so that I could observe a Damage Control exercise. My experience with the *Wren* led me to believe that the officers and crew of a reserve ship do not just *like* he Navy to the extent of giving up weekends, they *love* the Navy!

Reserve ships often lack the services of Destroyer Tenders and Shipyards on a regularly scheduled basis but the *Wren*, sometime before it joined our squadron before the Cuban Missile Crisis, was called to active duty and given access to those repair facilities. It was after the crisis that I was highlined over to the *Wren* from the *Hank*. Highlining is the process of being strapped in a metal chair and then manually pulled across the ocean between the two ships via a line stretched from one Destroyer to another. If the line sags, you can get wet; if the line breaks, you are required to wear a life preserver.

If, dear reader, you have read *Pages From A Journal 5 June 1961 To 27 June 1961*, Appendix E, you will know how difficult it is to keep a destroyer in tip-top shape in all things relating to Damage Control – every space accurately stenciled, Damage Control Lockers containing every necessary item, all compartments made air-tight and tested for that integrity, fire hoses and extinguishers in complete readiness, the Atomic Wash-down system fully operational with no broken parts, and Damage Control parties fully trained; I could go on endlessly.

As soon as I stepped out of the highline chair onto the decks of the *Wren*, I saw in an instant that here was a ship that would get a 100% perfect grade at the Destroyer Naval Training Center at Guantanamo Bay, Cuba. Every marking was accurately painted as though the *Wren* had just been commissioned! The Reservists from Houston spent their time well on their weekends. This readiness and expertise became obvious during the Damage Control exercise I graded. But even before that, as soon as I entered the Wardroom, I found a highly motivated, highly experienced, group of officers who were, on average, way above the officer ranks of the *Hank*; they were all Navy Lieutenants whereas on the *Hank* only the Operations Officer was a Lieutenant.

They spoke warmly about their Captain, the President of a large bank in Houston, Texas. When I met him I understood why. It was a pleasure to observe them in their Damage Control drills. Here was an entire ship with high morale, depth of experience in all things, motivated, and well versed in what might be called 'Naval Wisdom' and, of course, love, if not worship of the U. S. Navy. But what does this have to do with the Cuban Missile Crisis? More particularly, what has it to do with the *one* thing I *did* remember during that crisis?

The event I remember happened one night during the Crisis when we were plane guarding for the Aircraft Carrier *Independence*. At the time

I'm not certain that any of *Hank's* officers knew that Lyndon B. Johnson, Vice President of the United States, was on the *Independence*. He was flown out to join the blockade. President Kennedy had his hands full and, most likely, thought his Veep could add another close-up view to the complex decision making that he was involved in and that the world later found out about thanks to Presidential historians.

On that particular night I was approached by a radioman with a message board; he was required to get the initials of every *Hank* officer on an important message that just came in; maybe it was marked Operational Immediate! I sensed this was something important; how wrong I was! It was a hyped-up eulogy to the 'brave men of the USS *Wren*.' In a state of disbelief I read how the whole world, especially the wonderful citizens (voters) of the State of Texas, had their hearts and eyes focused on the *Wren*, and especially its Captain _____, President of the Bank of _____, in Houston, as he led this glorious band of Texans to preserve peace in the hemisphere, implement the Monroe Doctrine in the tradition of . . . I had the impression that the author of the message was speaking of the *Wren's* World War II exploits, but if that were so, not another ship was mentioned, yet it was sent to all ships present, many of which had distinguished WW II decorations. Then I realized that this message was a political statement from on high and very much in keeping with the ethic of 'The Lone Star State;' how could anyone fail to identify it as such? No doubt it was also composed from 'on high,' the Flag Officer's Quarters on the *Independence*.

But the time has come to shift our focus to my next home:

1950's West Coast On-Campus Dormitory Style
Engineering Graduate Student Residence
Architect Unknown
403B Crothers Memorial Hall
Stanford University
Opened September 24, 1955
Stanford, California

As we examine this shift from one coast to another, we need to keep an eye out for what, in my actions, was prompted by faith, intuition, authentic motives, and verifiable fact. As we pointed out earlier in the opening line, 'Can you believe what I am about to tell you?' perhaps you will detect elements of pure luck.

In this transition from After Officer's Country on the USS *Hank* to 403B Crothers Memorial Hall at Stanford University, we shall point out how what came before – Naval experiences, a Princeton Professor's answer to a question, a book read, entire classes taken, a transaction with an auto dealer in Barcelona, Spain, and other such preceding incidents – bore fruit in the sequence of events.

There is no question that the reason I applied to Stanford University during my third year on the *Hank* was due to the answer to a question that I posed to a Civil Engineering Professor during my Senior year at Princeton. It was a class called Advanced Strength of Materials and it used a text by Stephen Tymoshenko, an ethnic Ukrainian engineer from the Russian Empire who moved to the United States in 1922. At the time of my asking a question, I knew absolutely nothing about Stephen Tymoshenko except that he was the author of the Elementary and Advanced Strength of Materials texts. What I didn't know was that he was considered the father of modern engineering mechanics, that early in the 20th century he developed the theory of elasticity and the theory of beam deflection, and that from 1938 onward, he was a Professor at Stanford University; his contributions to the world were nothing short of being awesome!

I walked up to the front of the classroom and asked my Strength of Materials Professor, "Where do Civil Engineers go next for their education?" He replied, "many go to Stanford." I made a mental note of that and never gave a second thought to any other graduate school. Nor did I ever investigate, in any way, the classes that were offered. I did take the time, for purposes of the admission process, to articulate my intentions and I am certain that the letter, excerpted below, accurately reflects my feelings at the time; I called it *My Purpose and General Plan for Graduate Work*:

* * *

My purpose in graduate work will be to obtain two degrees, one in Structural Civil Engineering, and the other in Architecture. I feel that both the Bachelor of Architecture and the Structural Civil Engineering degree are necessary in order to fully develop the skills necessary for an independent, self-employed Architect/Engineer. I am encouraged in these feelings by my father who has both degrees from the University of Illinois and is an independent, self-employed Architect/Engineer.

During my undergraduate days at Princeton, I took as many electives as possible in the architectural/art areas. I feel, after reading Stanford's catalogue that I lack but a few courses to qualify for a degree of Bachelor of Arts in pre-architecture and that I could easily meet this deficiency through electives taken while studying for a graduate degree in Structural Civil Engineering.

First, however, I must still satisfy a desire to continue my technical inclinations in Engineering. Having majored in structures at Princeton, and having enjoyed mathematics and mechanical engineering electives, I desire to further my studies in mechanical engineering, and mathematics. I find Stanford's course descriptions and flexibility within various programs tailored to my needs.

On the humanistic side, I find that my previous architectural work has provided a necessary balance to my engineering studies. I also feel that the nature of the Architect/Engineer's work provides a great outlet for service to others and an opportunity to use my Naval experiences in dealing with many people from various walks of life in a position of responsibility.

In addition to my architectural courses taken at Princeton, I studied English, Economics, and Religion. During my years in the service, in addition to numerous professional courses, I took graded correspondence courses with the University of Chicago's Home Study program (Shakespeare, Plato and Aristotle, American English, and Introduction to Religious

Existentialism). I have found this latter method of study an extremely broadening, satisfying, and inexpensive way of study beyond formal education and intend to continue it for many years. It is for this reason that I feel ready to again resume formal technical pursuits in Graduate School without a feeling of off-balance.

* * *

There are any number of absurdities that, in retrospect, should be pointed out. The first is that I can't think of a letter that outlines more accurately what it would be like to follow in the footsteps of my father and grandfather, i.e., to be a Norwegian the rest of my life. The path outlined copies the wish to take some kind of program that would parallel father's 1929 degree in Architectural/Engineering at the University of Illinois. When we add to that the fact that at Stanford I did nothing whatsoever to implement the 'Purpose and General Plan' as outlined in the letter, it begs the question of what, actually, was going on when I chose my classes.

It is clear to me now that the Princeton Professor who pointed out that Princeton Civil Engineering graduates attend Stanford for more advanced study, was thinking about further classes along the line of those taught from Stephen Tymoshenko's texts. I had no idea that Stephen Tymoshenko was even alive, let alone was a Professor at Stanford; I certainly took no classes that extended my abilities in Structural Engineering unless one counts a class in Timber Design. Certainly nothing in the way of concrete structural design nor steel design was pursued at Stanford that took me beyond the classes in those subjects I took at Princeton.

I can't remember speaking with any advisor on the topic of goals and how to meet them. Presumably, the course catalog was my only assistance. But this is all of a piece with a set of traits that we will investigate shortly; it is very much a cut of the same cloth when I add that I had no idea that I was a veteran and was eligible for educational funds from the government; that knowledge came to me by accident several years later during a time when I was pursuing a second Master's Degree – a Master's in Business Administration at the University of Chicago – while employed by IBM, and a nearby colleague overheard me speaking of earning an MBA at Night School and asked me if I had received my subsidized government check for education!

But to continue. We will call the letter, *My Purpose and General Plan For Graduate Work*, a statement of my *ostensible* purpose, however flawed it became when compared to what I actually did. But was there another purpose, a non-ostensible one? In view of the fact that I never used, nor retained, any information from my Stanford Engineering classes – heavy construction, timber construction, tunnels, and others that I can't even recall. I do remember, though, one Professor who used the term 'Tunnel Stiffs' quite frequently. I retained more from an English class that I audited, and a graded class in computer programming using the computer language of ALGOL 60, a language that ran on a Burroughs B-5000 computer, it is important that we investigate this non-ostensible purpose which caused me to drive to Stanford for a MSE, Master of Science in Engineering.

Simply stated – and I have never wavered in making public this assertion – I went to Stanford to find a wife! This was my true intention, my purpose based on some kind of unquestionable belief or trust, i.e., faith, coupled with an intuition (knowing something without conscious use of reason (like statistics) – that reinforced my *non- ostensible* intention.

Toward that end I took, during my first quarter, several actions to further my goal. I enrolled in a class on Ballroom Dancing. I revisited one of my cousins, Sonja, a stewardess for Pan American Airways, with the notion that I might be assisted with discovering prospects. I hadn't seen my cousins, Sonja and Barbara, for many years – they came to visit us at Jerp House when they were both not yet ten years old. Nothing ever came of my visit with Sonja because she was always somewhere else in the world

My visit with Sonja's older sister, Barbara, was more propitious, if not lucky in a fashion that I could not have expected. Barbara was married but I happened to mention that I was looking for a dentist since I had not had a checkup during my time on the *Hank*. Barbara put me in touch with a High School friend, Carol, who graduated first-in-her-class at Northwestern Dental School, and was now practicing dentistry in Burlingame, California, where she was allied with an older, male dentist. I *did* need a checkup! It became apparent that I need two rows of three gold teeth, that's a total of six; in 1849 there was a rush to California for gold and I felt close to those souls who came all that way. Carol set to work and ended up giving me those teeth, her first masterpiece!

I say masterpiece because every dentist I have known since that time has exclaimed, upon viewing Carol's work for the first time, that they are absolutely exquisite! It is quite an uplifting (no pun intended) experience to have a dentist pronounce such encomiums just by looking inside one's mouth. Toward the end of the quarter, I invited Carol to attend a stage performance of *The Sound of Music* in San Francisco.

If I remember correctly, I did ask one of the young women in my Ballroom Dancing class, Cathy Pike, for a date; I only had coffee with Cathy but I found out that she was the daughter of the Episcopal Bishop of California, the fifth Bishop of that state, and, much later, came to know that he was a TV celebrity and quite controversial, being, as he was, an early advocate for: the ordination of women, racial desegregation, and the acceptance of lesbian, gay, bisexual, and transgender people within mainline churches! As we will soon see, there was, for lack of a better phrase, a kind of *Episcopal Destiny* that followed me around in California and this was to be the first act.

For the second act, we note that Crothers Memorial Hall, my Stanford Hall, a residence for Graduate Engineering Students, was named after Margaret Jane Crothers, by one of her six sons, George E. Crothers, class of 1895, a close advisor to Jane Stanford, and one of the benefactors who gave funds for a set of Carillon Bells for Grace *Episcopal* Cathedral in San Francisco. Professor Bigelow, my slide rule Professor at Princeton, would have given George E. Crothers an Engineering Bravo! For the third and final act, I would, ultimately, do my part by marrying an Episcopalian, Stanford Class of 1965! I know, blessed reader, that there is exactly seventy years between these two awesome persons, the first instrumental in putting Stanford on a solid legal and financial footing, and the second responsible for putting *me* on a solid footing!

But enough, now, about the effects of seven years of living in two environments completely devoid of female companionship; we must return to those antecedent activities that occurred during the time of transition between the *Hank* and Stanford. We begin with a Mediterranean liberty port, Barcelona, Spain. During the *Hank's* first six month Mediterranean period with the 6th Fleet, we were fortunate to berth at a location where we could step off the *Hank* directly into the bustling metropolis of Barcelona during the Christmas period. I don't mean to compare one city with another, "Comparisons are odious!" was another of my mother's epithets, but why would I rank Barcelona above Genoa, Italy, Marseilles, France, Naples, Italy, Djibouti, French Somaliland, Jidda, Saudi Arabia, Aden, British Protectorate, Bahrain Island, Assab, Ethiopia, and Malta? It had to do with culture.

A hundred feet from where the *Hank* was tied up at one end of La Rambla, we walked across the gangplank and encountered at our doorstep a tree-lined pedestrian mall street stretching three quarters of a mile! La Rambla was a major attraction of Barcelona. Both sides of La Rambla were lined with rows of Sycamore trees, a wonderful Christmas present.

A few blocks away from our berth in Barcelona, we easily walked to the Barcelona Cathedral of the Holy Cross and Saint Eulalia, which was surrounded by Christmas crèches which were extraordinary! A group of *Hank's* officers went to an opera, *Amahl And the Night Visitors* by Gian Carlo Menoti, and a large portion of the entire crew and officers of the *Hank* attended a Bull Fight. I toured Antoni Gaudi's Sagrada Familia and saw other Gaudi buildings, buildings I studied in my *Modern Architectural History* class at Princeton. Right at our doorstep, then, was a magnificent boulevard, a gateway to the city.

But it was a very tiny store with only a single doorway that was a mere seventy-five feet away from the *Hank's* quarterdeck, that became a very important shop to know about. This was the location of Navy Auto Sales of Barcelona. When the time came to leave the Navy I knew I could purchase, for $1400, a Red Volkswagen Beetle delivered to Norfolk, Virginia. Actually, $100 of that $1400 was for 'extras' required by US law. After picking up the car which was delivered to a dock not very from the Destroyer/Submarine Base, I could drive it to the Norfolk Volkswagen dealer and have the grease removed from the entire car – grease to keep away any salt spray during its transit – and install a high quality FM radio and rear speaker. Once the vehicle was ready I could pack my belongings and set a course for Jerp House and a summer break before the long drive to Stanford.

How did I occupy my time at Jerp House? There were still a few assignments left for my final University of Chicago Correspondence Course, *Introduction to Religious Existentialism.* I finished those assignments, typed them out and then, one by one, submitted them to the person who graded them in Hyde Park; my final assignment was sent from Stanford. You see, then, that those graded University of Chicago Correspondence Courses formed a kind of educational overlap; I started them early on the *Hank* and they carried me along until I was again in a classroom, not that I didn't take classes in the Navy. There were the Damage Control classes, a long Atomic, Biological, and Chemical warfare class in Philadelphia, Pennsylvania, and a class on decoding secret messages, and let's not forget those summer cruises.

In Jiddah, Saudi Arabia, I was fortunate to be selected by Captain 'Mad-Dog-Mallon' to attend a party at the U. S. Embassy. Why fortunate? Captain Mallon was a lawyer and I still remember his first Captain's Mast. I attended this session of non-judicial punishment just to see if there would be any change from Captain Dinwiddie's letting everyone off with a very slight punishment, a slap on the hands. The first man from the Engineering Department was there on a charge, if I remember correctly, of insubordination. Captain Mallon described what would happen to *him* if he was in the same situation. He recited the General Court Martial that would follow and all the extraordinary punishments: loss of command, reduction in rank, and more; he knew the Universal Code of Military Justice from memory! Then he threw the book at the man; reduction in pay, rank, etc. Within ten minutes after that first Captain's Mast, word flew around the ship that things had changed! From then on, Third Class Petty Officers were instantly obeyed.

But Mallon was also hard on his officers, especially the Gunnery Officer. For some reason, I was liked and never criticized. On the Mediterranean deployment's trip down the Red Sea, this had benefits like being invited to go to the U. S. Embassy for a dinner, and in Djibouti, French Somaliland, to be invited to accompany Captain Mallon and the Executive Officer to the Naval Superintendent's mountain summer place for lunch. I swam at Bass Lake but I enjoyed a swimming experience in Jiddah as well, even though there was no official liberty allowed. The U. S. Embassy arranged for a group of *Hank's* crew to use the Embassy's private beach on the Red Sea and I accompanied that contingent.

It was very hot and I couldn't understand why we loaded case after case of soft drinks into the rear seats of the bus. Upon arrival, everyone ran down to the water's edge and dove in to the bath-tub-like water, crystal clear, hot, and possessing tropical fish here and there – amazing! But even more fun was the ability to float effortlessly in the highly saline water, all you needed to do was lie on you back facing the sun, stretch out, and relax without moving a muscle!

But very quickly everyone *did* move their muscles. It took only minutes to recall those cases of cold pop. If you walked up the beach to the bus you could grab two bottles and then return back to the beach; it turned out there was one case for each person on the bus; when all the bottles were empty it was time to go back to the *Hank*, back home. On one of those returns to the shoreline I walked along the narrow beach path into an adjacent residential area that, I am certain, was 'out of bounds.' I saw no native citizens of Saudi Arabia. I reasoned that the stay-at-home mothers of young children either kept inside, weren't allowed to appear in public, or just didn't find swimming and floating that much fun.

So, back at Jerp House, I swam in Lake Michigan in the summer of 1963, but I was biased toward fresh, cold water where there were no tropical fish, only the minnows in the outlet that were carried across the dam that held back the waters of Bass Lake. But what about fishing in the Red Sea? Did the *Hank* do any of that?

On both six month assignments to the Sixth Fleet in the Mediterranean, *Hank* was assigned the independent duty of transiting the Suez canal, steaming to the bottom of the Red Sea – with stops at Assad, Ethiopia, Jiddah, Saudi Arabia, and Djibouti, French Somaliland, and Aden, British Protectorate. On the first Red Sea sojourn, the Executive Officer, Commander Faust, had the wherewithal to take on board a large quantity of fishing poles – enough to keep the crew happy.

We steamed at a speed that allowed us to get ahead of schedule and then anchored above a shallow piece of water at the bottom of the Red Sea, threw over all the fish lines and started catching Red Snapper! We were using Shark meat from a Shark that the Operations Officer, Mark Godfrey, caught earlier. Sailors who had never fished before in the ocean were now hauling in large, edible fish; they were put in an empty fifty-five gallon drum filled with salt water.

But the *Hank's* cooks didn't want to go to all the trouble of cooking up a fish dinner; pork chops were so much easier. After all, the entire crew knew we were steaming with only one boiler on line – cross connected so as to serve both engine rooms – but, more importantly, the boilermen tending that one boiler were required to 'come up for air' every fifteen minutes and take a lot of salt tablets – it was hot down in that boiler room and it was hot in *Hank's* galley. The Red Snapper were dumped overboard for the Sharks! This was providential in its way, it made up for the Shark that Mark caught to start the fishing frenzy that the *Hank's* crew enjoyed in the hot sun. We raised the anchor and continued on our way to Djibouti.

How different were those two visits to Djibouti. On my first visit, most of the off-watch officers attended a dinner party at the home of the

Naval Commandant. When we arrived at the address, there were huge wooden doors in the wall that separated us from what appeared to be a large, enclosed yard. The Gunnery Officer pushed on the doors and they opened. Up ahead and to the right was a porch leading up to the doors of the large residence. We walked about ten feet further beyond the gate which we closed behind us, when someone remarked about a sound that sounded like metal scraping metal. Where could it be coming from? Even more mysterious was that it seemed to come from above. Then someone spotted the cause! It was a pet Cheetah!

It sported a collar with a chain attached to it; on the other end of the chain was a metal ring; the ring was fastened to a wire rope that ran the breath of the entire yard from the far end to a fixture near the gate we just passed through. The Cheetah was exhibiting that trait for which it is known: high speed! And there was only one way to move – directly toward the *Hank's* officers in their civilian clothes. We began to panic; we couldn't get back to the gate, let alone open it, when competing in a race with a Cheetah; we all froze! Fortunately, just as we thought we were going to have an encounter, a fellow came out of the house and gave the Cheetah a sharp command. The Cheetah was trained, understood what it was told, and we quickly ascended the few steps up to the porch and into safety and our dinner.

On my second trip to Djibouti with Mad-Dog-Mallon as Captain, I accompanied the Naval Commandant, his wife, Captain Mallon, and the Executive Officer on a trip up into the mountains outside Djibouti where it was cool without Cheetahs, and we enjoyed French cooking while being entertained with tales of trips the Commandant and his family took into the valleys that we could see in the distance many miles away. In one of those valleys they hunted for, and found, geodes. But returning now to Bass Lake, I was to fulfill a desire that was anchored in a famous fishing story that had its antecedent in Professor Carols Baker's English course at Princeton.

Professor Baker was writing Ernest Hemmingway's biography and we, as might be expected, read Hemmingway in the class. One story we read was titled *Big Two-Hearted River*, named after an actual river called the

Two Hearted River, in Michigan's Upper Peninsula. Years earlier, I took my two younger brothers – six and nine years younger – on a canoe trip on the *Pine River* not so far from Jerp House. The *Pine River* was a fantastic river with beautiful scenery, and offered us many great rapids to run – all that one would want for a canoe trip.

Father told me to do this kind of thing with my brothers; I don't think it had anything to do with his tipping over in the aluminum canoe. Accordingly, I thought it would be a great idea to strap the old, number 96, Owasippie, aluminum canoe to the top of the Volkswagen Beetle, load it with all the gear, the three brothers, and seek out a place to put in on the *Two Hearted River*. The VW came through the trip from Norfolk, Virginia, with flying colors, and was scheduled to go to Stanford, California, in a very short time. I was certain that with all the baggage and the three human occupants, the VW would be able to cross the new Mackinaw Bridge with impunity, i.e., without being blown over!

As we pulled out of Jerp House the VW sounded a bit like a truck but we made the drive and located a put-in spot on the *Two Hearted River* – I was driving old logging roads, the kind that were used by the Owasippie Scout Camp drivers as they transported troops of scouts and their canoes through the backwoods forests of Michigan. Unlike these daring drivers who knew the unsigned logging roads like the back of their hands, I drove slowly and, when I finally parked the VW, I had no idea, nor even a map, to show me where to return to, nor, for that matter, did I know how to hire a taxi! You'll understand when I tell you that the *Two Hearted River* ran through wilderness and emptied into Lake Superior.

The trip downstream to Lake Superior was, unfortunately, uneventful – it *did not* have the exciting rapids of the *Pine River*! Quite to the contrary, it had log jams where I got out and pulled the canoe over the jams. We did not fish for trout; and unlike Hemmingway's Nick Adams after WW I, I didn't feel a need to erase my memories of the *Hank*, quite the contrary. On our last night we camped on the Lake Superior Beach where we encountered other humans.

Fortunately, I met an individual who was willing to drive to a point where we could begin searching for the VW; I say 'search' because we had very little to go on. All's well that ends well; I suspect that what we have here, tying things together, is the theme of transportation: the *Hank* through the Suez Canal twice, an Owasippie canoe down two rivers – the *Pine* and *Two Hearted* rivers – a Volkswagen on two long trips – Norfolk, Virginia, to Jerp House, and Jerp House to Stanford, California. The only thing missing, then, is that final leg: Michigan to California.

It might appear to you, my blessed readers, that there is a trajectory in the events so far discussed, that a kind of fixed path, dating from the senior year in High School – seven years of uncharted waters – is at play, the problem being merely how to stay in the center of that path so as to keep on a course to arrive at those goals which were intended from childhood. A case could be made that the end point was to be arrived at by persisting in the path that was set by Natal Ronneberg, i.e., becoming a third generation, self-employed Engineer. Certainly that letter to Stanford, *My Purpose and General Plan for Graduate School*, the so-called ostensible motive argument, would support this conservative notion. We can label this career drive the 'explicit' plan.

But we have observed a non-ostensible counterplan that is anything but explicit. In fact, it would not be out of place to characterize actions taken under the rubric of this counterplan as being random! The evidence for this randomness of action, this throwing of the dice of unknown, unexplored, options and its total lack of any forethought, I say, the evidence is legion. Who would take the recommendation of a single Professor as to what Graduate School to attend without giving the decision a second thought? This corresponds to an earlier ploy of applying to a single school, Princeton, sight unseen and never having heard of the school before, except through the mention of a $250 per year Eagle Scout Scholarship.

Since we are talking about evidence, I think we need to be precise. Strictly speaking, that reference about 'sight unseen and never having heard of the school before' is not, technically, accurate. My first *sight* of Princeton

University was on a Nightly TV News program; I should mention, in passing, that father insisted on having a TV as early as 1948! And I must add further that if having a TV is a Norwegian characteristic, then an early predictor of my *not* following *that* particular trait must be the fact of never owning a television.

But back to Princeton being on the TV news on the night of April 26th, 1956. Dr. Harold W. Dodds, Princeton's President, was interviewed as to why he would allow such a grievous act to occur on the campus. He replied to reporters that the Whig-Cliosophic Society, Princeton's Debating Society, like so many other student groups, was allowed to 'act on its own.' But what was it that was allowed? What was it that caused the Princeton campus to be heavily guarded? The Whig-Cliosophic Society, knowing that Alger Hiss was being released from prison, invited Hiss to Princeton to speak to the Society on Yalta. It could be interpreted as a celebration of his release from prison. Hiss was accused of espionage and went to prison on a conviction of perjury. The TV news showed viewers the streetlight near the Whig-Cliosophic Society's building; there were crowds all around the area. If the TV cameras were pointed one-hundred and eighty degrees from their TV news direction, I would have seen Witherspoon Hall!

We were discussing a conversation with an Advanced Strength of Materials class Professor. That Princeton Professor was, no doubt, intimately familiar with the life and work of Stephen Tymoshenko, the brilliant ethnic Ukrainian engineer from the Russian Empire, who was the father of modern engineering mechanics. Natal Ronneberg and scores of other Structural Engineers were affected by Tymoshenko's works in areas of engineering mechanics, elasticity, and strength of materials; the proof being that they are still in use after a hundred years. I hadn't the slightest idea that Tymoshenko was at Stanford, that he joined the faculty in 1938, the year I was born; that realization came decades later. While I enjoyed Tymoshenko's brilliance at Princeton, my classes at Stanford had nothing whatever to do with Strength of Materials! I could have chosen those classes on a random basis: heavy construction, tunneling, bridges, canals, and such like.

Who would listen to a single Chief Petty Officer, an unknown, to de-termine one's career ship for three entire years? These kinds of spur-of-the-moment snap decisions display a complete disregard for career planning; they are the actions of an unfocused individual who, for the most part, has no idea of what is going on even within a given academic pursuit; they are steps taken in *isolation* like leaving a Volkswagen parked in a wildness area of northern Michigan.

We must also characterize those first-quarter efforts of searching for a wife, the non-ostensible-reason efforts, as being scatter-shot as well. I at-tended Stanford using, for the most part, my own funds; I had no idea that the U. S. Government would pay me to attend Stanford after my NROTC Scholarship. Why was this? I never classified myself as a 'veteran.' A vet-eran was a military person who fought in World War II! To make matters worse, I never talked to a soul about these rather basic areas: the benefits that accrue to people who serve in the military. Of course, the Navy made no effort to inform officers who were leaving the service that such funds were available.

It is futile to pursue these dead-end topics any further. Let us re-turn to Crothers Memorial Hall and how I arrived at Stanford. In do-ing this we will, perforce, again focus on further random efforts, but regardless of that, we will introduce the trip to Stanford in the VW. But even before we narrate this same tendency for unfocused action in that cross-country trip, we must, out of fairness, offer counter-examples and their effect on this child wandering in the wilderness of modern life. And those counter-examples are such, that you, my reader, should insist that they speak to the theme of love! I say this because we will soon begin the third major chapter of this odyssey. Those chapters form the sequence: Memory, Home, and Love.

It so happened that while still attending Princeton, there was one day, an announcement made after a Mechanical Engineering class exami-nation, that there existed a device, a so-called 'Computer,' in the base-ment of the Engineering Building; hobbyists and others might want to view this object. I, of course, had no time for diversions – the English comedies at a nearby movie theater on Nassau street were much more to my liking – and so I only made a mental note of the statement. But once at Stanford, I did take an ALGOL-60 computer programming class because I sought diversion and regretted that I never made it down into the Engineering Building basement for a look-see. My intuition, hunch, whatever, was some kind of idle curiosity, perhaps I was also after some entertainment.

That throw-away class, however, was the seed that planted the non-Norwegian thrust, and growth, of my entire working career at IBM and even before IBM, a seed that grew into a fabulous, highly entertaining experience for thirty-four years, and we need to examine that in more detail to gain the perspective we are seeking for the counter-examples. The simple question is how such a throw-away class could have anything to do with love? During this pre-IBM period the whole idea of a computer kept coming into focus. The first time this happened was at Princeton; in the beginning there was the word but the word couldn't attract me. Here, from *Work – A Memoir*, is how that played out:

* * *

"I remember the first time I heard the word computer used. We just finished a final exam in mechanical engineering. I was thankful that my professor wrote the exams. He had conscience enough to at least discuss the issues that would make up the questions – it was a sense of fairness. There were other students taught by other professors; they took the same exams. They never saw the laws of thermodynamics applied in the same ways, and they, poor souls, had to think through the whole idea behind certain questions, by themselves, under the time limits of an exam. It was all pure luck for me; I was good at taking notes, memorizing things; but I digress.

"After the exam someone announced that a new machine was installed in the basement of the engineering building. It used punched cards;

you could join a club, it was like a hobby, like the flying club. It was an oddity, it was mechanical, it warranted some of your spare time; it competed with the movies in town – those English comedies that were so funny you had to yell at the audience in front of you because they were laughing so loudly you couldn't hear the dialog.

"After final exams, who had time for hobbies playing around with another invention? The only thing that mattered was knowledge that was in the course catalog, right?"

* * *

And then, in the Navy, on the *Hank*, it came up again when I realized just how old the *Hank* was:

* * *

"No. It wasn't until after three years in the Navy that the idea of a computer would catch up with me. Well, we didn't exactly lack a computer on my destroyer. She was built in 1944 and fought in World War II and the Korean conflict. I was Chief Engineer during the Cuban Missile Crisis, but that is another story.

"Down inside my ship in a compartment where some of the Engineering Department men stood watch – they were called 'IC' men because they looked after the interior communications, the sound powered telephone systems, and the gyro – there was a huge mechanical monster. It was a big computer operated by the Gunnery Department. It had little windows on the sides that allowed anyone to peek inside at the gears.

"During training at Guantanamo Bay (GITMO) jet aircraft would attack the ship and bearings and ranges would be dialed into this computer using little hand-operated cranks; the readings were passed down by voice from radar operators. The dials drove the gears inside the machine; it came to life, and the five inch guns were slewed around, pointed upward, and fired.

"The problem was simply that the planes were now fast – a lot had happened between 1944 and the early 1960's – and they were almost out of sight by the time the guns could rotate around toward them. I felt sure we could hit land targets and other ships but planes were another story. The Russians were sending missiles, not planes, during the Cuban crisis."

* * *

Finally, there was Stanford and the class in ALGOL 60:

* * *

"And oh, by the way, it was after the Navy, and it was only an afterthought that I decided to take an elective class in ALGOL 60 during my one year of graduate school at Stanford. ALGOL 60 was designed to be an international computer programming language, like Esperanto, which was intended to have everyone speak using one, universal language. It all sounded rational."

* * *

But what, exactly, was it that captured what I called the 'Romance of My Intellect?' We need to understand what truly trumped Engineering and the pursuit of my Norwegian legacy; we need to ask what new kind of *love* it was that came to be more intense, more exciting, and even more romantic than five years of Engineering studies.

* * *

"The Stanford class was equivalent to 'Computing 101 for Beginners.' We did things like find solutions to equations. You remember those algebra problems we had in high school? We solved things like $AX^2 + BX + C = 0$. Solutions were values of X which, when they were substituted in the equation, made the left side equal to zero. Using ALGOL 60 we found the solutions by incrementing values for X and then making the increments smaller and smaller as we searched for solutions. Ultimately we found the roots of the equations. If we weren't successful, we asked for help from the graduate student teaching assistants who were there in the lab.

"There was something practical, even exciting, in finding the roots of an equation with a machine that was so fast that it took only milliseconds. It was a new way; it was called an algorithm; it demanded creativity – like what to do when you went from a positive answer to a negative answer and neither were zero – it could be *elegant* as the mathematicians say; it was called *programming*; I seemed to have an affinity for it; it was fun; in that sense it did make for a good hobby; it was cumulative – the more you did, the better your skills were for the next program; it involved debugging – figuring out what went wrong.

"Debugging was like solving a mystery – it had lots of types of evidence – it challenged your powers of reasoning, the determination of which clues counted, where to look first, which clues had been corrupted and weren't reliable, how to step through your program – and even modifying it prior to a test run so as to print out numbers from inside the program to help you confirm what values your variables had at a particular point in the program. All these strategies appealed to the romance of my intellect!

"They caught my imagination unawares; they demanded more creativity than *engineering problems* which seemed rote by comparison. Programs always contained the germ of removing endless hours of boring work from human effort – think of accountants with their green eye shades – and the irony was that programs came about through human creativity and exciting problem solving during their development and perfection. The computer was the kind of machine that would revolutionize the world.

"But did I care about that? Of course not. I felt the promise that it would revolutionize work – my work – and that *did* seem worthwhile.

"But, of course, what can you do with ALGOL 60? This was a language that no one ever heard of. It ran on a Burroughs B5000 which I thought was an academic machine. I had no desire to become a graduate student in computer science and help students in *Computing 101* classes. All the same, the experience must have planted some kind of spark – a spark that just needed some tinder to bring out flame and sometimes that takes time. I knew of few maxims to live by but one was, 'Luck is when preparedness meets opportunity.'"

* * *

So we have examined the first counter-example; we move on to Example Number 2. Rather than drive back and forth to Chicago from Stanford for Christmas Break, I took a Stanford Charter Flight and, on the return trip, I sat next to my future wife: another random decision; I could have driven; I could have taken another seat – there were plenty of seats available just like there are on Southwest Airlines when you are in the 'A' group; I could have read a book; I didn't do that! Look again at that last phrase in the prior paragraph, 'Luck is when preparedness meets opportunity.' So I ask you, blessed reader, what other decisions in life are more important than a wife and a career? I haven't found any.

But getting back to my naiveté, my lack of planning, and the tendency to just run off and do something; those actions that are like taking a canoe trip without knowing how to return to the wilderness location where my car was. These character traits are no different than driving from Chicago to Stanford without adequate funds; they crop up at unexpected times and places. In the following excerpt we see this once again; the excerpt is from *Western Michigan Tales of Mystery and Adventure* in a story called 'Pentwater Beach Addition No. 1.'

* * *

He realized how naïve he always was when it came to such questions. When he drove across the country to Stanford he started to run short of cash. His plan was to cash a personal check at Yosemite National Park at Camp Curry but things were looking bleak in Nevada. He decided to stop in Reno, Nevada, and cash a check. As he motored down the city streets he looked up and saw a sign advertising a casino. Surely they would have funds there.

He parked, and went in the front door, and was directed to the pit boss, a guy who looked authoritative and was standing over a gambling table in back where the lamp above him made him stand out in the darkness of the patrons and tables around him.

Sherman asked the pit boss, "can you cash a small check on a Midwestern bank?" Sherman realized that the pit boss probably heard this a thousand times from patrons who were down on their luck; his look was a cross between disbelief, pity, and an internal disquiet at being interrupted.

"Try across the street," was his reply.

Sherman walked into the drug store that faced the casino, went to the counter, and found a grandmotherly woman who asked him what she could do to help. He explained that he was sent over from the casino by the pit boss because he wanted to cash a personal check.

"I see," said the woman, "have you any identification?"

Sherman took out his huge identification billfold and started to display his cards one-by-one: his driver's license, his Navy certificate of service card, several department store credit cards, his undergraduate ID card, and several cards from memberships in various organizations.

The grey-haired woman examined each card, turning them over as she went. Sherman was about to ask her if she could use a magnifying glass when at last she finished with a membership card in the National Audubon Society. "So you like birds?" she asked.

"Yes, I'd like to think I'm an amateur bird watcher. I need to get to Yosemite and maybe I can add a few more species to my life list."

"OK, I guess if you like birds I can trust you. I'll let you have ten dollars."

Sherman made out the check for the cash. He knew he could live on apples and peanuts with that amount and buy some gas as well. He thanked the woman and departed. Such was the naïveté that Sherman knew he possessed as he contemplated what to do with his new treasure.

* * *

The drive from Camp Curry in Yosemite National Park to Stanford, California, was uneventful and I moved into a room, 403B Crothers Memorial Hall, as an Engineering student. Carothers Memorial Hall was the most modern home I had lived in up to that time. Think, readers, of those Chicago, Silver Lake, and Michigan homes! Think of those 19th century dormitories – Witherspoon and Blair Halls. Or, if you like, imagine those several warships built during or just after World War II. Here I was, if you can imagine it, ensconced in a dormitory first occupied in 1955! Picture, then, a small two-person room with two beds, two desks, a pair of corner closets for storage and an entrance door off a hallway; open the door and at the opposite wall you sight a row of windows with a view – across the street – of another dorm.

I can understand the sympathy that arises within you, blessed reader; and all this after having climbed up one of those gorgeous trails at Yosemite, a trail that leads to an exciting waterfall!

No, the beauty of the Stanford Campus lies elsewhere; in the walkways dominated by Nature, in the hills behind the campus, in the Quad and Memorial Church, and even in Lake Lagunita when it fills with water in the Spring. I admired the perfume of the eucalyptus trees and towering palm trees. My first quarter roommate, Salvatore, was from Guatemala. Unlike my experiences as a freshman at Princeton with Frank Sinatra in the morning and Curt Weil at other times, I started to appreciate Salvatore's LP records, after all, we *were* learning the Cha Cha Cha and Tango in Ballroom Dancing class! Things like the Cha Cha Cha's Slide and the Tango's Magic Step. Salvatore told me about the incursions from Nicaragua and when he left Stanford at the end of the quarter after finishing his studies, he gave me two of his LPs: Manuel de Falla's *Ritual Fire Dance and the Complete Music of Manuel de Falla* and *Dazas Afro-Cubanas and other works by Lecuona* both records featuring the artist, José Echániz.

After I returned from my student flight from Chicago, the one where I sat next to my future wife, my roommate for the next two quarters was Salal Dumiyati from Beirut, Lebanon. Salal's father owned a soil testing firm and he was getting a degree in Soil Mechanics. Over the Christmas vacation I had gone from a Catholic roommate to an Arab roommate. I was not totally ignorant about the Middle East; my Naval career on the *Hank* helped to the effect that I knew about one tenth of one percent of what I now know. Where did that miniscule amount of information come from?

The *Hank* transited the Suez Canal twice; on our first transit I remember the Executive Officer, Commander Faust, telling us to count the number of Russian MIG aircraft at Kibrit Air Base as we steamed through the canal; we were to use the binoculars like we were looking at things a tourist would be fascinated with. So we told the starboard lookouts to pretend they were taken with the scenery and other sights and then, very quickly and casually, take a peek at Kibrit! I was on the Bridge during that first transit and the Executive Officer was not only concerned that we have an accurate MIG count to report to higher authorities, but he also was worried about his giving in to requests to have several 'bum boat' merchants come aboard with their wares, take up some space on the fantail, and sell items to the crew who could not have liberty in Egypt.

This permission was a generous gesture but Commander Faust made certain that they were to be watched; for example, trips to the head were to be 'escorted!' One of the members of R Division, my Division, came up to the Bridge to see me while on watch transiting the Suez Canal; this was a rare appearance as I never saw R Division personnel on the Bridge. The sailor who came up to me was a young man, I don't remember his name, but his mission was quickly stated: he informed me that there were lots of good 'bargains' on the fantail and asked if he would like me to have him haggle one of the bum boat merchants for a piece of 'Camel Hide Luggage.' I responded: O. K. After watch I was the owner of a piece of Camel Hide Luggage for which I reimbursed him $2.50.

Salal and I soon talked about Arab feelings with respect to the Middle East; Salal didn't have to be specific for me to understand him, instead, he gave me the spirit of his emotions. I knew the bare facts about Saudi Arabia; U. S. Ambassador Hart kindly came aboard the *Hank* and gave us a seminar in the Wardroom that related that history and our relationship with the Saudis – forged by President Roosevelt – and how Ibn Saud united the disparate tribes into the nation that became Saudi Arabia. This special relationship – we develop their oil and, in return, we protect Saudi Arabia with our military – was important to know when, later in our trip of independent steaming – Suez Canal-Red Sea-Arabian Ocean – we steamed up through the Straits of Hormuz and stopped at Bahrain Island in the Persian Gulf.

Once we tied up at Bahrain Island, the Wardroom officers went ashore and partied with the ARAMCO employees who lived in a town in the middle of the desert that looked exactly like small town America; they served tiny shrimp from the Persian Gulf and homemade booze that they made in their basements; they were starved for news from the United States. First they asked if we thought that their booze was good and, of course, we answered: Yes! Then they wanted to know where we were from; if you said New York, you soon had a group of ARAMCO employees who circled around you and, like the third-degree, started questioning you about what was going on in New York. In the middle of the party one of the Engineers received a call that required him to take a look at some equipment at the Refinery just outside town and asked if I would like to come along.

I agreed and that let me see the 'town' close at hand, not to mention the insides of the huge refinery. These tourist-like adventures were interesting but they were not what Salal and I eventually discussed: his relationship to Israel. I don't have to mention that relationship. On my side of the conversation, I pleaded with Salal that, if ever there was more fighting, he should not go and fight Israel. My reasoning came from those Confidential Documents I read while traversing down the Red Sea. "Even if every Arab country joins in to fight Israel," I said, "the Arabs will lose!" according to the Confidential information I had just read. I could never convince Salal but I did the best thing I could.

Love

And now, blessed readers, we must focus on a different word: love. "But wait," you say, "we have hardly finished with all those homes that you promised." My answer? Did I not continue with 'memory' when I segued to home? I did. So there is a carrying forward that is going on here: the past is prologue to the future. It is reasonable to expect, then, that this new love chapter will, in its way, continue the notions of memory and home; how else could it be? But there is much more to support this new perspective, this new focus: my world had changed! I would never again be the same; South Pacific had come to me on a Stanford Student Flight!

As I walked down the center aisle of that flight, I saw a stranger across the semi-crowded seats already occupied, 'And somehow I knew, I knew even then, That somewhere I would see her, Again and again.' Upon return to 403B Crothers Memorial Hall I instantly began the process that would reactivate the conversation that made the flight to San Francisco so brief. I would have three months; at the end of that time I would drive again to the San Francisco airport to put my future wife on another plane chartered by Stanford University, the plane that would fly her Stanford In France group to Paris – the undergraduate students and the two Professors, English Professor Albert Guerard, and Sociology Professor Sandy Dornbusch, and their families – and then on to Tours in the Loire Valley of France for a stay of many months.

As I left the parking garage I struggled to drive the red Volkswagen; emotionally I had never experienced a loss so profound, I needed all the strength that I could come up with and, physically, I had to concentrate on my driving; I felt I could not pull over, I had to go on, but neither could I stem the tide of tears that kept coming. A consoling thought, however, was already set in place through a simple strategy.

A few days before the departure – the force of which I never could have estimated – we parked the VW in downtown Palo Alto and walked into an electronics store on University Avenue. I purchased a portable tape recorder, the kind that takes those four inch diameter reels that I had been using for more than seven years. It used batteries, it used power from a 115 volt circuit, it could be used to access the French electrical system with an adapter. But all that was as nothing for I could *hear* my future wife across those months, and, even more importantly, she could hear me. After her return in the Fall she would know me better than before – all my foibles, all my plans to seek employment with an engineering firm with offices in Chicago *and* San Francisco. Now I could switch from one office, Chicago, to the other, San Francisco, while my future wife finished her Senior year at Stanford. If all worked out well, I would have a job waiting for me back in Chicago; I knew she wanted a Master's Degree in Social Service Administration from the University of Chicago.

I, too, would be able to hear her voice and stay in touch with her wonderful experiences in France and elsewhere for it would not be too long before her mother and two sisters would join her for a European tour. Oh, yes, there were letters exchanged as well. These letters I could read over and over again by myself as the months progressed but I could also put on the earphones and listen!

My family was at O'Hare Field when the Stanford In France flight stopped to refuel but Professor Dornbusch couldn't allow even a brief meeting; they would have to wait, just as I would. But, blessed readers, I think you can understand that now, every thought, every action, every plan, and every jog at a nearby Stanford track oval was, more or less, dominated by the anticipation of every tape and letter; how could it be otherwise? But what was it that made me *know*? Years later I would write a sonnet that I called *Stanford*. It was one of about 500 that I wrote during a short period of time. I analyzed all of those sonnets and culled down the entire group to the number of 365 – one for each day of the year. I attempted to make each sonnet's theme feel like it belonged on that day or, in most instances, within that particular month. I called the book that resulted: *A Love Affair With Flowers Fair*. The sonnet called *Stanford* was the one that ended up under the day for June 21:

Stanford

In this garden of poppies I found one
Unique, her dress a fragile feat so fair,
Brought softness to the air beyond compare
And joy discrete, orange prayer to my despair.

The jays made haste to pace this course of grace.
A morning rainbow found its place to arc.
The world once rough was soon made soft as lace
And hopeless thoughts receded to the dark.

But yet 'twas path to others led my way.
The sunrise of my day was not enough.
A bright bouquet of care had come to stay
With room for brothers, sisters in the rough.

And so today this bloom makes room for all
In gardens ever fresh despite our fall.

But there are experiences of love that are not expressible in words. And there are other kinds of love that do not involve persons. I think it's important to explain these claims before as we proceed any further.

* * *

A Digression
Being a Conversation Between a Fictional Author and Reader

"Why is that?" asked the Reader.

"The reason," answered the Author, "is that you must not think, my dear reader, that the entire tenor of the future narrative will be focused on the narrow cul de sac of matrimonial issues, a direction to which you might imagine we are tending. I ask your indulgence in some observations which, at this point in time, might not seem obvious."

"You have my indulgence, I am all ears," said the Reader.

"Very well. We have already examined certain character traits that, whether through genes, environment, or even something else, have come to lodge within, for lack of a better term, my personhood," said the Writer.

"Like what?"

"Think of that most recent example – the drive from Chicago to Stanford – with that idea of wanting to cash a personal check in Reno, Nevada. There's randomness there, lack of planning, and other tendencies already commented on; or the idea of always taking the advice of only a single person. I don't want to belabor things; my intention is merely to point out that there is a flip side of this topic; simply stated, there are already lots of other places, persons, and things that this Writer has fallen in love with.

"I'll go so far as to say that these things have been associated with the term 'romance,' but what's the difference? It seems to me that if we ask what motivates this guy – aside from his wariness about being a Norwegian all his life – we would have to answer that based on the evidence so far, the answer would be something like: this guy has to fall in love with what he is doing! That's his ruling motive."

"Ah, so! I believe there *is* a pattern there."

"So let's look at some of that evidence, then," said the Writer, "this guy has a love for *flowers*: he writes a book of poems – sonnets – and he calls the book *A Love Affair With Flowers Fair*. That's pretty explicit! And then, when he falls in love, what does he write about?"

"Let me see," said the Reader, "oh, yes, here it is: a garden of poppies, a bright bouquet, a bloom, gardens; it's all there."

"But many people love flowers even though few write 356 sonnets about them. But this guy loves all sorts of things. If we go from the sublime to the ridiculous, here is a fellow who has to love *Computer Programming*, of all things! You remember that bit about how working with computers appealed to 'the romance of his intellect?'"

"Right on!"

"And, of course, this kind of love for very specific persons, places, and things, began early in life. Take that piece about the Order of the Arrow. There was mystery in that bit about *The Coming of the Chief*, but the things that happened after that can only be described by saying that he *fell in love with the Ethics* of the Order of the Arrow!"

"Yes, and that explains why he had to memorize all those ceremonies, become such an active member, get elevated to the third level and all that," agreed the Reader, "it didn't have anything to do with not being a Norwegian, they don't have the Order of the Arrow in Norway."

"But there are some things in this guy's history that aren't so romantic to begin with; maybe they used to be but I can't say if they still are," said the Writer.

"I think I know where you are going," said the Reader.

"We just can't leave out Destroyers!" said the Writer, "before this guy ever set foot on a Destroyer, he likened his view of a nest of Destroyers — across a field, a hundred yards away — to the words of *Some Enchanted Evening* from *South Pacific*! If that's not a love affair at first sight, I don't know what is."

"I wonder," said the Reader, "if there's another kind of love that is lurking inside him? In those eighty-five billion brain cells. You remember that Indian Name he was given, Petachdonamen Weuchsowagan?"

"I do, it means *He who seeks knowledge*," answered the Writer, "and at first I thought that here was a guy going to Princeton after the ceremony, so the name seemed to fit that event; but, then, it turns out that he is interested in flowers, and when he has any spare time at Princeton, are you ready for this, he starts looking at the mosses that grow on those ancient stones that form the foundation of Witherspoon Hall. They weren't teaching any of that kind of stuff at Princeton, I think they called it Botany, even if he wanted to audit a class in that subject."

"That's right. So what does he audit instead? *Mediaeval Christian Theology*! He accidently finds this book down in the stacks of Firestone Library: Hugh of Saint Victor on the Sacraments of the Christian Faith *(De Sacramentis)* and decides to audit the Theology class," continues the Reader, "and he can't check out that book while in the Navy so he starts in with the University of Chicago Correspondence Courses; there you have it; it's a love affair with knowledge fair!" adds the Reader.

"But we have to cover all the bases," continues the Writer, "you know, people, *places*, and things. I think he's in love with Bass Lake; think of the square dancing, the moonlight on the lake, his father's plane circling the lake on Friday afternoon. Those kinds of things have their effect. And we have to introduce Scottie, a weekday father substitute for a six and seven year old male child. He learns a lot of things from Scottie, but let's not forget his own mother and father."

"No, let's not," said the Reader, "I suspect he has only given us a small portion of what he has 'locked in his heart' with respect to his parents."

"And to prove that, I just came across an example of your hunch. It's a piece from much later and has a different point of view. It is a tribute to his mother but it also shows how the *desires of a person he loves can cause him to love something*. We haven't seen a great deal of that except for his father's desire for him to follow in the family footsteps. But this piece takes something that we already know was *not* an object he was too keen about, the Clarinet, and turns it around to become the thing, the activity if you will, of the experience that he now counts as being responsible for some of the happiest times of his life. I'm tempted to ask: can you top this?" said the Writer, "it's about the love of a Band!"

"Let's hear it" said the Reader, "and that's not a pun."

* * *

All That I Am

"Some, I know, will accuse me of writing an excuse or an apology, and there would be a lot of truth in what they say. But I claim that when it comes to matters of the heart, you have to listen to both sides of the story. I think it was Abraham Lincoln that was credited with the words, 'All that I am, or hope to be, I owe to my angel mother.' I never looked on motherhood as being in need of any kind of adjective like *angel*. Instead, those haunting words set the bar for motherhood, but let me set you straight at the outset; you're not going to find out much about my mother, at least not directly.

"All this began, so I was informed, after World War II was over and I would have been seven years old at the time. Two brothers, both of whom could really play trumpet, returned from that conflict and, well, they wanted to spend more time with their instruments at their lips rather than at their shoulders. I couldn't blame them, and I really don't know what else they did with their lives, except that on Thursday nights, starting at 8 PM, all summer long under the band shell in Pentwater.

"There were a lot of others who must have felt the same way; fortunately they didn't all play the trumpet. Beginning in 1946 they called it the Pentwater Civic Band and they started something that really had no rules. It might have been in reaction to military discipline; I'm sure I don't know.

"What came into that void was a set of no rules. There was no conductor, there were no rehearsals; anyone could come and play if they had an instrument. The only fixed things seemed to be the day: Thursday, the time: 8 PM, and the length: one hour, or perhaps a bit more.

"I guess you could say that the music followed certain rules: there were lots of Sousa marches like *King Cotton* and *El Capitan*, but there were also lots of good marches from other composers like *Trombones Triumphant* and *The Footlifter.* There were novelty songs and popular songs from the past, waltzes and tunes for people who lived through the Depression and would know the words, songs like *Bill Bailey, Alexander's Ragtime Band, Let Me Call You Sweetheart, Pennsylvania Polka, The Darktown Strutters Ball* – the list was endless. The audience would tap their feet with the song while they spoke the words to themselves. And, oh yes, there was the college medley, a series of fight songs from the Midwestern big ten schools, but there were alma mater songs from other schools as well, like the University of Chicago.

"The Pentwater Civic Band played in a band shell located on the Village Green' which could easily contain 2,000 people sitting on the grass, on their folding chairs or, more appropriately, on their mats that were laid out on the grass. From the 1st clarinet section in the front of the raised platform, it always looked like an enormous crowd on all sides; there were parents, children, and lots of grandparents, and also people who were not attached to any children at the time.

"As soon as the concert began, young children migrated to the lawn in front of the raised platform and sat on the grass, like a group in school, listening to a story. Other, more precocious children, climbed up and hung on the railings, looking over the shoulders of the musicians, especially the 1st clarinet section that sat all along the south railing in a row, and eyeing the music which was printed on tiny pages about seven inches wide and five inches high. I always had the impression that there might be a young Mozart hanging on one of those rails, just behind me, a child that was capable of hearing a wrong note, but that was just an irrational fear of my own.

"But there always was an element of fear, just the same. Let me give you an example. If you had a friend, a flute player or saxophone player, for example, it didn't make any difference what the instrument was, and he or she was visiting you at your summer place, you could always encourage that friend to step up and play with the band on Thursday evenings: there were no rehearsals, no conductor, and everyone was welcome. The Catch 22 was in the music. If you have ever looked at a piece of music, essentially designed for a marching band when it comes to size, (let's use the *Star Spangled Banner* for an example), you'll remember that an enormous quantity of notes have to be squeezed on a seven-by-five-inch piece of paper.

"Your friend won't get to sit right in front of the regulars who play every week, but probably toward the end of the section, and may have a three foot distance through which to view those notes. Add to this the fact that almost all of the music is new, especially to an orchestra player. But this was true even to a band person because, by virtue of the vintage of the music it couldn't be duplicated. It came from 1946 and earlier. Now, you will begin to have a feel for the musicianship that few young, or even older players possess, but that was needed in the situation. Therefore, asking your friend to play with the band had an implicit touch of musical sadism in it. 'How did it go?' asked after the concert, always found your guest a bit deflated in their hesitant reply.

"In my own case, my humiliation was relieved somewhat by a strategy that my mother carried out. I should make it clear at the outset that, by the time I first tried to focus on the first clarinet part at a distance of three feet, the music itself, the actual printed pieces of paper, had become (I'll use another term of my mother's) priceless. In this context, all that it really meant was that you couldn't go downtown in Chicago to Lyon and Healy on Wabash Avenue and purchase any of it. Of course, if you merely looked at the books that had been pasted together for the band since time immemorial, and that had hand-numbered pages, you would see immediately that the music came from any number of original sources.

"The musician who choose what to play (this was another rule, the program or sequence of pieces to play during the hour, was completely determined on the fly by this person) (more about that later) would call out 'number thirty seven in the first black book.' Alternatively, he could call for 'number 123 in the binder,' which was a large, plywood covered collection held together by two large diameter key-rings. There were also, I should add, a handful of single sheet pieces stuck into the wooden box that held all the books for your section, and you just had to know what they were, which was no different than knowing which black book was the first and which the second.

"For years, my mother, who religiously attended the band concerts every week, encouraged me to join the band, citing the liberal rules of joining as an incentive. At a later time in life, I restarted clarinet lessons as an adult and acquired just enough courage to be humiliated. Fortunately, it was at the end of the summer season and I would have nine months to lick my wounds. But I had another strategy in mind as well.

"I told my mother, who stayed in Michigan beyond my own vacation times, to have Mr. Cook Richmond, the keeper of the wooden boxes, loan her the entire wooden box for the first clarinet section so that I could make copies of all the pieces for myself in Chicago. How she accomplished this task, I will never know. Post Office insurance would not help her argument; after all, by her own admission, the music was priceless. I think it must have been the fact that two boxes existed for the first clarinets at the time and here was a mother asking for a loan of one of them for her son. In any event, I can still remember standing at the Xerox copier one afternoon and making copies, and then sending everything back to Mr. Richmond, fully insured of course.

"This strategy made quite a difference. The ability to look at these tiny notes written on small pieces of paper, and also to figure out the markings, the repeats, where the trios started and which endings to use, helped a great deal, but even with that winter practice, I was never as good a player as Fritz, Mr. Johns, Rita, and Chuck, who sat beside me in the first clarinet section over the years.

"I always felt they tolerated me, and I realized that my early lack of lessons and rigorous practice during elementary school and high school could never be overcome by diligent lessons and practice as an adult. But I was a player in the spirit of the come-as-you-are tradition and ethic of the group, even though I spent hours during the winter months trying to avoid being perpetually humiliated.

"During the time before I joined the Pentwater Civic Band, I must also admit to another characteristic of my upbringing that influenced my having not even attended the concerts until such time as I could fully participate under the band shell. The short and the long of it was my need to use my time productively.

"As a child, I was always concerned with how I was spending my time during the summer, what accomplishments I had to show for myself, and show to others during the passage of any group of hours. I was goal oriented when the goals were felt to be worthy of my effort, and somehow, with all the people around me, the vacationers, only accomplishing the expenditure of their two weeks of vacation time by lounging around on the beach and otherwise being observers of life, or so I thought, I felt an antipathy to a certain life style.

"I fancied myself a summer resident, a person who had a different daily routine and responsibilities from those around me, and, if the truth be known, I also felt that designation bestowed upon me a degree of elitism. My mother's aphorism for this would have been, 'Nobility has its obligations!' I found it very difficult to spend any time in the numerous boutiques along Hancock Street in Pentwater, and I saw my participation in the Pentwater Civic Band as an extension of that tourist life style.

"But after I had played and been recognized as a contributor to an extraordinary component of the general public welfare of the Village,

I quickly reinforced my feelings of being elite by virtue of that status! Despite my inept background relative to other members of the first clarinet section, I honestly felt that when I bought a Blue Moon ice cream cone at Park Dairy, the young woman actually recognized me as a player and increased the size of the scoop. In short, summer residents in my mind now had responsibilities beyond vacationers. These attitudes might have been set in motion by the fact that my mother rented two cottages during the summer. The cottages that the family owned were in addition to their own place. The attitudes might have been engendered by her aphorism: 'Nobility has its obligations,' already cited, or by her worship of the music of the band–I have no idea.

"As a child, I acquired, almost by osmosis, a respect for the hierarchal nature of labor, work, and action discussed by Hannah Arendt. Labor, in this writer, tended to be conditioned by the necessities of life–renting cottages and looking after possessions, and that was my work as a child. But an action initiated a new process, being a band member, and had a political aspect, because I was a summer resident, one who had elected to live with the common goals of the ice cream merchants, gift shop owners, and people who rented cottages to the vacationers, namely, the entertainment of that transient group of people.

"But of course, I could not escape being enamored with the pleasures of labor: sawing logs, cleaning the boathouse, wooden boats, and such like, yet the pleasures of playing in the band were to overwhelm me with a pure form of multi-dimensional happiness that took me completely by surprise; the process, once started, had taken on a life of its own, a turn that was unpredictable, contingent, some would say, and came from a dimension of life that I had never experienced before.

"I have to be careful at this point because it is impossible to describe the pure joy I felt when I played the music. Even as I focus on just this one aspect of the experience, I recall many emotions at play. There was, of course, the feeling that I had arrived at a goal–even though I missed a few notes or even a sharp or a flat now and then. I could play, and keep up with the speed of the music–if you've never played *Galop-Go* at breakneck speed, you can't imagine the thrill.

"Close upon the heels of this feeling, there was the intrinsic nature of the pieces: nothing can compare with a Sousa march, but every piece was enjoyable; it was uplifting music per se. Hearing a piece on the radio of Pentwater Band music still brings back the shivers. I was having enormous fun while playing extremely listenable music and the audience was just as happy.

"Thirdly, there was an added element that came to me by virtue of the experience of playing something that listenable with others: people who I came to like–the other members of the first clarinet section. I can't even begin to count the number of times that Mr. Johns would remark to me after a piece and while the audience was still applauding, 'Now, that is a good piece of music!'

"There was an *esprit de corps* amongst the first clarinet players during and after playing; we enjoyed kibitzing between the numbers and we learned a lot about each other. We felt we were special. We thought there were 2,000 people in the audience who envied the fun we were having together, an audience that envied our friendship, our service, our expertise, our ability to amuse ourselves and, yes, maybe even who we were.

"And then there was the fact that I often chose the next piece or, let's say, perhaps fifty percent of the numbers. Butch, a baritone player, had the responsibility to call out the next number, but he made no doubt about the fact that he wanted help and made no plans prior to the concert. This must be another rule, since it fitted in so well with all the others.

"I memorized the numbers (and books) of all the best pieces for the clarinet section, you know, the ones where the brass are either intermittent or told to keep quiet, the pieces that were just plain super fun to play on that instrument and that sounded good. Sometimes it was having the melody to ourselves or the countermelody, sometimes it was the rhythm or the counter rhythm, or, as mentioned, just the fact that we could be heard as a group.

"As Butch paused while he searched for the next number, I became adept at calling out the suggested next number–'Number 37 in the second black book.' – I yelled out, and Butch invariably accepted my suggestion, and my fellow players relished playing that particular piece. 'Good number,' Mr. Johns would say after the piece, and I took it as a personal compliment.

"When the college medley was played, we had to be certain that both the University of Michigan and Michigan State University were included in the group; it would have been sacrilege to exclude either one; it might have caused a riot. I was able to get my mother's school, Illinois, in the medley, and I didn't have to look out into the audience to confirm that she would be standing and singing 'We're loyal to you Illinois.' With her right hand over her heart; she had a passion for the Illinois fight song.

"Once a year, there was a joint concert with the Scottville Clown Band, a legendary Western Michigan institution that traveled constantly and boasted a membership of hundreds of musicians to handle their requests for performances. For these concerts they encouraged the Pentwater Band Members to dress for the concert and my mother made a toga from two Chicago Symphony Marathon premiums: two towels with crossword puzzle squares in which were written the names of the great composers. I made a laurel wreath and a necklace with a rock from the shores of Lake Michigan. This joint concert used a conductor and the Pentwater Band rehearsed at the Pentwater high school. There was a lot of new music; it was often modern and used arrangements like *Hogan's Heroes*.

"The Clown Band used many busses to get around in, and during intermission at White Pine Village (that was where the joint concerts were held), I was able to enjoy a glass of beer on tap from the bar in their bus parked behind the band shell. The Clown Band was a raunchy crowd, dressed as they were in women's clothes and clown outfits. When on parade–their most frequent posture, as they all memorized their pieces–their leader, dressed in a ragged and scanty bathing outfit, led the group with a plumber's long-handled toilet plunger.

"Their theme song was *The Stripper* and one of the players, a guy with a feminine face, was also an expert stripper and he brought the house down as he teased the crowds by removing each piece of clothing. Back in Chicago I would tell my business associates (in white shirts and ties) about the kind of people I was hobnobbing with, the beer, the costumes, the stripper and the plunger. I relished their being shocked because it hinted at my true nature. And they thought they knew me! It gave me a postseason bonus.

"I remember Fritz, a retired clarinet player who played in several musical groups in Florida during the winter. He liked the group that played at the dog track, and he often joined the flute section, the only musician I've come across that played both those instruments. One year, a new clarinet joined the section and began playing the first clarinet parts. He had retired from the Cleveland Orchestra. One night he started showing me some clarinet fingerings for the prior piece. I nodded my head. Little did he know my origins!

"All this came together one day after I had stopped playing. I was writing a paper on John Stuart Mill after reading a great deal of his work. I felt his notion of happiness was much more complex, and in the paper I proposed to show that by first creating a short list of happy experiences, and then ranking them to see which rose to the top you could then say something beyond what Mill had said. As you might have guessed, playing with the Pentwater Band easily came to the top: there were just too many simultaneous activities, emotions, and conditions present all at once. My argument was that the quantity of all these happy inputs made the emotion much more complex than Mill made it out to be.

"There was public acclaim, the audience loved every piece, it was an integral part of their vacation heritage, and they were proud to come to

Pentwater in the summer and bring their friends to the Band Concert. The music was enjoyable to everyone and it had a beat; it was patriotic and fun to play, and the audience's enthusiasm matched that of the players. The blond piccolo player who stood and gave the solo in the *Star Spangled Banner* always received a huge round of applause. There was a feeling of solidarity between the audience and the players.

"The setting was idyllic: the band platform, the village green, the huge trees behind the band shell, and the sailboats lining the shore of Pentwater Lake just fifty yards away. Beyond this were the wooded hills along Lake Michigan and the channel to that lake. As the concert ended and the final, always-the-same trio of pieces were being played, the sun was setting and the nighthawks were flying overhead in the beginning of dusk that began to envelop part of the earth. You could feel the longing to continue this experience; for many it was the high point of the week, and to the musicians there came the feeling of responsibility for those thoughts and for the continuity from one summer to the next.

"It was the reinforcement of memories from the past, enhanced and carried forward into the future by the mind wanting to prolong and preserve something for the next generation, something free and patriotic and conjoining multiple generations. Here, surely, was purpose, community, something to relish in the winter and long for in the spring, and the joy of the flight of the nighthawks, like the colors of the setting sun, merely reinforced these emotions in players and audience alike.

"At the last concert of the summer, a woman rose to speak about ten minutes before the end. The Friends of the Pentwater Band would be passing through the audience for a collection to support the band. There was a band party in the fall. I attended the party with my mother on one occasion to see how the money was spent. Everyone brought their instrument. Before the sun went down and before members had too much to drink, the band went outside and played in Mr. Richmond's yard.

"I could see that for my mother, it was like a fall bonus. After resigning herself to hearing the band next summer, she could, for a brief moment, hear that sound once more, echoing across the homes of the tree-lined streets of the Village. It seemed a fitting event for fall and Halloween, another memory of sound to help with the cold winter ahead. The purpose of the party was to provide the musicians with one final feeling, one final catalyst to bring back those emotions, the complex conjunction of so many memories and associations that would never leave their inner sense of worth for the rest of their lives.

"So when my mother passed away, and I left the instrument alone during the winter, I could not pick it up in the spring and return, for I knew that even if I had, the tears would blind my eyes to the notes."

* * *

End of Digression

When a person falls in love he has experiences that cannot be expressed in words. Instead one can ask what it was that we did in those three months. That seems easier to say. At that time we were, of course, both students; don't ask me what classes I was taking for my Master of Science in Engineering. All I can remember is that after dinner, we studied together. When my future wife's residence house, Story House, had a party, we drove to Nancy Packard's Mountain View home built in the middle of an Apricot orchard. I spent time with my future wife and was only diverted by David Packard – the fellow who began the process that would lead to the computer I am using and the printer, as well – wandering about the rooms of his beautiful home in the capacity of a General Purpose Chaperone. Nancy Packard lived in Story House and so, for two successive years, I was able to enjoy these parties.

We drove to San Francisco to visit the night club called *The Committee*, an improv group like Second City in Chicago; it was fun. We drove up the winding road in back of Stanford to Skyline Drive and visited a State Park; we also drove to San Francisco on Skyline Drive – the scenery was so much better than Route 101. We drove all the way to Concord, California, and visited my Aunt and Uncle, Barbara and Sonja's parents. My Uncle Lars, a true Norwegian, flew the Pan American Clipper to the Far East. It was an eighteen day trip; he would have loved that take-off and landing we had as NROTC students in Corpus Christi, Texas; I say that, simply because he felt those vibrations constantly during those eighteen day sojourns. And, of course, Uncle Lars would have signed up for the Naval pilot program; the decks of aircraft carriers, while having that initial 'bump' when one lands after the tail hook grabs the aircraft, are much less bumpy than the water landing of a seaplane.

Pan Am was taken over by the Army Air Force in World War II so Uncle Lars was drafted, one could say 'in situ' and didn't even have to volunteer. Father wanted very much to serve during World War II but was rejected. Years later, with his experience as a Government Agent behind him, he found the Manila Folder in Washington where his request paperwork resided. Some Corporal had stamped the folder with the words "Too Valuable in Civilian Work" presumably due to his building of factories. In any event, as a child it seemed like father was in the Pacific theater.

This was because 7240 West Pratt Avenue was filled with artifacts from China before the war: Uncle Lars' gifts. I grew up with a huge, two-level, circular brass table in the living room. In a display case which mother referred to as 'The Fancy Cabinet' were carved ivory objects. These included figurines and those fascinating ivory carved spheres: the outside sphere is three inches in diameter and is carved with all sorts of iconic subjects, but there are lots of open spaces around the entire surface of the sphere. Inside the large sphere there are two more spheres and these also are carved. The result is that you can see all the way to the center where, like the Earth, the iron core can be seen through two carved crusts. Yes, I know, the real crust of the Earth is thinner than an onion skin because everything else is liquid. What I am trying to get at is that we can't see much beyond the crust, except for what comes up from a volcano and, like the earth, we can't see how anyone could carve those two, inner spheres!

We ate at places like *The Hippo Burger* in Menlo Park and in San Francisco and *The Spaghetti Factory.* We watched foreign films at Tresidder Union, a hangout on the Stanford Campus, and saw films like *Shoot The Piano Player.* My roommate, Salal, invited us to join his friends at a home-cooked Middle Eastern dinner party. I didn't have the opportunity to test out my mother's admonitions, you know, the ones about no woman ever marrying a man who cannot wash a floor, and the one about always going camping with your future wife before marrying her; nor was I able to know about my future in-laws except by word of mouth. I did the best I could by paying a visit to my old Scout Leader, Robert Nelson, who lived in a community on the way to my Aunt and Uncle.

But it is necessary that we return to that interim period, the time between my future wife's departure and her return in November. Once I recovered from my airport experience I waited for the mail to read and to listen to the events going on in Tours. I recalled my mother's saying that when you marry, you marry your spouse's family. How would I implement that? When back in Chicago I would write letters to my future in-laws; I would travel to Youngstown, Ohio, and visit my future father-in-law while the rest of the family – his wife and two youngest daughters – were visiting France and taking a tour in Europe with the eldest daughter. My future mother-in-law wanted to reciprocate coming to know her future son-in-law, the first of what might well be more son-in-laws. While staying in Paris she asked to make a tape recording to send to Chicago; the experience led to a family story.

After my future wife explained to her mother the workings of the small, portable, tape recorder, her mother asked to be alone in her room while she dictated her message to me. There was, of course, more of a personal touch in this request: she wanted to talk without anyone looking over her shoulder. As mentioned previously, the four-inch reels held only so much voice data depending on whether the machine was set to use the high speed or the low speed. After what seemed a fairly long time, the three sisters decided to knock on their mother's door and see if she was finished. Lo and behold, she was still speaking! The tape recorder was spinning around, as it was wont to do when the end of the tape was done and it required human intervention to turn the machine off. As a result I received a short written note alerting me to the fact that the enclosed tape was abruptly cut off in mid-sentence! Such are the origins of family incidents that are handed down from generation to generation.

But at the top of my list of things to do during this interim period was my implementation of my plan to take a job with an engineering firm in both Chicago and San Francisco so I could spend January through May of 1965 in California, living in Palo Alto, working in San Francisco, and spending every spare minute with my fiancée.

Oh yes, my fiancée accepted her ring at Christmastime in 1964. Parenthetically, I should mention that the large stone in the Engagement Ring came from my paternal grandmother's ring. Let me make it clear that my paternal grandmother, Natal's wife, was born in Norway, and, as previously pointed out, he was very successful in his career. But, again, I was oblivious to these things at the time since I was focused on working in Chicago and San Francisco, and so the attraction of wealth was not on my radar screen; there were other attractions.

But despite all of these digressions, the original ring, my paternal grandmother's ring, held a great degree of fascination for me as a child. Father, having survived the Depression, was, I am certain fearful of banks. I say this not only because he squirreled away things in hidden locations in 7240 West Pratt Avenue, but also because of the location of those items. For example, one day, father rolled out the bottom drawer in that huge three-drawer built-in set of drawers that was built into the tunnel; the handles to pull these huge drawers out of the tunnel and in to my bedroom were flush with the knotty-pine wall of my room. Once the huge drawer was out into the bedroom I could see that he had hidden the revolvers he used when he was a G-Man working for the Justice Department. The most famous revolver was at Jerp House in a gun rack; a judge gave it to him for his help in a murder case; it was chrome plated.

Guns were not that interesting to me at the time. Instead, it was a World War II Surplus Ammunition Case, the kind with a rubber seal. Father opened the Ammunition Case and inside were bundles of one-hundred dollar bills – just in case the banks started failing again – which, of course didn't happen due to the FDIC. But, in addition to building houses from which retirement income would flow, father had another place to squirrel money; he had a penchant for opening banking accounts at every Savings and Loan Bank on the entire Northwest Side of Chicago. Marie Christopherson would put money in as many as a dozen of these institutions; she held up a set of passbooks that looked like a deck of playing cards. A check arrived at the office and, assuming the payroll funds were in good shape, she asked father where to put the check. I can't exactly say how the decision was made; all I remember was that if father needed funds, it made no difference where he was; there was always a nearby Savings and Loan.

But, you ask, did my father keep my paternal grandmother's ring in an Ammunition Case from World War II? It was, after all, those Ammunition Cases that liberated Norway, but that was long after Natal was married, and long before World War I was even thought about. No, the rings – for there were several of them – were kept in a hollowed-out rectangular opening in the top of a closet door in a downstairs bedroom at 7240 West Pratt Avenue. I, as the eldest of three sons, was shown the secret enclosure; I used to stand on a chair and reach up there to see of the rings were still there, and they always were! I emphasize that fact because that purse and those rings were always with me, up there in the brain cells, i.e., my memory. In fact, that ring – there were three large stones in it, it was what mother called a cocktail ring – became central to a mystery story plot; the story is called *New Friends* and the first Chapter is 'Diamonds in the Rough.' This is a story about John Sherman, my fictional alter ego, who has finished picking blueberries at the top of a huge, wooded sand dune and, on his way back to Jerp House, stops to rest in a chaise longue at the top of a nearby dune. Sherman is twelve years old and just before he arrives at the chaise longue, from a distance, he sees another person leave the chaise longue. Here is the introduction to the safe hiding places in the first Chapter of *New Friends*:

* * *

Perhaps it was the fear of another run on the banking system that caused Sherman's parents to tell him and his sister about the valuables they kept at home. The family used a metal box with cash and valuables in it, in addition to a bank account and safety deposit boxes. Presumably, having cash at home added a feeling of security as cash would be on hand for contingencies. While most of the cash was put into a World War II army surplus ammunition box and hidden in a large storage drawer in an attic bedroom, many of the valuables were in another black metal box on a shelf in a first-floor closet. He was aware of there being coins and large dollar bills and other similar valuables, except that there was one type of valuable that was not stored in that box – diamond rings.

Several rings from his grandmother on his father's side were placed in a leather pouch, and this pouch was dropped into a hollowed-out cavity in the top of the closet door where the black metal box was kept. The hidden space was perhaps an inch wide, three inches long, and as many deep. In this pouch were many rings but only one cocktail ring which held, according to his mother, three one-carat flawless diamonds surrounded by many others. Sherman did not know why these items were not placed in a safety deposit box. Nor did he know whether or not they were carried to Michigan for two and a half months of summer residence.

* * *

And here are the final two paragraphs of the first Chapter of *New Friends*:

* * *

Sherman was picking blueberries in the afternoon on the hill he discovered when he found the saddle connecting it with the hill with the chaise longue. He wanted to rest before his descent, so he began the downward trek through the bushes to reach the chaise longue at the top of the adjacent blowout. He was halfway down the slope when he looked up and saw a man, or it may have been a boy, get up and leave the chaise longue by the path he had discovered years ago. He continued on negotiating the brush with the blueberry containers held tightly so as not to spill any, climbed up the short, slope and sat down, legs outstretched in the chaise longue. The stranger had disappeared, presumably down the path he himself would take.

His thoughts went to the pie or cobbler his mother would make and how large the berries were. He was just getting up and had grabbed the berry containers again when he looked down and saw, in among the blueberry plants beside the chaise longue, a small leather pouch exactly like the one his mother had shown him years ago in Chicago. Could it be the same? He picked it up, opened it, and there, among several other diamond bands, was the same three-stone flawless cocktail ring that belonged to his grandmother, the ring his mother told him would be used, should the day ever come, to construct an engagement ring for his own wife to be!

* * *

The story of how my working life in Chicago flipped back and forth from Chicago to San Francisco, and then back to Chicago, is, as with the diamond ring fictional story, best told through a series of excerpts. In those excerpts I am the narrator speaking to a group of IBM (The Company) retirees. I refer to the company I worked for in the two cities as *The Outfit*; the excerpts are from *Work – A Memoir*. The first excerpt relates how I set up the dual city deal that would take me back and forth between the two cities:

* * *

"It was through a strange set of circumstances that any opportunity came my way. I had to be a traditional engineer first and, in fact, I needed an Outfit with offices in Chicago and San Francisco so I could be with my future wife who was finishing her senior year at Stanford. I was only vaguely aware of the existence of The Company. As luck would have it, I accepted a position with the Outfit in Chicago in a department – the design of highways – about which I knew absolutely nothing. It was called the 'civil' department. I was soon switched to another department – the 'traffic' department. Their mission was traffic and parking studies about which I also knew nothing.

"But these were times when managers took risks with their employees. The other factor at play must have been that they were a large consulting engineering company – the second largest in the world – they were everywhere – they had sixty engineers in Bangkok! Sounds romantic, doesn't it? But I had all the travel I ever needed in the Navy; conning a destroyer through the Gulf of Suez with fifty other merchant ships to port and starboard; or through Windward passage in the Caribbean at a speed of over thirty knots during the Cuban Crisis and burning 5,000 gallons of Navy special fuel oil (NSFO) per hour. Guys who buy gas guzzlers like the Hummer can assuage their consciences with those kinds of numbers. Designing highways through jungles while being hunched over a drafting board in Bangkok held no attractions for me.

"The head of the Chicago civil department, a Mr. Boyd, listened as I told him my reasons for joining. 'I want to work in the San Francisco office from January next year through May. That way, I'll be with my future wife while she finishes at Stanford.'

"Boyd was a well-dressed fellow – the kind of guy who looked like he had just stepped out of a men's clothing store with a newly pressed suit, white shirt, and stunning tie. His shoes were polished and he looked like he was a candidate for the front office. Rolled up sleeves, suspenders, and sports jackets, were for the men at the drafting boards.

"He was not the kind of manager that made the rounds. Highways were tedious projects that took many years to design. I'm certain he felt it was best to incorporate the slow and changeable nature of these kinds of projects into one's management style. Only a few drawing boards away, a project was being laid out for an interstate highway through a portion of Washington, D. C. Each week the project manager – a fellow with a British accent – attended a weekly meeting in D. C. where all interested parties talked about where the road should go. Imagine trying to make progress through tradeoffs between moving a portion of a national cemetery vis a via taking a corner away from a park, museum or national monument – the project dragged on for years.

"'I see, we'll look into that when the time comes,' said Boyd."

* * *

I didn't have the two-city option in the bag when I was hired at The Outfit, all I had was employment in Chicago, the San Francisco part needed to be looked into! In the next excerpt we see what happened when that time rolled around and we looked into what I needed:

* * *

Change was inevitable; it was best to wait until the time came; promises, like everything else, would be subject to change.

"But change came before January and by that time at least three department heads were involved. I was switched over into the traffic department and was doing what could only be called 'grunt work.' I hadn't started programming yet. I was working for a very personable fellow. Interesting that his name also began with a B, Barry, Berry, or something like that.

"He liked to foster morale. He was upbeat, he smiled, joked, and walked around, taking an interest. His assistant department head was a jolly fellow who put on some weight. Barry or Berry was thin, taller than the man in the adjacent office, and when they got together there was a physical silhouette – large and small, thin and not so thin – that was implicit in their meeting before they even started talking. It added to the humor – the thin fellow was in charge but the other department head possessed his own kind of energy and always seemed to be rushing about, keeping busy.

"In early December I decided to walk over and ask Mr. Boyd if he had a job set up for me in San Francisco starting in January. He had said he would look into it. His office was spare by comparison to the traffic department offices which were always filled with stacks of papers – traffic studies, parking studies, and such like. 'I wonder if now is the right time to inquire about switching to the San Francisco office,' I asked.

'How's that?' he replied.

I reminded him of our first meeting.

'Oh, yes, now I remember,' he said.

'I want to be with my fiancée. She's been accepted at the University of Chicago. The wedding is in August.'

'I'll look into it,' he said.

"For a moment I thought he was going to look into the wedding. A week passed and I was called in and told there were no openings in the civil department in San Francisco. My reply was quick and decisive. I told him I would be leaving the employ of The Outfit at the end of the year and seeking employment in the San Francisco Bay area. I don't exactly remember the words I used. I rose and went back to my grunt work in the traffic department.

"The next day Mr. Barry or Berry called me in.

'What's all this I hear about you quitting?' he asked.

'It's true,' I replied and told him the whole story, the original request, why I joined The Outfit.

'What time is it on the coast?' he asked.

'I don't know,' I replied. Then he picked up the phone to call his counterpart in the San Francisco traffic department.

"I didn't know at the time that this was a small office at the end of Market Street. The traffic department was managed jointly by two fellows, Israel Gilboa and Jim Meyers. They didn't have window views from a sky-scraper on Wacker Drive – like the headquarters offices in Chicago.

'Gilboa,' began Barry, 'I've got this fellow on loan from Hugh Boyd in the civil department, says he wants to work in San Francisco next year until his fiancée finishes at Stanford.'

"Then there were a lot of small replies like, *yes, O. K., I think so*, and Berry ended the call. The upshot was that I had a job with the traffic department for the first part of the year. I thanked my current department head and went back to my desk.

"I walked out as though it was exactly what I expected. But inside was another story. I would be back on the West Coast, living in Palo Alto, seeing my fiancée every day! There was enough romance in that, of course, but now I would have the free time to enjoy San Francisco, the forests behind Stanford, the drive along Skyline Drive at the top of the hills to the west of the campus. I could take in *The Committee* night club, the ad lib, stand-up comedy group whose alumni came to coach Second City in Chicago.

* * *

After arriving at Stanford and unloading the VW at Story House, we went over to Tresidder Union and looked at the bulletin board, you know, the ones with tiny blurbs about anything and everything – things like baby carriages and one-room hideaways in Paris. The ones about renting rooms in Palo Alto had little 'tabs' of paper that you tore off, they had the address and the phone number you used to make contact. I made contact:

Palo Alto, California, West Coast Bungalow
Wooden Construction
Date of Construction Unknown
331 High Street
Palo Alto, California

What follows is the excerpt that relates my second home in California; it was different than Crothers Memorial Hall:

* * *

"For forty-five dollars a month, I took a room in Palo Alto – a block from the train and bus stops to San Francisco. Included in that monthly sum of rent was dinner for five days a week – the landlady's hobby was cooking. She had a bookcase of cookbooks. I shared a bathroom with Julio, a fruit truck driver who lived in an adjacent bedroom, but he was always on the road.

"I grabbed breakfast in the morning, pulled out the frozen portion of my lunch from the freezer, augmented it with the non-frozen portion – fruit and cookies – and soon was on the bus doing my correspondence class assignments. I still needed to learn about how to make highways and I studied statistics for the traffic studies.

"Was this the life? I was young still; I had seen the world and here was my plan working out to a T. And this was my first civilian job and I didn't know a single thing about highway traffic, parking studies, or the design of freeways! Pass the bottle.

"But I was still destined to do grunt work on the west coast. At least a big part of it was outdoors doing a traffic study in San Jose. I hired a fellow officer from my destroyer who just left the Navy and was living in Oakland. His brother and sister-in-law took us sailing on San Francisco Bay and we rescued a small sailboat that had tipped over but that is another story.

"It wasn't until I came back to Chicago that I was able to enlist the power of computers to free me from grunt work and the branches of engineering I had never studied even though I now had a master's degree – a master of science in engineering (MSE) to go along with my BSE. And, mind you, I still hadn't touched a computer for over a year!"

* * *

Mrs. Opitz, my landlady, lived with her son, Butch, in the house at 331 High Street. Upstairs, in the attic, she rented out a second room to a female graduate student whom I never saw or even spoke to. Presumably, my early morning breakfasts and bus rides to San Francisco were before the other lodger awoke. There were many distinctive features of the house on High Street but one stood out above all the others. Mrs. Opitz worked at Varian Associates and was always pressed for time; she took a bus to work. I, too, had to shop at a nearby grocery store to buy those items I needed for my lunches; the grocery store was about two blocks away. I was tempted to 'borrow' the distinctive feature to facilitate my own shopping, after, all, it was always parked in the middle of the front lawn!

What I am referring to is a shopping cart. In her haste, occasioned by her need to buy in groceries for a week, and her time constraints, what better way than to 'borrow' the cart for a week at a time? I felt that that cart was a marker, a sort of icon in steel, of a certain life style. I never borrowed it because I could easily carry my lunch-making ingredients in a single shopping bag but I still can see that shopping cart standing right in the middle of the often unmowed grass. Years later, at a time when our daughter was at Berkeley for graduate studies in their Public Policy School and we visited her, I became familiar with another marker that, for me, came to be the quintessential object for a front lawn in Berkeley. That identification began with the Bed and Breakfast that we stayed in. The Bed and Breakfast was a good place to stay; it was the back yard that intrigued me. I have never seen its like since.

On first venturing into the back yard path that began at our porch, one thought that the backyard was some kind of cultivated jungle. There were stones of every kind that were not the type that were purchased; rather, they were some kind of heterogeneous collection of found objects. Interspersed amongst these strange objects were plants of every description; some were flowers, some were plants that looked like they were planted as potential candidates for more serious cultivation, and, I suspect, some were just indigenous weeds that looked attractive. It was always a fascinating journey to walk twenty-five feet or more into this vegetative maze. But nothing in that overgrown yard became, for me, the quintessential object of a Berkeley lawn.

It was when we were driving out of Berkeley back to the airport that I spotted the object. After it was identified I played a game with those individuals who knew Berkeley, people who appreciated all those coffee shops, all those people sitting out in front of the shops drinking coffee and keeping their dog at their heels, and the coffee-drinkers who remarked on every child in all the baby carriages and held an ad hoc conversation with the pushers of those carts, the people who always had flowers from one or more of the flower stands that were on every street corner. I told the story to former Berkeley residents, people who knew the territory. I began with the Bed and Breakfast's back yard and my listeners nodded their heads in agreement. Then I popped the question: what is the quintessential object of a Berkeley lawn?

Everyone gave their opinion: some said there is no lawn, just flowers; others said there is no lawn visible because there are lots of protest signs; but no one could guess what the object was, yet, when I told them, everyone completely agreed – I never found a dissenter. That's because I began with telling them that the object stood in the middle of the lawn and it was surrounded at its base by a luxurious growth of high grass indicating it had been there for many years, in effect, it took on the characteristic of a kind of lawn sculpture that fit in with the ambience of Berkeley, it stood, if you will, for the Berkeley Ethic. The object was, of course, a Port-A-Toilet!

Our task, and I do understand it, is not to dally in Berkeley. Another Graduate School awaits in Chicago and another residence:

University of Chicago
Married Student Housing
The Gaylord Building
5316 South Dorchester Avenue
Apartment 418
Chicago, Illinois, 60615

But getting there, no matter how convoluted the route, is half the fun; we haven't even had a wedding, for heaven sake! My fiancée decided to forgo her Stanford graduation ceremonies so as to begin a round-about journey back to Youngstown, Ohio, where wedding plans and preparations could continue. But, blessed readers, we did, ultimately, attend a Stanford graduation! It happened a long time later and one of our children was responsible. Both of our children were admitted to Stanford and Princeton. Our son and firstborn chose Stanford over Princeton just like our daughter chose Princeton over Stanford. Since both children were accepted at both those schools, I have always wondered if there was a 'family' effect at work in these decisions.

This wonderment on my part – useless wonderment, some would say – is just a projection, a transference, of what we began with: my curiosity about what father actually thought and trying to figure that out from his actions. The difference here is the direction of that curiosity, i.e., father to child. Could it be that my daughter wanted to correct her father's Princeton experience in some way? No doubt she had heard pronounced at one time or another that her father was a 'Closet Princetonian,' a guy who not a soul knows ever set foot on that campus. I have no idea whether this was true; she majored in History. Could it be that my son knew of the joy his mother experienced at Stanford – both in California and in France – and wanted to duplicate that feeling, to follow in her footsteps? I have no idea; he majored in Human Biology.

But we are majoring in a return trip from Stanford to Youngstown, Ohio, and must refocus. That return trip would involve a passenger. My fiancee's younger sister travelled to California from St. John's College in Santa Fe, New Mexico, where she just finished her Freshman year – she was a member of the first class that matriculated from that school. The VW would carry three individuals and their necessary travel belongings on an itinerary that began at Stanford and then went on to Vancouver, British Columbia, Nanaimo, British Columbia (a city on the east side of Vancouver Island), Gabriola Island (a smaller island accessible by a thirty minute ferry trip from Nanaimo), Hebron, Illinois, (my sister's and brother-in-law's home), 7240 West Pratt Avenue, and, for my fiancée and her sister, continuing on to Youngstown, Ohio.

This sounds taxing – for the travelers, not for the VW – but it was not as taxing as that prior three-person trip to the Upper Peninsula of Michigan, the scene of the canoe trip on the Two-Hearted River. Nor would I ever lose sight of the VW in the forests of British Columbia. As previously mentioned, the Two-Hearted River trip was in response to father's encouraging me to take my brothers on such trips. The Canadian portion of this new sojourn was in response to my mother's admonition that when you marry someone you also marry her family! By going to Vancouver and staying with one of her Canadian families, I would begin to know four of my fiancee's thirteen Canadian cousins, not to mention her aunt and uncle. All of the cousins in this first family that we stayed with in Vancouver were young women. My own cousins, four in number – were all young women as well, but spread across two families, two cousins in each family – have already appeared; suffice it to say that with there being more than three times that number of Canadian cousins, I sensed that the sooner I started making their acquaintance, the better.

Who was responsible for all of these Canadians? Good question. My mother-in-law-to-be was a Canadian by birth; she grew up in Vancouver.

She met my future father-in-law on an ocean liner making its way to France. There are parallels here; I met my future wife on a Stanford Student flight from Chicago to San Francisco; after three months my future wife would leave for France. My mother-in-law-to-be retained her Canadian citizenship after she married an American, settled in Youngstown, and raised her family in Ohio. She took her three young daughters by train to Gabriola Island in the summers so as to be with her own parents; in the photographs of those young women they were always dressed in beautiful, *ironed*, clothes; I never understood exactly how she did it. While we are on that kind of topic, I would be remiss if I failed to mention that on the top of our Wedding Cake there was a commercial airplane on a pedestal that was covered with white glitter!

But equally important to know was the fact that Gabriola Island was, in the mind of my fiancée, an almost Holy place; my fiancee's mind was filled with wonderful memories of her childhood. Gabriola was *her* Bass Lake! So similar in certain ways of the heart – and that is what we are seeking to know – as well as differences – in the ways of geology, adjacent bodies of water, plant life, and so many other aspects of Michigan. This information exchange of childhood summer places was one of the many topics that were discussed during that Stanford Student Flight. On the occasion of a family reunion commemorating my fiancee's Canadian grandfather, and held on Gabriola in the summer of 2012, I put together a book of ten fictional tales from Michigan. I called it *Western Michigan Tales of Mystery and Adventure.* On the back cover I attempted to capture the common spirit that infused both of our summer residences:

* * *

Western Michigan Tales of Mystery and Adventure is a collection of ten stories assembled under one cover on the occasion of the Darling Family reunion on Gabriola Island, British Columbia, in August 2012.

Memorializing the summer residences of our youth through fiction that borrows from those landscapes of experiences that never leave our conscious reverence for all that life has to offer, is but another way of saying thank you to parents, grandparents, and all those who sustained that joyful legacy bequeathed to their heirs during those early times.

Even before this writer officially married into the Darling family on August 28, 1965, both parties to that event were acutely aware of how each partner was attached to the land, forests, waters, and the natural world that surrounded each other's idyllic summer retreat. Beyond mystery and adventure, a reader will find love, treasure, gold, silver, jewels, and the ever-present shorelines that offer so much in the way of excitement, history, and a never-absent past. And, given the backgrounds of the two parties, how could these stories be anything but uplifting?

It is appropriate then, in the context of a reunion that celebrates memories of the past, that stories written to carry forward the spirit of such a legacy, should be shared not just with friends but also with the relatives of one who came to share in the parallel gift of her spouse and encouraged the perpetuation of its memory in so many ways.

* * *

And so, after a two hour trip by ferry from the mainland north of Vancouver, to Nanaimo on Vancouver Island, and after a second, thirty minute ferry trip, from Nanaimo to Gabriola Island, the three travelers from Stanford arrived with another cousin, this time a male cousin, from the family of still another aunt and uncle. That aunt and uncle also lived in Vancouver, and we visited them as well; they, too, had four children, two boys and two girls; in a very short space of time, then, I came to know eight cousins and two uncles and aunts – that was fast work! David, for that was the name of our guide on Gabriola, opened the Panaboat, the name of the cottage as it was then called and which replaced the several dwellings of former times.

It took no time at all to see and understand the beauty that surrounded me on Gabriola Island and to mark the differences between that area and Bass Lake, the Lake Michigan beach, the high wooded hills that ran along the Lake Michigan shoreline between Pentwater and Ludington, in short, all those myriad features that I documented in the plots of the ten stories that I chose for *Western Michigan Tales of Mystery and Adventure.*

Along the shoreline of Gabriola Island there was a *tide!* I knew of tides from my three years on the *Hank* but I never had examined their effects from the standpoint of a child; my experiences on the *Hank* did involve the flying fish, dolphins, birds, and the brown growths of the Gulf Stream, but these were elements of nature that were observed *at sea.* When the tide was at its low point it exposed a multi-faceted rocky shelf that was filled with numerous ponds of salt water ranging from several inches across to six feet. These pristine depressions – like miniature aquariums – were filled with sea urchins, starfish, and other forms of life. They were absolutely fascinating; and for young children doubly so. I needed no explanation because they caught my attention and, when my own young children were to return years later, they, too, felt the same way.

At the top of these rocky shelves, just below where the vegetation of Gabriola Island began, the shelf was filled with huge logs that were arrested in their journey from lumbering operations; they came to rest at a point where they were a natural supply of wood for the stoves that were used for cooking and keeping warm. They were huge and required effort to cut and split – much more than the effort I expended at Silver Lake – but they were ubiquitous and an ever present feature of the entire Gabriola shoreline; they came from the Georgia Straits between Gabriola and the Canadian mainland to the east, and from Vancouver Island to the west.

Just beyond the junction of the shelf and the ocean's waves that broke against the rocky coast were beds of kelp. Those floating kelp balls, too, were of interest to young children. They reminded me of the buoys that somehow were detached from the Whitefish gill nets of the Lake Michigan fishermen; as I walked the Lake Michigan beaches, I collected the wooden buoys and the aluminum buoys. Years later, after my mother-in-law moved to Vancouver I became aware of beautiful glass spheres blown from transparent green glass. These appeared on the west coast of Vancouver Island and were used for home decorations. Where did they come from? From the nets of Japanese fisherman! The Japanese current that warmed Vancouver all year long brought them across the Pacific to adorn the living rooms of Vancouver and create conversation pieces for visitors. I would use them at the beginning of one of those ten stories in *Western Michigan Tales of Mystery and Adventure*, a story called 'Jack Archer,' that opens with John Sherman, my fictional counterpart, discussing several mysterious items with his grandchildren on the front porch of Idlewild, a summer home which will soon be discussed. The discussion brings the two worlds – Devil's Pond north of Bass Lake, and the west coast of Vancouver Island – together:

* * *

"When I found the third interesting thing, it seemed to me that someone was hiding at least two things, but, strange to say, if you found the first, that someone wanted to use it to help you find the second."

"Grandfather, you are talking in riddles now. I think you need to be more explicit."

"OK. It started one day when I decided to canoe into Devil's Pond. I've told you about that before. There's a creek that runs from the north end of Bass Lake to Devil's Pond, which is a tiny pond surrounded by a sphagnum moss bog.

"Well, I struggled through the bushes and enjoyed the quiet of the pond. There were some trees pushed over in a recent storm and I decided to paddle around the edge to get a closer look at uprooted trees lying on a bog.

"That was interesting, but, just as I decided to leave the pond and paddle back home, I caught a glimpse of a piece of green glass near one of the dead trees. I first thought it was a Seven-Up bottle someone threw away, but it was too big and round."

"Sometimes we think you make things up, Grandfather."

"I can understand that. Well, I didn't save the rudder, but I did save the green-glass object. I'll get it for you. I have it in a box on the top shelf over the below-the-stairs storage space in the downstairs Idlewild bedroom."

John Sherman left his grandchildren sitting on the front porch of Idlewild and returned with a cardboard box. He opened it. Inside was a green glass-globe about eight inches in diameter.

"It looks like a Christmas tree ornament, the kind they sell in gift shops."

"Yes, that passed through my mind as I climbed along the dead log, picked it up, and put it in the canoe. But the glass is too thick for a Christmas tree ornament and there is no place to attach a hook on it.

"My thoughts changed when I remembered that on the west coast of Vancouver Island, British Columbia, beachcombers find things like this – thick green balls. They are buoys that get separated from the top edges of Japanese fishnets and the Japanese current carries them to the Vancouver Island beaches. My mother-in-law, your great-grandmother on your mother's side, told me about them. She used them in her home as decorations. Hers were smaller though."

"Grandfather, are you saying that somehow a Japanese net buoy floated into Devil's Pond and got caught in the bushes? That's impossible."

"Yes it is, but the closer I looked at it, I knew something else was going on."

"So you went from a Seven-Up bottle to a Christmas tree ornament to a Japanese buoy to some fourth idea?"

"That's right. And you would, too. I might add that it's the mystery."

Sherman brought the ball closer to his grandchildren, "here, look inside. Do you see something?"

"It's a piece of paper."

"It does look that way, but I think it is a piece of parchment. Parchment is thicker than paper and doesn't burn as easily."

"But why put a piece of parchment in a glass ball?"

"Well, if you look at the parchment, you'll see why."

The eldest grandchild looked at the parchment first. She exclaimed, "Grandfather! Grandfather, it looks like a treasure map! There's a big X, two trees, and a circle that could be Devil's Pond. Maybe there's a treasure buried near two – I think it says tamarack – trees? Did you find a treasure?"

"I think it *is* a treasure map. I did think that when I found it and I still think so. It's just that every time I went back to look for two tamarack trees together – dead or alive – there were just too many pairs of trees. Also, have you ever tried to dig down through sphagnum moss? It isn't easy and you disturb the environment, which I don't think is a good idea anywhere, if it can be avoided."

"So, the real mysteries at Devil's Pond were complicated. Who put the ball there? Why, except to find a buried treasure – which seems ridiculous? And where is the treasure? What is it?"

"Well, children, Devil's Pond is a treasure. And I can still take out my green ball and contemplate why it got there."

* * *

Less than half a mile towards Vancouver was Entrance Island, home of the Berry Point Lighthouse, or so it was called by my fiancée and her family. We'll speak about that island and lighthouse in a moment. For now we shall only make a comparison between my mother and my mother-in-law with respect to how each obtained large fresh fish, more particularly, Whitefish from Lake Michigan and Salmon from the Georgia Straits. My mother drove to Pentwater to purchase a freshly caught Whitefish from one of the several fishing boats whose crews earned their livelihood by setting gill nets in the Lake Michigan waters. It was those gill nets that supplied the buoys for my buoy collection! I never could figure out exactly why there were wooden buoys and aluminum buoys; my only thought as a child was that there was some kind of advance in technology going on and that the wooden buoys became waterlogged whereas the aluminum buoys were impervious to that fate albeit that they were just as numerous implying that they detached themselves from the top of the gill nets just as easily as the wooden buoys.

When my mother-in-law wanted fresh salmon for her family she walked out on the exposed shelf that ran along the Gabriola shoreline and waved to the fishing boats to bring her a Salmon. There was always a helper who joined my mother-in-law and her three daughters; on weekends my fiancee's grandfather would take a break from his Vancouver law practice and take the two ferries to join his daughter and granddaughters; he kept a workshop of sorts near the shoreline and I am certain that my fiancée venerated him the same way that I venerated Scottie at Bass Lake. Like my own father, my fiancee's grandfather could get to Gabriola in two and a half hours – assuming good timing. The difference between the two was that father could not get work done while flying around Lake Michigan.

Meals at Gabriola were cooked on wood stoves which were fed by wood from those logs along the shoreline; water was fetched from a well – my fiancee's grandfather owned enough property so that in back, in the forest, there was a natural source of fresh water – but hot water needed to come from kettles that were also heated on the stove; vegetables came from a nearby farm which was even closer than the farm my mother used which was a mile away from Chris Cot and Jerp House.

During one summer the helper was a French cook! She noticed mussels along the shoreline. Most likely, she found them on certain sections of the shoreline that were still sandy. On the rocky portions of the Gabriola shoreline mussels were present in a more interesting fashion: they always seemed to be broken! How could this be? People in the know would tell the first-time-visitor just how those broken shells came to be: the gulls figured out that by picking them up, flying to the necessary altitude, and then dropping them, that they would break open! Clever!

In any event, the French cook, upon espying these delicacies, knew there was a serious oversight going on; she gathered the mussels up and soon added a new entrée for everyone's meals! There were, of course, differences between the two locations. For example at Gabriola there were many cabins devoted to different functions whereas at Bass Lake there was a central home. Returning to the brilliance of the Gabriola seagulls, I came to know of the brilliance of the Bass Lake crows. Along with this knowledge came the realization that the crows of Bass Lake possess a *sociology* that recalled the families at Bass Lake. These fascinating comparisons were put in a story called 'What's Past is Prologue' in the book *Western Michigan Tales of Mystery and Adventure*:

* * *

Sherman recalled an article he read in the spring 1998 edition of *The Living Bird*, a magazine he subscribed to for many years and was published by the Cornell Laboratory of Ornithology. The article was entitled *The Secret Life of Crows*. Written by Rachel J. Dickenson, it spoke of the research done by Kevin McGowan in the late 1980s. Sherman could not help comparing the groups of crows, which momentarily blocked his way, with the populations of Bass Lake families, many of which came to Bass Lake for generation after generation. Some of the characteristics had to do with group behavior. For example as the hours of dusk enveloped the lake, there were no crows around. Like the lake families, they retreat to congregation areas to prepare for the night's roost. Prior to that departure, there's a lot of talking back and forth and playing around.

Sherman remembered the family that came to reside in their summer home just to the north of Idlewild – an old home only seventy-five feet from Idlewild. Like the crows, where up to seven generations of siblings live on or next to the home territory, Sherman's neighbors spanned three generations but it was their constant late-night talking and playing around that marked them as very crow-like. There were countless families around the lake where nonbreeders or helpers associated with the territory leave for a while in the winter but eventually return to their parents and their home territories.

The crows, like many Bass Lake families, mate for life, and several generations of a single family can be found helping at a nest. This was Sherman's own story. Sherman recognized family parallels in which crows become breeders: They can leave home [Sherman thought of one well-known multi-generational family where the male children and grandchildren built new homes but one male child – a person that Sherman knew the best – remained in California.] They can wait for another crow in the neighborhood to die and then take its territory [Sherman thought of the situations where a Bass Lake family did not explicitly deed lake property to a family heir. The result was that the outside purchaser never had the attachments exhibited by members of the prior generation.] Crows can take over a portion of their parents' territory [The examples at Bass Lake were legion; the blond girl at the square dance was very typical of families where property holdings allowed expansion.] or crows can inherit their parents' territory when they die [Sherman and his older sister both inherited a summer home with property.]

Family groups of crows are dominated by males – male offspring tend to stay close to home (summer homes) whereas their sisters disperse. Sherman recalled a recent conversation where he congratulated a woman his own age – a childhood acquaintance – for having rebuilt her parents' cottage; he sensed her actions (as a female heir) as an exception and strongly reinforced it. A mere week after that conversation Sherman's wife, Dorothy, spoke to a male descendent of a family who was working on the family property on behalf of his younger sister – another of Sherman's square dance partners. But these musings on the social life of crows and Bass Lake families disappeared as Sherman returned from the Wishing Well with the New York Times because another real-time event, bordering on the unbelievable, captured his attention.

* * *

I have no idea of how the neighbors on Gabriola lived, all I *can* say, however is that I, too, came to love what my fiancée loved. Our family of four – five when my mother joined us – returned to Vancouver and Gabriola many times especially after my mother-in-law moved back to the city where she grew up after the death of my father-in-law; she had many relatives and friends – it was an excellent decision and our family always enjoyed returning. Collectively, all these visits opened my eyes to other aspects of nature: salt water nature, the towering trees, mountains, and islands. My artistic sensibilities were heightened by the Northwest Coast Indian artists, their totem poles, silkscreen work, jewelry, and sculptures. I partook of the legacy that was handed down from generation to generation.

The Darling reunion on Gabriola Island came forty-eight years after that first visit, the one where we motored in from Stanford in the VW. After all those intervening experiences, and associations, all of which were now a part of my life – in those eighty-five billion brain cells, each with up to ten thousand connections – I felt the need for an outlet; it must have been another way of saying thank you. Whatever the reason, I wrote the novel *Entrance Island*, a tale that focused on Gabriola, the Berry Point Lighthouse, the artistic aspects of Northwest Coast Indian art, and Canada. The back cover of that novel talks about the effects of an island on human nature:

* * *

Islands hold a fascination for mankind whether it be treasure, a retreat from civilization as a place where we can discover ourselves or just plain romance. Our imaginations run wild. The island becomes a catalyst for projecting our lives into the unknown. What would it be like to live there we ask and then we go on to imagine a paradise. But in this fantasy we never completely divorce ourselves from the past. We see this in those desert-island questions – what would you bring? and what music would you take with you? – questions anticipating some loss that must be planned for. Yet to the mariner, an island is a latitude and longitude that acts like a stake in the ground, a placeholder, except that it arises from water. If the island has a lighthouse or light tower then it possess even greater solidity. When once sighted, the mariner, the voyager, or even the traveler can use chart, parallel rule, a compass and binnacle to obtain bearings to predict exactly where he is and his progress through the water. Dead reckoning which cannot measure the currents and winds of fortune has been replaced by coast piloting. The island facilitates an entrance, another beginning, and new bearings for the future lives of those who have discovered its secrets.

* * *

The last line of that back cover captures this new dimension that opened for me; a transference of the spirit of a place occurred through Gabriola and its surroundings. This is why the last line resonates with my own experience: 'The island facilitates an entrance, another beginning, and new bearings for the future lives of those who have discovered its secrets.'

Again, blessed reader, it becomes necessary to take seriously that old warning about not seeing the forest for the trees. For us, the warning cautions us to put before us the perspective of the entire year of 1965 and pause, as it were, from examining those early growths of individual trees. Instead we need to see that 1965 was a *year of many beginnings*, and, having examined two of these – an engagement with a fiancée, and a location, Gabriola – what better time to examine the related character that ties together all of those *many beginnings* before we introduce them? For, as we shall see, they are as legion as the quantity of those *homes* which, by no means, have been exhausted.

We began the year with the mention of an engagement; we spoke of a fiancée, a term that replaced 'my future wife.' But the use of 'engagement' is not limited to the idea of a pledge and a binding by a promise of marriage sealed with a ring. The psychologists, who examine the aspects of the most satisfying ways to live, continually remind us of engagement as the human characteristic of being lost in a task, the kind of task that both attracts and holds one's attention. With that notion as our guide for 1965, the question shifts to how each one of these many persons, places, and things that were started – or continued – during that calendar year were engagements. Why is this the case?

First of all, we are interested in the longevity of the entire forest. Individual trees may come and go but there must be a huge quantity of those *endeavors* that stick around before we can claim to have delineated a forest, read *person*. The criteria then, is not just how many start-ups occur, but how many start-ups are there in a given year that stick around for a few decades or more. Secondly, we have those trees that had a jump start – they began earlier than this so-called special year – but that gives them no special status; they, too, will be judged by their longevity. But we, meaning us, blessed readers, have imposed further requirements.

We claim that there is this process called 'parental layering' that characterizes these beginnings or continuations, and if that is not enough, we are, ourselves engaged, in a chapter which has to do with love, albeit that we have previously defined this term as a many faceted jewel, extending across multiple kinds of engagements. Before we proceed to further engagements in 1965, I ask is there a better way to illustrate what we are talking about, than revisiting the two we started with? What are those, you ask. There seemed to be an engagement – that was reciprocal – between two individuals, a man and a woman. OK. What was the second? There seemed to be two long-term, engagements with two areas of the earth that were quite separated yet linked by being the summer residences of the selfsame man and women, and, oh, by the way, those residences exhibited the parental layering aspect we talked about. I'll let you off the hook when it comes to the love criteria.

So now, with the broader perspective in mind, we can assert that the claim can be made that the rootedness of that man and woman is akin to the Norway Spruce: two individuals receiving water and nutrients from the parent plant(s) while both are forming their own roots, to wit, the idea that the future husband and wife are both propagated plants! How does this work?

In our new focus it would be correct to point out that a visit to Vancouver, British Columbia, Gabriola Island, and the homes of eight of my fiancee's cousins – plus two aunts and two uncles – started an engagement that grew to many more visits to Vancouver and Gabriola, visits that would include our own family of two children and, even, my own mother. My mother's admonition that when you marry, you marry a *family*, would, technically begin on August 28th, 1965, but in terms of the personhood, the collective character traits, past histories, loves – in the many-splendored sense – the wedding, per se, seems almost an afterthought; there were just too many before-thoughts already in place!

Oh, yes, you assert, but you skipped talking about the engagement ring, except, perhaps, where that so-called flawless stone came from and how it became part of the plot of a mystery story! Quite right, it is always so easy to focus on what sparkles, and what sparkles more than a cocktail diamond ring? Even when separated from the adjacent stones. One way, then, to make up for this skipped aspect of the canonical definition of engagement, is to follow the lead of those two back covers that we have excerpted by excerpting still a third back cover from a recent novel, entitled, of all things, *The Gospel of Marriage*:

* * *

Oh, it's a long, long time from May to December | But the days grow short when you reach September | When the autumn weather turns the leaves to flame | One hasn't got time for the waiting game | Oh, the days dwindle down to a precious few | September, November | And these few precious days, I'll spend with you | These precious days, I'll spend with you. Time is stretched when the long year becomes fifty; each week now a year. The horizon of knowing the love of one's life becomes close enough to sense the change of autumn's flaming leaves to a golden anniversary. But the autumn breeze carries lines from within a prayer of Kierkegaard's, *to will one thing*, during those precious days: 'So may Thou give to the intellect, wisdom to comprehend that one thing; to the heart, sincerity to receive this understanding; to the will, purity that wills only one thing. . . . As the day wanes, may Thou give to the old man a renewed remembrance of his first resolution, that the first may be like the last, the last like the first, in possession of a life that has willed only one thing'. The lines do not arise from the motives of remorse and repentance, but gather up two elements that combine to confess the fiery point from which the transfiguration of the world can begin: love and marriage.

* * *

Now before we examine the key words from this back cover that make my point, I would like to apologize for an obvious question that I sense arises in many readers: "What the . . . is meant by *the fiery point from which the transfiguration of the world can begin*: love and marriage?" Good point! No pun intended. I admit my guilt in every aspect of the charge; I will further add that I have used the sentence before, the only difference is that I am now, in the spirit of living in Hyde Park, the home of the University of Chicago, prepared to document, in the fashion of a footnote, exactly where to go to answer that question. I will not put the answer in an Appendix of this book. I will not use any traditional footnoting protocol; I will merely state that to answer the question about *the fiery point from which the transfiguration of the world can begin*, you must locate an article taken from the Journal Put', feb. 1930, no. 20, p.47-79 by N. A Berdyaev, Studies Concerning Jacob Boehme, Etude I. The Teaching About the Ungrund and Freedom (1939 - #349) which article is prefaced with the following poem by *Angelus Silesius*:

["In water lives the fish, the plant in the ground,
The bird in the sky, the sun in the firmament,
The salamander must with fire be sustained,
And God's Heart is Jacob Boehme's element".]

What are, then, the words that make your point? Are they the words of the popular song that begins the back-cover piece? No, the words are 'Time is stretched when the long year becomes fifty; each week now becomes a year. The horizon of knowing the love of one's life becomes close enough to sense the change of autumn's flaming leaves to a golden anniversary.'

The words were meant to imply that the author is anticipating – from the standpoint of being within his 49th year of marriage – his fiftieth year, the year of his golden wedding anniversary. The book is written in anticipation of that celebration; you could say that by finishing it early, there won't be any pressure. The point, then, is that the engagement that began with a ring in December of 1964, exhibited longevity. But we must return to the second item, a location, Gabriola, which needs to be put into the context of the new perspective.

Very quickly – on the Honeymoon itself – the reciprocal engagement would occur and my fiancée, now as my wife, would begin sharing in the parallel gift of her spouse, the summer residence of her husband's youth and the spirit of such a legacy. The first part of that Honeymoon was spent at the Stratford Festival in Stratford, Ontario. But what are the precedents for that? You ask. There are precedents during the so-called BC, before children, period and there are many follow-on, post-BC trips, to Stratford with children.

The very first trip was made in 1955. You will recall that I square danced with Joan Craig, whose father was a dentist. Dr. Craig attended a conference in Canada in 1954 and went to the Stratford Festival that year. My mother heard of the Festival through Dr. Craig's wife who stayed all summer long at their summer home just above the dam over which the waters of Bass Lake poured into the final stretch, the outlet, before mixing with the waters of Lake Michigan. Mother resolved to drive her son to see *The Merchant of Venice* in 1955. We read the play so thoroughly that on the way we quizzed each other on where, exactly, certain lines came from, i.e., which acts and scenes; this was performed at Stratford's third season.

A mere ten years later, on our Honeymoon, we would see *Henry IV (Henry IV, Part 1), Falstaff (Henry IV, Part 2), Julius Caesar,* and *The Cherry Orchard*. But there was an intermediate BC trip. We have spoken of the Operations Officer of the *Hank*, Mark Godfrey, the officer who urged us on to win the question-and-answer competition of the Destroyer Squadron as we sailed to the Sixth Fleet in the Mediterranean. When the *Hank* went to Marblehead, Massachusetts, for that Fourth of July weekend, Mark's father invited the Wardroom to have dinner at Saugus, Massachusetts, in his back yard: lobster, clams, fresh corn on the cob, and such like, a real feast! When I took a vacation from the *Hank* in the summer of 1963, I went to Bass Lake, where else? and Mark asked me to purchase a bottle of Crown Royal Whiskey – 25 years old – for him in Stratford, Ontario; he thought it would be cheaper, and I thought it was the least I could do to repay Mark's family for their hospitality. On this trip with my mother and father, we saw that fantastic performance of *Timon of Athens* done in modern dress, the one that was brought to the New York stage after Stratford's regular season. The play, for me, was riveting; I can still see that red velvet jacket that Timon wore!

Subsequent trips with children occurred from the time our firstborn was a toddler to the time when both children were in High School. When it comes to memory though, who can possibly forget: Kate Reid, Christopher Plummer, Brian Bedford, William Hutt, Colm Feore, Douglas Campbell, Jessica Tandy, and Nicholas Pennell, to name a few?

After the Stratford Festival the red VW took us to, can you guess? That's right, Chris Cot for shelter, Jerp House for meals, and a new address for *work*!

Bass Lake Summer Cottage
Idlewild
Built in 1905
By
Chris & Justin Bortel
Of
Ludington, Michigan

A photograph taken during the Honeymoon period in Michigan records my wife helping with the task of winterizing Idlewild, i.e., taking down the huge screens on the large L-shaped front porch preparatory for the next effort: lifting up the wooden shutters, that replaced the screens during the winter, and securing them with the inside hooks that held them. We need to elaborate further on the sustained effects of helping with those screens.

During the Honeymoon in early September of 1965, the full set of responsibilities for Idlewild resided with the parent tree. The new growth layered onto a child consisted of the individual efforts to open and close what were now three summer homes: Chris Cot, Jerp House, and Idlewild, the last of which was purchased in the 1950s and was the home just north of Jerp House. A corollary of those individual work efforts was not only the acquisition of the necessary skills to winterize three dwellings (and also open the homes in the Spring), but also the skills necessary to repair and maintain them against the ravages of time, if not remodel them in accordance with the demands of modernity.

The distribution of these work efforts changed in 1973 when mother, now a widow, announced plans to deed Idlewild to our family. That single act triggered over forty years of effort across both kinds of skills and took as its goal the notion of keeping the house as close as possible to an aesthetic sensibility acquired by osmosis. One element of that sensibility was to maintain, as much as possible, the way in which it was in 1905, both internally and externally. This was facilitated by all of the antique furniture but also required extensive remodeling, all in the spirit of this ethic that seemed as if it came from nowhere.

Certain upgrades such as the replacement of threadbare porch rugs and canvas porch-drops that rolled down during thunderstorms on the inside of the screens, were easy to accomplish while maintaining the past; others, such as remodeling a kitchen, bathroom, and converting a garage to a guest cottage, required more thought. But despite the sense that these forty years of efforts across many different aspects of Idlewild seemed to come from nowhere, there was one source that pinpointed in clear and distinct words what, exactly, was going on; this source came from Hegel's *Aesthetics*:

* * *

"The universal and absolute need from which art . . . Springs has its origin in the fact that man is a *thinking* consciousness, i.e., that man draws out of himself and puts *before himself* what he is and whatever else is . . . This consciousness of himself man acquires in a two-fold way: *first*, *theoretically* in so far as inwardly he must bring himself into his own consciousness, along with whatever moves, stirs, and presses in the human breast; and in general he must see himself, represent himself to himself, fix before himself what thinking finds as his essence, and recognize himself alone alike in what is summoned out of himself and in what is accepted from without.

"*Secondly*, man brings himself before himself by *practical* activity, since he has the impulse, in whatever is directly given to him, in what is present to him externally, to produce himself and therein equally to recognize himself. This aim he achieves by altering external things whereon he impresses the seal of his inner being and in which he now finds again his own characteristics. Man does this in order, as a free subject, to strip the external world of its inflexible foreignness and to enjoy in the shape of things only an external realization of himself."

* * *

Sometime around the year 2005 an effort was made to set down what went on at Idlewild during thirty-five summers. This resulted in an unpublished document entitled *Instructions from Idlewild A Study in the Search for Authenticity.* It took one-hundred and fifty-five single space pages of prose and photographs to fully explore those years of effort. Since we are, at present, merely providing a perspective on the year 1965, I have, against my better judgement, placed in Appendix I the Introduction to that document. Why, you ask, against my better judgement? Let me briefly excerpt the first paragraph of that Introduction which, of course, speaks to the entire effort:

* * *

Introduction

It would seem logical that at the beginning of a text some kind of warning should be issued to the reader so that the waste of time spent in reading a text that has absolutely no relevance to the reader's circumstances or mental frame of mind might be avoided. This is so particularly true in so many ways that a valid claim could be made that the work you are about to read may apply to, at most, one or two readers. That would be at the outset. At the end, any such readers might be the first to agree that in fact the work has no relevance for anyone. Why would this be so?

* * *

The Introduction in Appendix I *does*, however, frame for you, blessed reader, a state of mind at a particular point in time and, as an historic perspective, is worthwhile. For anyone with the curiosity and the time, I suggest the perusal of Appendix I. For now, it seems fitting, in view of the size of the effort expended in writing such a useless document, that we give an excerpt, however brief, of what that picture of a just married bride helping her father-in-law remove screens from the front porch of Idlewild came to mean. The excerpt is from the book *Dawn* and the passage we will look at from that book examines a single Bass Lake poem from a collection of 365 poems already referred to: *A Love Affair With Flowers Fair.* Many of the poems are sonnets, one poem for each day of the year. Many of the poems are inspired by residency at Bass Lake during the summer months of May through September. The poem we are about to focus on is a poem for May 10th, a day that could mark the time when Idlewild is opened, or rather, a day when the multi-week process of opening Idlewild begins in the spring, reversing what the Honeymoon picture exhibits, i.e., the closing of Idlewild. We begin by excerpting the entire poem and then follow that with the commentary:

* * *

The brown leaves redeem each year I return.
Orchids greet with quiet simplicity
And joyous new life unfolds like a fern,
Blossoming holy authenticity.

The mind revels in the joy of labor
Bathed in the memory of ritual.
The past returns. Communion savor
Begets meaning, hope, individual.

Time slows its pace and serving yields beauty
Like a skirt of hemlock before the fall.
Love grows like a summer storm to move me
Piercing the heart like the whip-poor-will's call.

The tiny rock cress also knows of grace
And the secret happiness of this place.

* * *

As we proceed with Poetry and Prose, our intent is to put some order into these things; we are going to see what we are leading up to. Ironically perhaps, we are going to look at that poem, the one that starts with the brown leaves, and we will deconstruct it; that will be the poetry part. . . .

We are trying to describe the existential reality – as Milan Kundera would put it – of living a life where not just beauty, happiness, engagement, meaning, a sense of accomplishment, positive emotions, creativity, and relationships are present one-by-one in an activity, but a kind of activity where *all* those feelings of well-being, or many of them, are often simultaneously at play. Why does the poem serve as an entrée to this kind of pursuit?

> *The brown leaves redeem each year I return.*
> *Orchids greet with quiet simplicity*
> *And joyous new life unfolds like a fern,*
> *Blossoming holy authenticity.*

The child returns to Michigan in the spring and sees the leaves of the prior fall – flat on the ground, pristine in that only the snow has pressed down on them – no human has even walked upon that carpet. The origin of these brown leaves echo a line in Robert Frost's poem that begins with *Nature's first green is gold*, 'Then leaf subsides to leaf.'

> Nature's first green is gold,
> Her hardest hue to hold.
> Her early leafs a flower;
> But only so an hour.
> Then leaf subsides to leaf.
> So Eden sank to grief,
> So dawn goes down to day.
> Nothing gold can stay.

Nothing gold can stay; it is spring and if the leaves in the trees in Michigan are that delicate green and gold of early spring, then there is no grief mentioned in the child's poem, quite to the contrary; despite the carpet of brown, they are redeeming, despite being dead, they have *meaning*, they fulfill a promise, there is a religious awe awakened when months of city life gives way to the forest – the memories accumulated over a period going back to when the poet was six years old, the outlines of every leaf, the ubiquitous scent of lily-of-the-valley, the wind in the trees – there is a regaining of the possession of one's self, perhaps one's soul; the experience is emotional in a positive way; the leaves are a catalyst for the raising of feelings about the past in the next lines: quiet simplicity, joyous new life, holy authenticity.

The metaphors speak of the forces of nature that move the poet through his encounters: the quiet simplicity of orchids, the joyous new life of an unfolding fern. These displays of nature, dead leaves, blooming orchids, unfolding ferns, speak – even like a flower blossom – of authenticity; every meaning of the word applies: authoritative, genuine, real, trustworthy, true; they are all in accordance with fact or actuality.

The mind revels in the joy of labor
Bathed in the memory of ritual.

The child's mind, responding to his surroundings, begins an almost implicit reflection on his past: revels in – takes great or intense delight or satisfaction in – the joy of labor. Here is a pure statement about the shear satisfaction and joy of physical work; it carries meaning. It could be splitting firewood but it isn't. We need to take a cue from the idea of a return in the spring, the very first visit of the year.

The mind is bathed in the memory of ritual – the work that is done year after year at cottage-opening time: taking down the shutters, putting up the screens, sweeping the roof, priming the shallow well pump and turning on the water, raking the leaves, opening the fountains, putting up the bird feeders, restoring the screened front porch to its glory by moving to their places the cushions, the rugs, the pictures and other objects stored in the cottage over the winter. Each of these activities *are* rituals if only because they are repeated every year, but at a deeper level, every object has meaning, has a history, raises the *presence* of those who are no longer among the living.

A paragraph could be written describing the history of every single object that has been, over the decades, thought about, added to, remodeled, or otherwise repaired or restored. Every room rekindles memories started by the ritual of opening, fueled by the prior years of associations; restoring the front porch is no exception: how the futon was single handedly brought by the child from Chicago in the family car, how the porch floor rugs came from China through Marshall Fields' department store in Chicago and were paid for by one of the first royalty checks from a particular Field Developed Program authored by the child at IBM, how the antique gliders were rehabilitated with new canvas cushions for upholstery, their metal frames sand blasted and then painted white, how the dining table was refashioned by hand from an older table, how the missing rounded ends were restored by a carpenter in Ludington, an idea first suggested by the child's mother-in-law, how the wall cabinet with its yellow glass front was in Mr. Conrad's darkroom, how the Shaker clock was made from a kit, how the canvas roll-down drapes on the inner side of the huge screens were farmed out over the winter to make new drapes, how the original Franklin wood burning stove was restored and how its chrome pieces were re-chromed, how the Shaker chairs were hand made from kits from Shaker Workshops, why the light blue of the ceiling was chosen, where the several objects on the two tables came from as well as the objects in the wall cabinet, where every framed picture came from and which pictures belonged to Mrs. Conrad.

From room to room each 'how, what, why, and where story' implies meaning, memory, *presence*, ritual, the past, work – painting, preserving the spirit of the old with the appropriate new and honoring the imperfect antique glass in every window except for five panes that were broken and replaced with stained glass, their story then becoming who the glass artesian was and how they came to be.

> *The past returns. Communion savor*
> *Begets meaning, hope, individual.*

A communion in the sense of sharing or participation with, takes place with all of the people, now in the form of their *presence*, and with that memory, communion becomes something to savor – it holds the property of arousing interest by having the quality of indicating the *presence* of a distinctive but shared property. Mrs. Conrad and others come to mind by virtue of the personality of their tastes, the effort to preserve and maintain a home built in 1905 just as it was then. This gives renewed meaning to four decades of work; it reaffirms two of our most positive traits as human beings: the ability to *act* and to *hope*, the lack of which lead to despair. The cottage opening brings back the poet's sense of being a unique individual and awakens his memory of those persons who went before and who 'loved what we love.'

> *Time slows its pace and serving yields beauty*
> *Like a skirt of hemlock before the fall.*
> *Love grows like a summer storm to move me*
> *Piercing the heart like the whip-poor-will's call.*

The Golden Age, before the fall, is intimated by the slowing of the pace of life; however there is a new and important element: *serving that yields beauty!* Who is being served? First, it is the child's own family, wife, children – every effort of labor extends the experience of time spent in this magical world to the next generation – just as the poet's own parents gave him the gift of place and the myriad experiences that cannot be obtained without the past. Second, it includes the presence of others: neighbors, friends, and the older people who took an interest in you as a child, and sustained you in ways beyond the immediate family. But the child also feels he is serving his own parents, those who willed the legacy to him.

Every ingredient including the idea of a servant contributes to beauty that is linked to nature and conjugal love – a skirt of hemlock before the fall – the beauty becomes ubiquitous through the presence of love linked to positive emotions that range from: the wind, rain and lightning of a summer storm as it slowly approaches with thunder in the distance with no wind and then gradually builds, to the whip-poor-will's call at dusk on a quiet evening, plaintively piercing the forest to bring to our ears a quintessential tattoo as we begin to fall asleep.

The tiny rock cress also knows of grace
And the secret happiness of this place.

Grace because so much has been given, secret because the tiny rock cress knows and, presumably, has been an obscure witness to the generations who have attested to that bouquet of gifts by the only way they could describe the synergy of the components of so many elements – like the sense of accomplishment achieved through one's own labors – all joining together at the same time to produce happiness.

* * *

In a moment we will examine the claim made by, perhaps, some astute reader, that what is going on here is following the exact opposite of "Not being a Norwegian all one's life." That the seter, Idlewild, has taken over. But before that, I feel that another Appendix is in order, Appendix J, which is merely a list of activities that, over the years, were performed. By examining Appendix J, one can see that the activities are not, exclusively, all of one type; the picture is a mixed one. So what can we say about this claim of *being* a Norwegian all your life, of letting the seter take over?

If we associate searching for authenticity, as implied by the subtitle of the aforementioned document, and link that with the pursuits of perpetual maintenance at Idlewild, we dismiss, once again, the forest for the trees. The claim then gets more specific and is restated as follows: "The Norwegians built new seters from scratch and also fixed up those old farms up in the mountains, but when they fixed them up, they didn't have to keep up that effort for more than forty years, God forbid!" This restatement demands that we look closely at those summers and reexamine the concept of work itself.

The story so far, is biased by emphasizing the opening, closing, and maintenance of a 1905 summer house; what is left out is the transformation that occurs when two ethics are combined: work is *play*; as father would say, 'you are only happy when you work,' and *love* underlies, or motivates the engagement. There were, obviously, some of those activities in Appendix J that were for people. A sample would include:

* * *

+ Building a playhouse and picnic table *for his own children.*

+ Remodeling and restoring an old turn-of-the-century Evinrude mahogany rowboat – during a three-week work period – as a project jointly done *with his son.*

+ Converting a garage at Idlewild into a guest cottage *for his mother-in-law.*

+ Building a sliding-seat wherry that uses professional rowing sculls and enjoying *having his teenage children* row around the lake.

+ Overhauling an antique schoolroom clock where the initial overhaul was done by his *own father.*

* * *

But in a broader sense, almost every activity was for the family, especially mother, and the spirit of the former owner of Idlewild, Mrs. Conrad. We saw 'the work is play' ethic when examining Mr. Ronneberg, Sr., who never, ever, exhibited any other opinion with respect to his work; it was play, period! This notion informed my entire thirty-two years at IBM. In *Work – A Memoir*, the book that explores those years, the fictional John Sherman, now in retirement, speaks to several retirees at a series of get-togethers and relates, in the fashion of Marlow in Joseph Conrad's *Youth*, his story. At the very beginning, Sherman's listeners characterize who it is that speaks:

* * *

It was Sherman, the Systems Engineer, who seemed to have found romance in The Company, while the rest of us just plodded on, doing our jobs, reading our job descriptions once a year at the time of our annual performance appraisals, and watching our stocks grow, our families thrive, and knowing that somewhere our pension monies were accumulating toward some future and unknown occupation called retirement – a vague land where structure, corporate directives, and manager's manuals didn't exist.

Sherman, however, seemed taken up, fascinated one might say, with some kind of sense of fulfillment, of personal development, of excitement, that many of us never found, or, if we did, wasn't as pervasive throughout our working histories. So we sat back, filled our glasses, and listened to him because we all knew The Company and its history as only a daily worker at its myriad tasks could know it. We were fascinated with Sherman's view – it seemed to enrich our own lives, sharpen our memories, reignite the sparks that joined us in the solidarity of our past deeds – and, if the truth be told, seemed to add meaning to our lives as we negotiated the new, unexplored, and still vague land that presaged our ultimate destinations.

* * *

Much later in *Work – A Memoir*, Sherman speaks to the informal group of retirees about the years he moved his work to Idlewild:

* * *

"During those five years there was a question that was always asked by Company employees when I returned from vacation in Michigan. I occupied an office in a General Systems Division branch on the eighteenth floor of the new building and I knew many individuals in this office, other offices, and the education and data centers. It was the administrative manager of this eighteenth floor branch that had the dreaded job of inventorying my candy-striped confidential manuals; but I digress. The question was simply how I could return from a so-called vacation absence in Michigan and not have used any vacation days?

"They of course knew of the European trips that I took to teach in Paris, Mainz, Germany, and elsewhere. But those could not account for the strange phenomenon that showed up on my weekly time cards. The mystery was even deeper for my closer friends when I related the work I accomplished – things like converting the old garage to an insulated bedroom and bath for my mother-in-law who would come for ten days or so from Vancouver, BC, or my remodeling of the entire plumbing system in Idlewild, my summer home, which was built in 1905.

"The answer was that I brought my work to Michigan. My contact with my manager, Chuck, in Atlanta was by phone and could amount to a call a week, but one call does not add up to forty hours a week. Here is how I performed my work during those years.

"I opened Idlewild during the weekends prior to moving the family to Michigan for the summer. The move occurred after the Chicago public schools let out late in June. My classes were, for the most part, hands-on workshops. Writing a 200 page document, having nothing to do with a class, would also serve the same purpose as a class, but we will stay with a multi-day workshop class.

"Prior to moving my office to Michigan, I would have written all the hands-on class problems and executed them on a machine in Chicago or Rochester, Minnesota. I would pack up my source material – manuals, program listings, and the program execution results – in a cardboard box together with office supplies – typewriter, ribbons, paper, and rubber cement. To start with, a typical class would involve creating a complete double-spaced instructor outline. Adjacent to the text of each topical lecture would be the foil designation – usually a letter of the alphabet followed by a dash and then a number – that was to be displayed on the board using the overhead foil projector at that time. There could easily be several hundred transparent foils for a five day class.

"Before the children woke up, and after they went to bed, I would work on class material. There was, in addition, a student notebook of material that contained in-class exercises as well as the write-ups for the hands-on lab work done on the computer. A smooth copy of the annotated instructor solutions was given out at the teach-the-teachers class and they became part of the complete course document. Most instructors reviewed the solutions early on the following day.

"All of these various pieces were mailed to a woman in Atlanta who was the intermediate manager between the developer and the artists and word processing staff that transcribed everything into the format for publishing. She also assigned publication form numbers and saw to it that all the pieces were stocked in Mechanicsburg, Pennsylvania, where instructors and technical staff personnel could order their own copy. There was, of course, the announcement letter that had a complete course description and price. Once announced via that letter – which was sent to every marketing employee and systems engineer in the United States – the class was a priced product and any instructor could place the class in the curriculum at any regional education center. The announcement letter had to be composed, proofread set in type, and so on.

"When all or a portion of the material for a class – a set of lectures, a set of foils, for example – was ready, I traveled to the Pentwater, Michigan, post office and mailed a bundle to my contact in Atlanta. The woman had a delightful name, Gay Jolly! After Gay's staff had it in publishable format, she would mail it back to me and I would pick it up in my rural mailbox at the roadside when it was delivered in the early afternoon. I could start proof reading and the return of a subset of pages, foils, or whatever, to Gay; I could always phone her if needed.

"If I performed this work for six hours a day, seven days a week, I would have worked forty-two hours. That would mean that I would sometimes work when the children were driven to swimming lessons or were at the beach with their mother. When engaged on a large – 200+ page document – I could also perform all the work in Michigan merely by having brought up all the necessary reference material. In either case, I could have copies of the pictures I used to paste together for my classroom foils or diagrams I put in my documents, copied in Ludington and then cut and paste them before I made a back-up copy. For class foils, they would be sent to Gay in Atlanta for an artist to make the final foil.

* * *

So, one could argue, that the physical work efforts at Idlewild were a *diversion* from IBM, an occupation that encompassed many careers at the same time: Systems Engineer, Instructor, Education Developer, Consultant to Salesmen and Customers, Speaker, Software Developer, Author of Technical Papers, and Teacher to the technical IBM employees of Europe and elsewhere. But in that list of Idlewild Activities in Appendix J there are dozens of work projects that are, in reality, self-imposed, aesthetic creations/enjoyments. Take, for example, the planting of trees as recorded in *Instructions from Idlewild*:

* * *

. . . One positive result, what all this is leading up to in fact, was that I was exposed to the Hemlocks on the property (Pentwater Beach No. 1 property) for we walked it often and I fell in love with this species. When mother deeded Idlewild to us I knew there were a few large Hemlock trees in front of the property and I speculated that maybe they were left over from the lumber operations of the 19th century or, maybe, Mr. Conrad, the former owner, planted them. Next door, in front of the Ramsey cottage, there were lots of Hemlocks and I knew that Dr. Ramsey, the original owner during Mr. Conrad's time, must have planted them. Along the leaf covered road leading up to Idlewild there was a Hemlock tree with a branch that extended seventeen feet from an eight inch diameter trunk; the branch was five feet above the ground! And of course, in the Spring, when new growth occurs, the outer edges of every branch is a lighter green and aesthetically appealing with the way each branch bends throughout the tree, especially at the top. (At this point, the poem, *Hemlock Branch*, from the date of July 10th, is inserted.)

Hemlock Branch

Like lacy limbs of grace, you point the way
To where the feathered ferns would touch your hands.
The etching in this stretching makes us stay
To celebrate the joy of ancient stands.

The spring has dipped each edge in lighter green
And like a quiet needled wing of peace,
You bless the space, embrace the hope unseen
That all but beauty's face should ever cease.

Your touch like sphagnum softness heals the pain.
Beneath your bough, a benediction made
To rise and ever after know the gain,
The lazy mottled shadows of your shade.

Come, dripping rain make fresh the memory.
Brown needles join with snow to seek their sea.

* * *

The first use of Hemlocks brought to the Idlewild property was to reclaim a small piece of that property back to nature. During the years when Idlewild was rented and used as a benefit for father's employees, a small roadway ran from in front of mother's property to join the road leading up to Idlewild. We decided to return this small piece back to nature and planted white pine and five small Hemlocks transplanted from the back property in Pentwater Beach Addition No. 1. It was necessary to water these to get them to grow fast and, ultimately, to fertilize them in the spring. We included my son, Erik, who was old enough to lend a hand. The sheer beauty of the Hemlocks was too great and in 1993 I decided to begin a planting program on a larger scale, a program that would ultimately bring a distinct Hemlock forest effect to certain areas of the property.

There were open areas in the woods of Idlewild where small white oaks died or areas that were just void of trees to begin with. There were also many small white oak trees that seemed to get just so large, perhaps eight or nine inches in diameter and then die. It was in these open areas, surrounded by oaks, that we planted Hemlocks. By open area is implied just the forest floor; there was always a complete canopy above those open areas; the forest floor itself was also completely covered with all the ground varieties of vegetation and leaf decay from hundreds of years.

The effort led to the discovery of Paul's Tree Farm east of Ludington. Tom Paul was a second generation tree farmer and grew acres of beautiful trees. I received the impression that he let many acres grow undisturbed for the sheer beauty of the trees. Tom was a good baseball player, by reputation, for Scottville, Michigan. When I arrived in the morning he was telling off his crew and was upset with someone who took a corner too close and damaged a tree. Here was a man who loved all trees but he planted many fields of Hemlocks and he would dig them for me and I could haul them home and plant them.

The price was right and these were beautiful trees and I was planting for beauty. I asked Tom how to get them to grow and he said that if you took good care of them, by which he meant fertilizer at the right time and water, they would grow and the more you looked after them the better they would grow. Hemlocks love the shade and grow to over a hundred feet. They are easily identified by the two white lines on the underside of each needle.

In my first pick-up from the tree farm I loaded eight trees in the car as many times as necessary to transport all I purchased; this started the planting that extended into later years. (The 'extension' included more Hemlock in 1994, large quantities of White Pine, several plantings of Norway Spruce, and two species of Fir trees. All of the pine, spruce, and fir were from Needlefast Evergreens just down the road from Tom Paul.) In 2005 it took over an hour to water and fertilize with acidic Miracle Grow all of the large trees. (More recently the time is now two hours and, altogether, there are over six-hundred trees planted.) The early trees from 1993 are close to fifteen feet high (2005); many have multiple trunks and the graceful branches can be seen throughout much of the property. (More recently, they are nearer to twenty feet tall.) A park-like quality is added to the property with the full grace of a Hemlock occupying a space that once had no trees. This is a quality that one needs to discover on one's own initiative. Nothing suggests it except the physical arrangement of the trees, old and new, with respect to each other. Dead logs and branches lie near the Hemlocks, just as elsewhere, along with Bracken Ferns, Wintergreen, Indian Pipe, Squaw Root, Lily of the Valley, Huckleberry, native grasses, and several species of wildflowers such as cow wheat, jack-in-the-pulpit, white baneberry, and Helleborine orchids. (There is one granddaddy of the Hemlock species, a towering tree that pierces the oak canopy for its sunlight and is a mere twenty feet from the front porch.)

To keep the dead white oaks that still remain from breaking off in a high wind and falling on a Hemlock, a new method of taking care of these oaks was implemented. The top half of the oak is cut off and the dead upper half is placed on the ground. This leaves the lower portion, usually about eight to ten feet tall, standing and available for different kinds of woodpeckers (hairy, pileated, downy, red-bellied, and red-headed) white breasted nuthatches, and flickers. Dead trees on the ground from natural causes and white oaks that have lost their grip on the forest floor, all provide food for birds. With the four stone fountains strategically placed there is splashing water close at hand throughout the property and this makes for a form of wildlife refuge. There are always enormous quantities of chipmunks, black, gray, and red squirrels present at any time of day.

* * *

We continue looking at those activities that were not work. Already we have mentioned a man-made addition to the property and that is a contradiction to the ethic of leaving the property – and house – exactly the same as it was when it was built in 1905 or, more correctly, exactly the same as it was when Mrs. Conrad lived in the house. I knew what Idlewild looked like for, as a twelve-year-old, I raked leaves for her; Jerp House was next door. Let me remark that there were few exceptions to the ethic of leaving things the same. Strange to say, Mrs. Conrad left an outhouse structure 'out in back.' This was even after indoor plumbing; not that anyone used it, or even maintained it; it just stood there, a relic of former times. Of course it would take *work* to completely erase its presence and there was always more work that ranked higher on the list of to-dos.

One year, however, a year many years into Idlewild's new ownership, the old outhouse was torn down and the wood was taken to the dump. But a completely different situation occurred with respect to the children's playhouse. That began when a new pier was built at the lakefront – Idlewild always shared the Jerp House pier – and the old lumber looked good enough to build a playhouse. The playhouse was built with a screen door flanked by screened openings on either side of the door; there were large rectangular windows on the other three walls; it had two fold-up bunks and a small front porch. All the windows had shutters that were hinged – they were winterized in a minute.

So the playhouse was an exception to the rule. Out in front of the playhouse I put together a picnic table for the two children. Where did I get the knowledge to do that? You remember that Boy Scout Jamboree in 1950? We had to build a picnic table from scratch at that pre-jamboree camping experience, the one where I first heard *The Cremation of Sam McGee?* I didn't forget! There was another time when the work to keep something off the property was a bit more arduous. All these digressions, by the way, are a lead-in to the subject that we will soon pursue, the building of fountains. But first, since we have brought it up, we are going to talk about another arduous project.

Towards the time of the 35th year of ownership – give or take some years either way – we made a decision to purchase a Vermont Country Stove to replace the kerosene stove in the living room of Idlewild. This would allow a thermostat to be used, would cut down on the fan noise of the old stove, provide a more pleasing view through the glass of the stove, heat the house more efficiently, eliminate the filling of the kerosene tank in back of the old stove, take up less space, and would substitute a very fine stove – engineering wise – for a stove from the 1920s. I hope that is enough to justify the purchase. Whether or not it is, the decision was made that I should install the stove from scratch.

The implication of that 'from scratch' involved installing two LP gas tanks, installing all of the gas lines under the house – which proved to be an enormous effort as it had to be done without crawling under Idlewild where there was an air space but that space had not been entered since time out of mind. What does all this have to do with preserving the property in its original state? Excellent question!

The standard solution for the LP gas tank requirement is to place a large, white LP tank in the forest; that, by virtue of the ethic, was unacceptable. If you can, blessed reader, use suspended judgement for just a moment, I would like to indicate what happens to Bass Lake summer cottages when it comes to *not* using the septic system in place for decades. Every cottage that replaces an older septic system ends up cutting down several trees to the extent that a large, barren area, appears in the middle of the forest; by definition, an ugly scar. Suffice it to say that by proper maintenance efforts, I avoided that strategy and the only trees that are not those that were in place during earlier times are those trees that died a natural death or were struck by lightning.

Back to the placement of the LP gas tanks for the Vermont Country Stove. I noticed a trap door in the back porch deck and, on occasion, opened it and wondered whatever it was used for in past times; it had no apparent usage. It could, with a little digging, make an excellent location for two forty pound LP gas tanks which work in tandem with each other. With a third tank as a spare – and stored in an out building we call the 'woodhouse' from habit, it has no firewood – appropriately hidden; I would then be following the ethic. And so the tanks are accessible from above through the removable trap door!

These stories about the property have, if you'll remember, been related because of the fact that we are now going to talk about the fountains. The four fountains carried with them several aesthetic considerations, some of which are covered in the excerpt that follows. In a nutshell, those considerations are visible – their design, and the attraction of birds – and audible. You will recall those Architectural History classes that I took at Princeton? One of them, Renaissance Architectural History, was a tough class. Not only were there Art History majors taking the class but the pre Architecture students were in there too. Professor Coffin was a fantastic scholar and I had him for my precept, the small class that meets once a week for discussion. I worked hard in the class, received a high grade on my papers and for the entire course. It was particularly satisfying because of all the other art-oriented students I had to compete with. It would be like taking organic chemistry, or biology and competing with all the pre-med students and never going to Medical school. That's right, I was never to use the information except for a special trip that is coming up; that's called a preview of a coming attractions.

One building studied in Renaissance Architectural History was the Villa d 'Este in Tivoli near Rome, Italy. It is a wonderful example of Renaissance Architecture, a UNESCO world heritage site and, it is known for its *Italian Renaissance Garden.* I knew that garden; I listened to Professor Coffin talk about the *fountains* and there were a lot of them; they cooled the visitors to the Villa d 'Este just by their looking at and listening to those *fountains*. How could I get some mileage out of that high grade from Professor Coffin? Now it is time to look at the excerpt:

* * *

. . . I would also plant them (Cinnamon ferns) around four stone fountains which I would design, and build – using methods of construction that were self-developed – and then place out in strategic locations on the property. The fountains were made from granite beach stones. Why?

Any child at the Lake Michigan beach becomes instantly enamored with granite stones that can always be found in more or less abundance. Why so? First, they are dry in the sand but when one puts them in water they come to life and their colors come out. The children's parents who have taken a Geology class know that granite contains orthoclase or plagioclase feldspar, the former having a vitreous luster; one is pink and the other white. But granite also has quartz which is a brilliant mineral in its own right. Finally, granite has a black mineral which is either amphibole or pyroxene. (In a Geology exam when given a piece of granite to identify, the student needs to use a magnifying glass and estimate the angle that the black crystals make in order to know which black mineral is in the granite. In that sense, it's kind of like using a magnifying glass to distinguish between a Cinnamon fern and an Ostrich fern by looking at the backside of a tiny fern leaf and seeing if the veins are branched or not.) Granite can, therefore, be any color from deep red to pink to black and white and can also be dominated by quartz; the combinations are endless.

Second, for the child, the stones themselves are smooth to the touch. If they are flat they are easy to skip but many are rounded. Just holding a smooth granite rock in one's hand is a pleasant thing to do and would prompt a child to take such a stone home. All along the Lake Michigan beach such stones can be found but most of the beach is almost 100% sand with few stones except for certain, specific locations. One of these was Summit Park about a mile and three quarters north of where Bass Lake flows into the big lake. A second area was even further north where piles of granite stones exist and where the waves meet them even with a small wind from the west. There, the stones are constantly brilliant in the sunlight. Such a pile existed where the water of The Ravine – as I called it in a poem for June 11 – flowed into Lake Michigan. Before the water from the ravine entered Lake Michigan, the water encountered a huge pile of granite stones right at the beach and the vegetation arose from that pile as well. See Appendix K for the poem.

Given this exposure, there seemed to be no difficulty in understanding what the motive was for designing a fountain that would attract birds, provide for continuous water over granite stones in the sunlight – not to mention the sunlight coming through the transparency of the water itself – and also provide a sound, much softer than the Villa d 'Este outside Rome, Italy, but a sound just the same.

Granite

Crushed pillars in the wreckage others shun,
Numb to see how far you've come from quarry,
I found you on wet beach with sparkling sun
And knew at once the glory of your story.

I put you in my fountains just to see
The ever present colors of your face.
Your history spoke of cooling molten sea.
I set you on my desk to keep my place.

When dry, you never die but catch my eye.
Centuries ground you smooth and round on beach
Before my reach. Miss you the cry and sigh
Of seagulls high? What does the driftwood teach?

Your plagioclase and orthoclase engage
With quartz, black amphibole, or pyroxene
To keep my dream. I weaned you from the waves
A permanence to bring, my days fair sheen.

What I can't account for is precisely when the idea came to me of joining the stones from the beach into a fountain in such a way that the stones would be shown off. In any event one begins with a pedestal in which is embedded a copper tube. The pedestal is a tapering tube (three feet high, eight inches in diameter at the bottom and four inches at the top) of hardware cloth to which screening is attached on the outside. Prior to this the sculptor collects hundreds of small granite stones at the beach. Now, with both the pedestal and the stones in hand, the sculptor mixes up a batch of mortar and then, painstakingly, attaches those with mortar to that support structure. Surprisingly, with even a slight slant to the sides of the pedestal, the sculptor can work up the sides without having the stones fall out of the structure.

Once the stones are attached the pedestal is hollow but very strong by virtue of the mortar and the hardware cloth; it's like reinforced concrete in that respect. The next step, we are describing fountain #1, is to make a bowel (think of a large, circular mixing bowl, a foot deep and twenty inches in diameter at the top). The bowl is shaped with hardware cloth and screening in the same way as the pedestal was; the bowl is built upside down and the hardware cloth and screening at the bottom is anchored on its circular rim on a piece of plywood which is covered with wax paper. Starting at the bottom, circular rim, the stones are then applied in the same way until the entire bowl is covered with stones.

Once hardened, the bowl is freed from the plywood, turned up so that the bowl is facing upward, held in place with a wooden frame, and then, the inside of the bowl is built up, stone by stone, just like the pedestal, and a rim of stones is put in place at the top, circular edge. Ultimately, the pedestal and the bowel will be put together; when this occurs, the pedestal is filled with mortar and reinforcing rods that have been placed ahead of time in the bottom of the bowl, and that reach down into the soft mortar of the pedestal. The copper tube also sticks up through the bottom of the bowl. The purpose of the copper tube is to take water from a large, circular, eight inch deep and four foot in diameter bowl in the ground; the pedestal stands in the middle of the bowl.

For the bowl in the ground, think of a children's wading pool that is dug into the sand. Now, line that pool with stones that go up the sides, over the top of the rim and then back down to the forest floor. The pedestal will sit in the center of the bowl in the ground but a circular compartment is first built at the bottom of the bowl in the ground and then the pedestal is placed on top of the compartment. The compartment, which is also completely covered with stones, has an opening that allows a Little Giant Pump to be put inside; the pump connects to the copper tube and takes water from the bowl in the ground, pumps it up through the pedestal and the top bowl as well. The copper tube rises above the circular rim of the top bowl. When the pump is turned on, a column of water comes up, out of the end of the copper tube, rises up to eight inches above that end, falls back into the water in the top bowl, flows down the sides of the top bowl, continues down the sides of the pedestal, and collects in the bottom bowl only to be pumped back to repeat the cycle.

The top bowl holds water and so does the bottom bowl; they are both made watertight. Electricity is run underground from Idlewild with switches inside the front porch that turn on the Little Giant Pump. When everything is initially complete there is an exciting moment which is analogous to when astronomers turn on a new telescope for the first time; they call it "First Light." When the Little Giant Pump comes on for the first time, I call it "First Water." The bottom bowl is filled with water that runs, underground, in a length of plastic tubing, from a garden hose connection in the side of Idlewild; the plastic tubing has a small diameter and is winterized by blowing it out with a bicycle pump. Once the bottom bowl is filled, the Little Giant Pump is turned on, water rises up through the copper tube, comes out eight inches above the tube, falls back into the top bowl which, initially, fills the top bowl but, once filled, water then flows down the sides of the bowl and the pedestal and back for recirculation. But some of the water also drips down directly over the rim into the bottom bowl

All the granite is wet! Because the pump puts a fountain of water up above the surface of the upper bowl, that three-eighths of an inch diameter, transparent water fountain falls back on itself before it reaches the upper, horizontal surface of the upper bowl. Thus there is the wonderful sound of the water as it falls back, first into the top bowl, and then, secondly, as it drips from the edge of the top bowl, flowing over its edge and directly down into the bottom bowl. When, during the early morning or, later in the day when the sun is starting to set, that column of plashing water catches the rays of the sun and lights up to an even greater degree than during the day. Wherever there are drops of water falling through the air, above the upper bowl or dripping down from the upper bowl, the hummingbirds hover and catch tiny droplets for a drink.

So much for the first fountain; the others would all have different designs but four out of the five other fountains – two of those others are at Jerp House and my brother Peter's home on Lake Michigan – would have the recirculation of water with an appropriate Little Giant Pump. After many years the first fountain acquired a dark patina; all the stones in the pedestal and top bowl of the fountain were red granite. To keep that color ever present, a new set of winterization tasks was born: they were cleaned with water and a scrub brush, and then covered to keep out snow and ice. As mentioned earlier the underground water lines were blown out with a bicycle pump.

There was always a splash that left the fountains with a bit less water; it was easy to add water in the morning if necessary. The splash served to water the Cinnamon ferns that are planted just outside the bottom bowl; the fountains are also turned off at night. The joy of even a single fountain is way out of proportion to the effort, and there is a human identification with the birds and even other plants. When it comes time to close the fountains, sadness reigns, as caught in the poem *Fountain Closing*, a poem for September 30:

Fountain Closing

The chickadees were sad and I not glad
When I closed the fountain. Slippers long gone
Couldn't hold me with their song. Squirrels were mad.
When would next summer's spring come along?

The sassafras threw up their hands to stay.
A raucous blue jay caucus held no sway.
All knew I did not want to go away
Down a path so different from today.

A cool breeze from the lake was there to tease.
The hemlocks spread their limbs as if to please

And all the woods were pleading for my ease.
Each leaf and flower stirred my heart to seize.

Oh, the loss was felt that day I took the
Plashing joy away, all nature cannot say.

The summer home to the north of Idlewild, where Dr. Ramsey planted the Hemlocks in the front of his cottage, was owned by one of his daughters, Jane, and Fred, her husband, was a person I admired. My children went over and looked at Linus, the raccoon they found as a baby by the side of the road and raised as a pet. Fred was a manager in a starch plant in Indianapolis but he was also an expert tailor and he sewed suits during his vacation; these suits were for his own use. He, too, played clarinet hour after hour sometimes. For the second fountain, I needed help lifting the bowl onto its base. This was an enormous hexagonal bowl that sat atop of a large pedestal, there was no bottom bowl. A pump from just under the water surface lifted the water through nine spouts in a device that rose an inch above the water surface; the spouts all fell back into the single bowl to be recirculated. Fred helped lift the huge, and very heavy, hexagonal bowl into its wooden frame so that it would not be moved while the reinforcing rods from the bowl – inserted into the concrete-filled pedestal – would stay in place as the pedestal concrete hardened.

I felt an enormous loss when Fred died at an early age; a year later I saw Jane walking in front of her house; earlier, we were aware that the barred owl was back and when I talked to Jane she mentioned something about the spirit of the owl and Fred. Again, all this is captured in a poem that I gave to Fred's children who now own the house; the poem is not in *A Love Affair With Flowers Fair*:

In Memory of My Summer Neighbor

He helped me lift the granite fountain bowl
And then his clarinet stopped, our duets
Broken like all our hearts, and now the soul
Of Mozart and Weber brings us regrets.

He stayed up late into the night sewing
So he could feel the silence, wind or moon,
The conversation and laughter growing
Like his devotion to his pet raccoon.

As water brings out the granite color,
The lake revealed his character us.
The owl returned each year to discover
The missing quartz, the ever present loss.

Now our hope echoes, "He loved what we loved"
In an eternal lake summer above.

From a portion of the front porch at Idlewild a person can see the fountain that was built in front of Jerp House for my mother. I began with a bottom bowl and pedestal similar to my first fountain, but instead of a top bowl, a huge sphere over two feet in diameter and made of granite rocks sits atop of the pedestal. Out of the top is a small three inch piece of copper tube out of which comes an upward stream of several inches in height and which, falling back on itself, makes its way around the sphere and down the pedestal into the bottom bowl for recirculation by the Little Giant Pump. The sphere weighs hundreds of pounds and it took four men to lift it into the frame.

Unfortunately, the first time we lifted it, the frame was too weak, and it came crashing down! Now there was a need for emergency efforts as the hollow pedestal was filled with mortar that was beginning to set. On the second try, the wooded frame, which I reinforced, stayed up; the connection between the sphere and the pedestal was made joining the copper tubing pieces into a single copper tube path, and the reinforcing rods that extended down into the pedestal were successfully buried in the now hardening mortar of the pedestal. Mother received many compliments for this fountain and loved to look at it. I came to call it "Paul Bunyan's Golf Ball."

The third fountain on the Idlewild property was inspired by the movie, *2001 A Space Odyssey*, in which a huge rectangular block is seen rising out of the ground on a desolate planet. If a seven and a half foot tall "Point" fountain could be constructed, the same effect might obtain. The Point fountain would be about fourteen inches square at the bottom and then rise up to where it was about three inches round at the top. Regular "rebars," the kind used in highways and concrete structures, rose up to form the steel frame and then hardware cloth and screening was attached as with earlier fountains. The challenge was the very careful, and tedious effort it took to attach all the stones which varied from large at the bottom to smaller stones at the top. This effort was required because the four surfaces were almost completely vertical! Patience won out and I placed the Point fountain on a square platform in the middle of the bottom bowl, put in a powerful Little Giant Pump that could lift the water stream eight feet, and then we had "First Water."

How does the movie come into play? Since the Point fountain was about fifty feet into the forest, as you sighted it on the path – under which were buried the electricity and the tiny, plastic tubing to refill the fountain – it could easily be mistaken for a seven and a half foot dead white oak. Upon walking up closer, the person approaching it for the first time come to sees the colors of the outside surfaces and the small bubbling water fountain at the top. The stones are shiny and the fountain does not sound as noisy because a great deal of the water comes down the sides and quietly goes back into the bottom bowl. Nonetheless, there is a splash at the top and some water splashes off the stones on the side of the fountain for the hummingbirds to obtain a drink on the fly.

The same degree of unexpectedness in the movie occurs. Naturally, to all the hummingbirds, goldfinches, phoebes, tufted tit mice, and even blue jays and oriels, none of this would matter; they would just enjoy a drink or fly through the water fountain at the top or the spray to get a drink on the fly. Now, with three on the Idlewild property, the question was: would I get permission to build a fourth? The answer was yes.

For years a brush pile marked a section of the woods just to the north of Idlewild. The final fourth fountain on Idlewild property required that all the brush be removed. The fourth fountain was placed in that area. It is very difficult to describe the top which has four V-shaped compartments, a pedestal, and a bottom bowl that is oval. The top V-shaped set of compartments follows an origami-like paper folding that children make beginning with a square sheet of paper. In many ways, it is the most unique and interesting as water drops from many surfaces; it has a loud noise to attract birds and sits in a hollow surrounded by four foot high, newly planted Hemlocks with other ferns and pines planted around its edge to catch water.

For three of the Idlewild fountains, the forest comes right up to the fountains and wraps around them. At the Point fountain a set of ironwood trees arch above the fountain and, for the first fountain, sassafras trees have grown above the long, vertical column of water falling down upon itself. The origami-like fountain seems set amongst many trees as well. In addition to the light penetrating the transparent column of water, the shadows created at sunrise and, especially toward the end of the day are part of the attraction; the light and dark together with the water and the vegetation such as ferns and smaller Hemlock and White Pine trees growing around the lower Bowl, combine to further the matrix of dark and light textures.

* * *

But wait, somebody out there is raising her hand. We're trying to move from trees and fountains and get back to Hyde park and Married Student Housing. What's that? OK, we'll stick with fountains for a while longer; your question seems trivial. She says we've not talked about opening the fountains in the Spring. Well, all right, we haven't done that so we'll give it a shot. Yes, closing fountains is like a burial during the winter; you wrap them in plastic so they can survive the snow and ice. You hope the wind doesn't tear the plastic – or a falling branch – and that water doesn't seep into the fountain bowels and freeze.

There's no mystery, in the Spring it's just undoing what you did in the Fall; you, to use a metaphor, kind of bring the fountain back to life. Wait, she still has her hand up. You're still not satisfied. OK. You *want* a mystery. All right. No, wait everyone, we'll get back to 5316 South Dorchester Avenue in a moment. Let me think . . . good, I have it!

There occurred, on several occasions, an inexplicable event during the opening of the Origami Fountain. In the Fall the fountains are completely sealed so that snowflakes and raindrops can't get in. Now, the Origami Fountain *did* have a unique feature. When building the bottom bowl of the Point Fountain, I used an actual plastic children's wading pool. The whole bottom bowel was, of course completely covered with granite stones – very colorful – that ran completely across the bottom, up the sides, over the edge, and then back down to the forest floor – we've talked about that.

When it came to the Origami Fountain I resolved to use a large rubber, livestock drinking bowl for the bottom bowl. I spotted it in a rural hardware store and, for some reason, liked the idea. As far as achieving "winter integrity," a quality we referred to as "watertight integrity" for compartments on the *Hank*, it made no difference if the bottom was just stones, plastic, or rubber – the key thing was that it didn't leak. So what was it, then, that was inexplicable?

Well, truth to tell, there is always water in the Origami Fountain in the Spring – it has to do with the flat, outside edge of stones – the edge doesn't rise up like the Point Fountain – and the Spring rains leak into the rubber bottom bowl. No problem with rainwater however, the fountain is bailed out like a rowboat after a rain storm and then refilled from the underground water supply; I use tin cans for bailing and a large sponge to get at the last quart of water.

So when the inexplicable event occurred there was, perhaps, just an inch of water left to bail out and I was thinking about switching to the sponge which I always need to reach inside the cavity that holds the Little Giant Pump, and, all of a sudden I am taken aback! A live, perfectly gorgeous frog, jumps out of the cavity and pauses as though he is asking to be put free in the surrounding forest. There is no way that that frog – it is a Michigan Tree Frog but I don't look it up until after a couple of years of fountain opening – could get in; it had to be in there all winter! But no, this Tree Frog looks fantastic with its black stripes in front; it's beautiful; so that's the mystery.

I see you're happy now. So, you want to know what's going on; so did I and for two years I just had faith –'The just shall live by faith.' – Martin Luther. Then, after the third year's opening I went to my tiny paperback book of frogs, snakes, salamanders, and other, similar forms of life like toads. There it was, complete with the black stripes in front, and there was the answer. This particular frog can, upon sensing the coming of winter perform several tricks: one: expel water from its own, living cells, two: replace the water with its own form of anti-freeze, and three: survive the winter! This is not hibernation like the Grizzly Bears, heavens no! This kind of miracle occurs as well with fish deep in the cold depths underlying the arctic ice cap. It's like living in a suspended state. I see your hand is up again. Yes, that's it, it's like some kind of Cyrogenic Awakening. That also happened in the movie *2001 A Space Odyssey*.

That's also true. The frog in the Origami Fountain connected the Origami Fountain with the Point Fountain, a strange kind of relationship. They're both on the north side of Idlewild as well, very true. Yes, it's like those cryogenically frozen people except they have to be pronounced dead; these frogs weren't dead. No, we can't inject anti-freeze into our bodies; don't try it. In any event, these kinds of inexplicable happenings make for good *drama*. Yes, that's where we are going next: *drama*.

We go back to Hyde Park for the rest of the story; no, I didn't have that in mind when I started. It wouldn't be until we moved twice more beyond Married Student Housing to land – or jump, if you are still thinking about Tree Frogs – in a home that wasn't rented, or even a condominium; it was a genuine Hyde Park Red Brick Townhouse built in 1966. That owning of a home led Christiane's Aunt and Uncle to invite us to join the Midway Play reading group. This was another Hyde Park beginning; you could say it was deferred by several years. Christiane's Aunt was a volunteer who sat in the basement of the Gaylord Building when we moved in and Christiane's Uncle was a Professor of Philosophy, former Dean of Students, so we can't say that we were exactly ignored.

We needed to own a residence where we could have a sit-down dinner, every year, for thirty or more, fellow play readers. I distinctly remember one of those get-togethers at our townhouse when the play was very funny and the plot involved politics, the kind that takes place in the White House and thereabouts. The plot was not tucked away in my brain cells but the playwright was.

At the end of the reading – it was a short play because people have to get a night's rest – someone asked who wrote it!? Finally, George, a longtime play reader and Economics Professor at the University of Chicago, admitted he was responsible. We were all amazed and congratulated George for having made the transition from Economics to Politics and Humor; the play fit in so well with Washington, D. C., at the time, but I took everything at face value.

Not so many years later, I somehow acquired the urge to write a short play for play readers – I don't know if this was a Norwegian trait or not – if we use Ibsen as an example, that's not the kind of play I wanted to write. I didn't know if there are play reading groups in Norway, either. To keep the back row of the play reading audience awake, my play had to be: one, short, and two, funny. A short play is fine because, often, two short plays are produced or even several.

I thought of George and my resolve was to follow his lead; my first play worked well and my fellow play readers liked their roles and the audience had a good time; I continued writing more plays. In the middle of those fourteen plays, for some reason or other, I wrote the play which connects up with, you guessed it, the frogs in the Origami Fountain! And I gave the part – it was a monologue – to George; that tied things together. So, here it is, sit back and enjoy the show:

* * *

Cyrogenic Awakening
A Monologue in One Act

Cast: Mr. John Houston

Scene: A barren stage with the exception of a large Cyrogenic apparatus designed to preserve a single human on into the future. The apparatus bears no visual clues as to what might be called 'science fiction,' rather, the equipment looks as though it might be found in any hospital. The cover opens and Mr. John Houston sits up, gives a brief look around, steps out of the container, closes the cover and walks to center stage. He is dressed in a business suit and to the audience it appears that he has just been taking a short nap. He addresses his remarks to those responsible for this 'event' but he does not exactly know where they are because he cannot see them and, in fact, the scientists and technicians he talks to could be the audience but to him he knows they are there but never focuses on them.

"Made it! Made it! Made it! Been there, done that, got the tee shirt! Knew you guys would pull it off, just knew you'd make it. How nice to die and know that the whole thing is a big sleep. Wow! Thanks! Congratulations! Must have been a big project. That's the way. Science builds on one thing, one person's work, then another's? Must have taken years. Wonder how old I really am. Still using years?

"Remember the earth and the sun, the earth going around it? I started there. It would be logical to be somewhere else. Let me guess. Mars and Jupiter were in contention. Makes no difference. You are starting a new life; there's so much to learn; why not another place? 'Variety is the spice of life.' I'll miss earth. Life is the key thing.

"How much did it cost? I put a fair amount in escrow. Do they still have lawyers? Can't seem to forget Shakespeare. We'll talk about that later. I should be able to work again. I'll get a handle on this new body, new mind. Should be able to bring in some cash. Be some financial details to clean up. Bet I had some minimally invasive reprogramming already.

"Oh, by the way, you don't know anything about my wife. Actually, she was in a pretty bad way. Choices had to be made? It would be nice but, heaven sakes, life is more than the tip of the iceberg, it's the whole berg. Look at me. I'm going to need resocialization. Good opportunity to start over again. Never was one of those 'fraternity' men. Let me know the options. Hey, who's perfect?

"What about living? Machines, technology? I'm going to have to play 'big big' catch up. Hardly could bring up e-mail on my cell phone to say good bye to friends when all this started. But a whole lifetime? plenty of time. I seem to have all these memories floating around. That was no easy trick, all those neuron patterns. Let me guess. Stem Cells? I come from the dark ages; bloodletting. Eventually we got antibiotics.

"Best to think of the future. Must have lots of relatives, my children were the marrying kind. Genes don't change that fast. This is a new twist on the Makropulos Affair. I can't tell you what happened, nothing but a long nap. I'll recognize the family. Big talkers. You couldn't turn my father off. He'd be all for reprogramming. 'Parents of the world, don't sweat the details, just make certain there are suggestions for the second time around.'

"Speaking of starting over I kept a list of things I should have known but didn't. I never knew I was a veteran! Lost all those benefits. I never knew social security benefits were deductible on your state income tax. I didn't know the meaning of circumcision. But maybe you don't need to know this stuff anymore? I'll need that kind of information, updated.

"You're right, I haven't got the big picture yet. How in hell am I going to know how to live forever? Stupid! Bringing back old timers is nothing compared to living perpetually. That's a whole new ball game. Guys running around just to squeeze the last drop out of life, the last experience. Type A people. The only example we had were those Greek and Roman gods. Did they have the right idea?

"No diseases! What to people talk about? Hey man, would you believe, a whole new philosophy of life? 'The good life,' 'no regrets,' 'death makes life meaningful.' OK, top of the list: Philosophy 101: 'The unexamined life.' Going to be lots of time, no hurry. Wow! I'm glad I thought of that.

"There's got to be a lot of stuff like that. Some guy from a Brazilian jungle comes to Chicago. Life expectancy twenty years. Same thing. Reorientation! 'Time makes ancient good uncouth.' It's being going on. OK, maybe not as easy as it sounds. Flexibility. Social relations. I always felt intimidated by people who knew more than I did. Eighth graders whose parents took them to a black hole for vacation. There has to be a way to pick that stuff up. How do you relate to a guy who drove an automobile? History. This is a two way street. I don't want to be an anomaly!

"OK, you get up in the morning. Sleep. Do people sleep? Is there a pill maybe? All right, you start the day. No, you orient your mental framework so as to be aligned with what was in the old days some kind of time period the use of which was for setting an interval the purpose of which was to allow for some kind of human synchronization. You need that if two people need to start something together. All human activity needs this, a conversation, a meal, an appointment.

"Maybe these are all archaic words. Let's go back. How's this? The universe still has a finite life. An interval in a life is a time interval and requires two points, a start point and an end point. Subtract and you have the interval. Violà! Even though a human end lies out at infinity we still have to know when to schedule things, when to meet, how long to keep at it.

"Enough, enough. You know life was easy. It can't be harder! I don't want to be a vegetable. Utopia, OK, a good point to start with. Did anyone ever crack the code? Get full sign-off on what it might be? If so, was it implemented so that some of the big issues now seem ho hum? Food, diseases, wealth, political structure, housing, entertainment, whatever, self-fulfillment! There's a good one. What is self-fulfillment? History. Is there anything left to do? Anything left to create? Maybe there are no more sociologists?

"Suppose I can get away to music. Music! What about music? Had a hard time with mediaeval chants. Modern music not going my way. Can I live without Scarlatti? Maybe there's a group who listen to 'oldies.' Has to be a community, adapting, reorienting folks, friends who made it over. Willy Simpson. Is Willy here? Never liked Willy. Multiple groups. I hope he isn't in mine. Everything has a flip side. What about earth's wilderness, spiritual nourishment, pleasing landscapes, mental health affiliation with life, lifelike forms? Never felt that way about Mars. You had time enough. Bring earth back to wilderness, the whole planet one huge preserve. Stay as long as you want. Hey, reset to paradise, wow!

"I like flowers. My kind of flowers, violets, lady slippers. Hope I can recognize things. Chestnut trees from New York to the Mississippi. Good squirrel can make it all the way without touching ground! How much did it cost? Must have taken years. Some kind of primordial imprinting there, sunsets, clouds, butterflies.

"Oh yeah, I know, there's rage and fury in nature. 'The survival of the fittest.' How does that work now? I don't think you guys fooled around with my genes; I survived. You didn't even change my clothes. I can't believe they're still wearing these ties. 'Clothes make the man.' What's a button-down shirt got to do with survival?

"Still don't get it. What does an archaic word like survival mean anymore? History. We still had to have that routine. Motivation! That's what it's all about. People doing good works to become immortal. How does that work? The family, good paying job, trips to Europe. Kept us going. Maybe once in a lifetime you could camp in a wilderness. Now the whole earth. Are these things still a big deal? Seems like Eden is back in place.

"This is all too obvious. My problem is perspective. I'm using my own notions and haven't the slightest idea what actually caused all this to happen. Anthropological transference. Absurd. Louis XIV thinks everyone became a king but there are no kings. You guys know the emperor has no clothes, I don't even know what clothes are. Everything has to be reset.

"Sure, there used to be veterans. We have to start with what's inside. Quintessentially speaking, what is man? That's the question. Everything else is derivative. Gene patterns, neuron patterns, reprogramming. Once those are in place substantive follow-on questions can be asked.

"For sure, the physical world as no answers. It still needs taming and control but, of itself, no help there. Deep inside we look to see what those words used to mean, how they have changed and what they now mean. There's no predictable obvious progression, just a continuous stream of one probability following another. Hey, let's get started. Let me in!"

Curtain

* * *

You will recall, blessed reader, that we have taken this long-winded diversion to discuss the long term effects of my bride, on her Honeymoon, helping her father-in-law take down the Idlewild porch screens. There is no reason at this time to pursue Idlewild any further, not that there weren't many more fun/aesthetic activities that just couldn't be classified as work, the reason is that we must return to that Hyde Park address of the Gaylord Building, Apartment 418, at 5316 South Dorchester Avenue, and what awaits the newly married couple after their return from Bass Lake in early September of 1965. Yes, there *was* a wedding in Youngstown, Ohio; yes, there *was* a reception at the Youngstown Club; yes there *were* telegrams read and a toast given by the best man, my brother-in-law. And if we go back a bit further in time, on that trip returning from Vancouver, we stopped at Hebron, Illinois, a small town on the Illinois prairie, with a population of just over 700 people and a four-way stop sign marking the 'central business district,' the central business of the area being the growing of corn fields! I say that because on another trip at a later time, before the marriage, we visited Hebron and were given a tour of the surrounding farmland; the tour vehicle was a large corn-cob harvesting machine. We witnessed row after row of dry corn stalks being consumed by the machine which separated out the corn-cobs and caused them to be thrown, in a kind of corn-cob-stream, into a collection wagon astern of the mechanism.

Yes, there were wedding presents. How did the wedding presents get to Married Student Housing on Dorchester Avenue? A very good question. They certainly did not fit in a Volkswagen; imagine going through US and Canadian customs with a car full of wedding presents. OK, no, don't try to imagine that. Instead, an easier solution was worked out; the presents were driven back to Chicago – step one – and then my brother Peter, and his friend, somehow were given access to the apartment and were able to deliver the presents while the newly married couple were in Canada and Michigan. They also brought up dishes, pots, and pans. The furnished apartment was, at that time, rented from the University of Chicago for $85/ month! There are reasons for this. One of the reasons was given a paragraph in the book *Work – A Memoir*:

* * *

"Somehow I had been given a *cost-of-living* raise while on the West Coast and after the wedding I was given an extra fifty dollars a month to live on – after all I was putting my wife through two years of graduate school at the University of Chicago's School of Social Service Administration and living in married student housing.

"My new rent was eighty-five dollars a month. The building is still going strong at 5316 South Dorchester Avenue. My brother Peter and his friend brought up the dishes, pots, pans, and other wedding gifts while we were on our honeymoon at the Shakespeare Festival in Stratford, Ontario. It was a furnished apartment.

"It was on the top floor, the fourth floor, and it had a Murphy in-a-door bed. You opened two large wooden doors and pulled down a double bed that was hidden inside. It came down on hinges and springs that squeaked as it was lowered, and it filled up a good portion of the living room. The only downside was that one of the mattress springs came through and poked up to the degree that it was unpleasant if you tossed and turned. When you felt it intruding into your dreams it woke you up and thereafter you kept to your side of the bed, but I digress.

* * *

The other task we put before us was to show how that year of 1965 was a year of *beginnings*. You remember that, good. There were a lot of beginnings that occurred with that move to Hyde Park. We are going to look at a *condensed version* of those beginnings. This will be a test: see if you can list the beginnings from the excerpt that is taken from a book, *Black Friends*:

* * *

I never did go down the Mississippi with a black person of my own age – Norville would have been a good companion but our ways had parted. But my future *did* hold a river trip with one black adult and a group of black canoeists and it *was* an extraordinary adventure. I can remember putting that trip into writing with all the details but I can't find that document – it was B. C. before children – and that means it was between 1965 (marriage) and 1970 (first child). It is necessary that we see how this came about.

Returning from our honeymoon at the Stratford Shakespearean Festival in Stratford, Ontario, Christiane and I settled into the University of Chicago's married student housing building at 5316 S. Dorchester Avenue in the heart of Hyde Park. For almost forty-six years this community has been our home. We quickly became aware of our environment; we were living in one of the world's most successfully integrated neighborhoods. We will see how this legacy came about in the next chapter.

All around us were the institutions that would bring both of us into direct contact with black people – from the very poor to the wealthy. Almost kitty corner from us – at the northeast corner of Dorchester Avenue and 53rd Street stood the old Hyde Park YMCA. I did not know in September 1965 that, many years later, after the YMCA had been torn down, a new YMCA at 63rd and Stony Island Avenue would enter my life for a fourteen year period.

At this new Y I would arrive every morning before 6 AM and stand in line, waiting for the Y to open, and I would be the only white man in sight. This would occur until the University of Chicago built a fifty-one million dollar athletic center three blocks away from our home. We will speak of those friendships – which still exist – in our last chapter.

Nor could we have known for sure that our two children would attend Ray Elementary school and Kenwood Academy high school for twelve years. Kenwood was, at the time, eighty percent black and twenty percent white. Both children would be accepted at Princeton and Stanford, be awarded IBM Watson scholarship funds, and both would attend one of those schools – my son at Stanford and my daughter at Princeton.

Between that time in September 1965 and 2010, my wife would serve on PTAs and, for twenty-seven consecutive years, serve on the board of a major youth orchestra in Hyde Park. Two young black players from that group ultimately became principal clarinet and flute players at major symphony orchestras, the New York Metropolitan Opera orchestra and the Los Angeles philharmonic, respectively. Anthony McGill, the clarinetist, would play at president Obama's inaugural and, more recently, with Emmanuel Ax and Yo-Yo Ma at Chicago's Orchestra Hall, the latter now the Judson and Joyce Green Creative Consultant to that orchestra.

I would spend twelve years on the board of the Hyde Park Neighborhood Club – a mere two blocks away and situated in Nicholas park. In four of these years I would be president of the board of directors. This span of twelve years would give me a constant exposure to the other thirty-five board members – it was an integrated board – and, when president, take me through exciting times – a major building campaign.

The Neighborhood Club was a social agency founded in 1909; it served all races and all the levels of society through programs like the tot lot, summer programs, afterschool programs, the older adult day care center (which was 99% black older adults), golden diners, and meals on wheels. Awareness of and friendships with black friends that I could, formerly, count on my fingers, would now give way to entire groups. But the groups so far enumerated lay in the future and we must now return to the beginning period of our residence.

While in the Navy I began work on an Indian costume – principally on the long strips of seed beads made on a loom and taking – after many years – hundreds of hours of tedious effort. By the time we moved into married student housing I had enough of my costume finished so that I could participate in the yearly vigil ceremonies at Owasippe scout camps in Michigan. One close friend in the PhD program in English, lived next door to us on the fourth floor of married student housing. One summer he took a summer job with the old YMCA and I made a campfire appearance at Indiana dunes, a national park on the Lake Michigan shore, but I needed more to do than these brief excursions.

I began by examining the status of scout troops and cub scout packs in the area and came to the conclusion that many were well run – at least in Hyde Park. Accordingly, I became a scout commissioner – an advisory job, as I understood it – and I spearheaded a skill-o-rama for the Lake Shore district. This was a troop competition that was held in the gym at the Sinai synagogue located at 54th Street and Everett. (It has since relocated to the Loop.)

This was a competition that pitted individual scouts and teams of scouts against each other in events like: knot tying, life-line rescue, fire by friction, fire by flint and steel, and first aid. The key to implementation was a skill I learned from my own scoutmaster who made first, second, and third place wooden award plaques for all the events and for the winning top three troops. Using an architect's stencil to form letters with an India ink draftsman's pen, high quality plaques could be made by printing on a shellacked wooden plaque that was cut and sanded before shellac was applied and then varnished with a high gloss varnish after printing. My scoutmaster, George Simmons, Jr., made them for the Norwood-Edison Scout Leaders Association which held annual competitions in the Norwood Park district's gym in Norwood Park. I competed in at least two of these events.

* * *

Did you get all of the new beginnings? The list is not as long as that Idlewild List of Activities in Appendix J but that's because that list covers a range of years. Here are the beginnings I listed: The University of Chicago (which, itself, covers an enormous number of sub-activities), the community of Hyde Park (again, an enormous sub-category list could be made), living with the Black Community (the subject of the book, *Black Friends*), children, the South Side YMCA at 63rd Street and Stony Island Avenue, Ray Elementary School, Kenwood Academy, PTA's, a Youth Orchestra, the Hyde Park Neighborhood Club, friendships, and Scout Commissioner. There are some new beginnings that weren't discussed and that could not be predicted; one of these, for example, was our joining a play reading group; that would have to wait until we had our own townhouse.

I can't recall how many homes I promised to discuss; was it seventeen or eighteen? And then I seemed to shortchange the consequences of the wedding. There has to be a way to make up for those oversights. There are three more homes coming up in Hyde Park; then we counted those two eight-week cruises on the *Wisconsin* and the *Valley Forge* as homes. The point I am trying to make is that there is a post-wedding six-week home that should be counted. After all, if someone – actually a friend – hires you and your wife to go to France for six weeks, all expenses paid plus a salary, that counts for something!

Coming as it did one year after the wedding month, August 1965, it could be classified as a second Honeymoon. So what was this all about? It started way back while still living at 7240 West Pratt Avenue. You remember those Cub Scout Minstrel Shows where I was the interlocutor for one of them? You do? Good. In between the two acts of the Minstrel Show there was a Style Show. The reason I bring this up is that the woman that wrote the prose lyrics for the Style Show was my Cub Scout Den Mother, Mrs. Levin. Mr. Levin was a lawyer who, on one occasion, took a group of boys to Jerp House between Christmas and New Year; this trip occurred several years after my Cub Scout years. The story of that trip was memorialized in a short piece that I called *The Legend of the Car Ferry*. That legend appeared in a story called 'Pentwater Beach Addition No. 1' in the book *Western Michigan Tales of Mystery and Adventure*; in the story I describe the experience my Den Father had in Michigan with a group of teenagers who were now much older than Cub Scouts:

* * *

Sherman could remember those late December trips with his friends. His father would often accompany them as he insisted on the presence of an adult chaperone, but one year, one of his father's friends, a lawyer, Mr. Levin, volunteered for the job of looking after the group. Sherman retold the story many times and called it:

The Legend of the Car Ferry

Poor Mr. Levin! The trip across the lake was uneventful. Mr. Levin, the father of one of the boys, drove his Buick, and Sherman drove a much older Ford. Trouble began when one of the more obstreperous boys discovered, during his trick in the kitchen as one of the cooks, that Sherman's father, an architect by profession, stored about a dozen bottles of whisky on the top shelf of a kitchen cabinet.

Sherman's father was not a drinker by any means, but in a good year for business there would be at least a dozen bottles of whisky in fancy wrappers and beautiful bottles under the Christmas tree, and he ran out of space to store them all, despite the fact that some were always used at his annual office party. Plumbing, electrical, and general contractors seemed to think that whisky was the only gift for an architect, although some few shifted to fruit cake.

Sherman made lamps from the most exquisite whisky bottles by dumping their contents down the drain and filling all or part of them with transparent marbles, followed by the attachment of a fixture, lamp harp, and shade to the top, but there were limits in any household for only so many of these lamps. When one of Sherman's father's whisky-loving friends heard of this lamp-making being used for a bottle of twenty-five-year-old Crown Royal, he was said to have replied, "that's like pouring liquid gold down the drain!"

Mr. Levin found one bottle open with some whisky missing and assumed that one of the most unruly guests was drinking. As a lawyer and Methodist, he felt his responsibilities very strongly. This kind of thing and other situations plagued the stay, deprived him of some amount of sleep, and forced him to become a disciplinarian. He looked forward to relief in the Sunday car ferry trip back to Milwaukee. He was the lead partner in his law firm in downtown Chicago and had appointments on Monday. With luck he could have a nap Sunday afternoon after the drive of ninety miles between the two cities.

Sherman turned off the heat and the water on that Sunday and re-winterized the plumbing system in good time so that they boarded the car ferry before it left the slip and discovered they were almost the only passengers. They watched as the train cars were backed in, the few cars driven on, and the U-shaped barrier lowered at the stern. A final blast of the car ferry's horn indicated that the ship was underway.

The sky was overcast on the drive to Ludington. One never knew how rough a crossing was to be encountered until one arrived at an imaginary line drawn between Big Sable Point and Little Sable Point, a theoretical bow string that stretched between the tips of the bow, that concave archery-like profile of shore line between the two points. It was along this line that the wind was no longer protected by the land. When the car ferry crossed that imaginary line it began to wallow in earnest. The ship's purser came down and told Mr. Levin to keep his boys off the outside main deck, where he observed them playing hide-and-seek.

All day long on a longer than average trip, the car ferry met the waves of a Lake Michigan storm and wallowed in their troughs. Mr. Levin worked at keeping the boys inside, off the weather-exposed deck, and at peace. He longed to be within the Milwaukee breakwater. Then there seemed to be a particularly large wave and he almost lost his own footing. Soon after that the purser appeared on the scene and spoke with Mr. Levin.

"We didn't attempt to go through the breakwater even though we see it all clearly on our radar. The captain is afraid the high freeboard of the ferry will act like a huge sail and that with this wind we won't be able to keep her pointed straight on, in which case we might end up crashing against the lighthouse structures at the ends of the breakwater. We've turned around and are going back to Ludington. We'll give you all free staterooms and meals, but keep those boys of yours off the weather deck, please!"

"Can I call my wife and tell her to have my appointments cancelled for tomorrow?" he asked.

"Yes sir, you can use the radio telephone, right this way."

Early Monday morning the entire group awoke to a brilliant, sunny, winter day in Ludington. The car ferry began re-crossing the lake and had sunny skies for the entire trip. When the two cars were driven off, it was immediately apparent that the roads were as slick as ice. Mr. Levin's Buick crept up to each stoplight, cautiously using the brakes. At one of those early lights in Milwaukee city traffic, the front seat passenger in John Sherman's car quickly rolled down his window and lobbed an ice ball toward Mr. Levin's Buick, which crashed into the hard top of the vehicle with a loud thud.

This was the last straw! Mr. Levin defied the lined-up cars and the icy roads and the fact that the light changed to green. He walked back to Sherman's Ford, faced the culprit, and did what one of Sherman's friends called 'letting it all out!'

* * *

Mr. and Mrs. Levin had two sons. The first son was that fellow I mentioned earlier that spent a year in Mrs. Hoff's after-school classroom doing those long division and multiplication problems. You remember, OK, that's right, he went on to attend the University of Chicago. The younger Levin boy was, for me, one of those friends who are two years younger but, nevertheless, a friend. Reid Levin, the younger son, was a Groomsman in that Youngstown wedding in August of 1965. But we are getting ahead of our story. Mr. Levin, the Senior Partner of his law firm, used an exciting way to take a vacation with his wife. No! I don't mean going to Jerp House in the dead of winter, far from it.

When he wanted to travel with his wife, my Cub Scout Den Mother, he never revealed to her their destination until the very last minute! Mr. Levin or his travel agent made the arrangements, say, for example, a two-week trip to Paris, and his wife never knew where they were going until they came to the airport and were all ready to board the flight. The trip was always to some far-flung, romantic, destination, and it was always a secret.

While Reid, the younger son, was growing up, he accompanied his parents to France and, no doubt majored in the French language while in college; I'm not completely familiar with Reid's education. All I know was that on one of those trips to France – and there were many – Reid fell while exploring an archeological site, and the fall resulted in a broken leg. The accident caused Reid to spend an additional year in France. That year plus everything he did in France, both before and after the accident, made him an expert linguist – in the broadest sense of the word including playing French songs with his guitar – but also what can only be described as 'a lover of all things French.' So you see, we do have a love element entering this tale that goes beyond a wedding.

I lost track of Reid during my years in New Jersey, on the *Hank*, and in California, but we had enough contact to ask Reid to be one of our Groomsmen. By the time of our wedding Reid was a prestigious High School French teacher in a suburban school outside of Chicago. Reid achieved fame in several endeavors but Christiane and I were involved in only one of them. During our first year of marriage Reid and another superlative High School French teacher decided to bring ninety High School students to England and France for six weeks.

At the time, I was still working for The Outfit but I made a name for myself after I returned from San Francisco. We won't go into that, it's all in the first part of the book *Work – A Memoir*. Instead, I'll just excerpt the passage from that book about the opportunity that Reid and his friend offered us:

* * *

"I think it was after we had completed two of those toll bridge studies when a new outside opportunity arose, one that involved a special personal request from the traffic department. It was unexpected, involved learning, travel and we were given a salary with all expenses paid – it was too good to be true – and I meant *we* when I said it – it involved both my wife and I. It was the kind of thing that one couldn't say no to even if The Outfit was still a source of interesting work.

"An old high school friend, about two years younger than I, had spent years in France. He was a groomsman in our wedding and knew that my wife studied at Stanford in France. He needed our help.

"You may want to know why I bring this up. It's because I want you to know that I was treated well at The Outfit more than just once. I told

Mr. Barry or Berry that my high school friend and another outstanding high school French teacher were taking ninety students to England and France – one week in London, four in Quimper in Brittany, and a final week in Paris. They needed a chaperone couple for fifteen young women from as many schools.

"The request to the traffic department head was for four additional weeks off without pay which, when added to two weeks of vacation, would allow us to accept the job. I was to study French in Quimper, France. Mr. Barry granted my request.

"Maybe they thought I needed a reward – especially one with all expenses paid, a salary, and French cooking every day. On the charter flight to London, we studied the lengthy questionnaires that the parents of our fifteen wards had filled out for us – we felt we were true parent substitutes. We knew how to say yes or no to any special request that might come along.

"We were given a weekend off to visit Saint Jacut-de-la-Mer in Normandy to visit my mother-in-law's pen pal and her husband; we travelled back and forth by bus. While my wife sat in the most advanced French class given at the lycée, where we boarded, ate, and studied during the week, I sat in a beginning French class. We took side trips during the weekends to places like Mont. St. Michel. All the classes were taught by natives of France; my computer studies were put on hold.

* * *

What did I do to add to the programmatic aspects of the six-week trip? You'll never guess. I taught Architectural History to the students and called Square Dances. And, of course, we chaperoned the fifteen young women from as many High Schools. It was not difficult work and we were in Quimper, France, a major city in Brittany, during the Fêtes de Cornouaille. To this day, we still have a poster on the wall near the wash machine in the basement.

A young Breton woman, the Queen de Cornouaille, from 1965, stands with her lace coif in front of Quimper's Cathedral. The poster announces 3,000 costumes and 1,000 sonneurs, players of traditional music, which in Brittany was the bagpipe. During the Fêtes de Cornouaille, we watched the parade where we observed hundreds of lace coifs from every corner of Brittany.

We learned how to make Crêpes and the cooking at the lycée was fantastic; I can still taste the Celery au Gratin we had for a lunch. From our private room in the lycée, which was high on a hill overlooking Quimper, we watched the fireworks put on for the Fête. Below in Quimper we could see the Cathedral and the famous pottery firms of Herriot and HB Quimper where we purchased sets of dishes to take back to Hyde Park.

At Saint Jacut-de-la-Mer in Normandy we stayed in an Abbey where my Mother-in-law's pen pal and her husband, an International Law Professor in Paris, spent their summer vacations. We were put in private rooms! But the rooms were immaculate and we slept well. Paris, when the requests came in to teach while working for IBM, became my favorite place to teach in Europe. I taught a two week class I developed and two other one week classes there. On one of these occasions Christiane joined me and we stayed at the Hotel Scribe, just around the corner from Charles Garnier's Paris Opera, a building I studied in Renaissance Architecture. The stay at the Scribe and other teaching trips I took to Europe with Christiane made up for the separate rooms at the Abbey at Saint Jacut-de-la-Mer in Normandy and the very cold quarters we had when we visited Mont Saint-Michel. So our six-week sojourn to France in August 1966 prompts another entry in our pantheon of homes:

The Lycée Brizeux
29 S. Quimper
High on a Hill
Overlooking
Quimper, France
Brittany

After our return from France we began to live in a new apartment in Married Student Housing; we moved down the hall to Apartment 409. We were not moving up in the world, rather, we were moving horizontally. I should point out that before the switch to Apartment 409, the Married Student Housing powers *did* replace the Murphy Bed with a futon. That's not exactly correct; I should say that they added a hide-a-bed sofa near the door to the old apartment, 418, which allowed the Murphy Bed to be folded upward – there were springs inside the bed mechanism that, somehow, were involved in this (not the mattress springs) and that facilitated the Murphy Bed's ability to fold up into the wall so that the wooden doors that kept it out of sight – that is, the underside of the Murphy Bed – could be forever closed and the memory of rolling over the spring that protruded up from the mattress would no longer be a component of our dreams; this was progress with a vengeance. But the new Apartment had its own kind of excitement, it had, of all things, a view!

We wanted more in our new apartment so we paid more; our rent went from $85/month to $115/month. I should say, in passing, that the University completely remodeled all the Married Student Apartments in the Gaylord Building – when I can't say – and that parking alone, is now $75/month, but that is just an aside. Although I didn't know it at the time, back at The Outfit, I was getting very close to making a career change to IBM. More of that in a moment.

Apartment 409 was $30 more per month because of the extra room, a bedroom. An add-on plus was the view although I am certain that was not figured in to the higher rent. This view was toward the north; in Apartment 418 we had some windows but they offered nothing of interest to see. By looking down through the windows in 409 we were privileged to observe the back yards of several business establishments on the south side of 53rd street just west of Dorchester Avenue. The first item we observed was a piece of Nature, the trunk and growth of a huge Poplar tree rose up to and beyond the height of our room; this was a gorgeous sight that brought the seasons to us.

We became voyeuristic with respect to the individuals who operated or owned the shops below us, a small hardware store, Ribs-and-Bibs, a store on the corner which our neighbors at Apartment 417 claimed was a front for a bookie joint, and other businesses. It was fascinating to see when and why the individuals below us exited their places of work to enjoy their tiny back yards. Those individuals coming outside were a happening and no one ever knew we were, as it were, looking down from above. Often there were children and we reasoned that there were apartments above the storefronts.

We did our laundry on the north side of 53rd street and purchased Chinese take-out from the store adjacent to the laundry but we couldn't see those establishments directly because of the apartments above the hardware store. So much for the advantages of Apartment 409. What about the disadvantages. There *was* one disadvantage: the kitchen had no storage space to speak of. This is where a hardware store nearby comes in handy. It also is a good idea to grow up in a family that has a lot of homes to look after even if a lot of that effort is merely following your father as he makes repairs.

Without missing a beat, I quickly fashioned two narrow, multi-shelved, storage benches from wood; one shelf to the left and the other to the right made a kind of corridor but, together, they did the job. Looking back, it is interesting to note that there are *two* items in our current basement from 1966: the poster from Quimper and one of the kitchen 'structures' that I put together for Apartment 409! Both items survived three, further moves, a rental apartment, a condominium (first owners), and a Hyde Park Red Brick townhouse. Wonder of wonders!

I am told that Norwegians build things to last; this is certainly true of Natal Ronneberg, my grandfather. There are buildings he put up for Northwestern University and Apartment buildings as well as Laundries that are still going strong, albeit with different businesses. Like the upcoming change of career, we'll have more to say about building things that last when we return to Michigan. For now, we need to stick around Chicago a little longer. Towards that end, you would expect that an employee with only a very little career time – at The Outfit – would be extremely loyal to the organization especially after a six-week trip to France, at least such must be the popular sentiments of our society. After enjoying such a perk, then, the question is, *how*, in exactly two months' time, and *why*, would an employee, on his own, seek employment with IBM? This question is now on the table and, like most human actions, has an answer.

While all these kinds of things were happening in Hyde Park, there were a number of things happening outside Hyde Park. Chief among these was the transition, on November 1, 1966, of my employment to IBM. I'm speaking from the standpoint of the passage of time when I use the term 'chief.' Obviously, having children, was at the top of the list, just as having grandchildren now ranks right up there at the top. Here is the series of events that led to my seeking a job with IBM; the excerpts come from *Work – A Memoir* and they begin with our return from France:

* * *

"Upon our return I became aware that the computer department was looking to replace the 1620 with one of The Company's new machines, a 360. I was scheduled to attend a one week class in Basic Assembler Language (BAL) for the 360. Imagine! I had been around the Chicago traffic department for more than fourteen months since my return from San Francisco and now I was about to learn my third computer language.

"The thinking of The Outfit at the time was that 360 BAL was equivalent to 1620 SPS. This was, of course, only partly true – it was not clear that it would be necessary to know the machine level instructions for The Outfit's applications, but I was in France and couldn't be consulted.

"I interpreted the class as another reward – imagine! – time off for good behavior followed by another week of education to cap it off. Unfortunately, the class was not taught well by The Company educator. It made me wary; it suggested The Company was struggling to find people who could learn quickly – it was under pressure. It hinted at an environment of opportunity, of learning, of exposure to the laboratories and plant sites that developed the hardware and software both of which were rumored to be an exploding time bomb of unprecedented computing power that would affect all of society and ultimately lead to enormous leaps in human productivity.

"I compared the years it took to turn out plans for an Interstate highway against the fast paced environment of marketing computers. There were many competitors that wanted to replace the 1620 – it was a competitive situation. Everyone was in on the action – there were lots of young people working for The Company – in a year I would be seen as an old timer.

"All this appealed to my imagination, my sense of excitement. It felt like a call to leave drawing boards and engineering societies in my wake. There was the idea of teamwork and solidarity in belonging to a team where everyone was expected to be an executive, a marketer, a product specialist, a communicator, a fast learner, all at the same time. This was an environment where five week internal classes were a matter of course and where knowledge was being made obsolete at a fast pace.

"Like programming and the constant birth of new computers of all sizes, I sensed I had a natural attraction to the ethic, the life-style, the intensity of that kind of job – it was a fallback plan that never left my conscious thoughts."

* * *

"I'm certain we've all experienced that old adage of *too much of a good thing*. About a month before I left the Outfit – so different from my three years as a Naval Officer on a destroyer – I was asked to look at some FORTRAN gravity model code. A fellow in the Australian office tried to get a FORTRAN version running on a platform that ran that language. He had run into problems. It had to do with using external disk drives for data storage. The code was being sent to Chicago but before its arrival, Mr. Barry or Berry, called me in again. He wanted to reward me once more.

"My hunch was that the programming jobs for the traffic department were at a standstill awaiting the new computer to replace the 1620. In the meantime, I was being appointed as project director for a major study in Richmond, Virginia. Funny how people can ignore the basics. Hadn't I left the Navy in Virginia to go to Stanford and find a wife? Hadn't I already quit The Outfit earlier to be with my fiancée in Stanford? Even before I was married I was ready to quit in an instant.

"Travel to exotic places like Richmond couldn't hold a candle to the Red Sea, the Persian Gulf, and all the ports of the Mediterranean – the list was endless. If someone asked me at the time 'what is the worst job you could imagine?' it would have two characteristics. The first was that it took me away from Chicago – that would be like going to prison – and the second was anything that veered away from the trajectory I was on.

"Return to my fallback plan was instantaneous. I left Mr. Barry's office, went to my desk, looked up The Company in the yellow pages and found the nearest office. It was atop a new building on the west side of the Chicago Loop. I think the address was Riverside Plaza. The building faced the north-south branch of the Chicago River.

"It made no difference that someone there listened to my background and told me I belonged in the Hammond, Indiana, branch office. All it took was a short drive to Hammond, an interview with the Systems Engineering Manager, Denny, a programming aptitude test, a job offer at an increased monthly rate, a handshake with the branch manager, and I was ready to return to Wacker Drive and announce my resignation. Pass the bottle.

"How could I explain my notion of family life, my hunch that I was about to enjoy a new job a hundred times more than the old? Within a mere three months that latter feeling was obvious and whatever the number was, a hundred to one or more, things continued in that fashion for decades. There were, however, some amusing quirks associated with my departure.

"The first of these had to do with the competitive situation then in full swing. Many computer companies were vying with each other to replace the 1620. A young salesman from The Company – I had heard his name mentioned but never met him – was pitting The Company's 360 against many other machines. He was doing all the right things – inviting the front office people to seminars, marketing at multiple levels, visiting plant sites with The Outfit's executives, using literature, emphasizing The Company's multinational scope for an engineering company that, at the time, was the second largest consulting engineering company in the world.

"Just when the young salesman – I think his name was Mesh – felt he had a leg up on his competition, he was called into the front office of the executive vice president. He was expecting a signed order and a handshake as he walked down the row of offices to the corner office. As he entered there was a grim expression on the face of the vice president. Instead of a handshake and an order for a 360, he received an accusation: 'you are stealing John Sherman!'

"His reply and expression must have done the trick for, so the story goes, he answered his accuser with 'who is John Sherman?' I've always felt he would have been justified in answering 'who the hell is John Sherman?!' It's the kind of story that builds confidence in classes that train marketing people.

"I never ever walked the carpet to that neck of the woods – the corner office at The Outfit. No one doing grunt work would walk that way; it was assumed that only department heads went down that corridor. The Company at this time was desperate for people. There must have been instances of stealing technical people from customers. If the instances were proved to be true, The Company rescinded the employment offer. What else could they do? Everyone was a customer. Imagine! being thankful for using the yellow pages!

* * *

We were, at one time not so long ago, concerned with disproving those who claimed that all the Idlewild work was, in reality, a Norwegian trait. That in performing all that work for decades I could be accused of duplicity. We then talked about work as play, bringing up my IBM work during the summer, aesthetic endeavors, and so forth. We didn't talk about that imprinting that occurred during those formative years of age seven through twelve when father examined me on what was accomplished during the prior week while he was working in Chicago. It turned out that father, himself, wasn't as much to be pitied as those Muskegon Tower air controllers thought; you recall that conversational exchange about the heat and humidity being over ninety all week long. Why was that?

It is easy to imagine father having to do all the shopping, cooking, and dishes during those hot and humid days spent at 7240 West Pratt Avenue, days, I might add, that were devoid of air-conditioning. Things were not so bad. The Cub Scout pack enjoyed a waiting list for Den Mothers and Fathers and many of those prospective parents, not to mention existing Den Mothers and Fathers – who, with good behavior, could enjoy a three-year tenure – wanted to stay on the job or assure their being chosen. What better way, then, to achieve that goal than by inviting the Cub Master to dinner during those lonely days away from his family who were enjoying the cool breezes of Michigan?

When, during the Friday afternoon trip back from the tiny Ludington airfield, father recounted his weekly activities, he always included this litany of where he was invited to dinner! The Johnson's on Monday, the Zimmerman's on Tuesday, the . . . you get the idea. We could have gone on citing examples of why work at Idlewild was not work but at this point in our odyssey it is necessary that we return to Hyde Park on the south side of Chicago rather than digress to dinners on the northwest side. Once before, we returned to Hyde Park, and in an aside, mentioned still another Hyde Park activity: joining a Play Reading group. The name of the group was the Midway Play readers which was inaugurated in 1946 but our invitation to join came much later.

There is another way of going about this kind of thing instead of the random way of jumping in and out of the Hyde Park years in a back-and-forth manner. The alternative is to find some kind of all-encompassing category and follow it through from some starting point to the present. If we could find a category, by which we mean some kind of pursuit, interest, or hobby, that exhibited as many points as those eighteen or nineteen homes extending from way back – 7240 West Pratt Avenue – to a future point – 5508 S. Kenwood Avenue – then we would add an element of continuity to our narrative. The question becomes: is there such a category? Caution is needed to pronounce what it might be.

The category would already have made its appearance and, most importantly, would have to be the kind of thing that crosses into and out of all these arenas already travelled: arenas like 7240 West Pratt Avenue, Ebinger Elementary school, High School, Princeton, the *Hank*, Stanford, The Outfit, IBM, Hyde Park, Idlewild, and so on. It would have to exhibit some kind of ubiquitous presence that keeps cropping up. We need to make a case for it and that case needs to start back in the Middle Ages, if not earlier. So, let's get started.

You, blessed reader, recall that ceremony where candles were extinguished? Actually, the term used was snuffed. The first portion of the candle snuffing sequences mentioned 'Our duty to ourselves: to keep ourselves physically strong, mentally awake, and morally straight.' Even though they were snuffed, the hope spoken in the ceremony was that 'The virtues which they represent will glow the brighter in the hearts and consciences' of the audience. The time has come to look further into these words so as to locate this ubiquitous arena.

To a scout meditating on the meaning of these duties to the self, there was, ultimately, in my own case, the question of whether there was any priority implied in the *sequence* of the three items. This kind of question is all of one piece with those questions posed at the beginning as to what it was that father and mother truly thought; my excuse, of course, as time progressed, would be the consequences of understanding what it meant not to be a Norwegian all your life. To many young people who have grown up with a strong religious sense of direction, the sequence might be more in keeping with that upbringing if it were reversed.

Not being an expert across multiple, American, Christian denominations, nor even hoping to understand anything about other non-Christian faiths, I can only imagine that arguments in favor of this reversing school of thought would be Biblical passages like: 'But seek ye first the kingdom of God, and his righteousness; and all these things shall be added unto you. Take therefore no thought for the morrow: for the morrow shall take thought for the things of itself. Sufficient unto the day *is* the evil thereof.' Although never mentioned earlier, one of my mother's admonitions just happens to be within these words. Mother often used the phrase 'sufficient unto the day,' expecting her children to know the rest.

But despite these personal qualms as to the notion of reversing the three tenants of this portion of the Boy Scout Oath, the term 'morally straight' has a very specific meaning in the Scout Handbook: 'To be a person of strong character, your relationships with others should be honest and open. You should respect and defend the rights of all people. Be clean in your speech and actions, and remain faithful in your religious beliefs. The values you practice as a Scout will help you shape a life of virtue and self-reliance.'

Now there is another passage that seemed to crop up in my deliberations with respect to these three portions of the Scout Oath and that was the passage just prior to the one quoted in the last paragraph: 'Which of you by taking thought can add one cubit into his stature?' Many readers feel this applies to lifespan; others feel that thought is a matter of being worried or anxious. In any event, as a child, and extending much further beyond childhood, I felt that this passage had to do with pulling up oneself either physically, mentally, or morally by your own bootstraps. On the strength of that presumption, and as time progressed, I assigned great importance to the *sequence* of these duties to oneself.

As far as the Norwegians are concerned, I suspect that they would also agree with my endorsement of a meaning to the sequence as well as the import of the three phrases. To support that intuition I recall the skiers, the mountain climbers in Norway, the rugged terrain, the Olympic gold medals won by Norwegians, or even those Norwegians led by Joachim Ronneberg who led the raid against the Nazi heavy water plant in Telemark, Norway – a raid that took enormous physical prowess on the part of the members of the raiding party.

Despite father's far-flung interests, in my own upbringing, there was no emphasis on being physically strong. That emphasis would have to come through the genes of Natal Ronneberg, the grandfather I never knew, who, so I am told, played volleyball in the Loop, no less, every lunch hour no matter how many apartment buildings and laundries needed to be designed. And the Boy Scout definition of keeping oneself physically strong, seems to echo that important piece of information I took away from Stan Sieja, Princeton's fencing coach, who was also an Olympic coach at the time I was taking a fencing class from him. The information was the idea that you needed to have a sport for life, a notion reflected in the Scout Oath: 'To take care of your body so that it will serve you well for an entire lifetime. That means eating nutritious foods, getting enough sleep, and exercising regularly to build strength and endurance. It also means avoiding harmful drugs, alcohol, tobacco, and anything else that can harm your health.'

But there's a kind of reverse logic that comes into play in my family. I could not forget remembering the many, many times, that father gave me $2.00 to run down to the corner store on Pratt Avenue to purchase a carton of Camel cigarettes! I could not help being aware of those college pictures of father as a thin person. In my own time, father was not thin, nor did he participate in a regular exercise program. Instead, his early morning activity was with his stamps. Of course, at that time, as far as I can discover, no one had any idea of the carcinogenic effects of benzene. The reverse logic, then, was to incorporate the *opposite* kind of efforts towards physical exercise into my own lifestyle. The upshot was that, if father was a Norwegian in his non-pursuit of physical activity, i.e., exercise, then I resolved not to be a Norwegian, however much my father's lifestyle reflected that of most Norwegians. Of course, I was encouraged in this if only because I knew my grandfather Natal played volleyball every lunch hour!

A corollary of this kind of thinking was that I *did* take a lot of thought about my lifespan, and, to take it a step further, I came to feel that exercise aided a person's not becoming worried or anxious. I went on to read more into the *sequence* of the three duties to oneself; I felt the sequence was deliberate and significant. I quickly made it an article of my non-religious faith that being physically strong *should* be at the top of the list because it seemed that only when I worked out did I feel mentally awake in the fullest sense of the word. Now that *word*, with respect to being mentally awake is, from the Scout Oath: 'Develop your mind both in the classroom and outside of school. Be curious about everything around you, and work hard to make the most of your abilities. With an inquiring attitude and the willingness to ask questions, you can learn much about the exciting world around you and your role in it.'

So, in the ultimate reversal of the whole group that wants to *begin* with the 'morally straight' rule, I maintained – in my non-religious faith – the position that somehow, the stronger you are physically, the better you are able to remain mentally awake, and the more mentally awake you find yourself, the better chance you have to straighten out your life to make it morally straight. Let me say that before we go any further that I don't mean to go down that path of the third tenant, nor even pursue any kind of history of an attempt to stay physically strong. No, the reason for this elaborate grounding, this build-up, has to do with the 'mentally awake candle' that was snuffed and how it, for better or worse, glowed brighter in my heart and conscience. Not only are we in a section entitled love – and that Petachdonamen Weuchsowagan, *he who seeks knowledge* kind of aura – but there is a corollary that he who is characterized as such must have a kind of *love* for knowledge, but even more important at this point, is that this kind of seeking is the *thread* that carries us from the past to the present. How so?

If we take the trouble to list the *homes*, all eighteen of them:

7240 West Pratt Avenue
Chris Cot
Jerp House
Silver Lake
Princeton University
>Witherspoon Hall
>Blair Hall
>Blair Tower
USS *Wisconsin*
USS *Valley Forge*
Crothers Memorial Hall, Stanford
331 High Street, Palo Alto
Married Student Housing, University of Chicago
>Apartment 418
>Apartment 409
Quimper, France, Lycee Brizeux
Algonquin Apartments, Apartment 3B
Idlewild
Cornell Village Condominium, Unit 17A
5508 S. Kenwood Avenue

and then the classes and other experiences that, ostensibly, prompt one to be *mentally awake*:

Ebinger Elementary School
William Howard Taft High School
Princeton University, BSE Degree
NROTC Summer Cruises/Training
>Summer of 1957
>Summer of 1958
>Summer of 1959
USS Hank – Active Duty
>Course 401 Basic Damage Control

Course 402A Advanced Damage Control
Atomic, Biological, and Chemical Warfare School
Cryptography
American English – University of Chicago
Correspondence Course
Shakespeare – University of Chicago Correspondence
Course
Plato and Aristotle – University of Chicago Correspon-
dence Course
Introduction to Religious Existentialism – University
of Chicago Correspondence Course
Stanford University, MSE Degree
Palo Alto
Highways Correspondence Course
Statistics Correspondence Course
The Outfit
IBM Basic Assembler Class
IBM
Basic Systems Training – 5 Weeks
Develop/Teach Thirty Classes
Attend Other Classes – Too numerous to list at this
time.
University of Chicago, 190 MBA Degree
University of Chicago, Basic Program Certificate – 4 Year Program
University of Chicago, MLA Degree
University of Chicago Auditing Classes – Too numerous to list
at this point in our tale.

We arrive at a similar number but the *mentally awake* number is highly deceiving for several reasons. The most obvious concerns the case of IBM where every technical employee attends several classes every year, but, in my own case, my job description for many of those thirty-two years was developing and teaching thirty classes; in addition, I authored many Field Developed Programs and taught seminars on those software products, and wrote many Technical Papers.

Then, after the MLA degree, we have an ongoing series of classes audited at the University of Chicago. Life aboard the *Hank* was, in its way, a constant stream of learning experiences. But this kind of mentally awake stuff is not limited to the abovementioned because there are a number of self-education experiences: things like Fire by Friction – Appendix A, earning thirty-nine Merit Badges, developing a method to build stone fountains, beaded lamps, and to identify species of mosses.

This kind of thing was typical of my Norwegian grandfather, Natal Ronneberg, except that he was very good at acquiring languages as well as Engineering knowledge, not to mention being a good businessman. I was astounded when I read his article in The Norwegian Engineer publication in the early 1930s on the advantages of Apartment Living. The list of books he read in the first twenty years of the 20th century – to become more acclimated with American society – was impressive; those books were, in a sense, his merit badges.

Self-education, then, connected me with my Norwegian grandfather; but self-education also, in its way, made up for those BSE and MSE degrees that were never used. There was a third degree, an MBA degree, in that last list as well. I certainly treated it like a merit badge. The effort began around the time that I switched careers to IBM. Married Student Housing was behind us and we moved to:

Algonquin Apartments
Mies Van der Rohe
1617 E. 50th Place
Apartment 3B
Hyde Park, Chicago

The building was well known if only because the architect, Mies Van der Rohe, was famous. That fame would extend from Hyde Park to 330 N. Wabash Avenue where Mies built his last building, One IBM Plaza. By switching careers beginning on November 1st, 1966, and spending a majority of IBM years at One IBM Plaza, I could claim to, for a considerable period of time, have a Mies Van de Rohe origin or destination with respect to my commute!

Facts like that can be important. One reason to emphasize the trivial was that the two locations, one at 330 N. Wabash Avenue, and the other at 1617 E. 50th Place, Apartment 3B, were at two extremes with respect to *amenities*. The apartment was nothing to write home about; our next home, a half block away down Cornell Avenue, a condominium called Cornell Village (Apartment 17A), would outshine Apartment 3B by a huge factor.

Part of the problem was the view – there was none! just the other Mies apartments across the street. The furniture was very primitive until a short while after we moved in when the quality of the furniture moved up the scale from primitive to a bit less primitive. The event that caused this rise in our standard of living was the passing away of my brother-in-law's last, living relative. My sister and her husband were left with a truckload of Wicker Furniture; yes, I did say Wicker, and no, the apartment had no balcony. We received a phone call asking if we would accept it? Yes, of course, we weren't Goodwill Industries but we did need some basic pieces. My brother-in-law loaded up a truck in Hebron, Illinois, drove the truck to the back door parking lot of 1617 E. 50th Place, and we unloaded the Wicker pieces into the elevator, and strategically situated them around the apartment; our living room was now, in its way, filled with furniture.

The apartment was only a half block from the Illinois Central commuting line to Chicago's Loop which made it, initially, convenient for Christiane who was employed by Jewish Family & Community Services in the West Loop on Franklin; at the time, I was still driving to the Hammond, Indiana, IBM office and would not be promoted to the position of Instructor at the IBM Education Center at 18 S. Michigan Avenue, until November 1st, 1969. By the time of that promotion I had already started my Master of Business Administration at the University of Chicago's 190 Program on Delaware Street. This program offered the same classes as those MBA students took on the Hyde Park campus, the only difference was that it was taught after working hours.

If someone were to ask me why I started the program on Delaware Street, what do you think I would have replied? Yes, correct! I answered that it seemed that everyone was getting an MBA. It was no different than First Aid Merit Badge. But, for a certain group, the night school MBA was mandatory; this was true for new hires into Chicago's many banks. Not having an on-site MBA program of their own – which would have required hiring many professors with a varied group of specialties – the banks would hire new employees and then inform the new hires that they needed an MBA – majoring in Finance – and after they obtained that MBA – from the University of Chicago, Northwestern, or Loyola – let their supervisor know and, at that time, they could look forward to further progress in their career.

I, of course, ran into these young bankers as I put the coins in the vending machines that dispensed my dinners. Those machines make for a good conversation piece with current MBA students who attend the campus MBA program and have no problem paying their own way, i.e., they don't need to be employed. Many of these newer students drive expensive cars from garages near 1617 E. 50th Place; they live in a high rent district. When talking about my MBA I always emphasize how hungry I was for that can of hot corned beef hash that came crashing down after I pulled the correct lever. I drove the VW and later, after my promotion, I took public transportation.

But 1969 was important for several other events. Even before the summer ended, we knew that we would be expecting our first child in April of 1970. That forthcoming event made the construction site about half a block south, at 5201 S. Cornell Avenue, much more important to us. This high-rise condominium overlooking a lake-front park, marketed new units by constructing a replica of the condominium apartments on the site. We visited the replica and liked what we saw. Imagine! Instead of another Mies building across the street, we would see the sunrises across Lake Michigan 'from on high.'

The sunrises *were* spectacular and the view of the 'Point,' the park that extends out into the lake at the foot of 55th Street, added an extra dimension to the lakefront, but even watching the human activity going on in the parkland below us was fascinating. I began to keep a list of all the 'kinds of activity:' picnics, ball games, bicycling, baby strollers, sunbathing, walking, jogging, and sailing small boats on the waters of a huge pond, to name a few. After compiling a long list I felt that I would never spot a new entry, but that was not to be. "There's a woman sunbathing down there," I announced to Christiane, "she was just robbed! She doesn't know what to do," I added. I pulled out my list and added the new activity.

Before we moved out of our Indian Village apartment and into Cornell Village I asked father for a firm that would put down parquet flooring throughout Unit 17A. After our return from Bass Lake in the summer of 1969, we were able to see what a nice idea that was. The parquet floor included a huge dining/living room, a hallway and foyer, two bedrooms, and a large walk-in closet. Only the kitchen and the two bathrooms were not done as they were already tiled. The parquet was luxurious compared to the black floor tile of Indian Village. We enjoyed indoor parking, an outdoor swimming pool, a doorman, and inside washers and driers, not to mention saunas! This was *coming up* in the world and I mean that literally. The two bedrooms, one large and one small, as well as the living/dining area all had windows overlooking Lake Michigan; every window had a marble sill. The heating and air conditioning units were built in below the marble sills. Christiane's oriental rugs from Youngstown looked like they belonged on those parquet floors. Later, using parquet squares, I put down a parquet floor in the garage at Idlewild that I converted to a guest house for my mother-in-law. For now, an earlier deadline awaited me: to finish the MBA degree in March so as to be ready for the birth of our first child, a boy, in April of 1970.

The deadline was met with room to spare; the trip to Northwestern Memorial Hospital was a convenient one as we left for the hospital soon after waking up in the morning. The only glitch came when I went to bring Christiane and the baby back home; in my excitement I left the keys in the VW! I frantically asked around and the parking lot attendant knew what to do. I couldn't believe the tiny bill I paid – I used cash from my wallet – as we checked out; I was grateful for the IBM benefits; the check-out relieved my anxiety about the car keys, but back to the MBA graduation ceremony.

Did I want to attend a commencement? To pick up my degree? Who cares about picking up a diploma? I had picked up another 'commencement!' Mail it to me, please. I thus followed Christiane in not going to her Stanford graduation ceremonies. Besides, I had other things to attend to including the happiness of my parents and in-laws. Apartment 17A was a wonderful place to have a baby; we could walk holding our new family member and look out into the sunrise every morning; after all, a sunrise is a good metaphor for a baby, always gorgeous, always presenting something new with each day, and always challenging us by the miracle inside our home.

After moving in to Cornell Village, we kept the VW for a short time, it would get us to Bass Lake and Youngstown. The rest of our time the VW was used for my commute to the IBM office in Hammond, Indiana, or to customer locations all over the south side of Chicago and beyond; I didn't know it at the time but before the end of the year, that VW commuting would change to taking the Illinois Central commuter train downtown. There are, of course, an infinite number of stories about this period in IBM – from November 1966 to November 1969 – in *Work – A Memoir*. A reader of that book knows that there were three individuals who were promoted at the same time: November 1st, 1969. We enjoyed a triple promotion party put on by the office. The reason for three individuals, a Marketing Manager, a Sales Representative, and a Systems Engineer, leaving at the same time was simple: IBM, beginning January 1, 1970, was charging tuition for all of its customer classes, so-called fee-based education; everyone was wary.

As for my own promotion, during the three years at the Hammond office I acquired a wealth of hands-on experience with real customers; I wrote technical papers that were published internally by The Company, and started creating my own software – on the side – for which I earned royalties. The current Instructors in the Education Center lacked the field experience; many were hired immediately after graduation from college. They attended five weeks of training in Atlanta at a school called CST, Computer Systems Training, but that didn't provide the depth of handling real customer situations.

The Manager of the new fee-based Education Center at 18 S. Michigan Avenue was promoted from his position as Marketing Manager of the US Steel team in the Hammond Office; he knew me by reputation through my helping his technical team. The third promotion was a Marketing Representative in the Hammond office, a salesman who was promoted to a newly created position, District Education Sales Representative. He was given a quota that was measured by the amount of Education Center revenue that was achieved in the District.

I made sales calls with Jim, the new District Education Sales Representative, while in the Hammond office; we knew each other well. Naturally, the first thing IBM did was what it always does when faced with a new business opportunity: it held an Education Revenue Contest! We won! There was a booklet of prizes to choose from and I chose a large Stereo Set with lots of bells and whistles like a tape player, AM and FM radio, and many other controls.

You will remember, blessed reader, that we started these 'tales of movement' by introducing physical fitness activity. It's true that at that time, a lot of my physical fitness activity *was*, truly, movement: jogging. Despite the fact that father was not athletic and that I had to follow my grandfather, Natal Ronneberg, in his lunchtime volleyball games, in order to claim any affinity to a Norwegian Ronneberg, there *was* a lasting effect that carried over into my Hyde Park activities. You'll also recall that during those lonely weeks while father was in hot, sweaty Chicago, while his family was at Bass Lake, father was not to be pitied to the degree that one might expect. That was due to the fact that his Cub Scout Pack always had fifteen Dens with fifteen Den Mothers and Fathers, and, and this is important, there was always a *waiting list* for Den Parents. Hence it was that father enjoyed having dinner with existing *and* prospective Den Parents.

When schools started in early September, father would take me around to Den meetings – sometimes several in an evening – even though I was not old enough to join Mr. and Mrs. Levin in their basement for weekly Den meetings. I observed another activity in the basement of 7240 West Pratt Avenue, in that extensive Workshop Area that came about after WW II by virtue of the coal bin disappearing. In that workshop, all of the wooden projects for that small army of Cub Scouts were cut out. The upshot of these observations, and many others, I might add, *imprinted* me across seventeen consecutive years with what it took to run a Cub Scout Pack; I knew the business!

After surveying Hyde Park in the official capacity of a Scout Commissioner, I came to the conclusion that, with few exceptions, many of the Scout Troops did have excellent leadership; it was this observation that led me to inaugurate that Troop competition for which I made the award plaques using the methods of George Simmons, Jr., my own Scoutmaster, and the person who made plaques for the Norwood Edison Scout Leaders Association during my own career as a scout. But even before my twelve years on the Board of the Hyde Park Neighborhood Club – for four of which years I was the President – the idea came to me of becoming involved with Cub Scouts.

My strategy for what became two Cub Scout initiatives, was entirely different from what I observed as a child. First, I would go to a neighborhood where the Cub-Scout-Aged children were poor; so poor that it would be absurd to find a parent that could do the kinds of things that the Cub Scout Committee and Den Parents did for the Methodist Church Cub Pack. Second, there would be no church sponsorship, nor would any group sponsor my initiative, either secular, or religious. I would sponsor, finance, recruit, and otherwise completely support the group; all I needed was a meeting place and an opportunity to recruit members from that area north of 47th Street, North Kenwood. I found the place to recruit: Judd School in the heart of North Kenwood, and I found a place to meet: in a common room on the first floor of Public Housing just north of 42nd Street. With those two items in hand I began my first initiative. After that twelve years on the Board of the Neighborhood Club, I began a second initiative, in many ways much more extensive than the first. The excerpt below is from the book *Black Friends*; it describes my first Cub Scout group experiences which occurred before we had our own children:

* * *

I began by examining the status of scout troops and cub scout packs in the area and came to the conclusion that many were well run – at least in Hyde Park. Accordingly, I became a scout commissioner – an advisory job, as I understood it – and I spearheaded a skill-o-rama for the Lake Shore district. This was a troop competition that was held in the gym at the Sinai synagogue located at 54th Street and Everett. (It has since relocated to the Loop.)

This was a competition that pitted individual scouts and teams of scouts against each other in events like: knot tying, life-line rescue, fire by friction, fire by flint and steel, and first aid. The key to implementation was a skill I learned from my own scoutmaster who made first-, second-, and third-place wooden award plaques for all the events and for the winning top three troops. Using an architect's stencil to form letters with an India ink draftsman's pen, high quality plaques could be made by printing on a shellacked wooden plaque that was cut and sanded before shellac was applied and then varnished with a high gloss varnish after printing. My scoutmaster, George Simmons, Jr., made them for the Norwood-Edison scout leaders association which held annual competitions in the Norwood Park district's gym in Norwood Park. As a scout, I competed in at least two of these events.

I decided to take two further steps: I would mentor a scout troop that was meeting in the park district's building in Kenwood Park on Dorchester Avenue between 49th and 50th Streets and start my own cub pack. We will begin with the cub pack.

I grew up in a family where my father was the cub master at a Methodist church in Edison Park for seventeen years; I knew the business. It made sense to begin my own efforts in North Kenwood – north of 47th street – and meet in the ground floor meeting room in one of the huge, all black high rise City of Chicago housing projects that rose just north of 42nd Place east of Lake Park Avenue. I would have access to the lakefront park by crossing over the Illinois Central railroad tracks by using the pedestrian bridge at 43rd Street.

I began by interviewing the principal at Judd elementary school located at 44th Place and Lake Park. He gave me permission to present the program to the appropriate grade class rooms and I returned with my double trailer Indian bonnet and briefly spoke about cub scouts. I left a copy of the date and location of the first meeting. The principal also gave me a sign-up sheet with names and addresses of interested boys. I can remember following up with that list by going door to door in the surrounding area of apartment buildings which were demolished fifteen years later.

I didn't know it at the time but the huge public housing buildings, from which I also drew cub scouts and where I would take elevators up and down to encourage parents to send a child who had missed a meeting, would also be demolished – by dynamite – perhaps twenty five years later. And so I began my first Cub Scout group. I felt sorry for the sisters of my cub scouts whenever I came in contact with them. This occurred at Judd School and later, when I called at apartments.

Over twenty years later, at a time when I had finished my twelve years with the Neighborhood Club, I returned to North Kenwood and began another three year Cub Scout odyssey. It would meet at St. James Methodist church at 4611 South Ellis Avenue; recruitment would start at the Shakespeare School, 1119 East 46th Street, a couple of blocks to the east on 46th Street from the church, and softball would be played – during the spring – in the Shakespeare school playground to the south of the school. That later group involved many meetings of struggle as I did everything on my own. I also took groups of St. James cub scouts on trips – again on my own – and, travelling by Chicago Transit Authority busses, to places as far away as Lincoln Park Zoo. Those adventures must await a further chapter, Multitasking.

But now, in retrospect, I can compare the two experiences; there were similarities and differences. Aside from the shorter duration – only two years for the earlier cub pack, one important difference was that I often had at least one parent helping in my earlier endeavor. The meeting room was bland by comparison with St. James. I had a true architectural love affair for the old church and its rooms, its gym with a balcony, its spaciousness, and even its lighting fixtures. I had grown up in a Methodist church in Edison Park but it was nothing like St. James – I had a reverence for the environment.

The one parent was often a harsh disciplinarian and that was in sharp contrast to my own methods; I never wanted to shout no matter how unruly the cub scouts became. This made it particularly difficult for me at St. James. Another factor is somewhat difficult to explain. Let me begin by stating that I financed these operations entirely on my own in both locations; that included everything from craft projects, cookies and refreshments during a meeting to transportation costs and meals for a trip. I never wanted cost of any kind to prevent participation.

With my first group, I gave Cub Scout books to my scouts and that caused parents to purchase a uniform for their sons. When I started the second group years later I had the feeling that these boys were poorer than the first group. The total lack of parental involvement made me feel this way as well as the economic times. My hunch may have been correct or not, but no one ever came to a meeting with a uniform. I was not upset because for many boys it would have been too much and I was happy for the equality; I had too much empathy for those who would have stood out in yet another way and I wanted no reason for lack of attendance.

I did distribute Xerox copies of Cub Scout books to my second group but, in both groups, if a parent ever signed off on a requirement for a wolf or bear cub badge, I never knew it. I seemed to have more boys with problems in the St. James group but we will look at that in the later chapter.

Another difference between the two Cub Scout groups was that I purchased all of the craft projects for the first group. This removed the burden of thinking up a new project every week or so for the St. James group. On the other hand, the St. James projects were more interesting than store bought crafts and there was a greater degree of child effort involved, not to mention my efforts to teach boys how to do things and keep track of half-finished projects from one week to the next.

The front cover depicts some of these craft projects from the St. James group. In the appendix to *Black Friends* titled Front Cover, Appendix L, (*in our book*), I have documented exactly what these items are. Many came from very standard craft items that father made in his basement for seventeen years and for hundreds of cubs. There were items that could not be worked into the collage of the front cover because they were too big; these included a rope machine and all the pieces of a mobile.

One reason I remember so vividly the presence of uniforms in my first group is the photos I took when we took our only trip. I hired a school bus for a day at the Indiana dunes and everyone was in uniform. I took Polaroid pictures with everyone running up the first sand dune we encountered. I'm certain that many in that group had never encountered sand in that way.

But there was another common element in these two experiences. Within each group there was one boy that I identified as being particularly needy. It may have been the total lack of a father figure in the family – I can't exactly say – but, in both groups, the needy boys were children I paid particular attention to. I felt their need and they expressed it in different ways. I remembered their names while others have passed from my memory. I shall speak of Jeremy when we arrive at our story about the St. James group.

The child in my first group was Norris. Norris lived in neither the Chicago Housing Authority projects nor the apartment buildings in North Kenwood. His residence was a large home on the east side of that little piece of Oakenwald Street that ran from 4600 south to 42nd place in the north. The backyards in the rear of these homes faced directly onto the Illinois Central railroad tracks and the homes had seen much better times.

I became aware of his residence because Norris, after a time, wanted to be driven the short distance – his address was nearer to 4300 than

4400 – to the meeting place, perhaps less than a full city block away. Norris was an active, likeable child, unlike Jeremy who was likeable but shy and needed coaxing – all the way into his home – to join a social environment that might benefit him.

When a child is over solicitous of praise, can't seem to leave your side, and gives you the feeling that the next hour and a half will be a highlight way out of proportion to the rest of his week, there is something that clicks inside of you and all you can do is keep performing the work you have set out to do with the same kind of intensity and determination you have at the opera when the audience is silent, holding back their tears.

* * *

My second Cub Scout experience is a much longer story and did involve a church, St. James Methodist church, where I held my Saturday morning meetings. The entire chapter describing that period, a chapter I entitled *Multitasking*, can be found in Appendix M. But the time has come to return to Michigan. Not by any means have we exhausted the love affairs of Hyde Park. We have, for example, in passing, mentioned a Scout Troop, actually in the south portion of Kenwood, which caused a Michigan adventure on the Pere Marquette River with, you guessed it, the Grumman canoe and also with the loss of some second-hand cooking equipment purchased after the Boy Scout National Jamborees in 1950 and 1953, if you can imagine that. We'll return to that adventure later. We also alluded to a group called Midway Play Readers and, for good measure, mentioned twelve years on the board of the Hyde Park Neighborhood Club. The Neighborhood Club and the Boy Scouts go back to 1909; Midway Play Readers is young, by comparison, having been formed in 1946. Those previously broached subjects will have to take their place as we return to Idlewild, a place that seems to call out for recognition because of that early date of origin: 1905.

Going back that far suggests that we are privileging ancient, or rather antique, objects; that's true but in Michigan we do mean *roots*, the kind of objects you find when you dig down into the past. How does that come about? Well, digging for worms in the dry leaves of the forest can lead to an encounter with roots; little red salamanders as well, but we never use them for fishing – they are just too cute!

Although we began the journey to Idlewild with that poem that begins with 'The brown leaves redeem each year I return . . . ' we want to dig even deeper. Before we leave Hyde Park we need to mention that in October of 1972 while still at Cornell Village, Unit #17A, we were blessed with a second child, a girl. It was that year, too, or maybe early in 1973, that mother communicated her intention of gifting Idlewild to us. Our new goal is to examine the 'property' surrounding Idlewild and since property involves leaves, trees, and those kinds of things, we are going to begin with the first chapter of a book entitled *Dawn* which, in its own way, explores roots. In the excerpt the author is referred to as child:

* * *

Dawn

dawn *vi*

1: to begin to grow light as the sun rises
2: to begin to appear or develop
3: to begin to be perceived or understood
         <the truth finally *dawned* on him>

dawn *n*

1: the first appearance of light in the morning
         followed by sunrise
2: a first appearance: Beginning

It was a hot summer and the cicadas had been whining ever since the sun rose above the green line of trees that grew above the shoreline across the lake. Now the eastern sky above the dark green was a kaleidoscope of pink hues as if some unknown force was slowly turning the colors and clouds that used every shade of pink imaginable. The vivid oranges and reds that began the show were soon mottled within the buttermilk sky of dawn. It was a time of human silence – the scene changing at every moment – nothing would be the same ever again; the inevitability of the transition from the deep shades that rose out of the black of night itself would soon transform the heavens through myriad combinations of light, progressing until the sun completely obliterated all palettes like an artist washing his colors.

A child could sense that standing at the end of the pier was the best vantage point to witness the display. This same spot was the location for the nightly shows of sparkling stars as well, when the Milky Way spread itself across the cosmos from the constellation Cepheus to the deeply red color of Antares, the heart of the scorpion in Scorpius. As the display grew in intensity toward the total darkness of a moonless night with only the stars as pinpoints, the red of Antares, like our own sun, tinted the surrounding cosmic dust of the universe to a bright orange as if a reminder was needed for the coming of dawn.

What would it be like to place a sleeping cot on the pier platform and to fall asleep while counting shooting stars? Summer nights were short and the dawn light would come quickly like some power slowly rotating a dimmer through the direction marked dusk, and continuing beyond to the darkness called night. But pier-watching the sun peek over the far shoreline of forest was best observed through the lens of the forest itself. The oranges and reds, when viewed through and filtered by the green complexity of the woods enhanced the spectacle as though multiple objects of new colors and sizes were added to the kaleidoscopic mixture.

What does one do to follow this nightly show of heavenly splendor with its epilogue of humbling color? The solitude of walking through the fallen leaves of the forest beckons, if only because it, too, reminds of the transience of life. Like the newest blue stars forming out of the exploding remnants of those that have exploded before, so, too, the leaves, given time, recall the genesis of the nourishment of life to come. There are days for digging through and down into the rich legacy of our ancestors who have done nothing but to leave the earth itself alone as though they were aware of the lessons of this rich soil on their descendants; a black gold, more rewarding than its bright counterpart and not involving the alchemy of futility.

From that buried richness springs forth a cornucopia every bit as various as the heavens whose brilliance also arises from having sprung up from darkness. Objects created out of nothing except through light itself have arisen, once again, after millenniums of birth and rebirth, to dazzle the world with new forms and colors. All that is necessary to acknowledge this succession of miracles, is to recognize the process through our own reflection. The trees now grown to bring us shade and the rustling pleasure of their leaves are no less owed this reverence than the ferns that return each year with their crosiers, now a memory arising from the swaying complexity and variety of their fronds.

So many of the woodland objects arise from dust: the beautiful blue lichens – formed in the partnership of an algae and a fungus – begin with a fungus spore; the mosses arising from spores, tiny seeds that are distributed by teeth around the rim of their capsules; the millions of spores that form under a mushroom cap recall a microscopic dust power. Who has seen the spores that scatter from their cases below the fern fronds? The wind that brings us our peaceful sleep – either by moving the leaves or moaning by itself – distributes these dust-like spores while we rest. Surely, the complexity that arises from the objects we do see must compete with the dust of the universe, the pollen of every flower, and the bustle-like bloom of every orange hawkweed must be linked to the orange aura around Antares.

Beauty and the passing of time begin to connect these disparate elements. The spring rains glisten the dead leaves, continuing down to join the snowmelt droplets already at work to raise the green proliferation of plants that will be the first relief from the ubiquitous white of winter. But these same droplets descending upon the rugged and furrowed black bark of the oak create the background for the blue composition of the lichens that will come back to decorate that canvas with their own, more delicate and roughened texture. A circle of stems rises from around that oak tree scene like a green wreath but its glory comes earlier than the year's end. Tiny clusters of blue stemmed goldenrod buds quickly begin to form in the leaf bracts, building our suspense as the summer's nourishment finally achieves its purpose with a burst of bouquets of delicate yellow flowers, all up and down the arching stems as they wave in the winds of fall. Now the blues of lichen and stem, enhanced by the yellow clusters, both set off against the still dark and rugged bark, transport us back to the night sky – to blue-white Vega or the blue-and-gold double star Albireo – the most famous color-contrast double in the heavens – at the very tip of the head of Cygnus the swan, or at the very bottom of the Northern Cross. Even at an early age a child can reflect upon the two meanings assigned to the same basic pattern: a swan reflecting the large numbers of white visitors dotting the lake in the spring, and a cross reminding many of the Christian religion.

From this point we can, like a solitary hiker of woodland trails who responds to color and clusters, choose to take an older path back to Antares, an older star; or, like the clusters now blossoming up and down the arched blue stems, switch our focus to the open clusters of new, hot, blue, and young stars found within a chain of open clusters running in an arc from the spout of the teapot – Sagittarius – up and around to beyond the top of the pot. Like the yellow bouquets in each bract, the open clusters belong to us; they lie within our own galaxy, contain small groups of stars – dozens to a few thousand – and are young and gravitationally bound to each other – each cluster a mass of diamonds set out as though on a dark velvet cloth of a jeweler whose wares belong to all humanity.

As a child returns as an adult to the brown paths of leaves he has traversed for every year of life that he can recall, other sights and senses flood his memory along either of these pathways. Like *first light* when a new telescope is first activated, *first flower* focuses that memory on the first flower ever espied, orange hawkweed, with its bright orange bustle-like sunburst that hearkens to the feathered dance bustles of the American Indians, and to the equally intense curiosity to know its name and struggle with the heavy book of wildflower pictures – Homer D. House's *Wild Flowers* (1942).

But as the child grew he realized that beauty per se was not the only factor at work in his pursuits; a combination of other influences was present. The solution of which influences dominated, like a solved arithmetic equation, fixed the result: *what actions he chose to pursue.* Like digging down into the leaves to find the decayed accumulation of years of undergoing the complex natural processes within him, the child began to understand, for the first time, this conjunction of motives that were always in play. For what are leaves alone, lying alone, without water, and the connection to owner-ancestors who left the forest floor alone? He observed the effect during his search for fishing worms. The worms lay within the moist and flattened leaves of spring that looked like sheets of phyllo dough, and the rich, black soil, layered like veins of black gold, was already in abundance, a contrasting color to the glistening leaves and worms.

How could one explain the child's motive of wanting to name of every living thing – birds, trees, ferns, mushrooms, flowers, butterflies, stars, and even mosses? What factors led him to preserve the past, know and revere every square foot of ground, deepen his sense of place, and forgo what others saw as the pleasures of society for the sake of this other cornucopia of pursuits? Beauty was, no doubt, at the beginning, a motivator, but the ultimate causes were some set of forces that were, collectively, even more powerful.

Along the way the child decided to label these under the single rubric that he called *The Search for Authenticity* but he might just have used other words which were equally as inappropriate, like happiness. He tried to dovetail, as best he could, the complex emotions that went far beyond the confines of mere taxonomy, but there always seemed to be some pieces missing from the jigsaw puzzle, and he was never completely satisfied with his own, inward reflections. It was as though pieces – social, philosophical, and psychological – were revealed that advanced him forward in the mosaic that he was building but he lacked the complete unified field theory that would unlock the mystery of his own, internal, microcosm. Of one thing however he was certain: his search was not for *dark* matter — his elements, like the dawn, were made of light, uplifting themes.

Later, the child would be reinforced in his hunch for where to search for dawn-like, uplifting themes. The child would be influenced by one who defined further the notion of man as containing the universe *within himself*, Nicholas Berdyaev who had written: Man's *consciousness of himself as the centre of the world, bearing within himself the secret of the world, and rising above all the things of the world, is a prerequisite of all philosophy: without it one could not dare to philosophize.. . . he knows himself to be the absolute centre — not of a given, closed planetary system, but of the whole of being, of all planes of being, of all worlds.*

And so, as he walked through the woodland paths of brown leaves year after year, he continued to pay attention to the inner voices that seemed to direct his actions. He even reflected back upon his taxonomic motives, beginning with his study of bryology, hoping to probe beyond his fascination with families like the Mniums and Haircaps in an effort to find deeper meaning.

* * *

With the excerpt from *Dawn* serving as an introduction to *property* we will now look at that chapter called 'The Property' as it appears in *Instructions from Idlewild A Study in the Search For Authenticity.* Of course, all this preparation is for those who have continued on, those blessed readers who want to get to the part about a do-it-yourselfer who goes to the hardware store on vacation, who want to get down to the nitty-gritty details of remodeling, for example, a kitchen with an honest-to-goodness antique, wood-burning stove! Like so many things in life that involve a love affair, the idea here is that it is necessary to craft the setting; love is a many splendored thing; it has many dimensions; in this case the setting is like the first stage setting of a play or an opera, i.e., it speaks to us.

* * *

As a young teenage driver I was not sensitive to the feelings of an elderly woman who was almost eighty years old and whom my mother lionized. When her last trip was made *memory unafraid* – lines from the poem *Idlewild* at the end of Appendix I – Mrs. Conrad stayed with a friend in Pentwater and I picked her up and drove her to Glenn Ellyn, a suburb of Chicago, her home. Nor was I that enamored with her pristine 1937 Buick sedan and its excellent condition. My sister, who went to driving school in Chicago, taught me to drive using an old running-board, floor-shift vehicle that was equally as old; my lessons were in Michigan. After obtaining my driver's license, I was given the old Studebaker, but when it wore out I went on to drive one of the last Ford cars built during World War II, a vehicle that had no chrome but lots of vapor lock, an automotive malady that caused the car to stop un-expectedly and which I solved by keeping a bucket of water in the back with a sponge so as to be able to open the hood in traffic and cool the carburetor. The consequence of those experiences with what we called the 'pea green' Ford caused me to be impressed with the cleanliness of Mrs. Conrad's Buick and the fact that it did not stop unless instructed to do so by the driver.

When I wrote the words *memory unafraid* in the poem *Idlewild* sev-eral decades after this trip I had something else in mind. No doubt Mrs. Conrad, who never had children, was constantly in mind of the experiences she enjoyed while her husband was still alive during their summers at Idlewild – 1917 to 1933. By not returning to Michigan she would be leav-ing an atmosphere that would serve as a catalyst to such memories; I felt that she enjoyed many years of summers spent in Idlewild. Many might tie the words in the Biblical passage, *lo, I am with you alway*, and be closer to my suspicions. What I did have in mind when writing the poem was that Mrs. Conrad's principal loss was not being away from the huge wood-burning kitchen stove that she baked bread in, but the beauty that is, and that surrounds, Idlewild.

When one arrives for the first time in spring and steps on the forest floor of soft leaves of the prior fall, compressed by the snow that is now gone, one smells the forest for the first time and a flood of memories returns. The bouquet is a mixture of wintergreen, sassafras, bolete mushrooms, decaying leaves, and earth worms, often punctuated by strong doses of Lily-of-the-Valley that, at this time, grow in enormous patches. But the eye soon picks up even more clues than the sense of smell as one becomes accustomed to the new perfume. It is the effect of this initial experience that I attempted to put into the first lines of another poem.

> The brown leaves redeem each year I return.
> Orchids greet with quiet simplicity
> And joyous new life unfolds like a fern,
> Blossoming holy authenticity.

There are no smells in these lines because smells and sights during these first returns are quickly internalized to much deeper layers of experience and feeling.

The lines were written fifteen years ago at the start of a rather intense poetry writing period that extended for two years and included over five hundred sonnets; some poems like *Idlewild* were longer. Most of the poems were never read except by my mother but when I pursued them I saw that many were about Michigan and that some of them contrasted with life lived at Idlewild and life lived in the city of Chicago. From the IBM building at 330 North Wabash Avenue where I worked, there was a view of the Chicago River and beyond, following the river, Lake Michigan could be seen.

Two sonnets explored this dichotomy. The first, *Vacation*, was an attempt to contrast, using words in each line, the business environment in Chicago and the environment of Michigan, and the second, *Chicago Return*, continued in the same fashion using elements of the city such as city flowers, concrete, and the presence of people to do the same kind of thing.

Vacation

Where is the leading edge of quietness,
The mist that fills the bottom line of pine,
The value added from the nighthawk's tryst,
The strategy that twists red trumpet's vine?

No fern can forecast beauty's curving plan,
Nor violet inflict a deficit.
The leverage of each blossom's summer span
Remits the hummer's labor infinite.

The task force of the universe awaits.
The stars in overtime like diamonds shine.
Promotion through the world must now abate
To mine the profits of another clime.

It's time to spark the rally in our heart
Will fuel the fire we bring to all our art.

Chicago Return

Chicory in Chicago playing now,
But there are fields of purple knapweed come.
White clover 'long the sidewalk making bow,
But woodlands are the place I'd rather plumb.

The gulls cry o'er the concrete banks and soar.
Once more I'd try the sandy shores with pine
And even though the crowds applaud and roar,
I'd cheer the silent flowers, for they're mine.

At every block the river spans rise up,
But where are lilies white among the pads?

Come rising swallowtail and fill our cup.
Go find the spicebush, light these weary lads.

Replace exhaust with perfume sassafras,
Pipsissewa in pink for stone and glass.

I always knew that the major food plant for the Spice Bush Swallowtail butterfly was Sassafras; this was common knowledge. I expected to locate what I also considered would be a common plant around Idlewild – the Pipsissewa – and hoped that one day I would find it. There were Wintergreen plants all over the forest and my mother used to make terrariums using Wintergreen plants and moss. As a young child in the 1940s when mother encouraged me to find the orange flower, Orange Hawkweed, down by the Chris Cot mailbox, in Homer D. House's *Wild Flowers* tom of 1942, I saw the color photograph of Pipsissewa and knew, from an early age, what to look for. There are associations that come to mind in the alliteration of what must be an American Indian source name for Pipsissewa, the other name being Prince's Pine. The genus name *Chimaphila* is from the Greek *cheima* (winter) and *philein* (to love) according to the Audubon Society Field Guide. However romantic the Greek origin might be, it was always the Indian name that conjured up memories for me and these memories of the Idlewild woods were, strange to say, engendered on the ocean. Where else would one desire the woods around Idlewild than on the ocean itself?

After steaming for days in the USS *Hank* (DD-702) across a beautiful portion of seven eights of the world's surface without seeing a single green thing such as a tree or tuft of moss, instead of bright sunshine, blue water, and white wavelets, the *Hank* would rendezvous with and come alongside a Naval oiler, ships which the Navy always named after American Indian words or places. All of a sudden the *Mississinewa* would be sighted on the horizon and as Officer of the Deck reporting this to the Captain it was a joy just to speak the name. Once the report was made I could then dream of the woods, the Wintergreen, the Indian Pipe, the Bolete mushrooms, and all the other elements of the forest floor. Pipsissewa was so close to

Mississinewa that the colors of Indian feather bustles and dancing would come back to haunt the watch. Somewhere in all that wonderful color would be a pink that would match the delicate pink of the Pipsissewa and that pink contrasted against the wonderful shape and green color of the Pipsissewa's leaves became an antidote to the ocean if not the monotony of the watch for the leaves are sharply toothed, bright green and shining. Even a child would be the first to connect the flower of Orange Hawkweed, Devil's Paintbrush, with the bright bustle of a native Indian dancer.

How exciting, then, was the day when Pipsissewa was discovered on the grounds of Idlewild. Ultimately, it was found in two different locations. One of those locations also contained the distinctive leathery leaves and hairy stems of Trailing Arbutus, an endangered wildflower. At first it was the Pipsissewa's distinctive leaf and not the pink blooms which allowed identification; they differ greatly from the Wintergreen which is ubiquitous on the Idlewild property. Later, I was able to catch the blooms but the leaves and their pattern were enough to keep me looking for more and even document the plant by way of a sonnet before that time came. In actual fact, the poem *Pipsissewa* has it all wrong because in the northern states the flowers occur from the latter part of June until August and I wrote: 'They all must come and go by end of June.' It was my constant thinking that I *missed* the blooms that kept me from looking all summer long.

Pipsissewa, Prince's Pine

Pipsissewa, your name alone brings fame.
Ojibway must be jealous all the same.
They have Algonquin consonants to blame,
Your constant sheen for wintergreen's your game.

What's worse for me, I've never seen your bloom,
They all must come and go by end of June,
A month wherein vacation makes no room.
Would that the city's din would hold your loom.

So Prince, you see I pine to share your wine,
All summer see you grow near needles fine,
But only pictures show what you define,
So pink, so shy, so utterly refined.

And so each fall, I go where the sidewalks show
And dream one day when winter ends I'll know.

So what is the Instruction from Idlewild in all this? If there is a purpose to these various poetic digressions it would be to point out that if one is to value such experiences then one must not acquire a wooded piece of lakefront property, remove as many trees as necessary, destroy all the native species, and plant a lawn. When the old property markers for Idlewild were found they were buried beneath eight inches of thick, black soil, all of which was created by the decay from hundreds of leaves and other organic matter from the forest. Preservation of this legacy and avoiding the need to rape another area of its soil for a lawn would be the first corollary of this way of thinking, but there are many others that follow.

The forest is enriched by the decay of not just seeds, flowers, pine cones, dead ferns, and animal droppings, but also by branches and entire trees that have died and fallen down. If one has the opportunity to look at a Pacific Coast rain forest such as the one near Tofino on the west coast of Vancouver Island, one encounters layers of dead trees up to three feet thick and more; they are covered with moss and every kind of growth imaginable. Trees grow from dead trees! Enormous quantities of water are retained in this beautiful ground cover which can't even be penetrated by a human being without enormous effort as witnessed by the ingenious platforms that lead the visitor into this primeval paradise. Oddly enough, there is a beauty on Vancouver Island that accrues to the forest when the same rule is followed in Michigan.

Old limbs and entire trees come down, the bark comes off those trees, and enormous quantities of nutrients result. Complexity is restored to the forest floor and out of that complexity arises the beauty of nature. This can be seen where one Hemlock planted in 1993 – it had three trunks – was put near the long dead stump of a large white pine tree; the nutrients from the white pine tree accelerated the growth of the Hemlock vis a via the others planted during the same year. This complexity happens at the micro level and at the larger perspective of entire areas of the forest. By focusing on both levels at the same time I sensed this going on as I looked out from the porch of Idlewild at the forest floor between the porch and Bass Lake. As the sun was rising, it was the miniature complexity that surrounds Idlewild that seemed to drive the change in verse forms in each group of four lines in the poem *Morning Cobwebs*.

Morning Cobwebs

Silken forest floor, cobwebs in the light,
Who can tell us more, mist that ends the night?
Industry beyond manly dreams of might
Make us see futility in our fright.

They who stumble will be caught, quickly bound,
No safety net this gauze upon the ground.
This smoke brings fire to those who can't be found,
Grave an airy pyre with silk surround.

Link the leaves of green. Let me walk on air
Thinner than hair, rise, throw away despair.
The rigging of a million ships to spare
Will spring and wring my heart away from care.

Dead brown below then green between white sky
Of heaven's cirrus strands that fly across
The sands of years and logs of twig decay
To match this frozen time that starts the day.

Filter the pollen from the crisping leaves.
Sift the lowly breeze that sways the flower.

Spread your sense of ease across the carpet.
Blanket the new with past every hour.

Rise honeysuckle above foggy banks.
Your yellow blooms transcend this gauzy gray.
Raise up with bracken's palms, give higher thanks,
New life, the light that pierces leaf, new day.

But the rule of letting nature determine the landscape must be applied throughout every square foot of land. Like the house, where the spirit of the rooms remain the same, so, too, with respect to the outside for, if Mrs. Conrad were to return there as well, nothing would be that different except the thickness of the trees and additions that enhance the natural landscape. What is uglier than a huge metal tank, be it a kerosene or natural gas tank, occupying space in a forest? If a single jar can conquer the wilderness as it does in Wallace Stevens' poem *Anecdote Of The Jar*, then any man-made disturbance, however small, can disrupt in the same way.

Anecdote Of The Jar

I placed a jar in Tennessee,
And round it was, upon a hill.
It made the slovenly wilderness
Surround that hill.

The wilderness rose up to it,
And sprawled around, no longer wild.
The jar was round upon the ground
And tall and of a port in air.

It took dominion everywhere.
The jar was gray and bare.
It did not give of bird or bush,
Like nothing else in Tennessee.

For decades only the residents of Rochester, Minnesota, were plagued with resident Canada Geese. Now a lawn can become an invitation for perpetual feces throughout much of the United States, and the Canada Geese stay around during the winter months. The brown leaves themselves are a precious resource that go beyond the redemptive nature alluded to earlier in a poem. When raked away from a house in the spring for a foot of fire protection they become the necessary cover for the two parallel paths of the road up to the house, thereby transforming the road itself into a thing of beauty; a road like an old, moss-covered logging road in the deeper woods ready to be incorporated into an oil painting; a road that, unlike asphalt or stone of any kind, never interrupts the continuity of the forest from one side to another; a road that reminds us of two woodland paths that wind together into a paradise which derives from within us, as though planted there from some earlier presentments of memories we carry in our genes from experiences during a primeval period.

There is a difference between a sunrise on the ocean viewed from the bridge of the *Hank* and one viewed in the early morning as the sun rises across an inland lake and the light is filtered through green branches of many different species of trees and bushes growing along the lakeshore and between the lake and the viewer. Without this filter, which makes for a kaleidoscopic diversity from before the rise of the sun to long after, French Impressionism might never have been envisioned. It reminds the viewer of the glowing coals of a campfire in the night when some core of brilliant colors is constantly changing and being filtered through the logs and branches between the observer and the heart of the fire,

During the day, the patterns of light and shade on the forest floor that arise from the complexity of the filter in conjunction with the interaction of light and dark on the contents of the forest floor, like a sunrise through an early-morning complexity of green, cannot be adequately described; only an attempt can be made.

Forest Shade

So soft this forest floor with what is not,
A cooling invitation to the heart.

The patterned transformation of the wind
Enlightens feathered fern to instant art.

The slanting threads of morning thin to ray
And laser pierce the darkened, deadened fright
Till lengthened sunset shadows lead the way,
To mottled moonlight, sparkling suns of night.

Soft fall now guarantee of more to come
Stark skeletons of winter speak no mass,
Nor does the thirsty robin seek its run
When every branch makes shadow, broken glass.

So hide me now within the summer womb
Before the winter white marks all a tomb.

Before we leave this brief introduction to The Property the question should be raised about the effect of the white-tailed deer slowly reducing the diversity of even so small a piece of forest as the Idlewild property. It is certainly true that Pipsissewa is as rare as the leather-like leaves of Trailing Arbutus, and that Pink Moccasin flowers are deer food extraordinaire. How are we to cope with these losses? One possible way would be to use our powers, while we still possess them, to remember the loss.

Pink Moccasin Flower

When the wind wings fragrance from the forest,
Starflowers shining bright with their allure,
I find the reigning queen all glorious,
Pink upon her scape so slim yet still demure.

When jack-in-pulpit's prose and prayers are done
And ferns and hemlock boughs have said amen,

The Venus slipper's sepals all speak wanton
And make us young and lost to love again.

So from the past in unexpected place
Pose slippers one and two and more in grace
Than any plant or bird or man this day,
Beauty's testimony to a better way.

Now when winter snow reveals the withered
Capsule low, hearts have hope they too may grow.

A second way would be to mourn the loss.

Second Growth

I'll show you where arbutus grows
In rows where no one ever goes.
Along a logging lane of moss
I'll lead you till you sense the loss.

With ease did men erase the trees
That now would bring them to their knees
For then 'twas not a known disease
The lack of pine sap in the breeze.

Ah, what we would not buy for stumps
To reach the sky! Why did all die?
Did no one try, no single sigh?
Was gold that high in times gone by?

Were cathedrals never known
In the rough? Was life too tough?
Did no one brave to say enough?
Alas, the trees were merely stuff.

You, too, were devoured leather
Leaf. Help us stem today our loss,
Our grief that all will soon be dross.
Renew us with your fragrance sweet.

Fifteen years after writing those lines, Senator John Kerry used the same metaphor in a speech; I was able to relate to his words because of my own poems and experiences. Speaking of his mother Senator Kerry said, "She gave me her passion for the environment. She taught me to see trees as the cathedrals of nature."

Finally, I would suggest that if we apply the close reading of literary criticism to the forest floor, we discover new insights that will help assuage, with deer-proof certainty, an existing world with our discoveries. This occurred with respect to the Pink Lady Slipper or Moccasin Flower. Just before the Pink Lady Slippers had all but disappeared at Idlewild, my hopes were revived by a New York Times Science Times article that related that, in fact, Pink Lady Slippers propagated below the soil and that someday, exclusive of an eight foot fence, they might come back. At the same time I discovered Helleborine, another orchid!

For years I spied many lovely large – sometimes two foot high – stalks of flowers, usually drooping at the top like a fern's crosier to begin with, growing with an orchid leaf; they were deer proof and often ubiquitous, even in dry years. Close examination revealed that there were sometimes up to thirty blooms at the top of the long stem; these exquisite blooms were, in fact, orchids and there were, literally, hundreds of such blooms to view every summer. The blooms were not pink but multicolored, beautiful, and frilly like an orchid purchased for a corsage, and they were described in detail in Mr. Conrad's book *Our Native Orchids* by William Hamilton Gibson, Doubleday, Page & Company, New York 1905. There, above the bottom shelf that held the National Geographics of a decade later, was all I needed.

But even before the discovery of the species in Gibson's book, I had the good fortune to write down all that I could observe and to bring those notes to Barbara Plampion, a member of our Midway Play Reading group and an expert. She dropped her duties as principal host just when she was needed the most, went to her library and found the correct identification. What a gift to have another dimension to share with a woman whose company I enjoyed for so many years. But there was more reward to come in the discovery of Helleborine. I read Darwin's classic texts more than once but never had a tangible thread to connect his work with Idlewild. With the use of my magnifying glass I would now be able to make the connection for, on page 83, Gibson relates the story of Darwin's personal interest with Helleborine; I confirmed Darwin's observations with my own analysis. Here is what Gibson wrote.

"In Plate XXXV., Figs. 2 and 3, as seen in the front view as well as the side view, the flower projects well forward, and contains two pollen masses on its underside. Beneath it, with the sticky surface undermost, lies the stigma(s). The beak or rostellum is formed like a round knob, and projects beyond the stigma and underneath the anther. This knob is covered on its upper side with such a tender membrane that Darwin found he could prick it through with a human hair, and that when he did so, even without provocation, a slight viscid milk would ooze out, which would render the upper surface of the knob very sticky. He also found that the whole knob or rostellum would come off if it were shoved very slightly upward and backward, and that its underside was also adhesive, and would dry fast to anything to which it stuck.

"He examined flowers while still in the bud, and found that, before the flower expands, the anther opens, and exposes the pollen masses. These lie in round grains that stick together in fours. Each group of four is tied around by a fine elastic thread, and the sum total of all the threads is collected into a bundle that looks, under a magnifying glass, like a brown spot in front of the pollen. It is this bundle or knot of threads that becomes pressed against the knobby rostellum in the bud, the moment the anther opens. It sticks fast, and anything that will remove the rostellum will naturally pull the pollen masses out of their sockets in the anther.

"As the flowers stand out almost horizontally from the stem, the curiously shaped lip hangs out invitingly. The lower portion of it is rounded into a pouch in which the nectar lies, and the lip end is hinged and forms a landing place for insects.

"As the insect alights on this porch or clings to its swinging, hinged lip, he bends down into the honey cup and takes his fill, then flying out and upward, his head strikes the sticky under surface of the knob-like rostellum and drags off the cap, to the upper surface of which the pollen is adhering. . . .

"As some plants grew close to my house, I have been able to observe here and elsewhere their manner of fertilization during several years. . . . I thus saw the act of fertilization affected by the pollen masses being removed by wasps, and afterward carried attached to their foreheads to other flowers. . . ."

Following this analysis through one's own efforts bridges the early nineteenth century to the Idlewild property and the present. It joins the mind of one whose drive and curiosity remain to this day unparalleled, with one's own meager interest. There was another set of flowers on the Idlewild property which allowed me to celebrate the present, flowers that bloomed in bunches much like a small forest. There were many delicate flowers on fragile stems and the blooms were deer proof as well. A flower can be a difficult thing to identify especially when the blooms are small. After searching the Audubon Society Field Guide many times, I finally spotted Cow-wheat; by then, it too, was a favorite. I searched Edward G. Voss' three volume *Michigan Flora*, the bible for plants in Michigan, and was thrilled to discover that Cow-wheat was not only abundant but also ubiquitous for Idlewild and the entire state of Michigan.

What is happening here? The activities being described are those of an *amateur*. An amateur is a person who cultivates any study or art, from the standpoint of taste or attachment, without pursuing the art professionally. Darwin and Voss are professionals. The word amateur derives from French through Latin from *amator*, a lover, from *amare*, to love. This derivation marks these pursuits as belonging to a chapter on *love*. A pursuit can be enormous in scope, so complex that the love that initially sustained the effort can be dulled. This occurred with my taking up the study of bryology, i.e., mosses. I came to love mosses and wanted to learn about them and how to identify them. On the bottom shelf of the bookcase at Idlewild are many volumes of *Moss Flora of North America North of Mexico* by A. J. Grout, Ph.D. These volumes were self-published by the author throughout his life. Grout was one of the premier bryologists of his age. He also published *Mosses with a Hand-Lens and Microscope* and the smaller *Mosses with a Hand-Lens*. These books were published between 1900 and 1910. Grout left instructions in his will that any copies in his estate should be available for purchase from the Field Museum in Chicago *at the original price!* When pursuing a new field, what could be more encouraging than obtaining a set of beautifully illustrated books – about eighteen inches wide – at turn-of-the-century prices?

The further one delves into this moss library using both a microscope and a high-powered hand lens – 20X – the more complicated is the search. There is another, less complicated, level where the amateur doesn't need an extensive degree of expertise. Here is how that works with Cow-wheat. Voss reports that for Cow-wheat, the seeds have an elaisome which facilitates dispersal by ants. An *elaisome* is an appendage (modification of seed coat) on a seed, containing lipids attractive to ants (which are dispersal agents). The Greek *elaiodes* means oily substances which are insoluble in water and greasy to the touch. An *elaisome* thus pursued as an amateur connects a beautiful plant with an ant! When I observe ants at Idlewild I think of them below ground contributing to the spread of Cow-wheat.

The flowers resemble a snake's head but to my imagination the cluster of stems brings much more to mind.

Cow-wheat

Much like a tiny forest scene of green,
You stand serene with tiny banners out.
Devout, your manner's not to flout, you seem
A gentle scheme too delicate to shout.

Yet like a holy army vast, you stand
With ensigns at the mast. Across the hills
You blast the grass from yellow trumpets grand.
Your ordered ranks of frill instill with will.

But are you just a snapdragon at heart,
Small snake head never far from start of grace?
Your two-lipped flowers always are apart.
Does grimace on your face belie your lace?

Embrace us plant so spare, whate'er your race.
Your place so fair ensnares with its heirs.

It *is* possible to pursue the depth of mosses in a poem and use the technical terms that are discovered with a hand lens; this is done in the following poem.

The Spread of Moss

On a dry twisted seta held up tight
A capsule filled with spores is set for flight.
A peristome with teeth are set like bite
With cilia poised to filter life so light.

Operculum has long since sung its song.
Rhizoids throng below where they belong.
Each rock and tree has one-celled leaves so strong
To carry on the fight, their sight prolong.

The hygroscopic fringe begins its binge
Like hinges thrown open to impinge.
Sporangium's invisible infringe
Upon the lichens set for mossy singe.

And thus through dust we cannot see grows green,
Spread low across fair forest scene serene.

This first chapter of *Instructions from Idlewild* addresses the spirit in which the property is viewed. No doubt every family possessing such a piece of land will have their own way of following that spirit. In section Nine of the Sunday New York times for July 18, 2004, the leading article quotes a woman who is concerned about the life of her family: "I was pregnant with my second son, and we decided that the children needed to be in nature." And then she quoted her husband, "I think a lot of people are assessing their lives. What was missing was a spiritual component. It's part of a national re-evaluation." I ask myself if this is the way my parents spoke to each other in 1943, when they first began thinking about Chris Cot.

From the front porch of Idlewild one can sit in a comfortable futon and sweep one's head from left to right and back again. The span encompasses more than one hundred and eighty degrees. The lake, like the sunrise, lies beyond the green of many types of vegetation, from the forest floor to the sky, and complexity resides in the entire sweep. The Bortel brothers who built Idlewild, by lowering the distance where the large porch screens begin, allowed the front porch occupant to see the forest floor all the way up to Idlewild with the exception of a few feet. In the entire viewing space there are little, if any, man-made objects to be seen except the road that runs parallel to the lake shore. Even between that road and the lake shore there is heavy vegetation.

If one looks to the left and to the right for any other summer homes, the viewer again fails to see other manmade objects; there are, literally, no adjacent summer homes within sight! The end result of this positioning of Idlewild is that there is a synergism created by the conjunction of elements of nature together with the preservation of the house and the retention of, and increase in, the beauty of its contents and surroundings. This is a visual synergism wherein birds, squirrels, chipmunks, and the plash of water combine with all the other elements to preserve something of the past together with elements of our own time placed with the same sense of respect.

It is unfair to refer to the lake as though it was secondary to the property. Quite the contrary is true. The property extends all the way to the actual shoreline, i.e., the space between the road, Bass Lake Boulevard, and the lake shoreline is owned by the property owners. For Idlewild this strip is filled with bushes, trees, and plants of every description. Throughout the day a blue band of light comes through the complex band of green between Idlewild and the lakeshore. It dazzles at sunrise and sunset; the moon rises and a band of shining light comes through the now dark complexity of brush and trees, stretching on the surface of the water from far across the lake. The blue band extends to the north and south and can be seen in the wide sweep of more than a hundred and eighty degrees.

The smell of the lake when standing at the shoreline is very much part of Idlewild, as are the snails that mark their trails on the sand. The wind comes from the south and arrives through the whitecaps before you feel it on the front porch, sifted first by the pines, oaks, sassafras, and bushes. Idlewild and the lake are intimately tied to each other; the antics of kingbirds, the calls of kingfishers, the splash of bass, and the noise of flapping waterfowl – swans, geese, and ducks – can be seen and heard all day and at dusk, on a warm evening, the bats ply back and forth in the sky along the shore.

We will link these two – Idlewild and the lake – together with lilies, both white, one a quintessential representative of the spring, occurring in large patches on The Property and the other performing the same function in the summer on the lake.

Lily of the Valley

A patch of perfume locked away to keep
Across deep winter snows and memory

The gentle bonnets where the mist does seek
To cloud the mind with beauty's mystery.

Before the royal ferns have spread their wings,
A lowly flower sings of purity
And nods to all the humbleness in things,
The only source that brings security.

Like lace that reappears to be more dear,
The dreary face of forest floor erased,
The wedding whiteness bids us be of cheer,
So long a life as ours must have its place.

For if we leave such perfume on the breeze
The least of any wind will feel bereaved.

Water Lily

Where the black redwing's call to mate is heard
Near pink hairy willow herb, there lies
White star of word more bright than any bird,
A flower of Christ's parable so wise.

The fragrance of your way entranced Monet.
Your bouquet bloom of petals dispels gloom.
Where'er you settle there's no room for gray,
White bride of flowers, you can have no groom.

Where'er you rise you focus every eye.
World radiates around you when you're found.
You glorify and purify the sky,
With quintessential beauty you astound.

Exotic white aquatic, the world's your
Proselyte for you are sight despotic.

If you, blessed reader, have come this far in what may be called *The Idlewild Saga*, you may have observed that, so far, we have dwelt on the aesthetic elements: trees, flowers, preserving the forest as it always was, sunrises, fountains, birds, and ferns, to name a few. Yet the warnings, if you recall, have all been about the perils of the do-it-yourselfer, the guy who visits hardware stores. You *must* remember that bit in Appendix I about 3% outside help and 97% your own work? And all that business about sweaty work – changing of clothes three times during a workday – seems to have disappeared! The time has come to talk about the nitty-gritty! To follow in the footsteps of the worker, just as the worker followed in the footsteps of his father.

Only in this way can we, before we return to the relatively easy life style of Hyde Park, truly gage whether or not this guy is a Norwegian, assuming the Norwegians are as obsessed with home repairs and remodeling as he is. The question is what constitutes a normal human being? Is it normal to follow in the footsteps of the lessons of people like his father and Peyton Copas, and, to a lesser extent, Mr. Scott, as per Appendix D? We've seen that, career wise, another love, IBM and computers, eclipsed those educational pursuits that were followed so assiduously, which merely leads to the awarding of a degree. Most of the MSE engineering work was done in the pursuit of being with a fiancée in California. Will you be able to detect another kind of love going on in the Idlewild Tale of home repairs?

How do you measure motives? Can you rely on stated intentions as motive drivers? What kind of alternate life style was at play during those decades that began in 1973? For the psychiatrists and psychologists, these kinds of stories are case studies. Most of the practitioners of those professions – and we have an inordinate number of such as neighbors – don't get involved in *any way whatsoever* with what we will be the plain facts of the new direction we are now embarking upon. And for good reasons of their own, I am sure. So, let's take a look.

Sometime in late 1972 or early 1973 my mother, now a widow, informed us that she intended to give us Idlewild. We were in no hurry. Idlewild was rented or given free for vacations to the few employees of father's Architectural Engineering firm in Chicago, a firm that was no longer in existence. The old cast iron cooking stove that used wood for energy was still in the kitchen; the lumpy mattresses from the 1920s were still on one of the upstairs beds; the plumbing was cast iron and ancient. With the use of a crystal ball we could have seen that there were at least thirty years of projects to be worked on; many of these involved, refinishing, redecorating, repairs, and replacements.

At least the old piston water pump – which had to be torn down and worked on if one failed to remove so much as a pine needle from the priming water – was replaced by a Red Jacket Shallow Well Jet Pump. The problem was that it was in the bathroom along with the hot water heater and the very small, galvanized iron water storage tank. When you flushed the water closet, the pump came on loud. There *was* a refrigerator but it was on the front porch, a very ugly sight for what would become a much more beautiful space than we could ever imagine. In the summer of 1973 what kind of prospect was a summer home to a young wife with a three year old son and a daughter not one year old? Knowing what she did know relative to opening Idlewild and closing it, the prospect of owning a house built in 1905 was not a good one, especially when your husband had only three weeks of vacation. Peyton, the Bass Lake caretaker, had retired.

Interestingly enough, however, it was a talk with a woman we met for the first time in the summer of 1973 that crystallized our thinking. Perhaps I should say it was a catalyst to action for myself because my wife's thinking was already in good shape while mine remained amorphous.

We were visiting mother's Lake Michigan property north of Pentwater, which included Lake Michigan frontage as well as twenty acres behind it. At that time, a family, the McCall's, owned a half mile of pristine Lake Michigan frontage which contained only their own house and a guest cottage on the side. It gave you a good feeling when you estimated what the McCall's were paying in taxes! For some unknown reason, we walked down the beach to the north, looked up at their summer home and decided to pay a visit.

Mrs. McCall knew the name and showed us around; she was a gracious woman. When we came to the kitchen we were both utterly surprised! We, of course, kept that a secret. The sink in Mrs. McCall's kitchen was a match for the one at Bass Lake; the one in the Boat House that was at the far end of the Boat House, the one with the screen above it, the one which we used to clean fish using the hand pump on the right-hand side; the sink that was a relic from the 1920s and that my parents saved for their possible future summer home. It must have been put in the tunnel, covered up, or somewhere in the garage where I never explored for it. It was intended for a seter but all of father's sinks, excepting the fish-cleaning sink, were vast improvements over a 1920s sink.

The problem for the McCall's was not lack of funds – not with those taxes! If the house was accessible for grandchildren, it was also accessible for a dishwasher delivery. We made no comment. Even more amazing was the fact that Mrs. McCall told us: she had twenty-six grandchildren visit this summer. In effect, she was running a small camp for grandchildren and washing dishes by hand using an antique kitchen sink, the kind with a rubber stopper! Now, we too, knew that the Idlewild sink, stove, refrigerator, in fact the entire kitchen, was not up to what a young couple with two children needed. The tiny gas stove required outside tanks – which violated my principles. The refrigerator was on the porch, an eyesore. The cabinets were of the 1920s, the floor was wood, and the iron stove belonged in a museum, no matter how good the rolls and bread tasted.

There was a solution to these kitchen problems. Years before the need became acute, we noticed that the organization providing the solution, Style Trend Kitchens, occupied a prominent location in downtown Ludington; no less than on the corner of Ludington Avenue and James Street, a veritable landmark corner, the kind of prominence that brings to mind that old Realtor's line: location, location, location! I was particularly curious about such an enterprise having that spot. Why was that? It had to do with the prior occupant, Bach's Bakery. Bach's Bakery was a Ludington institution; my mother felt the pecan coffee cake could not be improved upon, but it was a row of Wedding cake pictures that were displayed on the wall behind the counter, that sealed the institution in my memory.

My mother-in-law often came to visit and she was attracted to the Wedding pictures; so much so that every time we visited Bach's Bakery she began a conversation with Mrs. Bach about those pictures. Comments were exchanged; it could be that she was thinking about the type of cake that might be necessary for her youngest daughter; I never knew. But all that is a digression. Early in the summer of 1973 we asked Mr. Hill, the owner of Style Trend Kitchens – he owned the factory in Muskegon that manufactured kitchen cabinets to order – to visit Idlewild. Mr. Hill pulled up in his camper a week later and explained all the points that made Style Trend Kitchens so successful. By the first week of October we had a paper plan proposal. By placing a deposit on the work I guaranteed the price even though the installation would be in the summer of 1974.

By the middle of February 1974 we received a beautiful color rendering of the entire kitchen; it was drawn in perspective so we could see exactly how things fit together. One of the key design points was to have a highlighting color; we choose red. That resulted in a beautiful red double sink; the floor tile would also be red. Our first task was installing circuit breakers and redoing the electrical service from the pole near Jerp House to Idlewild. The cast iron stove in the kitchen was picked up by volunteers from the Rose Hawley Museum in Ludington; they were ecstatic to receive such an antique; it became a highlight of the museum.

I gutted the kitchen. That effort included removing the small gas stove – and the LP gas tanks outside that serviced it – all the old cabinets, the sink, and all the cardboard that was between the studs. I did all the wiring. By reputation, we knew of Mr. Grover, a retired carpenter who lived on the opposite side of the lake. We engaged him; Mr. Grover would do the insulation, the large squares of ceiling tile, dry wall, and, most importantly, close up one window to the north, and install an Anderson window to the west directly in front of the red sink. He put in two new doors, one to the back porch and one to the L-shaped front porch.

These doors came with large sections of plain glass in them. Ultimately, I replaced all the smaller cracked panes of glass in Idlewild, and the very large plain glass piece in the door leading to the L-shaped front porch, with custom made stained glass from a stained glass craftsman who lived in Boulder, Colorado. He exhibited at the Hyde Park Art Fair and submitted designs over the winter, made all the panes, and then brought them to Hyde Park the next year. All of the windows in Idlewild were antique; you could tell by the imperfections in the glass. Five of the individual panes – there were four in each window – had a crack in the pane. This was due to all the putting up and taking down of shutters over the decades.

Rather than purchase antique glass and reglazing those windows, I decided to replace the panes with beautiful stained glass windows; the colors alone were gorgeous; the patterns were designed ahead of time and approved. When all the individual colored squares and rectangles were seen in conjunction with the numerous prisms, the windows became exquisite! The large stained glass window in the door matched the colors and designs of the five smaller windows. There are no other words to use except stunning!

Mr. Grover put up ceiling tile on the two sections of the kitchen ceiling that sloped toward each other and met in a long straight line. Finally, he leveled the floor with a new, solid under-floor. Now anyone can see that Mr. Grover did a great deal. What did that leave for me? Not knowing much about plastering, I covered the dry wall with Abitibi board, a covering that was washable. Next, I built a kitchen table from one of mother's old tables. I fashioned two leaves which would fold down if needed; they were hinged and allowed the table to expand to twice its usual size. I installed the tile floor. For the sloping, diagonal joint where the two sections of the ceiling met, I built an artificial beam and stained it brown, the same color as the third, antique door leading into the living room – which I stained. I installed an overhead, hanging lamp, as well as a hidden light over the sink. Before Mr. Grover began I did all the new electrical work.

The kitchen, then, had four doors: one to the back porch (new), one to the living room (overhauled and stained by yours truly), one to the front porch (new), and the fourth to the bathroom (also overhauled by yours truly.) With the window over the sink, the light was glorious from all points of the compass; we could see outside in any direction; through the kitchen sink window we could see the Arbor Vitae trees just beyond the window and a Hummingbird feeder on a small white oak tree about two feet from the window. Toward the north we could see the forest and Mr. Conrad's wildflower garden; through the living room window, we could see through the house and beyond, this was because the living room door to the front porch when left open added a depth of view that ran to the lake. In this sense the view through the house and beyond reminded the viewer of those Dutch paintings of the interior of a home, a device called *doorkijkje*. Through the new door to the L-shaped front porch, we could see the entire front porch and, beyond, the view to the lake. When that door with its large stained glass window was closed the light came through the gorgeous, exquisite, and stunning glass window with its colors of blue, plum, dark red, and purple, punctuated by prisms, all in a geometric design. Through the open bathroom door and the smaller bathroom window, we saw the forest to the south.

The kitchen was not at the center of the house, as some say the kitchen is with a Frank Lloyd Wright house; instead, we had a superior kitchen and it set the tone for everything that came after; rather, it set a standard; it was like a building foundation upon which the rest would follow. The refrigerator on the porch was removed and that corner was transformed through an antique, marble-topped, carved table; over the marble-topped table – an antique from Idlewild – we put a yellow glass, wooden cabinet – Mr. Conrad's cabinet from his dark room in an out-building known as the Woodhouse.

Style Trend very tastefully supplied integrated wooden cabinets to surround the refrigerator, the dishwasher and the electric stove. The electric stove was set at an angle in one corner of the kitchen; the other corner had a cabinet with a lazy-Susan with two circular shelves. This is why Mr. Hill named his firm *Style* Trend. Over the stove was a vent fan flanked by lights.

The refrigerator, dishwasher, and stove all had elements that matched the surface treatment of the cabinets. The cabinets were plentiful and luxurious. Every cabinet was designed to fit precisely into the kitchen; measurements were taken after the dry wall was installed, and all the cabinets were custom made in the Style Trend factory in Muskegon. By placing a deposit on the work in 1973, I saved $1,000 of price increases that went into effect in 1974.

The countertop material was a special material that Mr. Hill used for all of his kitchens; it took but a brief period of usage to pronounce it superior to anything else. I distinctly remember staining and finishing the inside wood of the Anderson window over the kitchen sink; why was that? It was during the time of Nixon's impeachment – Watergate! – and I was listening to Gerald Ford speak of what was to come. I was impressed with Gerald Ford but we now owned a new kitchen that was functional and matched our new Condominium in Chicago and, from the 17th floor of Cornell Village, gave us a splendid view of the lakefront. In both homes it was the sunrise that we saw when we woke up; in Chicago we saw that vast expanse of sky, clouds, and the effects of the sun from on high. In Michigan we saw the sunrise through the foliage as it rose above the forest across Bass Lake; it was impossible to draw comparisons, both led to spectacular displays of light. We knew that we did the right thing; we would not have to wash and dry dishes in the type of sink we used to clean pan fish, the one down in the Boathouse.

But, as with any element of change, there were extra steps that came with that change, some short-term, and some long-term. In the long-term group there were now special procedures for winterizing the dishwasher; the first year I was unaware of a bend in the copper line that supplied the dishwasher; like all good freezing winters, the cold air froze the copper line and I had to repair that and revise my closing procedures to include blowing the line out. This was a matter of breaking the connection below the dishwasher and blowing it out with my breath. A new, flexible connection, facilitated this blowing out – all it took was help from the friendly people at Briggs Hardware in Ludington who found the necessary fitting to solve the issue that made it work with fewer parts.

For the kitchen floor I went to Sears in Chicago and purchased beautiful red tile with a pattern and put it down with ease. Now the floor pattern kept the red motif color of the kitchen alive. After many years of usage – it was often polished with acrylic floor polish – the floor was professionally replaced with an exquisite high quality, red-pattern flooring, put down in two, large pieces with a joint where they touched each other; this piece and another, of a different color, which was put below the front porch dining table, are both fantastic improvements; I use a new additive to my wash water which is designed to enhance the surface.

The kitchen needed an oil painting! I went to the Pentwater Art Fair and purchased a small oil painting which was hung on the Abitibi board opposite the new Anderson window. In the picture, two small children are standing in sand dunes flying a kite but there are patches of trees and also large patches of snow for it is winter. There is a problem relative to scale that perplexes the viewer but the larger problem is one of context for there is a white house and behind it a red barn. The scene is viewed from above. How could a farm exist in such desolate hills? No other sign of civilization is in sight and despite the scale problems of the picture, the colors are well chosen and blend with the kitchen browns; the items are painted with skill, such as the various groups of forest, the house, and the barn. The viewer instantly feels for the two small children who must, even in the winter, resort to a summer activity in such a desolate area, and with such cold around them. They must create their own activities; they must develop self-sufficiency.

We couldn't imagine that visitors to Idlewild would see the two children in the kitchen oil painting as our own, or even more unbelievable, as the parents of our children at an early age! The oil painting made the viewer respect self-sufficiency; there were no objects in the painting that indicated any neighbors; the scene could be the wilderness area north of Ludington, a Federal Dunes area. Nonetheless, we did become more and more self-sufficient as we moved beyond the kitchen. As more rooms in Idlewild were completely remodeled, we stripped the furniture of Mrs. Conrad's ubiquitous gray paint and, once again, exposed the grain of the natural wood. Using kits I constructed Shaker chairs during the winter and the pendulum moved closer and closer to complete self-sufficiency – just like the pendulum in the Shaker Clock, also made from a kit, now installed on the front porch.

It went without saying that I would do all of the painting, plumbing, well drilling, and electrical work. We never employed a house cleaner to come in and vacuum or wash the windows, rake the leaves, or sweep the roofs. As the years progressed, the extensive remodeling that began with the kitchen, extended to the conversion of Mrs. Conrad's garage to a guest cottage, the remodeling of the Idlewild bathroom, and the complete consolidation of the entire fresh water system using PVC pipe – reducing the source of underground water to a single well – and a single, large hot water tank situated in the Woodhouse. There were, of course, many other projects like installing the Vermont Country Stove, re-installing the original Franklin wood burning stove on the front porch, putting a parquet floor and fireplace in the guest cottage – as well as a bathroom – and remodeling the front porch, the library, and the bedrooms.

What began as a split with Mr. Grover, the carpenter, doing the difficult carpentry work, became a permanent method of doing business. Some of the items for outside effort were easy to identify; these included stained glass windows, curtains for the Guest House – from Marshall Fields' – upholstering, replacement of all the drop-down front porch drapes, overhaul of the two front porch gliders which included sand-blasting and all new couch pads and pillows. The drop-down front porch drapes were torn and could barely keep out the rain when rolled down. By bringing them to a canvas shop for work over the winter months, we avoided having no rain protection in the summer.

There were many individual items that needed attention as well. I completely refinished a *wooden hammock*! Yes, that's right, an antique that not a soul ever imagined existed; it used wire rope as well. Mrs. Conrad's cloth curtains were converted to make small tablecloths, a Pentwater shop made bathroom cabinets, a Chicago firm made the base for the bathroom shower, four Tiffany style lamp shades were installed, and three back-lit pieces of glass – one of which was after Tiffany, the other two after Frank Lloyd Wright – were installed in the upstairs bedroom.

These kinds of things went on over the course of many years; the effects of yearly remodeling is not unusual. The do-it-yourself attitude was present as emergencies presented themselves; since we began with the kitchen, let's talk about kitchen emergencies. When the dishwasher was installed it was very easy to make the decision that the old drain that took away what plumbers call 'white water' should be used. This amounted to an open piece of six inch diameter drain pipe below the house. The water from the kitchen sink was directed to this pipe. By listening, we could hear water gurgling into this piece of what looked like an ordinary section of tile pipe in a vertical position that protruded six inches above the ground. Where that drain went to and how it got to that destination was a complete mystery.

I did have a memory from childhood of Peyton Copas digging between the two, small white oak trees which were now, more or less, outside the new Anderson window over the red sink. Those two white oak trees, however small, possessed hooks for that wooden hammock. The area between the trees held an additional attraction; it was filled with Blue Stemmed Goldenrod, a plant that, once identified, quickly became one of my favorites; the upshot of those wildflowers between the oaks was that it is the last place where I would want to dig! Why is that? I tried to answer why in my poem of the same name.

Blue-Stemmed Goldenrod

I watched your branches green all summer long
Like drooping willow weeds around the tree.
And then your gold exploded. I was wrong,
For you became the fairest thing to see.

So delicate each lazy arch became,
Eclipsing purple asters all their show.

I felt a magic spring had come again
To reign supreme in grace before the snow.

For nowhere could a color match your splay
Arrayed against the lichen blue of bark
And all was drab against your bold bouquet,
As though your death would leave the landscape stark.

October never knew a better sight,
Nor left us richer dream for winter night.

Thus it came to pass that when the first kitchen emergency happened, the area below the hammock was not dug into. The emergency consisted of water coming out of the six inch diameter open pipe drain when the dishwasher was running – simple enough – or I should say, 'hope springs eternal!' Even without twenty-six grandchildren an inoperative dishwasher needs immediate attention. Like Peyton, one of my role models, I picked up a shovel from the Woodhouse – an outbuilding about the size of a large garage where Mr. Conrad put a workbench, stored everything and put a darkroom in one corner for developing his pictures of nature – and began to dig. I discovered old, glazed drain pipes running deep down in the sand along the side of the house, i.e., between the Idlewild and the White Oak tree with the hummingbird feeder. I wasn't in the mood for any more sweaty digging and broke into the top of one of the drain pipe sections; immediately the rinse water began filling the ditch!

After this initial incident, there was no way of knowing that the entire length of the drain pipe was filled with grease; it looked like one of those pictures on the front of a bottle of chemical drain cleaner where the entire pipe is clogged. The ditch filled with dishwasher waste was a clue that a complete drain pipe replacement was in order as well as a great deal of digging below the hammock area to confirm that, yes, that is where a concrete, underground white waste water drain collection box receives rinse water from both the kitchen and bathroom, not receiving any waste from the water closet.

On the second dig, the Blue Stemmed Goldenrod plants were carefully dug up and placed on a piece of canvas; in fact all of the pieces of sod below the hammock area were treated the same way. Years later when I completely remodeled the bathroom, I would spend as many hours digging to discover the part of the white water drainage system running from the bathroom and replace that portion of the white water drainage system as well. Taking a cue from the pictures on the front of bottles of chemical drain cleaner, I began to use drain cleaner so as to avoid a third dig. My hunch was that drain cleaner was never introduced since time immemorial even though Peyton Copas could have done the work had he been asked to.

In response to the initial incident – the overflow from the dishwasher – I rammed out the pipe as it sloped upward, put a tight patch over the glazed pipe (the breaking of which might well be a sin to anyone knowledgeable, and I would be the first to agree.) and filled in the ditch with sand topped with sod. Alas, the ramming out was not the solution! I had to go at the sloping pipe a second time. For the second time around, I again dug down to the concrete catch basin or box. The catch basin was pumped out by an outside fellow who does that kind of work. Once the top of the catch basin was off I could run new PVC pipe to replace everything. I also ran PVC pipe up toward the bathroom in anticipation of a future remodeling of the bathroom and a complete replacement of all cast iron plumbing throughout Idlewild.

By the time that the bathroom remodeling was underway, Mrs. Conrad's garage was completely converted to a Guest House for my mother-in-law. In addition to its own fireplace, curtains from Marshall Fields', five Anderson windows, and a complete bathroom, the Guest House was given its own hot water tank, and shallow well pump – with a separate well-point driven by yours truly, and a platform bed that blended with the parquet floor. When the Idlewild main house bathroom was remodeled, the Idlewild pump, hot water tank, and cold water storage tank in the Idlewild bathroom were eliminated; the Guest House pump in the back of the Guest House now serviced both buildings; a new hot water tank, enlarged in capacity, was put in the Woodhouse, and all the plumbing, above ground and below, was converted to PVC.

We have not mentioned the presence of the underground septic tank that received waste from two water closets, one in the Guest Cottage, the other in Idlewild. I became intimately familiar with the septic tank for the water closets when I installed PVC drain pipe from the back of the Guest Cottage, under the full length of the cottage, and then proceeding further to an opening I made in the side of the septic tank; I made certain that the PCV pipe was sloped correctly along its entire length. The septic tank was further back in the forest about seventy-five feet from Idlewild. Its presence was apparent because there is a ram-out Y-pipe that allows a person equipped with a long coil of sewer-ramming wire-rope to clear the pipe. The Y-pipe surfaced where we parked. As I soon discovered, I would revisit the septic tank every seventeen years to install a new drain field. Suffice it to say, for now, that in the event of any problems along that seventy-five foot septic tank pipe, I performed the effort to diagnose and correct the problem with several sewer-ramming wire ropes; I never heard of a Roto-Rooter service until many years later.

But kitchen problems are not limited to water that won't drain from a dishwasher, heavens no! There's another source of water that can cause problems. Can you guess where that water comes from? That's right, from the sky, it's called rain water. Very early, in the beginning of the Idlewild Saga, we engaged a well-known, professional roofer from Pentwater to replace the entire 'lower roof' of Idlewild. This included the kitchen, bathroom, the huge L-shaped front porch, the library, and the downstairs bedroom. At that early date the old roof was removed and plywood was put down to reinforce the boards of the roof. Imagine my surprise when, after fewer than twenty-five years, I saw some tiny stain spots in Mr. Grover's kitchen ceiling. At the time, the roof covering for the kitchen and bathroom were rolled roofing; the professional roofer claimed that the roof was too flat for shingles.

I resolved to re-roof the kitchen roof myself! This would be my first venture into roofing; it sounds like I am going into the roofing business. You can imagine trying to live near a person, like myself, who professes a reverence for fern gardens and for every bracken fern that grew on the property. This kind of fetish, even for the natural, wild, bracken ferns, is noticeable; what you see is that when a bracken fern is bent, small sticks are used to prop up the bent bracken fern – the fern is tied up to the stick – and, in other situations, sticks are used as markers to direct traffic around bracken ferns that grow near the house. Bracken ferns grow naturally throughout the Idlewild property; they also resist transplanting hence they need extra care, especially when merely bent; transplanted Cinnamon and Ostrich ferns – which are easy to transplant – end up around fountains and in fern gardens. By doing my own roofing I would keep all the nails from falling on the ground and thereby prevent the damage of any green thing whatsoever. This reverence for things green can alienate individuals who see it as a form of mental disorder.

What insight! I mean by that the decision to reroof the kitchen. Within minutes I was at a lumber yard on a late Sunday afternoon telling the salesperson that if he could teach me in fifteen minutes how to roof an area of such and such a size, I would buy all the materials. He told me and I decided to do the bathroom which was also roofed with rolled roofing rather than singles. As I removed the old, rolled roofing above the kitchen, I was upset to find that the professional roofer, the one with a reputation, did not protect the wooden roof below the rolled roofing! His crew, no doubt, ran out of the under-shingle rolls of tar paper. What a discovery, exactly what I needed to cause me to spend two years reroofing the Guest Cottage. The story about not having enough slope for shingles wasn't a good tale, either.

So much for professionals. I purchased the new, rubber, ice and water shield rolls that once laid, are as waterproof as the shingles that you nail above that foundational layer. If you are putting on a new roof and it looks like rain the next day, all you need to do is get down that base layer of ice and water shield and you are home free! Yes, it costs a lot more than the old tar paper but when you do it yourself, it's worth it. So I ended up spending several days in the hot sun removing old roofing, hauling material to the dump in the car, one load at a time, and then putting down two beautiful sections of shingle roof that dovetailed beautifully with the old roofing, especially the diagonal joint which was directly above the wooden beam I constructed when the kitchen was remodeled. Another skill was added to my skill list, my dossier which was never used to land a job; not a leaf of any fern was touched let alone the stem of a Blue Stemmed Goldenrod. Like the oil based, white, semi-gloss paint that I was required to use on all the structures – Idlewild, the Guest Cottage, the Woodhouse, and the Children's playhouse, I was proud of the effort. Siding was, of course, verboten.

Other consequences of this do-it-yourself syndrome soon became apparent. Often, the best outside workers are not optional. Situations arise where you must work fast and not wait for people who charge more than Peyton, destroy plants, interrupt entire days, and force you to contend with their schedules rather than your own. Privacy is an important part of having a home and pick-up trucks are just as ugly as LP gas tanks, also very noisy; they fill up the driveway, tear up the brown leaf roadway, and have a habit of destroying green plants coming and going. Sometime the outside worker feels that playing his favorite AM radio station while on the job is necessary for his sanity. With two high quality FM radio stations available at Bass Lake all summer long – Interlochen National Music Camp, and Blue Lake Music Camp – playing Classical music most of the day, listening to AM radio is not a treat.

What can be more important than learning new skills, taking pride in your own work, and obtaining a sense of accomplishment as an amateur. Instead of buying a table for the kitchen and front porch, it was infinitely more satisfying to refashion and remodel two older tables, one from my parent's stock of tables, and the other from Idlewild. These came from a time before my own birth; they improved upon the tables that I started with; they would have made Mrs. Conrad proud. The kitchen table was custom designed to fit the kitchen, painted a red color, and given two hinged wings with a simple system of support for those wings.

The front porch table, an Idlewild original, was completely refinished. Mrs. Conrad's table was in need of an overhaul throughout, including all of the table-top wooden inserts and, for example, the pegs that kept the inserts aligned. It was my mother-in-law who suggested professional help after she enjoyed the refinishing. Christiane's mother commented that the ends were truncated, i.e., flat. She suggested I find a carpenter with an extensive wood working shop and have the carpenter fashion oak, curved end pieces. This involved using a router that matched the outer edges of the rest of the table, as well as pegging and gluing to strengthen these pieces that looked like a semi-circle of wood, one side of which was straight. Of course, there was the praise from my mother in preserving the past in creative ways and the pure joy of sweaty labor, the same joy that I discerned in Peyton as a child. Then there is the reinforcement of months and years of daily workouts and stretching that keeps one's muscles in tone; it is the knowledge that that kind of effort pays off when you can climb a ladder multiple times with heavy roofing and not need a week of recuperation.

Others would mention the cost. For a little over $5,000 we had a new kitchen! It was a kitchen I could identify with because I was engaged with so much of the effort. It was a kitchen I could maintain because I was both general contractor and worker. It was a kitchen that gave satisfaction every time I cooked and baked and I did a lot of that as the years passed. The red color motif blended in well with the sour cherry lattice pies I baked. When we entertained and made Blueberry pancakes for our guests, part of the satisfaction was working in this particular kitchen, because of its associations. I could look at the oil painting and feel that the two youngsters were children, not my wife and I flying a kite in pure innocence. This was because we conquered the problems and moved on to enjoy the efforts and we did this by sticking to principles relative to aesthetics and ecology. I experienced growth as a person. Perhaps I came to understand Mrs. McCall and what it was that she derived from having so many visitors.

But what can be the downside of this work ethic? Have you ever faced a tight situation where time was of the essence? Have you ever experienced problems with the work you did on your own? These are very important questions. At a later point we will examine out-and-out failures; for now, we'll stick with answering the questions. Suffice it to say at the outset, there is no denying that this drive to fix things takes over. This is especially true when it takes time to locate a repair person. During the summer season those kinds of people can be in demand and the motivated do-it-yourselfer acts, or so he is led to believe, quicker. So let's begin with what could, arguably, be called a tight situation.

After many years of flawless operation a small leak developed in the Sta-Rite shallow well pump which, by the time the leak developed, was in operation for decades. At the time the leak was observed, the Sta-Rite was the only pump supplying fresh water; the entire fresh water system was replaced with a single pump, the Sta-Rite, in back of the Guest Cottage, and all the pipe was now PCV. Anything wrong with a Sta-Rite pump was important because father mentioned that Sta-Rite was an outstanding brand. Father could have done architectural work for Sta-Rite, he could have used them in other locations, or he could have owned Sta-Rite stock; the important thing was that for decades, father was absolutely correct. Then one year, I observed a tiny leak at a point where the shaft of the pump enters the pump. My mental apparatus immediately was alerted: it said to me that I can't let even a small leak affect my opinion of a Sta-Rite pump.

This mental event occurred at the end of the season and before Idlewild was closed I called Kim at Tanner and Stark in Hart, Michigan. Kim, the resident guru, and, by now, a trusted helper, quickly pointed out that it needed a new pump seal and that I should order a kit from a supply outfit in Walkerville. I ordered the kit and received it before the end of the season. Not wanting to work on the only pump with closing such a short time away, I decided to overhaul the pump when I turned on the water the following spring. For some reason I remember being alone that spring when the overhaul was to be accomplished. Of course, I never overhauled a shallow well pump with a kit. The idea that if I did not complete the effort in a certain amount of time I would be quite thirsty was constantly in my mind. What I didn't know was that the pump would have to be removed from its pedestal and that a lot of unexpected steps were necessary, all of which required tools in hand or alternative improvisations.

Not only would there be no water to drink but I would be unable to take a shower, no matter how 'sweaty' the work was and, even worse, I might have to wait upon a professional to finish the work and get the water flowing. Originally, I knew that there was some kind of seal and that I saw water slowly dripping from that seal; the external symptom was not serious – it could easily have waited another year. The first clue that there was more involved occured when I looked over the pieces in the kit. The seal was the tip of the iceberg; the impeller and many other parts came with the kit! It was then I knew that I had a major overhaul to perform. There were many aspects to the struggle: getting at the pump, making it accessible to work on, working on bolts that were never, ever loosened, hoping I could reseal the pump, and if I had the tools. As the hours went by I looked at my watch constantly but with each new problem came a tiny bit of forward progress and, before I was too thirsty, I felt I was finished. I threw the electrical bayonet switch into the upward position after priming the pump and, like any good Sta-Rite, it came on and I soon had cold, fresh, Lake Michigan water filtered through a half mile of sand to drink. So much for a tight situation!

The next repair was with the lower element in the oven. Again, it was a matter of not having an oven for even a short period of time or, alternatively, having to have it serviced and then waiting for a part. Of course, it doesn't do much good to send in a warranty for a piece of equipment in Idlewild. Using an oven for, at most, three months per year, it takes four years before it has a year's worth of usage. After twenty years, what does a warranty do? You get the point. Once again, the drive to fix things took over; I called the 1-800 numbers in the booklet that came with the oven; I called an outfit in Ludington that, of all things, kept a small warehouse of old oven elements and was a great help on the phone; kind of a one-man inventory place.

The part was a used part but what difference did that make? When an element is red hot, a baker doesn't have to worry about the presence of a germ. In any event, I thought I had the tiger by the tail, installed the used part – it had a used part price as well – and turned the oven on. After two days of perplexing effort, the stove came on for a minute or two and then the circuit breaker would break and the entire stove was unusable. This failure, coming as it did at a time when I was in the euphoria of success, merely kept me on the job. I began making telephone calls for a second time; people can be extremely helpful when a *tough* challenge confronts their intellect. I discussed all of the symptoms, the wiring diagrams, the past history, and so forth. Helpers at the other end of the telephone analyzed the evidence and pinpointed loose connections made at the factory. The cause fit the diagnosis but no one could answer why the stove worked for twenty-eight years.

After long hours of conversations where the evidence was sifted and sifted, something that the man who sold me the used element said in our conversation, triggered my going upstairs to the circuit-breaker box, where I looked at the connection to the circuit-breaker for the stove, a connection that I made twenty-eight years ago. In those connections, once you place the wire below a set-screw you merely tighten the screw. I immediately called back the man who was so helpful. "You'll never guess what it was. At the breaker I had not tightened the connection tight enough. As soon as I twisted the set-screw a bit more, I knew I had it. Thank you so much!" Here was a situation that waited twenty-eight years to show up; it was like the build-up in the underground drainage pipe, only this time there was no one to blame but myself.

After the pump seal and the oven element at Idlewild I gained strength for more complicated problems in Chicago and repaired the sparker on one of the gas stove burners, and the heating coil in the clothes dryer in the basement. Then the Chicago stove needed a new burner part installed for the broiler, and the dishwasher a new rubber hose for the upper shelf, the hose that supplies the water for the propeller that revolves and throws the water everywhere inside. I concluded that Idlewild has effects that go beyond poetry. Only after it took me two years to replace the shingle roof on the Guest Cottage, did I finally relent to have outside help do the roofing elsewhere. There were three layers of shingles and rolled roofing to remove from the Guest Cottage before I could lay down the ice and water shield, the under-the-shingle rolled rubber protection, and then, finally, the shingles. I did half of the Guest Cottage roof one year and finished the other half the next year.

But the Idlewild ethic can also make a person cynical. To illustrate this I will copy into Appendix N a letter written to good friends, the couple that lived next to us in The Gaylord Building, Married Student Housing, during our two years in residence. They spent many days with us in Michigan and now live outside Philadelphia. The letter speaks of the term "Canuck" a six to seven gallon water closet purchased in Canada. Reading a philosophical work can cause one to reflect on life in Michigan and the next thing you know I am taking the evils of Bass Lake out on those who have no sympathies with my way of life. Woe is me! The other side of that coin of woe is the now common diagnosis of the disorder that I observed so many years ago in the Appendix N letter; it's called *Nature Deficit Disorder.*

Groups

It is time, once again, to return to Chicago from Idlewild. How does a person make such a return? Is it just a matter of closing Idlewild, packing up the car, and driving two-hundred and twenty miles to Hyde Park? Or is there something that can't even be entirely left? If that is true then it explains why poetry can be written from afar, why removal to a new location causes a period of reflection on the old. Or is there a sense of completion, bordering on finality, that occurs? A small voice from within that says it is time to move on, circumstances demand it, next year is another year, for now, new demands are awaiting in Chicago.

We tell ourselves that, "there is a part of me that says 'I can never live all year long in Michigan.' It would be frighteningly lonely: no opera, no theater, no chamber music, no restaurants, no University of Chicago, no Play Reading dinners, no auditing of classes, no Chicago Symphony, no Art Institute, no three-block bicycle rides to the place of a work-out at a gym, to audit a class, and to buy groceries without a nine mile drive. A familiar thing like Home Delivery of the New York Times can become a blessing way out of proportion to what it actually is when one needs to purchase the paper every day, and yet!"

There is, then, another life after Idlewild, a life of friends, a life of the mind with a different focus than home repairs, filling the five hummingbird feeders, four fountains, LP gas tanks, and constantly looking at that list of things to do written the prior year, a list of chores that there was not enough hours in the day to accomplish that year. How does one feel so confident about the next year possessing enough time? Just adjacent to that list entitled "Next Year" is a multi-page list of "The Current Year." It, too, will be added to the growing pile of yearly efforts. You look at the list for the current year and exclaim, "Ah, yes, I remember now how it started: that new, brass drain petcock for the pump – imagine, only $8.00 for a brass fitting like that – and that rotting piece of wood that needed instant repair – no problem using those left-over cedar boards from the new back fence at 5508 Kenwood, and yes, the Pileated Woodpecker bird house – I finally got to it!

There it is, way up in that huge oak, professionally installed by Kevin, the closest person to Peyton Copas. It was one of his twin daughters that asked when I would build it and not just express the idea as an intention to her father, an intention that she overheard. How could I let a nine-year old down? Kevin, who served in the one-hundred and first Airborne Division rappels up and down tree trunks like a tree frog; only Kevin could use pulleys to get the heavy Pileated Woodpecker house up that high. Now there is a tiny population of individuals who will look up there, beginning next March, to see if the mother and father birds have removed the wood chips through the four inch diameter entrance hole. If they have I can claim a success; if not, a failure.

Failures are a part of Idlewild living when it comes to birds, or even bats. There have been much larger failures in that category. But whoa, you say, slow down, you said we were going back to Hyde Park. That's right but we've switched to *groups*, and like everything else, birds live in groups; they call them colonies or flocks. How so? You must recall those crows we talked about earlier, the crows which, together, seem to emulate the residents of Bass Lake? You do? OK, well there are other groups that people cultivate. What are they? Bats and Purple Martins. You want to know how a person could fail with those groups? All right, we interrupt this portion of our program, our return to Hyde Park, to look at Bass Lake failures; after that, I promise you we will get back to Chicago.

Let me warn you though, we will preface the bat and purple martin failures with some other types that will involve that old friend, the Grumman canoe from Owasippie! Well, not precisely; the Grumman canoe participated in the failure, it was involved as an adjunct object to a fishing failure, and an inadvertent one at that. Then there was a bird feeder failure. After we look at those two we'll be able to talk about Bats and Purple Martins, but even before that, we'll give a brief look at a potential failure that occurred after the bathroom remodeling project. Here it is:

. . . The final problem came with the installation of the custom-made cabinet adjacent to the shower. I contracted this out and a beautiful cabinet was built that included room for the small electric heater in the baseboard – nice when you stepped out of the shower or, if it was cold outside – and two back-lit pieces of stained glass from the Metropolitan Museum of Art Gift Catalogue that were placed in the top doors of what was now a linen closet; they were copies of Tiffany windows.. The cabinet's top was slanted to follow the roof line of the bathroom and the entire space itself, was not square, so the carpenter/cabinet maker took lots of measurements. The shower tile was done by another professional and it, too, was not square but that was not a problem; he just spent more time cutting and fitting the tile.

But back to the cabinet. What the gentleman did not count on was that when built as a single piece, there was no way to jockey the entire cabinet into place without cutting up other parts of the bathroom that were already finished! He worked at this for quite a long time and then gave up, leaving me a note that he could not install the cabinet but that if I could, I could have the cabinet at cost which was quite a bargain as even the inside was lined with beautiful wood. Here was a case where I used an outside person with a complete woodworking shop but was left to finish the job myself. The answer was to cut the cabinet in half, horizontally, thereby separating the top linen cabinet with the stained glass windows, and the bottom section, which was for storage and had no stained glass. This left a small opening the size of a saw blade which was easily filled with putty and blended to the outside finish, not to mention the fact that the top two cabinet doors covered the putty work as well.

Failures

In thinking about the installation of the bathroom cabinet, the gentleman I contracted for the work made a mistake, a blunder. If the cabinet was scrapped the mistake would become a failure, i.e., a situation where some effort must be totally abandoned. In effect, my own intervention prevented a mistake from becoming a failure. Now we will turn our attention to look at my own efforts across various projects that are not merely mistakes but bona fide failures; cases where the desired result is not obtained. I should point out that in the contracting of projects out to experienced woodworkers, mistakes are rare. Mr. Grover's work always led to success in the case of the Kitchen and the Guest Cottage. Another woodworker from Ludington was contracted to copy, in walnut, curved trim pieces for large and small antique marble commodes as well as some non-curved pieces. These pieces were missing during Mrs. Conrad's time. This work was done with total success and allowed us to carry on a very decent restoration. This same gentlemen, using a router, added curved oak pieces to the two ends of the oak dining table on the L-shaped screened-in porch and the results were spectacular. Again, it appeared that these were broken off long ago and only through the suggestion of my mother-in-law was the need noticed.

There are also situations which I shall call "intermittent failures" or failures that, because of strong reasons, we are willing to live with and that merely cause extra labor on into the future. One of these, like the cicadas, occurs every seventeen years and another more frequently. For every failure there are hundreds of successes and, of course, there are major failures and minor failures. No matter what type or what frequency however, failures at Idlewild seem to carry a greater degree of poignancy and ridiculousness. This is due, on the one hand to the effort expended, the expectations one has relative to that effort, and the emotional attachment associated with it by virtue of the personal involvement in the work, and on the other hand by the fact that many of these situations involve man against nature.

Around 1859, nine years after she started writing poetry, Emily Dickenson wrote:

> Success is counted sweetest
> By those who ne'er succeed.
> To comprehend a nectar
> Requires sorest need.

Many of Ms. Dickinson's poems return to this topic. In my own case, Idlewild failures have not prompted such introspection. Perhaps, Ms. Dickenson could not laugh at herself; often that is all that remains to do after a failure. We begin with two of the minor ones, one early and the other late.

It was an absolutely dark night with total cloud cover. Even the lights on the houses across the lake were not bright. It must have been quite late for not even the hint of the sunset remained. The children were asleep and earlier I attached an additional hook to a fishing line, put two large worms on the hooks, and then cast the line out as far as I could. The drop-off, that point where the lake gets much deeper, was ten feet beyond the end of the pier and, as the cast was made in the dark, I was uncertain just how far it went. The purpose of the cast was to hook two bullheads for subsequent skinning and eating.

Bass Lake bullheads are delicious and taste like chicken. Mother would bread them and fry them with the pan fish when we pulled them up, often caught because we let the fishing line get too close to the bottom. Skinning was an art form. My son, a youngster at this time, would, much later, become an avid bullhead fisherman, staying up late and even riding a bike down to where the Bass Lake channel crossed under the lake road, i.e., right at the bridge, where he encountered raccoons who wanted to be represented in the action. In any event, this dark night was well before that time.

I cast from the end of the old pier, the pier that was eventually replaced and supplied the wood to make the children's play house. It rained a good deal during the prior week and the Grumman canoe was still about half full of water as no one turned it over after the rain. The canoe was in the weeds at the shore. I stayed up beyond the time I made the cast; under normal circumstances I would be in bed but I decided to take a flashlight and see what the bullhead line was doing. I walked down the road in front of Idlewild passing the seventeen foot long Hemlock branch on my right, and kept going to the end of the pier, lifted up the rod and felt a tug which would indicate that there were already bullhead(s) on the line.

Maybe I should try to get them off the line? This usually requires a pliers to get the hook out and is not an easy thing to do with a flashlight. I could put them in the canoe and, in the absence of a raccoon coming down for a drink – and a meal – the children could see them swimming around in the rainwater in the morning. If I caught two more there would be four to watch and enough for a meal if they were large.

We are talking about little effort here, except the additional resolve of staying up late; the tug on the line heightened my expectations. All these considerations happened in a flash and I instinctively began pulling in the line. The difference between what I felt and the effects of pulling in a bullhead line during previous evenings soon became obvious: something much larger than a bullhead was on one of the hooks! In fact, it must be a monster because the progress of pulling the line was quite slow yet nowhere near what one would expect if the line held a pike or a bass. Tucking the flashlight under my right armpit, I was able to continue the effort and now and then focus the beam out in the water where it was only two feet deep. I quickly saw the head of a very large fish; it was a huge carp!

Prior experiences with a huge school of carp came to mind. I always wanted to get my hands on a large carp. In early spring when they spawn, huge quantities come into the shallow water and make enormous froth as they frantically go around in circles with their upper fins thrashing the lake. I recalled the time that I quickly grabbed the ice fishing spear and a paddle and paddled the Grumman canoe to the middle of the white water; my thoughts at the time were that since there were so many, all that was required was merely plunging the spear down, it was impossible not to make contact. The effort was a complete failure as I jabbed at the moving bodies. The carp never seemed to stay in one place long enough or, alternatively, their scales merely deflected the spear. No one was watching the absurdity of this failure as I was surrounded by hundreds of carp that were making the water boil with fins and small waves; I never speared a carp.

I knew that Bortell's would smoke a carp for me if I could ever get one; at this time, out on the end of the pier, I didn't have that in mind. What I thought was that, one, I have a carp on the end of a bullhead line, two, if I could get the carp out of the water and into the canoe, I would, three, have a huge fish for the children to examine in the rainwater when they woke up in the morning. I didn't worry about a raccoon; implicitly, I felt that any cat-and-mouse activities between a carp and a raccoon in a rain-filled canoe, would favor the carp, after all, I failed with an ice fishing spear!

The problem was obvious but there were complications in the execution of any plan. First, the carp was on the hook at the far end of the line; the other hook was barren. This meant that as the line was pulled in it was necessary to keep track of that bare hook or get hooked myself. These efforts needed to be performed with a flashlight under my right armpit. I reasoned that if I could get the carp in close to the end of the pier without being hooked myself, once in that location, the next step was to get the carp on the left side of the pier, the side where the canoe was. Then, with the carp on the left-hand side, I would pull it toward the shoreline as far as I could; by that time the carp would be in very shallow water about eight inches deep.

I secured the fish line and ran to the Boathouse to retrieve a large plastic fishnet on an aluminum frame. This was a cheap net that we rarely used simply because pan fish don't require a net; in that sense, it was like the ice fishing spear that was used only once when we came up to Jerp House in the winter and used that ugly, aluminum-clad ice hut out on the lake. If I could get the carp into the net then I could lift the net, walk backwards on the pier – with the flashlight still under my right arm – raise the net with the carp high enough to get the net over the gunwale of the canoe and dump the carp into the rainwater. That was the plan. I maneuvered the fish to the left side of the pier and a bit towards the shoreline where the water was a not as deep. I cautiously lowered the net making mental note of where the extra hook was. I moved the net forward so that the huge nose of the carp was now in the bottom of the net, right up to the netting; so far, so good.

The tail of the carp extended beyond the rim of the fishnet! That made no difference, it was a big carp and eighty percent of the carp was in the net, eighty percent by weight, that is. The next step was to use the handle of the fishnet to leverage the lifting of the carp out of the net so I could start walking backwards. Accordingly, I lifted the handle and began leveraging the net upward. The handle began to bend like a bow! How strong was the net, anyway? There was no going back. I continued leveraging the carp up and out of the water and the handle kept bending. I was getting good at focusing the flashlight, and the fish line and rod seemed out of the way. A ray of hope crossed my mind. All of a sudden there was an enormous burst of energy – on the part of the carp!

By this time the handle and the rim of the fishnet were at ninety degrees to each other. I feared that the carp would get out of the net but the way I imagined its exit was not the way he choose to leave. The burst of energy was towards the shoreline! The carp put a huge hole in the *bottom* of the net; the force of that effort tore the hook from the carp's mouth and propelled the fish through the net as though it was made of lace, and I was left with a huge, bent fishnet with a large hole in the bottom. I went to bed without resetting the line.

Enough, now, about creatures under the sea, although later, we will return to another encounter in broad daylight. For now we will return to creatures of the air, more particularly, birds and bats. We begin with a minor failure before we segue to two major failures. The minor failure centered around the idea of hanging up a thistle feeder from a very large oak tree near the house, and in such a position that we could watch the goldfinches while at the dining table on the porch. Feeders at that location were used all summer long and they were continuously fascinating, only seven feet away from the porch table where we ate.

The idea for the minor failure germinated in Chicago as I spied a very beautiful, hand-blown, glass feeder from an Eastern European country. It was a thing of beauty that spoke to me from the pages of a mail order catalogue. When the thistle seed was partly, or even completely, eaten, the entire glass feeder would light up because the sunlight would come through the glass. Another feature was that it was large and the glass blower figured out how to make it look like a balloon where the center came to a narrow throat, and the bottom was flared up to hold the seed, altogether, a good idea on paper. The seed was kept in place by a huge, rubber stopper in the bottom and it was not clear how the thistle seed came out to rest on the circular trough at the bottom. Upon receipt of the feeder, that mystery was solved: there were three-eighths inch holes in the throat area to allow the Goldfinches to bring out the seed.

This was such a beautiful piece of glass that I ordered a wooden bracket from the State of Maine. When both items arrived I gave it to the family as an Xmas present and it was placed in a pile to be taken north on our first trip in the spring. Once Idlewild was opened and all the major things attended to, the bracket was mounted, the feeder filled, the rubber stopper put in place, and the entire ensemble was hung awaiting the arrival of the Goldfinches. The seed stayed inside the glass and it looked like it would take the beaks of the Goldfinches to get it flowing through the two holes down into the tray where it would be eaten directly. The sun came up across Bass Lake and we were awaiting success.

Later in the day I was working near that huge oak tree when I heard a noise. It was like grains of sand falling on dry leaves. I turned around and saw the thistle seed coming out of the feeder and down to the ground. The sun took the moisture out of the seed or expanded the seed, or both things happened. In any case, the seed poured out of the two holes, filled the circular tray at the bottom, overflowed that tray and, in a short time, like sand in the upper portion of an hour glass, emptied into the dry leaves! A classic failure had occurred.

This particular failure caused both a recovery and a further failure. The recovery was an easy one; I purchased two, tubular, thistle feeders, attached a wire hanger that allowed the two to hang from the single bracket from Maine, filled the feeders and watched as up to fifteen Goldfinches visited the feeders all summer long. At the cost of keeping the two feeders filled – there are always eight or nine Goldfinches at the two feeders – we entertained ourselves and guests who we always sit facing the feeders and who, invariably, remark about the Goldfinches.

But what to do with an expensive piece of glass? I decided to hang that feeder in the back. By hanging it in a sassafras tree near the Woodhouse, using regular bird seed, not thistle seed with the consistency of sand, perhaps a recovery could be made and the birds would slowly peck at the holes and bring down just enough feed to fill the tray. These would be Chickadees, Tufted Titmice, an occasional Cardinal, and whatever else might show up. This was quickly done and the beautiful glass feeder was given a second chance.

The next morning dawned and I was anxious to see if any birds were attracted to the feeder in the early sunlight when the rays of the sunrise are horizontal. To my surprise, some kind of *attack* had occurred against the fortress of the feeder! All the seed was on the ground in the leaves and much of the seed was eaten by the Black Squirrels who attacked. They knew what they were doing; first, they went after the rubber stopper and quickly emptied out all of the seed, much faster than the two three eights inch round holes! Further, the rubber stopper was nowhere to be found. I never knew squirrels used rubber for making nests. Thus one failure led to another. It is time to watch this occur on a much larger, more expensive, scale. This kind of thing extends across years and it involves a beginning *major project* failing, a recovery to recoup part of the loss by introducing a new *major project* using much of the pieces of the initial, failing project, and then the failure of the second *major project*!

I was always aware that there were bats in Michigan. On one occasion a little brown bat was caught in a screen; by removing the screen the bat was released. By merely looking up at the open sky through the trees during dusk as one walks along the road in front of Idlewild, the observer can see bats going after insects. There have never been any bats *in* Idlewild. It was this knowledge of the existence of bats and the literature from Bat Conservation International that ultimately convinced me that I should have a bat colony. I began with a small bat box on a white oak tree in the back of Idlewild where we parked but it never attracted bats. It was that failure that caused me to become a member of Bat Conservation International; through that organization I asked for more information, information like how to build your own bat house, and where to place it. Like every good Idlewild project this literature was sent to Chicago and I could read it and act on it during the winter months.

The first thing I learned was that you needed two colonies; a bachelor colony and a nursery colony. I decided to use the old, unsuccessful house for the bachelors and build, from scratch, a large nursery colony bat box. My ambition was to attract hundreds of little brown bats and to do that I would follow the instructions that arrived in the mail. It was insulated just like the specifications in the Bat Conservation International instructions, it had the correct dimensions between the plywood sections, it had plastic screening instead of metal screening, and it was a big house, three feet by two feet! Of course it was heavy. I varnished it on the outside and fixed it up with a small, asphalt, rolled-roofing roof. It took the entire trunk of our car to bring it to Idlewild.

The problem with the small Bat house in back by the parking area, was that it was not in the open, free standing, and not adjacent to a body of water. For the new location, I solved this by erecting a structure near the lake made up of four four-by-fours of treated wood. The major four by four rose about fifteen feet above the ground. At the top of this piece I placed the Bat house. I put the smaller, bachelor house, above the big Bat house. The location of the structure was a narrow strip of land that lies between the road and Bass Lake. In the front of Idlewild this strip is wide and has a lot of varied vegetation growing in it. There are huge white pines, lots of shrubs, sassafras trees, royal ferns, sweet pea flowers, and lots of other kinds of green plants. In short, it is a beautiful section of property. By a court ruling owners of property all along the lakefront were made owners of these strips in front of their land. At one point a huge oak rotted, fell into the lake and extended out into the water for twenty feet. Children liked to crawl along the now horizontal trunk or just sit on it. It was at the stump for that oak tree that I erected the structure to hold up the Bat house; the question is how could one person accomplish this?

The first problem was that long four-by-four pieces of wood are heavy. I started by building up a structure using three pieces of four-by-four posts buried in the ground and forming a triangle for the much longer four-by-four that would rise up twelve feet. The triangle effort failed because I was unable to get the height I wanted for the Bat house and the bachelor Bat house. My second attempt was the one I used; I dug two of the earlier pieces deep into the embankment at a distance of about four inches from each other; they projected above the ground four feet. Between these I placed a full length of a four-by-four by drilling a hole through all three and ramming a threaded rod through the hole. I could then swing up the long, full length piece, and drill a second hole and, using a second threaded rod, keep that piece upright. Finally, with a third piece dug in and rising about eight feet, I could tie the two upright pieces with wood pieces which gave stability. In the end, then, I did have a triangular base for stability.

The major construction problem was how to swing the long piece up to a vertical position. Drilling the three holes and placing the threaded rod that tied them together was easy. Now the long, central piece, could rotate on the threaded rod. The central piece was so long that when it was horizontal, it extended out into the road so that cars were obliged to use the oncoming traffic lane when proceeding north. Necessity is the mother of invention; the answer to the problem of swinging the central piece up and making it vertical was to use the old, wooden ladder to come up under the four-by-four and get it at an angle as high as could be done; that was the first step.

The next step was to use a rope attached to the top so as to pull it further up to the vertical position by using the old tree trunk that extended into the water. This was a delicate operation because care was called for not to pull it beyond the vertical; if that happened, the vertical piece would continue its rotation and rotate down toward the lake, the dead tree, and yours truly unless I could quickly jump into the lake! This required that I stop pulling before that happened and to lash the three pieces together – the rotating piece and the two, four foot high stumps – so that the second drilling could occur, the second threaded rod inserted and tightened about two feet above the first, and the third four by four dug in and tied to the piece that was now in place.

All of this was accomplished by one person and the structure was very stable; I received no complaints from any drivers. The only problem remaining was how to get the enormous Bat house to the top of this mast and make it fast so that the wind did not blow it down. I began by attaching a strong cross-piece at the top of the, by now, very high, four by four, and placed two pulleys on either side of the cross-piece. The plan was to use ropes through the two pulleys and raise the Bat house to the top. Making fast the pulley ropes while the Bat house remained at the top, one could then extend the wooden ladder to its fullest extent, rest it on the four by four, thereby allowing the climber to get to the top where the Bat house waved in the wind and then, using fasteners previously applied, attach the Bat house to the cross piece and the vertical four by four piece so that the ropes could be removed, not to mention the ladder.

This, too, was done with success by one person. Now it was the turn of the bats. They had to find this luxury condominium and make it their home. Following the guidance from Bat Conversation International, the older and smaller Bat house that was used in the woods, was attached to the top of the whole structure – by using the cross-piece – so that it rose above the roof of the New Bat house. We now enjoyed a pair of Bat houses that followed the guidelines of Bat Conservation International: high, near the water, a correctly built house, bachelor and nursery homes, the whole shebang! So how was it that the whole project became a failure?

From the front porch of Idlewild we could hear walkers in the know as they passed the structure. "See that structure up there, I bet you have no idea of what it is?" said the first walker to his companion. "No, I don't," came the reply. "That, my friend, is a Bat house!" "Ah, yes, I see!" This exchange went on many times during the summer. The problem was that year after year there was nothing to see. If you took a flashlight and shined it up into those luxuriously designed and executed quarters, there were no bats. Two doors away, a neighbor became interested in the failure and offered to bring dry, bat guano from her house in New Jersey when she went back in the middle of the summer. There was an attic in her old house and this was not a difficult task. After she returned, I thanked her for the precious guano, mixed it with water to reconstitute it so as to create what I thought would be the proper smell, climbed the ladder and painted it on the entrance section to the house. Nothing happened. People continued to walk by and make the same comments; as far as the walkers were concerned, it was enough to know that the huge structure was a Bat house. They didn't want to risk going into the brush at the base of the structure to look up to *see* if they could discover bats; besides this, they realized that bats aren't active during bright sunlight.

We waited and waited, year after year, and never supplied living quarters to as much as a single bat. I began to feel guilty. Passersby thought I was following the principles of good Bat citizenship by making a home for bats, hence contributing to the reduction of insects; their conversations implied these assumptions but all I was doing was fooling everyone since there were no bats. All the effort at building the structure in Chicago, hauling it to Bass Lake, installing it, and painting it with Bat guano from New Jersey had come to naught. What could it possibly be used for? I did, however, use it for one purpose.

During this period of years I was swimming laps in Bass Lake rather than in the Ludington High School pool and the West Shore Community College pool; while swimming back and forth just beyond the drop-off, I used the landmark of the huge Bat house as a marker to tell me when I was nearing the pier. It was a kind of end-of-lane marker. However, this didn't help me assuage my feeling of failure. I resolved that I would, in response to this rumination about how I was using the Bat house, use the failure to attempt another effort in attracting birds; I would transform the Bat house effort into a Purple Martin colony! By risking a second failure, you could say that I was in the position of having the opposite of back-to-back home runs, i.e., back-to-back failures!

The Purple Martin Society sent the same kind of literature as Bat Conservation International. Purple Martins love people so you need to attract a colony with nest opportunities that are out in the open, near a lake, high up, away from other trees and branches, yet near a house where people walked. The location of the Bat houses qualified when it came to all those criteria. Purple Martins ate thousands of insects, flew in from Brazil at certain times of the year that could be predicted by finding your zone in a chart that came with the literature. Once attracted, they keep coming back, year after year. The only problem is the first year.

In that first year you need to attract the juvenile males, not the adults who already know where to go from the prior year. You need to know precisely during what interval of time these juvenile males will come back to your latitude, and you need to be ready during that period. First, you open your Martin homes which have been closed up because you don't want other predator birds to colonize ahead of the juveniles. Second, you put up plastic decoys to make your colony seem like home – to fake out the juvenile males. Thirdly, you must play the Purple Martin Juvenile Dawn song on a continuous tape recorder one hour before dawn during this period. Here is how that works. Those juvenile males will be flying over your Martin homes and they will hear the song, come down to have a look-see, join up with the plastic decoys, enter your Martin homes and, ultimately, breed! You will then graduate to a higher status: a colony landlord. This promotion will entitle you to start keeping records; and, yes, there are explicit things you will want to mark down in those written records. Now if you, blessed readers, are sitting at home in Chicago during the wintertime, this whole scenario makes for idyllic reading.

I found that my plan of action was easy to formulate. First, the Bat house must come down, however difficult that might seem during a Chicago winter, and taken to the dump. Next, a decision has to be made on the type of Martin house you intend to use. At the time of putting my plan down on paper, white plastic gourds were all the rage. Based on the size of my pole, eight gourds would be the way to go. How was I to get eight white plastic gourds up in the air? When those juvenile males attracted a mate and began to have families, how was I to perform my record keeping? Did I want to climb up on the old wooden ladder to peek inside the entrance hole to gather the statistics? There had to be a better way; but let's take these armchair challenges in order.

In the basement at 5508 S. Kenwood Avenue, I built a wooden piece that fit precisely on the top of the four-by-four which, by the time I removed the Bat house, was just a stick of four-by-four sticking up in the sky. My collar would fit over that top end and would have two, long wooden rods, set at ninety degrees to each other, and each of these four projecting rods, one in each direction — north, south, east, and west — would have two gourds. So far, so good. To take statistics after the families started, each gourd would be attached with its own pulley. The pulley rope would be fastened on one of eight cleats at the bottom of the structure. There was only one, additional problem.

The Purple Martin Society made it clear that once your Martin families settled in, it was important to keep their front door — there was only one entrance — pointed in the same direction at all times, i. e., before, during, and perhaps even after their return from Brazil the next year. It was clear that, when you lowered and hoisted the white plastic gourds in your capacity as a Purple Martin Landlord, without some further invention, you could not control the direction of the front door after the gourd was hoisted back in place. By designing and adding constraints at the top of the gourds, I was able to keep all gourds in their original direction! This was important because once a Purple Martin Landlord, there was a need for weekly data gathering. Finally, I ordered the Juvenile Dawn Song tape for a tape recorder that we used for other purposes. The tape recorder fit on the cross bars, ran on batteries, and from its resting place and positioned one hour before dawn, it was easily pointed upward so that the sound waves would intercept the oncoming juveniles. I transcribed the tape from the Purple Martin Society into a continuous tape that went around in circles; I bought the continuous tape from Radio Shack — on a clearance sale — and then tested it; it was glorious to hear those juvenile males chirping away during that winter in Chicago!

All these preparations entered my daily thoughts. I began thinking about the fact that if I turned up the volume on the Dawn song, it might wake up the neighbors to the north. On the other hand, one of those neighbors brought the guano from New Jersey and others might not yet be occupying their summer home. Besides, what if a group of juveniles settle in? There's going to be lots of Dawn song from them! And I won't be able to do anything about it, year after year. By then, I reasoned, I would be a Bass Lake hero and walkers would have two things to comment on as they passed by Idlewild: the fountains *and* the Purple Martins. The real payoff would be when I reported my results to the Purple Martin society and then the joy of seeing my gourds occupied the following year. For that event I would, of course, clean out the gourds; it's a long way to fly, from Brazil, that is, and you certainly don't want to disappoint travelers from that far away.

All these plans came to pass after we settled in at Idlewild. As if by instinct, one hour before sunrise, and during the calculated juvenile return period for Idlewild's latitude, I would arise in my pajamas, put on slippers, walk to the Woodhouse, pick up the large step-ladder, carry it down to the road, passing on the right the Hemlock branch that was now seventeen feet long, set the ladder up against the former Bat house structure, now known as the Purple Martin structure, turn on the tape recorder to high volume, and set it, face up – with speakers pointing toward the heavens – on the support pieces which were now a tape recorder platform. Then I would walk back, put the ladder away, return to my warm bed and try to forget the noise of recorded juvenile Purple Martins as I attempted to get back to sleep before sunrise.

One morning, being in kind of a mental haze at this hour, I didn't realize that the sky was cloudy. I went through the ritual, by now, a very routine procedure. The tape was playing the juvenile Martin songs over and over as I settled into bed. But soon, another sound joined the songs coming out of the tape recorder: the fall of large drops of rain on the roof above the upstairs bedroom. I would have to rescue the tape recorder! This time I ran through the steps beginning with my running down the stairs from the bedroom. By the time I was out in the road moving toward the structure my pajamas were soaked. I could still hear the juveniles. Then, as I approached, I heard the familiar juvenile song except that it now sounded like the juveniles were drowning. As I approached the structure the song was transposed into gurgles and then, no more! I retrieved the recorder which was awash, turned it off, and brought it inside the Woodhouse. The recorder survived but it was necessary to purchase another continuous tape from Radio Shack – they were still on sale!

To make matters worse, I recalled that I purchased a yellow sign with a silhouette of Purple Martins on it that read "Caution, Purple Martin Colony." I was the one that needed to be cautious, not the passersby! By this time all the walkers knew what the eight plastic gourds were for. Elderly folks swore that there were Martins up there when they tried to focus on the plastic decoys. So what went wrong? There was, in fact, a conflict, or so I came to think when I tried to determine the cause of my failure. I felt that one principle of Idlewild had trumped the instructions from the Purple Martin Society, and it was my inability to execute a certain rule to its fullest extent that caused the failure. Here is how that analysis played out.

It was necessary to cut away brush at the base of the structure so that the Purple Martins didn't think that a raccoon would climb up and get at the young birds. I did cut away brush but I was hesitant because there was a lot of brush and I didn't want to ruin any plants. Another strategy was to install or make a raccoon guard, but it was further up that the problem occurred. The Society said that there should be a lot of clearance around the Martin homes, i. e., no tree branches around or near the Bat houses or gourds. I also did this and towards the lake and back towards the road there was lots of open space. In the southern direction a sassafras tree was too high and I trimmed it, reluctantly; it was a small tree. In the north, however, there was an Ironwood tree in full bloom for it was still spring; the blooms are white and gorgeous! I trimmed as much of it as I could but I felt it was treason to even touch one of these lovely trees, one of my favorites. At the time the entire strip was thought to be public property; at a later time an appeals court ruling was decided in favor of the property owners and the strip became part of the Idlewild property. Even so, I protected that strip from encroachment of any kind. I could not bring myself to remove any further branches beyond a certain point. In retrospect, I feel that this was a major cause of failure. Since the failure I have seen Purple Martin houses and gourds in pictures where there are absolutely no trees or bushes whatsoever. The problem is that the literature consists of recommendations, many of which I took; I felt that I could be less strict with one since I followed all the others.

After a long waiting period I took down the entire structure so that everything returned to nature. My brother, who lives on Lake Michigan and has a large beach area between his home and the lake, agreed to accept the gourds. But now, as promised, we must return to Hyde Park for there are other groups that await us. We will examine four of those Hyde Park groups. When we return once more to Michigan, we shall examine the important topic of Idlewild watercraft. We have, of course, explored that topic in the form of the Grumman canoe, but to dig deeper into the Norwegian aspects of watercraft, we must focus on how a particular water craft of the Norwegians made its way into the genes that expressed themselves at Idlewild. Can you guess what watercraft that is? Why yes, good guess: the craft the Vikings used to explore the oceans west of Norway. And we need to examine the use of sails, oars, and a craft that can carry many people. For now, that is getting ahead of things.

Returning, then, to Hyde Park, you will recall, blessed reader, that one of our themes is that Grumman canoe, the famous watercraft taken from the Owasippie Scout Camp system east of Whitehall, Michigan. For decades scouts from Chicago took the Chesapeake and Ohio Railroad train from downtown Chicago to a roadstead in the forest south of Whitehall to begin their two-week adventure. During that two-weeks some troops would canoe the White River, others would camp out for one or two nights, and some troops would do both.

Early in our own adventure called *living in Hyde Park* I became aware of a troop that never went to Owasippie. I discovered the troop in my capacity as a Scout Commissioner. The story of my adventure with that troop is told in the book *Black Friends*: it is a classic group tale.

* * *

We now return to the scout troop that met in Kenwood Park. As far as I can remember the cub pack activity had not yet started or, it may have been the other way around. In any case, when I first visited Mr. Barnett's troop in the Park District building I was impressed with the space; it had a certain old world – 1920's or 1930's – intimacy. It was not an architectural gem like the Blackstone library – a mere block away – but I liked it.

I did what I could to help with the program and not overpower the expertise of Mr. Barnett. His son was in the all black troop and there were boys from Kenwood – between 47th Street and 51st – but one boy, Greg, hailed from the other side of Cottage Grove Avenue. Like the trip to Indiana Dunes, there was only one outing and I can vividly remember it; it involved an overnight canoe trip on the Père Marquette river in Michigan, a river I canoed on many times.

I sensed that no one, including Mr. Barnett, was ever in a canoe before and I was right. My strategy was to hold a practice session in the east and west lagoons south of the Museum of Science and Industry. My brother-in-law made fiberglass canoes and I must have obtained two canoes from him for the training session. One was a large orange canoe that easily held three passengers and their gear but the second was an unpainted racing canoe; it had a very round bottom and was extremely tippy.

My plan was to have Mr. Barnett paddle stern in the orange canoe. I would have Greg, the elder boy from across Cottage Grove Avenue, paddle my family's Grumman canoe, an aluminum canoe. We would pick up this canoe at Bass Lake, north of Pentwater, Michigan, where it had been our family canoe since the early 1950s. With two adults, then, we could take seven additional scouts.

I set the practice period on a hot spring day and was upset when I learned that Greg would not be at the training session and, ultimately, not make the trip north. As I attempted to teach the J stroke to Mr. Barnett, I surveyed the other scouts and was disappointed in not locating a scout that could be trained to paddle stern nor had the strength to recover from mistakes made on a fast flowing river with lots of turns, above water obstacles, and other hazards like sunken waterlogged logs – left over from the 19th century lumber operations – and granite boulders lying just below the surface.

Beyond that, it was impossible to teach anyone how to 'read' the water so as to avoid these dangerous objects lying in wait to tip a fast moving canoe heading directly toward them. My fears on that hot Saturday morning were only assuaged by placing my hopes in the strongest scout and relying on pure luck. I was forced to ignore my old maxim that was on the desk of my High School principal: 'Luck is when preparedness meets opportunity.'

The day of the trip arrived and we loaded two canoes atop a station wagon belonging to one of my brothers and the convoy of two vehicles made its way to Bass Lake some 220 miles around Lake Michigan. At Bass Lake we loaded the Grumman canoe onto Mr. Barnett's car and then proceeded to our 'put-in' point on the Père Marquette River. We made camp, followed by dinner, and the next morning we woke up to rain. We had breakfast, broke camp, loaded the canoes, and pushed off.

I implemented a specific sequence for the canoes; I would have the aluminum canoe go first, followed by Mr. Barnett in the orange fiberglass canoe. I would take the rear position in case of emergencies, and use the racing, tippy canoe. Some might liken this to the 'clean-up' hitter in a three position lineup in a baseball game. Others would say it was more like Horatio Hornblower when, as a commodore, in *Commodore Hornblower*, he placed the flagship, HMS *Nonesuch*, in the rear of the column of his flotilla when he entered the Baltic in the first part of that book; both armchair observers would be correct.

I told everyone that we would meet again at a particular bridge that was quite a distance downstream. The idea was to have lunch together at that bridge. It looked like it was going to continue to rain and we could use the shelter of the bridge for that meal. My first intimation of the seriousness of my trusting to inexperience came very quickly. I soon came across Mr.

Barnett in the orange canoe. He was trying to extricate himself from being stuck in some logs along the shoreline.

He reported that he had helped the aluminum canoe. They ran into the shore and the bow paddler noticed a spider web a mere foot ahead of him. He stood up and yelled out, "It's a spider!" The canoe tipped. Fortunately they were able to reload and continue on. I helped Mr. Barnett get out of his jam, waited a short interval, and then continued. The next scene I came upon was much more devastating.

As we came around a bend I saw that the three scouts from the aluminum canoe were all standing with their gear on the right bank of the river. The aluminum canoe was stuck under a large tree that had fallen across the river and left a space on the left side that was only a few feet wide. I had no idea how any gear was salvaged. In any event, I could see that the terrain on the left bank at this point would allow walking an unknown distance to the bridge where we were all to have lunch. Mr. Barnett had gone ahead.

The large Boy Scout patrol cooking kit – a kit that my father had purchased as second-hand after a national jamboree – had been lost in the river. The two air pockets in the bow and stern of the Grumman canoe were keeping it afloat but it was caught in the branches of the tree. It, too, was a family heirloom and I made the decision to attempt a rescue of the canoe but first I had to unload my own canoe.

I began by unloading my two passengers and their gear to the left bank. I then returned to the right bank – all this done with the tippy canoe – and ferried the three aluminum canoe scouts and their gear to the left bank to join their fellows. I then returned to the right bank and grounded the racing canoe at the shoreline, pulling it up into the mud bank so it would stay put. Just at that moment I looked up and saw a beautiful water moccasin snake enjoying a snooze in the rain a few feet away.

Assuring myself that the water moccasin would stay put and not traverse the trunk and its branches, I then climbed onto the trunk and began my journey to a point directly over the stuck canoe. I felt the only way to free it was to jump on the stern and begin 'pumping' the canoe much like the fashion of competitors in the canoe jousting competitions at Boy Scout camp during a water carnival. In a jousting competition this kind of rocking also had the effect of moving the canoe forward toward your opponent who was also equipped with a long pole with a huge soft ball at the end; the objective was to push the other jouster into the water. Naturally, the jouster did not have to contend with live branches filled with leaves above and below the water.

After some initial experimentation I felt I gained the knack of it and was encouraged by seeing the aluminum canoe move forward a small distance. With a great deal of further rocking it was my joy to see the family heirloom completely free but, of course, my joy was short lived; the canoe was quickly caught by the fast river current and in a moment disappeared around the next bend.

There was nothing further I could do but return to the shore, avoid the water moccasin, and paddle across to the five scouts waiting for directions. My plan was to load the racing canoe with *all* the gear followed by my two original passengers. This caused the racing canoe to sink further but the water was not yet at the gunnels. I would have to deal with that.

Then I instructed the remaining three scouts to walk the riverbank downstream to the bridge and join the six of us who would be waiting for them. It was raining but the scouts had raincoats. I had no idea what they would encounter nor how long a distance they had to travel; at least the left bank at that point was not dense underbrush or swamp-like; snakes, if encountered, would have to be avoided. I was sending three city scouts into unknown territory; one of them reacted earlier to a spider by standing up and yelling, "It's a spider!"

I pushed off with a very heavily loaded racing canoe and started concentrating on what it would take to avoid overturning. We all kneeled and kept the center of gravity as low as possible. I resolved to do most of the paddling – since we were going fast with the current – and charged my passengers "To sit in the middle and avoid any movement that would rock the canoe."

We, too, encountered the rain but being wet was the least of my worries. I thought I would never see the aluminum canoe again. It had come into the family through the Owasippe Boy Scout camp system. My father paid the scouting organization the full price for the canoe and it was included in a group of canoes ordered by the Owasippe system many years ago. Upon arrival at the camp depot it was marked with the number 96; it was used by a troop during the first period when they took a trip on the White River; after that trip my father picked it up.

It was not only an heirloom; it also had a history. After arriving at Bass Lake my father took it out by himself to show us how he could paddle; he tipped over! It acquired a richer and richer history as the years passed; we took it out in Lake Michigan and rode the breakers in; we took it on canoe trips as far north as the Two Hearted River in the Upper Peninsula where Hemingway was inspired to write a story using the same name. We must return to our story.

After half an hour of paddling I came around a bend and there, nested against the plants growing along the right bank, was the aluminum canoe. It was as though it was magically stopped and just waiting for us. We came alongside, transferred all the packs to it, tied the racing canoe behind it and paddled on. We soon came across Mr. Barnett standing underneath the bridge to get out of the rain. We agreed that with the cooking equipment lost and with our sleeping bags wet, we should call off the trip and proceed back to Chicago after dropping off all three canoes at Bass Lake.

We were able to get our vehicles back from where we parked them – my mother assisted in this by meeting us at the bridge and driving the drivers to their vehicles. We alerted her that we would need lots of hot chocolate and food before we would start back to Chicago and she returned to Bass Lake.

Now came the worst part of the trip. Mr. Barnett may have had more faith than I – I had paddled the river and knew what grew along the banks – but after an hour of waiting under the bridge while the water poured down, we were both worried. I wanted something to do rather than just stand around; something that would take my mind off thinking about those three city boys from Kenwood following a river bank through unknown terrain. I proposed that I take one scout and drive back along the back roads – often logging roads – and take every road that led back toward the river's east bank. When we got as far as we could go on a road, we would roll down the windows and shout out the names of the three scouts who were looking for the bridge.

This went on for another hour and we returned to the bridge and reported no success. Now Mr. Barnett was getting as worried as I was and we had nothing else to do but keep waiting in the rain. I had not had a good night's sleep and that doesn't help with one's anxiety level. About half an hour later, one of the four scouts under the bridge yelled out "There they are!" Instantly, Barnett and I exchanged happy glances.

The three boys reported 'no problems;' they followed directions; it was an adventure and their morale was high. We loaded the vehicles with the three canoes, packed all the wet gear, and set off for hot chocolate and the meal my mother prepared. I guess you could say, "All's well that ends well."

* * *

So much for the Grumman canoe. As previously pointed out, we will return to watercraft when we revisit Michigan. It is time to fast forward in our Hyde Park Odyssey to a more recent period. The place we stop, in point of time, is just after the Master of Liberal Arts degree from the University of Chicago was a fait accompli and I resolved to march in the procession that ended in the Four Hundred Sixtieth Convocation, the Spring, Second Session of June Ninth A. D. Two Thousand. This gala event was held in the Harper Quadrangle. Hanna Holborn Gray, the *Harry Pratt Judson Distinguished Service Professor, Department of History and the College, President*

Emerita of the University, delivered the Convocation Address, "Getting The Third Degree."

Harper Quadrangle is an outdoor space near the old Harper Library. By renting a cap and gown to march to that site I would make up for missing two earlier Convocations: one for the Master of Business Administration completed in March 1970, just prior to the birth of our son – we had our hands full. And the other was the Stanford Master of Science in Engineering degree completed in May of 1964 – it was more important to return to Chicago and land that job with The Outfit so as to be able to move back and forth between Chicago and Palo Alto beginning in January, 1965.

A member of our Play Reading group, the Midway Play Readers, was the Vice-Marshal. A Professor of Business who served with me for twelve years on the Board of the Hyde Park Neighborhood Club was, for many years, *The Marshal*, no less. Finally, the husband of one of Christiane's closest friends, was an Assistant Marshal. I ask you if this trio of Marshals, albeit that one was recently retired, wasn't enough to motivate a MLA Graduate to march in black robe and cap in the hot sunlight of June 9th, 2000? Despite your answer, it *was* enough to move me.

Now the University of Chicago is, I am certain, not unique among institutions of higher learning in supporting various, little known, traditions. One of these has to do with a large in-floor medallion in the middle of a foyer in Mandel Hall where many activities are carried on, more particularly for us, the Chamber Music Series which, at the time, we had attended for more than thirty years. The superstition encapsulated in the tradition is never to step on the medallion.

Be that as it may, the Convocation tradition is an *administrative* rule emanating from the Registrar's Office. Simply stated, the degrees that are handed out are arranged in *strict sequential order*! This means that during the indoor lining-up period prior to the march in the sun, the sequential stacks of degrees are made to correspond precisely with the person-by-person queue of individuals receiving their degree and also, I would add, precisely in the same order as those individuals are seated in the front rows of the audience. Presumably then, the aforementioned distinguished marshals need only hand over, in order, the correct stack to the University President so that everyone receiving a degree returns to his or her seat with the correct document!

No, don't make any assumptions along those lines; I did receive the correct degree. My adventure came while marching to Harper Court, a distance of a mere two blocks. The adventure resonates with Hanna Gray's address: Getting The Third Degree. Here is the hard part for people who like to predict the adventure: you must also take into account that because of my adventure I had absolutely no idea of what Hanna Gray said! How's that for a clue?

Finally, after I returned with my Maroon Folder with my Master of Fine Arts parchment inside – the correct one – my seatmates to the left and right noticed that my folder contained a special, handwritten note from the Registrar's office. I shared the note with my adjacent seatmates and they were mildly impressed. So what, heaven sakes, *was* the adventure!?

June 9th, in the year 2000, was a hot day in Hyde Park. Despite wearing a black mortar board, I resolved to use sun tan lotion during the march. I applied the lotion inside the building where we were lining up and responding to our names so that the stacks of degrees were in perfect synchronization with our marching order. It was, of course, easier to apply the sun tan lotion while standing rather than marching. Once outside, however, there was the sun, in all its glory, shining with a vengeance!

I was soon sweating even though the march was a mere two city blocks long. Very quickly, before we made the left turn for the final stretch to our seats, I became aware that the sun tan lotion with the cooperation of my perspiration and conjoining together with that perspiration, had entered the corners of my eyes thereby causing a stinging sensation that also began to impair my vision. The natural response was to reach beneath the robe for my pocket handkerchief and do the best I could to alleviate the discomfort but there was still another block and a half to march. It would be sacrilegious to get out of line; think of the consequences: a huge mix up! Hundreds of graduates who worked for years on their degrees would end up with the wrong name on their degrees or even the wrong degree to boot. For some it would be a rude shock: getting a PhD instead of a mere Master's Degree.

I couldn't let that happen. I asked my fellow marchers for their handkerchiefs. Upon my returning them, they could be laundered, after all, it was only perspiration and sun tan lotion. With their help I made it to my seat but my eyes were still stinging. You see, I couldn't get all of the lotion removed from my face. I *was* able to march up to the platform and receive my degree – even the photograph doesn't hint at my problem. Upon return to my seat, however, I was still plagued. Thus it was that I could not listen to Hanna Gray's Convocation Address *Getting The Third Degree*. I was *experiencing* the third degree! But what was it that I found in my Maroon binder, the one that held my Master of Liberal Arts degree?

I was aware that one of the adult children of a Play Reader worked in the University's Office of the Registrar. You remember the Play Reader who stopped everything when I wanted to identify a new wildflower and she identified it as Helleborine? That's right, the expert; well, John, one of her sons worked with the Registrar; we knew each other from play readings at his home. His parents told him to look for my Maroon folder. He found the folder and inserted a congratulatory note. What a surprise! Especially coming, as it did, in the midst of my sun tan trials. When I shared the note with the people sitting to the left and right in my row, there were impressed. "We didn't get any personal congratulatory notes from the Registrar's Office," they remarked.

It made up for all the other discomforts of the Convocation. The question, however, was whether or not I was finished with my learning at the University with a third Master's Degree? I lost membership in the MLA group that met during evenings; how was I to recover, or rather replace that group with another? My friend, David, another Professor, candidly told me, "The last thing you need is a *fourth* Master's Degree!" I agreed and he then went on to explain that I could start auditing classes at the University – for free! This was good news; no more night classes! I was ecstatic; I could walk or bike to class. I hadn't enjoyed that luxury since I was taking the University of Chicago's Basic Program – the Great Books program – that was offered on campus just a few blocks away.

From that conversation there grew up a sequence of new groups whose membership extended across years and years of classes. I kept my mouth shut in those classes; if anyone asked me why, I maintained that my mindset was based on a parent that put two children through four years of expensive schools; what I meant by that was that paying customers, or, more correctly, the children of paying customers, should always be heard first. I qualify this because there were many times, especially in the smaller seminars, when I was encouraged to speak. Often I was given the nod after a period of silence became embarrassing. Again, I used an argument about why I decided to throw my answer – correct or not – into the ring, so to speak. I told the students sitting nearby that my efforts were *penalty free*! My young colleagues in learning seemed to like that reply.

There were all kinds of situations that are too numerous to examine in detail. The question that we are interested in, is, of course, was this auditing sequence a result of, say, genes inherited from my grandfather Natal? On the one hand, the answer is yes, he had a passion for learning, especially discerned in those long lists of books he read in the first two decades of the twentieth century to become acclimated to being an American citizen. On the other hand, his educational experiences were also linked to his profession; he needed to obtain greater depth into what moved and interested his clients, assuming that is even possible. If not possible, he could at least speak about common cultural ideas. My auditing, too, was like a profession as well; the University of Chicago calls that kind of thing "The Life of The Mind."

So, assuming one is curious, we can ask what, exactly, did that life consist of? Naturally, these classes were not entirely penalty free. I mean, of course, the occupied time, both before and after class, as well the purchase of numerous books; so numerous that bookcases began to proliferate in the basement. To explore in detail those experiences would take a goodly portion of a lifetime; there is a shorter way that, hopefully, contains the germ of what went on: the use of a list. Each entry in the list is a class where the material was read, notes were taken, class dialog was listened to, and subsequently shared with anyone else who cared to listen. Let's take a look at that list between the date of June 9, 2000, and the present. Each auditing experience took place in one of the three Academic Quarters: Autumn, Winter, and Spring. The Summer Quarter was spent at Idlewild. The classes are listed, roughly, in calendar sequence and are taken from the stacks of paper in the basement which, surprisingly, revealed more than anticipated when perused.

Classes Audited September 2000 to Present

History and Theory of Drama, I
Mill (John Stuart Mill)
Early Modern Europe
Renaissance Florence
Travelers on the Silk Road
Plutarch's Lives
The Philosophy of Visual Modernism
Dutch Art
The Historical Novel
Capitalism, Political Economy and the Early Modern State
Early Christianities
Renaissance Epic
Florentine Renaissance Art
Politics and Society in Nineteenth-Century France
Strange Shadows: Four Painters in Search of the Invisible
The Pre-Raphaelites
Skepticism and Sexuality in Shakespeare
Mediaeval Epic
Thing Theory

The Rise of Science Fiction

Eighteenth Century Novels

Chinese Tomb Art

Chekov

Hanna Arendt

Henry James: The Fiction of Crisis

Spenser

Sociology Class on Religion and Philosophy

Philosophy Class on Origins of Government

American Modern: Experimental Fiction

Modern European Novel

Comparative Kingship: Rulers in Twelfth-Century Europe

Perception and Action

Graduate Seminar on French History

The Bestseller in Twentieth-Century America

Hegel's Lectures in Fine Arts

Visual Art in the Postwar US

The Culture of Victorian War

Naipaul vs. Rushdie: Writing in the post-Colonial

Middlemarch

The French Revolution

The Production of Knowledge in Modern Europe

The US Civil War and Reconstruction 1846-1898

Introduction to Black Chicago

Stanley Cavell's The Claim of Reason

Forms of Philosophical Skepticism

Introduction to Heidegger

Machiavelli: The Prince and Discourses

History of Israel-Arab Conflict

History of Russian Civilization – 1

Somewhere in that list of audited classes there is a course that made up for missing out on the substantive content of Ms. Gray's address on *The Third Degree*. What could that be? A class taught by Hanna Gray! This was a history class that went back to Pre Reformation times; we read Erasmus, examined the effects of Martin Luther, and looked at Machiavelli's *The Prince*, among other texts. That class, and, of course, many others, affected another group: the Midway Play Reading group. I wrote the play *Luther's Parents* because of the reading in the class and actually *did* give a copy to Ms. Gray, the former president of the University of Chicago. And so, this is as good a time as any to segue to that group, the Midway Play Reading group.

We have already introduced this group; now we need to answer questions like: what, if any, was the effect of all that auditing on the Play Reading group? What, if any, did those auditing experiences have to say about being a Norwegian? And how, exactly, did the group operate? These are deep waters and we make no claims to be in tune with the many trained psychiatrists who live nearby. If we merely focus on Ms. Gray's class we can cite one play, *Luther's Parents*, that was inspired by the reading material of that class. Coincidently, the play also spoke about how children, like Martin Luther, might have acquired the traits that caused him to initiate the Reformation. But why talk in a vacuum; we'll talk about it after the show:

* * *

Luther's Parents

Characters:

> Luther's Father
> Luther's Mother
> Joe Peters, *A Neighbor*

Scene One:

> *A tastefully furnished middle-class apartment that could be anywhere between early 1950's décor to 1980's. Luther's Father is seen reading an evening newspaper in a stuffed chair while Luther's Mother is knitting in her chair.*

FATHER: No, no, no, it can't be!

MOTHER: What is it now, dear?

FATHER: I never thought I would have to start purchasing indulgences for that damn son of mine. After this, he's going to need a whole basket full of them!

MOTHER: What has he done now, dear?

FATHER: I told that kid that no one was interested in debating his theses. You remember – they were bad enough (*picks up a sheet of paper, reads*) – Proposal Number 46: Money should be retained for home upkeep vs. being squandered on indulgences. Proposal Number 86: The Pope's income is large enough to build his own Saint Peter's church with his own money vs. using that of indigent believers. Can you imagine academics – full professors, mind you – sitting around and actually debating whether or not the cross with the papal arms are of equal value to the cross on which Christ died? I thought they all were ridiculous. Now my kid is going to purgatory or worse yet and I haven't got the money to bail him out this time. I just don't have it, dear. We paid for his schooling and the church picked up some of his graduate costs but we just don't have it, dear. I thought we were home free – tenured faculty, nice university town. But it's beyond that.

MOTHER: What do you mean?

FATHER: He has been talking to the Princes now, nothing big, oh no, minor course corrections – eliminate all cardinals, no more pilgrimages to Rome, no kissing of the Pope's feet, eliminate or consolidate the mendicant orders, marriage for pastors and bishops, no more mendicant begging, no more festival days, except for Sunday – that kid is going to get himself excommunicated, or already has, for all I know. Look at this, he always loved making lists, here, Number 24, this is to the Princes, "Join with the Hussite's," – you remember what they did to John Huss.

Now you know how I reconciled myself to no grandchildren, but at least I thought I would have a son around for a while. That kid is going to get burned!

MOTHER: It's all due to Maria.

FATHER: Maria? Maria who?

MOTHER: Maria, the Peter's daughter down the block. Martin had a crush on her and it's starting to catch up with him.

FATHER: I never knew anything about this, nonsense.

MOTHER: It wasn't nonsense, and just because of that I didn't tell you. Martin thought you would fly off the handle you were so concerned for his career.

FATHER: You mean to tell me that because my son had or has a crush on Joe Peter's youngest daughter, the race is on to see whether he gets burned before either a premature death or after a long life as a national heretic?

MOTHER: Maria was a very attractive young woman. You see, you don't notice these things the way I do.

FATHER: But, but . . . (*flabbergasted*)

MOTHER: You don't remember how you were at Martin's age. He has all your genes, dear.

FATHER: So, let me get this straight. Our child, our little Martin, is going to take on the Pope, actually it's the entire Papal court and the curia he wants eliminated, anyway, our child is going to tell our national leaders how to manage the country, the universities, international diplomacy, whatever, all this just because he wants to marry Maria Peters?

MOTHER: Dear, you haven't been paying attention to the evolutionary biologists – everything we do is done to further the propagation of the species. Martin *has* had a very deep religious experience of grace to reorient him from good works, which, I might add, is probably due to those lists of chores you always gave him, but let's forget that for now. Anyway, despite this reorientation from good works to faith, deeper down, those genes are saying, "your parents need grandchildren," and Maria, whom Martin knew as a very dutiful and faithful child, needed to know that any children she might have by Martin would survive in the most important senses to her. Martin has now given her a fantastic demonstration of his potential, if not his actual prowess. He's not a total ascetic; we know that from the writings he has always published; he has your genes, as I said, dear, and women pay attention to these things. He's the ideal husband – sensitive, religious, knowledgeable of the pitfalls of raising children in today's world, civic-minded, educated – maybe he's too educated for Maria, but women are prepared to forgive that. If he can avoid the worst-case scenarios you have been ranting about, he has a great future.

FATHER: Well I never – grandchildren!

Scene Two:

The same room, the next day. The Luthers are seen at the opening welcoming Joe Peters who has dropped in.

FATHER: Joe, how are you? So nice to see you, how's the family, how's Joanna?

JOE: Oh, she's fine, Martin, visiting with her mother now – I'm left with the kids.

MOTHER: You know Joe, we do the same thing; we still call our children "kids." Martin is thirty-seven now and we talk about him here as though he were a teenager.

JOE: Well that's interesting, because I wanted to talk about Martin. He's getting into the papers a lot these days. Don't get me wrong, Joanna and I have already been to Rome and we really weren't thinking of making another trip anytime soon.

FATHER: It's a great place. Maybe a little too much construction is going on right now.

JOE: Well, yes, perhaps. Anyway, I wanted to talk about Martin and Maria.

MOTHER: Martin? Our Martin and your Maria?

JOE: That's right. You see, Maria is still at home with us and, I don't know if you knew, but for some reason or other she decided to sit in on some of Martin's classes at Wittenberg, not a degree program, just auditing. She has always had an interest in sacred theology – you know, she knew Martin in her earlier years.

MOTHER: Yes.

JOE: Well, I never knew just how keen Maria was on these things, I mean she has always been a good student and, well anyway, it seems that Martin, your Martin, thought she was quite keen, perhaps the best word is *proficient*, at this kind of thing, and Maria and he got to talking after class.

MOTHER: Yes.

JOE (*tentatively*): You know how these things happen; we all were young once. To make a long story short, Martin has convinced Maria that she was "predestined" to marry him. Maria says it looks like the government is going to back Martin with respect to all these lists of demands and practices, you know, the ones that we've seen in the papers, and one of those demands, I think it's Number 14 in that list that came out yesterday, says that Saint Paul in a couple of places endorses marriage – for clerical people –

something about a pastor not being compelled to live without a lawful wife. The upshot is that I think Maria is taking this as a proposal of some sort. I just thought I would stop by to see if you have heard of anything along those lines.

MOTHER: Well, it's better to have things out in the open rather than all those clandestine marriages in the clergy, people living together and even concubines. Don't you think so, dear?

FATHER: Joe, I guess I have been made aware that Martin was keeping an eye on Maria over these years, and maybe the feeling was mutual. But that damn son of mine! There is a difference between falling in love, making a formal proposal for marriage, publishing the banns – we went through all of that – there is a difference between that and telling a woman, after class, during what purports to be a discussion of "sacred theology" with an auditor – I guess that doesn't make any difference – in any event, there is a difference when one acts one way and when one talks about a theory of "predestination." If all this is predestined, then, as I understand it, it doesn't make any difference what the laws are, what we think as potential grandparents, or what the church, present or future, thinks. It seems to me Maria is joining herself or imagining herself joined to a guy who may well turn out to be a martyr. What I would like to know is whether this is love, sacred theology, or evolutionary biology? Who's in charge here? Whatever happened to the liberal arts?

MOTHER: Joe, didn't I hear you say that Maria has an aptitude, maybe just as good as Martin's, for this kind of thing?

JOE: Well, that's what your son says, but what are his motives?

MOTHER: Well, I don't think we can get anything from our Martin. Or let me say that I can answer for that – his motives are what the grace of God through His Word has revealed to him with respect to Maria. It is all of the same cloth; it's all knitted together as a single piece and you can't take away anything or make exceptions. He talks to me enough so that I can say that much. There is no need for clergy as an intermediate in all this – Martin thinks we can all "go direct," the priesthood of every believer, so there is no reason, in theory, why any of the "traditional" marriage or courtship conventions need to be followed.

FATHER: A father has a right to certain societal conventions. If this were our daughter and she came home and started talking about being predestined to marry someone, what would that say about her happiness, her ability to take a role in the secular world – where, I might add, everyone may not yet agree with the theological directions this "married couple" are taking? Is Maria prepared for the notoriety?

MOTHER: Joe, here is the way I see it. A woman has to make up her mind using an intuition, a set of values we probably haven't even talked about. We are not talking about teenagers any more. We have two responsible people here who have studied what the theological, secular, and other worlds have to say about things. But there is another world that is exclusively between the two of them, and of course the private world between each person, man or woman, and his or her Creator – and Martin has a lot to say about that – but it's not how well we agree or disagree with any old or new valuation of that but what Maria and Martin have to say to each other. I see a lot of good reasons why Martin would make a good father, a good son-in-law, and they have to do with his personality, his uniqueness as a human being, and not necessarily his belief system and how it conforms to belief systems that are being challenged by Martin himself. And, further, I don't think we can get at the real person from his writings in the newspapers.

FATHER: OK, dear, you have made your point. But let's not forget that this guy, our son, has lived a cloistered life. He's an academic, a very interior person. He's a fantastic catch, all right, but this marriage thing is going to put him back into a different sector of the real world – children, taking care of a sick child or a wife or even both – and I know our child has got that included in his new theology as well if I understand some of what he has written, but this is different. I guess what I want to say is that a man hasn't learned how to pray until he has had children, and he's telling everyone how it is already.

MOTHER: Joe, I've known Maria long time and I can't think of a more perfect daughter to have around.

Scene Three:

Same as Scene One.

FATHER: No, no, no it can't be!

MOTHER: What is it now, dear?

FATHER: I never thought I would have to start purchasing indulgences for that damn son of mine. After all this he's going to need a whole basket full of them!

MOTHER: What has he done now, dear?

FATHER: Excommunicated! This time he makes the headlines. And I thought that Leo was going to be so much better than Julius. *(Reads from the newspaper.)* Here it is, January 3, 1521, "It was announced today by a Papal Bull, *Decet Romanum Pontificem,* that Martin Luther of Wittenberg, Augustinian, Master of Arts and Sacred Theology, had failed to recant 41 errors in his writings outlined in an earlier Bull, 'Arise, O Lord, judge thine own cause.' Pope Leo X pronounced that his memory was to be wiped out. Much of Germany is still rallying to his side, however, including such nobles as Sylvester von Schaumberg, who offered him the protection of 100 Franconian nobles. Others such as Franz von Sickengen and Ulrich Hutten hailed him as the potential liberator of Germany." This paper does a good job, "all the news that's fit to print." Let's see, the Bull is being defaced in Germany; instead of burning Martin's writings they are substituting others. More demonstrations by students against the Pope. Well, I guess it's going to be hard to wipe out his memory.

MOTHER: I never worried about that, dear; after all, with children now, that's not so easy to do. You see, I was right about those evolutionary biologists.

FATHER: But maybe you didn't get the entire picture. Here's a human interest article on Martin in the same paper. They are quoting some of his views on marriage. *(Reads from the newspaper.)* "Marriage does not consist only of sleeping with a woman – everybody can do that – but keeping house and bringing up children." Bravo! That's quite liberal; everybody can sleep with a woman, that's good, very good. You know, dear, I wasn't certain he had it in him, but I think things are going to be OK. Here is more: "The father washing smelly diapers may be ridiculed by fools, but God, with all his angels and creatures, is smiling – not because the father is washing diapers, but because he is doing so in Christian faith."

MOTHER: While you may not have had faith in Martin's experience because of his age, I had faith in Maria's genes. A woman just knows that any man that has been through what our child has been through just has to be a good father – the future is all uphill.

FATHER: I just thought . . .

MOTHER: He still confides in me. Just yesterday he stopped in while you were out on your walk and he said that he was convinced that God had come to his aid by giving him Maria and vice versa. Marriage has given our son a glimpse of what the lost Eden must have been like – those were his very words.

FATHER: We can be proud of ourselves. Good upbringing, education, career-oriented. You know you can't say we neglected his religious studies or pointed him in the wrong direction – there was only one church at the time. You don't think he would fault us for that?

MOTHER: Don't worry; I'm certain he'd call it predestination!

Curtain

* * *

So, if Luther's parents are correct, it's our *genes* that count. Whoa! What about those experiences that led to those words in our opening paragraph? You know, the words about "The just shall live by faith." Surely the *environment* must have something to contribute to our actions, to Luther's actions. All this gets us back to that old quandary of environment vs. genes and the notion that maybe the answer is *both*. What about love at first sight? In order to stay within the confines of memory, home, love, and groups, while speaking of genes and environment, it seems clear that, very early on, those classes – both the MLA Degree classes and the auditing classes – were responsible for subjecting the Play Reading group to the effects of, well, living in Hyde Park – shopping at the Hyde Park Co-Op grocery store, being a Graduate student, writing papers, living in an apartment, and looking out for a potential mate. See if you can detect any of those environmental aspects in the play *Trouble in Tahini*. Two plays in a row? Call it a double-header.

* * *

Trouble in Tahini

Characters:

Ashley Farell, *a graduate student in English at the University of Chicago*
Penny, *Ashley's roommate, a graduate student in Religion & Ethics, The Committee*
On Social Thought, University of Chicago
Ralph Clark, *a law student at the*
University of Chicago

Scene One:

The Hyde Park Co-Op. Ashley and Ralph are seen in the same aisle, each pushing their own grocery cart. Ashley is scanning from top to bottom the produce on a shelf and is starting to use a methodical search. She is obviously flustered in her inability to find what she is looking for and having to work so hard for it. Ralph is more causal and minding his own business when Ashley backs into his cart.

ASHLEY *(apologizing):* Oh, I'm so sorry! And these aisles are wide, too; it's just that I have been looking for so long and I can't find the tahini.

Ralph is about to reply when the Co-Op announcer comes on and cuts him off:

ANNOUNCER: *Attention Co-Op shoppers! We have a special today in the fish department. Florida red snapper at $3.98 a pound! Take some of these delicious beauties home for the family.*

RALPH: Is Tahiti some kind of a fish from the South Pacific? Maybe they have it on sale along with those red snappers?

ASHLEY: No, and it's "tahini" not "Tahiti."

RALPH: OK, I've never heard of it. Why don't we look for it together? I'm new here and I could use practice becoming familiar with the logic behind these endless aisles. What is this stuff, Tahiti I mean, tahini?

ASHLEY: I'm making hummus and the recipe calls for a quarter cup of tahini.

RALPH: I love hummus. I think I saw some over in the deli area. It had all kinds of combinations: garlic hummus, olive hummus, herb hummus. Maybe they keep the makings over there.

ASHLEY: I don't think so. I'm making it from scratch.

RALPH: I see. Well, how do you make it? Maybe that will help.

ASHLEY: It has olive oil, garlic; the juice of one lemon, garbanzo beans, and tahini. You throw it into a Cuisinart, turn it on for five minutes, and *voilà* it's done!

RALPH: Sounds delicious. You mean to say you have located Garbanzo beans and can't find tahini?

ASHLEY: Actually, I haven't tackled the beans yet.

Ralph is again cut off by the announcer.

ANNOUNCER: *Attention, Co-Op Shoppers! We have a fresh supply of mangoes just in from South America, only $1.98 a pound. Get them while they last in the produce department!*

RALPH: Now, let's see, where do they make hummus?

ASHLEY: It's a Middle Eastern food.

RALPH: That's right, so they must have a Middle Eastern food section somewhere. Let's stroll through these aisles until we see something.

Ashley and Ralph begin to stroll up and down the aisles looking for Middle Eastern food.

ASHLEY: You know, I do feel like I am on a trip when I shop here. It's not just the things like mangoes, but I see olives and I am in Greece, chutney, and I am back in a London Pub. The other day I was picking out pasta and I was back at Florence and Milan. One day, they had fresh snails and I swore I would go back to Paris to that restaurant where I had them in butter and garlic.

RALPH: I can see what you mean. By the way, I'm Ralph Clark, I just entered the Law School here.

ASHLEY: Ashley Farell, I'm in the English department, hoping that the subject will still be taught by the time I get my PhD.

RALPH: Here we are, Middle Eastern! Now, let's see, hummus, hummus, no, that's not it, Tahiti, Tahiti, no, no, tahini, tahini! Ah, here it is, white stuff, comes in a bottle—what is it anyway?

ASHLEY (*reading label*): Tahini is a miracle food. Made from ground sesame seeds, it is highly nutritious and packed with amino acids, calcium, B vitamins, vitamin E, essential fatty acids, iron, manganese, phosphorus, potassium, sulfur, and zinc, yet it contains no saturated fat and no cholesterol.

RALPH: Brother! It sounds like you don't need any vitamins. Let me at it! I can't wait till we find the garbanzos.

ASHLEY: It looks like this side is all ethnic. Hey, down here in the Mexican section. I found them.

RALPH: Let me see. On one side it says garbanzo beans and on the other chick peas. That's quite something, two names for the same thing. They don't look like small peas and I haven't the slightest idea what garbanzo means. Let's see. *reading* At low cost and beneficial in their whole-food content, they are one of the best sources of cholesterol-lowering fiber, almost as high as bran in cereals. They also are excellent sources of complex carbohydrates, high-quality protein, vitamin A, B-complex vitamins, and minerals, including iron, calcium, phosphorus, and potassium. *He stops reading.* Another winner! Did you say you already have your garlic and lemon?

ASHLEY: Yes, that was easy, but you can help me with the olive oil.

They continue searching the aisles for olive oil.

RALPH: You know, I have to hand it to those Arabs, I never would have dreamed they dipped their veggies in such dynamite. I don't mean to sound prejudiced, but I always thought Yasir Arafat was a bit on the heavy side.

ASHLEY: Here it is. Now what kind?

RALPH: Oh, I would take the extra-virgin; that's always the best.

ASHLEY: Really, you're kidding; no wait, there was a Co-Op health article on that in the Evergreen just last week. *She reaches in basket to pick out Evergreen News sheet.* Here it is; let me see. *Reads* Cold-pressed extra-virgin olive oil, made from the first pressing of the choicest olives is the one exception with respect to cholesterol. In Greece and southern Italy, where this oil is consumed in quantity, people have much lower blood cholesterol levels and a much lower rate of heart disease than people elsewhere in Europe and in the United States. A large amount of the fat they consume comes from olive oil. *She stops reading.* So, you are right, the other stuff is bleached and subjected to a denaturing process. Well, now I will be able to make my hummus. You've been such help; thank you. *She offers her hand.*

RALPH: No problem. I just wish I could taste some of that hummus. It sounds great for after a workout.

ASHLEY: Well, why don't you come over? We were just going to have a small party. How is six o'clock?

RALPH: Well I, don't want to intrude.

ASHLEY: We English majors need some lawyers around to bring some reality into the conversation. Here, I'll write down our address. *She quickly scribbles down address and hands it to Ralph.* See you tonight.

Scene Two:

The inside of a typical walkup Hyde Park apartment. Ashley is on the phone and Penny, her roommate, is sitting on a couch reading but obviously unable to concentrate completely.

ASHLEY (*speaking on the phone*): No, I had searched all over for the stuff and I didn't know they had anyone to help – A courtesy desk? Is that where all those announcements come from? That's a misnomer if ever I heard one. – No, I didn't pick up another graduate student. I just backed into his cart and he needed an orientation so we searched together. Then, when the hummus sounded so good, I invited him over. – No all I know about him is that he works out and is in the Law School. – OK, so we will have one more tonight. See you later. *She hangs up phone.*

PENNY (*mocking the Co-Op's announcer*): Attention, Co-Op shoppers! Will the lovely young lady who can't find a date at our main store remember we now have two more; that's right, two additional stores to keep trying with, the Kimbark Plaza store and our new store on forty-seventh street. But hurry, young unmarried law students don't last.

ASHLEY: I swear there's a conspiracy going on here. An accidental frustration leads to assistance and I am being accused of going after strangers, of having no judgment of character, of being overly sociable. The next thing people will say is that I am doing financial planning for when my grant runs out!

PENNY: Ash, we're just trying to put some reality on the table. Imagine yourself shopping again a few years from now where you know where everything is and know everyone. You are still working on that thesis, doing all the housework, catering to a former law student who is now putting in seventy hour weeks, six days a week, and then he convinces you that you need to search out some disposable items in the paper products aisle and give up reading Trollope and Dickens.

ASHLEY: Well, at least such a relationship would have started when we were both members of the proletariat. Have you ever thought about the consequences of been courted by a member of the bourgeoisie? Despite what MacIntyre and Williams may say, that class seems to start with any capital you might have left in the bank. Then they go on to assign some points for social capital, discounting for any cultural capital you may have picked up on the south side of Chicago; throw in some credit for imagined sexual capital or otherwise, but may not add much for any spiritual capital you have picked up in the Divinity school. Assuming the result is positive and dovetails with your career plans and, God forbid, relatives and associates, you may become a bourgeois yourself.

PENNY: All any of us is trying to do is to reinforce what you say when we point out that some of these guys seem to be interested in a woman's use value, but they often end up thinking about exchange value, and we want to protect you from that; you're just too unique.

ASHLEY: And all I'm saying is that I'm not interested in any person who thinks I am a commodity with any kind of value or any kind of capital no matter how you define it.

PENNY: OK, we believe you. Now maybe you had better mix up some of that stuff with the extra-virgin olive in it or we will have a roomful of troubled people here tonight and need to save some to calm the waters.

Scene Three:

The same room later in the day, now full of young people, mostly graduate student types, talking animatedly, and dipping veggies in hummus; each holding a glass in his other hand. More prominent now is a floor-to-ceiling bookcase that takes up one entire wall. Penny, dressed very attractively in a red dress, is looking for texts in much the same frustrated way that Ashley was looking for tahini at the Co-Op. Ralph has apparently found a text and is reading when Penny bumps into him.

PENNY (*apologizing*): Oh, I'm sorry! I don't seem to be able to remember the scheme I used to organize these bookshelves and I can't find the books I need for my paper.

RALPH: That's perfectly all right; today's my day for being bumped into. You must be Ashley's roommate—we met earlier in the day—I'm Ralph Clark.

PENNY: Hi, Ralph I'm Penny. Ashley told me, I think, you met while she was shopping.

RALPH: Yes, this party reminds me of the Co-Op, all of the people running around and all of the food, very effervescent. I bet you haven't any idea how good garlic is for you?

PENNY: Not exactly.

RALPH: Here. *He nods to the text he holds.* I knew if those Arabs were smart enough to use garbanzo beans, tahini, and olive oil, they must have known something we don't know about garlic. *He reads.* Garlic stimulates the production of the amino acid Glutathione, a powerful antioxidant and detoxifier. Allacin, a sulfur compound in fresh garlic, has antibiotic and antifungal properties. It protects against heart disease and stroke. It contains the compound adenosine, a smooth muscle relaxant that lowers high blood pressure. It lowers cholesterol, relieves rheumatism, cleanses the blood, prevents clots and boosts the immune system, suppresses tumor growth in animals and contains phosphorus, potassium, calcium, protein and significant amounts of vitamins B and C. *He stops reading.* Now I know why I feel like a new person ever since I stepped into this apartment; I have been energized by hummus! What's the topic for your paper?

PENNY: Love.

RALPH: Love? That sounds like a great topic. Why don't you let me help you? I mean, find the books you are looking for. Which ones are you going to use?

PENNY: Well, there's a little paperback here somewhere on Plato's *Symposium.* I think it has a blue cover.

Both search the bookcase.

RALPH: I think I've found it, yes, here it is. It looks quite marked up. *He reads.* But what I am trying to say is this — that the happiness of the whole human race, women no less than men, is to be found in the consummation of our love, and in the healing of our dissevered nature by finding each his proper mate. *He stops reading.* Great source material for your paper. *He reads.*

He makes the dispositions and the hearts of gods and men his dwelling place – not, however, without discrimination, for if the heart he lights upon be hard he flies away to settle in a softer. *He flips a page.* But there's a divinity in human propagation, an immortal something in the midst of man's mortality which is incompatible with any kind of discord. *He stops reading.* OK, what other author are you going to need? *He hands Penny the text.*

PENNY: There's a small red book, Kierkegaard's *Works of Love.*

Both continue the search.

PENNY: Here, I have it.

RALPH: What is it you like there?

PENNY: Well, it's a little hard to put in a few words but first there's the examination about the consequences of the statement "Thou shalt love thy neighbor as thyself." That's from the first essay, *"Thou Shalt Love"* and then some of the ideas from the second essay *She reads.* Love covers a multitude of sins. For it does not discover the sins; but the fact that it does not discover what still must exist, insofar as they can be discovered – that is hiding them. *She stops reading.*

RALPH: I'll have to read that.

Ashley steps into the conversation.

ASHLEY: Ralph, I'm so sorry I haven't been able to get out here; I've been in the kitchen. This is Penny, my roommate; I guess you've met.

RALPH: No problem. Yes, we've met. I've been helping her get together the books for her paper, fascinating topic.

ASHLEY: Good, well, I didn't want you to feel neglected. Actually, I have to get back to that Cuisinart; things are going fast around here. See you later.

Ashley leaves.

RALPH (*looks at watch, then to Penny*): I should be running too. I think that's going to be a great topic. I'd love to read it when you finish. We law school students need some love, I mean we don't study that type of material; we're more concerned with actions, torts – not the kind you eat, negotiable instruments and that sort of stuff.

PENNY: OK, give me a call in a week or so. I'd love to read it to you *She writes down number and hands it to Ralph.* By then I hope to have come up with something. See you later.

Scene Four:

The same as Scene Three, only the next day. Penny is by herself on the phone, talking to a friend.

PENNY (*speaking into the phone*): No, well, yes, it was really more Ashley's party, but she had to spend a lot of time in the kitchen. – I thought I would get a jump start on my paper; things seemed to be running smoothly. – Right! So he started helping me find some of the texts I needed to review. – Well at least I didn't ask him to look for the Kama Sutra! (*Ashley comes in through the door*) Here's Ash now. Talk to you later.

ASHLEY: Was that Ralph on the phone?

PENNY: You know, Ash, I think he's looking for someone, anyone, but I think you found out more about him than I did. He eats, he works out; he goes to school. He seems lonely, somewhat naïve. I told him he could read my paper when it's finished.

ASHLEY: If you do that, he'll be in your arms before the bibliography and you'll be married before graduation.

PENNY: Well, I've always wanted to marry someone with lots in common: someone who loves hummus, shops at the Co-Op, went to the same school. It's those things that lead to real intimacy, like breathing, sleeping, speaking English, being a U. S. citizen. For all I know, he might even live in an apartment.

Lights fade.

Scene Five:

The same apartment Penny is alone and working on her paper. Books are spread out and she is wearing glasses.

PENNY (*reading slowly*): "So we have seen that praising love as Agathon does in *The Symposium* still does not explain its existential power. Nor does Socrates associating it with the good, beautiful and longing for immortality explain how things get started. Although much has been written in the New Testament and in Kierkegaard's works on the love for mankind as a duty and the highest emotion we have toward others, romantic love still eludes us. Nor does romantic love seem to have any necessary moral force associated with it. We see this in the Middle Ages in cases when the knight must obtain the wife of another and the more impossible the quest, the better. What then constitutes the essence of love?"

Telephone rings. Penny picks it up.

PENNY (*speaking into phone*): Penny. Oh, yes, Ralph. That's right, we did talk about that. Well, as a matter of fact I was just been proofreading it as you called. Sure, come on over. Ashley isn't here right now. OK.

She hangs up phone.

PENNY (*continuing to read*): "Love at first sight is too common an experience to be ignored, yet we find little scientific literature on the subject.

There is something contradictory about love at first sight simply because so many of the sources we have reviewed seem to place the essence of love in the acknowledgement of the unique, almost divine personality of the loved one and the reaffirmation of that spirit or force in a relationship that ultimately joins two into one. How can love at first sight accomplish this seemingly time-consuming process unless there is some love particle, like a photon or a graviton, or a yet undiscovered massless particle that transmits more than just visible information?

"Thus we see that the extent to which we have to draw on the imagination is a measure of the mystery we are probing. If the image of the beloved from across a crowded room causes instantaneous free association then we would expect elements of the unconscious to well up into the preconscious and merge with every thought and feeling already there, building and reinforcing a catharsis in a process that might well last a lifetime. The synergism of this process when coupled with physical desire might well explain the phenomena."

Doorbell rings. Penny goes to the door. Ralph and Penny look at each other and then embrace.

Scene Six:

A typical walkup apartment in Hyde Park. Ralph and Penny, as a married couple, are more conservatively dressed. Penny is feeding a baby in a high chair. Ralph enters with a briefcase in hand as the scene opens.

PENNY: Have some hummus, dear. He's eating so much now, it's taking longer to get dinner on the table.

Ralph takes off his coat and comes over to watch the baby and Penny. He picks up a veggie and dips it into a mound of hummus on the table.

RALPH: I see what you mean.

Ralph plays with the baby during feeding.

RALPH (*to baby*): Hello there, are you happy to see me? You are, yes, you are! Oh you want to grab my thumb? But you have food all over your hands. You don't care, do you? Well, neither do I. *He puts hand out.* Oh, how strong you are! Is that fun? Oh, you're still hungry. Here, try some hummus, it's so good. You like that, do you? So do I, so do I.

Curtain.

* * *

Now that we've looked at a couple of plays the question arises "What was Play Readers really like; how did it function, i. e., how, exactly, did the whole thing work? There were multiple aspects: the dinner before the play, the producer who chose the play or plays to read and cast the parts amongst the members, and the audience reaction. All that kind of thing was rolled up in a third play, *A Meeting of the Migraine Play Readers.* We'll put that play in Appendix O and let it go at that.

Much of the background and the route by which I became associated with the Hyde Park Neighborhood Club is summarized in the book *Black Friends.* Our intent is to divide the review of that particular group into two portions; the first portion will include some of the fun we had. It includes the skills at making wooden awards, the one I learned from George Simmons, Jr., as a scout. We saw that skill being used in a Skill-O-Rama that I spearheaded in Hyde Park as a Scout Commissioner. It seems to come in handy when dealing with groups. Another fun activity was a skit that we performed at an auction fundraiser held at the Hyde Park Bank lobby. The final piece was a humor piece I wrote for entertainment at an annual meeting of the Hyde Park Neighborhood Club, a monologue that I gave during one of the four years I served as President of the club. It was patterned after the Garrison Keillor monologues on the Prairie Home Companion radio show. The first portion is excerpted below:

* * *

After residing in our town house home for eight years, I was encouraged by my wife's aunt – a Hyde Park resident since 1947 and wife of a University of Chicago Professor of Philosophy – to accept a nomination by the nominating committee of the board of directors of the HPNC for a position in its thirty-six member board. The Neighborhood Club was founded in 1909 in a storefront and it grew out of the settlement house movement in Chicago. It occupied a one story building on the south side of Nichols Park which is bounded by Kenwood and Kimbark Avenues – east and west boundaries – and 53rd and 55th streets – north and south boundaries.

During my twelve years on that board I always felt that the reputation of my wife's aunt was at stake and I applied myself assiduously to my duties. Before I was elected president of the board for four consecutive years, I was secretary and chairman of various committees such as membership and development. I made friends with the thirty-five other members of the board as well as employees and volunteers who worked for and at the club.

Through those friendships I slowly became an advocate for its programs. The by-laws stressed the goal of offering programs that would not overlap with other organizations and the club truly pursued that goal by serving the community with programs that other agencies did not offer. The Tot Lot, at this time was unique; it offered a service to many University of Chicago graduate student families. But that task of offering programs that did not duplicate others in the neighborhood was no less true of the Older Adult Day Care Center – one of the first of its kind – Golden Diners, outdoor/indoor summer programs for children of many ages, afterschool programs, and others.

Once having been elected president of the board during my seventh through tenth years, the powers that be came to the conclusion that a Capital Development campaign should be announced with a goal of millions of dollars so as to raise funds for a building campaign that included a gym and other functional spaces. A professional staff was hired, a wealthy businessman in the community was recruited to be the chief volunteer fund raiser and my chairmanship of the board of director's development committee was continued while also serving as president. The fund raising began.

There was no lack of talent involved in the campaign. One of the individuals who served under the top professional fund raiser has just been elected to chairman of the Cook County Board, easily one of the most important jobs in the Chicago area, and rose to that position after being – for many years – one of the most outstanding aldermen in the city. Another woman, the 25th district representative to the Illinois General Assembly since 1979, supported the campaign with great enthusiasm and is now Illinois' first female Majority Leader in the General Assembly.

With this kind of professional and volunteer support behind the campaign we devised numerous strategies for earning the good will of the neighborhood. Using a sequence of slides from the club's archives I developed a script for a slide show; this could be used at 'coffees' that were held in the homes of people who invited neighbors over – much like those strategies used during political contests. We sponsored a walk-a-thon and had T-shirts for all participants. This was a very public event that took walkers along the lakefront. We held auctions with high priced items in the lobby of the Hyde Park Bank; the president of that bank and another officer were on the HPNC board.

During one of those bank auction events, we put on a musical to entertain patrons. Robert Ashenhurst, a business school professor and board member wrote the original music for it as well as the script. It was called *Goodnight Irene*; Irene was the paid executive director of the Neighborhood Club. One of the catchy tunes he composed for the musical was the *Good Neighbor* song which we all sang while Bob played the piano. I can still remember some of the lines from the song:

> If you saw someone in trouble
> Somehow you'd help if you could,

It's everyone being a good neighbor
That goes with a good neighborhood.

If you had something to offer
Somehow you'd feel that you should,
It's everyone being a good neighbor
That goes with a good neighborhood.

Chorus

Toddlers all play in the tot lot,
Teenagers practice their hot shot,
Seniors also have a lot got,
There's a place in the sun
For each and every one.

As the campaign progressed, one of the wealthiest board members, a black businessman, Neil, lobbied for a very high class auction. He quoted the very large sums that were raised by other boards where he was also a board member. As board president and development committee chairman, I was also the official liaison between the development committee and the board. The development committee now consisted of community members, board members, the professional head of development, the businessman, white, who accepted the job of chief of the campaign, and the HPNC executive director, Irene.

I had to give a lot of thought to these kinds of issues and tended to agree with Neil, a fellow I liked a great deal and respected for his support of the black community. On the other hand, beginning with my first year on the board, I was aware of the inordinate amount of time and effort that was put into some of the traditional fund raising events – rummage sales, tag day solicitors, auctions, and a pancake breakfast with an accompanying plant sale. What I saw were many people involved for extended periods of time, good attendance, but very small amounts raised relative to the total yearly budget.

Neil's idea was too rich for the board to be approved – too many people felt that the club's supporters would not go for the additional commitment. Already, the annual dinner at the Quadrangle Club was an expensive affair. Taking a clue from the Good Neighbor song, we created *The Good Neighbor Award* and awarded an individual at the annual dinner. This tended to bring additional individuals and groups to the dinner to support the honored good neighbor.

We decided to start the development campaign with a kick off dinner held at the restaurant that was then on the top floor of the Hyde Park bank building. I decided to present 'awards' at that dinner even though the campaign hadn't yet officially started. I made wooden award plaques – the same way I used for the Boy Scout Skill-O-Rama plaques in 1967. The awards had humorous designations yet were appropriate to the character or efforts of the person designated as the winner of the plaque. I kept the idea completely secret and took the audience by surprise when it came my turn to speak; it was a successful part of the kick-off dinner and was a subtle way of getting things going with an upbeat atmosphere yet still alerting everyone that there was hard work ahead.

As the campaign progressed the board's objection to Neil's lobbying for a high class auction seemed to be playing out in another direction: as people gave to solicitations at campaign 'coffees' held in private homes and contributed to a walk-a-thon, regular contributions to the club's operating expenses began to lag – a budget deficit was in the making; I sensed this was my responsibility.

As mentioned, I agreed with Neil's fundamental premise: pancakes and rummage would not do the trick. Already we had capitalized on Robert Ashenhurst's Good Neighbor song by encouraging the community to help nominate and celebrate the designation of the good neighbor of the year award. I now developed a plan to attack the deficit that would also grow out of the song; I would finance the manufacture of several hundred gold and black square lapel pins. They would have the logo of the club, the letters H, P, N, and C, set in gold on a black background on a three-quarter inch square pin bordered in a gold strip that was the same width as the letters. The logo of the club which appeared on the outside wall and on the letterhead was made up of the four letters arranged as follows:

H P
N C

The logo also had the cross bar of the H extended across to the bottom part of the half circle of the P. In addition to that, the right vertical line of the H extended down to the right hand vertical line of the N. The C stood alone. None of the letters had any frills – they were all made with pure lines.

The qualification to receive one of these beautiful pins consisted in making a contribution – for a given year – of either $500 or $100 – I can't exactly remember; of course you could give more. In addition, your name would be joined with others under the rubric of 'The Good Neighbor Society.' The members of this society would be published in various printed media and, further, a brass name plate would be added to a plaque in the entryway to the club. In a subsequent year I financed another pin that was circular but used the same idea as the square pins.

Finally, to spur regular operating fund donations, I set up, at my own expense, a matching grant – from an anonymous donor – which would supplement a certain percentage of the contributions until my funds were exhausted. Many board members probably guessed where the funds were coming from but the public didn't know. I always felt that the best way to get operating fund contributions was to ask for money with no strings attached – and we did have yearly telethons to call and ask former donors to keep on giving. What I wanted to avoid were those kinds of activities that were equivalent to hundreds of hours of collecting and sorting rummage. I was right in my surmise; the pins and matching grant worked and we did not run deficits during the campaign.

My success in these events emboldened me to singlehandedly provide the entertainment for the annual dinner at the Quadrangle Club. The summary of the last year's program was always printed and handed out with the program which included the awarding of the good neighbor of the year award. There was a person who gave a short speech announcing the award winner and his or her qualifications. My part was the president's report.

No one knew what to expect; there was only the short speech to award the person chosen as good neighbor of the year. In prior years, there might have been a musical group for entertainment. When it came to the president's report I stood up and began:

'Well, it's been a quiet week in the Neighborhood Club, my home club. I think it was Monday; no it was Tuesday when Clarence Bunsen walked into the Older Adult Day Care Center and told Polly the whole thing was ridiculous. "What's ridiculous?" she asked. "The whole thing, this whole thing: day care for older adults. When I grow old, I'll just up and tell my children to take care of me. I took care of you, now it's your turn to take care of me, so here I am." "But what if your children are in Los Angeles, Clarence?"

"Why then, I'll go down there." "I see," said Polly, "well that's your choice." "That's what's wrong with this country today; too many children aren't willing to take care of their parents." "I guess you're right."

'It was Wednesday night when the rummage club came in to work over the rummage. The rummage club in my home club has become somewhat of an institution in itself. They once petitioned the University to grant a PhD in rummage. The president wrote back that she would consider a degree in the history of rummage but that the science of rummage was too complex an issue and, in any event, other universities already had such a lead that the University of Chicago didn't think they could catch up. This made the rummagers, as they call themselves, even more militant in their pursuit. You see in my club, rummage is not just a job but a way of life. When someone gets a Christmas present that doesn't fit they don't return it. "That'll make great rummage, put it in the basement." People don't stop to think that rummage means used. About fifteen years ago the rummage club distributed small magnetic signs for refrigerators and strips for the bottom of the basement door that said "Think Rummage."

'So the rummage club met to sort rummage on Wednesday evening and you could hear the usual conversation: "Beautiful blue blouse, three dollars." "Are you kidding, I saw a blouse like that at the St. Paul sale two months ago with a gravy spot that went for $3.50" "OK, four dollars." This year they nominated another member for the 'Good Rummager of the Year' award.

'Irene was sitting at her desk that morning when the phone rang. She picked up the phone; it was an irate auction person. Two years ago she had bid on a free home cooked meal, cooked in your own home for a party of ten people but had never opened the envelope to find out that the offer was good until September 1987, providing one call and arrange for a final date before May 15th. Well May 15th was a long time ago and this woman felt entitled to have someone from the club come over to her dinner party, which was next weekend, and just happened to have ten people including her aunt from Boston who liked clam chowder and another relative from the east coast who was on a salt free diet, and when would the neighborhood club send over the chef? Irene gets these kinds of calls every day. She said that the club doesn't have a chef in its employ. "Who cooks for those golden diners?" asked the woman. "Those meals are prepared by the city by an outside group." "Well, why not arrange for delivery of ten meals from that group next Saturday?" This woman was determined. "Well, that would be against the contract," said Irene. "Well, I want my money back with interest," said the woman, "money and interest or ten meals." "I can't do that either," said Irene. "Well, then I will just have to call the police." Irene could see the picture on the front page of the Hyde Park Herald: Neighborhood Club Deprives Widow of Food by Caroline Hirschman. The alderman's office reported today that the Hyde Park Neighborhood Club had deprived an elderly woman of seventy-eight years of ten meals prepared in her home for which she had paid the club in advance two years ago. Other members of the board were unavailable for comment but a club spokesperson said that the club never intentionally deprives anyone of anything and that the matter would be referred to the special events committee." OK said the woman and she hung up.

'It was Thursday night when the development committee met. Now the development committee has had a problem. It wasn't too long ago when a new board member attended his first committee meeting and asked "What are we supposed to develop?" this gentleman had hoped he could get in some weight lifting but realized when he walked in the door and people were not in swim suits that perhaps he had chosen the wrong committee. "We develop fund raising strategies – contributions," Eleanor had explained. "You mean like rummage sales?" he replied. "No, money with no strings attached – cash contributions." He had never associated cash with development. "Perhaps I'm on the wrong committee." "Well, it's too late now the committee list has been printed," said Eleanor. "We are here to develop funds not to spend them on new lists." Everyone agreed so he had kept quiet.

' "Why don't we just assess the entire neighborhood?" one woman asked at the start of the meeting. "How would that work?" "Well, we'd send bills for services rendered and if they weren't paid we turn them over to a collection agency." "Good idea, I know a great collection agency," one of the members suggested. "Aren't we missing something? Won't people be upset when we turn their account over?" "We'll get them to fill out a pledge card first – with a signature." Irene could see the headlines on the front page of the Hyde Park Herald, Neighborhood Club Assesses Common Citizens for Ostensible Services Rendered by Caroline Hirschman. The state representative's office reported today that the Neighborhood Club had fraudulently printed bills equalized across the Hyde Park Kenwood area for assessments for each single family residence. The state's attorney's office has decided to investigate. Political scientists at the University of Chicago said that the University had tried this once before, failed, and was now recommending automatic electronic funds transfer. Help was being sought from the Hyde Park Bank.

'On Friday, Irene looked out the window where a large construction truck was just squeezing its way out of the narrow driveway that was being used for delivery of material to the new building. It had jockeyed for forty minutes and was finally near its freedom but a Chevy had just pulled into the nearby space and was complicating the removal. Coming toward the club was a fire department inspector. Irene remembered the summons to show cause about the new alarm system. Something would have to be done to prevent the club from being closed down. She pondered setting off the old evacuation alarm but could see the headlines in the Hyde Park Herald, Neighborhood Club Cripples Two Older Adults in False Evacuation Alarm by Caroline Hirschman. In a ploy to sidetrack a fire inspector from the city, Neighborhood Club director Irene Smith caused a panic leading to a frantic evacuation of the club. City health inspectors are reported to be considering closing the club until further notice.

'No, wait; it was just a bill collector for food services for Head Start. This would be easy. "How are you Mr. Appleby? So nice of you to stop by. Yes, I know we are nine months behind but there's been an election, things have stopped for a while at city hall but we expect movement soon." The development committee had set up an 'in extremis' fund and she pondered using it but was afraid of the headline in the Hyde Park Herald, Herald Detects Neighborhood Club Bribe to Food Service Contractor by Caroline Hirschman. Caught red-handed with not-for-profit funds, the Neighborhood Club has been using under the table payments to keep away bill collectors from city food service agencies. A Federal investigation is hinted at by a state senator's office.

'It was time for a walk. The construction crane was just now removing the old corrugated roof. But wait! It had gone over the Park District's designated ten by thirty foot rectangle and was crushing the grass blades outside the approved strip. Irene could see the Headlines in the Hyde Park Herald, Neighborhood Club Invalidates Park District Agreement, Friends of Nichols Park Picket and Sue Club by Caroline Hirschman. Vice President Quale arrives as envoy for Bush to investigate environmental destruction; asks for directions to Nichols Park.

'No, the best thing would be to ask the crane operator to move back four inches. Irene rushed to the crane and explained the situation and then realized that it was lunch hour and the crane had been commandeered by a member of the Older Adult Day Care Center, a guy who had worked cranes some thirty years ago. "Don't worry about me, I can handle this as well as anyone," he yelled from the cab. Again, it was another headline in the Hyde Park Herald, Neighborhood Club Self Destructs Old Building by Caroline Hirschman, An unexpected runaway crane collapsed into the existing structure of the club causing extensive damage. Insurance authorities' preliminary findings indicate that coverage does not apply.

'What would tomorrow bring? She recalled that old play done in the Hyde Park Bank Lobby "Good Night! Irene." And that's the news from the club where all the women are strong, all the elderly men are good looking, and all the children are above average.'

I received a large round of applause at the end and had the satisfaction of knowing that I had provided the entertainment. It was a time when Garrison Keillor was very well known throughout the United States. What surprised me was the comment that Bob Ashenhurst made to me as we were leaving. Bob was a talented writer and musical composer for the University of Chicago Revels, a comedy musical review that was put on in the same location as the HPNC annual dinner; Bob said that "it was the best thing he had heard all year!"

The additions to the HPNC were built – not as luxuriously as originally anticipated by some, but adequate. Bob Petty, a well-known TV personality and a black friend who lived a few doors away was master of ceremonies for the dedication in the new gym. Bob is lean, tall, and good looking. He threw out the first basketball; a large audience was on hand.

It had taken some doing, machinations which do not belong to this story, but I would be remiss if I did not credit Max Jacobson, a fellow board member and chief of engineering at the Harris Bank. Without Max rolling up his sleeves and taking charge of construction issues by quickly putting to sleep the issues that revolved around how to maximize the money we did have in hand, we would never have succeeded.

* * *

The second part that speaks to my involvement in the Hyde Park Neighborhood Club is more serious. I use the term serious because it talks about an IBM teaching experience in South Africa. More to the point, it relates a short speech I gave to the board after my return from that trip. This portion of my involvement with the HPNC group is in Appendix P.

But now, as promised, we make our return to Idlewild and the subject is *watercraft* in the context of *fact* and *fiction*. You might think that the subject will include fish. Why would that be the case? If you recall that Natal's father, my great grandfather, opened the Ronneberg Canning Factory in Stavanger, Norway, the second factory of its kind, or you may remember those fiskeboller that were sent to Chicago from Norwegian relatives, or even the sardine tins with the number 246 on the bottom – bristling, as the Norwegians call them. On the strength of those recollections you would be perfectly correct to assume such things.

What you will soon see is that the *fictional* portions of the watercraft adventures do involve underwater objects in Bass Lake on the part of both craft: an iron safe that is felt to possess a treasure, and an under-the-lake monster that attacks from below! We pursue the creation of these two watercraft, a large wooden rowboat, and a single-scull wherry, to examine how that Norwegian passion, call it the *Viking* passion, did, through Norwegian genes, make its impact felt. The Viking ships were an open craft, carrying a single, square sail, multiple pairs of oars, and a broad steering oar.

How very appropriate, then, is the Bass Lake rowboat! Think of the common elements: the Bass Lake rowboat was built in 1905 – from a past era, just like the Viking ships. It was built by the Evinrude Boat Company – now no longer with us in that boat-building capacity, just like the manufacture of Viking ships. The Bass Lake rowboat was fitted with three pairs of oars – fewer than fifteen in some Viking ships but then, Bass Lake *is* smaller than the ocean. The Bass Lake rowboat was built from Mahogany – not unlike the oak of the Viking ships, just more expensive. The Bass Lake rowboat sported a single mast with a single, large, square, canvas sail that was fixed at the top with a cross-piece hoisted up to the top of the mast, and anchored at the bottom by two side-ropes, one to port and one to starboard, that kept the sail spread out. This, too, was just like the Viking vessels which were managed in an identical fashion so as to catch the wind. The Bass Lake rowboat was steered by a stern rudder, an old sailboat rudder found in the Idlewild Woodhouse, and the rudder was attached to the stern of the Bass Lake rowboat – exactly analogous to the Broad Steering Oar of a Viking ship – and both were handled by a single crew member.

The Bass Lake rowboat began its new life when it was overhauled in the Idlewild Woodhouse, a three-week effort that was performed by my twelve-year old son and yours truly. The only subtraction from the effort was the replacement of the mahogany floorboards. Here, then, is the story of the overhaul excerpted from the book *Stories of Groups*:

* * *

Sherman and his wife Dorothy felt that concentrating all their efforts on a single piece of property, Idlewild, was better than the Monopoly-like efforts of Mr. Sherman. Our focus will be on the story of the mahogany craft that Sherman saw early in his childhood at Chris Cot; it came into view through several preliminary circumstances.

Sherman's mother was hesitant to part with any property of sentimental value. She resisted offers to sell Chris Cot until a veterinarian, Dr. D., a renter who loved the lake and shared many of her values, made it clear that he would cherish the house. Sherman remembered how Dr. D. treated a pet ferret. His efforts made him an instant hero with Sherman's children. Sherman's sister and brother-in-law were given the property with Mr.

Waite's cement block shop that Sherman and his sister explored as children and which Mr. Sherman purchased from a prior owner who converted the shop into a summer home. Sherman's sister and brother-in-law tore down the cement block house and built a new year-round home on the property.

Sherman's brother-in-law, Elmer, asked Sherman's mother to have the mahogany boat from Chris Cot. He was given the craft. He turned it upside down on a low structure in the midst of bracken ferns outside his own shop where it experienced many snowy winters. Perhaps twenty years later, when Sherman's son was twelve years old, Sherman asked to have the old boat for a three-week project.

Sherman and his son completely overhauled the craft. The plan was to completely scrape and refinish the Evinrude mahogany rowboat. Sherman and his son made major decisions at the beginning. They postponed replacement of the floorboards. Because the entire stern was rotten, they replaced it with a new stern fashioned from oak boards left over from an old dining room table. Instead of laboriously removing the boat's paint, father and son scraped the exterior hull. (Sherman took the USS *Hank* (DD-702) through two shipyard overhauls in which the entire exterior of the underwater portion of the hull was sandblasted and repainted and, not owning a sandblaster, he did not want to spend years on the outside hull effort.) They left the original caulking between the planks of the hull in place. When they placed the craft in the lake in the spring, they let it soak for several days to swell so as to make the seams watertight.

Once these decisions were in place, it was easy to add several extra items to the agenda. They added a third pair of oars for the front seat, bringing the total pairs to three. To fulfill Sherman's dream of being rowed around the lake like a passenger in a Greek galley, they also added a stern rudder operated by the backseat passenger. Ultimately, Sherman added a single mast with a single square canvas sail.

With these latter additions, three to six rowers and a person manning the rudder could quickly row across the lake against the wind, hoist the square sail, and return with the wind at high speed, even creating a bow wave. In three weeks of effort, Sherman and his son transformed the beautiful family heirloom from a semi-rotting hull to an old-world craft that caught the attention of onlookers as they rowed it like Cleopatra's barge down the lakeshore and through the channel to the beach.

With his two children rowing the back two pairs of oars and his wife rowing the new, front-seat pair, Sherman stretched out on the luxurious back-seat and steered the craft with beach towels and pillows to cushion his ride. Time and again, onlookers addressed themselves to Sherman as his family rowed him in what was arguably the best-looking craft on the lake. As this watercraft, with the lines of a boat that looked like it was designed for a *Treasure Island* movie, came rushing past a pier, bystanders shouted out: "You've got the best seat!" "Nothing like putting the family to work!" "You have it made!" "That's the job I want!" Sherman wrote a poem to commemorate the reappearance of the triple-oared beauty:

> For years she lay captured by the bracken,
> Her stern rotting in despair of freedom
> And thirst for paint and water unslakened,
> Sixty years of past memories frozen.
>
> Then summer sweat of labor unthawed her,
> Restored the mahogany ravages
> Till romantic beauty, slackened painter
> And waves envied the red buoy's nearness.
>
> Now when three pairs of oars yoked her freedom
> She gave the present more than ancient form,
> The joy of family labor now our kingdom
> We rowed to the future, memory reborn.
>
> My yoke is easy and my burden light,
> Pulling over the waves pushed back the night.

A *Treasure Island* craft was an adequate comparison for more reasons than one. The mahogany craft was anchored to a red buoy just beyond the drop-off. In this position it swung around the buoy with the wind. Automobiles driving along Bass Lake Boulevard slowed down to catch sight of the newly restored beauty with its sloping stern, rudder, and classic lines. But there came to be another dimension to the notion of an island treasure, a dimension that not only would fire the imagination of scoundrels like Long John Silver but also any of the ordinary citizens of the lake who yelled friendly words of approbation as Sherman glided past their piers.

* * *

And now we move on to the *fictional* portion in our tale of the Bass Lake rowboat, the part where a treasure was spied on the bottom of Bass Lake and this part *did* begin with a fishing trip. Here is how that happened:

* * *

It all began one day when Sherman decided to test a sea anchor. Sherman always enjoyed trolling for pan fish as a child. On a day with light winds, the methodology was simple: row or motor upwind, arrive at a starting position, and do not drop the anchor. The old Jerp House plywood boat caught the wind with its broad sides and began to drift. Now, several fishing lines were put over. It seemed to the young John Sherman that this was the way to catch the largest crappies.

Years ago, Sherman's father landed a seventeen-inch crappie on a plug he had cast. When he looked it up, he said it was almost a record size catch for a silver bass, as the species was sometimes called. Sherman always trolled hoping to catch a silver bass close to seventeen inches, or even longer. A large worm or night crawler would probably do the trick as well as a plug. There was just one problem with the mahogany boat: he felt he needed to slow down the speed of drifting. So he decided to make a sea anchor.

But a sea anchor needed testing. What better way than to test it on a high-speed, drifting return from across the lake? Sherman knew that great pressure would be placed upon the sea anchor. But with some weights added at the bottom, he could lower it and keep the ring vertical. Floats would keep the top pointing up and weights would keep the ring bottom vertical. The idea was similar to the fishing nets used in Lake Michigan.

Sherman sewed a tapered canvas cone around the ring. It tapered to a small opening much like a wind sock telling pilots which way the wind is blowing. Sherman remembered the day he tested the sea anchor. Sherman and his children began by rowing across the lake against the wind. Once across the lake, they ceased rowing, hoisted the huge square canvas sail, and fastened its ends to make it act like a spinnaker. Sherman took up the tiller and steered to point where the craft could run with the brisk wind. His children sat on pillows placed on the floor to lower the center of gravity. The mahogany boat was travelling at a fast clip.

"I'm going to test the sea anchor!" Sherman yelled out.

"OK," came the reply.

Sherman threw the anchor off the stern beyond the rudder and saw it sink and then stretch out behind him. The mahogany craft slowed but was still running with the wind.

"Looks like it is working," he yelled again. "I'm going to pull it in."

"OK," came the reply.

Sherman put the tiller between his knees. As he began pulling the anchor something pulled and then he sensed an abrupt interruption. It felt like the bottom ring got caught on something. Sherman had no idea what it could be, but whatever it was, it pulled the line for the anchor out of his hands. He thought the line would snap, but luckily he attached two nylon lines to the ring bolts in the stern.

Instead of losing the sea anchor, the mahogany boat lost its forward momentum. If they were going at full speed, one of the nylon lines might have parted. In a moment, the boat was permanently anchored to something below the surface.

"I'll pull us back to whatever it is and see if I can get us free!" Sherman yelled to his son and daughter.

"OK," came the reply.

Sherman leaned over the new broad stern, the oak stern he and his son rebuilt from the old dining room table, and pulled on the lines against the force of the wind and waves until the sea anchor was below the stern.

"Man the oars and reverse-row until the anchor is free!" yelled Sherman.

"OK," came the reply from his children. They quickly fitted the oars back into their rowlocks and rowed in reverse.

For a brief moment Sherman peered down into the water, now calm, and saw an amazing sight. Rowing in reverse managed to release the bottom portion of the sea anchor's ring. He quickly hauled this piece back into the boat. This went exactly as he hoped. What he didn't expect to see was the obstruction catching the bottom part of the sea anchor ring.

In an instant, before the seaweed returned to cover the object, Sherman saw what looked like the L-shaped handle of the kind of metal safe in which a small business keeps its cash. This was confirmed by a combination lock adjacent to the handle.

In a way, it made perfect sense: only something with the weight of an iron safe and possessing a strong handle could stop a speeding and very heavy craft with so much momentum. On the other hand, it made no sense at all. Who would go to the trouble of rowing out a perfectly good, very heavy thing like a safe, just to dispose of it when the safe would be worth something even if it was empty, at least for the scrap metal?

As he hauled up the sea anchor and his children took in their oars, Sherman grabbed the tiller once more. Only this time, he gathered mental bearings to objects along the shoreline that marked their starting position. It was not like having a pelorus with its calibrated compass ring similar to the ones used on a destroyer, but it was better than nothing and, with luck, he might find their exact location again.

As they returned to full speed, Sherman felt even more exhilarated than when he threw over the sea anchor and watched the mahogany craft slow down. Handling a fouled anchor was an important element of seamanship for every sailing ship. He performed the test well: the anchor was safely aboard.

But other connotations came to mind from the incident. Since the defeat of the Spanish Armada in 1588, a fouled anchor was the seal of the Lord High Admiral of Britain, a position presently occupied by Her Majesty, Queen Elizabeth II. As they struck down the sail, stowed the oars, sea anchor, mast, and sail into the canoe for return to the boathouse, Sherman could not help but wonder if his seamanship would now make him as rich as the Queen.

* * *

The question of how Norwegian influences from the past affect actions in the present times, remains active throughout our pursuits. In our case, that old saying about the fruit not falling far from the tree is implicit when we recall that we began with the notion that, for a Norwegian Spruce, the layering phenomena of nurturing goes one step further: nurturing occurs while still attached – externally – to the parent plant and only later, is a break made and a new plant produced. We will pursue this analogy once again as we examine the next watercraft: a

Wherry. In one sense, the analysis is complex because of the presence, as previously alluded to, of a monster occupying the, so to speak, second half of our tale, the *fictional* portion.

It is always a good idea when beginning a new tack, to explore the genesis of the object under discussion; thus it is that we seek to locate what Norwegian associations resonate with the building of this particular Wherry and then, later, explore why the choice of a monster attack against a Wherry and its occupant – innocently rowing around Bass Lake – could have anything to do with Norway. These *are* deep waters – no pun intended. Like any scientific study, it helps to document the growth of the analysis.

After considerable thought, then, it was felt, due to the complexity of the issues, to address the two issues through two, separate, answers. First, we examine the Wherry, i.e., where did it come from, how was it built, how was it used, and what were the motives – both before and after the sixty hours of effort that it took to construct it by hand? The excerpt wherein we pursue these questions is all *factual*. The second portion, the monster portion, then, is the *fictional* piece.

We preface these two sections with a reminder. As with so many of these prior fictional diversions, we remind you, our blessed readers, that, yes, there *are* excerpts that tie in to our overall strategy of examining the consequences of that admonition 'Don't be a Norwegian all your life!' But within those *fictional* excerpts, there is one thing we have never done, and that is, resort to *supernatural* explanations of the fictional events. There always is, albeit it is in "The rest of the story" a purely logical answer to those cliff-hanging scenes that have been, heretofore, variously employed to make some kind of point in the plot. This rule is no less true with respect to the underwater Monster that attacks the Wherry; there is no need to imagine the impossible nor even wonder why such an abrupt path was taken.

Returning, then, to the *facts*, the first part of the Wherry story. By looking at the first excerpt, a superficial set of ideas come to mind: the object is principally made from Honduras mahogany, the same material as the Evinrude Rowboat from 1905, only much, much thinner. The term superficial is used because the material, mahogany, has nothing to do with Norway. In fact, the argument is just as silly as trying to connect up an old, 1905 Rowboat with an older, Viking vessel! We know, or will know, shortly, that the sixty hours of work effort it took to construct the Wherry from a kit, was done quite recently, in point of time; the kit was put together by a business still in existence in Bellingham, Washington.

Another false start is brought to light when we realize that the Wherry is made from expensive, virtually indestructible, materials: expensive varnish applied over epoxy coated mahogany on the inside, the finest white, marine paint applied over epoxy coated mahogany on the outside, and bronze rivets wherever needed. Any attempt to make some kind of connection with those well-preserved Viking vessels dug up in Norway, might be tried but, that, too, is a blind alley. The Norwegian Vikings had no idea that their vessels, now in museums, would last that long; archeological preservation, when examined, is accidental. And it is not clear at all that, at the time of the Vikings, the Norwegians were interested in single-scull rowing craft either to build muscle – in the fashion of a work-out – or to engage in individual competitions for rowing as with the Olympic or even the Pan American games. Of course, it is true that a Viking ship could get up to ten knots, but that was with sail and thirty rowers; we're talking about a single pair of sculls and no sail!

So where does that leave us? I think we can link the drive to build and row a Wherry to two Norwegian cultural interests: craftsmanship and beauty. Under the concern for beauty we include the surrounding beauty of Bass Lake – as noted in the excerpt. Both these notions have to be experienced; one has to visit a Viking ship and marvel at the craftsmanship, the lines of the craft with its curving bow, sail, and stern. A visitor must see the carvings incorporated into the Viking wood, which brings out the conjunction of craftsmanship and beauty at the micro-level of observation, in addition to the macro-level.

As for the Bass Lake Wherry, all that can be offered is our first excerpt from the book *Stories of Identity* in the first part of the first chapter in a story called *Where We Walk to School Each Day*. So here it is:

* * *

John Sherman bent forward at the waist and drew the sliding seat of his single-seat wherry closer to the flat stern of that craft by bending his knees. With his arms fully extended and his knees drawn up to his chest, he was now in a position to apply power to the beautiful pair of wooden sculls that would propel the craft forward over the mirror-like surface of the lake.

Like so many actions in life, the next sequence was by now automatic. First came the counter-clockwise twist of the wrists, the left hand above the right hand. The twist would place the two curved blades at the end of the sculls in a position perpendicular to the surface of the water, where, with a quick lowering from their already extended position toward the bow of the wherry, they would be ready to bite into the lake's surface in preparation for the pull of the sculls forward. Following this, the back would be straightened, the arms drawn inward, and then the legs extended, the latter movement moving the sliding seat toward the bow as it rolled along the metal runners of an Oarmaster rigging made of anodized aluminum and stainless steel and snapped into the bottom of the wherry.

It was hard to rank which element of pleasure dominated one's sensibilities in this effort of propulsion, there were just too many of them all present at the same time. Not the least of these was the beauty of the craft itself. The interior of the wherry was an uninterrupted surface of five-thirty-seconds-inch-thick Honduras mahogany marine plywood that was varnished with the most expensive varnish John could buy. The slim form of the craft, pointed at the bow, was a sight to behold from the shore as it cut the water like a knife. The pure white outer finish was applied from a can of the finest marine enamel available. It went without saying that both of these surfaces, inside and outside, were impervious to the ultraviolet rays of the sun.

One could look at the laminated gunwales to remind oneself of the painstaking effort that was expended in building the craft by hand. A three-sixteenths-of-an-inch thick strip of white basswood was laminated between the two mahogany pieces of the gunwales. All three of these pieces were formed to the shape of the tapering hull. The outside edge was rounded and then, with proper tapering, the three pieces were joined at the bow in a sharp point, altogether making for an example of exquisite beauty and old-world craftsmanship that was enhanced by the silicone bronze fasteners that attached the gunwales to the mahogany plywood's upper edges of the wherry. The entire wherry was a never-ending source of aesthetic pleasure to Sherman, who labored for sixty hours during a hot summer, so as to guarantee that the craft would be a joy to look at.

The mahogany from Honduras was shipped to Israel where three-ply Okoume marine plywood, four millimeters thick, was manufactured to make the five-thirty-seconds-inch-thick plywood that formed the hull. From the Middle East, the plywood traveled to Bellingham, Washington, where it was laser-cut to multiple pieces that formed the bottom and sides of the hull. By coating every single piece of the hull with epoxy before construction started, the resulting product was entirely waterproof and virtually impervious to the effects of aging, it could literally be buried in the ground and then dug up decades later. If so, only the varnish and paint would be ruined, the wood itself would still be protected from rotting.

At the start of construction, the pieces were wired to each other so as to form the sides of the craft. The bottom and sides were then bonded to each other with epoxy and fiberglass tape.

Temporary plywood framers facilitated the shaping of the hull. These were like the internal framing pieces in the old balsa wood model airplanes of John's childhood, which, gradually growing smaller toward the tail of the aircraft, were responsible for shaping the fuselage. On the outside of the wherry, epoxy and fiberglass tape were again used to strengthen the seams and then to finish the outside joints to a smooth and seamless hull that left no evidence of how the craft was constructed. From Washington

State to Michigan, a large oblong box was shipped with all the various pieces packed with care between layers of plastic foam. On top of the pieces
rested a large comprehensive assembly manual of instructions.

The result of Sherman's earlier efforts in making the wherry was a
watercraft that he could easily lift; the hull was forty pounds, as light as a
feather. The hull design also made the wherry as strong as iron. It could
be rowed in waves of considerable size without the bad effects that were experienced in choppy water by the collegiate single shells that were rowed in
competitions. With a typical load of 232 pounds (including a twenty-three
pound Oarmaster unit), the wherry was a mere twenty-seven inches at the
waterline, compared to thirty-eight inches at the gunwale.

John learned the sequence of movements that best propelled the craft
forward. As previously outlined, the rower would bend the back from the
forward bent position. Next, the rower pulled his arms toward his body, and
finally extended his legs to their full length from their anchored position in
the front of the metal frame where John's running shoes were held in place
by Velcro straps. This sequence propelled the craft perhaps twenty feet and
initiated a glide that continued the forward motion during the time that the
recovery motion was in progress: the lifting of the sculls, the feathering of
the sculls (making the blades at the end of the sculls horizontal to avoid the
ill effects of the wind), and the return of the sculls to their bow position. All
this was accompanied by the undoing of the rower's three earlier efforts, ending with his back being bent toward the stern, his legs bent (returning the
sliding seat to the stern), and his arms, once again extended forward.

The aesthetic effects of the rower's labors were now conjoined with
their more immediate counterparts. In addition to the aerobic effects of
the exercise, arms and legs were exercised, as well as the back and the
muscles of the stomach and wrists; some claimed that every muscle in the
body was exercised. Instead of seeing the inside of athletic facilities like
the gyms and health clubs he was forced to use during the winter months,
Sherman felt the glorious beauty of nature accompanying him as he progressed across the glassy surface of the lake.

In the early morning, the sunrise in the sky competed with its reflection on the water. Sherman could never determine which version of the sky he liked best, for each often presented a kaleidoscope of fiery red, purple and orange clouds set against the dark green of the trees that grew at the shoreline, and both these versions were pierced by the blue of the sky and the white of clouds that somehow had not been painted by the rising sun.

Ducks and white swans competed with jumping bass for attention while, along the shoreline, the pink of hairy willow herb, jewelweed, and the fragrance of white water lilies vied with the red-winged blackbirds and the antics of kingbirds, as they acrobatically went after early morning insects.

Sherman knew that kingbirds wintered in almost every country in South America, as far south as northern Argentina (below twenty-five degrees south latitude), immigrating through Central America and the West Indies before arriving at their breeding grounds, which ranged from the southern tip of Florida to the southern portions of Yukon Territory, Canada (above sixty degrees north latitude). He wondered if they rested during that migration in Honduras near where the plywood of his wherry was harvested. Despite the kingbirds antics and Herculean distances, it was the great blue heron that always seemed to dominate, stealing attention as it froze in the shallow water of the shoreline, and elegantly pausing until the wherry passed on.

Even if one deferred his exercise to a time later in the day, when nature might be said to be more disturbed, John could not but feel that the wherry itself made a statement. It was not a noisy, gas-guzzling, and polluting power-boat, pulling water-skiing, fun-loving, and noisy vacationers across and around the lake. Instead it was a unique and quiet statement of beauty, undisturbing to nature, almost a part of nature in that it blended in with the natural surroundings; the blue herons did not fly away from it but seemed to watch it instead.

The wherry resulted from one's own manual skill and effort. Its coming into being reflected values like patience, persistence, and aesthetic sensibilities. These, in turn, were linked with the ethic of exercise, the cultivation of health and well-being, both physical and mental that somehow seemed to eschew the gaudy consumerism of the age and instead embrace old-world values of tranquility and peace that harkened back to Longfellow:

> The world is too much with us; late and soon,
> Getting and spending, we lay waste our powers:
> Little we see in Nature that is ours;
> We have given our hearts away, a sordid boon!

But John *was* grateful for the control of the old-world weeds, curly leaf pondweed and Eurasian water milfoil. Without the lake management program that was now in full effect, the ease with which the sleek wherry cut the water would be interrupted by weeds that reached to the surface of the lake.

* * *

Many readers who have been following these excursions/excerpts might be prone to say that the nature of our pursuit seems tenuous. The time has arrived where what is called for is that earlier ploy, a digression involving a fictional author and a reader. Well, OK.

* * *

Being a Further Conversation Between
A Fictional Author and A Reader

"I don't quite understand where we are and where we are going," began the Reader.

"How is that?"

"We started with that rowboat thing, you know, the reconditioned Evinrude/Viking vessel, and, yes, there was some kind of inadvertent, for lack of a better term, 'resonance with the Norwegians,'" said the Reader.

"I can imagine some kind of connection forged in those eighty-five billion brain cells, each with their ten thousand connections, as responsible for the connection; after all, the science of the brain is still in its infancy."

"OK," agreed the Author.

"But now, we seem to be on a different tack," said the Reader, "and I don't mean a sailboat tack."

"Yes, a different tack, and it is different."

"Let me see if I understand this. We are going to encounter a monster: the monster hasn't anything to do with Science Fiction; it's going to attack the Wherry and there's going to be some kind of further, Norwegian connection."

"I heard the same thing," said the Author.

"I suppose the connection, like the Viking ship/rowboat analogy, could go back many centuries?"

"It could, but it's hard to imagine the Norwegians making watercraft that looked like single-scull, sliding-seat Wherries," agreed the Writer.

"That's part of it, but the other part is that the rowboat was real, you could touch it and feel it – and the office safe was real, even if its presence on the bottom of Bass Lake was inexplicable. Now what we have is a fictional monster that we're to believe is every bit as real – I suppose it has claws – and it seems like things are getting out of control; I have to use suspended judgment across two realms of disbelief!"

"As I understand it," began the Author, "We're not going to completely understand the monster unless we read the story where it is described. It's called *Red and Green*. If I'm not mistaken the monster story is a continuation of the tale that began with John Sherman the day after the incident with the lucky shot that caused his Hummingbird feeder to fall to the ground."

"Yes, I remember, Sherman grabs a neighbor's canoe and takes off for Devil's Pond," said the Reader.

"And we have no idea what that first part is all about; somehow, at the last minute, a noisy paraglider picks up the fugitive and that's the end for us," said the Author.

"So you're saying it's the same guy?"

"I have no idea. These two events could be completely random, and unconnected; I can't imagine any connection, they seem bizarre! If they keep on going, I would be more convinced that some disarranged person has some kind of grudge against Sherman but Sherman, himself, can't figure out what is happening, so my hunch is as remote a possibility as any other guess," said the Writer.

"OK, OK, We'll give this the benefit of the doubt."

* * *

It is appropriate that we immediately excerpt this Bass Lake encounter with a monster, before any kind of Norwegian/analysis/conclusion-drawing takes place, one way or another.

* * *

Sherman was as perplexed as ever the next day when he decided on two things. The first was not to report the incident – what further information would the sheriff's office have beyond what he already knew? It would just be a waste of taxpayer money. If a license plate had been taken down, maybe some further clue could be had but renting a powered paraglider was as routine an activity as the day is long. The second was to row his wherry around the lake, in case something came up.

Sherman lost himself in the rhythm of his single sliding-seat rower, stopping only after two hundred pulls of the sculls to take a drink of Gatorade from his Stanford University red plastic exercise drink bottle. He calculated later that it was on his third stop that the incident happened. He was off the entrance to Quinn creek on the opposite side of the lake from his own home, Idlewild. He always kept beyond the drop-off in deep water and let the sculls drift in their sockets in the Oarmaster unit while he refreshed himself with Gatorade. He was pressing the top back on his red Gatorade bottle, when what could only be described as a sea monster reached up out of the lake with two large green scaly arms and grabbed the right-hand scull.

In a moment, Sherman realized the monster, or whatever it was below the surface, was grabbing the scull with the intent of overturning the wherry. Perhaps the creature wanted to steal the craft, as it was easily the most desirable watercraft on the lake; it took sixty hours to build and was solid mahogany with laminated gunwales, yet it only weighed forty pounds. Alternatively, the monster could be the same person as yesterday's gunman, returning now in the disguise of an undersea creature to make a direct threat, a reminder not to pursue any further the Devil's Pond incident of the prior day.

No matter what the reason, vengeance now coupled with the drive to defend his prized possession rose within Sherman. He still had control of the left scull, and by using both hands and by striking with full force, he could launch a counter attack to the frantic efforts of the undersea creature. Sherman pulled back the scull, dug the blade deep into the lake, and gave it all the force he could muster. The wherry began a strong turn in response to this effort, and the green arms seemed caught unawares. The creature had all it could do just to hang on.

Sherman thought of detaching the left scull and using it to clobber the claws grasping the blade of the right scull. The problem would be that the creature might grab both sculls and pull one from Sherman's own grasp. The Oarmaster unit would keep the right scull from being taken simply because it would have to be carefully removed from that unit; in effect it was locked in place with the usual embrace between the Oarmaster unit and the wooden scull.

Instead, Sherman decided to reverse the thrust of the scull. He flipped it one hundred eighty degrees in the brass holder at the end of the Oarmaster, and then dipped the scull into the water at the stern and pushed the scull in reverse. Now, the wherry turned sharply in the opposite direction and it looked like he would throw off the monster.

Soon after, Sherman was giving two strong pulls in one direction, then flipping the scull and pushing back for two more pushes; it was like the zigzag course he had followed during antisubmarine maneuvers in the Navy, where all destroyers in the screen inserted the same plastic zigzag cam into the mechanism that directed the helmsman's steering. With the wherry, Sherman was giving a random amount of effort for each set of pulls. He reasoned that this would allow the intelligent force under the lake no idea of how best to achieve its own ends of upsetting the wherry and that it would soon tire.

Sherman continued the random zigzag pattern and it was working. He was giving the sea monster a run for the money; it was all it could do to keep its green arms attached to the right scull. Finally, with one long and hard pull, Sherman saw the arms let go and fall below the surface of the lake. He quickly regained use of the right-hand scull and recommenced his rowing; there was no time for a Gatorade break, no matter how much his electrolytes needed replenishment.

Sherman's plan now was to regain the pier, grab a pair of his best Zeiss birding binoculars, and scan the lake to discover the monster surfacing. He felt free from the sea monster's upsetting efforts to steal one scull, to swamp the contents of the wherry, and to make off with his craft. Toward that end, he gave the sculls as much power as he could, imagining he was rowing at the Pan-American Games for the USA, or better still, at the Summer Olympics. There remained only one problem; no matter how hard he rowed, he knew he was not going as fast as he should be. He liked to think he could put the wherry into hyperdrive at will, but now another will seemed to be at play.

This suspicion was reinforced by air bubbles rising and breaking the surface just beyond the middle of the wherry, below the right arm of the Oarmaster unit. There was no doubt about it, the creature had attached itself to the bottom of the craft, perhaps using a lamprey-like sucker, and was riding the underside as a freeloader, just waiting to resume its prior attack!

This was no different than a submarine riding in the wake of a destroyer where sonar could not pick up the contact. What Sherman needed now was a two-ship attack, a brother-sister attack, with the brother destroyer making the attack, using depth charges or hedgehogs, while the sister destroyer maintained sonar contact with the sub from a distance. Sherman was the radiotelephone operator on the bridge during antisubmarine exercises in the Mediterranean. He wanted to get more training and the radiotelephone exchanges were both fast and exciting. Using two-character code words, the ship controlling the attack would announce, without need for a reply: "I am brother, you are sister, one three zero, three zero zero, twenty."

In such a communication, Sherman would make his own ship the attacker, assign a listening role to the companion destroyer, and then give the bearing, range, and speed of the contact. But there was no companion wherry on the lake! Sherman would have to handle the attack on his own.

He needed to devise a new tactic and implement it with the same instantaneous effect of a brother-sister destroyer team. He decided to pull up both sculls; that would give the green-armed sea creature the option of grabbing either the Oarmaster unit or the wherry itself. As soon as it extended an arm toward either of these, Sherman would strike out at it using a scull as a club. The strategy was to send the thing, now wounded from the scull, to the bottom of the lake to nurse its pain; he would try to use the thin blade of the scull like a knife.

The wherry slowed to all but a halt, underway with no way on, as Navy jargon would have expressed it, and Sherman saw the sea creature's bubbles going out to the tip of the Oarmaster unit. Then, all of a sudden, the arms reached out of the lake and up, grabbing the end where the brass oarlock, or scull lock, was fastened. But Sherman was ready; he saw the bubbles and knew what was coming. No sooner had the creature's fingers grabbed the metal arm and brought it down, in an effort to swamp the wherry using the full leverage of its body, than Sherman struck back with a blow soft enough not to hurt the beautiful scull but fierce enough to injure the wrists of the monster. Sherman could feel the blade hit the monster's soft wrist, where scales and bone were probably strongest, and then felt elation when the creature gave up its hold.

But Sherman was now helpless should the monster attack more directly, lunging out of the water and grabbing the gunwales on either side of the wherry, or even the small, flat sternpiece, about seven inches wide. In this way, an upsetting motion could occur without any warning and it would be awkward to use a scull, if only because it would have to be positioned for a blow and there just might not be enough time for that.

And then the monster came. Before Sherman could think through any defensive strategy, two claws grabbed the right front gunwale and tipped the wherry, flooding it, and throwing Sherman into the water.

Somehow his feet came out of the Velcro straps at the back of the sliding-seat Oarmaster unit. He knew that the unit was locked to the bottom of the wherry and would not be lost. As he surfaced, he also remembered that the sculls would float. He had never exposed the inside of the wherry to lake water and this desecration raised his ire once again. Now the wherry replaced the hummingbird feeder as the catalyst for his vengeful desires, even though the feeder was old, jury-rigged, and had been repaired to last many lives while the wherry was new, painted, and coated with epoxy so as to last for decades under any condition.

Nonetheless Sherman grabbed a scull, mounted the overturned wherry, and began paddling toward the shore. He soon saw a line of bubbles approaching, coming right at him like a torpedo wake, and he took evasive action. He paddled the wherry so that the sharp point of the bow, a mahogany point, directly faced the advancing line of bubbles. He speeded up. Ramming was always a good offense. He knew that the Oarmaster unit's arms now extended underwater, arms of steel to port and to starboard, ready to hang up a perhaps oblivious sea creature.

And it was the sea creature's ignorance that brought Sherman safely home. The creature avoided the pointed bow but was soon caught in the starboard Oarmaster extension. Now there was enough time to wield the scull down toward the aggressor and keep the creature from again using the leverage of the Oarmaster arm to roll the craft over, throw Sherman back in the water, and equalize the odds between them.

Again and again, Sherman felt the blade taking effect on the body of the beast. He was thinking of reversing the scull and using the heavy, grip-end of his weapon for greater effect, when suddenly the monster fell away. Sherman saw the bubbles disappearing; the attack was defeated. Now the plan would be to right the wherry, retrieve the other scull, store everything away, and then scan the lake for the possible emergence of a green creature.

Back ashore, no sooner than his precious wherry was safe in its sling, wiped dry with a towel, cleaned and put away with the Oarmaster unit and sculls, Sherman returned to the end of the pier to scan the lake. He was glad he acted so fast. In his first sweep with the Zeiss binoculars, he saw the scaly green back of a large gorilla-like object emerge from under the shallow water at the estuary of Quinn Creek, directly across the lake from the pier. He would have to paddle fast, but perhaps it had a lair in the forest between the lake and old Route 31, Père Marquette Highway. There was no time to explain to Dorothy why he needed more exercise after rowing around the lake, let alone why he was seeking any more adventures on a day that already had its share.

* * *

In relating the search for Norwegian influences with respect to the question *why a fictional monster* we need to take a broader perspective. What would have been the result of never having heard those words *Don't be a Norwegian all your life?* Is the dilemma introduced into a child's mind more important than whether or not that child can actually adopt the country of his or her grandparents? Mother often mentioned a Norwegian benefit that accrued to my older sister. What was that about?

There was some kind of Norwegian-based social welfare benefit that could be claimed by my sister; the benefit didn't extend to males, nor did one have to live in Norway; the only requirement was to be a female descendent of an honest-to-goodness Norwegian. Presumably, taking advantage of the program required residence in Norway – a kind of second-generation reverse migration. Although asserted as gospel truth to us as children, it was, in its way, every bit as perplexing as the caveat about continuing to be a Norwegian the rest of your life. Residence would have required a language capability even though most Norwegians now speak English. Proof of the sincerity of the benefit seemed, for a child, to be close at hand. Why so?

A frequent visitor to our home at 7240 West Pratt Avenue was a woman we all referred to as 'Aunt Cora.' Aunt Cora, a relative, lived nearby in the adjacent community from our own, Norwood Park. After learning to drive I could pick up Aunt Cora for a Christmas dinner, or any gathering, for that matter. The designation of her residence became my version of where I would end up if anyone asked me where older Norwegians ended up; Aunt Cora lived in the Norwood Park Norwegian Old People's Home. Even at a much later age when making a point about the future, I would, on occasion, draw upon this institution for certain effects that made my point.

This digression suggests that a healthier form of reflection arose due to the earlier warning not to be a Norwegian that far into the future. That earlier admonition triggered a search for meaning. There was, too, a kind of ritual *search for meaning* that was a template for searching for Norwegian meaning. This process, and it was more a process than a ritual, was put into motion whenever a letter arrived from a Norwegian relative.

Despite the modern-day English language proficiency of Norwegians – exhibited by an IBM Norwegian, a young woman, in one of my European classes, and her sharing with me that she knew of a genuine *Norwegian Ronneberg* employed by IBM Norway – during childhood the letters from relatives in Norway were all written in Norwegian. Mother became aware of the letter after the postman dropped it off, but she could not understand its content. Father, upon returning home from the office, could not understand the contents either! I grew up in a family where it took two to tango. Mother read and pronounced the words of the epistle, and father, hearing the words, understood what was being said! Call it cooperative translation. The process certainly makes clear that it was the oral understanding and use that father returned with when that long visit was made to Norway and he was demoted back to kindergarten!

The search for some kind of monster antecedent is just as bizarre as needing two people to understand a letter; there just had to be a connection. I began with *Beowulf*, a monster tale, if ever there was one, from sometime between the middle of the seventh and the end of the tenth century of the first millennium. *Beowulf* hails from the land of the Geats, or what today is known as Southern Sweden. What does *Beowulf* have to do with anything Norwegian? Hang in there! In the poem called *Beowulf* he sails over to the land of the Danes to help them get rid of a man-eating monster called Grendel and, I should add, Grendel's mother. Again you ask, what do the Danes have to do with Norway?

The answer is that the Danes have a lot to do with Norway. It just so happens that for four hundred years Denmark and Norway were united. I felt I was on my way to establishing the connection I was looking for.

Grendel had *savage talons*, Beowulf, when fighting Grendel's mother comes to rely on the *might of his arm*. At another point when Beowulf locates a sword in Grendel's mother's armory and uses it to bite *deep into her neck-bone*, I of course pictured John Sherman using his scull to cut deep into the Bass Lake monster:

"He decided to pull up both sculls; that would give the green-armed sea creature the option of grabbing either the Oarmaster unit or the wherry itself. As soon as it extended an arm toward either of these, Sherman would strike out at it using a scull as a club. The strategy was to send the thing wounded from the scull, to the bottom of the lake to nurse its pain; he would try to use the thin blade of the scull like a knife." – "Then, all of a sudden, the arms reached out of the lake and up, grabbing the end where the brass oarlock, or scull lock, was fastened. But Sherman was ready; he saw the bubbles and knew what was coming. No sooner had the creature's fingers grabbed the metal arm and brought it down, in an effort to swamp the wherry using the full leverage of its body, than Sherman struck back with a blow soft enough not to hurt the beautiful scull but fierce enough to injure the wrists of the monster. Sherman could feel the blade hit the monster's soft wrist, where scales and bone were probably strongest, and then felt elation when the creature gave up its hold."

These revelations were encouraging but I sought more evidence. Now let me emphasize that this kind of correlation pursuit after a Norwegian dragon, was entirely new; I never even dreamed about such things! Imagine my surprise when I came to know more. Picture this situation: you are searching for a connection between this fictional monster and you come upon a creature of Scandinavian Folklore with the following characteristics: it dwells in *fresh* water, it is a spirit that is *dangerous* and *clever*; it is known to lure victims in leaky boats (read: easily tipped, light weight Wherries) so as to draw them down to the *bottom of the water*, and, this is very important, this creature is a *shapeshifter*, he changes into a *man* to lure his victims to him:

"Back ashore, no sooner than his precious wherry was safe in its sling, wiped dry with a towel, cleaned and put away with the Oarmaster unit and sculls, Sherman returned to the end of the pier to scan the lake. He was glad he acted so fast. In his first sweep with the Zeiss binoculars, he saw the scaly green back of a large gorilla-like object emerge from under the shallow water at the estuary of Quinn Creek, directly across the lake from the pier. He would have to paddle fast, but perhaps it had a lair in the forest between the lake and old Route 31, Père Marquette Highway. There was no time to explain to Dorothy why he needed more exercise after rowing around the lake, let alone why he was seeking any more adventures on a day that already had its share." Q. E. D.

Mathematicians add Q. E. D. as a final flourish to their proofs calling everyone's attention to what has come before – it is done, I have shown you that *which was to be demonstrated or proved*! And oh, by the way, the water creature is a NØKK, and yes, John Sherman *is* lured into Quinn Creek!

* * *

And so, I presume, that Erling Berg, my father's employee, the one-armed worker that helped build Jerp House, saw the value of challenging his employer's son with the task of trying to understand "Don't be a Norwegian all your life." as, hopefully, the beginning of a child's introspection from which would arise a humility for what we have been given, a touchstone in the sense of a test of the genuineness of our humanity.

Appendix A

Fire by Friction

Note: in this appendix I refer to myself as John Sherman.

John Sherman was paying attention to his adult leader with more than the usual amount of enthusiasm. The Norwood-Edison Scout Leaders Association was sponsoring a fall competition held in the Norwood Park Field House gym. Prizes would be awarded for individual efforts – like, fire-by-flint-and-steel – and team events – like, the life-line rescue and knot-tying relay. Troops would receive awards based on total points accumulated in all events, but perhaps, and most importantly, he knew that Mr. George Simmons, Jr., his own leader, and his father, Mr. George Simmons, Sr., had always been active leaders in this local organization, and it behooved Sherman to carry on the efforts of Troop 849 as it entered its 25th year of continuous operation. It produced many notable graduates, and Sherman felt he owed it to the men and their predecessors who invested so much time and effort in developing the skills of people like Sherman, even though he was only twelve years old.

One of the more difficult individual events that needed a volunteer to compete for Sherman's troop was the fire-by-friction competition. When indoors and working on a large piece of cardboard placed on top of the wooden gym floor, the objective was to rub two pieces of wood together in such a way as to produce a glowing coal, and then nurse that coal, together with adjacent tinder, into a flame. The first contestant to produce a flame took first place, and three plaques would be awarded for 1st, 2nd, and 3rd place individuals as judged by a team of adult judges.

Sherman never studied this skill in any depth before he volunteered. He was aware that it was mentioned as a possible elective requirement for the camping merit badge. He also knew that in outdoor competitions, the range of skills were broadened by adding the requirement to use the flame to ignite a fire – the sticks for which were built up from scratch ahead of time – that would burn a piece of grocery-store string stretched between two stakes at a height of eighteen inches above the ground. In this outdoor variation, each contestant was provided with a fourteen inch piece of two-by-four wood from a lumber yard, and was allowed to use an axe and knife to prepare kindling from that piece.

Still another outdoor variation did away altogether with the need to burn a string. Instead, the fire was used to cook a pancake. Once browned on both sides, it was necessary to run with the frying pan to a point fifty feet away where a clothesline was stretched between two poles. To win, it was necessary to run to the clothesline, flip the pancake over the line, catch it in the frying pan on the other side of the line, and then return to the fire.

Sherman asked his father to purchase a standard fire-by-friction kit from the Scouting store in the Loop; the kit came with a set of instructions. The kit served as an introduction to the basic elements of the methodology that Sherman felt was the most propitious path for obtaining a flame. It contained a bow, a piece of flexible wood with a handle at one end. When a leather thong was attached through holes at the top of the bow and just above the handle, and further, when simple knots were placed in the thong so as to allow for five and a half inches of slack on the bow side, one envisioned how a spindle was captured by the slack portion of the thong.

The bow, like the bow in a bow and arrow bow, would bend in the same fashion, and the thong would become taught just like an archery bow. The spindle, (which in this way caused the thong to tighten), was unlike an arrow; nor was the power of the bow, once the spindle was captured, transferred to the spindle in the same fashion as an arrow. In the first place, the spindle was an octagonal piece of soft wood with eight flat sides, fourteen inches in height, and just over an inch thick.

In the second place, to conjoin the slack of the thong around the middle of the spindle, one placed the spindle in the middle of the leather thong and then rotated it one hundred and eighty degrees, a half circle, until the thong went around the spindle just once. In earlier times, on sailing ships, this would be called, taking a single turn.

The ultimate destiny of the spindle, after the top and bottom ends had been whittled into points, was to have these pointed ends placed into two very different pieces of wood. The top piece, a handheld piece of wood, was small and could easily be held in the grip of the left hand, if you were right-handed. The top portion was curved so as to lie comfortably in the grip of the left hand, and the piece was less than two inches wide, only three inches long, and only an inch and a half deep.

In the bottom of this rounded-on-the-top-hand-held piece there was a half inch diameter hole drilled to a depth of one half inch. In the bottom of this hole was a piece of metal and the top of the spindle, which was vertical when driven to spin by the back and forth horizontal sawing motion of the bow driven by the right hand, spun against this metal and never changed either the width of the hole or its depth.

The bottom anchor plate for the spindle was an altogether different piece of wood from the top piece. In size, it was about a foot long, from two to three inches wide and about three-quarters of an inch thick. Each anchor plate had carved into it multiple anchor points, one of which was used to accept the bottom, pointed end of the spindle. The design and carving of a single anchor point will be described shortly.

The anchor plate was placed upon a wad of tinder, usually very fine like the lining of a bird's nest; it was a very dry set of fine fibers made from the strands of the inner bark of a tree that was pulverized to create what might be described as a pad of steel wool, the obvious exception being that it was organic material. The material was called tinder because it was highly flammable if touched with an ordinary sulfur match, more of that aspect later.

The anchor plate was made of soft wood, much like the spindle itself, because, like the spindle, it was intended to create a compact nugget of hot, black, wood powder when the spindle and anchor plate disintegrated under the pressure that was applied vertically from above, by the left hand pressing down on the top piece, and the intense heat of the friction generated by the spindle's rotation in one of the anchor points.

Before describing an anchor point, it is well to note that the anchor plate was held in place by the left foot pressing down upon the anchor plate and the vertical pressure from above, transmitted through the top piece by pressure from the left-hand grip of that piece. To facilitate this vertical pressure and steady the entire left arm, the wrist of the left hand was pressed against the left leg for support.

That same left leg support kept the spindle vertical as well, pressed as it was within the anchor point in the anchor plate and the hole in the top piece. The leg support which gave a vertical stability to the spindle, and its two wooden holding pieces, was necessary because that support resisted the horizontal back-and-forth effects of the bow that was spinning the spindle, first clockwise and then counterclockwise in an alternating fashion, as the right arm, like a violinist's bow arm, went back and forth.

The instructions that came with the kit pictured a three dimensional diagram of how to carve an anchor point. Using an electrical drill press, or hand drill, and a saw to explain what an anchor point carving looked like, one would begin by drilling a three-sixteenth hole through the anchor plate about a half inch in from the edge.

Next, one would use a countersink to create a downward tapered crater as though one was going to put a large flat-headed, V-shaped, three-sixteenth inch wood screw or bolt into the hole. This tapered crater received the lower end of the spindle, which was whittled to a point that fit into the crater.

The final step in carving an anchor point was to create an upside down, elongated "V" shaped opening below the crater, about one half inch deep, measured from the bottom of the anchor plate upward, and extending to the outer edge of the anchor plate. In this open space, created so as not to weaken the anchor point to the extent that the anchor plate would in any way fracture or split under the vertical pressure, the nugget of hot, black power would accumulate, in the upside-down and elongated "V" just above and lying on the tinder.

When properly breathed upon – more of that later – or otherwise exposed to an air current – more later – this hot black nugget of wood power was discovered to be a hot, red, glowing coal. The black outer surface disappeared instantly, as if by magic, and, when properly fanned in conjunction with the tinder below, would cause that tinder to burst into flame.

Sherman's task then, was to discover and overcome all the myriad pitfalls involved in this ostensibly straightforward process, both those implied in the foregoing and those yet to be discussed. He volunteered to master a task that would take daily practice and experimentation across a period of two months. This practice, time, and experimentation, was absolutely necessary before he felt completely comfortable to display his skills prominently in a public competition with any degree of anticipated success.

In this effort, easily the most quintessentially heuristic endeavor of his early years, he could discern three distinct phases. All of his efforts were performed on the basement floor of his home during after-school, weekday hours, and on weekends when the family was in Chicago.

The first phase was marked by a struggle to use the bow, thong and top piece that came with the kit while, at the same time, teaching himself how to properly make anchor points in the anchor plate, and then developing the best strategy for holding the entire apparatus in an upright and rigid fashion. This later strategy included such things as how best to place both hands and feet, how to brace the left arm against the left leg for increased stability and strength, what amount of vertical pressure to apply to the spindle, how much slack to maintain in the leather thong prior to the 180 degree rotation so that after rotation, the resulting tension in the thong, together with its grasp on the eight-sided spindle would, in fact, cause rotation rather than slippage, how to keep the spindle from slipping out from either of its upper and lower end holding cavities and, assuming all those skills were in place, when and how best to stop the alternating rotating process with the bow and begin the blowing or fanning process which would nurse the black wood powder nugget accumulation into a glowing coal. Failure in this last item, stopping the bowing, could lead to a destruction of the nugget in several different ways.

Sherman remembered the words of the first degree of an Indian ceremony he ultimately memorized where the new candidates were being told of their efforts prior to being initiated into the first or ordeal level of the organization, "None of these things will be easy; none may be taken lightly by you. Upon your faithful performance of them depends your achievement of the Ordeal." Another appropriate phrase from the Scout law, a phrase that Sherman's mother often repeated to him on many types of occasions, was a reminder that ran, "And defeat does not down him."

In all of the first phase skills, there was a need for simultaneous perfection. Any lack in one skill would lead to failure. In addition, many would require further levels of expertise beyond this first phase, for there were multiple levels of knowledge and skill that were built upon earlier proficiencies. Learning the violin by oneself would begin to describe the task, if it were seen as a single set of skills, but Sherman felt there was no complete analogy, one required an accomplished violinist to learn that kind of bowing but with respect to bowing for making a fire-by-friction, and all of the other associated skills, no person existed who possessed the skill to teach him anything.

But there was the further requirement to always build upon all of the simultaneous skills that were going on at the same time and that went beyond bowing to things like grasping, pressure, holding the mechanism in a certain way, smooth stopping, picking up the anchor plate and tinder a unit, and items peculiar to his goal, like analyzing smoke, breath con- 'ending down and returning to an upright position, the development of the coordination of all muscles, and particularly the strength needed in several muscle groups.

Sherman was fortunate to obtain, early in the process, replacements for two pieces of equipment that were inadequate to the job, and that had come with the kit. Perhaps the new items were as important as having a quality violin and bow. Years later, he was confirmed in this hunch when he bought his daughter a bow made by John Norwood Lee for use with her violin. The idea suggested itself because of the early struggle with the kit bow.

The length of the kit bow was too small, resulting in many back and forth bow movements which quickly sapped the strength of Sherman's right arm. In addition, the kit bow was defective with respect to the strength with which the thong held the spindle, i.e. the grasping ability of the leather. The spindle slipped no matter what the thong tension was.

Sherman was fortunate at the time of this early phase to be given a new bow, thong, and top piece from his leader, George Simmons, Jr. With the new bow, it was clear that the leather thong was vastly superior and the bow was at least 50% longer. The effect of the former was to prevent spindle slippage, even when the thong was tight, and the effect of the latter was to cause an increased number of rotations for each of the forward and reverse motions of the bow and a resulting reduction in strength needed in the right arm. The new bow was made from the branch of a tree and was slightly curved to begin with and, it was more flexible than the kit bow, a quality that Sherman felt contributed greatly to its performance.

The top piece was infinitely more comfortable to hold in the left hand, and that allowed Sherman to apply more vertical force. After using the new top piece, there were no more instances when the top of the spindle slipped out of the piece. The bowing became smoother and the bow handle was more comfortable.

The combination of all these additions caused Sherman to feel that he would be able to further develop his arm and leg muscles so as to obta the necessary degrees of coordination and strength. Even with his first us-age of the new bow, he sensed increased power in his hands being transmit-ted to both the spindle and anchor plate for the same expenditure of effort.

The final problem solved in phase one was the breaking of the anchor plate. At first, anchor points were too close together and the wood between anchor points broke off due to the narrow bridge of wood between their respec-tive holes. This was corrected by purchasing a quantity of anchor plates and spacing out the distance between anchor points in each plate. Certain anchor plates were also deemed to be cut from wood that was too hard; this led to too much time and arm strength being outputted in order to build up a nugget.

Spindles, too, varied in the density of wood and Sherman became an expert in purchasing both high quality anchor plates and spindles. Wood that was too soft (close to a balsa wood) or too hard (close to a hard elm) were unacceptable, the latter because it took too long to cre-ate a wood-powder nugget and too much bowing strength to heat the nugget.

A corollary to the anchor plate problem concerned the size of the elongated V-like open space below the crater; too large a space weakened the plate and too small a space affected both the size of the nugget and the speed of its development, as well as the temperature rise, by virtue of its proximity to the end of the spinning spindle. Sherman felt that ex-perimentation in all these techniques, parameters, and interrelationships, allowed him to begin a transition to the problems of phase two.

The development of strength and coordination across all aspects of the project was an ongoing task throughout the effort. With a new top piece and bow, adjustments became necessary, but chief among the chal-lenges of phase two was the knowledge of when to stop bow action and begin the nurturing of the nugget into a glowing coal.

In the poem, *The Cremation of Sam McGee,* by Robert W. Service, the ˇvhen he arrives at the marge of Lake Le Barge, faces a completely opposite situation. After he lights the boiler fire, an entire furnace of glowing coals develops. He then burrows a hole in the glowing coal and stuffs in Sam McGee.

Stopping bow action too early would lead to failure due to either no nugget developing or a nugget that was not hot enough to be on the threshold of being fanned to a red hot coal. The spindle, to be sure, obscured the nugget, and the upside down V-nature of the anchor plate cooperated in this by further hiding all but the small top of the nugget. The only reliable thing to go on was the quality of the white smoke that began to pour forth from the intersection of the spindle and the anchor plate. This quality, used in conjunction with the knowledge of how long to keep the bow motion going, were all based on prior experience.

It goes without saying that tactics to avoid exposure to or the breathing of this smoke became instinctual, and, in fact, the bending at the knees and return to the upright position, a repeated sequence of actions characteristic of phase three, was a ploy, one of the main purposes of which was to clear away the smoke from those two human organs: eyes and lungs, the other purpose being a need to fan the glowing coal to flame without extinguishing the coal by the moisture inherent in the human breath, but more of that later.

Sherman became an expert at knowing just how long a certain quality of rich, white smoke was needed to pour forth before he stopped bowing. Pressure from above was a factor that determined this quality; too little pressure generating low quality smoke and a concomitant lack of heat was bad and too much pressure leading to muscle fatigue or breakage of parts was equally unacceptable.

In this latter category, it must be recalled that the anchor plate, held in place with the left foot, rested upon a pad of dry tinder. There was an inherent instability in this. The pad pushed up against the most fragile part of the anchor plate, the part where it was weakened by drilling and' sawing of the elongated V-like open space. Downward, left-foot pressu' to keep the anchor plate from moving horizontally due to the force of the bow, caused corresponding up-thrusting forces to be transmitted through the tinder pad to this weakened portion of the anchor plate.

There was, of course, a risk that the tinder pad would be compressed to such an extent that the fluffiness required of tinder, per se, would be lost and, in the fanning step, could not be restored simply because Sherman did not have four hands. This risk was avoided by having the pad extend beyond the anchor plate so as to have a non-compressed portion. A further requirement of phase three became that of bringing, if necessary, this extended portion of tinder into play during fanning.

Phase three then, was principally concerned with the all-important task of nursing the hot, black nugget of wood powder into a glowing coal, and then causing that glowing coal to ignite the tinder into a flame. It was necessary, at the start of this final phase of the entire process, not only to stop the bowing at the correct time, but also to do this without any jerking or disruption of the fragile powder nugget – it must be kept intact – and this requirement dictated that the anchor plate and tinder must be picked up together as a single unit and held in the identical position, one to the other, that they enjoyed when bowing was gracefully stopped.

The most efficacious holding position could be described as cupping the combination of the two items in the outstretched palms of both hands held together near the little fingers and both hands facing upwards. The two thumbs were used to maintain positioning of the anchor plate and tinder pad in a fixed relationship. This configuration had to be quickly put into place because no time was to be lost in starting the fanning effort. The basic physical movements during this phase, bending down and then up in a repeating fashion, have already been alluded to, only the logic behind them need be further described.

It was first necessary to assume a standing position from the semi-ʻng posture used during the bowing phase. This not only relieved ʻnts of their kinks and pain, but also, when upright, allowed for a ʻwing from a bent over position to the upright position, easily an arc of one hundred and forty degrees. Very early in his experimental efforts during this final phase, Sherman became aware that blowing the hot nugget into a glowing coal was not effective; the breath, especially after the exertion of bowing, contained too much moisture and continuous blowing quickly became counterproductive and extinguished the coal-to-be and any hope of achieving success.

Instead, the body was bent down and, as it returned to the full upright position, through the larger arc of extended arms – the dry air that the nugget encountered in that rapid, circular return performed the fanning function. Once having arrived at the top of the arc, the two hands could then be drawn inward to a point where a breath would reach the nugget and then, while bending down quickly, human breathing would carry on the further fanning until the body was once again fully bent at the waist, the hands extended and the process repeated over and over.

Phase three thus involved a cycle that implied good balance, coordinated breathing, an exercise pattern of bending at the waist, arm motions, and the usual strategies of avoiding smoke, unless one performed the effort outdoors in the presence of a wind. Indoors, a slight rotation at the top end of the cycle took care of the smoke or, alternatively, a quick side step.

Once this cycle was mastered Sherman was rewarded with a glowing red coal, and with careful efforts so as not to drop the coal to the ground, the red glowing coal could be made to quickly enflame the nearby tinder, or the tinder moved under it from the outside, which, as previously alluded to, was not greatly compressed, judgment being used here.

The only further skill was separating the anchor plate from the tinder so as to leave a cradle or nest of tinder wrapped around the glowing co: Once this was done, further, smaller, bending movements soon caused t tinder to break into flame in what might be described as a flash – QEI

Sherman recalled how proud George Simmons, Jr. was when I the fire-by-friction individual competition at the Norwood Park fie! No other contestants were able to make a flame, and the 2ⁿᵈ and award plaques were not presented. This differed from the fire-by-flint-and-steel contest where all three awards were presented.

Not only was George Simmons, Jr. one of the principal officers of the organization and a co-organizer of the entire event, carrying on a tradition started by his own father, but George hand-made all the awards, and Sherman's winning helped Troop 849 accumulate total points to the extent of being the troop that won as the 1st place troop.

George Simmons, Jr. constructed the awards by cutting wooden plaques, sanding them and then giving them an initial coat of shellac to fill the grain. Phase two in this process was hand-lettering, using a stencil, a draftsman's black India ink, and pen, with the words appropriate to the event, its sponsor, the date, and success achieved, first place, second place, and so on. In the final step, a clear varnish was applied.

The result was a gorgeous award that was produced at low cost and in keeping with the skill nature of the event. In his adult life, Sherman made many such awards for organizations he belonged to, and he considered plaque making a bonus skill that he learned from George Simmons, Jr.. George Simmons, Jr., as the leader of Troop 849, was thus able to retain in his own basement the fruits of his own plaque making efforts, where he kept all the Troop awards, and near the location where he made them.

This first competition, however, was not the most memorable. Not long after the indoor event in Norwood Park field house, at a district camporee held in a forest setting on a fall weekend, and involving all the troops ⟨in⟩ the district, another leader of Sherman's own troop, Mr. Nelson, an orga-⟨nizer⟩ of all the competitions, was to witness the results of an outdoor fire-⟨by-fricti⟩on competition. Mr. Nelson was the chief organizer of the entire ⟨eve⟩nts.

⟨There⟩ were several rules in effect for the fire-by-friction com-⟨petition. Each indivi⟩dual was situated in a grassy field about ten feet apart ⟨from anothe⟩r. The goal was to burn a piece of grocery store string stretched at a height of eighteen inches between two slim poles at each station. Each contestant was given a piece of two-by-four wood about fourteen inches long and could use his own axe and knife to prepare kindling for a fire to burn the string.

Spindles and anchor plates were to show no signs of previous usage but anchor points could be cut ahead of time in the anchor plates. Contestants were to supply their own tinder. A piece of cardboard was supplied by the judges to place on the grass; a small, circular section of sod was removed directly below each string for later replacement after the contest. To win, the string had to burn into two pieces. The other condition in play, though not outlined in writing to the participants and their leaders, was that the contest was to be held during a "light rain!"

Sherman felt that if he was asked to write down an example of what it meant to "Be Prepared" he might use this event for source material. He kept his tinder in a plastic bag and his anchor plates and spindles were also protected from precipitation. After the whistle blew, indicating the start of the event, he quickly prepared his kindling and built a tepee-like fire structure with long, pointed pieces from the two-by-four pointing up, thereby remaining as dry as possible, especially on their undersides within the tepee, but also well arranged to carry a flame an additional four inches above the top of the points to where the string hung. He prepared a large quantity of small kindling sticks using his knife and protected them from the rain.

His plan was to use his raincoat to cover the bowing operation and then count on the paucity of raindrops and statistical luck to keep his powder and subsequent nugget and glowing coal dry until the tinder burst into flame. He would shove the flaming tinder wad through an opening in the tepee, a triangular shaped void that looked like a tepee door. Once inside the tepee, the small sticks would be quickly placed on top of the tinder to carry the flames upward to the pointed members that were stable by virtue of their conjoined support and anchorage in the soil below the piece of sod that had been removed.

All this worked as planned and Sherman was rewarded by seeing a large crowd of men and boys gathered around his site and by hearing that crowd break into cheering when his string burst into two flaming fragments as the string parted. Again, he rewarded the efforts of one of his own leaders, Mr. Nelson. He won once more and could relax and even monitor the success of others. He had no idea of what to expect from the other contestants.

After an additional half hour, it was clear that no one else would achieve a fire by friction. The judges agreed that no further progress would be made by any other contestants; perhaps it was preparation, speed of execution, strategy, the rain or a combination of all of the above. In any event, Sherman remembered that each of the remaining contestants was given two sulfur matches and told to finish the competition.

Sherman reasoned that Mr. Nelson wanted to award the 2nd and 3rd place points and awards for this event, he never knew for sure. He discovered that many contestants, all but a few, failed with their attempt to burn the string using matches!

Sherman reviewed the circumstances that led to his fire-by-friction in these contests and also to lighting the fires of his passion for success. His parents encouraged him and purchased the kit and subsequent supplies. George Simmons, Jr. gave him two pieces of superior equipment. George Simmons, Jr. and Mr. Nelson, two of his own leaders, scheduled indoor and outdoor competitions, and finally, his mother put up with smoke in the basement while he practiced. He concluded that in all *these* things his path was frictionless.

Appendix B

Information about Natal Ronneberg

The following information is taken from the *Norwegian American Technical Journal*, Vol. 3, No. 1, dated Chicago, Ill., February, 1930. That issue, beginning on page 3, contains a major article entitled "Some of the Elements Entering into the Planning of Modern Apartment Hotels" written by N. Ronneberg. As fascinating as that article is, we excerpt the biography on page 5 of that issue; it reads as follows:

"Mr. Ronneberg was born in Stavanger, Norway, in 1876. His father was the owner and founder of the T. Ronneberg Preserving Co., the second oldest canning factory in Norway.

At the age of sixteen Mr. Ronneberg graduated from the Storms High School (Middel Skolen). He then went to England, where he studied English, German, and French, also English business methods, at Scranton College, Liverpool.

On his return to Norway he entered the Bergen Technical College, from which he graduated in 1896. He then studied mechanical and electrical engineering at the Technical University, Darmstadt, Germany, remaining there for two years, and graduated in 1898.

After graduating from Darmstadt, he came to America in order to get some practical experience and obtained a position in the Mechanical Engineering Department of the Westinghouse Electric & Mfg. Co., at Pittsburgh, where he remained two years.

He then came to Chicago, where he joined his brother, Trygve, who had also come to this country and had a position as engineer with Purdy & Henderson. On arriving in Chicago he became connected with the Engineering firm of E. C. & R. M. Shankland. While at this office he became acquainted with Soren Anker Holt, who also was employed there and who had considerable experience in engineering, and in the early part of 1901 they started an engineering office, under the name of Holt & Ronneberg, in the Security Building.

Later, when Mr. Holt was called away to take care of some special experimental work, Mr. Ronneberg went into partnership with O. J. Westcott, former chief engineer for the Illinois Steel Co., under the name of Westcott & Ronneberg. During the nine years they were engaged in business together they did the engineering work for numerous buildings, both in and out of Chicago. Among other things, they were the engineers for more than fifty theaters, numerous office buildings, warehouses, hotels, factory buildings, and bridges.

In 1910 Mr. Ronneberg sold out his interest to Mr. Westcott and went back to Norway for a much-needed rest. On his return, a half year later, he started in business again with one of his former draftsmen, R. G. Pierce, under the name of Ronneberg & Pierce, and for seventeen years they had offices in the Otis Building. During this time Mr. Ronneberg devoted his time to planning and financing industrial buildings, and among other projects he planned and financed more than sixty laundries, being considered one of the foremost authorities on modern laundry construction.

Two years ago Mr. Pierce, who had been Mr. Ronneberg's partner for the last seventeen years severed his connection with him. Mr. Ronneberg then organized the firm of N. Ronneberg, Inc., into which he took his son, Earl F. Ronneberg, who recently received his engineer's degree from the University of Illinois.

During the last few years Mr. Ronneberg has been very active in planning and financing modern up-to-date hotels, apartment hotels, and large apartment projects, in addition to his industrial engineering work. Mr. Ronneberg has just returned from a month's trip to California, where he had just completed the work on four factory buildings for Durkee Famous Foods,

Inc., a division of the Glidden Company. These four buildings comprise a copra warehouse, a refinery building, hard butter, and margarine buildings.

Mr. Ronneberg's brother, Trygve, who is also an engineer, with offices in San Francisco, assisted him in the work on these buildings in California.

Mr. Ronneberg's office at present is in the Otis Building, where he has been since the building was erected."

* * *

The following information is from a marketing pamphlet which, from the dates of the pictures, covers a timeframe of 1915 – 1920.

Ronneberg, Pierce & Hauber
Industrial Engineers
And Architects
10 South LaSalle Street Franklin 4415
Chicago, Ill.
Description

The first and senior member, Mr. Natal Ronneberg, a licensed structural engineer, is a man of very extensive experience in building and building construction, mainly in Chicago and vicinity. He is a Civil Engineer, having graduated from engineering schools in Norway and Germany.

Of the twenty years spent in this work, ten was as a member of the firm of Westcott & Ronneberg. This firm of structural engineers did some of the most important and largest work, not only in Chicago, but of the entire country. While in this work, Mr. Ronneberg was able to acquire some very valuable experience in building construction. The work being done by various architects, he was able to get an insight into the methods used by all. The last ten years has been spent as the head of an engineering and architectural firm.

* * *

Towards the end of this marketing pamphlet – which is principally pictures, below which are lines of text – there is a sequence of bungalows.

Page 41, Bungalow "The owner of this building, a builder, was so well pleased with the results that he has repeatedly returned to have Ronneberg, Pierce & Hauber design and prepare plans for his buildings."

Page 42, Bungalow "Another example of the work turned out for Mr. Erickson, the builder mentioned on preceding page".

Page 44, Row of Bungalows "The above illustration shows a row of bungalows erected in Colonial Gardens, Chicago, for William Zelosky, one of Chicago's greatest sub-dividers and realtors."

Page 44, Home and frame bungalow "The D. O. James home on North Shore (left picture), A frame bungalow of the Queen Anne style."

Page 46, "Floor plan of a five-room bungalow."

Page 48, "Floor plan of a five-room bungalow with side entrance. Plan of a five-room bungalow, front entrance, sun parlor and breakfast room."

Appendix C

Chris Cot

John Sherman and his older sister Julia were playing in the sandbox behind what their mother originally called the Christopherson Cottage. In the spring of that year, John's father took him on the Chesapeake and Ohio Railroad's car ferry across Lake Michigan from Milwaukee, Wisconsin, to Ludington, Michigan, to check out this cottage.

After the car ferry docked, Mr. Sherman Sr. drove his car nine miles south of Ludington to Bass Lake to locate the cottage that he wanted to rent for the forthcoming summer season. John owed the first three of his Michigan summers, all spent in the Christopherson Cottage, to a woman very close to the Sherman family. John's father's secretary, Marie Christopherson, spent her childhood summers in the summer home that grew to be called Chris Cot by the Sherman family. Mr. Sherman Sr. was looking for a place where his young family could stay all summer when his secretary suggested an answer.

"My brother, Sydney, has been living in the Bass Lake cottage ever since he was given an early discharge from the army," Marie told her employer one day in the office of his architectural and engineering firm, J. Sherman and Company.

"Now I remember – he was wounded and he inherited the place where the Christopherson family spent all their summers," replied Mr. Sherman. "But does he want to rent it for the summer?"

"I think he does. Take the car ferry to Ludington, drive down to Bass Lake, and talk it over."

"I'll do just that and I'll take my son with me."

John Sherman remembered that trip. Many years later he was writing a memoir. He called it *Instructions from Idlewild* with the subtitle *A Study in the Search for Authenticity*. Our focus is not on that study but the opening paragraph of that work mentions this very trip:

"When I was six years old, father took me on a trip to the location that would become the locus of all the dreams, aspirations, and yearnings of my subsequent life. We must have driven from Chicago to Milwaukee and caught the Chesapeake and Ohio car ferry across Lake Michigan to Ludington but the excitement of those myriad impressions did not remain. What did remain was the image as we approached the south end of Bass Lake north of Pentwater and I saw along the roadside spikes of cattail waiting to be cut and held like a magic spear, a brown softness that hearkened back to some primeval bond that was instantly awakened."

During the summer of that first year, Sherman remembered that trip as he dug in the sandbox. His father located the Proctors, a retired couple who lived next door to Sydney Christopherson. Mr. Proctor pointed to a house that stood fifty feet from his garage. Sherman accompanied his father as they walked over to the large set of windows that ran across two sides of the cottage. They peered inside and saw a young man reading a book. There were bookcases along the back wall as well as a huge iron wood stove that looked like a boiler that was five feet in diameter. In front was a screened in porch, part of which John's mother was to call a sleeping porch.

Sherman remembered only one thing about Marie's brother Sydney: he owned a movie projector. During the visit, he turned it on and showed a film in the living room of Chris Cot. It was one of the first movies he saw as a child. He remembered much more about the Proctors.

He watched this couple through the windows that ran along the entire dining area where the Sherman family ate all their meals for three consecutive summers. As he ate, he saw that Mr. Proctor had an interesting hobby, a hobby that sparkled like gold. John became aware of the glittering treasure on a day when Mr. Proctor opened one of the two garage doors behind his home.

Hanging from the ceiling rafters inside this garage were row upon row of gleaming brass chandeliers. Although made of brass, they were polished to a near-gold finish that caught John's attention. Even more eye-catching were the crystals that hung from the brass rings. These pendant crystals caught the light like prisms, dazzling Sherman with the colors of the rainbow. Atop the ring on each lamp was a hand-painted glass piece and every conceivable type of object from the world of nature was painted on them – flowers, birds, trees, ferns, and combinations of these items. The young Sherman boy wondered how Mr. Proctor, a retired railroad employee, could have earned enough money for these treasures.

This was the question John asked his mother after the garage door was closed and they returned to Chris Cot.

"Ten years ago, many people living in Mason and Oceana Counties had no electricity," began Mrs. Sherman.

"Even today, we have no electricity for our kitchen stove and for the icebox," remarked Sherman.

Sherman knew that the stove his mother cooked on used kerosene; she used matches to light the burners' circular wicks. Sherman smelled the kerosene when the stove burners were lit. Every week the iceman came to Chris Cot in his truck. Using ice tongs, he grabbed a big block of ice from inside the truck and carried it inside the cottage and heaved it into the top of the icebox.

All the ice from a week ago had melted and disappeared down a drain pipe into the sand below the house. There was usually only a small piece of ice left. On some delivery days, the new block wouldn't fit and the iceman used an ice pick to make the block smaller. When this happened, John liked to suck on the ice chips that were chipped off the big block. He wrapped them in a paper towel so his hand would not get cold.

"But how does not having electricity have anything to do with Mr. Proctor's treasures?" asked Sherman.

"I'm coming to that," said his mother. "When the electric company put in electricity for the farms and orchards in Mason and Oceana Counties, they strung the new electrical lines for one road at a time. With the coming of electricity, everyone bought lamps and light bulbs to replace their old kerosene lamps. In Mr. Proctor's garage we saw kerosene bowls made of glass. There was one in each lamp and a cotton wick extended into the bowl to soak up the kerosene just like the stove in the Chris Cot kitchen. In the lamp the wick extended into a clear glass chimney and the flame was at the top of the wick, inside the chimney."

"Mr. Proctor cleaned and polished the bowls and chimneys to look like new," said John.

"That's because his hobby is collecting kerosene lamps and making them like new. He drove down each road where the electric line was just put in. He stopped at each farm and offered to purchase the old lamps to add to his collection."

"So that's how he bought his treasures! I bet he didn't have to pay very much for those old lamps," remarked Sherman.

"Yes, that's right," said his mother. "And they could use the money to buy more bulbs and electric lamps."

"Now I understand."

There were other activities at Chris Cot that were unlike city life in Chicago. Instead of putting the garbage in a concrete container that faced the alley, at Chris Cot the garbage man came to collect the garbage once a week. He drove up in a horse-drawn rig. Tied together on the rig – a flat platform – were multiple fifty-five-gallon steel drums into which he dumped the kitchen garbage. Sherman thought the flies were just as bad as the smells. He couldn't wait until the garbage man turned around his rig in the small space in back of Chris Cot and went on his way. Sherman's mother said that the garbage man fathered seventeen children! It was impossible for Sherman to imagine having sixteen brothers and sisters living in the same family.

But an even worse situation occurred when the Sherman automobile was caught behind the garbage man's rig as both vehicles were on their way to Pentwater. If you rolled up the windows, the car got very hot; if you rolled them down, passengers had to contend with flies and smells until the automobile could pass the rig. The problem occurred because the Bass Lake roads were very narrow with lots of turns, and the garbage man drove right down the middle of the road. For a long time you just had to bear whichever choice you made – heat or smell. During the war years, Sherman's mother travelled to Pentwater to purchase extra ice for his baby brother with rationing coupons. On these trips, while Sherman bore the smells, flies, and heat, he thought about the pieces of ice he could suck on the way home as his reward.

Sherman and Julia soon learned that there were other things to explore in the woods beyond the sandbox. The first of these were the blueberries and huckleberries. They picked them into containers and put them on their cereal at breakfast time.

Appendix D

Warmth

Note: in this appendix I refer to myself as John Sherman; Chris Cot refers to Christopherson Cottage.

"Mother, mother, I'm going over to Scottie's," yelled the young John Sherman as he finished his breakfast at Chris Cot. The year was 1945 and in the next month, September, Sherman knew he would be seven years old.

"OK, dear. Now don't bother him; he has his work to do," remarked Mrs. Sherman.

Sherman picked up a small, artificial leather quiver containing six arrows, put it in his left hand and an unstrung bow in his right hand, and raced out the back door of Chris Cot. He crossed the single lane road that ran between the properties of Chris Cot – where his family was renting for the summer – and the summer home of Mrs. Kelly.

All summer long Scottie lived with Mrs. Kelly. He slept in a huge, upstairs bedroom that occupied the entire second story and had a north-south peaked roof that intersected with an east-west peaked roof thereby forming a symmetrical cross when seen from above. Under each peak was a window – four in all – so that breezes from any direction would enter Scottie's bedroom.

As he crossed the road he could already see that Scottie had started part of the day's work; he was tending a small fire of leaves that were smoldering in a rusted fifty-five gallon drum. A circular piece of hardware cloth rested on metal rods that ran through the drum – there were four rods about six inches above the bottom. Looking down into the drum when it was empty, Sherman could box the compass by using the point where each metal rod came out – N, NE, E, SE, S . . . and so on. Scottie served in the Navy and taught Sherman the compass points. Below the rods and hardware cloth were holes in the side of the drum that let the air in and kept the smoke rising.

Sherman ran up to Scottie and was almost out of breath as he spoke, "Scottie!" The answer from the tall and lean person who was leaning on the wooden end of his rake was always the same, "Whattie?"

"What are we going to do today?"

Scottie was Mrs. Kelly's fulltime, live-in summer help. The rest of the year Scottie lived in Saugatuck, Michigan, and Mrs. Kelly went back to work in Chicago where she was employed by Cook County. Sherman, however, guessed there was more to it than just being a handyman-in-residence. His mother told him that Mrs. Kelly was a widow – she had lost her husband – and that Scottie and her husband were friends. One day he spoke his conjecture to his mother.

"Mother, I think I know why Scottie spends the summer with Mrs. Kelly."

"What do you think?" replied Mrs. Sherman.

"Well, Scottie and Mr. Kelly were friends and before he died, Mr. Kelly asked him to look after Mrs. Kelly if he should die first."

"That's a very good reason and it makes sense."

Sherman could see Mrs. Kelly in the kitchen which had a window that looked toward the woods in back. Scottie didn't refer to her as Mrs. Kelly; he called her "Lady."

"I don't want you to get me in trouble with Lady," said Scottie, "so why don't you begin by practicing with your bow and arrows?"

An unobstructed path extended from the back of Mrs. Kelly's cottage through the trees to a cardboard box that was propped against the side of a small hill about twenty-five yards away. Scottie taught Sherman how to hold the bow, how to place the arrow correctly, how to aim the bow, how to release the arrow, and how to adjust the aim when the arrows went above the box and were hidden in the oak leaves or fell short and buried themselves in the moss and sand in front of the box.

Sherman remembered the day when Scottie introduced the sport to him. "This is a fletching machine," said Scottie as he took out the device he used to put feathers on his homemade arrows. "The machine holds the feathers precisely in place against the arrow while the glue dries and it also grasps them to keep them perfectly flat."

It was good to begin by showing Sherman how an arrow was made. Now Sherman knew that there was only one way to put the arrow to the string – it was important that two of the three feathers lay flat against the side of the wooden bow. Reversing the arrow caused one feather to be perpendicular to the bow, scrape against it, and that would soon cause the feather to fall off no matter how well glued it was.

Later in the summer Scottie told Sherman about the bow and arrow clubs in Chicago that he belonged to when he was younger. "Was there anything like the Double Eagles that you used to win when you hit them with your slingshot?" asked Sherman. Sherman was asking about the story Scottie told him. Adult men placed the Double Eagle coins between the wooden sidewalk planks and every boy in the neighborhood quickly lined up at a distance to take turns and try to hit the piece. The boy who hit it with a stone got to keep it. Scottie told about the cries of pain he heard from everyone behind him in line when he was first in line as the competition started and Scottie hit the Double Eagle on his first shot.

"Yes, there was," said Scottie as he answered Sherman's question. "We used to place small balloons in the center of the archery target. The first arrow to hit the balloon and burst it with a loud noise won the prize." Sherman didn't have to go back in time to imagine Scottie's younger years to be impressed with his skill. The first time Scottie picked up his powerful bow, nocked an arrow into the bow string, and pulled it back, Sherman sensed the strength of his elder friend through the iron like steadiness with which he held the bow and arrow with no movement. His skill was obvious in the long pause while he concentrated while aiming and then releasing the arrow, and in the straight-line flight of the arrow, and the force with which it hit the center circle of the target with a loud noise as it buried itself into the cardboard up to the feathers.

"We're going to have to get some bales of hay," was Scottie's remark and a few days later Scottie took Sherman with him to a nearby farm and they returned with two large bales strapped to the fender of his coupe. But Sherman always aimed higher than the target, no matter what it was. His bow and his own muscles were not powerful enough for a "straight line" flight. Aiming higher caused a few arrows to fly above the straw and Sherman searched beneath the oak leaves on the hill behind the target for the telltale signs of the colorful plastic nock pieces fastened at the string end of the arrow and into which the bowstring was inserted. Sherman's father kept buying new arrows to replace the half dozen in his quiver. After searching for half an hour Sherman was ready to recite the first lines of Longfellow's poem:

The Arrow and the Song

I shot an arrow into the air,
It fell to earth, I knew not where;
For, so swiftly it flew, the sight
Could not follow it in its flight.

"I'm going to shoot a line over that dead branch so I want you to stop practice," said Scottie as he took up his bow and arrow. Sherman witnessed the operation many times. The arrow had a string attached and Scottie could shoot it up and across the limb.

"Stand back," Scottie cautioned as he drew the bowstring back and pointed the arrow up. Sherman saw the arrow rise and the string uncoil and follow it as it neatly passed above the limb and then fell into the path near the target.

"Good shot," Sherman yelled.

Scottie attached a stronger cord to the string and pulled it across and down. He tied a rope to the stronger cord and soon he had achieved his purpose.

"Now I can pull the limb to where I want it to fall," Scottie told Sherman as he put tension on the rope and tied it to the bottom of a tree. Then Scottie placed a ladder against an adjacent tree and used a curved saw blade on the end of a long wooden pole to saw through the limb where it met the trunk. In a moment it was on the ground; not a single live leaf or branch of any other tree was destroyed – the limb lay along the path to the target.

"You can trim the small branches," Scottie informed Sherman, "but remember to stand on the opposite side of the trunk from the branch you are trimming. Use the hand axe so that you swing it toward the tip of the branch, cut the branch near the trunk, and don't forget to look for symmetrical "Y" pieces to make good sling shots."

Sherman remembered how Scottie taught him new things. He trimmed the fallen branch and Scottie piled the dead pieces in a pile where either he or Sherman would chop them up for kindling in Lady's wood stove. The chopping block was another experience where Scottie coached Sherman in how to stand, how to hold the branch, how to cut on a diagonal, and how to avoid being in the way if the axe glanced off what you were working on. Sherman also knew that Scottie kept his axes razor sharp. He was too young to learn that skill but when he was older and had learned how to sharpen the Sherman family axes, he tried to keep them as sharp as Scottie's – it was another important element of safety.

"This looks like a good, 'Y'" said Sherman as he held up a Y shaped piece.

"Yes, I think so. Put it on the back steps to the kitchen."

"Are we going to raise the weather vane?" asked Sherman as he finished trimming and handed the razor sharp hand axe back to Scottie.

"O. K. we have a breeze."

Scottie built a weather vane from two long bamboo fishing poles. One pole was fastened to and went straight up the side of a white oak tree. It had metal rings that stuck out every three feet. With a pulley at the top and a cord that ran from the bottom of the inside-the-rings second pole, up to the pulley and down the outside to a cleat at the bottom of the oak, Scottie could pull the inner pole up above the top of the oak where it would catch the wind about five feet above the crown of the oak. On the end was a small wind sock that rotated and – like the larger wind sock on an airfield – pointed to the direction of the wind.

Scotty pulled the bamboo pole up until it was above the tree. It reminded Sherman of an arrow being slowly shot vertically through loops that looked like those on a fishing rod. At the top of the wind sock was the arrow point – it was bent at a right angle just like a fish line at the end of a fishing rod – but it also rotated with the wind unlike a real arrow point.

"I think it's coming from the southwest," said Sherman when the wind kept the small sock pointing in that direction.

"Yes," said Scottie, "when your father flies up on Friday, he'll have a tail wind and might get up here in less than two hours."

Sherman spent much of the day with Scottie in the back of Lady's cottage. At other times he would join him on the screened-in front porch and watch Scottie as he made fishnets and carved wooden boats. On Fridays he still longed to hear the drone of his father's plane as it circled the lake. From the moment he woke up on a Friday morning he listened until, sometime as early as three o'clock in the afternoon, he recognized the engine, quickly ran home, grabbed a towel and rushed to the end of the pier with his sister to wave at the plane as it circled Bass Lake. He soon knew the two towels were seen when his father leveled off and was heading for the Ludington airport.

Sherman didn't need to run back and tell Scottie that he was driving to Ludington to pick up his father. Lady and Scottie watched the Friday afternoon ritual many times. In one sense, they had no child of their own and they felt Sherman's absence during the weekend but in another sense they did have a child.

Mr. Scott

My best friend at six was sixty-three.
Jealous I was because he seemed the best
Of everybody. He trimmed trees, taught me.
Made sailboats, fishnets, bows and arrows blessed.

He was thin and tall, I was small withal.
His smile and twinkle bright let me know that
I was liked and he raked leaves from the fall.
Sling shots, ships, turtle traps were all his chat.

Who was this pipefitter that smoked and spat,
Spoke of wooden sidewalks back while tending
Worm farm fat near a homemade black fly trap?
To my constant "Scottie?" he said "Whattie?"

His memory never gone, that pure love
So strong, I answer, remains all lifelong.

Appendix E

Pages from a Journal

Having been aboard the Hank for a year and having been through the Norfolk Naval Shipyard at Portsmouth, Virginia, for a regular overhaul and then to the Training Base at Guantanamo Bay, Cuba, I found an old Journal one day that was started by an officer who was still aboard. Being in a rather odd position since our training was interrupted in order that we could proceed to the Dominican Republic due to an uprising there, I was attracted to the idea of keeping a journal and began one for the next twenty-four days.

* * *

Monday 5 June 1961 – Still steaming off the Dominican Republic on special operations. Have been plane guarding for the Randolph. At this rate we will never get back to GITMO (Guantanamo Bay, Cuba, U. S. Navy Destroyer Training Center) for our Operational Readiness Inspection or even Key West. Finished tentative leave schedule and posted it in R (Repair) Division compartment. Shipfitters seem to be picking up somewhat, but just don't have the optimistic spirit towards work. Chief Cox things I should be more of a hard-nose. Stood 12-16 watch in Combat Information Center during Holiday Routine; rather boring except for new messages concerning a Change of Operational Control to Commander Task Force 120. Looks like they are sending another carrier at least plus more Destroyers in case we have to go in. Received typhus shot and had a small headache. Have the mid-watch in combat (Combat Information Center) tonight, really feel qualified now to work with a carrier. Must remember to have something to do for Shipfitters every morning at quarters. Finished hull report; spaces have been neglected somewhat since we have been at Guantanamo.

Tuesday 6 June 1961 – Today saw the arrival of three more carriers: Intrepid, Boxer, and Shangra-La in addition to Lind, Barton, Soley, and other ships of Destroyer Squadron 2. Spaces still in need of much work. One man, Cuthbert, Fireman, is giving trouble because of a sixteen hour working day. Everyone must tow the line though. Spending many idle hours with Repair Division people to see to it that all work is recognized. Miller and Regnier working late tonight on Low Pressure air compressor. Mounts says that liquid overflow in reefer compressor has boiled oil into the cooling pipes where, upon being cooled, it stays to coat the walls of the tubes. Claims Glazer put in lots of oil when thermostatic expansion was improperly set. Sounds like a good idea, but requires shutdown of two and a half months of chow in the reefers. Reviewed Bureau of Ship's Chapter 58 on reefer machine, also charged ice cube machine today. Because of large volume of crypto (cryptographic) traffic, Archie (Supply Officer) was put on Crypto watch. Brockman now Junior Officer of the Deck and McClure, Radarman 2nd Class, stands Combat Information Center Watch Officer. Shipfitters continue to crank out work. Must begin letter of commendation for Raby. One crypto message had a tape fifty feet long. Intelligence summary very informative today, also read wire service giving latest news predictions that we will be here another week.

Wednesday 7 June 1961 – Still plane guarding in Station #3 for Randolph together with Dealy. Looks like situation will hold its own, however, we have enough ships here now to either evacuate the U. S. Nationals or fight another WW II. Have now been out one continuous week. Actually more; we had a one and a half day stop at San Juan two Mondays ago and left for Culebra on the 26th of May. Learned more details on how to operate Electronic Counter Measures gear; analyzed pulse from SPS-10 surface search radar. Made fudge for wardroom using one and a half cups milk. Came out good but mushy. Found out how difficult it is to cook with sea conditions. Having difficulties with Raby, Fireman, but hope the oil of tact is spread. Work continues by all hands at a moderate pace. Preparing now for Captain's Material Inspection on Saturday. Still, no mail has arrived. Have night in tonight so will watch Ocean's Eleven Movie. Traded with Randolph while refueling today for six good movies. Observed fueling procedures at forward fueling topside. Powell, Boatswains mate 2nd class, had to cut a two inch line when he couldn't let it slip away. A good emergency trick. Baked bread now being cooked in galley is delicious.

Thursday 8 June 1961 – Randolph departed with Dealy today and Hank gets transferred to Commander Destroyer Squadron 2, Commodore Stencil, and all the old ships of the squadron. Hank screens the amphibious group. Big meeting of the minds and all ships at 1700 today. Spaces coming up, material inspection tomorrow. Must keep men extra busy to take their minds off going back. Bobbitt, Fireman, Absent Without Leave, San Juan, Puerto Rico, flown in by helicopter; will transfer to deck force as soon as possible, post court martial proceedings. Morale is low and will probably go lower prior to picking up to a big peak upon arrival at Norfolk, Virginia. Randolph goes back to Guantanamo to continue training. Will this happen to Hank after the 'Dominican Campaign?' Captain says that his orders to crew to 'stay off life lines' and 'wear white hats' have affected morale. Beat Jones, beat, my-eye, skunked Jones at Cribbage. Captain claims we were mediocre and bragged we were good. Now, after Guantanamo, we are just getting good and must prod onward to get to be hot-shots. A good theory, but what about the fundamental problems of keeping the ship going and repairing things that fall down?

Friday 9 June 1961 – Continued steaming with Commander Destroyer Squadron 2 and rest of Destroyers down here. Join up with amphibious group at night for screening. Had Captain's material zone inspection today and came out good except for Ram Room. Living compartment received an excellent. Had trouble with Meyer sleeping in late. Tonight we inaugurate the new 01 level movie screen which Raby made. Babbitt got a Summary Courts Martial from Captain today. First Lieutenant refuses to accept him (on the deck force) in exchange for Huskins. Jonesy (Gunnery Department Head) says he will give us Huskins when he can, in return for no one. High lined Guard Mail with Barton who just finished her Yard Overhaul. Her numerals are off, men scroungy and would have received a Low Unsatisfactory from Guantanamo (Destroyer Training Center) on her high lining technique. All this in contrast to Hank who has white hats on all men, shirts buttoned (and on) and uses Guantanamo technique. Engineering plant has developed several bad steam leaks now that we are steaming saturated steam versus superheated steam. Things are falling into a routine pattern and Key West begins to look more and more out of the picture. Tomorrow is Captain' personnel inspection. Mid Watch in Combat tonight where will carry out more training for Supply and IC division personnel.

Saturday 10 June 1961 – Commodore Blair, Commander Destroyer Division 22, came aboard and was transferred to USS English from USS Lind. He seems to be a rather easy-going fellow compared to the young whippersnapper, easy going, Evers. Spent time preparing for Protestant divine services tomorrow. Will see if attendance gets above sixteen of two weeks ago. Doc Rossell and Braqeau helped conduct the service. Did some work but slept most of the morning after the mid watch. Probably Chaplain Cook will come aboard tomorrow and all efforts will be shot. Working now with the Intrepid and Commander Task Force 121. Commander Destroyer Division 22 says that Commander Second Fleet wants Destroyers to return to Guantanamo to complete refresher training. I seem to be the only officer who thinks this is a good idea. We have been getting somewhat of a workout down here. Dief (abbreviation for next Chief Engineer) is writing his relieving letter and he found many discrepancies in the battery tray records. Captain's personnel inspection was canceled due to high lining at 0600 tomorrow. Crew was really mad at all that wasted work. I'm sorry to say, it was a bad maneuver. Twenty-nine midshipmen due to arrive shortly, mostly from NROTC.

Sunday 11 June 1961 – Steaming now with Shangra-La which appears to be squared away. Chaplain Cochran, Protestant, came aboard this morning for church services thus my preparations went for naught. Gave a sermon on God the Father Almighty. Slept most of the afternoon. Bill Sweet (Communications Officer) went back with the Chaplain via helicopter to get copies of missing messages. At 2000 refueled at night from oiler. Used new red refueling lights. Oiler accused Hank of cutting their messenger, but it only parted. Steaming now with Newport News and other Destroyers for Atlantic Fleet Exercise. Posted page and a half of single spaced, typewritten jobs for Shipfitters to accomplish. Did one inch of beadwork and slept all night.

Monday 12 June 1961 – Arrived at Culebra at 1300. Half the Atlantic Fleet came right with us or immediately behind us. Next exercise scheduled for Wednesday. Received eighteen bags of US 2nd class mail from AO-55 (oiler), no 1st class mail since 31 May. Had chits for tools brought into Dief., $30 Shipfitters, $30 Auxiliary Gang, and $20 for Electricians. We really are in a bind for money. Spaces are coming up, Low Pressure air compressor is back in commission and Shipfitters accomplished some things today. Looks like we will fire Wednesday; may depart for San Juan, Guantanamo, Norfolk Virginia run starting today. Will know for sure tomorrow after conference. Expect Auxiliary Gang's paperwork to come up now. Read Time magazine and letters from home and noted that I haven't written for quite some time. Captain requested a stop at Guantanamo only, but I want two more weeks to make up for lost training. Hope to get full night's sleep tonight. Have been exercising fifteen minutes at odd intervals, other than that, accomplish next to nothing.

Tuesday 13 June 1961 – Moored at Culebra until about 1700 today when left to join Task Unit 123.2.2 as part of a ten Destroyer screen to begin a big amphibious exercise. Work seems to be coming along. Word is now that we go back to Guantanamo for one week and then to Key West as a school ship for another. This will be good training experience but will lower morale tremendously. Damage Control drills had unsatisfactory improvement the last two weeks at Guantanamo. I imagine that we will fall flat on our face in Damage Control.

Wednesday 14 June 1961 – Steaming with nine Destroyers, Boston, and Newport News. Making shore bombardment runs on Culebra early in the morning and late at night, thus gaining no sleep until 0400. Al Haggerty (former Chief Engineering Officer) was relieved by Bob Diefenbacher as Chief Engineer. Haggerty is now planning a smoker for Saturday. Haven't seen my men for quite a long time as I am check sighting in Gun mount 52. Gun mount 52 is clean by comparison to Gun mount

51. We fired star shell illuminations until 1045. The watch in Combat is really tired. Looks like we will refuel Saturday and arrive at Guantanamo Sunday, late, in time for some frozen Daiquiris at the Club.

Thursday 15 June 1961 – Very tired up to 1000 as had only two and a half hours sleep. General Quarters at 0545 to fire call fire mission on Vieques Island, Puerto Rico. Auxiliary Gang is painting their shop. Looks very good. Chewed out Archie (Supply Officer) for milk in reefer decks during defrosting. Meyer wants me to put $50 in safe; will put in liquor locker. Thompson, Engineman 3rd class, lost Identification card. Executive Officer wants to exchange a particularly good movie tomorrow for smoker. Fired until 1000 this AM on call fire. Chief Cox made fudge, very good, for me this day. All Officers said 'Now, this is good fudge,' referring to the last wardroom batch. One man in screen being transferred to Newport News for appendix operation. Pay day today, was paid $49 of which $35 went to wardroom for mess bill. This is the second month of a high mess bill and reasonably bad food. The crew is almost ready to petition Congress for the bad chow. Example: Iced Tea for breakfast, lunch, supper, for last two weeks. Also poor ham and mutilated steak. The bread is very good. Shipfitters I guess are working but I haven't seen much of them. Haven't written home in an age. Tomorrow is D-Day and we go in on exercises after which Marines land on Vieques. Must get lots of sleep tonight in preparation for 04-08 Combat watch tomorrow.

Friday 16 June 1961 – Everything went wrong today. First, we go back to Guantanamo for three days more of training, two of which are Operational Readiness Inspection days, Tuesday and Wednesday. None of the fire stations throughout the ship are satisfactory. Inoperative fittings have been reduced but we still can be caught badly. In addition, there was little accomplished today. Commander Destroyer Division 22 is turning out to be as bad a leader as my results would indicate I am. Finally, a valve in the forward officer's head gave out and we have no flushing water. I have two men on Mess Cooking, three men in the holes (engine rooms and fire rooms) standing watch and one compartment cleaner. Dief has given the hole watch standers exempt privileges to sleep-in. This complicates things.

Let it go on record here and now that 1. The old Engineering Officer told me not train (told, ordered!) and 2. Do not! Set up a system of division Damage Control Petty Officers. I have been dumped on and a messenger boy for one full year. I guess this is my own fault for not complaining <u>more</u>, but I always understood that in a military organization, you do what you are told; this is part of the game, so to speak. We had firing this morning and put out 108 rounds in fifteen minutes. We then took off to Guantanamo with the USS English with Commander Destroyer Division 22, the new Commodore who says that the <u>ship</u> will lose one hour of liberty per man he sees on the Hank with improper uniform. This is the hard-nose, threat-of-punishment attitude. Maybe it works, it is for sure that there are many softer schemes that don't work. I guess we get hurt for having no water wash-down system also. This is my fault combined with a two or three page typewritten report as to the history of why the job was never completed. Also there are unsanitary conditions in the after crew's head. I just don't think we will begin to pass our Operational Readiness Inspection in any way, shape, or form. The smoker for tomorrow night has been canceled until after the Operational Readiness Inspection. At 1230 the Captain called everyone together to push clearing up the small items left at Guantanamo. Needless to say, I have a full share of said items – discrepancies of seven weeks ago still not done. I am trying to go to the Civil Engineering corps again, but I think they want more in-service time from me which would cancel any hope for the program.

Saturday 17 June – Another bad day. Just saw a large cockroach crawl across the deck. I am convinced that the Navy is not for me. I should request transfer to a shore job. Being a leader isn't so great after all. It is just a lot of crap. There is no challenge here, no co-operation. The whole thing appears to be organized, but it is just one big mess. Engineering, studying, the thinking life has its virtues. Let glory, leadership, smartness, alertness, and all that rot go with the boys who want it. I'll take a good book any day. Then there are two other kinds, those who go with the crowd and the crowd leaders. All of the officers on this ship with one or two exceptions, are not leaders, individuals, who stand on principles. Essentially their philosophy is: 1. Be flexible, stay loose, don't get a bad reputation, 2. Don't get into anything you can't get out of, 3. Be not the first nor yet the last, 4. Co-operate politically, don't forget your date of rank, 5. Have social, group goals, forget about why the Navy, why I am doing this, why this must be done this way, 6. Forget about thinking, don't try to get behind things, 7. Change your tactics, mix your subordinates up, keep them guessing, 8. Allow no time for training, then chew people out because they don't know their job. Arrived Guantanamo at 1700 today and will depart Thursday for Norfolk after a Tuesday and Wednesday Operational Readiness Inspection. Spent 8-12 watch in Combat Information Center and 12-16 hours in fixing up fire stations. Shipfitters just don't have any spirit except when I work with them. This whole year has been one big miserable flop. The Operational Readiness Inspection will be a Waterloo for sure. A tragic comedy, no a comic tragedy. We lost a red devil portable blower today, just disappeared. The Executive Officer seems to enjoy things and works very hard including backing me up by paperwork which no one reads and terse statements to other officers which go unheeded. Boy, if I could only get off the Hank. I really feel sorry for my men who must feel the same way. Nothing is deferred, everything is operational immediate so that it will get done right away, today. Twelve different officers with twelve first priority jobs equals twelve immediate jobs. Held fire drill for Section III and they were like a herd. Again: 1. No time to train, 2. Resentment to drills after hours, 3. No other officers recognize their responsibility for training their own men or, 4. Even recognize the need for fire and collision drills.

Sunday 18 June 1961 – Had the 8-12 watch on quarterdeck this morning. Last night we lost many gallons of fuel oil over the side and today they had to go after it in the small boat which was filthy after many hundreds of pounds of carbonized sand. Watched two movies today, 'The Black Orchid,' with Sophia Loren and 'Zorro.' Also accomplished miscellaneous paperwork. D-day is Tuesday. D for Damage Control. My fingers are crossed. Williams and Morris worked on inoperative fittings and Chapman mimeographed new Emergency Assistance and General Emergency bills. Also ate the noon meal with the crew and wrote a blast to the Captain via the Supply Officer and Executive Officer denouncing the whole mess hall, the preparation as well as the way in which the food is served. Had fresh milk for the first time in almost two weeks. Commodore Stencil arrived to-day, but he has not visited Hank yet. It looks like we will go alongside the Sierra when we get back to Norfolk. Things should calm down somewhat. Still get next to nothing done, just sort of drifting along. Have lost most of my old bounce. Don't care much for any other officers down here.

Monday 19 June 1961 – Tomorrow is D-day, D for Damage Control drills. This is just like the night prior to a big exam. The ship went on gunnery and Anti-Submarine Warfare drills today south of Guantanamo. Went to General Quarters twice. Spirits are high but how high is knowledge? The Wardroom air conditioner is out with a leak in the salt water cooling line. They worked continuously all day, just put it together and one electrical box chatters and there are now two larger leaks in the same line. I set up a patrol to check condition Yoke until General Quarters. Fire stations should be ready. We will be very weak on in-port drills and battle preparation discrepancies. It will be a miracle if we set a good Yoke or Zebra. I have the same feeling that I know I will flunk this exam tomorrow. The only thing in our favor is our loss of training time down here and our being away for two weeks. Chief Cox always manages to keep in good spirits though. He certainly is a great guy. Received first class mail postmarked 16 and 17 today. Getting up at reveille tomorrow. It's almost like the In-service inspection except there, the Captain was really trying to win.

Tuesday 20 June 1961 – Today we flunked the overall Damage Control phase of the Operational Readiness Inspection, tomorrow we get three in-port drills. Repair III with Turner, Ship fitter first class, was particularly bad. Reported only one item out of twelve in their hit and took twenty minutes to put the fire out. He and Shinault should, 1. Never have been put together, and 2. Never have been rated. Leadership, spirit, co-operation, and teamwork were bad. They just didn't want to move. Six Yoke and nine Zebra discrepancies knocked us down in material condition. They were minor discrepancies like loose sounding tube caps and air test caps and main deck doors not in a locked position. I am (with the exception of Guantanamo standards) almost satisfied with material condition. During the Atomic/Biological/Chemical attack, McMillin was back at after steering trying to help out. He was our key 'word-passing' man on the bridge and with casualty power about 80% rigged when the atomic hit went, I was worried. Went to the Officer's Club tonight and saw Russ Stratton, one frozen daiquiri, and swimming pool with girls doing winter ballet. Engineering and Gunnery and Operations were bare satisfactory, a bit worse than I had expected. In order for Hank to get an overall satisfactory, we must be outstanding in Anti-submarine Warfare and Damage Control drills tomorrow which looks impossible. Man overboard drill was excellent. Tomorrow we leave for Norfolk. The Captain has put up a big sob story about our being called away and only getting three weeks of training as our reason for doing so poorly, but I know it is more than this for Damage Control and put all the report forms on the R division bulletin board. Talked at the pool with the first Lieutenant from the Barton, Flagship of Commander Destroyer Squadron 2 and he gave us the big Squadron, squadog, picture including information that two out of three ships in Destroyer Division 21 were unprepared to start training on the arrival inspection. My arrival inspection discrepancies were 83% completed and this left only a few 'knit picking' items. Have something to work for now and am a much better qualified Damage Control Assistant than before. When we go to the Mediterranean, we must continue training. I might take leave starting 1 August. Also must work out a new leave schedule for division as soon as possible.

Wednesday 21 June 1961 – Today we completed the Anti-submarine Warfare part of our training and Damage Control in-port drills. Anti-submarine Warfare was unsatisfactory with an overall grade of 40.5. The collision drill was a high satisfactory, fire about 10 points, and the emergency assistance detail was unsatisfactory because the P-60 (portable fire pump) was water bound from the fire drill. All-in-all it was a big flail because we refueled, replenished, offloaded and onloadeded ammunition, and loaded much liquor that was purchased at Guantanamo. These drills make the whole ship unsatisfactory, of course, and the Captain flew into a rage after we did so poorly on the Anti-Submarine Warfare portion. I am standing independent steaming Officer of the Deck watches and had the first dog watch coming out. Repair lockers have to be really straightened out after these drills. Tomorrow is the Guantanamo good-bye party on the fantail. We are having charcoal broiled steak, salad, ice cream, soda, French fries, and entertainment. Ace Haggerty is in charge. The Commodore came aboard and wants thirty-four nine inch tent pegs. He is an ardent family camper, very fat and sort of out of it.

Thursday 22 June 1961 – Completed leave schedule today and everyone will get leave. The Executive Officer held a lecture with in-port Officer of the Decks and came up with an outstanding talk. Today the Commodore wants his carburetor fixed upon arrival. The Wardroom air conditioner still leaks and we are going to DEVCON it. Tonight, during the party, I have the watch and will pass over the One MC (public address system) "Now this is a drill, this is a drill, the Mobile Canteen is on the pier." This morning the Executive Officer talked of job rotation aboard ship and I guess this the first real action being taken on the bad job I am doing. With the new Destroyer man's School for Officers in Newport and the possible discontinuance of the Destroyer Atlantic Fleet Engineering School, Chief Engineers on Destroyers will probably come from career motivated officers who sign up for the six month Destroyer Atlantic Fleet Engineering School and two more years of service. As a result they will probably ship in another guy and make me Anti-submarine Warfare officer or something else. (This did not happen, I was given the Chief Engineer's job 29 May 1962.) Auxiliary Gang has their gear in good shape now with a few small exceptions and will begin spray painting. Jones wrote a Guantanamo Good-bye song for the officers to sing first and then for the crew to join in. The Shipfitters have cut a large fifty gallon drum in two and have added legs so that steak can be charcoal broiled. They also built a tripod for the microphone. A large Guantanamo good-bye sign was painted by one of my men and a Gunner's Mate and put on Mount 53 amid signal flags. Chiefs Johnson, Brown, and Cudd are doing the cooking on the gratings from the galley ovens. These grates fit over the half barrels. Entertainment tonight includes Middleton and Mr. Swift as well as various singing groups. The movie on the torpedo deck using the new movie screen is "Psycho" by Alfred Hitchcock. We are transporting fourteen movies from Guantanamo back to the Norfolk Movie Exchange. Had two hours of sleep this afternoon and now have a small headache. Am trying to identify a new bird with a very long tail, believe it to be a tropic bird.

Friday 23 June 1961 – Had the 08-12 watch this morning which was rather boring. Spent the afternoon profitably. Changed Cuthbert's, Regnier's, and Meyer's leave periods. Made an inspection of all spaces and routed same, did hull report and brought records up to date. Checked all four work logs and noted much progress this last week including four satisfactory air tests. It looks like we will go to Baltimore for the 4th of July and will have a tender period until then. Am planning my leave for the first ten days in August already. Must check to see how flights to Chicago and Ludington run. The Commodore's last tour was with the Bureau of Personnel and he says that no people from the Ivy League stay in the Navy and that they hang on to some only because of political reasons, interesting. Beat Sweet at two out of three games of Cribbage and also beat Jones. This can't be luck. We play cutthroat and I lost my first points today because I failed to count correctly.

Saturday 24 June 1961 – Arrived at Norfolk, Virginia, at 0900 today and all the brown-baggers (married men) were off loaded. Moved to the high rent district (after officer's country) and found my new diggings very pleasant with lots of new room, a safe, and a desk combination that is spacious. There is also adequate fluorescent lighting and file cabinet space. Received much mail from about one month ago including a write-up on man-o-war birds. The Commodore finally went down to the machine shop and helped Dief cut out his tent pegs. Jack Brockman's car was inadvertently taken out of storage, driven, and slightly smashed up by a Mr. Lewis, a lawyer. We went, I as a witness, to question him and try to find out why only 215 miles extra were on the speedometer when the accident was in Lancaster, Pennsylvania. We didn't find out. After dinner, Jack and I took a drive to the airport where I found out that they were stopping night coaches to Chicago. I think now that I will take the train instead because of the cost involved. After this, went to Virginia Beach to see the tourists and have something to eat. Jack told United Services Automobile Association that his car would be in storage and must now explain the incident.

Sunday 25 June 1961 – Wrote home today and outlined leave schedule from 2 to 13 August. Went running at McCormick Center and found myself to be in bad physical shape. McCormick Center is still a rat's nest. Tomorrow I have the 8-12 watch on the quarterdeck and will break in Bob Purcell who reported aboard from Virginia State University yesterday. He is a history major and is still unassigned to the Hank's jobs. Made out maintenance schedules for all fire plugs, hatches, doors, scuttles, and the like. Once mimeographed they should help towards a better Damage Control maintenance program. Will set up a lecture with Damage Control Petty Officers and go over what I want done, then check up on the job. This is the recommended Guantanamo method for doing things. Finished my logs (bridge logs) to pacify the Executive Officer. Bill Sweet is on leave and wrote an incorrect log which I found. Read for about an hour in Carlyle's *French Revolution* and then stepped into the Wardroom to watch the end of 'On The Beach' with Gregory Peck. Also read an outstanding article in the Princeton University Alumni Weekly by Eric F. Goldman, "The First 100 Days" of the Kennedy administration. May read it again tonight after I get the steward to bring me some blankets because the high rent district is cold.

Monday 26 June 1961 – Stood 8-12 watch this morning on the quarterdeck and 'broke in' Bob Purcell. Had holiday routine this afternoon. Observed Hydro on #2 boiler, economizer hand-hole difficulties on #1 boiler, and helped rig red-devil elephant trunk for suction into B-10. Reginer is mad because he can't go up for 3rd class Petty Officer. Other than him, however, have ordered exams for every man who is possibly eligible. MS-4 (a steam valve) is going to the yard on a yard tech. We leave for Baltimore Saturday and leave on the 5th to arrive on the 6th and then have another full tender period. Read a good deal in *French Revolution* this afternoon and went down and shook up the troops for having a dirty compartment. Cox, Turner, and Carnes are on leave. Shealy, Williams, and Miller were in charge today as Mounts was on Special Liberty. Tomorrow I had better crack down a bit. Also received today a new Machine Repair Fireman Apprentice by the name of Peebles from Pennsylvania. Just exactly what the doctor ordered as Stuck's understudy. Am very low now on supplies and must order many things prior to the Mediterranean.

Tuesday 27 June 1961 – Spent a full day in port. Things seem to be going downhill rather rapidly. Hayes, a Fireman Trainee, is now up to a Special Courts Martial for attempted larceny. He tried to break into Archie's safe last night and broke into Tom Luter's Top Secret file in looking for the safe combination. As a result, an investigator from the office of Naval Intelligence came aboard and took finger prints and asked questions. My Damage Control First Class, Williams, gave us the clue when he told me at quarters that Hayes had borrowed the bolt cutters but had not returned them. The door to the Supply Office had a cut lock and the safe had marks on it. Went running and read more of the *French Revolution.*

Wednesday 28 June 1961 – Another day in port, progress is slow, the yard is having difficulty with MS-4 and lighting off and getting underway will be close. Too much time in port, I can see now, is really bad. The Mediterranean will be a Godsend. Revised watch, quarter, and station bills, also General Emergency and Emergency Assistance bills. Worked a bit on service records. Meyer, Shipfitter third class, is Absent Without Leave and will probably be busted, then a mess cook as far as I am concerned. His attitude, just like Bobbitt's, is terrible. This supports the hard fact that I have some of the worst the Navy can offer, all in one group. Auxiliary Gang's work is slow, after steering is being painted, also the Shipfitter Shop is being painted.

Appendix F

... When returning from his leave, Rostóv felt, for the first time, how close was the bond that united him to Denísov and the whole regiment.

On approaching it, Rostóv felt as he had done when approaching his home in Moscow. When he saw the first hussar with the unbuttoned uniform of his regiment, when he recognized the red-haired Deméntyev and saw the picket ropes of the roan horses, when Lavrúshka gleefully shouted to his master, "The count has come!" and Denísov, who had been asleep on his bed, ran all disheveled out of the mud hut to embrace him, and the officers collected round to greet the new arrival, Rostóv experienced the same feeling as when his mother, his father, and his sister had embraced him, and tears of joy choked him so that he could not speak. The regiment was also a home, and as unalterably dear and precious as his parents' house.

* * *

From *The Shadow-Line*

"Captain Ellis (a fierce sort of fairy) had produced a command out of a drawer almost as unexpectedly as in a fairy tale. But a command is an abstract idea, and it seemed a sort of 'lesser marvel' till it flashed upon me that it involved the concrete existence of a ship.

"A ship! My ship! She was mine, more absolutely mine for possession and care than anything in the world; an object of responsibility and devotion. She was waiting for me, spell-bound, unable to move, to live, to get out into the world (till I came), like an enchanted princess. Her call had come to me as if from the clouds. I had never suspected her existence. I didn't know how she looked, I had barely heard her name, and yet we were indissolubly united for a certain portion of our future, to sink or swim together!

"A sudden passion of anxious impatience rushed through my veins, gave me such a sense of the intensity of existence as I have never felt before or since. I discovered how much of a seaman I was, in heart, in mind, and, as it were, physically – a man exclusively of sea and ships; the sea the only world that counted, and the ships, the test of manliness, of temperament, of courage and fidelity, and of love.

"I had an exquisite moment. It was unique also.

". . . He laid his hand on my shoulder and gave me a slight turn, pointing with his other arm at the same time.

"There! That's your ship, Captain," he said.

"I felt a thump in my breast – only one, as if my heart had then ceased to beat. There were ten or more ships moored along the bank, and the one he meant was partly hidden away from my sight by her next astern. He said: 'We'll drift abreast her in a moment.'

"What was his tone? Mocking? Threatening? Or only indifferent? I could not tell. I suspected some malice in this unexpected manifestation of interest.

"He left me, and I leaned over the rail of the bridge looking over the side. I dared not raise my eyes. Yet it had to be done – and, indeed, I could not have helped myself. I believe I trembled.

"But directly my eyes had rested on my ship all my fear vanished. It went off swiftly, like a bad dream. Only that a dream leaves no shame behind it, and that I felt a momentary shame at my unworthy suspicions.

"Yes, there she was. Her hull, her rigging filled my eye with a great content. That feeling of life-emptiness which had made me so restless for the last few months lost its bitter plausibility, its evil influence, dissolved in a flow of joyous emotion.

"At first glance I saw that she was a high-class vessel, a harmonious creature in the lines of her fine body, in the proportioned tallness of her spars. Whatever her age and her history, she had preserved the stamp of her origin. She was one of those craft that, in virtue of their design and complete finish, will never look old. Amongst her companions moored to the bank, and all bigger than herself, she looked like a creature of high breed – an Arab steed in a string of cart-horses.

"A voice behind me said in a nasty equivocal tone: 'I hope you are satisfied with her Captain.' I did not even turn my head. It was the master of the steamer, and whatever he meant, whatever he thought of her, I knew that, like some rare women, she was one of those creatures whose mere existence is enough to awaken an unselfish delight. One feels that it is good to be in the world in which she has her being.

"That illusion of life and character which charms one in men's finest handiwork radiated from her. An enormous bulk of teak-wood timber swung over the hatchway; lifeless matter, looking heavier and bigger than anything aboard of her. When they started lowering it the surge of the tackle sent a quiver through her from water-line to the trucks up the fine nerves of her rigging, as though she had shuttered at the weight. It seemed cruel to load her so . . .

"Half an hour later, putting my foot on her deck for the first time, I received the feeling of deep physical satisfaction. Nothing could equal the fullness of that moment, the ideal completeness of that emotional experience which had come to me without the preliminary toil and disenchantments of an obscure career."

Appendix G

26 September 1961

From: Mr. Ronneberg

To: R Division

Subject: My Policy and Ship's Policy Concerning Duties and Liberty in the Mediterranean

1. I desire every man in R Division to get the maximum out of the Mediterranean tour. By maximum I mean:

A. Maximum liberty as scheduled for the *Hank*

B. Maximum advancement in rate

C. Maximum use made of tours, activities scheduled ashore, and, for in-port time, ship's library and correspondence courses

D. Maximum job satisfaction – This has always meant, for me, putting into the job you are assigned, only your best efforts.

E. In short, the best use of time on board and off ship, and I mean <u>both</u>.

2. Already, each man has a copy of 'Military Smartness of the Engineering Department.' I consider the most important points as follows:

A. Appearance at quarters each morning

B. Smartness at quarters and for entering and leaving port

C. Being in the correct uniform for entering and leaving port, and for replenishment or fueling exercises. Remember dungarees are not allowed after working hours in the 6th Fleet.

D. Appropriate remarks concerning uniforms must be corrected immediately – waste no time.

I intend to make appropriate remarks in the 'remarks' section of the quarterly marks sheets concerning uniforms. Men who are below par will not be recommended for rate. Petty Officers third class and second class are required to look better than firemen; this is part of their job and explains why they are paid more.

3. Compartment regulations as posted must be followed. Considerable improvement is now underway. Keep it up – cooperate!

4. Security Watch – A smart security watch that salutes the Officer of The Deck and knows its duties and isn't afraid to report violations or violators, who are in a good-looking uniform, are the only kind of security watch that we can afford to have. Some additional points are:

A. We will have sentries almost all of the time in the Mediterranean, it is your duty to check up on them.

B. You are my personal representative to check condition X-Ray and Yoke. Use the closure log to see whether people have obtained correct permission. Report violations to the Officer of The Deck.

C. The watch that hoists the Ensign and observes colors must be in whites with neckerchief. Be at the quarterdeck ready to go.

D. After your rounds have been made, stay at the quarterdeck and assist the Officer of the Deck. I have always been especially proud of favorable comments from my fellow officers concerning the security watch.

E. One final word about security. Foreign ports, visitors, and foreign Naval personnel, make your security checks an <u>absolute</u> <u>must</u>. The consequences of an unattended crypto shack or a safe broken into and not discovered are extremely grave.

5. Liberty

A. Each man will be required to have a liberty card, ID card, and a Geneva Conventions card before going on liberty.

B. Standby chits will be submitted in <u>duplicate</u>. One copy will be retained by the Ship's Office, and one copy by the man going on liberty. The Officer of the Deck will ask for this chit.

C. Only Mr. Patterson will exchange money. No money exchanges on the beach will be used. This will be done between 0900 and 1000 on the mess decks every day. You must plan your purchases. Mr. Patterson will not take any money back. There are three seamen in jail right now who traded on the beach and got counterfeit money.

D. If you are caught on the beach during bad weather, report to the beach guard. Be back in the first morning boat or expect to be Absent Without Leave.

E. Put your liberty card back in the box when you come off liberty. Don't expect any special favors from me or the Executive Officer if you lose your liberty card.

F. There will be an officer on the quarterdeck twenty-four hours a day. He will inspect the liberty party for:

1. *Hank* patches.
2. Proper rating badges.
3. Haircuts.
4. Shoes.
5. General condition of entire uniform.

The Officer of the Deck will inspect Officers, Chiefs, right on down the line. I intend to be hard-nose about this and so do the other officers.

G. Seamen and Firemen enter the boat first and debark last. Move smartly. Don't grumble if the boat is full of Officers, Chiefs and 1ˢᵗ Class Petty Officers on the first run – start working to get ahead the next day.

H. Chits will be in by 1100 daily. Other chits will be considered on an emergency basis only.

I. Boat gongs: 3 gongs – boat leaves in 10 minutes, 2 gongs – boat leaves in 5 minutes, 1 gong – 1 minute prior to departure. Boat capacity maximum, fair weather, 21 including crew of 3. 50% reduction during bad or unpredictable weather. Boat Engineman, be sure to check for fuel, don't delay the Captain or the Executive Officer because of fueling, think ahead.

J. Conduct Ashore – every man has read and signed the Statement of Understanding by the Sixth Fleet. The Communists capitalize on every little slip we make: drunkenness, four language, unfriendliness, black market operations, illegal use of cigarettes. Any man who ruins the reputation of our great country is detestable to me and should be to you.

K. Remember and follow the Confidential Instructions given at quarters concerning emergencies.

6. The R Division can perform work in backward countries which will have international significance. This is because of our skills and resourcefulness in helping the less fortunate and because of our helpful spirit. Projects for churches, orphanages, schools, and other backward areas are already being contemplated by the Commodore, Captain, and Executive Officer. When the time comes, let's be ready.

7. One final note on exercise – Daily exercise is highly recommended to improve one's mental outlook as well as one's physical condition. Try it.

E. F. Ronneberg

Appendix H

My final efforts were rewarded when I could write this letter to R Division. If leadership is to be defined as making people do more than what they themselves believed that they could have done, then my efforts, despite a bad start, had proved successful.

To: R Division
From: Mr. Ronneberg

1. The recent examination results indicating that thirteen R Division men are to be promoted to Petty Officer Third Class and Second Class next month are extremely gratifying to me. It is an accomplishment that rates with the Captain's comment to me after the Commander Destroyer Division 22's inspection in the Mediterranean. After this inspection, the Captain said to me that R Division was the finest looking division he had ever seen on a Destroyer. These results bring the total men advanced the past year to seventeen. Of the nine remaining in the Division, seven were not recommended. The two men who took exams but failed, I believe, were taking the most difficult exams out of all those given.

2. I am particularly optimistic about the quality of Petty Officer leadership in this Division despite the personnel changes and transfers that will occur in the future. I say this because I know that:

A. Every man has had outstanding Leading Petty Officer examples with which to compare his own personal leadership.

B. Appearance, with only a few exceptions, has come up tremendously.

C. There is an increasing tendency to look for and grasp responsibility.

D. There is an increase in pride in work despite the extra time and pain this takes, there is better utilization of manpower and there is more cooperation within the Division and between other Divisions.

3. Second Class Interior Communications, Engineman, and First Class Engineman and Shipfitter exams will be tough, I guarantee it! Norfolk summers are hot and uncomfortable; our operations will continue, there is still much work to do. There is nothing so assuring as getting things done ahead of time.

> Let us then be up and doing
> With a heart for any fate.
> Still achieving, still pursuing.
> Learn to labor and to wait.

E. F. Ronneberg

* * *

Another measure of my success as a Division Officer for R Division was this Letter of Commendation for Miller, Engineman Third Class.

* * *

Toward the end of the Mediterranean trip, I began recognizing certain individuals who were making more than an average contribution. The first of these persons was Miller. The Executive Officer was extremely pleased with the first draft and wrote 'excellent' on the side. The Captain wrote 'I concur, let's go on this!!'

3 December 1961

From: R Division Officer
To: Commanding Officer, USS *Hank* (DD-702)

Via: Executive Officer

Subject: Letter of Commendation for Miller, Fred, E. Jr., 532 90 68, Engineman Third Class United States Navy

1. During my tour of duty aboard the *Hank*, I have observed this man perform the type of work described in the paragraph below. His recent overhaul of one of the ship's P-500 pumps moved me to write this letter. His thoroughness and attention to detail on this particular job brought to mind the many other jobs that he has performed in the same manner for the past year and a half. He is a man who loves his work and takes a great deal of pride in what he does. He is very adept at using Instruction Books, Coordinated Shipboard Allowance Lists, and Supply Catalogues in achieving the results that the manufacturer calls for on the machinery that he works on. I have written paragraph 2, below, with the intent that it be included in a letter of commendation to be prepared by the Ship's Office subject to your decision in this matter.

2. By this letter you are hereby commended for the performance of your duties while on board USS *Hank* (DD-702). During this time you have demonstrated a willingness and a technical ability which are rarely excelled by persons of equivalent time in service and rate. These qualities have been demonstrated time and time again in repair and maintenance you have conducted on pumps, compressors, diesels, auxiliary machinery, and on the 150 lb. steam system. In addition to this, you have the skills of an expert craftsman on the machine lathe, having turned out many difficult and badly needed parts for electronic as well as engineering plant equipment. By your 'can do' attitude and skills, you have added materially to the fighting readiness of this ship. Your preparedness and qualifications are representative of the highest traditions of the Destroyer Navy, Backbone of the Fleet.

Very respectfully,

Earl F. Ronneberg, Jr.
Ens, USN

Appendix I

Introduction

It would seem logical that at the beginning of a text, some kind of warning should be issued to the reader so that the waste of time spent in reading a text that has absolutely no relevance to the reader's circumstances or mental frame of mind is avoided. This is so particularly true in so many ways that a valid claim could be made that the work you are about to read may apply to, at most, one or two readers. That would be at the outset. At the end, any such readers might be the first to agree that, in fact, the work has no relevance for anyone. Why would this be so?

The text purports to be a set of instructions for the care of a summer home built in 1905 and subsequently altered or maintained in a certain fashion. Obviously, only the owners of the home, Idlewild by name, would expect to receive any practical value from those instructions. But it is in another dimension, beyond the house and grounds, that I expect there will be found a non-existent population of relevance for these instructions. This dimension or realm might be termed the mental or even spiritual realm. Others might to choose to call this second realm the lifestyle realm and include all the thought processes and notions that cause one to spend a portion of life circumscribed by such a lifestyle. Let me try to explain this pitfall as well.

One way of looking at these instructions is as an outline for a vacation. Depending on the public or private nature of the employment world, one can expect, over a lifetime, to have anywhere from two to six weeks of vacation. This is a very small set of weeks and perhaps, the most common idea of how best to enjoy this time is to place oneself in an environment that optimizes free time, time to do what you want to do. A desire for a maintenance-free condominium or a resort or ship where every need is catered to by others seems to be currently in vogue. Travel to a new place is also implied together with the excitement of shopping, meeting new people, and observing foreign ways of life. Without belaboring the point, the furthest one could possibly imagine as the opposite of such an 'optimal free time' vacation would be one involving the need to read and live these instructions or one's own version of them.

In order to take a vacation at Idlewild or even three months of retirement living, one must have some kind of mental drive that justifies the effort. To the outside observer, viewing things over the long term, the kind of continuous activity implicit in these instructions will seem irrational. What could be more irrational than continuous labor, often requiring multiple changes of sweaty work clothes in a day, isolation to a relatively small area of wooded property, one that was familiar to you as a child of six, and has been visited on a yearly basis ever since? Even Thoreau went into town to visit and talk; certainly his trips to a hardware store were rare. Furthermore, the effort is anything but short term. Planting and fertilizing trees, for example, can only be truly satisfying over a minimum span of ten years. A great portion of these instructions then is an explanation of the mental frame of mind necessary to endure these self-imposed indignities, a frame of mind that seems to have worked for the writer.

Another aspect of these instructions is that they involved an appeal to what people in the hardware business call a 'do-it-yourselfer.' The instructions assume that problems will arise similar to those of the past twenty-five years, and that instead of spending thousands of dollars on having others do the work, the reader will want to do it him/herself. This is not absolute; there are times when a skill is absolutely necessary, for example in certain efforts of carpentry, tiling a shower, or the making of stained glass windows, but the instructions will stretch that line a great deal toward the reader and away from the paid worker.

The upshot of this extraordinary mix of owner effort (perhaps 97% owner vs. 3% outside, paid help) will be a very strong emotional attachment to the physical results. But it will not be the kind of attachment eschewed by the poet who wrote: *The world is too much with us; late and soon, Getting and spending, we lay waste our powers. Little we see in Nature that is ours;* quite to the contrary. In many efforts the work will be performed with Nature close at hand and will involve nature in all its forms. Then, too, even with that 3% where, for example, in an artistic decision, where the work is done by an artist or skilled worker, the planning of the work will involve design, choice, installation, and a host of creative aspects independent of the artesian, not to mention one's own efforts and ongoing maintenance.

The result of all these endeavors will be very strong attachments to these former efforts. After ten years it is possible to sit in a room or stand at a location outside in the woods and describe a history of personal involvement in every tree, leaf, plant, or element of effort in a room inside Idlewild. Thousands of memories and experiences are awakened as one moves from one location to another. Relating those associations to another person would take weeks of continuous talking. It is highly likely that no one will be interested in what you say, a situation that brings to mind Wallace Steven's poem, *Continual Conversation with a Silent Man.* For some this is bearable but for others, I suspect it may not be.

In many respects what these instructions will relate is an artistic lifestyle that involves all the aspects of a life as well as specific artistic endeavors which cannot be performed by a unique owner artist. Preserving artistic elements from the past is part of that game, a game that also includes building upon the creative beginnings of others. If William Morris's *art is the expression of man's pleasure in labor* could sum things up with respect to Idlewild my task at warning the reader about the mental or even spiritual aspects of these instructions would be easy indeed. The problem is that there are so many other dimensions simultaneously at work.

We have already alluded to the sense of place that is necessary to understand these instructions. Such a sense is often quoted by nature writers. Not only is it necessary to know every fern, tree, flower, bird, and animal by name, but is also necessary to know the history of every natural object. This can be illustrated with a simple example. The unfenced property of Idlewild is subject to the predations of hundreds of thousands of white-tailed deer that have taken over the forests of Michigan. Nevertheless, there is a memory of the paper map drawn some ten years ago, of almost a hundred pink lady-slippers that grew ubiquitously throughout the property, some in clusters of six flowering stems. They, like the bush honeysuckle, have all but disappeared but the mental map has not. One cannot walk without being aware of the loss, for at each location plotted on that paper map, the memory of those flowers is reawakened. This sense of loss is part of having a sense of place, a kind of reverence for what is gone but not forgotten, together with a heightened appreciation of what remains.

But even more poignant are the memories of people. Oddly enough, for Idlewild, it is the memory of the former owner, one Mrs. Conrad, whose husband of 1917 acquired Idlewild in 1913, and who, as a long-time widow – from 1933 on – became a friend of my mother in the early 1940s by virtue of my father having built a summer home, JERP House, on the adjacent property. I say 'oddly' simply because her character, as it affects the content of these instructions seems more imprinted on my psyche and more influential, at times, than those of my parents. Even one of Mrs. Conrad's renters, a man named Vaughn, a brilliant University of Chicago physicist, who came with his parents and who left traces of his mind on Idlewild and its surroundings, belongs on this list of influence. And although Mr. Conrad, a naturalist, who died long before the 1940s, was unknown to anyone in my family, his photographs, his darkroom, his workshop, his books, and stories of his interests, all seem to call out in as poignant a fashion as the whip-poor-will's call we heard at dusk as children but hear no more.

A history of memories that are tied to the natural world and to people and their effects on house and property, then, seems to be part of the mental perspective that rides along, as it were, life as it is lived at Idlewild. It would be the deepest folly to expect such things to accompany any new owner but yet, ultimately, as time goes on, a *presence*, makes itself felt. I use *presence* in the following sense: 'The link of *my life* within the depths of time is an introduction to the mystery of family. Taken from the angle of *depth*, my life no longer appears as the terminus of various biological series, but as an endowment; the kinship between father and son therefore implies a mutual recognition and the impossibility of disassociating the *vital* from the *spiritual*, for the *spiritual* is only such on condition that it be bodied forth.'

Another example might help. Mr. Conrad obviously started the wild-flower garden that now contains hundreds of jack-in-the-pulpits and white baneberry plants. That patch of ground is somewhat sacred, not only because Mr. Conrad was a naturalist by profession, but also because he married a woman who was revered by my mother. Is my own fern garden based on Mr. Conrad's efforts? Perhaps. Are the numerous hemlocks planted since 1993 a result of appreciating the few, by comparison, now towering conifers that he planted? Perhaps. How many times did my mother remark to me that what I had done either inside or outside Idlewild would be appreciated by Mrs. Conrad? Many, many times; it was her chief way of complementing both my preservation of, and augmentation of, the house and the property.

So the spirit of Mrs. Conrad – and even of her husband – became a guiding principle for all the effort that was done. Mrs. Conrad was a relatively poor widow; almost all of the items in the house are antiques and these were all retained. Other items like rugs and mattresses were replaced. But Mrs. Conrad, in an imaginary return, could still visit Idlewild and she would recognize her own spirit throughout; in a sense, nothing is changed. The downstairs bedroom that she used still has the cast iron frame bed, the marble-topped, mirrored dresser, and the cardboard sign by the bed that reads *Lo, I am with you always*. Mrs. Conrad's Bible, where that line came from, is still in the downstairs library cabinet along with National Geographics from 1914 through 1916; this kind of enumeration could go on and on.

An enumeration of what Idlewild is not will also serve to delimit readership. A brief history is in order. In the late nineteenth century, after much of Michigan was cut down, enough white pine, oak, ironwood, and sassafras trees remained around Bass Lake, three miles north of Pentwater, Michigan, to encourage various church groups to spend time along the shores of the lake. Ultimately, this led to the building of summer cottages for individuals from faraway places like Lansing, Michigan, and Chicago. A handful of homes including Idlewild, were built by the Bortel brothers and those homes are said to be influenced by the homes of the Pennsylvania Dutch.

Bass Lake was particularly attractive in that it was a large lake (two miles long by a mile across), had a natural channel to Lake Michigan which was a beautiful, winding route, twenty-five feet across and a half mile long, that ran through exquisite property as it twisted and turned. On one side the channel flowed at the base of Eagle Top, a huge wooded dune, and one of three such consecutive dunes which mariners on Lake Michigan refer to as The Three Sisters. At the end of the channel, it flows over a dam into a meandering stream-in-the-sand called the outlet which, in turn, enters Lake Michigan; to the north and south of that entry point, the beach stretches for miles of sand that is pure, white, and very fine. The outlet is warm and flows into a crystal clear Lake Michigan that is cooler than the Bass Lake water. For many decades the beaches stretching north and south were literally, uninhabited, except for about a half mile north of Pentwater. In former times, a train to Pentwater allowed passengers to follow an old logging road north to Bass Lake or, alternatively, a small boat could be motored north to the outlet and then, using the outlet and channel, taken further to a summer home on Bass Lake.

In 1905 the original owner of Idlewild purchased a piece of property roughly 154 feet wide and 350 feet deep on the northwest side of the lake and the Bortell brothers built Idlewild. The Bortell brother's signatures – they used Justin and Chris Bortel at the time – and the date of construction were written in pencil on the wall behind an antique mirror on the east wall in the upstairs bedroom. One of these brothers was the great great grandfather of the current owner of Bortell's fish establishment about a mile and a half north through a forest that is, for the most part, completely uninhabited. Bortell's fish establishment operates during the summer months for the retail sale of fresh and cooked fish; no other such place exists for miles around; the establishment is operated by the 4th generation of Bortells; during the rest of the year the Bortell family smokes fish for grocery stores.

Before the lampreys made their way through the Eisenhower locks and spread to the Great Lakes – Lake Superior excepted, due to the cold temperature of that lake – and killed off the whitefish, perch, and chub industry, several fishing boats went out on a daily basis through the large Pentwater breakwater and set out gill nets; this was true of Ludington as well. It was those gill nets that supplied beachcombers with the wooden and aluminum buoys for buoy collections.

Bass Lake was soon occupied by many summer homes. In the 1920s and 1930s the trip from Chicago was a long one, at least eight hours by car; teachers, who enjoyed a long summer of vacation time, found the lake attractive. This was the case with Mr. Conrad who, unmarried at the time, purchased Idlewild in 1913 when the Summit Township taxes were $5.06 per year! Mr. Conrad taught botany at Crane Jr. College in Chicago and photographed nature in Michigan and elsewhere. His Idlewild darkroom was an enclosed corner in one of the large out-buildings, and his photographs remain in the Idlewild bookcase library.

From this brief history much can be understood. First, the homes are very middle class and very few people have, traditionally, lived permanently on Bass Lake. The homes are not modern day condominiums. Initially, many homes had outhouses in back and there was no electricity. Hand pumps, wood stoves, and alternative forms of refrigeration, made for fairly primitive living. Finally, electricity did come to the area; shallow well water systems were installed using large, piston pumps, and indoor plumbing even though many owners kept their outhouse in back for nostalgia purposes. As these instructions will point out, much of Idlewild is now remodeled in a fashion that preserves the past and elements such as certain systems, like the septic system, are still in use, the only difference being that the earlier septic system is now used by a modern kitchen and two bathrooms.

Many of the summer homes are now rented. Where a third or fourth generation family passed down a home to the current owner, rental does not occur. Families come to Bass Lake because it is in their past, or, more accurately, in their memories from childhood. Wealthy newcomers build new homes on Lake Michigan north from Pentwater all the way to Ludington for about fourteen miles. Pentwater is a tourist town – it shrinks to less than 25% of its population in the winter – and Ludington, nine miles to the north, is where people shop for staples. There is no formal entertainment at Bass Lake; the square dancing of the past is no longer; Camp Morrison has morphed into a trailer park!

Within a family that has come to Bass Lake for generations, there can be little to do once the grandchildren have finished their visit. This is especially true if the kinds of things discussed in these instructions do not keep the owners busy or, if they hold, they are of little attraction to them; older couples often change their homes to turn them into residences that don't require the efforts that Idlewild still demands. Many new homes exist on the opposite, east side, of Bass Lake, and some homes are permanent residences for older couples who spend only six months in residences. For individuals not particularly enamored with work or the lifestyle implicit in these instructions, and for whom extensive remodeling has not cut down the effort, the only recourse for entertainment might be to host perpetual teams of friends and relatives all summer long, or return to the suburbs of major cities for golfing and city attractions.

Father managed to keep his family of four children at Bass Lake all summer long and still be with them by using his single engine plane to commute to Ludington on the weekends; this began in 1944 when there was no wartime rationing of aviation gas. This reduced his travel time from over eight hours one way from Chicago to often less than two hours, depending on the wind. In 1959 when Mrs. Conrad was approaching eighty, she sold Idlewild to father for $6,000. As a young driver I chauffeured her back to a Chicago suburb in her 1937 Buick. The real question is how did Mrs. Conrad accomplish all of the tasks implied in these instructions? She had electricity, a bathroom, and a large cast iron wood kitchen stove for baking bread and her meals. Who removed the shutters – they are heavy – stored them away, put up the screens, turned on the water, painted the house, and had it cleaned before she drove up from the city? How was it possible for a woman in her seventies?

The answer lies in the availability of a caretaker that served the entire lake, Peyton Copas, who kept the keys to every summer cottage and had, as it were, the opening and closing instructions for every cottage in his head. Peyton was a bachelor who lived in the woods with his sister's family and chopped wood during the winter months. To activate his services an owner like Mrs. Conrad merely sent him a post card a month or so before returning that specified the date of return and any specific instructions. Peyton would sweep the roof, remove and store the shutters, put up the screens, wash the windows, arrange for a local woman to come and clean the home, and turn on the water; any additional tasks could be specified. Perhaps a dead tree or limb needed sawing; perhaps a new septic tank needed to be dug, a water pump taken apart and overhauled, a new well-point driven, or the house needed painting, or the pier needed more paint before it was set on sawhorses and placed in the lake. It made little difference. As a child I observed this very gentle and hardworking man drive up in his pickup truck and get to work. He had muscles of iron, a bronzed smile, and he was a role model.

In later years I realized that Peyton was just like Alek Therien, a wood-chopper that Thoreau found near Walden. The lines that Thoreau wrote and that linked Peyton with Alek were: 'A more simple and natural man it would be hard to find. Vice and disease, which cast such a somber moral hue over the world, seemed to have hardly any existence for him. . . . He interested me because he was so quiet and solitary and so happy withal; a view of good humor and contentment which overflowed at his eyes. His mirth was without alloy. . . . A wood-chopper and post-maker who can hole fifty posts in a day.'

My father, who ultimately came to own three homes on the lake – Chris Cot, JERP House, and Idlewild – became worried one year when he realized that Peyton never sent him a bill for this kind of work. He decided to visit Peyton's living quarters; Peyton was away working but his sister opened Peyton's desk drawer; there were hundreds of bills stored inside the desk – work of every conceivable type of effort. With the help of Peyton's sister father collected all those past due for his three homes so that he could get current. "When would these have been sent out?" he asked Peyton's sister. "When he needs a new truck!" was her reply.

After Peyton passed away there was no one to perform these kinds of services for the lake. Mrs. Conrad's handwritten instructions in beautiful script, written on such topics such as how to light the oil stove and turn on the water thus became the seed for ongoing instructions that were revised as necessary. It also was appropriate that when we spent part of our honeymoon at Bass Lake, ten years before Idlewild was given to us by my mother, now a widow herself, one of the photos taken in 1965 would be my bride helping father remove the screens from the long L-shaped front porch of Idlewild.

If I could summarize this excursion into family and regional history for the reader I would suggest that the purpose is to have the reader examine his or her own upbringing. It seems to me that in order to relate to these instructions one has to be programmed from childhood with certain ways of thinking and certain habits. Further, I might add, that even within a family of four children there is no guarantee that any one child will be so programmed. If I can relate how this worked in my own case then the reader might well reject any further need to go on by virtue of being raised with a disposition that is completely opposite to what is necessary to carry out the kind of lifestyle in *Instructions for Idlewild.*

. . . The world seemed divided into two groups, perhaps four. First, there was the division of those who took vacation and those that did not. In the latter category was father who only took weekends, and people like Peyton, and Mrs. Tryan who, with her husband kept a farm about a mile away where mother could buy fresh chicken, vegetables, and raspberries. In the second group there were those who took vacation but who worked on their vacation. I counted myself in this group. Sure, I would accompany my older sister to the Lake Michigan beach and swim out to the second sand-bar and lie on a towel for a minute or two. But there were more interesting things to do and there was a reconciliation to be done with a list come Friday when father returned: the railing down to the boathouse needed work or one of the log steps needed replacement.

At JERP House it was fine for my sister to play her 45 rpm records but that was not for me. In a dry year digging for worms in the leaves was a task and took skill. One needed to feel, by instinct, where they were, and it was hot and dirty work, every bit as dirty as scaling and degutting the fish late into the night when mosquitoes were out. Sure, I would hike back into the wooded hills between Lake Michigan and Bass Lake, and climb up into the barren sand patches at the top and look out and admire the huge white pine trees that marked the shoreline where Idlewild stood, but, more often than not, it was to pick the wild blueberries in the hot sun from the bushes that lined the fringes of those sandy depressions.

It seemed that happiness was dependent on work. Thus it was that mother, who saw her own mother in Mrs. Conrad – mother's mother passed away when mother was seventeen – was more than happy to volunteer me to rake Mrs. Conrad's leaves and use her old banana cart because, as a child, mother remembered that kind of cart being used in Chicago on the corner of Clark and Diversey.

. . . In a sense, then, my mother's role was to supply a philosophical support for the ethic which both parents followed. . . . There also was a population of older adults who spoke the same language.

In this latter category, and somewhat unique, was Mr. Scott who was a live-in handyman in the next-door summer home from our first three years of renting.

. . . Was this a romantic attachment to the past that was being de-veloped? All these activities and homes were old. Even the stories Mr. Scott told of his youth were old. I can remember his story of how Mr. Scott and his young friends purchased gunpowder ingredients, each going to a separate drug store, mixed them together in the proper proportions, placed them in an envelope, and put the envelope on the street car tracks resulting in extra work for the conductor when a car was blown off the track. Was I being trained in the cultivation of nostalgia while at the same time constantly holding up work as some kind of idol?

These are the questions which you, the anticipated reader of the instructions to follow, must ask yourself. Unless you have some kind of spiritual kinship with these notions, there is little point in going further. If that is the case I will now quote a poem about Idlewild that I wrote many years after the events just spoken of. This Introduction should explain all the references in the poem which to others, not so well prepared, might seem strange. It is, however, but a poor consolation for having come this far and no further.

* * *

Idlewild

A group of white pines tall does mark the spot
Where woods not lawn preserves the past a lot,
Like slippers, cow-wheat, rock cress, and the rest,
But buildings bring the people back the best.

Within these walls lives happiness and grace.
Perhaps the prayers of former worshippers
Sanctified the place with white curtained lace.
In any case the mood's not his but hers.

She cooked her bread on iron-woodstove grate
Into her widowed eighties late. Her Guide?
"For lo, I am with you always . . ." was by
Her bedside, her smile warm, bright, and wide.

Her friends seemed saints to me who raked her leaves
With wheeled banana cart àl la Clark and
Diversey at turn of century. All
Antiques remain witness to her industry.

She must have brought nature to her Sunday
Class back home, for her husband taught it, too,
At school. The wicker rockers on the porch
Much wear have shown during gracious teatime, too.

The shop had corner darkroom with ancient
Bottles white and brown, ice tongs, washboard, oarlocks
All hung down, a box of coal on wooden
Floor with tons of things, like a hardware store.

And out in back? Well, I won't mention that!
Except to say that slippers marked the way.
A gothic pump quite strong had come along
With Victorian tub on legs. Hooray!

The garage contained a pristine car not
Driven far, a '37 Buick
In the shade! I drove it to Chicago
When her last trip was made, memory unafraid.

The trees are wider now, the bushes in
The wildflower garden thicker, boats on
Lake, and we run quicker, but unchanged still
Lives white pine tall, the slipper and the wicker.

Appendix J

Idlewild Activities

Astronomy
Baking bread
Butterfly Identification
Botany
Boat Repair/Restoration
Birdhouse Building
Bird Feeding
Beading
Bat House Building
Bird Study
Bryology
Blueberry/Raspberry Picking
Biking/Maintaining Bikes
Bathroom Remodeling
Building Children's Picnic Table
Chain Sawing
Cooking
Clock Repair
Clock Making from Kit
Clarinet Playing
Canoeing
Children's Play house Building
Cleaning Fish
Digging Worms
Driving a Well by Hand
Electric Wiring
Electric Stove Repair
Ecology/Preserving/Enhancing Forest

Exercising
Fireplace Installation
Fly fishing
Furniture Repair
Furniture Refinishing/Stripping
Furniture Making
Fountain Building
Geology
Gardening/Perennial/Fern/Wildflower
Games (board)
Glazing Windows
Gas Stove Installation (Vermont Country Stove)
Guesthouse Project
Hemlock Tree Planting
House Maintenance
Historic Preservation
House Painting
Hiking
Installing Parquet Floor
Installing Tile Floor
Jogging
Kitchen Remodeling
Lamp Making
Leaf Raking
Log Stairway Building
Landscape Design – Planting/Fertilizing 600+ Trees
Mildew Removal
Mushroom Farming
Making Platform Bed
Making Shaker Chairs
Purple Martin Project
Painting
Planting Trees
Poetry
Plumbing – Overhaul/Maintenance

Preserving
Perennial Garden
Pump Repair/Overhaul of Pump
Photography
Roofing
Rowing
Redecorating
Rent Rabbits
Stove Repair
Swimming
Sculpture
Septic Tank Maintenance
Skinning Bullheads
Screen Repair
Stove Installation (Wood, LP Gas)
Splitting Wood
Transplanting Trees, Ferns
Tree Trimming
Tree Removal
Tile (Drain Field) Installation
Table Building
Washing/Waxing Floors
Wildflower Identification
Wherry Building (From Kit)
Watering/Fertilizing Trees

The Ravine

Like a butterfly in flight I'm drawn to
This site, a canyon of great height, breezes
Fair and flowers there to renew all sight,
A jungle of the past, frozen delight.

Approach is through high meadow dew, then the
Wood with yellow blossoms, sunflowers bright,
The edge abrupt as path is steep, zigzag,
Erect to keep as one descends the deep.

But soon the sound of waterfall comes out
The sandy canyon wall emerging neath
A tangled pile of logs and leaf, so fresh
And wild, takes all my grief in disbelief.

For here for sure past nature pure as this
Filtered, gurgling stream can be seen, unchanged
Like ancient dream, surrounded now by leaves
Of every shape and shade of leafy green.

And in the crevice where mild moss and
Wood and rock are blessed to blend near water
Bright, the warbler slakes its thirst so slight, a
Tiny jewel of landscape set in scene of might.

And as one follows down the path, the noise
Of big lake waves in crash does mingle with
This stream's modest splash until a balance
There, logs and rocks and waterfalls and clash.

The arbor vitae, trees of life, do rise
From massive tangled logs so great in size
To force us wise, so short our spate, so late
To realize nature's beauty and our fate.

The early meadow rue is wide in view,
Reminder true of all our debts past due.
For who in spring would think this life so short
A thing when all around rebirth we sing?

For all who take this steep path up and down,
Who fear the end but see not yet the crown,
Take from these yellow blooms and breast so bright
Hope for memory, kept so true, so right.

Appendix L

This appendix is an explanatory document that describes the various craft projects that were used during the period described in the Chapter on Multitasking in the book *Black Friends*. The sequence begins in the upper left hand corner. The reader of *Don't Be A Norwegian All Your Life* will have only the description to get an idea of the projects I used while with the Cub Scouts at St. James Methodist Church, Appendix M.

Item #1 – Dinner Party Name Tag Holders. Two circular pieces cut from a white birch tree limb, sanded to a smooth finish, and then sawed so as to create a slit for the insertion of a name tag (as shown) for use at a dinner party after the upper surface is varnished.

Item #2 – A personal sanding block. A rectangular piece of wood is rounded at each end. A piece of plywood is sanded and then attached with two wood screws. A long piece of sand paper is held in place by wrapping it around the block and holding it tight through tightening the two wood screws.

Item #3 – A tic tack toe board played with clear marbles of two kinds, for example blue and green vs. red and yellow.

Item #4 – A small magnetic compass that can be used in any number of craft projects.

Item #5 – A polished rock from the Chicago Field Museum shop which makes a good Christmas present or prize for a game.

Item #6 – A circular decoder board with the alphabet on the outer circle. Given the combination of a number and a letter of the alphabet, the inner circle is aligned with the outer. It now becomes a secret code decoder. A secret message can now be written with numbers instead of letters and decoded by another person with the same device and who is given the combination and the message.

Item #7 – Key Chain Charm. A thin slice of a circular tree branch. Nine holes are drilled. Six holes are drilled for ball bearings. One hole is used to attach it to a key chain. Two center holes about three-quarters of an inch apart are used for grocery store thread. The thread allows high speed spinning of the disc, first in one direction and then in another. For the two dice below this item, see the description of Item # 19.

Item #8 – A pyramid game where the object is to remove all the ball bearings except one.

Item #9 – A varnished clothespin that can be decorated to make a clothespin person for decorating a Christmas tree.

Item #10 – Wooden Rubber Band Wooden Trick Device. A rubber band comes out from the bottom of a wooden block. The block has a hole drilled in it from top to bottom. The top piece is rounded and has a wooden rod that has a v-shaped cut in the end. The top of the wooden rod is the top of the wooden block which has been sawed off after it has been rounded. The apparatus is a magic trick. The magician claims to be able to grab the inside portion of the rubber band in the v-shaped cut in the end of the rod. He inserts the wooden rod and pretends to be working at grabbing the rubber band inside by twisting the rod and inserting it in and out very carefully. He holds the rounded top between his thumb and his finger next to the thumb as he pretends. Finally, he claims to have it and very slowly withdraws the rod about an inch. The proof of his claim is that when he lets go of the top it snaps back with a loud snapping noise as the top piece hits the bottom piece. In actual fact, he has caused the snap by squeezing the rounded top between his fingers in such a way that it is forcibly powered toward the bottom block.

Item #11 – Parts to Construct a Mobile. Another circular piece of a thin piece of wood cut from a branch. The wood is sanded and then varnished. A piece of string is attached and this marks it as being one of several items in a mobile that has four items hanging down from it: the circular piece, a pine cone, a shell, and a small piece of wood (lying on top of the boat at the bottom) which has a metal cub scout pin attached.

Item #12 – Wooden Puzzle. A long piece of wood with three holes. A piece of cord or string is threaded through the holes in such a way that two loops are made. Each loop has a metal washer. The trick is to try and get both washers in a single loop. The problem is that the washer does not fit through the center hold. By moving the center knot through the hole and then joining the washers on a single loop, the task can be accomplished.

Item #13 – A group of Christmas songs for group singing.

Item #14 – A peg board with a single Shaker peg. Four holes allow attachment to the wall.

Item #15 – A Turk's head knot used for a neckerchief or as something to have in your pocket. Made from plastic covered clothes line.

Item #16 – A scrapbook with front and back plywood covers.

Item #17 – A necklace strung with plastic beads and used as a mother's day gift.

Item #18 – A Wooden Boat. A rubber band is stretched at the rear and a paddle (not shown) is placed in the rubber band and then twisted. When placed in water, the untwisting of the rubber band causes propulsion.

Item #19 – Five dice made from square pieces of wood that are sanded and then marked with the usual markings for dice. The two dice between Items #7 and #10 are used as a sample to use when marking the dice. They have drilled holes instead of pencil markings and are stained.

Item #20 – A game. Three posts made from match sticks lie across the diagonal. On the upper right post are several rings of thick paper each larger than the one below. The object of the game is to move the several circles to the lower left post without ever having a larger ring on top of a smaller ring.

Appendix M

Multitasking

The word multitasking is used in computer systems to refer to the apparent capability of a computer to execute many programs (tasks) at the same time. This, of course, is an illusion simply because most computers have a single central processing unit (CPU) or engine. When one program must wait for information – such as a record from a hard drive or disk – that function can be started with a separate, additional, specialized computer, one that handles input and output operations. While that lengthy input or output function is being performed, another task can be using the central processing unit until it, too, needs a time consuming input or output operation.

From the point of view of the single engine or central processing unit, the processor is never idle – its function becomes one of getting one task moving on its own time consuming activity (usually an input our output operation) and then quickly switching to another until each is served and the round robin efforts begin all over again.

This description of a computer is a metaphor for the efforts we are about to describe. I was destined to perform this kind of servicing for an hour and a half every Saturday morning at St. James Methodist church where up to ten or more Cub Scouts – analogous to individual tasks – all simultaneously vied for my attention and with only a single central processing unit, myself, available. Once a boy or group of boys were working on their own it was as though their efforts were, collectively, the separate, additional specialized computer(s); I was still multitasking with all of the others that needed attention. We will soon see that the portion of the program where every boy was engaged on making an individual craft project was only one part of the meeting time that required me to multitask.

Trips to Chicago cultural institutions like the Lincoln Park Zoo, Shedd Aquarium, the Field Museum, and even the baseball field adjacent to Shakespeare Elementary school in north Kenwood, also required the skill and even extended to periods of time spent on Chicago Transit Authority (CTA) buses and in cafeterias. Even games and special events like a gold rush were not exempt from requiring the skill – but that is getting ahead of our story.

We must begin from the time that I resigned from the Neighborhood Club board. Many will disagree with my actions – after twelve consecutive years on the board. There were those who, at the time, considered a HPNC board job as a lifelong commitment. But I had other ideas. I accomplished much in those twelve years – four years as president. The new building was up and running; the organization did not go bankrupt even after I was no longer president – two years – and reverted to being just a member of the board.

I no longer worried that my wife's aunt would be criticized for proposing me to the membership committee. The Good Neighbor Society was still going strong and donor's names were still being added to the lists that stretched out below the years on the plaque in the lobby of the club. But I longed for more direct program involvement with the needy.

I wanted to get involved in a situation where I could not obtain parental help; I sensed that, given the community, I would be unsuccessful in this second venture with respect to parent participation. I can be criticized for these feelings simply because Cub Scouting is a parent based activity but my hunch was that the parents of my fifteen new Cub Scouts had their hands full with other children, shopping, and other activities during a Saturday morning. In any event, I had plans for a broader and longer term program than the one twenty-two years ago. At this point in my IBM career I could well afford to spend funds on trips where transportation and meals needed to be purchased.

After my recruitment visit to the Shakespeare elementary school, I did not visit as many apartments or homes as I did earlier but from those

I did visit and from the children who came to my new group, I felt my hunches about parental help were correct. As previously mentioned the neighborhood *seemed* to have changed – perhaps black families that could rise in the economic scale moved away – certainly the old, large apartments were torn down.

I was encourage by an article I read in the New York Times by Daniel Goleman from the year 1990 entitled *Child's Skills at Play Crucial to Success, New Studies Find*:

"Games of 'house,' mock battles of schoolyard Ninja Turtles and other diversions of young children have come under intense analysis as scientists studying the roots of social skills find that ability in interpersonal dealings can be crucial for academic achievement and success throughout life.

"Understandably, children who cannot read the feelings and intentions of playmates and who lack a natural sense of timing and smoothness in social interactions are among the least popular in any children's group. But new data reveal more dramatic costs of such early awkwardness: these children are more likely to fail academically, drop out of school or get into trouble with the law.

"As a result, educational researchers are designing programs to help social failures, a new curriculum meant to bolster children's social intelligence. . . . Beyond preventing problems in school children, enhancing social intelligence builds a set of skills that may be among the most essential for life success of many kinds, psychologists say.

"'People with a high social intelligence are enormously qualified for life,' said Howard Gardner, a psychologist at the Graduate School of Education at Harvard University. Dr. Gardner's 1983 book 'Frames of Mind' (Basic Books), in which he proposed that there are several other important kinds of intelligence beyond abilities for math or language, has been highly influential in the new appreciation of social intelligence.

"Social intelligence, Dr. Gardner said, allows people to take maximum advantage of the resources of others. 'We're finding that much of people's effective intelligence is, in a sense, outside the brain,' Dr. Gardner said. 'Your intelligence can be in other people, if you know how to get them to help you. In life, that's the best strategy: mobilize other people.'

"He added: 'If you have social intelligence, you know that this only works if there's some kind of mutuality. If it's all one way, people will end up feeling you've exploited them.'"

I wanted to create an environment where I could foster types of social intelligence:

Types of Social Intelligence

Observations of the roles taken by children at play reveal four kinds of social intelligence that are the roots of social talents in later life.

1. The Leader

First boy in a group: "I want to play mad scientist, but nobody else does."
Second boy: "O.K., you get to choose who the leader is, but you can't choose yourself."

The second child excels at organizing, initiating, coordinating and maintaining group activities.

2. The Mediator

First girl in a group: "Everybody wants to be Cinderella."
Second girl: "let's just play we're all pretty ladies at the ball instead."

The second child negotiates solutions, prevents social conflicts or resolves them.

3. The Friend

First boy, as others run off: "I fell and hurt my knee and all the other kids ran off."

Second boy: "Ouch! I hurt my knee too!"

The second child connects with others, starts and nurtures relationships and responds appropriately to others' feelings.

4. The Therapist

Girl observing two others playing: "She looks like a friendly person when she plays with that other girl. I'll ask her if she wants to be friends with me, too."

This child analyzes social situations and understands and reflects on others' feelings, motives and concerns.
<End excerpting>

I think it would be the deepest folly to claim that my program succeeded in these aims. All I can claim is that an out of school environment was created in which the opportunities existed, the soil existed, if you will, for planting the seeds.

When I announced the new initiative at the Shakespeare school – again with my Indian bonnet – I was once more impressed by the classroom discipline. Nonetheless, I never wanted to yell; I remembered my parent helper from the earlier experience. There was something to be said for a group environment of freedom – freedom from siblings, parents, and teachers. As I think back, my true problem was that I lacked the training that would have given me the awareness to quietly point out the lesson opportunities that came up. If I possessed more hands-on experience I would have stopped relying so exclusively on my actions in getting things back to normal and spoken out; but in my own defense, I did work at explaining the Cub Scout Promise and Law.

I passed out a flyer in my visits to the Shakespeare classrooms – as I did earlier – only now, I was meeting at a church. At the first meeting I took photos on a Polaroid camera and made a photo board with my own picture in a scout shirt and neckerchief – I always wore the top half of a scout uniform. I passed out Xerox copies of the requirements for the Bobcat pin. The first two pages had the Cub Scout Promise and Law:

Cub Scout Promise

I, ... , promise to do my best
To do my duty to God and my country,
To help other people, and
To obey the Law of the Pack.

The Law of the Pack

The Cub Scout follows Akela.
The Cub Scout helps the pack go.
The pack helps the Cub Scout grow.
The Cub Scout gives goodwill.

There was some kind of resonance in these simple lines with the Good Neighbor song, a song written by Bob Ashenhurst for a show we put on at the Neighborhood Club to raise funds. I am thinking of those lines like:

"If you saw someone in trouble
Somehow you'd help if you could,
It's everyone being a Good Neighbor
That goes with a good neighborhood.

"If you had something to offer
Somehow you'd feel that you should,
It's everyone seeing a Good Neighbor
That goes with a good neighborhood.

"There's a place in the sun
For each and every one."

I began the meetings with the group reciting the Cub Scout promise and ended it with the Law of the Pack. I did devote time to explaining the meaning of the promise and the law. I felt successful if I could include all of the following program elements: a song, a story, a game, a craft project period, refreshments and an ending where we formed a 'living circle' and recited the Law of the Pack. During all these program elements there were a group of interruptions or difficulties that gave me additional tasks.

The first of these difficulties was my inability to understand what a child was telling me. For the first time in my life I desperately wanted know and needed to know what the problem or frustration was but all too often, no amount of repetition could clarify the issue. I could not go beyond two requests for repetitions in my attempting to understand. First, I felt it was demeaning to the child and second, there were others who needed my attention – my multitasking could not come to a complete stop with a single task.

This inability, under duress, to understand what a child was saying was one of the most frustrating aspects of my new group. I never remember it being so acute in my first group of cubs. It occurred when a child was working on a craft project or when a child was telling me what he wanted to eat when on a trip and I was compiling a list of items to purchase. At a certain time in the early summer we met outdoors and the problem seemed to disappear due to the common jargon of softball for which I was thankful.

Discipline, of course, was always necessary to a certain degree but there was another aspect – allied with discipline – that I sensed partook of another element. It occurred when we sat down in a circle in the middle of the large gym and I wanted to read a story. I should point out that playing a dodge ball game while standing in a circle or a more aggressive game while standing in a circle exhibited the same need for discipline but not to the same degree. The more aggressive game involved using a long, eighteen inch canvas cylinder about two inches in diameter that had been stuffed with cotton.

The child that was 'it' walked around the outside of the circle and dropped the cylinder in the hands of another cub, all of whom were facing inward with their hands behind them, open, and ready to receive the cylinder. Once dropped, the cub that dropped the cylinder would run around the circle once, attempting to avoid the blows of the child who received the cylinder. Safety lay in returning to the open position in the circle – formerly occupied by the boy doing the whacking and who was the next person to be 'it.'

The problem that occurred with the story reading was that there were always one or two boys who could not sit still and listen; it was as though they were never read to. My stories were good ones and I don't think that was the issue. This added to my frustration.

There were, of course, emotional problems that surfaced and I had to handle those as best as I could; I expected these. My own problem was always the multitasking issue and the exacerbation of issues that needed to be looked after. On occasion I did have a child who wandered off on his own to some corner or room of St. James church but, by putting out refreshments and cookies at the end of the meeting, I knew that return would be made.

In this latter category – that of wandering off – I never anticipated the ultimate frustration – wandering off or separation of two boys while on a field trip! It was every bit the equivalent of those three boys from Mr.

Barnett's troop who had to walk the Père Marquette River bank on their own. It happened on a CTA bus trip to the Lincoln Park Zoo.

It was necessary that we changed buses in front of the Shedd Aquarium; we needed to catch a bus to the north side. I shepherded everyone into the bus – these trips were always well attended – the bus pulled out into the outer drive, and I started counting out the bus transfers for the driver when I looked back and spied the two boys who had deliberately held themselves back. It was obvious that these two didn't want to go to the zoo but begin their own adventure! There was nothing I could do except add their names to a new list – the 'anxiety' list – that formed in the back of my mind as we motored north to Lincoln Park.

Another ongoing problem was what I came to call the 'basketball problem.' On occasion, I would stretch the church's volleyball net across the middle of the gym and play volleyball for the game. This game, perforce, exposed the volleyball as part of my equipment, some items of which – like the volleyball – I attempted to hide in a balcony at one end of the gym. There was an irresistible drive on the part of several boys to search out that volleyball – no matter where I concealed it – and start shooting baskets at any time of the meeting. I took to keeping the gym doors closed while we worked on craft projects outside the gym in the huge hallway but merely opening the doors for forming a circle for a story or another game caused the basketball problem to appear.

I should mention the need to involve many children in activities; this took the form of some kind of inherent indifference to what the rest of the group was doing. I sensed the lack of some kind of parent reinforcement or motivation; it could have been a way of trying to get attention in a passive fashion – I never exactly knew.

There was one child, Jeremy, a child who I recognized early in my work was a child who very much needed socialization but who failed to attend the meeting altogether. I took to visiting his home, the first floor of a three story walk-up building very near St. James church. This I did before the meeting in much the same way as I did with Norris in my earlier group. I reinforced his mother's pleas to go with me and enjoy the meeting. I had to take him under my wing, convince him to come with me, get into the car and drive the final block to the church. As I look back on the Polaroid pictures I see he strongly resembled a young Bill Cosby. He was the only child I can remember taking by the hand.

The most difficult strain on my ability to multitask came during the crafts project portion of the program. The reader can obtain a feel for the nature of these projects by referring to the Front Cover Appendix with its accompanying description of the items pictured. There were other projects that were too large to include in the photograph. These included a rope machine that allowed the creation of a length of braided rope from, for example, a ball of grocery store string or used kite flying string. This project included two pieces of wood that had to be sanded, finished, and joined together as well as a handle that was connected with three pieces of coat hanger wire appropriately formed, inserted in three holes, and then bent so as to incorporate the handle.

Another project was a tin tapping project where a pattern (provided) was traced using carbon paper onto a rectangle of aluminum sheet metal which was attached to a piece of plywood; this created a wooden frame around the aluminum. By using a nail and a hammer, indentations were made along the lines of the pattern.

Every project required adult help by way of directions and even to the determination of when the next step was in order and what exactly that consisted of. Having one or two children shellacking or varnishing while others were still gluing, sanding or sawing, will only begin to suggest the myriad demands that came simultaneously as I struggled to service one child after another while coping with one or more of the difficulties aforementioned.

At the end of the craft period it was necessary to mark the projects with names so that they could be resumed a week later, and then store them away. Baseball when it came in the early summer was a 'piece of cake' by comparison to the indoor meetings the rest of the year. I was always interested in knowing on which team I would play when the two team captains began choosing sides and how soon I would be chosen. Let me say that I was not chosen first by any means.

Before we examine what might be termed 'the anatomy of a field trip,' it is well to examine two outside events which I felt to be successful beyond my expectations. To kick off the start of the Cub Scout year in my father's Cub Pack on the northwest side of Chicago in Edison Park, it always began with a fathers' and sons' picnic. To examine the extent that seventeen years of being a Cub Master father had on the eldest of his three sons, I copy the appropriate description of the events of the beginning of the Cub Scout year from my earlier book *Stories of Identity* from pages 10-12. In this excerpt I refer to myself using the fictional name of John Sherman. My father is Mr. Sherman and his friend is a name named Orlebeck. The excerpt also, at the end, describes the baseball playing that began in the fall.

* * *

Orlebeck and Sherman's father ran the Cub Pack, together with adult members of the Cub Pack committee. Orlebeck was chairman of the committee and Sherman's father was Cub Master. During the school year there were often as many as fifteen dens that met each week, and there was always a waiting list for den mothers and fathers.

Sherman could remember the map sessions held in the living room of his home in early September. A large street map of Edison Park was used and each member was marked with a colored pin at his place of residence, one color for each age. Each lucky den mother and father's residence was marked with a pin of a different color. Once the pins were in place, penciled circles were drawn around ten or twelve pins so that a den was formed with nearby scouts. A continuity check was made from one year to the next to keep scouts with the same den parents for three years.

The fall season began a series of activities: weekly den meetings, the fathers' and sons' picnic, Cub Scout softball competition, extensive rehearsals and preparation for two nights of the Minstrel and Style Show, and finally, the Christmas Family Dinner and party. The weekly den meetings always involved a wooden craft project, and hundreds of pieces of wood were cut in Sherman's basement using the machines there to expedite the process. Each project needed a finished sample to work toward and Sherman's father often visited four den meetings in a single night to facilitate the distribution of projects, books, and badges that were earned, and pass on information of activities yet to come. Sherman accompanied his father to these meetings as a six- and seven-year-old child.

The major event of the fall season that began things was the fathers' and sons' picnic at a nearby forest preserve location. A huge fire in a stone forest preserve sheltered fireplace was lit and it allowed hot dogs to be roasted along with marshmallows. After dinner there was a program that included singing. One of the most popular parts of that singing was a competition known as *Throw It Out the Window*. To prepare for this competition, the audience was divided into two groups, fathers on one side and sons on the other, and each group had its own song leader.

Each side had to think of nursery rhymes that had not yet been used; to repeat a rhyme meant that your team lost. You could also lose by not being ready with a new rhyme when your group's turn came. The first group might begin:

Tom, Tom the piper's son, stole a pig and away
Did run, and he threw it out the window, the window,
The second story window, high low, low high, threw
It out the window.

The opposite team, by now, would have a rhyme and would quickly reply:

Jack be nimble, Jack be quick, Jack jump over the
Candlestick, and he threw it out the window, the
Window, the second story window, high low, low
High, threw it out the window.

The songs now went back and forth between the two groups, and no repeats were allowed. While one side sang, the other struggled to find a new rhyme, and things got more and more frenetic when one side felt that the other side was laboring to come up with a new rhyme, so they would sing their own rhyme faster and faster until a true delay occurred, or a duplicate was detected, and then they would claim victory.

During this portion of the program, some of the committee members were distributing a bushel basket full of smooth stones painted gloss-yellow a few days before. They would scatter them all over a large field of grass across the road from the shelter. It now being completely dark, and all of the songs finished, someone would announce a treasure hunt, and everyone's flashlight was turned on as boys ran to the field, spread out, and began searching and pocketing yellow stones that were found. Boys announcing a "find" would only quicken the intensity of the search by everyone else, much like the final stanzas of the "Out the Window" competition. This went on until no more pieces of treasure were found; then the picnic things were packed up and everyone drove home.

But of course the fall program was only just begun. In addition to the weekly den meetings, there were competitive softball games, played with several teams, and played between different Cub Packs from the entire neighborhood and adjacent neighborhoods as well. The coach, the father of a boy who had long since graduated to the church Boy Scout troop, became a revered person for the patience, coaching help, and good sportsmanship he always displayed. People learned what to keep track of, where to throw the ball, when not to throw, and basic things like keeping your feet together as you fielded a grounder.

* * *

Managing the idea of a picnic was a bit too much to imagine but I spotted an empty lot kitty-corner to the Shakespeare school property where we played softball. It was overgrown with weeds and flowers. I determined to have a 'gold rush' followed by hot dogs, refreshments, and desert, to celebrate the 'find.'

I collected a large quantity of small but very smooth stones on the Lake Michigan beach during the prior summer. It took no time at all to paint them with yellow gloss enamel paint. Finding one of them would excite any child who discovered such an object in so unlikely a location. Although the lot was crisscrossed with several pedestrian paths, I felt that few of those users would discern my 'gold.'

Accordingly, early in the morning of that softball playing Saturday, I carefully planted my 'nuggets' throughout the lot. The weeds and brush provided a perfect cover and the gold could only be detected by a person looking straight down. I avoided placing the gold near the paths and although there were other objects in the field – some glass and soda pop cans come to mind – my scouts had dealt with glass all their life. In fact, we always cleared the baseball playing field of these kinds of objects before a game.

Just as we finished baseball for the morning, and everyone was expecting me to fetch refreshments from my car; I intimated that I heard that there was some kind of secret message stuck in the schoolyard chain link fence. This took everyone's mind off the fact that my car was not parked in its usual place. My wife had dropped me off with the balls and bats so that she could return with the picnic.

Everyone rushed to the chain link fence and the secret message was discovered and read aloud. It had information about someone finding gold and instructions to the 'gold field.' The entire group dashed across the streets to the lot and started searching for the nuggets and putting them in bags I had passed out. The timing of my wife's return was perfect, for just as the last nugget was found, Christiane drove up with the lunch. It wasn't dark and we didn't have a fire that had burned down to coals nor even sing the song *Throw It Out The Window* but it didn't make any difference. I felt that I had taken an element from my own childhood and transformed it into the life of other children; the memory of this event went a long way toward making up for my struggles to multitask during the making of craft projects.

There was one other event that I borrowed from my exposure to having grown up with a Cub Master for all those years – the annual Christmas party. The Christmas party for my father's Cub pack – as near as I can recall – was really a family dinner; there must have been entertainment – I think it might have been a movie as well as some other type of fun – and a visit from Santa Claus with gifts distributed to all the children in attendance.

However vague the actual details of my own experience of the Cub Scout Christmas party as a child are, my experiences of the IBM Christmas parties – which were held for my own children a few years back from the time I was working at St. James – were quite vivid. These always included professional entertainment like a magician and rather lavish gifts for children. In effect you submitted the names, sex, and ages of your children and the IBM Club did all the effort to purchase and wrap the gifts. There were extensive refreshments and a Santa Claus. These events motivated me to have my own party for my Cubs.

There was no visit from Santa Claus and parents and siblings were not in attendance. Nonetheless, at the end of a regular Saturday meeting, it was announced that Santa *had* made a visit the night before and a Cub Scout was told where to go to discover a white bag stuffed with presents. I would purchase items from the scout trading post in the Loop, wrap them, and label them with the names of each boy. I often included several items like a polished rock from the Field Museum, a game or a medallion on a key chain – anything that appealed to that age group.

Once the bag was found and brought back, I could form a circle and personally withdraw an item, read the name, and distribute it. In this way I could keep any item for a child not in attendance but there were few of these because I had hinted at a visit from Santa during the prior week. After the gifts were distributed we had Christmas cookies and refreshments, sang Christmas songs from sheets like the one on the front cover of this book, formed the 'living circle,' recited the Law of the pack in unison, and adjourned.

We now come to that part of my overall program which I referred to as 'field trips.' We certainly went to Lincoln Park Zoo several times as well as the Field Museum and Shedd Aquarium. By focusing on a zoo trip, the general idea of what went on should be conveyed. A week prior to a trip I distributed an information sheet that outlined when it would start, when to be at St. James, how we would travel – by CTA bus – where we would catch our first bus, how long the trip would most likely take, what to wear, and the fact that all expenses would be paid. I wanted no excuses for not coming due to finances. We met at the church at the designated time, waited a brief interval for any stragglers, and then walked down 47th Street to the corner of 47th Street and Lake Park Avenue to catch our first bus.

I became adept at getting a group of children onto a CTA bus, getting everyone seated, and then paying for all the fares and collecting the transfers. We exited from the first bus in front of the Shedd Aquarium and caught a bus that took us to the zoo – there may have been a second transfer but I cannot recall it now. It was on one of these trips that I realized that two boys had 'bowed out' of the trip. I will not keep the reader in suspense any longer but merely say that both made it home safely – they had their own return bus fare. I suspect they were just exhibiting their own independence in view of the fact that one boy was nearing 'Boy Scout' age.

In any event, we exited the bus to Lincoln Park Zoo near the 'Farm in the Zoo' buildings and explored that thoroughly before moving beyond to the rest of the animals. There were always chicks that were hatching out of eggs and horses that could be seen at close hand. After a while everyone began to get tired and we stopped for lunch.

There was a Park District restaurant on the side of the lake not far from the Farm in the Zoo and it presented little difficulty by way of getting orders in and back to the children; there always seemed to be fewer patrons than the Field Museum. At the Field Museum we ate at McDonalds and getting the orders in and back to the Cubs was another story altogether.

It began with keeping track of what each child wanted. McDonalds was noisy – there was no easy way of speaking to the personnel as there was at Lincoln Park. I had to keep track of what each child wanted, and that could give rise to not understanding exactly what a child was telling me. I wrote this down and also noted which scout wanted which items for lunch. I then consolidated the items for ordering. Finally, I found one or two tables and left my group at these tables while I proceeded to tell the McDonalds person my entire order.

McDonalds was always crowded and I looked back at my charges to make certain they were behaving while I waited for the trays of food – yes, it took more than one trip. After I paid for the food, waited, and began my return trips, I always was aware of nervous looks from the largely white diners nearby; but I always thought that no one else could boast of such a family!

My other encounter with potentially disgruntled whites came when it was time to return home from the Lincoln Park Zoo. We would now be boarding a return bus at a time when wealthy white shoppers from the near north side – Lincoln Park – were headed for the Michigan Avenue shops – an early Saturday afternoon on a sunny spring or early summer day. Here was a group – my group – that would delay forward progress if only to get the fares collected and everyone seated, or appropriately standing in the back of the bus. I can remember the looks of the other passengers as I walked back for my own seat. It always reminded me of a scene in the movie *The Graduate* with Dustin Hoffman.

At one point Dustin Hoffman breaks into a church at the point of time where a wedding is going on and has almost been consummated; the bride does not want to marry the groom because she loves Hoffman. After breaking into the church Hoffman calls out the brides name from the rear of the church and she leaves her groom and runs to him down the aisle. The parents of this 'arranged wedding' immediately get terrible looks of revenge on their faces but the entire congregation seems equally mad – think of all the waste of money for those wedding gifts!

The groom joins everyone else in the congregation as they all run to catch the pair that is now eloping. Hoffman, the interloper, knows they will all be after him in a moment so he grabs a cross and jams it in an entrance door mechanism. We see all his pursuers with angry faces trying to break through the door but to no avail. The 'stealer of the bride' in plain clothes and tie and the bride in her wedding dress run down the street, stop at a bus stop on the next corner, and then board a bus that just happens to be coming down the street.

Just as the angry crowd finally makes it out of the church we see Hoffman fumbling for change. The pair makes their way to the back seat of the bus, sit down, and face forward in an effort of obvious relaxation. We now see the bus passengers who have all, slowly, turned around to see the pair that has just taken their seats; the passengers all have faces of utter disbelief.

As I walked to the rear of the CTA bus that would take us back from Lincoln Park to Hyde Park, I, too, received looks of disbelief and maybe even a look or two like the outraged parents and groom as they struggled to escape the church and muttered oaths under their breath; but on *my* bus there were others who wore a smile!

So how have I come to feel about those that would disagree with my multitasking actions? I would smile, like those few on the bus, and say that, on balance, I gave some children a good time that they might not otherwise have received. And what evidence would I offer to that effect? I would tell them to read the next chapter, a story about fourteen years of going to the YMCA at 63rd Street and Stony Island Avenue where they will see that for those years, at 6 AM, I was the only white man around as we waited for the Y to open. The friendships are the subject of the next chapter and belong in a separate narrative.

But one incident that occurred at that YMCA *does* belong in this chapter for it is a piece of evidence that I would offer to answer the question. It occurred on a Saturday when all the black young men of Woodlawn and points elsewhere came to play basketball. I was walking up to the door using the sidewalk from the parking lot. I could see the large crowd ahead of black youths gathered together and exchanging stories.

A black youth separated himself from his friends and walked, almost ran toward me shouting "Mr. Ronneberg, Mr. Ronneberg!" No other person I have known has ever had such an experience. It was Jeremy, now no longer resembling Bill Cosby to the same degree. He was concerned that I had forgotten him. I assured him that I had not.

Appendix N

Greetings from Bass Lake,

Some tourist outfit used to publish *Carefree Days In West Michigan* and mother would distribute it to her renters with great expectations that they would take in most of the magazine. In addition to the beach, you would pursue dune scooting, fishing, blueberry picking, take in the movies at Pentwater, and swim — eat the foods, go to the band concert, even try to catch the Scottville Clown band — which celebrates its hundredth birthday this year — and, of course, arrive and depart by Car Ferry refreshed and so on and so forth. This was supposed to be the Bass Lake life style, a mythical notion that reflected, somehow, Hegel's notion of the wise person as "one who is capable of answering in a *comprehensible* or satisfactory manner *all* questions that can be asked him concerning his acts, and capable of answering in such fashion that the *entirety* of his answers forms a coherent *discourse*."

For those of us who were not <u>tourists</u>, god forbid; for those of us who were summer residents, a more difficult set of questions would be asked. On us were laid the tasks of cottage maintenance: opening and closing, painting, septic work (before the days of the "Canuck"), cleaning, driving a well-point, and turning on the water, roofing, and so on and so forth. We, perforce then, must be wiser. We would have to stay up late and identify the stars in the heavens for the renters just as we pointed out the flowers of the woods. We would have to pretend that there was no alternative life style to this brand of West Michigan leisure and that cottage rentals were what Jefferson really meant when he spoke of "life, liberty, and the pursuit of happiness" and not what everyone before him knew he should have written "Life, liberty and the *protection of (preservation) property*." People who rented cottages would have to bemoan their own wretched fate and build up the well-deserved destinies of those who could live the carefree life, the privileged who were never meant to sweat.

Imagine the grandchildren and great grandchildren of my mother's kin then, weaned on TV, given water skis, and noisy Sea Doo's before they can swim, never knowing what it means to wash and dry dishes, bored with games like hearts, Tripoli, and Cribbage, never having to seek out and grapple with that difficult task of entertaining oneself, let alone, cleaning a toilet bowl. To this generation there is the *green world, water,* and *the city.* One tree or flower is pretty much like another; Bass Lake and Lake Michigan are like each other in that they are wet; and the city is the place of choice due to rock concerts, lakefront fireworks crowds, and massive and expensive entertainment alternatives which don't involve the development of curiosity; the initiatives come from one's friends and are *neat* and *cool* by the same criterion.

Picture now the new separation; the child who walks along the road and sees the hummingbird feeder but never the hummingbird; the confused mind that cannot grasp the fact that anyone with a paint brush may not be electronically uninformed; the sunbather who never catches the sun through the burst of pine needles or on the backside of a fern or resting on the light green tips of a Hemlock branch as it points lazily in one direction and then another as the wind gives it motion. These and hundreds of other images must be experienced through the eyes of a professional photographer else they do not exist. So while some search for a coherent discourse others are unaware of the meaning of the word.

So what does it mean to watch the woodpeckers, the nuthatches, robins, and chipmunks gather around and fly to and from a fountain in the woods? Is this all a matter of taste which changes with age or are there certain archetypal images passed through the genes as it were from time immemorial and which form a visual heritage for mankind and are ignored at one's risk of losing something important to humanity itself? Where is the bottom line in all this? If that question cannot be asked and answered, then Hegel's premises are wrong for no one can "realize the *encyclopedia* of possible kinds of knowledge" so as to be able to answer all questions and be *perfectly* self-conscious, i.e., *omniscient.* Beauty, or what have you, must be strictly in the mind of the beholder and the water skier must be just as majestic as the slanting sunlight in the woods illuminating every form; the call of the pee wee and the catbird must be just as thrilling as the sound of a car alarm out of control or the incessant yelling of children being pulled on a plastic tire behind a powerful and noisy, oversized boat.

So long as no one knows exactly what the "dark matter" is, will everything be up for grabs? Will we continue to be divided into various "worlds" just as in Lindsey's *Voyage to Arcturus* or in Tolkien's *Lord of the Rings*? Some few of us will attempt to create or own Lorien and plant Larches or even Hemlock to preserve the delicate needles and green into winter. Others will never know a larch from a launch nor why Carl Fabritius' European Goldfinch of 1654, *Carduelis carduelis*, differs from *Carduelis tristis*. Yet in all this it does seem safe to say that those that never build fountains will never even see the birds let alone a proliferation of species. And we might add that those that are shown Arcturus as opposed to being prompted by their own curiosity may never remember how to find it again or remember that it is the fourth brightest star in the entire sky, bright enough for its yellow-orange color to show even if it is thirty-six light years from Earth.

One wonders if the forces of proliferation are themselves being ignored. Is the Milky way merely a cloud? When thousands of Little Wood-Satyrs bounce around by day on every blade of grass and leaf, begging for identification with their colorful yellow-rimmed eye-spots and fireflies light up the woods at night when the Satyrs have calmed down, pulsing yellow phosphorescence, is it only firecrackers and noise that can waken mankind? Is this the only jolt left from the numbing TV? Are we talking here about the basic distinctions between light and darkness, a distinction that goes back to the big bang which had to wait some three hundred thousand years before light itself was born, or Genesis if you will, and are we saying that new insidious forms of light have come to distort vision itself?

We return to Hegel who presupposes the existence of the *Philosopher* for at each dialectical turning point there must be a *Philosopher* who is ready to become *conscious* of the newly constituted reality, it is only he who wants to *know* at all costs where he is, to *become aware* of what he is and who does not go on any further before he has become aware of it. The others close themselves up within the range of things of which they have already become conscious and remain impervious to new facts in themselves and outside of themselves. For them the more things change the more they stay the same hence every tree and flower are alike.

Appendix O

A Meeting of the Migraine Play Readers

Cast

Mildred, *the elected secretary of the group*
Ralph and Edwina Falconberg, *hosts – only Ralph speaks*
John and Mary Ann Swizzle, *co-hosts – neither speak*
Jackson Caruthers, *a member of the play-reading group*
Jane Williams, *a member of the play–reading group*
Hickory Jones, *a member of the play–reading group*
Hillary Smith, *a member of the play-reading group and producer of the evening's play*
June Buckland, *a member of the play-reading group, asked to read as producer*

Cast of the play *"Prisoner of Passion:"*

Shelia Brighton, *heroine, played by Hillary Smith*
Mrs. Brighton, *mother of the heroine, played by Jane Williams*
Carlton Minor, *a suitor, played by Jackson Caruthers*
Luther Morris, *a rival, played by Hickory Jones*
Wilhelmina, *a well-to-do young woman – does not speak*

The scene is the living room of Ralph and Edwina Falconberg, one of the host couples of the Migraine Play Readers. The members reading parts sit at the front of the room. The remaining members form the audience and sit at the rear.

MILDRED: I hope everyone is here and that we have all had a good dinner. I think it's time to thank our hosts, the Falconbergs and the Swizels. Has anyone seen the Falconbergs and the Swizels?

JACKSON: I think they're out in the kitchen.

HILLARY: Hey, call 'em in.

JACKSON: Naw, let 'em be. They won't like the play.

MILDRED: Not *thank* our hosts?

JACKSON: They ran out of salad. I didn't like the dessert.

HILLARY: I didn't either, but that's no reason. It was better than last year.

JACKSON: Listen, let's get on with the play. The damn thing is too long.

HILLARY *(defensive)*: I cut the play.

JACKSON: All that stuff about unrequited love gives me a nervous tic.

MILDRED: Here they are.

The host couples enter.

MILDRED: We'd like to thank our hosts.

Mild to no applause.

RALPH FALCONBERG: We're going back to the kitchen.

MILDRED: Our next meeting will be co-hosted by Jackson and Hillary. And now for tonight's play, for which our producer is Hillary.

HILLARY: Since I have a part, I have asked June to introduce the play.

JUNE: Tonight's play is called *Prisoner of Passion.* This is a piece from the early nineteen hundreds. The characters are Shelia Brighton, a young woman in her early twenties who sews at home with her invalid mother, played by Hillary Smith; Shelia's mother, Mrs. Brighton, played by Jane Williams; a Suitor, Carlton Minor, played by Jackson Caruthers; and Luther Morris, a rival and villain, played by Hickory Jones.

The scene opens in a sitting room at the Brighton home. Shelia is sewing an elegant dress of silk and flowers for what must be a very wealthy customer. Mrs. Brighton is knitting in a rocking chair off to the side with a shawl wrapped around her.

MRS. BRIGHTON: Shelia, dear, make certain you don't crush those lovely flowers. No woman wants to go to a dance with wilted flowers.

SHELIA: I know, Mother.

MRS. BRIGHTON: And make certain those stays don't fall out. I think Wilhelmina is going to the ball with Carlton Minor this year. I'm certain she will want to look her best.

SHELIA *(aside)*: Oh, to think I am sewing this so that Carlton can enjoy the arms of a Wilhelmina! Curses!

MRS. BRIGHTON: Haven't you gone out with Mr. Minor, dear?

SHELIA: Yes, Mother.

MRS. BRIGHTON: I think he is very marriageable.

SHELIA: Yes, Mother.

MRS. BRIGHTON: He seems to have very good taste.

SHELIA: I know, Mother. *(Aside)* Except for choosing Wilhelmina. Curses!

JUNE, *reading a play direction.* A knock is heard at the door. *The audience hears this sound, too.*

MRS. BRIGHTON: That may be Wilhelmina coming for her dress.

SHELIA: I'll get it, Mother.

JUNE, *reading a play direction.* Shelia stops the sewing, goes to the door, and admits Luther Morris. *Shelia does this.*

SHELIA: Luther, I'm so glad to see you. Come in.

MRS. BRIGHTON: Well, maybe you two want to talk. I'll go into the kitchen.

JUNE: *Mrs. Brighton exits.*

LUTHER: Working as usual, Shelia?

SHELIA: You know, someone has to put food on the table.

MILDRED (*interrupting*): Hillary, this is bad, bad, bad! The Johnsons are already asleep. Where did you get this play?

HILLARY: At Regenstein Library.

MILDRED: I didn't know they kept plays that long. It must have been very dusty. Hillary, did you really cut this?

HILLARY: Yes, it took me hours.

JACKSON: It's too long. Let's get going.

HILLARY: It gets better.

JACKSON: No, it doesn't.

JUNE: Let's give it a chance. I had to read it. If I can stand it, so can the rest of us.

JUNE: Silence from the audience!

JUNE *(continuing* Prisoner of Passion*)*: O K, Luther has just entered.

LUTHER: Shelia, I came to ask you to the ball. Will you come with me?

SHELIA: I haven't anything to wear. I don't wear clothes like these.

JUNE: *Shelia points to Wilhelmina's gown.*

LUTHER *(aside)*: I think I can fix that gown so Shelia won't worry about being embarrassed with what she has.

LUTHER: Shelia, you can wear that blue dress you wore a few years ago. Go get it. Let's take a look at it.

JUNE: *Shelia exits to get the gown.*

LUTHER: Now, just a few cuts here and there from an expert like me and this gown will come down after the first dance.

JUNE: *Luther makes some very professional cuts to the dress and places Wilhelmina's dress back on the sewing machine.*

LUTHER: There!

JUNE: *Shelia reenters carrying the blue dress.*

LUTHER: Gorgeous! I'll bring you a new shawl, some flowers, and you will be the belle of the ball. Will you come now?

SHELIA: Oh, Luther.

JUNE: *Shelia pauses, thinking about her true love, Carlton.*

SHELIA: O.K. I'll go.

LUTHER *(going to the door):* Don't you worry, Shelia. I guarantee you that Wilhelmina won't think she has anything on compared to you. See you later. *(Luther exits.)*

JUNE: *Shelia puts Wilhelmina's dress back in its box. Mrs. Brighton reenters.*

MRS. BRIGHTON: That was a short visit.

SHELIA: Luther has asked me to the ball.

MRS. BRIGHTON: I thought you wanted to go with Carlton.

SHELIA: Don't worry, Mother. I want to go and not stay home.

JUNE: *A knock is heard at the door.*

MRS. BRIGHTON: That may be Wilhelmina coming for her dress.

SHELIA: I'll get it, Mother.

JUNE: *Shelia stops packing the dress. She goes to the door and admits Carlton Minor.*

SHELIA: Carlton, I'm so glad to see you. Come in.

MRS. BRIGHTON: Well, maybe you two want to talk. I'll go into the kitchen. *(Mrs. Brighton exits.)*

CARLTON: Working as usual, Shelia?

SHELIA: You know, someone has to put food on the table.

MILDRED: Hillary, you said that things would get better. The Johnsons are snoring. I'm having trouble hearing the play.

JACKSON: I haven't even had a chance to read my part.

Hillary begins to cry.

JACKSON: Now look what you have done. When you produced last month, we had to listen to some guy who had no idea of what he was doing, what he was saying. The whole thing made no sense.

MILDRED: That's just because you have no appreciation for the theater of the absurd.

JACKSON: It was absurd all right. At least this thing has a plot.

HILLARY *(stops crying):* Oh, Jackson, you defended me. That play made no sense to me, either. Do you really want to take Wilhelmina to the ball?

JACKSON: Those aren't the lines. I'm supposed to come in and ask *you* to the ball. Where are you getting those lines?

MILDRED: Look, the Johnsons are awake. They want to know what's going on.

JUNE: Let's give it a chance. I had to read it. If I can stand it, so can the rest of us. Is this a play reading or some kind of a lovers' consciousness-raising session? *(The audience silences.)*

JUNE *(continuing):* OK. Carlton has just entered.

CARLTON: Shelia, I came to ask you to the ball. Will you come with me?

SHELIA: I thought you were going with Wilhelmina.

CARLTON: Wilhelmina has been called out of town. She won't be going to the ball.

SHELIA: I haven't anything to wear. I don't wear clothes like these. *(Shelia points to Wilhelmina's gown)*

CARLTON: That looks like Wilhelmina's gown. Why don't you wear it? I'm sure she won't need it on her trip and you are both the same size.

SHELIA: But someone else has asked me.

CARLTON: Why don't you just call the other person about an hour before I pick you up and say you are sick? Whoever he is, he won't be able to find anyone and we can go together.

SHELIA *(swoons):* Oh, Carlton! I feel we'll have such a great time.

CARLTON: Gorgeous. I'll bring you a new shawl and some flowers and you'll be the belle of the ball.

SHELIA: Oh, Carlton. *(She pauses, thinking Carlton is her true love.)* OK.

CARLTON *(going to the door):* Don't you worry, Shelia. I guarantee you that no one will catch people's attention compared to you. See you later. *(He exits.)*

JUNE: *Shelia puts Wilhelmina's dress back in its box. Mrs. Brighton reenters.*

MRS. BRIGHTON: That was a short visit.

SHELIA: Carlton has asked me to the ball.

MRS. BRIGHTON: I thought you were going with Luther.

SHELIA: Don't worry, Mother. Not anymore. Carlton has asked me.

JUNE: *A knock is heard at the door.*

MRS. BRIGHTON: That may be Wilhelmina coming for her dress.

SHELIA: I'll get it, Mother.

JUNE: *Shelia packs the dress away. She goes to the door to admit Wilhelmina.*

SHELIA: Wilhelmina, I'm so glad to see you. Come in.

MRS. BRIGHTON: Well, maybe you two want to talk. I'll go to the kitchen. *(Mrs. Brighton exits.)*

Before Wilhelmina can ask "Working as usual Shelia?" and Shelia can respond "You know, someone has to put food on the table," Mildred stands up.

MILDRED: Break anyone? Break? The Johnsons look thirsty. Let's go to the kitchen and have some water.

The group exits to the kitchen for water, leaving Hillary and Jackson.

HILLARY: Oh, Jackson, you defended me and you didn't like the dessert. I don't love Luther. You know that.

JACKSON: Shelia *(he catches himself)* — I mean, Hillary — what are you talking about?

HILLARY: Don't you see this play is for us, about us?

JACKSON: Shelia, that is absurd.

HILLARY: No, that was last month's play. Tonight we have a real plot. Didn't you see? Even the Johnsons were subliminally affected.

JACKSON: Maybe the water will sober them up.

The play readers return, offering Hillary and Jackson plastic glasses of water and taking their seats.

MILDRED: June, since we have had our break, why don't you skip to the second part of the play? If we need to know what Wilhelmina and Shelia say to each other, we can stop and look back at the script. O.K? *(June yawns.)* Fine.

JUNE: *Act Two. The scene is still the Brighton living room, but the time is now after the ball. Mrs. Brighton is in her rocker as before, knitting.*

A knock is heard at the door. Mrs. Brighton stops knitting, goes to the door, and admits Shelia. Shelia enters with a tablecloth wrapped around her like a skirt. Tucked into the skirt and worn like a blouse is the top half of Wilhelmina's dress with its roses and flowers.

MRS. BRIGHTON: Why Shelia, you are back early. What happened? Why are you wearing a tablecloth?

SHELIA: Oh, Mother, it was wonderful, so exciting!

MRS. BRIGHTON: You mean it was so wonderful that you had to hurry back and tell me?

SHELIA: No, the ball, Mother.

MRS. BRIGHTON: Tell me.

SHELIA: Well, I called Luther and told him I was sick. He was mad, but then Luther is Luther.

MRS. BRIGHTON: OK.

SHELIA: Carlton picked me up and we had our first dance. I think it was a fox-trot.

MRS. BRIGHTON: Go on.

SHELIA: Well, Carlton went out for some water and cake. Mother, you'll never guess – Carlton and I have the same tastes! We both love devil's food cake.

MRS. BRIGHTON: Amazing.

SHELIA: So, I am waiting for something to eat and drink, and who comes in but Luther.

MRS. BRIGHTON: No. You mean he found someone on short notice?

SHELIA: Not at all! He came to see if he could pick up someone!

MRS. BRIGHTON: Well. And then what happened?

SHELIA: He came up to me. He had a bad look. He was about to talk when I think I turned away slightly and then it happened.

MRS. BRIGHTON: What happened?

SHELIA: The entire lower half of Wilhelmina's dress fell to the floor! People began to stare. Luther fell back.

MRS. BRIGHTON: I think we had too many visitors while you were working on that dress, Shelia. But you weren't doing anything with the dress that would cause it to fall apart.

SHELIA: Yes. Well, just at this time Carlton was coming back with cake and punch – he couldn't find water. He sees Luther and my condition and assumes that Luther has attempted rape in the middle of the dance floor. He doesn't give him a chance to talk, but delivers what I will always call a one-two punch. Oh, Mother, it was wonderful!

MRS. BRIGHTON: The one-two – what did you say? You mean he gives Luther a drink?

SHELIA: Punch, Mother. First he throws both cups of punch in Luther's face and then he gives Luther a punch with his fist and Luther is down.

MRS. BRIGHTON: And then what happened?

SHELIA: I don't know. Carlton whipped off a tablecloth, wrapped it around me, and hurried me to the restroom. The rest of the dancers were attending to Luther. Oh, Mother, do you think we can keep it?

MRS. BRIGHTON: Keep what, dear?

SHELIA: The tablecloth, of course. Every time we eat dinner, it will remind me of Carlton.

MRS. BRIGHTON: And then you came home?

SHELIA: Carlton took me home. But, Mother, there's more.

MRS. BRIGHTON: I suspected that.

SHELIA: Carlton has asked me to marry him!

MRS. BRIGHTON: I see.

SHELIA: Yes. He said that when he saw me there in distress and with not much on, he just had to say what was inside him. The only reason he had asked Wilhelmina was that two years ago he had promised. He had to keep his word.

MRS. BRIGHTON: Carlton seems very much a knight in shining armor. First, he rescues you from a rapist, insults the man, knocks him out, finds you emergency clothing, spirits you away from the crowd, and then he proposes that you live happily ever after on devil's food cake. And he is a man of his word.

SHELIA: Yes, Mother. Can you imagine my new name? Shelia Minor. Doesn't it sound good? You know, we had a distant relative by that name. He was in the army – Major Minor.

MILDRED: Curtain, curtain, enough, enough. A wonderful ending. Thank you so much for producing.

HILLARY: You do like devil's food cake. I've seen you help yourself to seconds many times.

JACKSON: Yes, but we're the only unmarried people in the group. It will put a tremendous crimp on a producer's flexibility.

HILLARY: Other groups manage. But just think how much more efficient co-hosting – even hosting – will be. As a married couple, we will count as a single host. You can do the salad and I can do the cake.

JACKSON: Yes, I guess that's true if it's OK with Mildred. But I don't need any references made to your military relatives.

HILLARY: That's a deal. I'll even make a tablecloth skirt.

JACKSON: That sounds very interesting.

They embrace.

Curtain.

Appendix P

But if I could write a Lake Woebegone monologue aping the fashion of a Prairie Home Companion piece set at the HPNC, I could also get seriously emotional about the community that I now called home. I invested myself in a small way compared to many others and my attachment grew beyond how I felt about that un-air conditioned, fourth-floor apartment in married student housing.

I have already written a story of the trip to South Africa that prompted me to give a short speech to the board of directors after I returned from Africa. I shall copy the text of those events from my book *Work – A Memoir.* In the text, like the earlier piece from *Stories of Identity*, I refer to myself using the fictional name of John Sherman. The story starts on page 207 and begins with a class for the System/38 computer that I developed for IBM, my employer at the time; education development was a major portion of my job description at that time in my career. The excerpted section begins with my mentioning experiments that I made and which became the basis for a hands-on performance measurement class for the System/38.

* * *

"By initiating any number of these programs to operate simultaneously, I was able to model a System/38 that was lightly loaded all the way up to a heavily loaded system. To develop the class I ran many experiments. I used all the tools, System/38 commands, and displays that were difficult to understand and interpret. By holding some variables constant while varying one or two of the others, I could isolate the performance consequences across a broad range of tuning options. I could then draw graphs and use the displays that resulted when System/38 commands were executed; these commands displayed the results of the success or failure of changing parameters during a sequence of environments. They were difficult to use and comprehend without a system running at or near capacity and already tailored by the initial user choices of resource allocation.

"My experiments carried over into my lectures and the lab problems – they became the basis upon which the course was developed. Students could use the same programs I used – they were learning vehicles and were explicit in their characteristics – known quantities as distinct from unknown customer programs. The student would be better off learning principles rather than get bogged down with jobs borrowed from real life and which were unlike his or her own environment.

"Somehow, word got around of my experiments; my intention was to make a class for customers, drawing upon my familiarity with some of the necessary internal, under-the-cover operations that would be of value to systems engineers. My manager at the time, Frank, received a letter from an Advanced Systems Development manager in Rochester. Rochester wanted to review the objectives, outline, and content of my class. This was unusual high-level attention.

"Later, I remember getting a call from Rick, one of the principal performance gurus in Rochester. It so happened that, at the time he called me, I had already accepted an invitation to teach a teach-the-teachers class for the System/38 Measurement and Analysis class outside London to a group of European technical specialists. The London class was one that included a great deal of internal information that would not be put into a customer class. I had also accepted an invitation to teach a four day Advanced Program to Program Communications class in Paris in July of the same year. Christiane would join me in Paris. I rarely accepted more than one overseas invitation in a year.

"It was after the point in time when these April and July classes were set in place that Rick called. He received an urgent request to teach System/38 performance classes in South Africa. His schedule was completely filled. Could I go and fulfill the request? Aside from this being my third trip abroad in one year, the agenda looked interesting.

"The first class would be a two-day intensive class for systems engineers that would compress what I taught outside London in April. The second class would be a three-day customer class – pretty much what was announced for customers in the United States in June. In between the two classes my host, a South African IBM employee and his fiancée, would take me to Kruger National Park, an enormous game preserve, for three full days.

"I thought of that line in Shakespeare's *Measure for Measure*, that line of Lucio's about our doubts being traitors, and I accepted. Mind you, this was a time when apartheid was in full swing! When I left on my twenty-five hour flight to Johannesburg, a black man, Harold Washington, was running for mayor of Chicago; he lived in my neighborhood, Hyde Park.

"South African Airlines was not allowed to land and refuel in Africa. In the middle of the night, the 747 I was flying began its approach to land on one of the Cape Verde islands in order to refuel. The passenger sitting next to me and I both looked out the window; all we saw was a single light. It looked like a water landing up to the last few minutes; then two rows of lights came on all at once and we saw the single-lane runway as we made our final turn. I told my seatmate that it reminded me of landing on an aircraft carrier. We disembarked, stretched our legs and spotted Cuban soldiers who were enroute to another destination in Africa.

"I never lived in the south. Norfolk, Virginia, where my destroyer, USS *Hank* (DD-702), had its home port was a Navy town; black sailors were evaluated on their merits, just like everybody else. As engineering officer on the *Hank* during my third year of active duty, a second class petty officer, Rhodes, was a young black member of the crew who performed the job of *oil king*. He kept track of the contents of every single fuel tank; it was called Navy Special Fuel Oil (NSFO). He held one of the most important jobs in the department; it was on a par with the evaporator men who distilled 700 gallons/hour. Rhodes never made a mistake; he was one of several I would have called my *right hand men*.

"Hyde Park was one of the most successfully integrated communities in the United States. Both my children went to a high school that was 80% black, 20% white; they both were accepted at Princeton and Stanford. In Johannesburg I saw the white/black signs above the washrooms when the classes I was teaching took a break. On our way to Kruger Park we stopped at a roadside gas station to buy some soft drinks. I went up to the counter that was for blacks and bought refreshments for my two hosts; something inside me rebelled. We drove away and my host warned me not to do that again.

"Earlier, during the two-day class for systems engineers, I spoke with a young black systems engineer during a break. When The Company hired her, her father quit work and retired; his daughter could now support the family. But these memories pall by comparison to what my eighth-grade daughter said when I made my safe arrival call to Chicago.

"The call was delayed by a day. Before I placed it, I had already taught for a day and I was sitting in the lobby of my hotel waiting for my pick-up to class to arrive. I was reading a local newspaper and on the front page was an article about a public beach in Cape Town where blacks were excluded and an incident had occurred — the details I can't completely recall and it makes no difference; all I can remember are my emotions.

"It was later when I placed the call to Chicago that the tears came to my eyes, and I think they still come. My daughter picked up the phone and she didn't say 'How are you?' or 'How was your flight?' no, her first words were 'Washington has won!' Those words made up for the newspaper which I threw in the trash earlier in the day."

Sherman paused and reminded his audience that he included a short speech that he read just after he got back from Johannesburg. At the time, he was serving on the board of the Hyde Park Neighborhood Club during one of those twelve years he was their president.

Short Speech to Neighborhood Club Board

Irene has asked me to make a report on the Good Neighbor fund drive and there is little more to say than that only with an enormous effort will we reach the $60,000 of this year's goal. Whether or not we make that goal, may I share with you briefly my larger perspective on the future?

Often we don't appreciate what we have until we lose it. Some of you may not feel the loss of the YMCA because you may never have participated in its programs. But there are things we all experience and share: our city, our neighborhood, and our club.

When I leave this country on a trip I am always intrigued if I will feel these lines upon my return:

> "Breathes there the man with soul so dead
> Who never to himself hath said,
> This is my own, my native land!
> Whose heart hath ne'er within him burned,
> As home his footsteps he hath turned
> From wandering on a foreign strand!"

And sometimes I find that emotion not as strong as years ago. After the Good Neighbor night I went immediately on business to South Africa and I was just as intrigued about my return feelings. There were some clues given me while I was there. As I sat in my Johannesburg hotel lobby reading a newspaper that seemed as incredulous as though it was from outer space, there was a small article that stood out in sharp contrast to everything else being said in the entire paper for it said: "Washington had won.!" And when I made my $50 safe arrival telephone call home, the first thing my daughter said was not "How are you," but "did you know, Washington has won!"

But what were my feelings when, after about twenty-four hours of continuous travel, I entered the taxi at O'Hare for the last leg of the trip? Little did I know how my emotions would quickly overtake me for here was a black driver, a stranger, yes, but a free citizen of my country, and my city. I wanted to affirm his freedom, and his personality, and at last, talk to an equal, black person.

After only eleven days of loss, I felt the need for that relationship, and conversation, just as Scrooge wanted to return from his glimpse of the future. And never was I happier, and prouder to be going home nor did my heart burn more as I realized that we both knew where Kenwood Avenue was for it's in Hyde Park near the center, where the Neighborhood Club is.

The world does know where Chicago is and we support a beacon institution within a beacon neighborhood of that city. We should make certain that now, as well as in the future, we always stand out in sharp contrast.

Other Books By Earl Ronneberg

Short Stories

Old Friends and Other Stories
Stories of Identity
Stories of Groups
Western Michigan Tales of Mystery and Adventure

Nonfiction

Work – A Memoir
Black Friends

Poetry

A Love Affair with Flowers Fair

Philosophy

Dawn

Eclectic
Fiction/Nonfiction

Forms of Life

Novel

Entrance Island
The Gospel of Marriage

Made in the USA
Charleston, SC
13 January 2015